CW00801153

Eleanor of Castile

of

Castile

The Shadow Queen

SARA COCKERILL

AMBERLEY

For my parents, Lilian and Alan, with love

First published 2014

Amberley Publishing
The Hill, Stroud
Gloucestershire, GL5 4EP

www.amberley-books.com

British Library Cataloguing in Publication Data.
A catalogue record for this book is available from the British Library.

ISBN 978-1-4456-3589-7 (hardback)
ISBN 978-1-4456-3605-4 (ebook)

Map and table design by Thomas Bohm, User design.
Typesetting and Origination by Amberley Publishing.
Printed in the UK.

Contents

Maps and Family Trees

Family Tree 1: Five Weddings

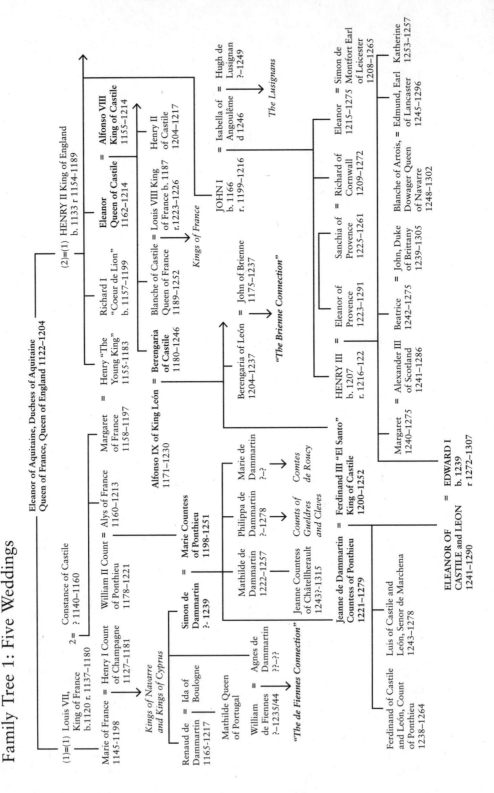

Family Tree 2: The Brienne Connection

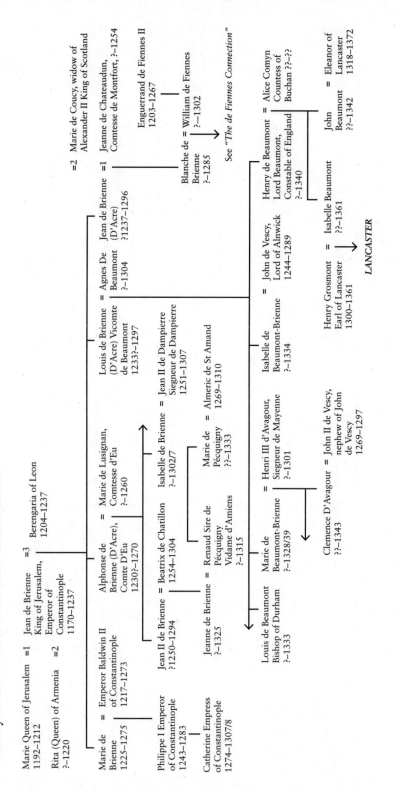

Family Tree 3: The de Fiennes Connection

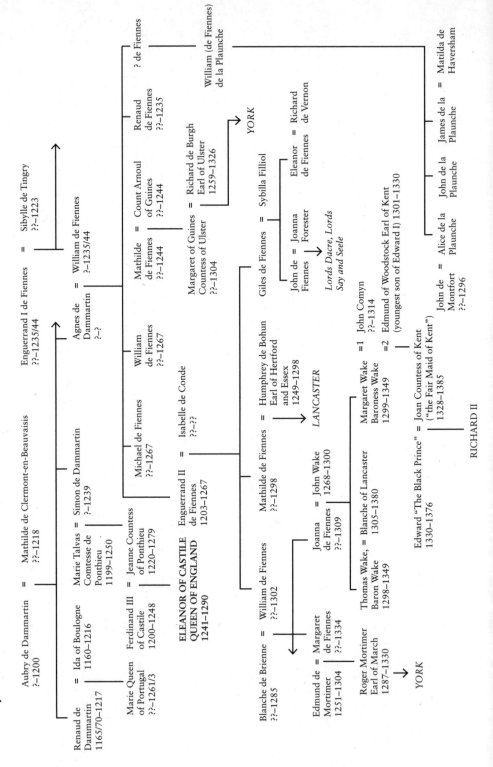

Family Tree 4: The Dynastic Web

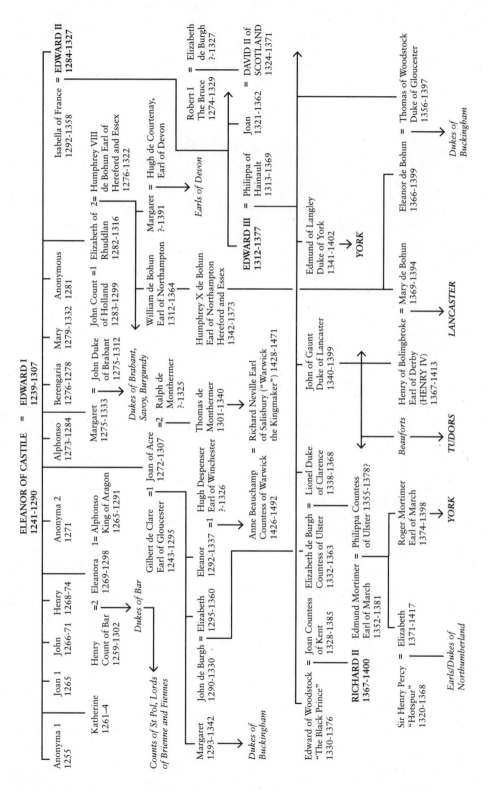

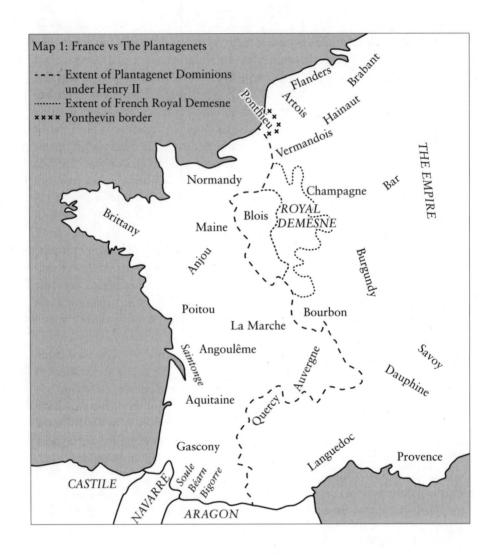

Map 1: France vs The Plantagenets

---- Extent of Plantagenet Dominions
      under Henry II
········ Extent of French Royal Demesne
×××× Ponthevin border

Flanders
Brabant
Ponthieu
Artois
Hainaut
Vermandois
THE EMPIRE
Normandy
Champagne
Bar
Brittany
Blois
ROYAL DEMESNE
Maine
Anjou
Burgundy
Poitou
Bourbon
La Marche
Angoulême
Savoy
Saintonge
Auvergne
Dauphine
Aquitaine
Quercy
Gascony
Languedoc
Provence
Soule
Béarn
Bigorre
CASTILE
NAVARRE
ARAGON

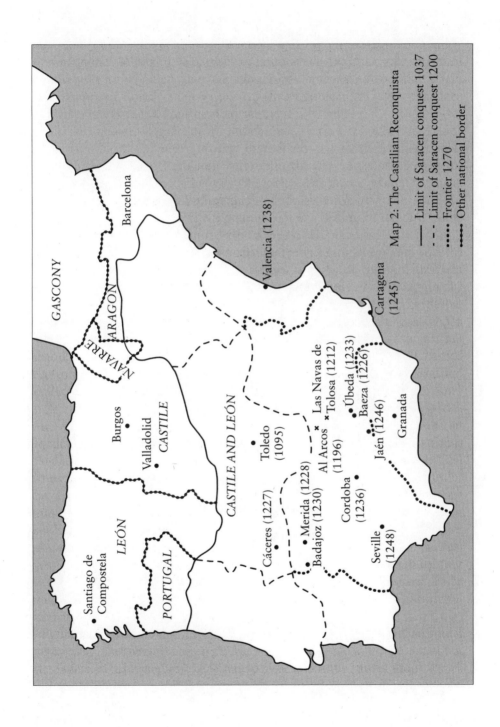

Map 2: The Castilian Reconquista

——— Limit of Saracen conquest 1037
— - — Limit of Saracen conquest 1200
• • • • • Frontier 1270
•••••• Other national border

GASCONY

Barcelona

ARAGON

NAVARRE

Valencia (1238)

Burgos

Valladolid

CASTILE

Santiago de
Compostela

LEÓN

CASTILE AND LEÓN

Toledo
(1095)

Las Navas de
Tolosa (1212)

Úbeda (1233)
Baeza (1226)

Cartagena
(1245)

Al Arcos
(1196)

Cáceres (1227)

Merida (1228)
Badajoz (1230)

Cordoba
(1236)

Jaén
(1246)

Granada

PORTUGAL

Seville
(1248)

Map 3: Gascony

POITOU/AQUITAINE

Châtellherault

Poitiers

Île d'Oléron
SAINTONGE

Saintes

Limoges

Angoulême

Soulac

Bourg

Blanquefort

Libourne

Bordeaux

St Foy La Grande

Cadouin

Castillon

Monpazier

La Réole

GASCONY

Belin-
Béliet

St Macaire

Uzeste

Bazas

Villeneuve-sur-Lot

Roquecor

Agen

Dax

St Sever

Toulouse

Bonnegarde

Bayonne

CASTILE

Pau

Luq

Béarn

Oloron

Bigorre

NAVARRE

Mauléon

Canfranc

Soule

Urdos

Burgos

Jacca

ARAGON

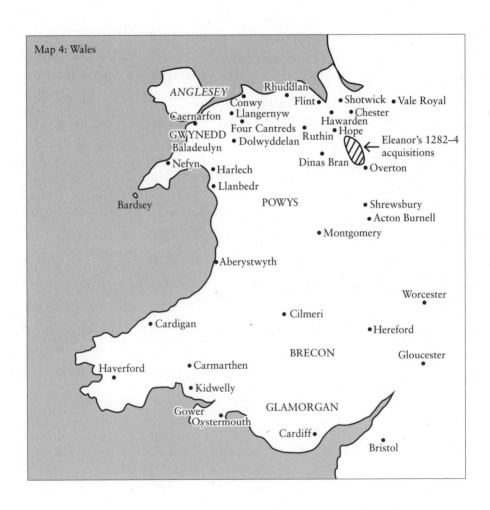

Map 4: Wales

ANGLESEY
Rhuddlan
Conwy • Flint • Shotwick • Vale Royal
Caernarfon • Llangernyw • Chester
Hawarden
Four Cantreds • Hope
GWYNEDD • Dolwyddelan Ruthin
Baladeulyn
Nefyn • Eleanor's 1282–4 acquisitions
• Harlech Dinas Bran • Overton
• Llanbedr

Bardsey POWYS • Shrewsbury
• Acton Burnell
• Montgomery

• Aberystwyth

• Worcester
• Cilmeri
• Cardigan • Hereford

BRECON Gloucester
Haverford • Carmarthen
• Kidwelly

Gower GLAMORGAN
Oystermouth
Cardiff •
Bristol

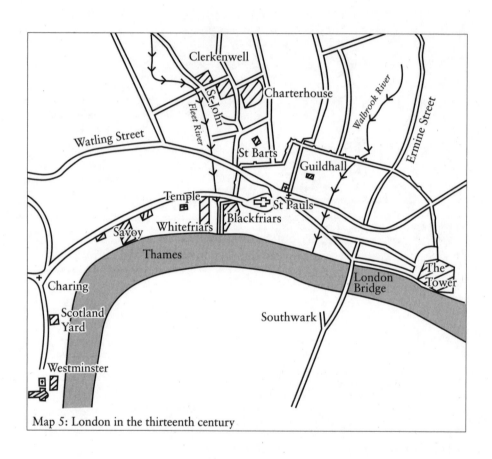

Map 5: London in the thirteenth century

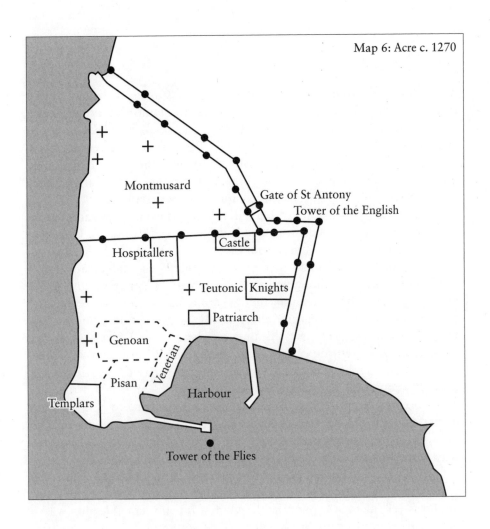

Map 6: Acre c. 1270

Montmusard

Gate of St Antony
Tower of the English

Castle

Hospitallers

Teutonic Knights

Patriarch

Genoan

Venetian

Pisan

Templars

Harbour

Tower of the Flies

Preface

If you know anything at all about Eleanor of Castile, you may count yourself in the elite minority. By far the most common question I have been asked during the course of writing this book has been (with a puzzled frown) 'Who was she, exactly?' Perhaps one in ten of those asking has made the connection that Eleanor was the wife of England's greatest medieval monarch, Edward I. And they are hardly alone. In a recent bestselling popular history a full-time historian and his editors managed to assign Philippa of Hainault to the first Edward, rather than the third; numerous other historians have also 'lost' Eleanor of Castile.[1]

The second most common question has been why I decided to write this book at all. The real answer is that I was labouring under a misapprehension. I thought that the record on Eleanor needed to be put straight and the perception that everyone had of her corrected. But it seems in fact that 'everyone' did not have a perception of her at all. Few knew that for centuries Eleanor has been wrongly lauded as the epitome of quiet retiring queens, with Botfield and Turner, upon whose work that of Agnes Strickland was substantially based, describing her thus: 'No equivocal reputation is associated with Eleanor of Castile. She never swerved from the position which fortune assigned to her, or failed to perform the gentle and peaceful duties which belonged to it. The memory of her unobtrusive virtues and worth passed away with those who witnessed, or were the objects of her care and solicitude.'[2]

So why does Eleanor of Castile deserve to be rescued from the scrapheap of history? One very good reason is because she was far from unobtrusive; she was a remarkable woman for any era. Eleanor was a highly dynamic, forceful personality whose interest in the arts, politics and religion were highly influential in her day – and whose temper had even bishops quaking in their shoes. Highly intelligent and studious, she was incomparably better educated, and almost certainly brighter, than her husband. She was a scholar and an avid bookworm, running her own scriptorium (almost unique in European royal courts) and promoting the production of illustrated manuscripts, as well as works of romance and history. Equally unusually she could herself write and she considered it a sufficiently important accomplishment that her own children were made to acquire the skill.

She also introduced numerous domestic refinements to English court life: forks, for example, first make their appearance in England in her household and carpets became sought after in noble circles in imitation of her interior design style. She was a pioneer of domestic luxury: she introduced the first purpose-built tiled bathroom and England's first 'fairy tale' castle – both at her own castle of Leeds, in Kent. She revolutionised garden design in England, introducing innovations – including fountains and water features – familiar to her from Castile.

Perhaps most interestingly she was also in many ways the obverse of the traditional mid-late medieval queen, who was expected to be humble and intercessory. She emphatically rejected the paradigm of submissive queenship, insisted on having a real job to do and was devoted to that work. As well as acting as part of Edward's innermost circle of advisers, she also took on her own shoulders a whole department charged with accumulating properties for the Crown and acquired, through her own efforts, a major landed estate. In modern terms one might well see in Eleanor a parallel with Hillary Clinton – a real dynamic power behind the throne.

At the same time Eleanor was still a highly effective and discreet matchmaker in the way expected of medieval queens. For anyone with an interest in later medieval history the feat she achieved of quietly inserting members of her family into most of the great houses in England is breathtaking: practically all the Wars of the Roses claimants descend from her wider family as well as the English royal family.

Another powerful reason for bringing Eleanor into the limelight is that she had one of the most varied and interesting lives of any of England's queens in any era.

The daughter of a famed Crusader and international hero, Eleanor of Castile was brought up partly in the most intellectually and culturally sophisticated court in Europe and partly in the vicinity of the battlefield; for Castile was a country very actively engaged in military affairs, with her father and brothers constantly riding off to battle during her childhood. Eleanor's childhood was, in effect, spent on campaign or among the work involved in the aftermath of a campaign. As a result she had imbibed first from her Crusader father and then from her academic prodigy of a brother much important theoretical and practical knowledge of war, government and the role of a king.

She married the future Edward I aged twelve and bore her first short-lived child aged only thirteen. By the time she reached England a year later, the marriage alliance was considered a liability by her father-in-law, Henry III, and her position at court was extremely difficult. This was hardly improved by the arrival at court of a landless brother seeking subsidies from her new family; or the fact that she and her mother-in-law, Eleanor of Provence, never formed a warm bond as they battled for influence over Edward – a battle that Eleanor of Castile won. From her earliest days as a wife to the English heir, her hand can be traced guiding him in asserting his independence from his mother's tutelage and in assembling the skills he would need to be both a great king and an outstanding military man.

In the Barons' Revolt, which ensued soon after her arrival, Eleanor chose to stay in England when the queen and the ladies of the court fled to France, preferring to face the chances of war with her husband, to whom she was completely devoted. She oversaw the defence of Windsor Castle on her husband's behalf and, once forced to yield it, she suffered a terrible year in effective captivity; a time that encompassed the deaths of her next two children, complete destitution and real fears for Edward's own life.

After the war, Eleanor encouraged Edward to go on Crusade to the Holy Land, and accompanied him, leaving her young children behind for three years and encountering the physical hazards that killed a number of the crusading party, including the King of France and one of her childhood friends. While in the Holy Land she almost certainly witnessed a violent assassination attempt on her husband and reputedly (though not in fact) saved Edward's life after it. She bore still further children in Acre while effectively on campaign, losing one of them. All in all she was to bear Edward somewhere in the region of sixteen children, of whom only six survived to adulthood.

Towards the end of the Crusade, news arrived of the deaths of both the King of England and Eleanor's own eldest son. The new king and queen, however, took two years to return home, enjoying a prolonged and triumphant reception as they passed through Italy and a lengthy stay in Gascony where a new son was born.

As queen, Eleanor was placed by Edward in charge of one of his central policy goals – the reinvigoration of the Crown property, which had been much dissipated under his father. She therefore turned property developer, building up by her own direct endeavours a massive property empire equivalent to a major noble landholding. Her property interests often directed the movements of the court, since she was a 'hands on' manager but would not stray from Edward's side.

Eleanor also accompanied Edward again throughout his Welsh campaigns, bearing her final child, the future, catastrophic, Edward II, amid the building site that was Caernarfon Castle, assisting in the resettlement of Wales and promoting the 'Arthurian' myth that surrounded Edward's court in this period of triumphant conquest.

Eleanor encouraged the plan for the marriage of their eldest daughter to the King of Aragon, a project that carried the royal couple to Gascony in the late 1280s and kept them there for three years – again without their children. To save the marriage they had to bring about the King of Aragon's rehabilitation in the eyes of the papacy following the European war that had flared up between Aragon, France and the papacy. During this time, although her health was failing, Eleanor played an active diplomatic role internationally, and acted personally as a mediator in disputes between local noble houses, in the same way that a prince might.

Ultimately it seems likely that she worked herself to death; with her health failing, she was still pushing on with her habits of active acquisition and management of property and superintending litigation, as well as organising weddings for her family and dependents. She died, aged only forty-nine, in a stranger's house, having been taken so ill on her travels that the house of friends, a mere four miles distant, could not be reached.

Her death blindsided the formidable Edward, who had throughout their marriage loathed being parted from his wife. A part – but only a part – of the extensive tribute by which he marked his grief for her loss is the series of 'Eleanor crosses', the most complete and ornate set of monuments to a beloved spouse ever seen in this country and very possibly in Europe at large. To this he added a tomb in Westminster Abbey, which is considered by many to be the high-water mark of the English Decorated style, along with two other lesser tombs and a myriad of other charitable and religious memorials.

Still the reasons for telling Eleanor's story are not exhausted. For one thing, through the details of her property empire we can catch rare glimpses of the more humble lives of medieval people. There are the servants rewarded with smallholdings, the farmers caught between the clashes of great nobles and great abbeys, and unsure to whom to pay their rent; there are the fat bullyboy bailiffs who would not be out of place in a modern tabloid, turfing families out of their houses to weep by the side of the road. We can also catch some sense of the academic climate; we can see at close range, through Eleanor's own links to one school of thought, the beginnings of religious controversies that would rumble on until the Reformation; and religious practices, such as the rosary, which hold sway to this day.

Why, if the story is in itself so interesting and there is scope to correct the received picture this radically, has there been no biography to tell the true story? This has often astounded me during the course of my research. However, the answer is simply this: Eleanor has proved a highly elusive character. The materials that mention Eleanor specifically are so fragmentary as to give one little to get hold of. The Canadian historian John Carmi Parsons spent years in research apparently in preparation for such a work, but appears ultimately to have considered the project impossible. In connection with one of the best remaining sources, Eleanor's *Liber Garderobe* of 1289–90, which provides a day-to-day account for that period of all messengers sent and items purchased, he completed an exhaustive examination of the materials but concluded that the materials did not enable a picture to be brought to life, lacking any sense of her actual thoughts or reactions.[3]

While I would not entirely endorse these views – I think there are numerous points when Eleanor does vividly peek out of the records – there is certainly force in them. Moreover, even the limited 'Eleanor-specific' evidence that exists is difficult to use with confidence. What exists is a fairly complete *Liber Garderobe* relating to the final eighteen months of Eleanor's life, a near-illegible roll of household expenses for 1287–8, a partial roll of household expenses for 1288–9, an account of the inquest into her properties after her death, and casual mentions in the 'chronicles' and in Edward's records. One can therefore readily see that what remains in any detail relates to small portions of her life, so that there is a real danger that those portions (and particularly the inquest) get magnified out of all proportion, producing a distorted image. Thus the one modern popular historian to have attempted a short pen portrait of Eleanor concluded that she was a horrible woman with a vile temper, whom no one but her husband liked.[4]

However, more general material can do much to fill the gaps. The amount of writing which went on at the Castilian court about events, theories of kingship, education and the upbringing of princes is considerable, and I have concluded that a reasonable picture of the circumstances of Eleanor's life up until her marriage can be discerned, even if it rests on inference from the general to the specific in some places. In the years prior to the Crusade her moves have to be traced through Edward, but the inference that Parsons was prepared to tentatively make as to her role in positioning Edward can be supported by some specific personal links between events or people and Eleanor. After Edward's accession the material becomes slightly fuller, but I have made one important assumption. Although itinerary material for Eleanor only survives from the short period covered by the *Liber Garderobe*, I have inferred that, except where she is vouched for as being elsewhere, or it is obvious that she must have been elsewhere (e.g. when Edward was on active duties during the Welsh War), Eleanor was with Edward. I regard this as a permissible inference based on their notorious devotion, the almost complete correlation between the two itineraries for the period where itineraries for both Eleanor and Edward exist, and the fact that where Eleanor is vouched for by the chronicles, by surviving correspondence, or by Edward's wardrobe records, she is almost always to be found with Edward. I also consider that this inference is supported by the fact that so much of Edward's itinerary seems to dovetail with Eleanor's properties. One of the oddities of Edward's itinerary has always been that he travelled to some very out-of-the-way places. However, a cross check between the itinerary and Eleanor's properties very often reveals that the court was actually staying at one of Eleanor's properties or a few miles from a prospective purchase.

In researching this book I have found not only a very different picture to that which is generally seen, but also a very different one to that which I originally imagined I would find. I certainly expected to find Eleanor far more interesting and more dynamic than her press allows; maybe that she would even be a worthy foil to the greatness of Edward. What I did not expect was the sheer range of Eleanor's talents and influence. Nor did I anticipate the full extent of the dynamism or the hardness which she plainly had. To give one example, I had thought it likely that, given her background, coming from Castile where Christian–Jewish relations were very much more friendly, enlightened and sophisticated than in England, she had acted as an intercessor for the English Jewish population; the more so since the Jewish expulsion occurs in the year of her death. The reality has proved markedly less attractive. There is in fact no sign of any closeness to the Jewish community or real empathy with their problems. Eleanor used her familiarity with Jewish religionists in being happy to deal with the Jews (as some other magnates in England were not), and blithely acquired numerous debts from them while resolutely defying disapproval from the Church – characteristically on well-thought-out doctrinal grounds. But there is no sign of any meaningful intercession by her or promotion of her Jewish business partners' interests unless they were hers too. Her relations with her Jewish colleagues were strictly business; and in business she played hardball. Ultimately it would appear that she had no compunction about expulsion once an economic case for the Jewish population ceased to be compelling.

The result of my review is perhaps a less attractive figure in conventional terms than I had expected, but it is certainly more attractive than either Strickland's milk-and-water heroine or Hilton's grasping harpy. The picture, as it presents itself to me at least, is a startlingly modern one. Eleanor emerges as a woman of many interests and many talents, which she pursued with energy, while nonetheless embracing her role as a wife above all others. She was a woman who would not be penned in by the circumstances of her birth and marriage to a particular destiny, but who tried – to a large extent successfully – to utilise her abilities and education to carve out an interesting and demanding role for herself. One might say that seven hundred years before the feminist movement made this a goal, she succeeded in having it all: a strong, devoted marriage, an extensive family and a fulfilling high-level job. Hilton regards her as an awful woman. I beg to differ. After several years' acquaintance with Eleanor, the word that springs to my mind is awesome.

Sara Cockerill, 2014
www.saracockerill.com

Acknowledgements

There are three people who must imperatively be thanked for their contributions to this book.

The first is Michael Prestwich, whose work on Edward I actually led me to introduce myself to Eleanor. It was his mention of the change in the character of Edward's reign after Eleanor's death which first set me wondering whether there was more to a woman who had appeared in most of what I had read as a very quiet, traditional queen. So without him, this book would most certainly never have been written. I also owe him immense thanks for his kindness and patience in reading through the entire book in draft and providing many insightful and helpful comments.

The second person to whom thanks are indubitably owed is John Carmi Parsons who, any reader of the notes will quickly appreciate, had done a very great deal of detailed scholarly research on Eleanor. That research provided me with a huge amount of the building material for putting Eleanor's story together. I have been awed repeatedly by the meticulous nature of his researches. Had his work not been available I could never have done the job which he did, and the book would be immeasurably poorer for it.

Finally, unending thanks must be given to my husband Nigel, who not only brought those key copies of *Edward I* and *The Three Edwards* into my world, but discussed my early tentative theories with me; and was a model of patience in listening to the immense amount of Eleanor-related trivia which has seemed fascinating to me as I progressed with the writing process.

I would also like to thank Colette Bowie for releasing to me an advance version of the relevant sections of her book on the daughters of Henry II and Eleanor of Aquitaine, and Suzanne Lewis for confirming her future approach on the Trinity Apocalypse. Thanks are also due to the very many kind people at Westminster Abbey, the British Library, British Museum, Bodleian Library, National Archives and Bridgeman Art Library who helped me to put the illustrations together.

Finally, many thanks to Jonathan Reeve and Nicola Gale at Amberley for being prepared to take a chance on an author with no pedigree in writing history!

1

The Backdrop

On 1 November 1254, a fifteen-year-old boy was married to a twelve-year-old girl in the elegant Normanesque abbey of Las Huelgas in the northern Spanish town of Burgos. The couple had been formally engaged for some months but they had met for the first time only a matter of days before the wedding. Both were unsupported by their parents at this major event; the bride's father was dead and her mother had recently fled the country, while the groom's parents had chosen not to accompany him, and would only see the new couple for the first time over a year later. Such a wedding hardly seems auspicious. But this unpromising start was the beginning of perhaps the most successful royal marriage in England's history, for the bride was Eleanor of Castile and the groom was the future Edward I. As he became one of England's greatest and most successful kings, his wife was never far from his side and his devotion to her has become a byword, reinforced by the multiplicity of touching images of her he raised to commemorate her death, some thirty-six years into their marriage.

Yet though by those images and her splendid tomb – hailed as one of the masterpieces of the Decorated style – she is perhaps the most visible of the medieval queens of England, the opposite is the case when it come to the facts about Eleanor of Castile. She leaves almost no trace in the main records. In the process of reconstructing her life I have frequently felt that she hides away among the shadows of history. So elusive is she that there has never been a full biography of her life and there are no easy answers to the obvious questions: Who was she? Why was a Castilian princess married to an English prince? Did she influence Edward at all politically? And why was that marriage such a huge success?

To answer these questions it is necessary to take a step away from the facts one can know for sure about Eleanor. There are almost no verifiable facts about Eleanor's childhood, for example, and yet her story cannot possibly be said to start on the day she married Edward. At nearly thirteen years old she had a wealth of experience and knowledge already available to her, which must have coloured who she was. What is more, the fact that she was the daughter of one of Spain's greatest kings, an international hero and a future saint, is by no means irrelevant to the reason why the marriage came about, or to the assumptions about the role of a king which she will have brought to the marriage and communicated to her husband.

So where does one start? Even commencing at Eleanor's birth will not answer, for three reasons. The first is that the question as to why an English prince was marrying a Castilian princess cannot be answered without looking much earlier; although the marriage of Eleanor and Edward has come down to us as a great royal love match, the truth is that it was in all senses an arranged marriage, which existed only because it was politically the most suitable match available on both sides. The reasons which made it so appropriate derive principally from family and political factors, some of which reach back a full century before the wedding. Therefore the match itself is incomprehensible without some grounding in that backdrop.

Secondly, the importance of family to royal and noble individuals in this era must not be underestimated. Family was what fundamentally made you what and who you were. Family was what brought the privileges of rank and wealth, when the opposite was all too visible every day. Duty to family was a central part of the education and indoctrination of noble children – and particularly girls, who would be used as human links in a chain binding different family interests together, and who would be expected to bear an active role in promoting the relationship which their marriage was to facilitate. As Henry III put it, in the context of negotiations for Edward's marriage to Eleanor, 'friendship between princes can be obtained in no more fitting manner than by the link of conjugal troth'. In the interests of family, complex relationships developed through generations; and frequently women were the prime movers in the business of maintaining or supplementing historical family ties.

For Eleanor herself, the careful husbandry of family interests later formed a very significant part of the business of her life. Like most royal and noble women of this era, she appreciated the value of noble blood and alliance and would carry in her head the ancestry of her own family and those surrounding it – unto the third and fourth generations. She would then deploy this knowledge in forming alliances for children, friends and dependents. One illustration of this sphere of knowledge is the way in which papal dispensations would permit marriage 'within the fourth degree of consanguinity', i.e. with anyone who had a common ancestor four or more generations ago. Thus a common great-great-grandparent was permissible, but a common relative more recent than that was not – unless special dispensation was obtained. The number of ramifications which a family tree can gain in the intervening period can be imagined; particularly with second marriages, which were common if a first spouse died, a not infrequent occurrence given to the dangers of childbirth and battle. Yet in the world in which Eleanor moved, people, and particularly women, would be expected to know precisely such details. Ultimately one of Eleanor's great achievements was to surround her immediate family with supporters from her wider family, and to do so in a way which avoided negative comment from interested parties. The subtlety of the job that she did in interweaving her family into England's aristocracy cannot be appreciated without some perspective on the broader family ties that she brought with her.[1]

Finally, the fact that Eleanor is a woman who makes few positive appearances in the records means that direct evidence of her qualities and interests is very incomplete. We cannot unearth those facets of her without looking at the context and probabilities.

Therefore this chapter has to cover some broader family background, following Eleanor's family through four generations. This sets the stage for the political rationale for the marriage, as well as for Eleanor's own place in the world. It also begins the process, which the next two chapters will complete, of gathering such material as there is about the family backgrounds and early experiences for each of Eleanor and Edward. By looking in this chapter and the succeeding ones, at the family backgrounds of each and their upbringing, it is possible to form some views about the events and interests which affected each and moulded them into the two young people who stood at the altar in November 1254.

This is a story which can best be told broadly as the story of five weddings spanning four generations. At either end stand the marriage of Henry II of England and Eleanor of Aquitaine, which is the blood link between Eleanor and Edward, and the wedding of Eleanor's father, Ferdinand of Castile, to her mother, Jeanne of Ponthieu. In between lie on Ferdinand's side that of Alfonso VIII of Castile and Eleanor of England and of their daughter Berengaria of Castile to Alfonso IX of León; on Jeanne's side there is the marriage of her mother Marie of Ponthieu to Simon of Dammartin (the relationships discussed are illustrated in Family Tree 1: Five Weddings at p. 4). Each wedding forms part of the context for the marriage of Edward and Eleanor, and each has relevance to Eleanor's later life and interests.

In political terms, the first marriage is key. It is possibly the most famous of all medieval marriages: that of Henry, Count of Anjou, the future King of England and Duke of Normandy, and the greatest heiress of her generation, Eleanor, Duchess of Aquitaine and Countess of Poitou in her own right. It is key in one sense because it provides the blood link which existed between Eleanor and Edward – both were direct descendants of this marriage. But in political terms this marriage created the situation in which an Anglo-Castilian alliance made sense. It is therefore actually an understatement to say that the course of events leading to the marriage of Eleanor and Edward can be traced back to this event. In fact it is vitally necessary to go back to this date to put the later marriage into any form of context.

The Anjou–Aquitaine marriage took place a little over a century before that of Eleanor and Edward, on Whit Sunday, 18 May 1152. It was effectively an elopement, coming only eight weeks after the annulment of Eleanor's marriage to King Louis VII of France. It had two other hallmarks of an elopement: it was celebrated in a somewhat perfunctory style, the chroniclers disapprovingly describing it as having taken place without the ceremony that befitted their rank; and it took place without the consent, which should have been obtained, of the parties' mutual overlord – the same King Louis.

The reason no consent was sought and the marriage was rushed on was not raw romance; the protagonists had probably only met once before the wedding, albeit that some commentators considered that Henry made a noticeably good impression on the queen. It was because it changed the balance of power in Europe at a stroke. What is particularly ironic, given that the reasoning behind the annulment was Eleanor's failure to provide Louis with an heir, was that the notable fruitfulness of the marriage ensured that it continued to do so for future generations.[2]

Two major political effects were created. The first was in making the English power block the primary cause for concern for French monarchs for generations to come. The marriage made the succession of Henry to the throne of England virtually a certainty and therefore linked (either at the time or for the future) England, Normandy and the Norman possessions in northern France, Anjou, Poitou and Gascony. Prior to the marriage England's status had fallen low, with the civil wars that had followed in the wake of the death of Henry I without a direct male heir. This marriage ensured that England ceased to be perceived as of little concern; instead it became a major power. What is more, the English Plantagenet power block was, in terms of territory, far greater than that of France, and it hampered the French king's traditional means of maintaining power by fostering dissension between his powerful vassals. From this moment on it would therefore be imperative for French kings to look at all times to means of destabilising the Plantagenet empire and chipping pieces of territory or influence away from it as they could.

The second political effect was one within the Plantagenet empire itself, and it reflected the disadvantages that came with this massive empire. Henry's lands stretched from the north of England, west to Ireland and then south to the middle of France. Eleanor's lands then stretched from the middle of France to the Spanish border. It followed that there were many neighbouring interests involved in such an empire, all of

whom would have their own axes to grind – and most of whom would
be inclined to take advantage of any weaknesses or lengthy absences.
Although Henry moved fast – often faster than his enemies anticipated –
the sheer distances involved, as well as the economics of warfare, meant
that the iron fist alone could not provide an adequate safeguard. A
journey to Gascony would take weeks – and longer if the weather in the
Channel was unfavourable. Hence, as regards the southern reaches of the
empire, the Plantagenet approach was to maintain the position as much
as possible by alliances; principally by marriage alliances. Each generation
of Plantagenet princes which followed Henry's marriage to Eleanor
would duly make a marriage alliance with a power near to the borders
of Gascony. Edward's match with Eleanor was simply the latest example
of the policy. Thus Richard I had married Berengaria of Navarre, John
married Isabelle of Angoulême and Henry III Eleanor of Provence.[3]

The first of these southern marriage alliances, and one of the most
significant politically, was the second marriage, which forms the
background to Eleanor of Castile's story. This was the marriage of
Eleanor of Aquitaine's daughter and namesake Eleanor of England to
Alfonso VIII of Castile. The idea of this marriage was to bring Castile,
the dominant power in the Iberian peninsula, into harmony with the
Angevin interests and avoid the need for too much attention to the
southern border, since Henry had much with which to concern himself
elsewhere. Conceptually the plan was sound, and on one level at least
the alliance was a great success. This was the personal level: the marriage
was famously harmonious, with Eleanor actively ruling alongside her
husband, who actually specified in his will that she was to rule alongside
their son in the event of his own death. In the event, Eleanor of England
died only twenty-eight days after Alfonso in 1214, and was buried at
his side. Their graves were and still are in the Abbey de Las Huelgas, in
Burgos, where, just over forty years later, Edward and Eleanor of Castile
were to renew the alliance between England and Castile.[4]

On a political level, however, the marriage may be said to have been
less idyllic. This is because the most important single issue, which later
drove the marriage of Eleanor of Castile and Edward I, is the Castilian
claim to Gascony which arose from the earlier Anglo-Castilian marriage.
While the marriage of Eleanor of England and Alfonso was performed
to secure the Gascon frontier, Alfonso was too canny a politician and
too ambitious a monarch not to capitalise on his advantages. During the
lifetime of Eleanor of Aquitaine he held his fire. Her control over her own
patrimony was always significant, and her relationship with her daughter
and son-in-law was apparently very good – she stayed with them for a
long visit in 1201 and helped arrange the marriages of their daughters.
But following her death in 1204 King John of England was troubled
elsewhere by French advances on Anjou and Normandy, and this was too

good an opportunity to miss. Alfonso launched an invasion of Gascony, citing a claim to Gascony which derived from Eleanor's dowry – the validity of which claim is still debated.[5]

However valid or tenuous the claim, the invasion was a fact and although it was ultimately abandoned, this was not formally done until 1208; in the intervening four years Alfonso had at times actually held most of Gascony except Bayonne and Bordeaux and had issued charters styling himself 'Lord of Gascony'. As a result the claim raised by Alfonso was very much in play between the two countries and was not formally relinquished until Eleanor of Castile's marriage nearly fifty years later. As the English Crown progressively lost the vast bulk of its French lands under John and failed to regain them under the decidedly un-martial Henry III, the importance to England of the remaining territory, Gascony, increased – and so did the question as to the English throne's title in the area.[6]

The marriage of Eleanor of England and Alfonso is also important in the influence which the achievements of their reign had over Alfonso's effective successor, Eleanor's father, Ferdinand III. Those achievements therefore form the background to the situation and culture in which Eleanor was brought up, which is considered further in the next chapter. Principal among these were three factors: the resumption of the fight against the Muslim invaders (the Almohads), the centralisation of Spanish power in Castile and a cultural and intellectual renaissance.

So far as the fight against the Islamic invaders was concerned, most of the Iberian peninsula had fallen under Islamic control in the ninth and tenth centuries and a powerful and sophisticated caliphate had developed around the town of Cordoba. The process of winning back the land (which the Muslims had called Al-Andalus and which gradually became called Andalucia by the Spanish peoples) had begun then, and was to continue until 1492, when Isabella of Castile and Ferdinand of Aragon conquered Granada, the last outpost of the Muslim invaders. In Al-Andalus, Iberian attempts at reconquest were initially held in check by Yusuf ibn Tashfin of the Almoravids and later by the Almohads; both Berber dynasties originally based in North Africa.

But toward the end of the century the Iberian nations had fought back against the invaders, to the extent that the peninsula was now roughly divided into the Almohads in the south and west with the Iberian nations of Portugal, León and Castile in the north (reading from west to east) and Aragon in the north-east. Until the middle of the twelfth century León and Castile had been one kingdom, with León the dominant element, but the countries split after the death of Alfonso VII, with much resultant feuding. It was Alfonso VIII who began the process which was to push the Almohads back and who also put Castile in pole position as the dominant country in the peninsula.

The process was not entirely a smooth one: Alfonso suffered a great defeat with his own army in 1195 at Al-Arcos, when he attempted a gallant but hopeless attack against a numerically vastly superior force. Reputedly the foundation of Las Huelgas abbey, where Eleanor and Edward were to marry, can be traced back to the Al-Arcos defeat; according to some accounts, Eleanor of England persuaded Alfonso to found the new monastery to make up for any default in religious duty which might have accounted for the result of the battle. In fact, while it seems likely that she was indeed the driving force behind the foundation of the abbey and its constitution as a female institution, the date of foundation of the abbey, 1187, suggests that the link to Al-Arcos is a mere romantic story. More practically, after the defeat Alfonso ensured that the fight against the Almohads received support from the papacy, who, crucially, designated the work of reconquest a Crusade. With this support, Alfonso was then able to form a coalition of his neighbouring Christian princes: Sancho VII ('the Strong') of Navarre, Alfonso II of Portugal and Peter II of Aragon. It was this coalition, assisted by miscellaneous foreign Crusaders, which Alfonso led to victory in the Battle of Las Navas de Tolosa in 1212.[7]

That battle was a bloody and decisive encounter. After some disagreements among the members of the Christian coalition, Alfonso managed to cross the mountain range that defended the Almohad camp, sneaking through the Despeñaperros Pass – guided by a shepherd boy, according to Spanish folklore. Some accounts suggest that the Christian coalition caught the Moorish army completely by surprise, but more reliable ones indicate that it was a much closer-run thing. Differing accounts predictably give credit to different members of the coalition for the ultimate success of the battle, with at least some offering that accolade to Alfonso for a critical charge at the head of his reserves. But in any event the battle was a complete victory for the coalition, with the Almohads suffering immense casualties: figures between 70,000 and 200,000 were reported at the time. The battle was a victory of such significance that in Spanish history Alfonso VIII, as well as being called 'the Noble', is described as 'El de Las Navas' (He of Las Navas). It is credited as marking the effective end of the power of the Almohads in the Iberian peninsula. But, as important, it put the central part of the peninsula into Castile's control, thereby creating a platform for Spanish union.[8]

Alfonso VIII was also the first of the martial kings of Castile to foster the idea of Castile as a centre of culture and learning. He was the founder in 1208–9 of the first Spanish university, the *studium generale* of Palencia, where Italian and French teachers taught theology, canon law and the arts. While this institution did not survive him, it is hugely significant to the wider world of learning in that during in its existence it provided the training ground for St Dominic, who studied there for ten years. Palencia can thus claim credit for the origin of the Dominican Order, which flourished in Spain from shortly after its inception and became very influential at the Castilian court as well as overseas – with Eleanor of Castile later being one of its greatest patrons in England.

Culturally in this period the court was also considerably influenced by Eleanor of England, who, like her sisters, encouraged the poets and troubadours familiar to Eleanor of Aquitaine's Poitevin culture, with the Castilian court becoming a recognised haven for such artists. In all probability she was also involved in fostering some knowledge of Arthurian literature. A copy of Geoffrey of Monmouth's *Historia Regum Britanniae* is likely to have accompanied her to Castile on her marriage and there was certainly an Occitan Arthurian romance, *Jaufré*, written at the contemporary court of Alfonso II of Aragon. The Arthurian tradition seems to have continued into Eleanor of Castile's own generation; her eldest brother, Alfonso X, refers to Arthur, Merlin and Tristan in his own Galician-Portuguese poems, indicating a considerable familiarity with Arthurian romances. Eleanor of England also introduced to Castile the veneration of her family's own martyr St Thomas Becket, endowing an altar in his memory at the cathedral of Toledo.[9]

Alfonso's reign also saw a move towards cohesion in the states in the peninsula. Politically and militarily the Kingdom of León was very much the odd man out, while Castile drew closer to Aragon, particularly with the military alliance which resulted in the victory at Navas de Tolosa. However, dynastically, closer union with León was brought about by marriage ties, specifically the third of the five weddings in this chapter. As we shall see below, Alfonso's eldest daughter, Berengaria, reluctantly married Alfonso IX of León and thus became both the means of uniting the Castilian and Leónese thrones and the grandmother of Eleanor of Castile. Two other daughters, Urraca and Leonor, married the heirs to the kings of Portugal and Aragon. Finally, further strengthening the prestige of Castile over that of the other Iberian nations, Alfonso and Eleanor's most famous daughter, Blanche, married Louis VIII of France. She became the mother of St Louis (Louis IX) of France and an iconic regent of that nation in his troubled minority and later in his absence on Crusade. Some historians consider that she deserves to be counted as a monarch of France in her own right.[10]

The third wedding – the marriage of Berengaria of Castile and Alfonso of León – is significant in Eleanor's story for three reasons. First, it shows the circumstances which moulded Eleanor's remarkable father. Secondly, it shows the woman who was undoubtedly held up to young Eleanor as her role model: Berengaria 'the Great'. And thirdly, it sheds light on Castilian princesses' expectations as regards property.

The marriage was not a great success and ended in divorce. Alfonso IX, a Leónese nationalist, was deeply hostile to any link with Castile; indeed, he had even allied with the Almohads, and plundered the border fortresses of Castile after Alfonso VIII's defeat at Al-Arcos. He was only brought to contemplate the marriage under heavy pressure from the papacy, which in 1196 excommunicated him and placed his entire kingdom under papal interdiction, with indulgences being offered to any Leónese citizens who took up arms against him. This sanction was prompted by two defaults: his raids on the righteous Castile, and his incestuous marriage. The marriage, which Alfonso had refused to abandon even after it was annulled by the Pope, was to his first cousin Teresa of Portugal and had been entered into in furtherance of his anti-Castile stance. It resulted in two daughters and a son.[11]

Nor was Berengaria keen on the match, but she was persuaded by Eleanor of England that it was her duty as the only realistic means of securing peace – or at least its semblance – in the form of peaceful borders. This was to be achieved via the requirement for Alfonso of León to tender strategic border forts as part of Berengaria's dower. It is important to note that, at marriage, Castilian and Leónese queens and noblewomen traditionally received a dower or *arras* from their husband's property which was assigned to them for life. This approach, derived from the Visigothic legal tradition, is a very different one to that which operated in England at this point. In England the concept of dowry, or gift from bride's family to that of the groom at the time of the marriage, was certainly well known, if not ubiquitous; and any dower, or provision for the wife by the husband's family, was suspensory and did not come into effect until after the husband's death. In Castile, by way of contrast, dowry was rare, and dower operated from the time of marriage. Thus in receiving these properties as dower, Berengaria would actually effectively own them and have power over them at once, providing Castile with the security it sought.[12]

The marriage, which took place in 1197, resulted in five surviving children: two boys and three girls, the eldest son being Eleanor's father, Ferdinand, later Ferdinand III of Castile and León. While with the benefit of hindsight the match was therefore successful, it was at the time more or less disastrous. In the first place, this marriage to Berengaria was also within the forbidden degrees of consanguinity and again performed without a dispensation, which was seen as contumelious behaviour by the papacy. So Alfonso of León, instead of being reconciled with the papacy, was placed under a personal interdict for the rest of his life.

Even more seriously, the absence of a dispensation meant that the marriage was annulled by the Pope, leaving no clearly legitimate heir to the throne. This decision was campaigned against by joint Castilian–Leónese delegations for some time, but the Pope was immoveable, despite his predisposition towards Castile for its attempts against the Almohads. Berengaria initially stayed with Alfonso in defiance of the Pope, perhaps because she herself was not initially excommunicated, being somewhat laughably regarded by the papacy as a mere pawn in the hands of her menfolk. However, at some point her personal involvement became clear and she too was excommunicated. Most seriously, the Pope expressly declared that any children she would bear to Alfonso would be illegitimate and would have no right to inherit anything of their father's. So, in late 1203, Berengaria left Alfonso and returned to Castile – pregnant with her last child by him. As soon as Berengaria had left, Alfonso promptly returned to his first wife and the two countries were up in arms against each other again within months. In 1212, Alfonso of León still refused to join Castile against the Almohads unless Berengaria's dower lands, still being controlled by her, were first restored. This was not done and the Leónese army therefore missed out on the glory of Las Navas de Tolosa.[13]

So Eleanor's father, Ferdinand, should never have been King of Castile or León at all. So far as Castile was concerned there was at least one heir ahead of him throughout his childhood. As for León, not only had he been declared illegitimate and unable to inherit by the Pope, but until 1214 he had an older brother by his father's first marriage; and his own father was adamant that he should not inherit. However, owing to three quirks of fate, by the time he was eighteen Ferdinand was, despite the questions over his legitimacy, the acknowledged King of Castile and also the obvious heir to León. The first quirk of fate came in 1211 when Fernando, the eldest son of Alfonso VIII and Eleanor of England, died on campaign just before Las Navas de Tolosa – with the result that the crown passed on Alfonso VIII's death in 1214 to Berengaria's ten-year-old brother Henry I of Castile. Then, in the summer of 1241, Ferdinand's older half-brother Fernando of León died. Thirdly, Henry of Castile then died prematurely in 1217, bizarrely enough from a tile falling on his head, shortly before he was due to marry his cousin Sancha of León.[14]

In Castile the direct heir was, of course, Berengaria, not Ferdinand. She had been a prominent figure in Castile since the death of her parents, leading the mourning for her father when her mother was unable to do so by reason of her own grief, and acting as the guardian of the young king despite strong opposition from the prominent de Lara family. But on Henry's death Berengaria formally renounced her rights of inheritance in her son's favour and Ferdinand became king. However, Berengaria, notionally a nun at Las Huelgas since 1204, did not retire from the scene. Far from it; she advised and assisted Ferdinand throughout his reign until her death, standing in for him in his absences on campaign, and acting as an effective quartermaster in assembling men and materiel for his needs, particularly in relation to the campaign for Cordoba. Indeed, she was technically co-ruler with him, issuing decrees in her own name. Although less celebrated than her sister Blanche, she was in effect one of the most powerful women in Europe.[15]

Thus, in 1219, it was on his mother's advice that Ferdinand contracted his first marriage with Beatriz (or Elizabeth) of Hohenstaufen, the possessor of one of the most fabulous pedigrees in Europe, being a granddaughter of Emperor Frederick II and also of the Byzantine Emperor. The reasoning behind this match is a little mysterious and has been much debated. One strong possibility is that the masterful Berengaria had in mind the fact that Beatriz would bid fair to be a submissive wife – her mother, Irene Angelina, was famously described as 'the rose without a thorn, the dove without gall'. The couple went on to have ten children, including Eleanor's half-brother, the future Alfonso X 'el Sabio', a name variously translated as 'the Wise' and 'the Learned'. The latter, as will become apparent, is the more accurate designation.[16]

Meanwhile, the relationship with León remained fractious. Alfonso IX wanted to avoid the union of the two countries that would follow if Ferdinand inherited. Therefore in 1224 he invited the famous warrior John of Brienne to marry his daughter Sancha and inherit the Leónese throne. Brienne was a French aristocrat from a relatively well-connected but not overly wealthy family. He had gained celebrity status similar to that accorded to the great English knight William Marshal by virtue of his prowess in tournaments and in actual war, assisted to some extent by his personal charms. His impressive stature is well attested – he was said to tower above other men and to have the physique of Hercules – and to this he apparently added considerable good looks. This winning combination had made him an obvious candidate when King Philip of France was asked to nominate a husband for the young Queen Marie of Jerusalem, and later attracted the young Princess Rita of Armenia, who anticipated having to fight her half-sister for her crown. To add still further to his attractions he had, since the death of his second wife, distinguished himself on Crusade. He would therefore have made a truly formidable candidate to oppose Ferdinand. However, Berengaria was not so easily defeated. She intercepted John on his way to León and, with support from her sister Blanche, who could promise great benefits in terms of French goodwill for his whole family, persuaded him that the better course was to marry her daughter Berengaria instead, thereby making him an ally, rather than a threat. This was effectively Alfonso's final throw; although he willed León to the still unmarried Sancha on his death in 1230, he knew that his dream of an independent León was over.[17]

After the very early years of his reign, when some domestic disaffection had to be overcome following Henry's turbulent minority, Ferdinand III remained on campaign almost non-stop throughout his first marriage and acted in partnership with his father Alfonso, despite the continuing issue about the future of León. This partnership led to key victories in the south at Cáceres in 1227 and Mérida and Badajoz in 1230, opening the road for a future reconquest of Seville. However, the victory at Badajoz was Alfonso's last. He died in September 1230, doubtless aware that, despite his best attempts, Ferdinand would assume the leadership of the reconquest on behalf of both Castile and León.

And indeed, despite some continued resistance to the idea of a united León and Castile, Sancha was easily set aside by Berengaria and Ferdinand following Alfonso's death. Berengaria negotiated a treaty, known as the 'Treaty of the Mothers', with Teresa of Portugal whereby Teresa's daughters recognised Ferdinand's rights as King of León in exchange for a very comfortable allowance. Ferdinand then returned to campaigning with huge success, capturing the town of Úbeda in 1233 and keeping up the pressure against the Almohads on a broad front. Finally, in 1236, he took Cordoba itself.[18]

Meanwhile, however, Queen Beatriz had died in late 1235. Her death brings us to the final marriage in our chain, which was Ferdinand's second marriage, in August 1237, to Eleanor's mother, Jeanne of Dammartin, later Countess of Ponthieu.

The match seems highly implausible – Ferdinand was a great and successful king, whose first wife had been of the highest imperial descent, whereas Jeanne of Dammartin was only the heiress to a small county in north-eastern France, which was of no interest to the Kingdom of Castile. However, under the surface there were good dynastic, political and personal reasons to consider the marriage suitable.

Dynastically, for example, Jeanne was actually of royal descent – through her maternal grandmother she carried the bloodlines of the royal houses of both Castile and France. That grandmother was the notorious Alys of France, the daughter of Louis VII and Constance of Castile, who had been the cause of one of the longest-running international incidents of the late twelfth century. In 1169 it had been agreed between her father and King Henry II of England that Alys should be betrothed to Henry's son Richard (later to find immortality as 'the Lionheart'). Aged just nine, she was therefore sent to England to be raised at court. Alys grew up, but no marriage took place and it was widely reported that her father-in-law elect Henry had taken her as his mistress – and even that she had borne him a child. While the reports, usually doubted by modern historians, may have been fuelled by political considerations, the failure to proceed with the marriage became an international scandal. Nonetheless she remained unmarried and in Henry's care until his death in July 1189. Her fiancé, Richard, had now succeeded to the throne and finally terminated their engagement in Messina in March 1191, according to some accounts on the grounds that she had borne a child by his father. Alys was probably entirely innocent, but her reputation was ruined – her own immortality is in Churchill's much-quoted summary that 'except for her looks, the tales were none too good'.[19]

The unfortunate Alys was finally sent back to France, aged thirty-five, in 1195 and was speedily disposed of by her brother. On 20 August of that same year he married her to the teenaged William III Talvas, Count of Ponthieu, who was doubtless brought to agree to the match in large part on account of the dowry she brought – the county of Vexin. This county had long been an issue between France and the Plantagenets, since the two counties of Ponthieu and Vexin form a useful strategic block. Philip therefore probably had it in mind that, since Alys was eighteen years older than her husband, the marriage would be childless and Philip would thus gain control of Ponthieu, a small but strategically important county. If he did, the plan misfired. Alys and William had one child, a daughter named Marie, born sometime before 1199.[20]

The marriage of Marie, half-royal and heiress to two strategically important counties, was arranged while she was still young, in 1208. It forms the fourth marriage in our chain because it would provide the political impetus for the marriage between Eleanor's parents. The groom was the thirty-year-old Simon of Dammartin. His claim to fame and to such a distinguished marriage rested entirely on the fact that he was the younger brother of a remarkable man called Renaud of Dammartin, who likely figured as a tragic hero of romance in tales told to Eleanor as a child.

Up until 1190, the family of Dammartin had a proud heritage but held only a fairly small county near Paris. Their daughters married other members of the minor northern French nobility – de Tries, de Saint-Omers, de Gourneys and (significantly for our story) de Fiennes. But in that year the family began a rapid ascent to influence and power by virtue of Renaud of Dammartin's exercise of one of the less distinguished traditions of the era – the abduction and forced marriage of an heiress. The heiress in question was one Ida of Boulogne, the sole surviving granddaughter of King Stephen and Matilda of Boulogne and hence the heiress to both the Norman county of Mortain and the county of Boulogne. Ida was a massive matrimonial prize – and also chronically unlucky in the matter of husbands. By 1186, when she was twenty-six, she had already lost three husbands. It appears that she thereafter had plans to marry her own choice: Arnold II of Guines. However, at this point Renaud of Dammartin intervened. He sought Ida openly, but when her uncle refused to consent to the match, the intrepid Renaud simply abducted Ida and carried her off to Lorraine. Ida seems to have been reconciled to the match, to the extent of reportedly colluding in Renaud's later imprisonment of Arnold of Guines. They had one child, who in due course became Queen of Portugal.

Ida's apparent readiness to acquiesce in her abduction may be explained by the fact that Renaud was far from being a simple adventurer. He is described variously by contemporaries in superlatives and four-letter words. He was 'cultivated, ambitious and versatile' and, among other things, a noted patron of the arts. More to the point, so far as material advancement goes, he appears to have been one of the most able military men of his generation. He campaigned successfully with Richard the Lionheart against Philip of France in the late 1190s but defected to Philip shortly after Richard's death. He was then apparently instrumental in the vital French propaganda victory in 1203 – the taking of Richard's beloved and supposedly impregnable Chateau Gaillard.

The link between Renaud of Dammartin and this attack is strongly suggested by the fact that, very shortly thereafter, Philip created him Count of Mortain, Varenne and Aumale. Nor was this the end of Philip's gratitude, for he then appears to have sided with Renaud when he contrived to fall out with his neighbour in the Pas-de-Calais – Alys's husband, William Talvas. Through Philip's influence and Renaud's high standing with him a reconciliation was brokered, the key point of which was the marriage of Simon, Renaud's nearly landless younger brother, and William Talvas' heiress, Marie. The land issues which had brought the row into being were compromised and Renaud agreed to give Simon some of his Norman lands and possibly also his own county of Aumale. The deal was sealed by the marriage, which took place in 1209.[21]

But within ten years Renaud, at the best of times difficult to live with, had overreached himself and brought ruin not only on himself but also for a time on the county of Ponthieu. By 1212 it was clear that he would gain no further promotion from Philip; he therefore sought refuge with his cousin, the Count of Bar, and threw in his lot with King John, who promised him further counties in the Pas-de-Calais–Somme area, some of which he earmarked for Simon. The acquisition of these counties, together with the future occupation of Ponthieu, would have given Renaud control over virtually the whole of the strategically vital Pas-de-Calais area and made him one of the most important men in France and England.[22]

Accordingly it was on John's side that Renaud, Simon and their de Fiennes in-laws fought at the epochal Battle of Bouvines in 1214, while Simon's father-in-law, William Talvas, remained loyal to the throne of France. Renaud fought brilliantly, repelling charge after charge, but eventually his formation was wiped out by sheer force of numbers. Simon escaped the field of battle, but Renaud was taken prisoner in the melee. He and Comte Ferrand of Flanders, who had defected with him to support John, were held in the castle of Goulet for thirteen years; according to some picturesque reports, Renaud was chained to the wall by a chain half a metre long for all this time. It is then said that, on the release of Ferrand in 1227, Renaud was told that he would never be released, upon hearing which he committed suicide, choosing the anniversary of Ida's death for the occasion.[23]

Meanwhile, Simon escaped to England, where he lived for some time without his wife, who remained with her father in Ponthieu. Inevitably, in the light of the betrayal by Renaud, his and Simon's assets and titles in France were confiscated by King Philip. Thus at the death in 1221 of William Talvas, although Marie was his heiress, the title of Count of Ponthieu was confiscated to France. Philip had guardians appointed for Marie, who lived at Abbeville on a small pension from the king. However, the separation from her husband in this period was perhaps not as absolute as the records might suggest. Her eldest daughter, Jeanne, Eleanor's mother, was apparently born in around 1220, six years after Bouvines, and three other daughters followed – at least one of them being of marriageable age in 1236 and therefore inferentially born in the early 1220s. It would seem therefore that one or the other of the couple managed to sneak across the Channel for occasional conjugal visits.

Reconciliation with the French Crown followed in stages. First, in 1225, Marie concluded a treaty at Chinon by which she acknowledged the Crown's right to take her lands and in return she was restored to her father's lands. Simon, however, remained *persona non grata* until five years later when a second treaty, concluded at St Germain en Laye, finally allowed him to return from England and reconciled him to the French Crown. But the treaty had teeth. Not only did he have to endorse the seizure of his lands, but critically he also agreed not to marry either Jeanne or her next sister to any enemy of the king or kingdom. Thereafter Simon and Marie held Ponthieu jointly until his death in 1239, and Marie held it alone until her own death in 1251.[24]

By 1233, Jeanne was of marriageable age. She was a reputed beauty – she was later described by Roderigo Ximines de Rada, the Archbishop of Toledo, as 'a princess who excelled as much in modesty as beauty ... enriched with all sorts of good qualities'. She was also the heiress to a county, which was vital if the English Crown was going to maintain any form of challenge to the French in Normandy. Finally, her family, which had suffered considerably in the service of King John, might well be seen as having a claim on the English monarchy for some considerable benefit. For one or more of these reasons, in 1233 Henry III began to negotiate a marriage with Jeanne. These negotiations progressed to the stage that, on 8 April 1235, Henry and Jeanne actually pledged themselves to each other by proxy by the *verba de praesenti*, an exchange of vows couched in the present tense, which was widely taken as being a binding marriage. The marriage between Henry and Jeanne was therefore seen as a done deal, subject only to obtaining a dispensation from the Pope allowing people related within the prohibited degrees to marry. The intention appears to have been for the formal marriage to take place quickly – possibly as soon as 27 May 1235 – and a letter was promptly sent to the Pope seeking a speedy dispensation.[25]

Of course we know that this marriage did not ultimately take place; by 22 June Henry was instead suggesting to the Count of Savoy a marriage with Eleanor, daughter of the Count of Provence; and by October this suggestion had materialised into a definite marriage contract. In the end Henry married Eleanor of Provence and became father of Edward I, while Jeanne married Ferdinand III and became Eleanor's mother. What prevented the original plan from coming to fruition was some constructive collusion on the parts of the formidable sisters Blanche of Castile, Dowager Queen of France, and Berengaria of Castile, Dowager Queen of León.

That collusion was necessitated by Blanche of Castile's political agenda. For Blanche, who had ruled a somewhat restive France throughout her son's minority, this proposed marriage between Henry and Jeanne created a real problem. The principal attraction of the marriage for Henry was the strategic importance of Ponthieu, which would give England a key foothold in north-east France – as the Battle of Crécy en Ponthieu was later to prove. This would be a loss of prestige for the Crown which would encourage disloyalty as the new king, Louis IX, found his feet. Moreover the history of the Dammartin family would have indicated to Blanche that trouble might well be expected from them. Blanche was therefore determined that this marriage should not take place and invoked the term in the reconciliation between the French Crown and the Dammartin family. Although the marriage to Henry arguably did not fall foul of this provision, the threat of invoking this penalty was enough to ensure that the marriage did not proceed.[26]

But having deprived Jeanne of a splendid marriage, with a king as a husband, Blanche was in honour bound to find a very good alternative. It was here that what might be termed Berengaria's personal problem offered a solution to Blanche's political one. Berengaria's problem was relatively simple: Ferdinand III was now widowed. There might have seemed no pressing need for him to remarry since he had an extensive and relatively healthy family – including seven living sons – by his first wife, and there can be no doubt that his mother was more than capable of arranging for the upbringing of these children. However, she was concerned lest he contract liaisons which were unbecoming to his dignity. Whether this was a real concern can never be known, but certainly the number of children produced by his two marriages (he was to add a further five by his second marriage to his tally of ten children from his first marriage) suggests a partiality for feminine company. In addition, Berengaria will have been aware that if Ferdinand resembled his father at all, there might well be a tendency to collect mistresses: Alfonso had acquired at least thirteen illegitimate children during the course of his two marriages.[27]

A marriage between Jeanne and Ferdinand was therefore ideal for both sisters' purposes – it was of sufficiently high status to placate the Ponthevins but moved Ponthieu away from English alliance. It also kept the heir to Ponthieu under Blanche's control, albeit at one remove, and it strengthened the links of blood between the Castilian and French crowns.

Meanwhile, from Berengaria's point of view there was that Castilian blood link. She was banking a favour with France, and if Ferdinand had a keen eye for feminine charms, a young wife of great beauty was just what was required.

Seventeen-year-old Jeanne was therefore betrothed to King Ferdinand in the summer of 1237 and married in October of the same year. The marriage seems to have been a success – Ferdinand was very fond of his new wife, taking her with him on campaign, and giving her extensive gifts of property. In dynastic terms, too, the marriage was productive; the couple had four sons and one daughter. The eldest child was Infante Ferdinand, later Count of Aumale, who was born in 1239 and died in around 1265. Their second child was Eleanor.[28]

2

Eleanor's Early Years

Nearly thirteen years of Eleanor's life passed before her wedding. According to St Ignatius' view of education, her nature was formed long before she stepped onto the English stage. And yet before the date of her marriage with Edward we know nothing for certain about Eleanor. There is no record of her date of birth. There are no stories of her childhood. There are no letters by her or about her. She is named by no contemporaneous chronicler. About the only thing of which we can be sure is that she was at her father's deathbed in 1252. The process of unearthing her childhood is therefore by no means straightforward.

Mercifully, however, Eleanor grew up in a country which was full of activity and which placed a premium on written record. From these records we can piece together three different perspectives on Eleanor's childhood, each of which will show powerful influences which acted upon her and inevitably affected who she was. The first view we can get is the political record; it is possible to trace in outline the major events which punctuated her childhood and which provided the major talking points of those years. As Eleanor's family was at the heart of these events, this shows us the circumstances in which she grew up, the major themes which occupied those around her – and the figure which dominated her childhood.

The other two perspectives are essentially cultural. One is broadly so, considering the administrative work which her father, King Ferdinand, was doing, in which his model of kingship and the multicultural aspects of the Iberian peninsula which made Castile such a different place to England, had considerable influence. The third is more intimate: to try to conjure up some kind of picture of the day-to-day life of a princess of thirteenth-century Castile. This can be done predominantly by considering the facts which we do know about her family and the culture of the Castilian court.

The first perspective must start with Eleanor's own birth. There is no record of the date, simply because it was not a great event in Castile.

Ferdinand already had plenty of children, and to the commentators one more was neither here nor there.

Eleanor's birthdate has traditionally been given as 1244 or even 1246, thus suggesting that she was under ten years of age when married. There are still modern accounts which follow this orthodoxy, but it can now be convincingly rebutted by three pieces of solid evidence which show that Eleanor was in fact born in late 1241 and that she was thus just under thirteen years old at the time of her marriage.

The first piece of evidence as to the date of her birth is the fact that, in 1254, after their marriage, not only did Eleanor accompany Edward to Gascony, but they also set up their own household for about a year, rather than joining his parents in returning to England. It was, of course, absolutely normal practice for underage brides to be handed over to their future families, but the expectation was that they would then be educated and trained in the home of their new parents, rather than commencing married life. Children had to be raised and educated to fill their station in life, and even as they reached canonically marriageable age it appears to have been well appreciated that the risks of early childbirth were to be avoided if possible. Therefore the usual age at which a princess or high-status bride would be expected to enter onto married life was not earlier than fourteen. So to find Eleanor and Edward despatched onto married life with her aged only ten would be almost unheard of.

It would be completely unthinkable given that the queen to whom Eleanor was entrusted was Eleanor of Provence. Edward's mother has received (in part justifiably) a fairly hard press over the years. However, one positive thing which is quite clear about her is that she was a very caring and dutiful mother, very much beyond the norms of the day. She had herself the unhappy experience of being married at a very young age, having been twelve years old when she was married to Henry III and having suffered from the pressures put on her to produce an heir. There is evidence that she had formed the view that even twelve was a young age for marriage. Therefore, had Eleanor been as young as ten, there is simply no way that she would have been left alone in Gascony for the first year of her marriage.[1]

The second piece of evidence is an impeccable, near-contemporary record of the birth of a daughter Eleanor to Ferdinand and Jeanne at an earlier date than 1244. Rodrigo of Toledo, who was chancellor of Castile and Ferdinand's principal adviser for many years, writes in March 1243 in his great work *De Rebus Hispaniae* that Ferdinand and Jeanne had three children: Ferdinand, Eleanor and Louis. The fact that Eleanor is named second in this list raises a strong inference that she was indeed the second child of the marriage – particularly as it was frequently the case that sons be listed before daughters. The inference that she was the middle child chronologically also appears to be supported by external evidence: there is a three-and-a-half-year gap between the two sons first appearing as witnesses to Castilian royal charters. This rite of passage effectively marked the princes' emergence into political society and was likely to have been undertaken at more or less the same age. So the fact that Ferdinand first appears in May 1252 and Louis in October 1255 indicates that there was a gap of more than three years in age between them.

The third and perhaps most conclusive piece of evidence for the approximate date of Eleanor's birth is that at her memorial service in 1291 there was a procession of forty-nine bearers with candles. This being a slightly unusual number, it gives rise to a strong inference that it related to her age at death.[2]

It is possible to narrow the dates slightly more by considering these last two pieces of evidence together. The evidence of the candles strongly suggests an age at her death of forty-nine and hence of birth in 1241. However, if her age at death on 28 November 1290 was in fact forty-nine this would indicate that Eleanor must have been born before 28 November 1241. Counting back from this date would suggest that Eleanor would have been conceived by about the first week in March 1241. The Castilian evidence shows that it is unlikely that Ferdinand and Jeanne were cohabiting for a period of thirteen months prior to nearly the end of February 1241; he is recorded by the reliable *Primera Cronica General* (which he part authored) as being resident in Cordoba, assisting the Christian population of that city against the Moors of Seville, and being 'reunited' with Jeanne on his return to the north. A baby conceived at this period would be (premature births aside) born in mid- or late November 1241. One can therefore tentatively give Eleanor's birthdate as somewhere from mid- to late November 1241.

This date also fits in well with what we know about the birth of Louis, whose appearance in the charters in late 1255 suggests a birthdate not later than late 1242, while he is referred to by Roderigo of Toledo as being very young (*parvulus*) in early 1243.[3]

As for pinning down an actual day, there is no way of doing this for certain. In the late thirteenth century more mind was paid to the anniversaries of people's deaths, when memorial services were held, than the anniversaries of their birth. There is therefore no record of birthday celebrations to point the way. The only birthday which appears to rate a mention is 'Domine Natalis' – the Lord's birthday. However, in my view there is some reason to suggest 23 November. This is because, as we shall see, both Edward and Ferdinand were to deliberately schedule important events for this date.

It therefore appears likely that Eleanor's birth took place at Valladolid, where Ferdinand was staying in the winter of 1241/42. One thing we do know, however: Eleanor was named after her English great-grandmother

Eleanor of England, wife of Alfonso VIII and daughter and namesake of Eleanor of Aquitaine.[4]

The political backdrop to Eleanor's childhood, and particularly her early childhood before the death of her father, was indubitably predominantly the reconquest of Spain. This was an issue which informed all aspects of life in the Iberian peninsula at this time. Ferdinand's progress in the 1220s and 1230s has already been outlined. Following Eleanor's birth, the work of the reconquest still continued apace.

The immediate target in Eleanor's first years was Murcia, which was taken in 1243 with Alfonso (and likely a good selection of the family) attending for a solemn entry into the city and consecration of the city's mosque as a cathedral. Thereafter Ferdinand visited Palencia and Toledo, dealing with complaints and abuses raised by their citizens, before returning to Burgos in September for the veiling of his only other daughter, Berengaria, as a nun at the abbey of Las Huelgas.

The next year he was back on campaign, leading the attack on the territories round Jaén and besieging Arjona, which fell, along with Mula and Lorca, in the course of the year. During the course of campaigning he broke off to visit Andjar to see Queen Jeanne and escort her to Cordoba, where she lived during the Siege of Jaén, which continued until 1246. In 1245, with the siege still ongoing, Ferdinand took Cartagena. Jaén itself was finally taken in April 1246 and Ferdinand was substantially based there for eight months afterwards, 'ensuring the prosperity and security' of the newly conquered territory.[5]

Meanwhile, the formidable Berengaria died in early November 1246. She was buried alongside her parents, Alfonso VIII and Eleanor of England, and in the sight of her eldest granddaughter at the abbey of Las Huelgas. Eleanor will almost certainly have attended her deathbed and funeral, and while (still being aged under five) her personal memories of her grandmother will have been vague, the honour in which Berengaria continued to be held by the entire royal family will have ensured that she was presented to Eleanor throughout her childhood as a paradigm of what a Castilian princess should be: intelligent, capable, astute, regardless of self in her devotion to her duty and fiercely loyal to her family. For instance, Berengaria is recalled in the *Primera Cronica General* as 'a very wise lady and a great expert and sharp in political affairs and [who] understood the risks of government'.[6]

Once Jaén was settled, the primary focus for Ferdinand and his elder sons, who had by now joined him on campaign, was the conquest of Seville. This occupied the majority of attention throughout 1247, although Guillena and Gerena were taken in 1247 with the support of the Emir of Granada, now a vassal of Castile. Seville was at this time the largest, most populous and best-defended town in Spain, with a ring of defensive fortresses and state-of-the-art twelfth-century walls and moats.

Consequently its conquest was a long and bitter fight. For the defenders there were all the horrors of famine within the city as the siege tightened; accounts describe the defenders eating leather once all food had run out, and emerging with their health utterly shattered. And, lest anyone think that in Ferdinand's family campaigning was a spectator sport, the accounts left by Alfonso X of his own direct involvement are supported by the death, during the fighting for Seville, of Ferdinand's third son, the twenty-three-year-old Fernando.

By the latter months of 1248, however, the end was in sight. On 23 November 1248, terms of capitulation were signed. This was probably deliberately timed to coincide with Alfonso's twenty-seventh birthday, but it is possible that it also coincided with Eleanor's seventh birthday, which must have fallen very close indeed to this date. On 22 December, Ferdinand, carrying a statue of the Virgin Mary, made his formal entry into the city – symbolically and again doubtless designedly, on the feast day of the translation of St Isidore, Seville's patron saint. The entire royal family and Peter, the brother of the King of Portugal, were present for the procession to the mosque. Like the mosque at Cordoba, this was now reconsecrated as a cathedral. This day, marking her father's great triumph and attended by the entirety of her family, will undoubtedly have been one of the high points of Eleanor's childhood.

Following the conquest of Seville Ferdinand made that city his base, superintending the works which he had in hand there and, in essence, attempting to remake this major city as an equally affluent Christian city. This was a considerable administrative process involving legal reforms (to which we shall return), granting houses and lands to suitable settlers and bringing artisans to work there, as well as building bridges with the existing community and the flourishing resident Jewish community there.[7]

At the start of December 1249, Eleanor's eldest brother, Alfonso, was married to Yolande/Violante of Aragon at Valladolid. For future reference the latter name, which seems to suit her temperament better, will be used. This was an event at which Ferdinand was accompanied by Queen Jeanne. It is likely that Eleanor, too, will have been present on this occasion.

The year 1250 marked a return to campaigning; Ferdinand and his troops took swathes of towns near the Guadalquivir and Guadalete rivers. By winter he was starting to plan a North African Crusade, since, with the treaty of truce and co-operation concluded with the Emir of Granada and functioning well, there essentially remained nothing to conquer at home. Ferdinand was again generally in Seville for the years 1248–51, except when dealing with the pacification and security of the towns recently taken. It seems very probable that Queen Jeanne was likewise based there and that between the ages of seven and ten Eleanor, now of an age to be more at court, will likewise have spent the majority of her time there.

However, in the spring of 1252 King Ferdinand became ill with dropsy, which apparently progressed rapidly. The cause of these dropsical symptoms is unknown, but with heart problems evidenced in the Castilian royal family this seems a likely cause. By the end of May Ferdinand was plainly nearing his death and the entire family was called to his deathbed at Seville. Alfonso X left a detailed account of this event, which he says was attended by all Ferdinand's children except Sancho, the nineteen-year-old Archbishop of Toledo, who was unable to attend; possibly because he was still studying at university in Paris. The *Primera Cronica General* actually mentions Eleanor and her brothers by name as being present.[8]

Ferdinand was confessed and then asked to be stripped of the trappings of royalty and to adopt a penitent's clothing. Having done that, he called his queen and children around him. Ferdinand blessed Alfonso first and then each of his other children in order of age, making the sign of the cross over them and making them answer 'Amen' to his blessing. To Alfonso he gave a more detailed charges than to the rest. Three points in his instructions are of particular interest. First, he urged him to stand in place of a father to his siblings and to procure for each an establishment worthy of their birth. Secondly, he exhorted him to hold Queen Jeanne in the same affection and respect as if she were his own mother and give her all honours due to her; a pointed injunction which reflected certain disputes which had already arisen between the two.

He thirdly, and again rather pointedly, gave his charge for the future to Alfonso, saying,

> I leave you all the lands on this side of the sea which the Moors won ... one part of it conquered and one part laid under tribute. If you should manage to hold it all ... then you are as good a king as I; and if you should enlarge it, you are better than I; and if you should lose any of it, you are not as good as I.

Ferdinand died on 30 May 1252. On 1 June his body was transferred from the Alcazar of Seville to the church of Santa Maria, where it was buried two days later beneath the statue of the Virgin Mary which he had carried into the city on his triumphal entry in 1248. On the same day Alfonso was acclaimed as King Alfonso X of Spain and accession celebrations were held in the Alcazar.[9]

The mourning for Ferdinand was widespread and seems to have been very genuine. The successes which he had achieved in the reconquest placed him at the forefront of Spanish warlike kings – indeed, of warlike kings worldwide. His respect for justice and his personal affability made him well respected even by those who had been his enemies, such as the Emir of Granada, who had become his loyal ally. Formally, he was remembered annually with a memorial service. Informally, it appears that his memory was constantly in the minds of his family.

The main events of Eleanor's childhood thus have a predominant theme – war – and a predominant figure – her father. The death of Ferdinand offers a good perspective from which to judge the way in which he would have been seen by his daughter and the influence he would have on her as she grew up. The victories which he won were the fabric of her childhood. They should by no means be understated; they certainly were not by contemporaries or by historians. The achievements of Ferdinand as a campaigner were very significant indeed. He is still regarded as one of the great soldier kings of history, particularly in Spain where his feast day is still observed on the anniversary of his death, and his beatification was at least in part as a Crusader, the reconquest having been given Crusade status.

In practical terms his conquests added enormously to the size and the prestige of Castile; in effect, on his watch Castile expanded from covering a seventh of the peninsula to sprawling across the larger part of it, including gaining a corridor to the Mediterranean at Murcia. As for the national impact of the reconquest which Ferdinand achieved, even the somewhat terse *Primera Cronica General* confirms the sense of national fulfilment in the detail with which it recounts the entry into Seville and the terms in which it lauds the '*sancto et noble et bienauenturado rey*'. Further confirmation of the international repute which Ferdinand gained as a result of his conquests comes from the lips of the usually tart English chronicler Matthew Paris, who declared of Ferdinand 'that king has done more for the honour and profit of Christ's church than the pope and all his Crusaders ... and all the Templars and Hospitallers'.

It is therefore inevitable that Ferdinand's achievements, revered not just throughout his country but through Europe, would have been impressed on Eleanor from a young age. Equally it seems certain that, coming from a country with a warlike past and present and with a father famed around the world as a military leader, she would regard the business of war as being a central part of a king's job.

Ferdinand's influence will not have stopped there. Aside from his qualities as a warrior, Ferdinand was plainly an impressive personality. A Muslim writer, who obviously had no cause to think well of Ferdinand, described him as 'a kind man with great political sense'. Alfonso, whose relationship with his father was not always smooth, described him as a handsome man with truly regal presence, well spoken and courtly as well as decisive, knowing the moment to act. The reference to his regal presence may well refer in part to his height; certainly at least one of his grandsons overtopped six feet two.[10]

Alfonso's verdict also speaks to his good manners; but Alfonso's experience of him, as well as that of his opponents, pays eloquent testimony to the iron fist in the velvet glove. A good example is the deathbed exchange recorded between the two above; Ferdinand's guidance to his son was interesting and somewhat chilling. It shows a clear sense that goals had to be set and aspired to and that even kings had to be judged by their achievements.

This brings us to the second aspect of the life which Eleanor lived as a child: her opportunities to study the business of kingship at close range. One respect in which Ferdinand appears to have excelled as a ruler is in understanding the limits of military success unless consolidated with a view to peace. In this there is a surprising contrast with his bookish son Alfonso, who might rather be expected to emphasise this aspect. As can be seen from the outline above, each conquest made by Ferdinand appears to have been followed by a period of administrative activity while the new conquest was resettled and brought somewhat into line with the existing territories. Thus, after the conquest of Jaén he spent eight months there, turning the mosque into a cathedral, repairing fortifications, planning the next stage of the campaign and establishing privileges for Christian colonists. After the conquest of the important city of Seville, he spent at least a year on the business of resettlement and made it his base for the remainder of his life. At each of these administrative halts it is inevitable the court and his family would have assembled and spent time in the new location. Eleanor would thus have had a front-row seat to appreciate how the administrative business of kingship and conquest might be done.

What would Eleanor have seen? Under Ferdinand, the business of administration proceeded on a twofold basis. The first and most pressing part concerned the defence and population of the added lands. His technique here was to act quickly to place fortified sites – as well as certain civic and strategic buildings – under royal control, to increase or improve on their defensive capabilities where necessary, to distribute land among a range of his victorious troops and to introduce laws and incentives designed to facilitate permanent settlement by the Castilians in his train and other future economic migrants.[11]

The second part related to attempting to bring the legal systems in the various territories onto a similar footing to that in his existing Castilian lands. It would appear that Ferdinand appreciated that this was a matter which had to be approached sensitively, and it is here, in particular, that his sense seems to have exceeded that of his son. The law prevailing in the Iberian peninsula at the time had its source in the survival, after the Muslim invasion, of a modified version of the Visigothic *Liber Judiciorum*, which, crucially, appeared under different variations in different regions. Ferdinand's technique was to grant (or impose) a specific *fuero* (a code or charter of privileges) to localities that lacked a known juridical tradition or whose laws were confused. But – and this is a key point – he would tend to select the *fuero* to be applied so as to reflect differences required by local circumstances. Thus, while limiting the degree of legal disparity among the various municipal codes, he made the imposition of new laws easier to swallow by respecting certain local aspects of the existing laws. So there were in operation in different localities the *Fuero Juzgo* as operated at Toledo, the *Fuero Cuenca* and the *fuero* of Cordoba.[12]

Ferdinand was also a thinker on the subject of the role and duties of kingship. He was the initiator and probable part author of the *Setenario* or 'mirror for princes' which was the forerunner of Alfonso's more famous *Siete Partidas*. Both reflect an elevated view of the role of kingship and of the duties of a king, being intended as a didactic tool to assist the king in doing good and avoiding evil. After his death Alfonso continued his father's work, writing extensively on the duties of a king. In particular he describes justice as the 'mother of all good', which unites men and says that a king should not desire to do anything contrary to law, referencing Justinian – 'whatever he could do with justice constituted his power' – and Solomon – ' a king who is just and loves justice governs his country and he who is too covetous destroys it'. Therefore during the course of her childhood Eleanor will have heard plenty of discussion on the subject of the nature of and requirements of kingship and will have imbibed the views that a king should be actively engaged in the promotion of justice, that he should do nothing contrary to right and that he should be involved in the making of good laws designed to promote the prosperity of the realm.[13]

The debate about legal systems and modes of kingship was a manifestation of a more fundamental aspect of life in Castile, which was in stark contrast to the world which Eleanor would find when she left the country on her marriage. In England and France stable boundaries and relatively peaceful times had enabled the development of a more structured society. The Iberian peninsula, by contrast, had been a mass of shifting borders for centuries. Castile, which had become an independent country fairly recently in the course of the struggle, was particularly geared to constant warfare and shifting of frontiers. It has in fact been repeatedly described as 'a society organised for war'. Indeed, it was the castles which accompanied the warfare in the peninsula which gave Castile its name – and its coat of arms. Big, brutal red-brick and stone castles of the most functional variety were common, and while some were essentially trading and administrative bases, many were built for defence, or to mark the attacking line of the war as Castile advanced.

Reflecting this warlike emphasis, the kings of Castile thought also about military theory; in particular, in Part II of the *Siete Partidas* they set out a series of injunctions about military practice, which demonstrate that the work of the Roman writer Vegetius, whose work *De Re Militarii* was a handbook of best military practice probably compiled for the Emperor Theodosius, had been thoroughly studied and approved in Castilian military circles.[14]

Another effect of the pre-eminence of warfare was that in a number of respects Castilian society was much more fluid than was the case in other European monarchies. While noble rank and privileges were, here as elsewhere, largely for the warrior caste, the fact that more of the population was involved in warfare enabled more people to have access to joining the noble caste. In addition, the process of reconquest and its economic imperatives had forced the Catholics of Spain into close contact with Muslims and Jews and enabled them to see at first hand that these religious minorities were about as far from being ignorant or uncivilised as it was possible to be.

As regards the Muslim invaders, they had centuries before established in southern Spain an advanced agrarian economy involving complex irrigation systems which were novelties in Europe. Such innovations had given rise to prosperous towns and cities. For example Cordoba, often described by Arab historians as 'the jewel of the world', was the largest town in Western Europe, with a population of at least 100,000 in the thirteenth century – and this total was considerably down from its apogee when it reputedly accommodated 500,000 – a figure, it should be noted, that London did not attain until the eighteenth century.

The Muslims in Andalucia also had a much stronger intellectual heritage than did the Christian nations. Islam's conquests of former centres of the Roman Empire had ensured that it was the heir to the knowledge of Europe's Greco-Roman past – not least in terms of custody of books. All sorts of knowledge that would otherwise have been lost was saved, guarded and worked upon by Muslim scholars. For the rulers of Andalucia in the ninth to twelfth centuries did not just save the books, they patronised intellectuals and learning to a liberal extent. The result was that in the late twelfth century and early thirteenth century, if you wanted a piece of out-of-the-way knowledge, you were best to look for it in the libraries of the Iberian peninsula; in the thirteenth century, Gerard of Grenoble went to Toledo when he wanted to get hold of a fundamental work on astrology by the Greek astrologer Almaget. Castile was therefore a treasure house of intellectual resources.[15]

Nor was Muslim culture the only thriving culture in the peninsula. There was also a flourishing Jewish population both in Castile and in the reconquered Muslim territories. Overall, the Muslim incursion was probably a factor in pushing Christian–Jewish relations into a much more congenial framework than in any other country. But also in reconquered territories Christians, Muslims and Jews had already been living together in relative harmony – a tradition of *convivencia* wherein the Muslim rulers had offered both Jewish and Christian minorities considerable opportunities to flourish and to take part in public life. Overall, there was a closer and warmer relationship between Christians and Jews than was found elsewhere in Europe. Formally, as elsewhere, the Jewish population were the property of the Crown, and modern writers have suggested that *convivencia* was a mere fig leaf which does not do away with the reality of legal dependency. Yet a contemporary Jewish writer stated that in affairs of everyday life this vassalage was hardly felt. The Jewish population was well established and prosperous in a number of Castilian towns.[16]

From this population came a number of very well-to-do and well-educated men who distinguished themselves in the royal service. One example very close to home is that Queen Jeanne's own personal physician was Jewish. However, there are records of many other Jewish luminaries at the courts of Ferdinand III and Alfonso X in the roles of advisers, secretaries and even ambassadors – operating at such a high level that they were gifted by the Crown with lands including houses, vineyards, olive groves, fields and mills – all in perpetuity and under their absolute control. For example, Eleanor's brother Alfonso gifted the whole of a prosperous village called Paterna Harah outside Seville to a number of his favoured Jewish officials.

One particularly notable example may be given: Don Sol ibn Zadok of Toledo (Don Culema) was entrusted by Ferdinand III with collecting the tribute to be paid by the King of Granada, and later become both chief tax collector and ambassador under Alfonso X. On his death his extensive property included vineyards, olive groves, houses and warehouses 'full of goods' scattered throughout Seville, Carmona, Ecija and Toledo. His son Don Isaac thereafter became Alfonso's chief financier until 1278. These men were true courtiers, with their own retinues, and were treated with great respect by the Christian community who feted them as men of great wealth and influence. So Todros Ben Judah Halevi describes a journey with Don Isaac and his retinue, travelling in regal style, showered with gifts by interested parties and dancing with well-born young ladies.[17]

Castilian kings had also encouraged Jewish businessmen to act as the vanguard of resettlement in recently reconquered areas, for example by the granting of tax breaks. More generally, the Castilian monarchs fought the corner of their Jewish subjects against papal interference. One particular bone of contention was the requirement under the Fourth Council of the Lateran in 1213 that Jews wear clothing to distinguish them from Christians. This was opposed both by Ferdinand III and Cardinal Archbishop Roderigo of Toledo; interestingly, however, and chiming with the modern doubters of *convivencia*, they did so effectively on economic grounds. The Jews, they said, would simply move to Muslim territories and take their affluence with them. The result was a concession in 1219 that exempted the Jews of Castile from the requirement to wear a distinguishing mark.

The second vista over Eleanor's childhood therefore shows us a world in which she saw the role of a king as both a soldier and as an administrator in the interests of the nation. The well-being of the country and the development of a cohesive national spirit was key. And, in this cause, interaction with those of other faiths as a matter of business or in the realm of the intellect was a matter of small moment.[18]

The third perspective over Eleanor's life concerns the actual day-to-day surroundings and doings of her life.

It appears highly likely that her earliest memories were formed at least in part on campaign. As we have seen, Ferdinand was busy about the business of reconquest during this period. It appears that Jeanne accompanied Ferdinand on campaign most of the time, as his first wife Beatriz had also done and as Berengaria had done with both her husband and her son. Jeanne's presence is specifically recorded in Andalucia in 1244 despite a perilous military situation; she was moved nearer to the field of operations in 1246 and she is also recorded living in camp at the Siege of Seville in 1248. One of Ferdinand's biographers reports that he did not like to separate himself from Jeanne but took her on campaign and installed her somewhere safe but near enough the battlefield for him to visit. This, of course, would be entirely in keeping with Berengaria's desire to ensure that Ferdinand did not 'lower the tone' of his reign by taking up with mistresses. While it is unlikely that the principle that an accompanied husband is less likely to stray would have been actively present to Eleanor's mind in her early years, the idea of royalty – including royal women – on campaign would certainly have been a part of Eleanor's accepted norms.

Whether we can conclude from this that Eleanor herself was directly familiar with the exigencies of campaign other than from passing visits is less certain. It is well established that in general children of royal and noble houses in this period were not likely to enjoy anything which the modern reader would recognise as 'quality time' with their parents. In their early years at least, contact was likely to be periodic and relatively formal. In addition, frequently children were substantially raised away from their parents, in an environment which was thought likely to maximise their chances of survival, since courts were justifiably considered in general unhelpful to this aim. However, the details of such fostering, even for royal heirs, are extraordinarily scanty; to use a case in point we have almost no material about Edward I's upbringing and in particular his early years; and equally scholars lament the black hole of information about the early years and education of Alfonso X. What is known is that Ferdinand's sons were brought up by surrogates in spartan conditions far from home; the future Alfonso X (later accompanied by his siblings) was sent to be raised in the Arlanzon lowlands near Burgos to ensure a healthy upbringing and direct contact with the people he was to rule. This served a dual purpose – the healthy upbringing in the country was there to promote survival, and the spartan conditions as a reflection of the warrior mindset of Castile, where pampered princes were not welcome.

It is doubtful that Eleanor, whose upbringing was not required to produce a warrior, was sent to the same spot as that chosen for Alfonso and the other sons, but it is quite likely that her early years were spent substantially in some pleasant country spot under the supervision of a governor, very likely with other royal or semi-royal children as part of the household. However, it is almost inevitable that she would, during a long campaign, have made visits to her parents in camp, and may well have moved her main residence to be within easy distance of operations. One way or another, therefore, we can be confident that she would have been familiar with the dislocations of campaigning, and also intimately familiar with military camps.

But equally she saw a life of almost unimaginable luxury. The campaigns were punctuated by stops in the major towns of Castile and Jeanne is attested spending considerable periods of time both at Cordoba and Seville. The former was not only huge by medieval standards, but had many beautiful fountains and hundreds of public baths; the figures range from around 300 to 900. Its streets were paved. At night they were lit and patrolled by guardians of the peace, a system not introduced in England until the nineteenth century. The cathedral-mosque is still regarded as one of the beauties of the world, with UNESCO World Heritage Site status, and was still more so until defaced by the sixteenth-century renovation which so appalled Emperor Charles V. Commentators speak breathlessly of the forest of multi-coloured columns of jasper, granite, onyx and marble, supporting red-and-white arches inspired by the Dome of the Rock, of the intricate decoration and of the beautiful courtyard. The markets of the city were plentiful, offering a wealth of meats and fruits: oranges and lemons, of course, but also figs, cherries, pomegranates, pears and apples. In addition spices, nuts and herbs were abundant. All in all, such was the reputation of Cordoba as a prosperous area that when it was reconquered, it was inundated with Spanish settlers.[19]

Seville, the Almohad centre of culture and development for the century previous to its conquest, was also comfortably more affluent and artistically brilliant than any Christian town in Europe. It had been on the receiving end of a huge programme of building and improvements including palaces, towers, quays and dykes, a repaired and improved Roman aqueduct, and extensive and busy warehouses on the bank of the river, served by vessels from all around the world. Its defences had been entirely reconstructed and two magnificent centrepiece buildings had been completed within the last century. The first was the Alcazar, commenced in 1171, guarded by a tower of gold on the banks of the river. The second was the mosque (later the cathedral), built in the last thirty years of the twelfth century, which rivalled even that of Cordoba. It boasted walls painted many colours and embellished with Persian battlements and arcades and it looked onto a courtyard planted with orange trees, which combined their fragrance with the sound of constantly playing fountains. Inside the viewer was overwhelmed by the sight of hundreds of marble columns ascending to a roof comprising domes of wood and stucco, elaborately decorated. The interior was further blessed with gilded mosaic pavements and elaborate alabaster lattices. More generally, the Arab writers of the time praised Seville for its luxury and plenty, overflowing with fine foods, lovely women, talented musicians and poets. Indeed, so well provided was it that it gave rise to a proverb: 'If you were to ask for bird's milk in Seville you would be able to get it.'[20]

So, although on the whole detailed records do not survive of the design and decorations of the palaces which fell to Ferdinand as part of the Reconquista, we can therefore expect that they too would have been ravishingly beautiful and boasted the last word in modern luxuries. Elegant palaces which took the local Hispano-Roman and Visigothic idiom and transformed it with subtle shifts of elevation and complex decoration, courtyards of finest white marble, stucco latticework of the most breathtaking complexity, delicate friezes in Kufic script, running water, luxurious baths and jewel-bright ceramic tiles – all were present and would have been familiar to Eleanor.

But what is certain about these palaces is that they had the most amazing gardens, and in particular water gardens; gardens marked out with flowing streams of water, derived from the sixth-century Persian concept of the 'paradise' (*pairidaiza*), a walled garden with a water axis. While in Spain the gardens were some way short of the full wonder achieved further east, the records show clearly that beautiful gardens did exist, principally of two sorts: the 'pavilion on pool' type and the 'courtyard with a central pool' type.

The palace at Seville inherited a wonderful set of Islamic gardens from its former owners. Records survive of one part of the gardens of the Alcazar of Seville where a sunken bed surrounded four watercourses which came to meet in a central circular pool – those four watercourses being designed to echo the supposed four rivers of Eden, a not unusual concept in Islamic gardens and one which was known as *chahar bagh*. As modern commentators have noted, this assists the viewer in perceiving the space around him or her; thus the garden is not merely beautiful, it is also harmonious and inspires a sense of peace and relaxation. This sense of harmony would be contributed to in many cases by the use of topiary, with trees trained and clipped into double or triple decked shapes and arranged in geometric patterns.[21]

Other wonderful ideas were also deployed. Recent excavations have revealed in the Alcazar gardens another garden, the patio of the Qasr al-Mubarak, with parterres 5 feet below the water channels and with the walls beneath shaped into a continuous arcade which was stuccoed and painted. Thus a person walking on the path, or seated in the pavilion which overlooked it, would be above the flower bushes and even, possibly, the fruit trees, but walking below among the trees there would be cool shade and beautifully decorated walls, with the sound of water all around. The effect of the sunken beds next to the watercourses would be, when viewed from above, to give the effect of a live carpet. The full effect of these breathtaking gardens has not survived; for example the existing, much-lauded, Patio of the Doncellas at Seville gives only the most distant impression of the loveliness of the earlier gardens.[22]

Sometimes the use of water would not simply be confined to simple flowing streams; fountains, and chutes involving noria or waterwheels would be included to enable water to be moved from a lower level and then tipped out on a higher level, to demonstrate man's mastery over this most valuable of commodities. Such devices were apparently very popular in Spain, being mentioned in poems as giving sounds like the wails of parted lovers. Less poetic descriptions liken the sound to a distressed camel.

Still more wonderful features appeared in some gardens; the garden at Toledo of Ismail al-Mamun, which may have survived to Eleanor's day, had a gold-encrusted stained-glass pavilion at the centre of a lake which could be covered in a cascade of water. Another very common feature in Islamic gardens was the use of 'zoomorphic' fountains: fountains shaped like animals, often lions. The Fountain of the Lions in the Alhambra, which may date in part to the eleventh century, is one example, but there was another at the Munyat al-Naura near Cordoba which boasted a gilded lion fountain with jewelled eyes, the water entering at the back of the lion and cascading from his mouth.[23]

Eleanor thus grew up among wonderfully lovely gardens designed to create a sense of harmony by considered use of the features of shade, scent, formal planting and flowing water. A description of the effect is given in relation to a famous garden in Cordoba:

> The courtyard is of pure white marble, the stream traverses it, wriggling like a snake. There is a basin into which all waters fall. The roof [of the pavilion] is decorated in gold and blue and in these colours are decorated the sides and various parts. The garden has files of trees symmetrically aligned and its flowers smile from open buds. The foliage of the garden prevents the sun seeing the ground; and the breeze, blowing day and night over the garden is loaded with scents.[24]

If these were the external surroundings which formed Eleanor's horizons as a child, what of the other aspects of a child's life – family, education, play? We can come to some conclusions on this from looking at the childhood of the most prominent of her siblings, Alfonso X. His biographers note that his early spartan rearing was tempered by family security, extensive education and cultural opportunities, and that while he served an apprenticeship in war from a relatively young age he was also allowed much time for affairs of the mind. These factors, all important in a child's experience, can be considered in turn.

The mention of 'family security' indicates that the royal family did at least meet as such on a regular basis. The closeness of the family bond implied by this phrase should perhaps not be overstated, given the quite spectacular, not to say murderous, way in which the sons of Ferdinand fell out in later years. However, there were plenty of members of the family with whom to form a relationship.

In the context of Eleanor's experience of family, one point should be noted; the immediate family who would have been at least in regular attendance at court was predominantly male. Only one of Ferdinand's daughters by his first marriage survived into adulthood, and, as noted above, she became a nun at Las Huelgas not long after Eleanor's birth, having been resident there for much of her childhood after a miraculous escape from death. By contrast, Ferdinand's sons almost all survived to adulthood. Her formidable grandmother died before Eleanor was five years old. Accordingly, it is unlikely that her childhood was one which was dominated by female ties, although she may well have been close to one cousin, Beatriz, who was very nearly the same age. It is correspondingly likely that she learnt to interact well with boys and young men from a young age and, given the warlike society of her country, that she learnt to appreciate the preoccupations of the warrior male.[25]

Among her brothers, her closest contacts would probably have been with the older ones rather than the younger ones, as the younger ones would be largely being raised away from court in a different location to her. Thus, her eldest half-brother, Alfonso, already twenty at the time of her birth, was an integral part of the campaign team and would be seen whenever she visited. Likewise, her next brother, Fernando, formed a part of the command structure until his death in 1248 and the third, Fadrique, was finishing his training in arms also. The other brothers who would be likely to have been close contacts are Enrique and Sancho, who were respectively ten years and eight years her senior and would have emerged from the schoolroom by the time she was old enough to form impressions. Hindsight confirms that these brothers were her closest contacts; they are the only siblings who ever visited Eleanor in England after her marriage, and it is with regard to these brothers and Fadrique that she appears to have exercised her influence both with Alfonso and elsewhere in later life.

However, this is certainly not to suggest that Eleanor was not close to Alfonso: it seems clear that Eleanor, either during her early years or after her father's death, did have enough close contact with Alfonso to be very close to him as well; although never a playmate, he was plainly a beloved older brother and mentor and on the intellectual front, a friend.[26]

It was not only her immediate family who may well have formed the social circle around her at court. Her aunt Berengaria of León, who married John of Brienne in 1224 and moved to Constantinople, where he became regent for the young Emperor, appears to have maintained ties with the Castilian court until their deaths in 1237. Her daughter Marie married Emperor Baldwin II of Constantinople. However, her sons, Alphonse, Louis and Jean, though somewhat older than Eleanor and primarily based in France from 1244, certainly maintained close links themselves with the Castilian court. All of them are noted as relatively frequent features in Alfonso X's witness lists, which indicates a close relationship. They will therefore have been known to Eleanor from her earliest years, and Jean in particular was probably fairly close to Eleanor in age.[27]

There was also plainly, given the presence of Peter of Portugal at the celebrations in Seville, some contact with other royal families in the peninsula. In particular, frequent contact was likely between the royal families of Castile and Aragon. King Jaime of Aragon (himself a distant cousin of Ferdinand) had a number of daughters near to Eleanor in age. Violante, who married Alfonso, was some five years Eleanor's senior. Costanza, destined to marry Alfonso's brother Manuel, and Isabelle, the future Queen of France, were respectively about a year older and two years younger than Eleanor. Also close to Eleanor in age was Jaime's heir Pedro, who would later become Pedro III of Aragon. Violante's marriage to Alfonso was celebrated at the end of December 1249 and Eleanor will have seen a good deal of her in the next five years until her own marriage. Whether in these early years the unhappiness of the Castilian royal marriage was already apparent cannot be known. However, at some point in those years Eleanor will have learnt about her brother's growing family of children by his mistresses, a reinforcement to the lesson on which Queen Berengaria had been so keen, to keep one's husband close.

One thing which was plainly central to the upbringing of the Castilian royal family was rigorous academic study. As we have already seen, Castile had acquired, through the Muslim invaders, a rich resource of learning and Eleanor's ancestors were keen to foster intellectual study, with both Alfonso VIII and Alfonso IX founding universities and Ferdinand III continuing their work. Ferdinand III did not merely appreciate and encourage learning in the abstract, however, but also ensured that his children were participators in it. Alfonso X's devotion to study was noted by observers from the time he emerged into open view in his early teens, and this implies that he was already well grounded in learning at that age. Thus Ferdinand plainly ensured that his children had good teachers from a young age. This is consistent with Alfonso's own writings, which suggest that seven is the age for commencement of serious study and advise the choosing of good teachers for princes.

Ferdinand was doubtless encouraged in this by the Dominican Order, whose emphasis on the importance of learning was an important part of their religious outlook.[28]

As for the substantive content of that learning, we know that the education which the children pursued was not narrow, nor purely religious. Instead their studies covered a broad humanistic base, and at least three of Ferdinand's sons, Felipe, Sancho and Enrique, were sent for further study to the University of Paris. Alfonso himself actually left a description of the range of learning which a well-educated man should, in his view, have, and this can obviously be inferred to mirror his own. In his *General Estoria* he states that such a person should be learned in the seven liberal arts. The first three (or *trivium*) were rhetoric, grammar and logic – the three roads to teach the young mind how to get somewhere. The remaining four (*quadrivium*) are arithmetic and geometry, music, astrology, physics and metaphysics. As for languages, Alfonso wrote and spoke several, and was clearly able to read Latin well, even if the evidence for his writing in that language is thin.

There is yet further clear evidence that Ferdinand was very keen that his children should receive a good education. This is found in his commissioning of a book of the 'mirror for princes' variety called the *Libro de Doze Sabios* (*Book of the Twelve Wise Men*), which places in the mouths of twelve wise men statements from the Bible along with fables from Eastern didactic works, a fine example of the synthesis of cultures in play at Ferdinand's court.

Raised in this rich academic tradition, in his turn Alfonso had the hunger for knowledge and for books that marks the intellectual and became world-famous for his intellectual curiosity and willingness to patronise scholars. From the start of his reign he employed distinguished academics of all disciplines and from a wide variety of countries and religions in a scriptorium at his court. One purpose for this was to translate as many books as possible from Old Arabic to Spanish so as to make accessible to himself and others the learning of the classical era, which then only existed in Arabic. Considerable original work was also done by his academics on mathematical and astronomical questions, and they produced under his guidance the primary set of astronomical tables in use until the late sixteenth century.[29]

In language, poetry and music, the family seems to have been particularly well taught – and matched their education with talent. Alfonso himself was in part at least the author of the *Cantigas de Santa Maria*, a set of devotional poems set to music which borrow heavily from the tradition of the troubadours. Enrique of Castile, meanwhile, though less of an intellectual polymath than Alfonso, was a noted troubadour as well as being a soldier. He has recently been identified as the author of the distinguished tale of chivalry *Amadis de Gaula*, the story of the star-crossed love of King Perion of Gaul and Elisena of England and the adventures of their lovechild Amadis (the hero worshipped by Cervantes' Don Quixote). It has been described as the foremost work of Spanish chivalrous literature of the age. The achievements of the two brothers therefore demonstrate again the level of education and culture which was current in the children of Ferdinand. This was the atmosphere in which Eleanor was raised.[30]

Fantastically enough, we have almost a first-hand account of the principles on which Eleanor's later education would have been based. This is because Alfonso wrote extensively on the subject of learning, and indeed the upbringing of royal children. Since his accession, when Eleanor was just over ten, coincides with the time when Eleanor would be expected to be moving into more demanding education and spending more time at court in order to become familiar with the currents of political thought, one can expect her education to have been conducted entirely along the lines of Alfonso's opinions and views.

The starting point here is that Alfonso had a passion for didacticism, both from his own inherent love of learning, and as an endeavour which in his view took man nearer to God. As he put it in his *General Estoria*, 'every man who is full of virtues and knowledge resembles God, because through him all things come; and the more knowledge he has, the more he resembles God and the closer he becomes to His nature'. Therefore it will have been drummed into Eleanor that learning was next to godliness.

But Alfonso actually set out in his *Siete Partidas* the education which should be given to a prince, and to a princess. Interestingly, he considered that a princess should have the same tutors as a prince, thereby indicating that he considered that they should be as highly educated as their brothers. One can therefore (save as regards martial training) regard the rules for princes as being equally applicable to the princesses, and hence to Eleanor's experience of education.

Generally Alfonso's list of the training which a prince should have, in Title VII of Part II of the *Siete Partidas*, may be likened to that to be expected of a well-behaved Victorian child. There is an extensive litany of behaviour and deportment issues. Those raising the children should pay careful attention to their rearing – the children should be very pure and refined in all their actions and kept in the company of pure and refined people only. Their tutors (of good family and judgment) should teach them to be elegant and clean and to eat tidily. They should be taught to speak properly and politely. They should not speak loudly, or in a very low tone, and they should not speak either very rapidly or very slowly. They should speak with no gesticulation and should use neither too many nor too few words. They should not listen with mouths open, and should walk gracefully, without dragging their feet or raising them too high. (It is interesting to see how universal are such preoccupations on the part of parents, even at a gap of several hundred years.) As for formal education, children should be taught to read and write, how to learn to know men and how to talk to those of all stations in life.[31]

For princesses there are special injunctions, doubtless to be attended to while their brothers gained proficiency in arms. They should be brought up with much greater supervision, to ensure they formed good habits as they would have a greater part in raising children in due course. 'The most important thing in the world … is that for the sake of loyalty they should respect themselves and their husbands and consider carefully everything else which they have to do in order that they may have good habits and offer a good example to others.'

Interestingly, their supervisors 'should especially prevent them from yielding to anger for … it is the one thing in the world which most quickly induces women to commit sin'. Indeed there is also considerable focus in Part V, which deals with a king's attributes, on the importance of suppressing anger – there are two laws dealing with this alone. Even without the corroborative evidence of later events, which demonstrates that both Alfonso and Eleanor had on occasion very lively tempers, this would suggest that the royal family of Castile was very prone to anger, and that it was considered important to keep that unattractive trait controlled, or at least hidden, so far as possible.[32]

All in all, therefore, Eleanor will have had the finest education available to a child at that time, and one which will have emphasised the importance of both style and substance. Deportment was highly valued but so too were more substantial attainments. Eleanor's education, like Alfonso's own, will have covered the seven liberal arts. But one can also assume that a healthy knowledge of theology will have been part of the programme, since in Alfonso's view (perhaps more so than his father's) the purpose of an understanding of the liberal arts was to better understand the holy scriptures. Eleanor's education is therefore likely to have been such as to naturally promote in her an independent and intellectual interest in doctrinal matters and a view that it was important, if one could, to study and attempt to understand as much as possible as a route towards God. What is more, Eleanor could herself write (a very unusual skill at the time). This fact is explained by the fact that Alfonso considered that this was necessary 'in order to learn more easily what [one wants] to know, and to be better able to keep [one's] secrets'.

Very much to the fore was the importance of discipline in learning. This learning will not have come without effort; the habit of work will have been inculcated early and emphasised repeatedly; and it will have been reinforced by the examples around her, particularly with her father and brother, who were unceasingly at work, and over no small range of material.

But the Castilian court was no narrow intellectual hothouse. The evidence establishes clearly that Ferdinand enjoyed a wide range of

cultural pursuits and games. In the *Setenario* Alfonso pays tribute to
his father as the perfection of a Christian knight and humanist prince,
evoking the educated and sophisticated atmosphere of the court:

> He knew well the art of hunting all game, as well as playing board games
> and chess, and other varied table games; he liked the singing of men and
> he himself knew how to sing; likewise he liked courtly troubadours and
> singers and jongleurs who could play instruments well. He liked all this
> very much and he was a discriminating connoisseur in this matter.

The fondness for the playing of troubadours and jongleurs is also reliably
attested elsewhere. A number of well-known troubadours were associated
with his court, and a troubadour-style composition of his own has been
identified. The strong troubadour influence is reinforced both by Alfonso's
later devotion to wider culture, including music and poetry, and Enrique's
unmasking as a talented poet.[33]

Alfonso, too, was fond of games: he was a generous patron of chess
experts, and on his death he was writing a book about pastimes and
games. As for Eleanor, it seems safe to assume that the taste which she
later had for chess was acquired in childhood, possibly even playing with
her father in his illness. One therefore gets the picture of a court very
full of business, but also very full of sophisticated diversions when the
opportunity presented itself.

Nor were the diversions all sophisticated. As noted above, in
summarising Ferdinand's character, Alfonso emphasised his father's
passion for hunting. This passion is one Alfonso plainly shared. He
writes in the *Siete Partidas* of the importance of physical fitness for a
king. Hunting is then particularly singled out as an important part of a
prince's and king's regime, although the intellectual justifications for this
are a little thin; one rather senses that hunting was a very popular pastime
indeed with the Castilian royal family and simply could not be left out.[34]

So at this point it is possible to review what we know about Eleanor
at the time when the possibilities for her marriage first began to be
considered. As a provable fact we know practically nothing, but from the
wealth of material about the Castilian court it is possible to make some
very strong inferences.

Eleanor was familiar with the most beautiful things that humankind
could then create, in homes, decoration and gardens. She was used
to the rich and varied diet available in the warm climate of her home
and in some of the most affluent towns on earth: oranges, lemons, figs,
pomegranates, spices – including, of course, saffron.

At the same time she was familiar with and used to a fairly peripatetic
life, often 'following the flag'. She was very used to the preoccupations
of the warrior male and to a male-dominated society; and knew how to

thrive in such an environment. She had been afforded a ringside seat at a key point in her country's history and been enabled to see the importance of both the active and administrative sides of conquest, and to absorb a positive and detailed high-level debate about the role and duties of the ideal king, in particular the importance of justice.

Eleanor was educated to the very highest level, well beyond the usual limits of female education or even those of a prince. As for religion, devoutness was a given in that age, and with her education at the hands of the Dominicans and latterly under the influence of Alfonso X she was trained to believe in and to exercise an intellectual rather than emotional approach to religion. In terms of personal style, she was encouraged to adopt a decorous, discreet style somewhat different to the lively, probably flirtatious style approved in France and adopted by her mother.

However, Eleanor was no one-dimensional bookworm or would-be nun. In line with her family habits, she also regarded cultural amusements such as board games, music and poetry and physical ones such as hunting as an integral part of life.[35]

Finally what of her expectations for her future husband, an inevitable preoccupation for a royal princess? It is clear from the glowing terms in which Alfonso speaks of him that Ferdinand's memory was constantly celebrated and venerated at the Castilian court. To Eleanor, Ferdinand was surely a hero and the perfect Christian knight. We can safely assume she worshipped her father and that, as the question of marriage began to be mooted, what Eleanor would hope fate would bring her would conform roughly to that ideal, possibly along the lines of the following list: tall, handsome, a great king (or one in the making), an intellectual, a sound administrator, a mighty soldier and a Crusader – and with something of a taste for hunting and the arts. Well educated as she was, she surely appreciated that she would be fortunate if half of the items on her wish list were fulfilled.

3

The English Side of the Equation

But what about the English side of the equation? What were the personalities and political currents which faced Eleanor on her marriage?

The picture must naturally start at the top, with Henry III. In 1255, when Eleanor was first to meet him, he was forty-eight years old and had been king for nearly forty years, having acceded to the throne in 1216 at the age of just nine, on the death of his father, King John.[1]

As a king, Henry was in almost all respects highly unsatisfactory. The political story which follows will illustrate why without need for much further explanation. However, he had two limited plus sides: he was a distinguished patron of the Church and of the arts, and he had a talent for showmanship. His taste for and appreciation of beauty and his profound piety induced him to be largely responsible for the magnificent building of Westminster Abbey. He also oversaw extensive redecorations in most of the southern royal palaces, including the Tower of London, which included paintings and carvings of the very highest quality. He adored metal and jewel work, pictures and sculpture; moreover, he had both good taste and an ability to communicate his vision of how things should be done to the many workmen who sought and gained his patronage.[2]

As for his 'set pieces' of monarchical showmanship, these were plainly masterpieces; even the cynical chronicler Matthew Paris, who writes only to find fault, admired them. One which had recently taken place at the time of Edward and Eleanor's marriage was the marriage of Edward's sister Margaret to Alexander of Scotland in 1251, and a consideration of this conveys not just a sense of Henry's talent in this department but also something of the atmosphere of the English court. The focus on the great event was plainly considerable. In his determination to produce a magnificent and memorable display, there are a good 130 orders evidenced in the administrative records, scattered over a period of months prior to the wedding. These come from the king directly, and cover all manner of clothes, gifts, catering and decoration. So we can see that the king and queen wore heavy silk robes furred with ermine, while twelve-year-old Edward and his companions went through at least three costume changes over the day. The edited highlights are Edward's violet twilled-silk tabard embroidered with three gold leopards front and back and trimmed with miniver (squirrel belly), another made of cloth of gold, again twilled with miniver, and a third with a particoloured tunic of chequered cloth of gold and plain coloured cloth, to be worn with a brightly striped shirt underneath. One can only imagine that Edward had to be forcibly inserted into these garments by his companions, Ebulo de Montibus and Nicholas de Molis. The young Scottish king was presented with a sword with a silk-covered scabbard and a decorated silver pommel and silver gilt spurs. Margaret departed to her marital home bearing, aside from her own trousseau of clothes, ten cloths of gold for religious offerings, a costly bed, a number of ornate saddles and over £300 worth of jewellery, including thirty-five brooches and 173 rings. The feast featured (among many other items) salted fallow and fresh roe deer, a multitude of hams, 10,000 haddock and 500 conger eels plus over 12,000 gallons of wine. All in all, very little expense was spared to give the impression that a great and powerful king was in charge of events; but the records show the reality – an aesthete more concerned with catering than politics.

On Eleanor's arrival, another of these set pieces was put in place – a well-conceived and well-executed show to emphasise the importance of the royal wedding and, through this, the status of the royal family. In this way Henry III was perhaps a forerunner of Henry VIII, with his keen eye for the well-staged and publicised shows of kingship and the well-thought-out dynastic painting. In the 'keeping up with the Capets' aspect of kingship he was therefore not without talents.[3]

In almost all other key respects, however, Henry was spectacularly untalented. He had none of the Norman or Angevin military talent. While he was apparently tutored in the military arts by distinguished knights, the skills seem never to have taken with him. Matthew Paris, mocking his crusading ambitions, described him as a 'petty king, untaught in military discipline, who has never galloped a horse in battle, wielded a sword and brandished a spear'. His one major military expedition was into Poitou in 1242, where he attempted to reclaim some of the territory which Louis IX had been steadily gaining there. In sole command of the campaign for the only time in his life, he advanced northwards along the Charente from Saintes – neglecting the obvious precaution of taking the fortified castle of Taillebourg which lay en route. While King Louis may well have been the least militarily talented member of his own family, he knew better than this. He promptly proceeded to Taillebourg, cutting Henry off from his base and coming very close to capturing him. Henry was forced to take advantage of a brief truce to flee back to Saintes – leaving Louis to turn the English retreat into a costly rout. The result? An expensive five-year truce and the loss of Poitou. At home, his lack of military skills would later help to prompt the resurgence of problems in Wales at a time when the lack of clear succession to the leadership of Wales should have enabled the English king to make hay.[4]

Henry also appears to have been almost totally devoid of political sense. The first and key charge against him is his playing of favourites. Throughout his majority rule he tended to seize on a person or group and elevate them to undue prominence, while acting with ill grace or ingratitude to other key players on the political scene. As will be examined in more detail below, this tendency was politically disastrous. His choice of non-English favourites in particular was inflammatory, because it eroded the political status of powerful families with powerful interests to defend, and it was particularly ill timed as the loss of the Plantagenet foreign empire, and with it the nobility's related landholdings in those areas, created a more inward-looking, nationalistic society in England.

So Henry's favouritism created hostility in the powerful nobles whose support he needed. His lavish gifts to his favourites exacerbated that hostility, and they also materially damaged his own position by impoverishing the Crown and limiting his ability to offer patronage elsewhere or to deal with crises as they arose. Ultimately, much of Eleanor's life's work became to make good some of the damage wrought in this respect by her father-in-law.

If further drawbacks to kingship were needed, Henry also blatantly lacked any interest in the legal and administrative work which Henry I and Henry II – and also to a certain extent his father, John – had established in English minds as the duty of the king to the country. Henry had no interest whatsoever in the workings of the system of justice in the country or in the abuses which caused dissatisfaction among key sections of the population. He was not even prepared to buy popularity by the easy means of his presence – he travelled as little throughout his dominions as he could, basing his court at a small nucleus of favourite palaces, largely southern, for the majority of his time. Here he would stay for weeks at a stretch, attending to the ceremonial and religious aspects of kingship and moving only when an extraordinary reason demanded it.[5]

Finally, although plainly not without personal charm, he lacked the politician's instinct for the correct use of charm, and even more importantly the ability to select and use people of talent. He was also apparently (in the Angevin way) prone to fits of temper, but never learnt to use them to impress, as Henry II had and Edward would. Henry appears to have had a tendency to lose his temper to the point of irrationality, generally with someone to whom he owed gratitude or a favour, and this tendency showed him to be no politician. Worse, it alienated people he needed – usually just at the point when he needed them most.[6]

Some excuses for Henry can be found. He had no model of kingship to follow in his early years; King John died when Henry was only nine years old and had been much occupied with political and military crises in his latter years, sending his wife and children away from him to safety. Unlike Louis IX, who also lost his father young, Henry had no great regent in his mother. Louis, of course, was sheltered and trained by the redoubtable Blanche of Castile. In England, Henry had no parent at all. In the wake of John's death, Henry's mother, Isabella, countess of the politically important – but vulnerable – Angoulême, left England and her children and returned in 1218 to her territories. There she contracted a territorially impeccable marriage with Hugh de Lusignan, the head of the most dangerous set of her neighbours. The Lusignan approach will become apparent, but by way of introduction they had on more than one occasion tried to kidnap Eleanor of Aquitaine, their nominal overlord. On one occasion they merely killed the Earl of Salisbury and took the young William Marshal hostage. At a later date they succeeded in kidnapping Eleanor herself and took the county of La Marche as the price of her release. Following her second marriage in 1220, Isabella settled down to raise a further, large, family – which was to prove more than a little significant in the decade after Eleanor arrived in England.[7]

All in all, however, when one looks at the English court under Henry, he appears as one of the people least naturally gifted in the skills required of a king. Even before Edward emerged as king in waiting, there were quite a number of other people who might have discharged Henry's job with more credit.

One of them was his own wife, Eleanor of Provence. Despite her name, her most significant familial heritage was from Savoy; her mother, Beatrice, came from the sizeable and talented ruling family of that region. At the time of his marriage in 1237 Henry may not quite have appreciated what he was getting, given that Eleanor was only twelve. In time she herself proved quite a formidable political operator, and her family still more so. For the first few years of the marriage Eleanor's role was conventional: she was, it seems clear from the descriptions, beautiful, which appealed to Henry's aesthetic sensibilities. Being so much younger than Henry she was initially inclined to idealise him, which soothed him. She shared with him a love of arts and romance – and he showered her with presents and remodelled apartments for her in at least nine royal residences. One of his rare forays outside his usual round of castles was a trip early in their marriage to Glastonbury so she might see the site celebrated in Arthurian romances.[8]

Eleanor also fulfilled her primary function: Edward was born on 17 or 18 June 1239, when she was about sixteen years old, and he was followed a year later by Margaret, with Beatrice and Edmund following in 1243 and 1245 respectively. So, for the early years of her marriage she was simply the beautiful, adored young queen and mother of a growing family, and her relationship with Henry seems to have been idyllic. Bolstered by her popularity, Henry adopted her relatives (known as the Savoyards) as his first significant group of foreign favourites and established them in a variety of positions of power. But Eleanor had an eye to her financial affairs and to power, too, and by the middle of the decade she had begun to flex her political muscles, ably advised by a her politically acute relatives, sometimes in opposition to her husband. Their main battleground, the question of relatives, will be examined in more detail later in the chapter, but there is certainly evidence that by the early 1250s Henry had begun to find some of Eleanor's assertions of her rights a little wearing. In particular, in early 1252 she even forced him into litigation over a dispute regarding the right to present a clergyman to a living, and had the unforgivable cheek of being found to be in the right. The relationship between Henry and Eleanor in fact deteriorated to the extent that, later in 1252, just a couple of years before the marriage of Edward and Eleanor, Eleanor of Provence was actually banished from court by her husband and her finances frozen.

Although the banishment lasted only a couple of weeks and the couple reconciled after this, producing one more child (a daughter Katherine), and despite the fact that she was entrusted by Henry with the regency in early 1254, the adoration of Eleanor which observers marked in her early years as queen seems to have gone by this stage. Whether the rift was ever fully mended may be open to doubt. There were almost certainly no more children after Katherine, although Eleanor's fertility was proved; she was only just approaching her thirties at this time and there were no lengthy enforced separations for some years after this. As both Henry's mother and Eleanor of Castile herself demonstrate, it was quite usual for a woman in a flourishing marriage to keep producing children well into her forties – Henry's mother had ten children by Hugh de Lusignan after her thirty-third birthday, and Eleanor of Castile was bearing children up to her mid-forties. It therefore appears that there may have been a degree of estrangement in the marriage, due to Henry's dislike of having to face Eleanor's abilities and determination.[9]

Eleanor of Provence may well have taken such estrangement in her stride as, tutored by her Savoyard relatives, she had determined on an important political role for herself in controlling Edward as the heir. A Savoyard, William de Dya, was appointed joint custodian of Edward, along with the Englishman Hugh Giffard, and Bernard of Savoy was appointed keeper of Windsor Castle, where the children spent most of their time. With her people in place even when she was not present, Eleanor could trust that her children, and in particular her son, were being raised to mind her priorities.[10]

Aside from her political role in managing the royal heir, Eleanor carved out for herself a rather greater wifely role than had become traditional, following the disgrace of Eleanor of Aquitaine and the succession of two non-interventionist queens in the form of Berengaria of Navarre and Isabella of Angoulême. In particular, impelled by necessity, she established something of a financial powerbase for herself during Henry's life. The means by which she did this was the provision to her by Henry of a succession of highly remunerative wardships and her attempts to increase her own prerogative income. Both of these steps were controversial. The wardships which she acquired were high profile, and were then exploited by her, in a fashion which her own biographer concedes was ruthless, in pursuit of quick and substantial returns. Her attempts to expand the ambit of her prerogative income, including an ambitious attempt to expand the incidence of the tax known as 'queen's gold', were controversial both at a national and local level. The former can be seen in the fact that questions were asked at the Oxford parliament of 1258. As for the latter, the queen's gold issue provoked a very serious hostility to Eleanor among Londoners in particular, and this hostility was to come home to roost in later years.[11]

It seems likely that Eleanor was a warm person who got on well with other women and formed strong friendships; Howell found evidence of long correspondences with more than one intimate friend, and on reading her letters a lively, charming person speaks through the years. To add to her beauty she obviously also had a keen interest in style and dress. Howell notes that her wardrobe records a wide variety of beautiful and luxurious items of clothing: gowns in vibrant colours trimmed with borders worked with gold or silver thread or decorated with pearl buttons, capes trimmed with fur, indoor slippers and goatskin boots. Overall, they present the impression of a queen for whom style was an indispensable aspect of queenship.[12]

Another major player in the English political world was Henry's younger brother Richard of Cornwall. Richard appears also to have lacked any great interest in or aptitude for martial endeavour. Although he did go on Crusade with Simon de Montfort in the earlier years of Henry's reign, he does not appear to have returned with any great reputation as a soldier. The reputation with which he returned was far more as a politician, supported by a number of actions on Crusade, including the conclusion of an advantageous truce and negotiation of the return of numerous high-ranking hostages, including Simon de Montfort's brother. But there is no reason to doubt his courage. The debacle at Saintes in 1242 illustrates both his bravery and his political abilities: he crossed the River Charente to the enemy camp armed only with a pilgrim's staff to make a personal appeal to King Louis for a short truce, which was granted. Powicke concludes that he was in better control of his temper than Henry and that he made better use of his wits.[13]

In the early part of Henry's majority reign, Richard was a powerful force in arguments for administrative reform, speaking on behalf of influential barons. He was also very good at business, accumulating a large range of estates, often as the price of his agreement with his brother at difficult moments. He worked hard at the management of his properties, becoming, largely by his own efforts, one of the richest men in the kingdom. By the time of Eleanor's introduction to English politics in 1255 Richard was, in a quiet way, a great man at court, married to Eleanor of Provence's sister Sanchia – a marriage to which he was reconciled, characteristically, by a large grant of money. Richard's biographer makes the good point that while Henry and Richard were both tied by their marriages to the Savoyard faction, Henry impoverished himself by giving them gifts – whereas Richard made them loans, which he ensured were repaid.[14]

The third relative who had abilities better suited to kingship than Henry was in many ways the most important: Simon de Montfort, Earl of Leicester. De Montfort was the son of the famous general of the Albigensian Crusade against the Cathars in southern France. As a younger son, Simon had arrived in England with next to nothing and had been warmly welcomed by Henry, presumably on the strength of his great charm and his equally considerable reputation (the origins of which are mysterious) as a warrior. As to his charm, the records provide clear evidence of that most ephemeral of characteristics: his 'pleasant and courteous way of speaking' is noted by one chronicler and its effect can be traced in his personal conquests of other, perhaps better, judges than Henry, such as Robert Grosseteste and Louis IX. It can also be seen from the records which remain of his 1253 trial, where both partisan and non-partisan chroniclers were plainly swept away by the force of his advocacy, and also from both his ability to get people to act against their own interests and his ultimately well-placed confidence that he was a fit match for one of the greatest heiresses of his day.[15]

However, he had gradually come to cast a very uncomfortable shadow over Henry. To add to his reputation as a great warrior had come two important additions: status and money. In terms of status, he was already very well born; although it is conventional to describe his father as coming of the minor French nobility, he was in fact descended from William the Conqueror via one of Henry I's numerous illegitimate progeny. He also had a claim to the prestigious, though impoverished, English earldom of Leicester, which he made good by purchasing the claim and persuading Henry III to endorse it. However, to this he added hugely by his marriage, in 1238, to the king's own sister Eleanor, widow of William Marshal the younger, Earl of Pembroke (following some attempts at other, even more stellar, heiresses).

Eleanor herself, it should be noted in passing, has a tolerable claim to being a better candidate for king than Henry based on pure ability.

Powicke considered her the most able of the daughters of John – who included the Queen of Scots and the Holy Roman Empress. Recent scholarship, particularly that of Wilkinson, has highlighted her considerable abilities as a politician in her own right in networking for her family and in fighting the cause of her dower rights, as well as some military ability in holding Dover Castle in 1265. Certainly, the picture of her which emerges suggests a rather tougher personality than Henry could claim to possess.[16]

The Montfort marriage was not a marriage designed by the king. It appears that he was probably charmed into it by de Montfort and Eleanor and that he consented without appreciating the political storm it would cause for him. The possible alternative is that Henry's hand was forced by a suggestion that the couple had anticipated the ceremony. This alternative, though romantic, is generally considered unlikely, given the favour in which the pair remained immediately after the marriage. But however he was cozened into it, Henry was still casting recriminations about the circumstances of the event some time later: in 1239, while in a rage, he openly accused de Montfort of having seduced Eleanor before the marriage – one classic example of Henry's unpredictable and misplaced rages referred to above.[17]

However it was brought about, not only did this wedding bring de Montfort very near the throne in kinship, it also, notionally at least, brought him considerable wealth. Eleanor's first marriage, to William Marshal, entitled her to a third of her late husband's lands for life by way of dower. These vast lands had substantially come to Henry III's childhood regent, the great warrior William Marshal the elder, through his marriage to Isabel de Clare, heiress to the earldom of Pembroke. Eleanor's rights had also been increased by the dowry given her by Henry on her marriage. Overall, Eleanor was therefore entitled to over £500 per year in respect of the Marshal lands in England and £400 in respect of their Welsh and Irish lands. This was nearly double de Montfort's own income as Earl of Leicester, and transformed him in one swoop from a mid-ranking noble into a considerable magnate.

In the years which succeeded his marriage, de Montfort's star continued to rise. He was acknowledged as a military leader internationally as well as in England; he was offered the post of Governor of Jerusalem, and later that of Constable of France. To add insult to injury, so far as Henry was concerned, de Montfort was one of the few people who distinguished himself at Saintes in 1242, fighting a rearguard action to protect Henry.[18]

All of this led to a relationship where Henry depended upon and violently resented de Montfort in roughly equal measure, and where it is likely that de Montfort's contempt for him was never entirely absent from the king's mind. He appointed de Montfort to Gascony in 1248 to protect the area for Edward and yet refused to back his actions there, instead embracing the chief noble of the region, Gaston de Béarn, whom de Montfort had sent to England in chains, recalling de Montfort and putting him on trial. The result was that de Montfort was acquitted in circumstances which were humiliating to Henry. And yet, even after this, in the run-up to the wedding of Edward and Eleanor, Henry was again asking for help from de Montfort, which de Montfort gave – as was his way, at a price.[19]

So much for the key personalities within the royal family. What of the wider political context? In truth, England was notionally secure but politically fraught; in marked contrast to Castile where, in recent years, faction had largely been buried in an exterior focus: reconquest. Many different issues fed into the English situation, and any full treatment of them lies well beyond the scope of this book. However, there were effectively three key themes: issues of local governance and justice; resentment at the costs involved in Henry's scheme to procure the throne of Sicily for his second son, Edmund; and the issue of 'aliens'. It was this latter issue, which encapsulated resentments arising out of Henry's adoption of a multitude of foreign favourites, which was probably the single most burning problem underpinning the considerable difficulties at the English court at this time. It was also an issue which hovered over the marriage of Eleanor, an 'alien', to Edward.

As mentioned above, in the wake of Eleanor of Provence's marriage to Henry there had come to England a very sizeable contingent of her maternal relatives from Savoy. First came William of Savoy, who was already rising fast in the Church. He was quickly in Henry's confidence and became the first target of the anti-foreigner lobby when Henry attempted to force his election to the wealthy and prestigious bishopric of Winchester. Death intervened to prevent further advancement of William, but he had left behind him a certain number of other Savoyards, some of whom remained in England. The most notable of these was Peter d'Aigueblanche, named for the area of Savoy from which he hailed. By 1239 he was Archdeacon of Shropshire and he became Bishop of Hereford in 1240. Shortly thereafter, two further uncles arrived. The first was Peter of Savoy, who became Eleanor of Provence's primary adviser and the head of the Savoyard faction at court. The second was another cleric, Boniface, whose election as Archbishop of Canterbury Henry forced through in 1241. The timing of their arrival was propitious for Henry: both Richard of Cornwall and Simon de Montfort were absent on Crusade at the time and would remain so for some time. By the time they returned, the Savoyards were ensconced at the heart of court and had already been richly provided for. Peter of Savoy, for example, was knighted by Henry in early 1241 and thereafter given a wide range of lands, honours and posts of influence, including the honours of Richmond and Pevensey, the custody of most of the key south coast castles, of the lands of the late Earl Warenne, Lord Warden of the Cinque Ports.[20]

At this point, the patronage for the most senior Savoyards was not a particular issue. They were useful men, and by virtue of a number of magnates dying without heirs Henry had sufficient land in hand to indulge them without treading on anyone's toes. But the problem was a cumulative one. In the wake of these 'headline' Savoyards came wave after wave of smaller fry. Ridgeway has identified well over 150 Savoyards who enjoyed Henry's patronage in the years after Eleanor of Provence's arrival as queen. Although only a minority became resident in England, and many entered the households of Savoyard magnates, there were a significant number who remained at court.[21]

Particularly significantly, many of them were 'seeded' into Edward's household and later into his group of companions, thereby (theoretically) ensuring that the Savoyard faction kept control of their most important asset – the heir to the throne. Two examples will suffice. One of those who accompanied Edward to Gascony after his marriage was Ebulo de Montibus, who came, as his name suggests, from the Savoyard mountain regions. He was a protégé of Peter of Savoy and was placed by him in close contact with Edward in the early years of the 1250s. He witnessed many of Edward's Acts and was one of those who appeared with Edward at his sister's wedding.[22]

A second example is Otho de Grandison, who was to become one of Edward and Eleanor's closest companions. He was of a Savoyard family whose interest was needed by Peter of Savoy in the Pays de Vaux. Otho appears to have been put into Edward's household during the schoolroom years for Edward later referred to Otho as having given 'faithful service from his earliest youth and our own'. Otho was probably born in 1238, and the date which has been identified for his likely arrival (1247) corresponds with the period when Edward's household was set up. It also seems likely, from three facts, that his family, though noble, was impecunious. In the first place, his father was given a pension of £20 per annum for the services of his sons. In the second place, the fact that he would part with Otho, his eldest son, indicates that there was not much to look forward to at home. Finally, the fact that Otho for years appears in the records simply as 'Ottonin' – even after his father's death made him Lord of Grandson, and he became a knight only some seven years later, indicates powerfully that the Lords of Grandson did not have enough money to support the knightly state. Otho, as will become apparent, rose to considerable wealth and rank on the back of his strategic placement with Edward in childhood, although his loyalty was to Edward, not to the Savoyard faction.[23]

But it was not merely or even mainly in the question of patronage that the Savoyard influx was offensive. Three Savoyards were married, at Peter of Savoy's behest, to three of the most wealthy Anglo-Irish heiresses, whose marriages were in the gift of the king, removing this source of wealth from the English and Irish nobility. To cap this, following an Anglo-Savoyard treaty in 1246, the male heirs to major English honours began to be picked off by the queen for her relatives. The queen's cousin Alice de Saluzzo was brought to England in 1247 to marry the underage heir to the earldom of Lincoln. With her came another relative, to be married to the male heir to the substantial Irish honour of Connacht. Next was the lordship of de Vescy, which at that time controlled Alnwick and much of Northumberland. The Vescy heir, John (another future close friend of Edward and Eleanor), was married to Alice of Saluzzo's sister Agnes. Then came the matches of Eleanor of Geneva to Alexander Balliol and Margaret of Savoy to the heir to the earldom of Devon. Still further examples can be given. Each of these marriages represented control of vast tracts of land and revenue and affected the running not just of these territories, but their neighbours and those in the affinity of the family for years to come. Thus, although a number of the marriages were happy, and the Savoyards did assist in maintaining peace in difficult areas, feeling ran high over these marriages. It can be seen from Matthew Paris' reports in his chronicle that the practice was and continued to be resented and the marriage of English heiresses to foreigners was a key issue for the barons in 1258, when the tensions beneath the surface of the English court came to the surface.[24]

Had matters stopped with the Savoyard interest, however, all might just have been manageable. There was a limited number of sufficiently ranking Savoyards. However, in 1247 Henry invited four of his de Lusignan half-brothers and his half-sister Alice to come to England and live under his patronage. They were later supplemented by a couple of his de Lusignan nieces. The third of the visiting brothers, William 'of Valence', was then married to the heiress to the lordship of Pembroke and was also given a pension of over £800 per annum. An attempt was made to install the youngest brother, Aymer, who was probably in his late teens at the time, as Bishop of Durham. When this attempt was not successful, he was given a rich living in Wearmouth and in 1252 was installed in the even richer see of Winchester – at which time he was still being educated at Oxford. The older Lusignans, Guy and Geoffrey, who remained largely in France, were given rich pensions. Meanwhile, Alice was married to the heir to the Earl Warenne (Surrey), while her cousins were married to the heirs of the earldoms of Gloucester and Derby.[25]

Predictably, with these new aliens came their own protégés and soon they too were installing themselves as constables of strategic castles or within the royal household. Equally predictably, the new aliens were unwelcome both to the English nobility and to the Savoyard faction. So far as the English nobility was concerned, this new influx of foreigners and their preferments fell into the account which was gradually being prepared against the king. So far as the old aliens were concerned, there were naturally rows, the most severe of which prior to Eleanor's arrival is worth recounting.[26]

In late 1252, a quarrel arose between the queen's uncle Boniface, Archbishop of Canterbury, and the king's half-brother Aymer, the bishop elect of Winchester, concerning the appointment to the post of prior of the hospital of St Thomas at Southwark. Boniface was away and Aymer installed his own candidate. An official of the archbishopric pointed out that the archbishop's confirmation was necessary, and when his advice was ignored he took it upon himself to excommunicate the new prior. At Aymer's instigation the prior elect ignored this interdict, and was then seized and imprisoned in the archbishop's prison. Aymer consulted with his brother William who, in true Lusignan style, despatched a bunch of armed men, ransacked the prison and surrounding manor and sprung the prior from his prison. They then rounded up the archbishop's official, who was beaten up and then dropped in the middle of nowhere with instructions to walk home.[27]

The king was plainly placed in a most uncomfortable position, but was principally annoyed with those who had taken to complaining about the Lusignans – foremost among them, the queen. Nothing was done immediately on the actual dispute, but Henry suspended her control over all her lands and banished her from court, sending her to Winchester. On the other side of the equation, he simply suspended or diverted monies payable to William of Valence. The row rolled on for weeks, but was eventually patched up in early 1253, with Aymer swearing that he had been no party to the raid and being given the kiss of peace by Boniface. Officially the matter was over, but the huge fault lines which had rapidly opened up at the heart of the court, and which had proved so difficult to close, showed just how unstable the position was.[28]

Aside from the political aspects of the English court, it is worth considering the royal family life. The key point is that Henry III and Eleanor of Provence were devoted parents, and indubitably made themselves beloved by their children. Henry was capable of great charm and generosity, particularly towards those who were no threat to him, and one can imagine that this made him a delightful father. Having lacked a settled childhood himself, he was keen to see that his own children had what he had missed. Many records remain of his concern for his children. In October 1242, he contacted the constable of Windsor to say that he had heard that the children had no good wine to drink and instructed him to present them with two of the best tuns to be found in the castle. (It should be understood that this was not a case of encouraging underage drinking – diluted wine was drunk to ameliorate the health risk posed by unclean water.) Later the same year, Henry instructed the sheriff of Gloucester to send fifteen lampreys, a much-prized though disgusting-looking eel-like fish, to three-year-old Edward – who we may imagine had confided how very much he liked lampreys. He sent fur-trimmed scarlet robes and special 'two-seater' saddles for Edward's first attempts at horsemanship. It is also likely that Henry and Eleanor were comparatively 'present' parents: Windsor, where the children seem to have been largely based, was second only to London in the list of Henry's most visited locations in the years 1236–41, and most of his other favourite palaces were a sufficiently short distance to enable the children to visit their parents far more frequently than was common with royal children.[29]

Meanwhile, Eleanor, from a notably devoted family, was well placed to recreate that ambience in her own nursery. Nor did she spurn the maternal role; for prolonged periods in every year of her children's childhood she would base herself at Windsor with them. While Henry minimised his travel, she travelled even less, choosing to stay with her children for parts of the year rather than accompany her husband. So between July 1252 and July 1253 she was at Windsor for thirty weeks of the year, with the rest of the time spent at Clarendon, Marlborough, Woodstock and Winchester for about a fortnight at a time, and with only two flying visits to the capital.

Despite the king providing a separate fund for the children's household, her wardrobe records provide clear evidence of her closely overseeing their dress, with a detail which bespeaks intimacy. She chose gowns for Beatrice, a tabard of Ypres silk for Edward and – a fact which will resonate with any parent – apparently innumerable pairs of children's shoes. Her close presence in her children's lives is also attested by her gift giving to their nurses – in 1253, eleven-year-old Beatrice was given a brooch to give to her nurse from Eleanor's accounts, and the nurse was also given a brooch directly by Eleanor. Brooches were also given to Edward's former nurse Lady Alice, and to the nurses of John de Warenne's daughter Alice de Lusignan, Richard of Cornwall's son Edmund and Alice de Saluzzo's son Henry. Inferentially these children were all being brought up with the royal children at Windsor, and Eleanor had formed warm ties to them all. As Howell notes, the picture which emerges is of an establishment which placed children and their wellbeing at its heart – a child-centred household which would not seem out of place today.[30]

No contemporaneous detail remains of the way in which the children were looked after from day to day, but a vignette from the nursery later run by Eleanor of Castile at King's Langley shows the level of comfort which the children enjoyed. In 1286, the Queen's Remembrancer notes that young John de Warenne (the grandson of John de Warenne and Alice de Lusignan) had two new robes a year, one at Christmas and one at Easter 'as the sons of great lords are accustomed to have'; two palfreys and three sumpter horses with men to keep them; five squires, their horses and three valets. For dinner he was allowed three pennyworths of bread, three dishes from the kitchen, a pitcher of wine and two of beer; for supper his allowance was a little larger. At night he had one torch to burn as long as it lasted, and twelve candles.[31]

What else do we know of the Windsor establishment where Edward was brought up? As in Castile, so also in England, hunting, predominantly in the form of falconry, was a favoured hobby: the queen ordered gloves for this pastime for Beatrice and Edmund. But while that would remain his favourite form of hunting, Edward seems also to have taken to hunting with hounds, being given permission to hunt in Windsor forest in 1247. Chess was certainly played as it was in Castile, but more informal recreations seem to have been favoured. Music in particular was a favourite; there are records of dancing and minstrels to play for the children. Indeed, music was so very much enjoyed that in 1242, when the king and queen went to Gascony, 'Richard the Harper' was retained for the comfort of the royal children, who were then only two and three years old.[32]

Windsor therefore would have been to the royal children very much a family home. However, from quite a young age Edward would have been accustomed to a degree of itinerant life with the court. It is likely Henry had his family around him for Christmas in Westminster or Winchester, and at age seven Edward was with his parents at the consecration of a new abbey church in Beaulieu in 1246 when he fell ill. There are also records of Edward having chambers at a number of the royal castles and palaces: Woodstock, Oxford, Silverstone, Guildford, Havering and Gillingham, for example. Overall, it seems to have been a much more relaxed, and rurally based, upbringing than Eleanor enjoyed. War was far away, not an ever-present reality. Armed camps were unheard of; so too was the prospect of losing a near relative in battle. Administrative business, never a favourite of Henry's, was predominately carried on away from the children. Life as a royal child in Henry III and Eleanor of Provence's nursery establishment must have been very much a life of ease and pleasure.[33]

The upbringing of all the children, and of the future king Edward in particular, is of course likely to have involved a very great deal of religious observance and doctrine, though little theological debate. Henry III was not a speculative theologian, but an emotional devotee of the cult of St Edward the Confessor – the un-martial king upon whom he had seized as the appropriate model for his own kingship. Similarly, Eleanor of Provence corresponded with theologians, but for her moral guidance rather than from a spirit of intellectual inquiry or debate. Thus the feast of St Edward the Confessor on 13 October was a major event for the Henrician court; Henry was almost always at Westminster for the celebration of this festival and also frequently for the anniversary of the Confessor's death on 5 January. Even when he could not be there – as, for example, in the year of Margaret's marriage to the King of Scotland

– he ensured that the festival was kept with magnificence in his absence. Further, while travel as a whole was not much in favour, travelling for the purpose of pilgrimage was very much a feature of the court under Henry. One or other of the feast days of St Thomas Becket was often held at Canterbury, and for at least half of the years 1234–41 Henry organised tours of pilgrimage into Norfolk to Walsingham, Bromholm and Bury St Edmunds. Edward will have been present for a good number of these visits of pilgrimage, at least once he passed the 'danger age' of about seven and began visiting the court more frequently. The result of his early religious training appears to have been to produce in Edward what Prestwich has described as 'unsophisticated piety', with a taste, albeit more limited than that of his father, for pilgrimages and devotional visits.[34]

A theme which emerges from the household records is that Edward was by no means as robust as a child as he was as a man. As an adult he seems hardly to have known a day's illness until his latter days. But as a child he was considered more fragile in health. Reference has been made above to the obviously sudden and severe illness of Edward aged about seven at Beaulieu in 1246, which necessitated his staying for three weeks, accompanied, in defiance of Cistercian rules, by his mother – and doubtless a good handful of nurses and waiting women. Records also exist of his being ill at Westminster and Windsor. However, he seems to have gained in strength as he grew, and in his later childhood, as in his adult years, he seems to have enjoyed good health.[35]

Edward's companions were not confined to his siblings, not least because the two siblings nearest to him in age were both girls – Margaret and Beatrice. His only brother, Edmund, was nearly six years his junior. Around 1247, various boys of roughly his age were brought in to make up his household and his schoolfellows. Money was frequently assigned by Henry for the expenses of Edward's household 'and the other children dwelling with him at Windsor'.[36]

Practically no record remains either of the identities of these companions or the course of education which Edward and his friends followed. However, some small traces remain. Despite the closeness in age, and family ties through his aunt Eleanor, Edward was not educated with Simon de Montfort's similarly aged boys, Henry, Simon and Guy, all born between 1238 and 1240. They were apparently educated under the aegis of Robert Grosseteste, the saintly and academic Bishop of Lincoln. Henry of Almain, the son of Richard of Cornwall, to whom Edward was very close and who was his father's eldest son by a number of years, is likely to have been one of the group at least for some period of time after the death of his mother in 1240; Henry was over three years older than Edward and may have graduated from the schoolroom earlier.[37]

The gift of a brooch to Henry's younger brother's nurse suggests that Edmund of Cornwall was part of the household, but his age (he was born in 1249) makes him a more likely companion for Edward's own brother, Edmund. Similarly Edmund de Lacy, who went on to marry Alice de Saluzzo, the queen's cousin, and whose son's nurse was gifted in 1252, may well have formed part of the Windsor group before his marriage, though nine years older than Edward. Within Edward's household from a very early stage and part of Edward's own group was Otho de Grandison. Likewise Ebulo de Montibus, who was almost Edward's contemporary in age. Other possibilities for the group, at least in its latter stages, are John de Vescy, the heir to the Lord of Alnwick, who was married to the queen's Savoyard relative Agnes de Saluzzo; Edward's close friend Robert Tybetot; and James, son of the seneschal of Gascony, Nicholas de Molis. Almost certainly present were the sons of Bartholomew Pecche, who was appointed to be Edward's guardian when Edward was seven. They accompanied Edward and their father to Spain for Edward's wedding to Eleanor. Some more humble children are also recorded as forming part of the household, including the two sons of one Ferrand, a crossbowman.[38]

As for what the boys learnt, it will certainly not have been as academic an upbringing as that which Eleanor enjoyed. There was no comparable tradition of scholarship at the English court, nor were there such academic resources. On the whole it is thought that Edward, unlike Eleanor, could not write, though it is considered likely that he could read and had some knowledge of Latin as well as fluency in Anglo-Norman French and English. He was not the first English king to speak English – King John wins that title, and Henry II is reputed to have had a limited English vocabulary. Moreover, speaking English was no great sign of scholarship, it being the language of the lower classes and therefore not deemed a subject for study.[39]

In further contrast to Eleanor's childhood, the books which would have surrounded Edward and his companions are not likely to have been very scholarly; aside from religious works, they were probably largely confined to the stories of knightly chivalry which his mother is known to have read, and for which his father also had a fondness. Eleanor of Provence was educated, and read and corresponded with one of the great religious men of her day for spiritual guidance. But there is no whiff about her of the bluestocking; she was in essence a 'people person'. Her books were acquired for her from booksellers such as Peter and William of Paris and appear to be prettily bound romances, or poems of chivalry like John of Howden's *Rossignos*, which recounted tales of Hector, Troilus, Alexander, Caesar and the Knights of the Round Table. That Edward also read these tales can be inferred from the fact that he possessed at least one such in his adulthood. He was thus raised to be, and became, literate, but not bookish.[40]

Another reason for the pull of the romances which were the backbone of his reading is that they were entirely compatible with a major part of his education as a king's son: knightly skills including horsemanship, weapons training and hunting, both with dogs and hawks. Bartholomew Pecche would have been primarily responsible for this training, but the reported presence of the Nicholas de Molis who had been with Edward at the Scottish wedding indicates that this gentleman, elsewhere referred to by Matthew Paris as 'a distinguished knight', probably coached Edward and his companions in knightly skills.

Both mentally and physically, then, Edward was raised to believe in and to attempt to embody the knightly ideal. To add to this, with Richard of Cornwall's children present or often visiting the Windsor establishment, it is inevitable that Edward will have heard from Richard his crusading tales, similar to those which the earl told Matthew Paris; and the entire household is likely to have participated in the crusading fever which overtook the court in 1250 when Henry III took the cross in imitation of Louis IX, who had departed for the Holy Land in 1248 and had recently taken the port of Damietta in epic style. Queen Eleanor's copy of *The Song of Antioch*, a romance history of the First Crusade, was probably quickly dog-eared and formed the subject for discussion and play throughout the nursery.[41]

However, though the ideals of knightly attainment were very much to the fore, it seems doubtful that Edward's training was very rigorous in practical terms. England was at peace, and intended to remain so. Eleanor of Provence would be against any training which was hazardous to her precious eldest son, and so too would Henry III, who himself had no time for fighting, or even for hunting, and regarded tournaments as almost criminal. It would therefore seem that Edward's knightly training, though doubtless correct and thorough, will have been largely formal. It is highly unlikely that it was anything like as intensive as that which the sons of Ferdinand, raised in fairly spartan conditions, surrounded by active warriors and expected to take to the field in real engagements in their early teens, underwent.

At fourteen, it therefore seems that the young Lord Edward, as he was known, hardly seemed likely to be the dream match for the scholarly daughter and sister of Castile's very active soldier kings.

4

The Marriage

The origins of Eleanor and Edward's famously harmonious marriage lie, ironically enough, in deep disharmony. This is because the first seeds of the idea of the marriage can probably be found in the miserable time experienced by both Gascony and its seneschal or governor, Simon de Montfort, in the years 1248 to 1252. A soldier of huge talent, he was certainly at this stage in his career more reminiscent of his intransigent father than the hero of representative politics often portrayed in modern accounts. His approach to the task in hand in Gascony was therefore of the iron-fist-in-iron-glove type, with little sensitivity to local customs and politics. These tactics had not at all suited the Gascons, who had never fully reconciled themselves to being part of the Angevin Empire rather than *pares* in a *primus inter pares* arrangement with the dukes of Aquitaine. His period of rule culminated in the trial, referred to earlier, of charges brought against him by numerous disaffected Gascon nobles. Although a short-term truce was patched up following the failure of that trial, it was obviously apparent that the situation in Gascony was very much open to opportunist meddlings by those averse to the Angevin rule – including Castile.[1]

The timing of this unrest was very unfortunate for Henry. Ferdinand III had died in May 1252 and Alfonso X, new to the throne and with his father's dying challenge ringing in his ears, was not slow to pick up the baton in this regard, very possibly encouraged by Gaston de Béarn, who will have been well placed to tell tales of Henry's weakness. Straight after de Montfort's trial, Alfonso accepted the homage of Gascon families alienated by de Montfort's harsh policies – including the influential Gaston, who, although cousin to Eleanor of Provence, was never averse to mischief making for the Crown. Soon word began to filter through that Gascon wine merchants were seeking out new markets in Castile – doubtless also with the encouragement of Alfonso and Gaston.[2]

In this context, Henry felt that it was necessary to promise a visit to Gascony by himself and Edward, now titular duke. However, the timeline shows that, in parallel, he began to investigate the possibility of a marriage between Eleanor and Edward, as a deal which would keep Castile out of Gascony. He was reporting his intentions to go to Gascony in April, and by 15 May 1253 he had accredited William of Bitton, the Bishop of Bath and Wells, and former chancellor John Maunsell to seek the marriage. This step was reported by the chroniclers with some confusion as to the identity of the lucky princess; some suggested that it was the daughter of Alfonso who was to be the bride, but Alfonso as yet had no daughter. However, the uncertainty over the bride's identity illustrates how low was Eleanor's profile.[3]

A number of commentators dating as far back as Matthew Paris have speculated that the claim to Gascony by Alfonso was merely a tactic designed to entice Henry into the marriage. However, modern scholarship has rejected this analysis. Alfonso may not have had a strong belief in the claim, but some sort of claim was there.[4]

The fact that the English marriage was not Alfonso's goal in meddling in Gascony is also borne out by the delays which he imposed upon the negotiations. Two particular sticking points appear in the records. The first was the demand that Alfonso knight Edward, an important point of honour, particularly in the militaristic ethos of Castile. This would be a difficult issue in terms of pride; Henry would normally have expected – and did expect, despite his own lack of military prowess – to knight his son himself, as he had knighted the King of Scotland. It was also an issue in terms of security, since Edward would make the perfect hostage. The second issue was dower and dowry. Alfonso offered nothing by way of dowry but instead expected Henry to provide generous dower for Eleanor, rejecting Henry's first offer of 1,000 marks per annum.[5]

In fact it appears that, initially at least, Alfonso was using the English marriage negotiations as a stalking horse to bring another bridegroom to the table. So while early progress was made, with a draft treaty being in the hands of John Maunsell by summer and one of Eleanor's cousins, William de Fiennes, being added to Edward's household on 5 July 1253, Alfonso then appears to have deliberately stalled negotiations. Meanwhile, he entered into negotiations with Navarre for the marriage of the new King Thibault, aged fourteen, to Eleanor.[6]

In many ways the Navarrese marriage was of more utility to Alfonso. There was a disputed claim to feudal supremacy over Navarre which dated back to 1134, when Garcia VI of Navarre had sworn homage to Alfonso VII of Castile. Navarre also had designs on Gascony and offered access for Castile to Gascony via the Pyrenean passes, which would be of great use if Alfonso intended to act on his claims. A Navarrese marriage was not out of question in status terms; one had been considered for Alfonso himself at an earlier stage. Further, there was a suitable dynastic connection on two sides, first through Blanche of Navarre, who had married into the Castilian royal family in the previous century, and secondly via Eleanor of Aquitaine's daughter Marie, who had married Thibault of Champagne, great-grandfather of the present king. Moreover, the Navarrese marriage was a particularly ripe plum at the time, since Thibault was not yet of age, and there was therefore a decent prospect of Castile effectively annexing the kingdom.[7]

However, scenting danger – and probably rightly so – Queen Marguerite of Navarre instead submitted herself to the protection of the less acquisitive Aragon, who, as junior partner to Castile in the Iberian peninsula, was also keen to rein in Alfonso. Thus, she undertook in August 1253 that Thibault would 'never at any time in his life, marry the sister of the Lord Alfonso, king of Castile, daughter of the Lord King Ferdinand and the Lady Queen Jeanne'.[8]

So by late August 1253 Alfonso was back facing the English marriage, with Henry, who had left England in late July, on his way to back up diplomacy with force. Negotiations are likely to have awaited the event somewhat, since Henry's military history might well lead Alfonso to believe that his hand would strengthen as Henry floundered. As it was, however, Henry did surprisingly well, combining the diplomacy which de Montfort had scorned to employ with military action where necessary. The success of this latter aspect can probably be traced to the assistance of de Montfort, who came to Henry's aid – but only after both payment by Henry and intervention from Robert Grosseteste.[9]

Obviously forming the view that his hand was unlikely to improve in the near future, Alfonso came back to the table at about the end of 1253. Thus by 8 February 1254 John Maunsell went back to Castile, this time accompanied by Eleanor of Provence's close associate Peter d'Aigueblanche, the Bishop of Hereford.[10]

It appears by this time that Henry was absolutely determined on the marriage, since the envoys were empowered to offer generous terms including a provision that Edward would have lands worth £10,000 (15,000 marks) yearly and Eleanor would be dowered 'as fully as any queen of England had ever been'. Given that the envoys cannot have set off until after 14 February, matters must then have proceeded apace, for by 31 March the Castilian envoys announced that peace was made and that Alfonso would abandon his claims to rule in Gascony; a treaty of alliance was promulgated the next day in Toledo. On dower, Alfonso had sensibly insisted on a rather more specific promise than Henry's vague platitudes. Henry's initial offer of 1,000 marks was raised to £1,000, to be increased by 500 marks at Edward's accession. Henry's concession on this front may well reflect the fact that he was already aware, from his own wife's financial difficulties, that £1,000 was miserably inadequate to a modern queen's needs.

The terms of the treaty bear some examination. The financial promises referred to above were considered by many in England to be so extensive as to denigrate Henry's own status – Matthew Paris said they made Henry a 'mutilated kinglet'. Plainly they were also considered significant by Alfonso, who in summer 1254 insisted upon a little due diligence, inspecting original grants of land to Edward and requiring that they be reissued with Henry's Great Seal. However, in reality the grants were not absolute, leaving Henry able to interfere substantially in the territories ceded to Edward, and the fact of the grants was even of positive benefit to Henry in some areas, shoring up dubious claims to overlordship.

Henry did concede the knighting issue – Edward was to be knighted by Alfonso on or before the next Feast of the Assumption – and he also agreed to seek commutation of his earlier vow to go on Crusade in order to assist Alfonso with an invasion of North Africa. However, neither of these concessions were of much substance. Henry also agreed to help impose Castilian supremacy over Navarre, but this agreement would only 'bite' if Alfonso ever got anywhere close to supremacy. Otherwise, as part of the unpicking of the Gascon troubles, Henry agreed to restore losses suffered by Gascons who supported Alfonso. The marriage of Edward and Eleanor was also to be backed up by a reciprocal marriage of Henry's daughter Beatrice and one of Alfonso's brothers.[12]

On the other side of the fence, Alfonso renounced all claims to Gascony and promised to return all lands seized from Henry in the Gascon troubles. He also promised that, once he made peace with Navarre, any Gascon lands seized by the kings of Navarre would be returned, and that Henry should have a half share in the lands conquered in any African expedition. It should be noted here that suggestions that Alfonso did give some dowry, or that Eleanor had dowry in the form of being heiress to Ponthieu, are inaccurate – there is no record of her bringing any dowry and she only became heiress to Ponthieu on the death of her older brother Ferdinand, more than a decade later.

There were therefore a number of 'pie in the sky' elements of this treaty – the North African expedition never happened, Henry was never absolved from his crusading vow and Navarre never did come under Castilian rule, maintaining its somewhat marginal existence until the sixteenth century. Putting these to one side, it is at first tempting to say that Alfonso did very well out of this treaty, in that he got a royal marriage for his sister at no cost to himself. But to regard this absence of dowry payment by Alfonso as a win for Castile is a mistaken approach.

Eleanor, even with no dowry, was no bad deal for Henry and England. To get a princess at all was a point of considerable value. But Eleanor represented rather more than a 'mere princess'. She was the daughter of a great crusading king and the sister of a king who, at this stage in his career, promised to be a leading light in international terms, both through the affluence brought about by Ferdinand's conquests and by reason of his own scholarship and Imperial connections. A Castilian connection was therefore very valuable. What is more, Eleanor was the only daughter of Ferdinand to come on the market; the only other daughter to live to adulthood became a nun. Further still, although Eleanor was not actually heiress to Ponthieu, she would have influence over her mother, who was now the regnant countess on Henry's doorstep.[13]

Nor was this Henry's only gain from the deal. On top of Eleanor's personal claims, Henry got back lands which he had lost in Gascony; and most of all he got as near a guarantee of peace in Gascony as he could expect, given the nature of the Gascon nobles, especially Gaston de Béarn. He was certainly now safe from Castile, and also from Navarre, which would inevitably go down to the combined might of Castile and England, if it got out of line. The value of this guarantee was of almost inestimable value to him. Nor was he the only one to appreciate its value; the peace which the marriage brought bore fruit in the crucial relationship with France. Once the marriage was agreed, Louis IX realised he would be unable to foment useful discord in Gascony, and ultimately acknowledged Henry's claims in Gascony by the Treaty of Paris in 1259.

In fact, a better question is, what did Alfonso get out of the deal? It must be recalled that he would see none of the money for which he had fought so hard. All he definitely got, in exchange for a dubious but valuable claim to Gascony, was the honour of knighting Edward and the further honour of a royal marriage into the English royal house – not the prize it might have seemed in Henry II's time. Otherwise, his gains were speculative. Certainly Spanish historians have reproached Alfonso soundly for his stupidity in abandoning the claim for so little return. All in all, Alfonso appears to have obeyed the letter and the spirit of his father's injunction as regards Eleanor and done his very best to ensure that she was well provided for.

From the beginning of April, implementation of the deal began: a safe conduct was issued for Edward at once, and on 22 April Alfonso ordered the Gascons to return to their allegiance to Henry. By 18 July, the final details were falling into place: the date was set for some time within five weeks of Michaelmas; Henry typically hoped for the Feast of St Edward the Confessor on 13 October. Two days later, Edward assigned dower lands to Eleanor: the towns of Stamford and Grantham, the castle and town of the Peak and the manor of Tickhill. On 23 July, John Maunsell was ordered by Edward to conclude the marriage by proxy; the letter refers to Eleanor's 'beauty and prudence', of which Edward has heard by general report. Interestingly, this letter seems to be the only extant reference to Eleanor's beauty, and its combination with 'prudence', as opposed to 'charm', *debonairité* or 'sweetness', is an unusual one, suggesting that her serious nature had been mentioned to Edward by the envoys who had met her. In August, a Castilian embassy headed by Garcia Martinez, a diplomat who appears to have been appointed Eleanor's *ayo* (tutor or governor) for the purposes of finalising the negotiations on her behalf, arrived in Gascony to accept the dower assignment.[14]

In all of this business, it will perhaps have been noted that Eleanor's mother, Dowager Queen Jeanne, seems to have played no part. This apparently reflects the *actualité*, and the reasons for this shed light on Eleanor's relations at this time with her immediate family. The truth was that by 1254, Eleanor's mother and her eldest brother were embroiled in a very serious row – and her mother was also playing a starring role in a scandal of no mean proportions. The combination of the two was to place Jeanne firmly outside the circle involved in arranging the match and even to make her continued residence in Castile impossible.

Alfonso's relationship with Jeanne seems to have been stormy for some time, as Ferdinand's injunction to Alfonso on his deathbed hints. The reasons behind this are interesting. In the first place, although the relationship between a stepmother and stepson of approximately equal age was never likely to be very easy, Jeanne had apparently had cause to resent Alfonso from even before her marriage. The original plan of Blanche of Castile had seen Jeanne marrying Ferdinand and her younger sister Philippa marrying Alfonso; papal dispensations for both marriages had been obtained. However, Alfonso had very strong views indeed about the nobility of his descent, which can be seen in the *Cantigas*, where he trumpets his noble descent by reference to his mother and states that his first great advantage was that Ferdinand III had given him life 'through a woman of great lineage'. Alfonso therefore flatly refused the marriage, and made much of the noble descent of the wife he eventually took – Violante of Aragon.[14]

The slight and the huge loss which the marriage represented to the position of her family was not likely to be lost on Jeanne. A second royal marriage would have improved her family's political importance immensely. As it was, Philippa did not marry until comparatively late and then married (as his third wife) the Count of Eu, a lesser member of the prolific de Lusignan family, and, after his death, a scion of the House of Coucy; both respectable but by no means brilliant marriages.

To add to this original point of friction there was a considerable dispute about property, in particular the dower which Jeanne held as queen. As noted in Chapter 1, the Castilian concept of dower involved the wife entering into ownership of the property at once, and not merely on the death of her spouse. While the approach whereby dowry, the gift from the wife's family, outweighed or replaced dower was prevalent elsewhere in Europe and was gaining ground in parts of Iberia (including in Alfonso's own plans), it had not yet established itself in Castile. Queens in Castile therefore held and ruled substantial portions of the royal demesne as their own, as, for example, Berengaria had done with the disputed border forts. This gave them greater personal wealth and opportunities for patronage than was common elsewhere.[16]

It was common practice for queens to swear fidelity to the king and to his heir in respect of such property. Jeanne, however, refused to submit her properties to Alfonso's authority. Alfonso then took a hard line about whether certain other properties gifted by Ferdinand to Jeanne were properly alienable from the Crown, and he refused to acknowledge her rights to them. Attempts were made to resolve the resulting disputes, but by 1252 there are records of litigation between Jeanne and Alfonso. This ongoing dispute explains Ferdinand's charge to Alfonso on his deathbed to treat Jeanne with the same affection and deference as if she had been his mother and give her all the honours which were her due. There is doubt whether Alfonso respected his father's wishes in this regard. Ferdinand's will left certain lands to Jeanne, including some at Cordoba and Jaén, but Alfonso denied her seigniorial rights over them and may also have actually withheld their benefits from her as well.[17]

At odds with Alfonso, Jeanne found a sympathetic ear close to home. There was no firm principle of primogeniture established in Spain, and it was therefore possible for younger sons to have hopes of the throne. Doubtless with this in mind, the colourful Enrique – reputedly the best soldier and diplomat of all the sons – had refused to recognise Alfonso as Ferdinand's heir in 1246. Once installed as king after Ferdinand's death, Alfonso in turn refused to recognise the grant of certain lands to Enrique under his father's will, a move which pushed him into rebellion.

Jeanne and Enrique sympathised with each other over their problems with the intractable Alfonso and Jeanne even attended a meeting which Enrique held with his allies at Burgos. This closeness led to rumours that the two were lovers. The commentators suggest that this is unlikely to have been true – Jeanne, although only thirty-two at Ferdinand's death, was still a good ten years older than Enrique. However, it is obviously possible, and two factors suggest that it may indeed have been the case. The first is Jeanne's later choice of a second husband of limited means, which suggests that she had a taste for handsome or charming men. The second is the storyline of Enrique's later work *Amadis de Gaula*: its theme is a forbidden love between a penniless prince and a queen. Certainly there was very considerable gossip about them at the time, as traces of it still survive in the fragmentary records.[18]

Ultimately, Jeanne's relationship with Alfonso seems to have reached a point where her position was totally untenable. She was apparently not consulted by him over Eleanor's marriage and she did not even attend the wedding, choosing to leave Castile in the summer before the wedding, even though by this stage all the arrangements were in place. The ostensible reason for her departure was that she was to assume her position as Countess of Ponthieu after her mother's death. However, since her mother had died in 1250 this was a very threadbare excuse indeed, and the probability is that her disappearance at this stage was intended to embarrass Alfonso.

Two interesting points regarding Eleanor emerge from this little byplay. The first is that Eleanor cannot have escaped being aware of the difficult relations between her mother and Alfonso throughout her childhood and yet she apparently managed herself to maintain good relations with him. He certainly went to considerable efforts to ensure that she was well provided for, though this could not benefit him, and possibly the less that was asked on Eleanor's behalf, the more he could himself have gained. And certainly she felt more than simply dutiful to him: her correspondence with and support for him in later years might just be put down to familial imperatives, but the christening of one of her sons as Alphonso (an outlandish name to the English ear) vouches for a very real affection.[19]

Part of this may be linked to the second point emerging from this story: this period will have provided Eleanor with an object lesson in the importance of the rules which she had been taught on the maintenance of good habits, of quiet deportment and, of course, of suppressing her temper; and the difficulties a queen who abandoned these principles might attract. It is a lesson which she appears to have learnt to admiration. In later years, although associating very closely with many of her husband's unmarried friends, not a whisper ever appears about her. It appears that, on this point at least, she saw her mother's approach as the worse course and preferred the teaching of Alfonso. Indeed, given this obvious closeness of view and affection between Alfonso and Eleanor, and Jeanne's decision to leave Castile and not to support her young daughter through her marriage, one may well infer that the bond between Eleanor and her mother was not particularly close.

It is worth noting at this stage, as it was a precursor to later problems in which Eleanor tried to assist Alfonso, that Alfonso's troubles with Enrique and Jeanne in this period did not come in isolation. The chief nobles of Castile chiefly fell into factions behind the two pre-eminent families of de Lara and de Haro. The latter family had been in the ascendant since the days of Berengaria's regency. However, Ferdinand had been tolerably even handed with the de Laras, keeping them happy enough to be peaceful. Alfonso, however, openly favoured the de Lara faction. Unsurprisingly this resulted in a good deal of disaffection, at a time when the nobility were no longer gainfully employed in the reconquest. The result was an alliance between Enrique, the de Haros and Jaime of Aragon, which hampered Alfonso's control over both Seville and the north. In 1254, Enrique and Jaime agreed an alliance by the marriage of Enrique to Jaime's daughter Costanza, the sister of Alfonso's own queen. However, within the year Alfonso, chiefly through Queen Violante's intercession with her father, had brought an end to this proposed marriage and the appearance of peace had returned. The price of Alfonso's speedy rejection of his father's modus operandi would come later.[20]

Meanwhile, Jeanne left Castile with her son and heir apparent, Ferdinand. Her younger son Luis (who was probably only just eleven years old) was left behind in the custody of Alfonso, who, in fulfilment of his vow to his father, made provision for him, investing him as Señor de Marchena and Zuheros. This was probably because he had practically no inheritance prospects in relation to Ponthieu. Henry issued safe conducts for Jeanne and Ferdinand on 16 July, they spent some time at Bordeaux with the English royal family in August and she was back in Abbeville, capital of Ponthieu, on 31 October, the day before Eleanor's wedding.[21]

Meanwhile, what of the groom? He set out on 29 May 1254 with his mother, the Archbishop of Canterbury and a large company of knights, magnates, officials and courtiers. The size of the expedition can be gauged by reference to the scale of the preparations which were made for it: bridges and hurdles were ordered for 300 ships, ships were requisitioned, including all the ones in London capable of carrying sixteen horses. The honour of providing the ships for the main passengers had been divided among the Cinque Ports and Yarmouth, Winchelsea drawing the queen and Yarmouth drawing Edward. However, when the ships were assembled the men of Winchelsea were enraged by how much better Yarmouth's ship was and attacked it, killing some of the Yarmouth men, carrying off the (obviously superior) mast and fitting it onto their own vessel.[22]

Edward and his entourage arrived in Bordeaux around 10–12 June. He was housed separately from his parents, his mother staying in a house which she had used on a previous visit. Henry was absent; he was still reducing the troublesome fortress of La Réole, where the hard core of resisters had congregated. However, he had provided for suitable donatives (three gold cloths each) to be ready for his wife and Edward to offer at the churches of St Andrew, St Sever and Holy Cross.[23]

Edward did not set off for Castile at once. He went to join his father shortly after his arrival and it is likely that he spent much of the summer being brought up to speed on how things stood in Gascony and what he would have to do on his return after his marriage. We know that some letters were issued in his name at this time which indicate that, while he was giving some orders directly (for example ordering William Longespée to invest the chateau at Bourg-sur-Mer), otherwise an administration over which he had little control was being put in place. He did meet his mother and brother-in-law elect as they passed through on their way to Ponthieu in August, giving him a chance to learn a little about Eleanor before their meeting. He was then at La Réole after the surrender of the town later in August.[24]

Somehow, everything became delayed and somewhat less glorious than was suggested by the huge send-off in England. Although Edward's knighting had been set for 13 October, he did not arrive at Burgos until after this date. The reasons for this are unclear; certainly Henry was by this point settled in Bordeaux, which would suggest that Edward's presence was not vital. It seems possible that Edward's commitment to being involved with the administrative issues arising out of the La Réole dispute were the cause, for we find him in September making arrangements for settling some points arising from this. A commission was constituted and approved by Edward on 15 September and by the king on 29 September, and a peace based on forgetting the past was declared by Henry in Bordeaux on 7 October, when he counselled the contending parties to make up their differences by marriages, as he had done with Alfonso.

Another possible reason for the delay emerges from the documentation of Edward's stay in Bayonne around the start of October. The plan had been for Edward to be escorted by a distinguished retinue of English magnates, but in fact the companions he took were mostly Gascon, and had to buy clothes for the wedding in Bayonne. It may be, therefore, that the late arrival of his retinue prompted a delay, and in the end Edward was finally forced to set off without them.[25]

Whatever the reason, Edward left Bayonne on 9 October and arrived in Burgos on 18 October. This, and the fact that Alfonso was making his first visit to Burgos since his own accession, doubtless provided an excuse for entertainments on a considerable scale. Certainly for the rest of the year Alfonso dated his documents by reference to the year in which the Lord Edward visited Castile, which indicates that in his eyes the visit had been a great event. With both Castilian and English royal families fond of hunting, it is inevitable that some time was spent in this diversion, and this will have provided an easy way for the young couple to get to know each other and enjoy the discovery of the first of their common interests.

Prior to the wedding there will certainly have been a visit to the venue at Las Huelgas, which resonated with the bridal couple's shared family heritage. It also provided a suitable meeting point for the two because architecturally Las Huelgas was predominantly a French Gothic construction, which referenced the architecture and layout of the Plantagenet pantheon at Fontevrault. It will therefore have seemed familiar to Edward and set the context for Eleanor's forthcoming change of countries. There will also have been an opportunity to pay their respects at the tombs of Alfonso VIII and Eleanor of England, which probably did not at the time bear their current, heavily heraldic appearance, and that of Queen Berengaria, who had recently been reburied, at the instance of her granddaughter and namesake, in a magnificent decorated tomb chest featuring Gothic arcading and carvings of the Virgin Mary with Christ.

What would the young couple have made of each other at these first meetings? Edward's appearance in later life is well attested by Nicholas

Trivet, a chronicler who wrote for Edward and Eleanor's daughter Mary and appears to have been given a good deal of inside information by her. He tells us what later archaeological investigations confirm, that Edward was indeed unusually tall, standing head and shoulders above most men, earning his nickname 'Longshanks'. He also tells us that Edward was golden haired in his childhood but as he grew older his hair changed to dark brown, and that he shared his father's characteristic droop in one eye. He also had a slight lisp, although Trivet assures us that this in no way hampered him in argument; one may perhaps here call to mind the slight lisp which has been no hindrance to Sean Connery's acting career. Marginal sketches of Edward in later life show that he had a very decided, square jaw and suggest that the clean-shaven look which was then the accepted mode was not easy to maintain, with suggestions of five o'clock shadow in more than one representation.

The latter characteristic was probably not much in evidence at just fifteen; at this stage he was a mere sketch of the man he was to become. Probably dark haired (just), there seems every likelihood that he was tall, thin and not yet done growing – in the awkward, half-fledged stage of the teenage years. As for Eleanor, who also probably still had a couple of years of growing to do, it seems likely that she had little of adult beauty, except possibly her fine eyes. However, her training to interest herself in her husband's affairs, and her genuine passion for horses and interest in music, probably made her as acceptable a female companion as Edward could reasonably have hoped for.

With introductions and preliminary celebrations out of the way, sometime in late October Edward and some of his companions were knighted by Alfonso, and on 1 November the marriage was performed at Las Huelgas. Edward was fifteen years old, and Eleanor was still a few weeks short of her thirteenth birthday. On the day of the wedding, Alfonso formally abandoned his claims to Gascony in favour of his new brother-in-law and thereafter there would have been some days of further festivities. But it was not long before the couple set out for Gascony.[26]

On 11 November, the newlyweds are recorded as being at Vittoria in Spain (about halfway between Burgos and Bayonne), but by 21 November the records show their presence in Bayonne, and one of Edward's clerks described him in a charter as 'now reigning in Gascony as prince and lord'. One might fondly imagine that all would be easy going at this point; however it is clear that problems will have been apparent to Eleanor from the very start. Edward was completely out of money: Trabut-Cussac describes how the newly married couple's route back to Bordeaux can be traced by the IOUs left in their wake. This was not a significant problem at the time – there were plenty of takers, with the security of future tax and trading revenue, as well as those from confiscated goods and justice. But it demonstrates that Henry III had left the province in a parlous state financially and had abandoned Edward to sink or swim – without leaving him enough money even to pay the soldiers notionally left for his security. Furthermore, the bad feeling left by the recent disputes was far from dispelled – Edward and Eleanor's retinue was reportedly abused by locals on their arrival from Spain. On the honeymoon, therefore, all emphatically did not smell of roses.[27]

It is almost certain that Eleanor met neither of her parents-in-law at this stage. Certainly neither of them attended the marriage, and records suggest that Henry left Bordeaux on 3 or 4 November en route to Cognac and Fontevrault and that he first received news of the marriage having taken place on 20 November, when he was at Marmoutier. Although Howell speculates that the two Eleanors would have met on the return to Gascony, this seems unlikely as it was in this period that Henry and Eleanor together made the first of their peacemaking visits to Paris. Henry had sought permission from Louis IX for himself and his queen to travel back from Gascony by way of France, and the records indicate that they set out together in late October. Further, it is unlikely that Eleanor would have been late to join a visit which she (as sister of the French queen, Marguerite) had probably played no small part in arranging.[28]

Given the ages of the two protagonists – Eleanor not even in her teens – one is bound to wonder whether the marriage was consummated at this stage. As indicated above, the age of marriage for girls was generally fifteen or older owing to the risks of juvenile childbirth. Yet at the same time numerous child marriages took place, with the young bride being brought up as a member of the groom's parents' household. Examples of this approach include Marguerite of France, wife of Henry the Young King, and Alys, her sister, both of whom were brought up from a very young age at Henry II's court. In such cases, the consummation of the marriage was generally delayed until the age of about fifteen.[29]

However, more difficult questions arise in cases like that of Edward and Eleanor, when the parties were above canon age but younger than usual. It is certainly the case that some young marriages were consummated. For example, Margaret Beaufort was only thirteen years of age when she bore the future Henry VII, and the marriage of Mary de Bohun (aged twelve) to the future Henry IV was consummated in order to guarantee her vast inheritance. However, it appears that it was more usual for conjugal relations to be delayed in such cases; for example, Isabella of Angoulême was married aged twelve in 1200, but did not have her first child until seven years later. The knowledge that she obviously had no fertility problems, since she was to bear John at least five children in a nine-year period and then go on to have at least another six by her second husband, indicates that consummation was delayed until her eighteenth year. Likewise, Eleanor of Provence, who had at least five children, did not bear her first child until over three years after her wedding, aged a little under thirteen. Again, Mary de Bohun, although required to consummate the marriage for political reasons at twelve, then lived apart from her husband for about four years, bearing her first live child more than five years after the marriage.[30]

So into which camp did Eleanor fall? Certainly the evidence of Eleanor's later fecundity (estimates of the number of children she bore Edward range from nine to nineteen, but the best evidence suggests at least fifteen children) and the fact that the first verifiable child born to Edward and Eleanor was sometime between 1262 and 1264, would tend to suggest that they were not regularly cohabiting in the early years of their marriage. However, politically it would seem probable that from the English point of view the marriage required to be put beyond doubt so no legal quibble could be taken at a later date, especially in the light of the fact that Alfonso had already given evidence of being tricky. This approach would also be consistent, and is only really consistent, with leaving Edward and Eleanor together in Gascony for a year; if the marriage was not to be consummated, she would have been more likely to be put in charge of Edward's parents, or have a separate establishment created for her.[31]

Confirming this is the slight, but significant, evidence of the child Parsons calls Anonyma. In a book of controllers' accounts for the king's wardrobe in 1286–7, there is a record showing that the queen provided a gold cloth on 29 May 1287 to the Dominican priory at Bordeaux to mark the anniversary of the death of her daughter, who was buried there. There is extensive material for the king's and queen's wardrobes in 1286 and none shows any sign of a child dying at this time, nor do any of the documented children at this date 'go missing'. Accordingly, this was not the first anniversary, but an anniversary of a death longer ago. This leaves two possible years in which a child could have died in May when Edward and Eleanor were in Bordeaux: 1255, and on return from Crusade in 1274.

One can effectively eliminate the latter possibility. Since Edward and Eleanor took none of their children with them on Crusade, the only child who could have died in 1274 was one born on their travels. There were three of these: the unnamed child who is recorded as being born and dying in Acre in 1271, Joan 'of Acre' and Alphonso. Both of the latter two were alive and well in 1274, and for some considerable time thereafter. Therefore, unless either the child born at Acre completed the long journey back to Gascony and survived nearly six months before dying (Edward and Eleanor were certainly in Gascony by November 1273) or they for some reason brought the body of their child back to bury, the child buried in Bordeaux was one born in 1255. As for these alternative possibilities, the former seems to be ruled out by the accounts for the children's household, which indicate that only two children (Joan and Alphonso) were with their parents in Gascony in 1274. The latter is just possible, but seems highly improbable given the conditions in the East and the length of time taken by them on the journey back.[32]

Thus there is a compelling case to be made for the birth of a child as a result of the early consummation of the marriage in 1255. This is entirely consistent with the probabilities. Yet again there is a parallel with Mary de Bohun. She bore a dead child – the result of the premature consummation of the marriage – in 1382 and cohabitation ceased after this until she was of an age to enter on childbearing safely. The attentive reader will of course have deduced that Anonyma cannot have been a full-term child. A marriage consummated on 1 November would not generally produce issue until late July. Anonyma would therefore be a stillbirth some weeks short of the due date, possibly caused by an accident, an illness or some problem with the baby herself. This hypothesis also fits well with the known itinerary of Edward in mid-1255: the records show that he was based around Bordeaux much of the time, and was recorded there both in mid-May and at the beginning of June. In mid-May he went to conduct business in St Emilion, and was at work there on 27 May. Thereafter there is an abrupt gap in the records until 1 June, when Edward is found at Bordeaux. The administrative records therefore echo an anxious young husband awaiting the outcome of his even younger wife's first labour, a sudden dash to its premature commencement and a sad outcome.[33]

One final piece of evidence in support of this conclusion as to consummation is the attitude of Edward and Eleanor to the marriages of their daughters. Despite heavy political pressure, Eleanor begged her husband not to send their daughter to Aragon at the age of thirteen and to instead wait at least eighteen months; she succeeded. While there may have been other political considerations which fed into this specific stance, it is also the case that not one of their daughters was sent away to be married before she was past fourteen; one married younger, but was kept at home until she was past fifteen – and her husband had to beg to get her even then.[34]

There is therefore good reason to suppose that the marriage was consummated at once and a premature child was born and died in late May 1255 – when Eleanor was only thirteen and a half years old. The premature daughter, who must have died at birth or very shortly afterwards, was probably given no name; usually commemorations recorded in the wardrobe accounts identify the person by name.

This unsuccessful pregnancy was obviously a traumatic event for a thirteen-year-old to endure and may well have had implications for Eleanor's health for some time. It is possible that, as with Mary de Bohun, cohabitation did not then resume for a few years, but on balance this seems unlikely since the pair do not appear to have been kept apart at all on their return, but resided at court. More probably a degree of caution was exercised by them to avoid conception until Eleanor was somewhat older.

There are a number of other threads to note from the very limited material available in relation to this first year. The first is to understand something about Gascony, both because it played a significant part in the politics of the English court and because it was a place of importance to Eleanor and Edward.

Gascony was the most substantial remaining part of Eleanor of Aquitaine's territories. Like all of those territories it was emphatically a southern French territory, having its own distinctive language and traditions. One important aspect of this which is easy to forget – both for modern readers and for the Angevins and other northern French, for whom feudalism was the natural way of things – is that it was not a feudal territory at all. Its towns and nobles had far more independence than their English counterparts, and many of the nobles held their lands freely, and were not subject to any feudal service. The result was that it was impossible to rule Gascony by routes which would seem intuitive to someone used to the English or even the northern French way of doing things. The truth, as indicated earlier, is that the Duke of Aquitaine did not by any means have the power of a ruler with full feudal authority. If he asked one of his nobles to jump, the answer was unlikely to be 'How high?' – it was more likely to be unprintable.

Adding to these difficulties was the fact that it was itself a disparate territory, covering not only the sophisticated and prosperous cities of Bordeaux and Bayonne, which were commercially dependent upon trade with England, but also large stretches of almost undeveloped countryside and the rugged mountainous regions of Soule, Béarn and Bigorre, each of which effectively controlled a route over the Pyrenees. There was no recognised body of law or custom which prevailed across the region; different counties had differing traditions and laws. Internally it had its own conflicts, borne of both the different interests represented by its various areas and the natural rivalries and factions which sprung up within each area. Notable among these was the almost non-stop strife which was carried on between certain individuals and families. Examples include the festering dispute over the county of Bigorre between Gaston de Béarn, probably the most powerful single noble in the territory, and his neighbour Esquivat de Chabanais. Then there were the disputes between Arnaud Odon and Gerald of Armagnac, between the Viscount of Soule and Arnaud of Tardets, and between Gaston de Béarn and Auger of Soule (the heir to the Viscount of Soule).

Nor were the cities free of trouble; a constant feature of Bordeaux politics was the internecine strife which prevailed between the factions of Colomb and Soler. These were generally old-fashioned, visceral disputes about dominance, not sophisticated political disagreements which were likely to be amenable to mediation. Moreover, they radiated outwards owing to the complicated interrelationships within the duchy.

Another complicating factor is that at no time until Edward's accession was Gascony actually managed by someone with ultimate authority; until then, including when Edward resided there in 1254–5, the authority held was subordinate to that of Henry III, who was well understood by the Gascons to be out of touch with the minutiae of the region. Accordingly, any decision to which exception was taken could be, and was, simply appealed to England, thereby ensuring delay. The result was that it was practically impossible to carry out any wide-ranging reforms. This tension was more or less exactly what hamstrung Simon de Montfort – and resulted in his trial by Henry III.[35]

The net result was that there were only two practical routes open for governing in Gascony – to proceed by consensus, guiding rather than commanding; or to take sides, recruiting the forces of one party to keep the other down. Henry naturally favoured the first – but, as can be imagined, in these circumstances governing by consensus resembled herding cats and offered little room for pushing forward reforms. Equally naturally, Simon de Montfort in his incumbency as seneschal favoured the latter, siding with the Colomb faction in Bordeaux against the Soler family and with his nephew de Chabanais against Gaston de Béarn in the dispute over the succession to the central county of Bigorre.[36]

The second strand to pick up is to briefly evaluate the work which Edward was doing. In truth, although Edward did involve himself closely with the governing of Gascony, he was not entirely left to sink or swim: a number of his mother's Savoyard advisers, including John FitzGeoffrey and Stephen de Salines, are among the advisers who were with him in this year. Eleanor's relative Michael de Fiennes (brother of William), who was also one of the party and became Edward's first chancellor, also had some Savoyard connections.[37]

But even allowing for this advice, Trabut-Cussac has traced the work which Edward was doing throughout the year in the local rolls and gives him a very good 'end-of-term' report. He concludes that, with a seriousness surprising for his age, he worked hard to forge a definitive peace and to recreate a normal administration in the face of constant financial problems. He also records that Edward managed to procure many submissions from men who had a year before been in rebellion and that while he still left Gascony poor, it was enjoying a lasting peace and a reasonable administration. This conclusion is borne out by a study of the local records which show that from the time when the young couple arrived back in Gascony in late November Edward was apparently busy issuing orders, pardons, restoring goods, and sitting in justice, considering matters both great and small which were brought by locals to his court.

This approach is very interesting in that it resonates with the interests Edward would come to show later as a king.[38]

In terms of approach, consensus together with limited administrative reform was the order of the day. Looking at the various acts issued, a good deal of what was being done was effectively unpicking the most controversial steps taken by Montfort. He encouraged the mediation of other disputes, successfully disposing of some (for the present at least). Building blocks were also put in place for a more sensible and cohesive administrative system: a constable of Bordeaux was appointed, and he gradually became the chief financial officer of the city, thereby reducing the status of both the Colombs and the Solers (whose prominence had stemmed from their direct financial dealings with the Crown) and taking much of the political sting out of their intractable differences.[39]

In addition, Edward commenced his military experience during this period, as money problems caused unrest. Gascon seneschals traditionally struggled financially on two fronts. First, they had to get the necessary co-operation of the local lords in persuading their tenants to pay the tax on agricultural holdings, which was estimated according to the number of cattle maintained. Secondly, revenues always fell short of English expectation; there was an entrenched mindset in England that Gascony made a considerable net financial contribution to revenues – which may well have underpinned some of Henry III's disputes with de Montfort. This had almost certainly been true back in Henry II's day. However, we now know that in fact at this point Gascony was a net drain on English resources. Edward's position was worse than that of the usual seneschal, in that the consequence of the past upheavals was that normal revenues were considerably down even on historic levels.[40]

He therefore decided to levy an extraordinary tax, which was dressed up in part as the traditional levy on the occasion of his being knighted. In the context of general austerity following the civil unrest of the past year or so, and when the papacy was seeking a tax of a tenth in support of Henry III's supposed intention to go on Crusade in Sicily, it needs hardly be said that, however much good Edward was doing in managing individual grievances, this was a step which was hugely unpopular and provoked further unrest.[41]

Quite how serious this was is unclear: Henry III had a tendency to 'spin' facts (or even invent stories) to suit his convenience. One should therefore perhaps not give too much credence to his announcement in April 1255 that he had to send reinforcements to Edward. However, it is certainly the case that military steps were being taken on a number of fronts, which indicates a fairly tense situation; in July Edward was besieging the fortress of the Comte de Gramont and he also reinforced Fronsac, occupied Guiche, and improved the fortifications at Bayonne (sending for materials from his territory in Ireland).[42]

Finally, in looking at what was done during the course of the year, the records of Edward's travels, in which he was probably mostly accompanied by Eleanor (when the vicissitudes of pregnancy allowed) already show signs of a more active style of government than that of his father. Henry's year in Gascony was relatively static, with a number of stops for between two weeks and a month. Edward, however, was constantly on the move, albeit with a number of bases to which he made regular returns, such as Bordeaux itself and Saint-Macaire, a pleasant fortified village just outside Bordeaux which housed a substantial priory dedicated to St Sauveur. It is highly unusual to see a stay of longer than a week at any location; far more common are two-night stops as he repeatedly visited Bayonne, Dax, Saint-Sever, Bazas, Castillon, Bergerac and other major towns throughout the region – as well as stopping in La Réole to see how it was settling down. This is consistent with Edward's much more active style generally, with his interest in administration, which would encourage him to see the details on site.[43]

Having marshalled the evidence for this first period of government, one is forced to wonder whence came this interest and this active approach, so different from that of his father. One credible answer is not far to seek – this approach was consistent with the hands-on style of government which was the norm in Castile. It is probably too much at this stage to look simply to Eleanor, but in the weeks surrounding the marriage Edward had ample time to consult with the experienced and didactically minded Alfonso, to assist in forming his views as to how he would manage his first solo venture. Alfonso, too, will have been within easy reach for correspondence in this first year. But Eleanor had also been brought up in this school of thought, and had witnessed her father's administrative business at close range; she will certainly have wanted to see her husband develop as a ruler in the style of her father. It therefore seems probable that Edward's first foray into government was inspired by ideas received from his new Castilian family, and supported by Eleanor.

Meanwhile, for Eleanor the year will have been an important learning curve too. Not only would she have to familiarise herself with a new court and way of doing things, and a complete new cast of characters, she will also have wanted to begin to bring her Anglo-Norman French up to scratch – the French that she spoke with her mother will almost certainly have been Picard. It is likely that between this, her pregnancy and illness, the discussions which she shared with Edward as to the infinite series of Gascon problems and her natural concerns about Edward's first military forays, time will not have hung heavy on her hands.

Apart from the learning which each had to do during the year, it appears clear that this was a very important time for Edward and Eleanor as a couple, providing them with a relatively unsupervised period in which they could build a relationship in a normal fashion. In this, the sojourn seems to have been a thoroughgoing success, laying down some of the ties which held them together so firmly in later years. In both these respects one can perhaps discern a very modern parallel; in today's English royal family, both the queen and the Duke of Edinburgh and the Duke and Duchess of Cambridge vouch for the importance of just such a period of relative normalcy before joining full-time royal duties. The success of the year is reflected in the considerable fondness which both developed and later manifested for the area – which is apparent in the fact that they returned more often than appears to have been necessary to Gascony in the years ahead, with visits in 1261–2, 1273–4 and 1286–9. It is also vouched for by Trabut-Cussac, who prior to his death studied Edward's Gascon endeavours more closely than any other scholar. He describes Edward as having a particular fondness and solicitude for Gascony.[44]

The pair seem too to have established close relationships with a number of those who were around them at the time, forming the nucleus of what would become a stable and harmonious domestic court. Otho de Grandison and Ebulo de Montibus were of course present. So was an English Montfort, Peter, and very possibly John de Vescy – both of whose families later allied with Eleanor's. Guy de Lusignan, too, is frequently glimpsed as present in the records, and may have met his future wife, Eleanor's cousin, Jeanne of Châtellherault, during this year.

With so much going on and being learnt, it might seem puzzling that Edward and Eleanor did return to England so soon. However, the answer is simple: it was not their decision. On 17 August, Henry III had sent in unequivocal terms to recall Edward from Gascony, indicating that he should go to Ireland and announcing who should take charge in his stead. Although Edward had notionally received Gascony as part of his provision on marriage, Henry had not actually renounced his title as Duke of Aquitaine to him; short of rebellion, Edward therefore had to leave Gascony. One can readily imagine that he did so reluctantly – indeed, the period of time which he spent crossing i's and dotting t's before he finally left on 29 November speaks for that, as well as for his enthusiasm for the administrative side of his job. So too does the position as regards Peter of Savoy. It was intended that Edward should hand over the reins in Gascony as soon as possible after the arrival of Peter of Savoy, appointed by Henry as seneschal. Edward, however, did no such thing. Peter arrived in September, but Edward did not leave Gascony until late October, continuing to do business via his own appointees (including Eleanor's cousin Michael de Fiennes) until late in October; Peter of Savoy's name is notable by its absence from the records.[45]

One final point can be noted. There is every sign that by the end of the first year Edward was already devoted to Eleanor. The evidence for this comes from the documents surrounding his return. It was certainly Henry III's idea – in fact his command – that Edward should not return to England at all at this time, but instead go to Ireland until Easter 1256 to see to the affairs of his second territory. But when Edward did finally leave Gascony, he instead followed Eleanor back to England, flouting the instruction to go to Ireland. In Edward's open defiance of his father's command we can see a strong desire not to be too long away from Eleanor. For the next thirty-five years, only dire necessity would keep them apart.[46]

5

The First Years in England

Eleanor, now just under fourteen years old, arrived in England at Dover early in October 1255. She is reported as having come with a large retinue, probably composed of a good number of their English court from Gascony, but without either Edward or adequate smart clothing. This last lack immediately provides another insight into the how the compatible tastes of Eleanor and Edward had already manifested: while the Henrician court was a very dressy place, Edward as king eschewed royal purple or rich clothing, preferring more everyday clothes, and Eleanor also seems to have lacked a taste for expensive clothing. For her formal entry into the court, the plain attire she had brought with her was deemed completely unacceptable, and the costs of making good her wardrobe were met by her father-in-law, Henry III, who wanted her to make a good impression – not least perhaps because his own stock was currently rather low, with heated debates occurring at the October parliament over his demands for funding for his Sicilian project.

Henry therefore sent her 100 marks to purchase what she needed, and a choice of decent palfreys to ride upon. It seems likely that Henry had originally wanted to welcome Eleanor in time for the feast of St Edward on 13 October, but her late arrival and inadequate supplies made this impossible. Instead, Henry put her in the charge of the castellan of Dover Castle, Reginald de Cobham, asking him to look after her and escort her to London by way of Canterbury, where she was to spend St Edward's Day instead in the company of, among others, Edward's old tutor in arms, Nicholas de Molis. As well as his other gifts, he sent her a variety of offerings to be made at Canterbury 'and other shrines along her road': a silver alms dish, which he had ordered as long ago as July, two gold brooches for offering at the shrines of Edward the Confessor and Thomas Becket, and twelve silken cloths, six of arras and six of gold. A stop at Canterbury will have been congenial to Eleanor too, as affording an opportunity to visit the shrine of Becket, whose veneration had been introduced to the Castilian royal family by Eleanor of England.[1]

Following this programme, Eleanor arrived in London on St Etheldreda's Day, Sunday 17 October 1255. The London to which Eleanor came was a place which is difficult for us to picture, with the vision of the enormous modern city embedded firmly in our minds. Contributing to the difficulty is the absence of any contemporaneous description of the city as a whole – the nearest description is that given by William FitzStephen, Becket's biographer, some century earlier. To bring it up to date, the best that can be done is to add details of buildings which are known to have been built in the intervening period, and vignettes which emerge from London's administrative records.

Approaching the city as Eleanor will have done, from the south, the first thing to note is that there was effectively no London south of the river. With the exception of one or two sizeable buildings and gardens in the ownership of the Church or monastic orders, the countryside ran right up to the river – or at least to the commencement of the marshland which abutted on the river in many places. For London in the thirteenth century was a much lower-seated and more watery place than its modern incarnation, where the many streams which meandered down to the tidal Thames have been enclosed and the banks of the river built up to make flooding an almost unimaginable contingency.

The route over the river was by boat or by London Bridge – the route Eleanor will likely have used. However, the amazing view which this structure (a massive version of Florence's Ponte Vecchio) ought to have afforded did not exist, since it was built up on either side with shops, whose rents, notionally at least, paid for the upkeep of the bridge.

On the north side of the river, the city fell effectively into three parts. The first, and only recognisably urban part, was the City of London itself, which was still substantially bounded by the Roman walls, in which six gates – Aldgate, Bishopsgate, Cripplegate, Aldersgate, Newgate and St Paul's Ludgate – provided the routes in from outside the walls (Moorgate had yet to be put in place). Outside the walls, some wharves and shipyards now extended east along the bank of the river, and some commercial development had also begun in the north-east segment, in the area known as Houndsditch. This was a rather marshy area, which attracted crowds for skating during the winter months. There were also some more elegant developments a little outside the city wall to the north, before the commencement of fields, pastures and watermills leading to the great forest of Hampstead, which contained deer, boar and even wild bulls. The Knights of St John, the Benedictines and the Carthusians had all set up substantial priories to the north-west towards Clerkenwell, and we know that at some point in the thirteenth century the bishops of Ely and the earls of Gloucester built their own palaces at Ely Place and Clerkenwell.

On the eastern boundary of the city stood the Tower of London, which was, in 1255, very much in the course of improvement by Henry III. His works included luxurious private quarters for king and queen, with a great hall between them, and an expansion of the boundaries of the Tower. The king's quarters were sited on the first floor of Wakefield Tower (then known as the Blundeville Tower) and there was a private watergate east of that tower for royal use. The queen's chambers apparently resembled a bower, with roses painted on a white background. Other features of the improvements included new curtain walls, crowned with a range of new towers, completion of an inland moat and a sparkling coat of white paint on the White Tower. In addition, the Tower featured a zoo or menagerie of some size. From early in the 1240s the Tower had housed the odd wild animal, such as the three leopards sent by Emperor Frederick II. But in 1251 the main royal menagerie, then sited at Woodstock, was moved to the Tower. Among its inmates were leopards, lynxes and a camel, but the *pièces de résistance* at the time of Eleanor's arrival were the polar bear, presented by King Haakon of Norway in 1252, and the elephant, which had recently been sent as a present by Louis of France following the successful meeting between the two kings in December 1254. The polar bear was kept on a leash and allowed to fish in the Thames. The elephant was housed in a house (prudently designed so that it could be put to other uses if required) some forty feet long and twenty feet wide; it died in 1258. After this, its bones were used to make reliquaries for Henry III's increasing collection at Westminster Abbey and its house was used as a place of imprisonment, *inter alia* for Jews accused of coin clipping.

In contrast to the Tower's burgeoning importance, the castles which held the western end, Baynard's Castle and Mountfitchet Castle, were in a state of considerable disrepair, their destruction having in fact been ordered by King John and at least partly carried out. In due course (and with Eleanor's active support) these sites would be given to the Dominicans or Black Friars for their London establishment.

To the west of the city walls flowed the substantial River Fleet, powering mills where Turnmill Lane now stands, and descending into the huge valley of modern Farringdon Street before exiting into the Thames. Some sense of its scale can be obtained by standing on Holborn Viaduct, the site of the old Holborn Bridge (named after the stream of the Hole-burn, which joined the Fleet near this point), and envisaging the two small islands which stood in the stream between the banks at the base of Fleet Street, forty metres asunder, and which provided the base for the lower river crossing, which Eleanor would have followed. The river was navigable as far as the bridge – at least periodically – for the effluent from the Smithfield slaughterhouses and the nearby tanneries tended to silt it up. Through the City also ran the smaller, but still significant, River Walbrook, which entered the city by what would later be Moorgate, with banks at (appropriately) Bank and Mansion House, reaching the river slightly to the east of the modern Cousin Lane. This river was crossed by means of a substantial bridge in the vicinity of Poultry, which can have been no pleasant business, because it was reported at about this period to be no better than an open sewer, full of dung and refuse.

The glory of the city was St Paul's Cathedral, sited much where the existing building lies but probably resembling a slightly larger version of Salisbury Cathedral. It had one of the tallest spires in Europe, a majestic nave and exquisite stained-glass windows. At the time of Eleanor's arrival, it was undergoing an extension which would see it enclose the nearby church of St Faith's, and replace its roof with new wood – a decision which was to doom the building four centuries later.[2]

The second coherent part of London lay round the dogleg curve of the Thames to the south-west. Here was a substantial enclave which was built up around the royal palace of Westminster and its neighbour Westminster Abbey. Around these major centres were dotted satellite dwellings and palaces. The kings of Scotland maintained a house, known as Scotland Yard, and some of the major courtiers also had houses in the near vicinity of the court – in later years, Otho de Grandison would have a house near Westminster of such size that a parliament was held there. Quite how large Westminster was at this stage is unclear. In the eleventh century there were fewer than a hundred dwellings here. By 1300 that number would have risen to around 3,000. At the time of Eleanor's arrival it probably therefore presented the appearance of a small town in its own right. Dotted nearby were small villages and farms, such as the grouping right opposite the turn in the river known as Charing, in which some houses and gardens had been granted in the 1230s by the Marshal family to the Augustinian priory of St Mary at Roncevaux. In the intervening years these had been converted into the priory and Hospital of St Mary Rounceval.

Between the two London centres of the City and Westminster lay the Strand and Fleet Street, along which ribbon development was in the process of occurring. The first colonists appear to have been the Knights Templar, who in the late twelfth century abandoned their base in Holborn for a large compound between Fleet Street and the river, just west of the city walls. Their church housed the body of William Marshal and his sons, and had originally been destined to be Henry III's own final resting place. Their compound was also used as a safe deposit for valuables by many. They were bordered by the Carmelites or White Friars, whose establishment was slightly nearer the City walls. Then followed more palatial developments. The greatest of these was the palace of the Savoy – owned, of course, by Peter of Savoy, on land gifted to him by Henry III. It was later to become the home of the earls and dukes of Lancaster. Another palace known to be in existence at the time was York House, the residence of the Bishop of Norwich, built sometime before 1237 and whose watergate can still be seen in the Embankment Gardens.[3]

Eleanor arrived to a considerable welcome, Henry having given orders that 'she should be received with the greatest honour and reverence'. The king, his nobles, the lord mayor and a crowd of citizens went out to meet her, dressed in festive clothes and mounted on caparisoned horses, and she progressed through the city by Cheapside and the Strand to Westminster, along roads hung with coloured cloth in her honour. There also appear to have been illuminations, ringing of church bells, singing 'and other displays of joy' to accompany the procession, as well as processions of all the clergy of St Paul's and Westminster Abbey.

Despite all this brave jollification, London is unlikely to have made a good impression on Eleanor. The dank of an English autumn will hardly have helped to add glamour to a city which boasted few of the beauties and civilisations of Cordoba or Seville – or even some fairly basic amenities such as running water. There was, of course, plenty of water flowing through the city or standing in its numerous marshy areas, but at this point in time it was generally dirty, insanitary water, fit only for industrial processes such as tanning. The wells which had recommended the city to eleventh-century chroniclers were now unfit to use and London possessed only two water conduits which were regarded as somewhat wondrous. Those who could not access these had to venture outside the city walls to find clean water. To the denizens of London, the idea of a city owning multiplicities of public baths would have seemed utterly incomprehensible. To Eleanor, the capital city of her new country must have seemed a stinking and uncivilised little town.

At Westminster Eleanor was conducted to her rooms, which Henry, advised by Eleanor's brother Sancho, had decorated in the Castilian style, with tapestries on the walls – a mode of ornamentation then only familiar in churches. Moreover, as Matthew Paris reports in shock, 'even the floors were decorated in this manner' – this being the first reported instance in English history of the use of floor carpet instead of rushes. Following her reception, Eleanor made rich offerings at the shrine of St Edward, to whose cult Eleanor was introduced by the gift of a life of the saint. At the same time, Henry may well have offered a rich cope of samite at the Confessor's shrine, seeking a favourable outcome to the Sicilian business.[4]

Despite the effort made, it is likely that Eleanor will have found the level of comfort available in even her renovated rooms in the palace of Westminster somewhat disappointing. The cool weather, hardly excluded by thick stone walls, will have been an unpleasant novelty; the decorations which Henry had done for Eleanor of Provence in her rooms there with the figure of winter 'portrayed with such sad looks and miserable appearance that he may be truly likened to winter' would seem all too apposite. What is more, while Eleanor was used to roughing it to an extent, she was also used to the luxury and beauty of the Spanish palaces. Even at their best, and with all Henry's work, English palaces were in a different league. Again the most obvious difference to her would probably be the lack of running water. In Spanish palaces, running water was such a given that it was used to decorate gardens for fun. In England, it was more or less unheard of.

The gardens themselves, even with Eleanor of Provence's influence, were much simpler and more functional than the 'paradises' to which Eleanor was accustomed. The older queen's tastes seem to have run more to herb gardens than paradises. She had a walled garden at Clarendon and herb gardens adjacent to her apartments at Winchester, Kempton and Windsor. At Woodstock her herb garden was beside the king's fishpond. Perhaps the best gardens were those at Everswell, within the grounds of Woodstock, originally designed by Henry II for his Fair Rosamund. Here chambers were set out in the garden for the king and queen, among the pools and the gardens, and in one of them Henry planted a thousand pear trees, which will have looked lovely in blossom in spring time. There were probably no gardens at all at Dover and those at Westminster seem not to have received much attention.[5]

So on arrival Eleanor had to start to deal with a new home in a new and very different country – and one where political difficulties lurked, in particular for a foreigner. In some ways, life was less difficult than it might have been. She had apparently already established a good rapport with her husband and many of his close companions. She was already fluent in French, the working language of the court. The king was minded to be very welcoming to her, as is evidenced by the trouble he took over the decoration of her rooms and the pardoning in December 1255 of a Jew for murder at the instance of Eleanor's *ayo*, Garcia Martinez (evidencing the greater sympathy with the Jewish community which was apparent in Castile). Finally, her mother-in-law, with whom she would be in close proximity, would be minded to be very kind to her: she was not only a woman who was devoted to her family and children generally, she was also – by a labyrinthine route which both women would have understood – actually kin to Eleanor.[6]

Yet, as will become apparent, it is likely that any such cossetting by Eleanor of Provence was either of short duration, or was rebuffed – or both. Despite the natural closeness into which they were thrown, the evidence suggests that the two Eleanors never became remotely close. A good amount of Eleanor of Provence's correspondence has survived – but none of it is with her daughter-in-law. In later life she corresponded often with her son; but her correspondence with Eleanor appears to have been confined to short notes about domestic issues. Likewise, the correspondence of Eleanor of Castile which comes down to us is not with her mother-in-law. In part the lack of closeness is not unnatural: one of them was, after all, destined to succeed the other in the exercise of ultimate power.

But also the two women's personal styles were sufficiently different that there was never likely to be great natural sympathy between them. Eleanor of Provence was elegant, beautiful, feminine and in tune with the traditional requirements of queenship. Though in many ways a forceful woman, she was nonetheless very traditional in her style. A medieval noblewoman was valued for her looks and her charm, for her ability to provide an heir for her husband and for maintaining links between her blood family and her family by marriage. In all of these roles Eleanor of Provence played her part to admiration. Her beauty and *debonairité* are repeatedly mentioned in the sources, and she plainly played along with her husband in his enjoyment of creating a pageant of kingship. In short, she looked and acted the part. She also made no bones about playing the formal role which was assigned to the queen, in interceding for petitioners with the ultimate source of power. So far as her role as mother of the heir was concerned, it is plain that this was the primary role by which Eleanor of Provence defined herself. As regards her role as a bridge builder between her family and her husband, the earlier chapters will have shown clearly that in this respect she succeeded perhaps as well as any queen in history; almost certainly rather too well.

'Our' Eleanor defines herself to us in the contrasts which she presents to her mother-in-law. Let us start with looks. It is highly unlikely that she was anything other than, at the least, a very handsome woman: her images on her tomb and the remaining Eleanor crosses show a woman of elegant features, as would be expected of the daughter of the handsome Ferdinand of Castile and the noted beauty Jeanne of Ponthieu. There is no suggestion that Edward, who could have commanded the most beautiful mistresses had he been so minded, was ever unfaithful to her in thirty-seven years of marriage; this too suggests that she was, and remained, a well-favoured woman (even the notably devoted Edward III strayed from Philippa of Hainault as she grew older and stouter). And yet she appears never in her lifetime to have been defined by her appearance. Apart from the half-hearted report before her marriage of her beauty, no one ever describes her looks. Even on her show-stopping entry into the city, not one single word in praise of her beauty finds its way into the chronicles. From this we can be tolerably sure of one thing – that she was not the sort of woman who traded on her looks. This, of course, is consistent with her upbringing under the watchful eye of Alfonso X. The conclusion is supported by her state on arrival in England, when the view was obviously taken by Henry that she did not have a wardrobe remotely fitted to her position. It is unimaginable that a woman who considered appearance a priority would enter upon a period of life when others would be called upon to judge her without a suitable armoury of dresses. In other respects, too, Eleanor was not a natural companion for her mother-in-law, being much more bookish and infinitely more fond of outdoor activities.

So while the two Eleanors undoubtedly formed an adequate modus vivendi, Eleanor will not have been a daughter-in-law Eleanor of Provence could take to her heart. But most significantly, Edward stood between them. Once Edward returned, the queen wished him to remain essentially under her wing; and at this point it will have become very apparent that Edward was no longer amenable to this, and was supported in his bid for independence by Eleanor. The spectre of this difficulty may well have appeared with Eleanor herself, and the news that Edward would follow her to London, rather than going to Ireland. Friction between the two women was therefore probably present from early on, and this will not have made Eleanor's transition into English life any easier.

Indeed, it is probably fair to say that Eleanor got off to a very uneasy start in England and that her first couple of years there were difficult in the extreme. The reason for the marriage was the treaty with Alfonso. As it was, many English people did not see this treaty (which principally concerned Gascony) as being of much significance. To make matters worse, by the time she arrived in England in late 1255, the treaty which had brought about her marriage was already running into difficulties.

The co-operation envisaged by the treaty was not proving straightforward. Pardons of those involved in Alfonso's incursion did not proceed speedily, the proposed African Crusade was making no progress and Henry was dragging his feet over the second marriage contemplated by the treaty. It was actually for this reason, and not as a comfort to Eleanor, that her brother Sancho was in England; Alfonso had already despatched a high-level mission including Garcia Martinez to press the various issues which had arisen, and they were still trying to make progress when Eleanor returned.[7]

In January 1256, Henry sent Peter d'Aigueblanche and John Maunsell to Castile to talk to Alfonso, but the terms which they carried were not accommodating. Henry refused to make restorations until Alfonso threw his full weight behind the ducal administration. He also refused to progress the marriage of his daughter to Alfonso's brother Manuel until he had details of Manuel's endowment and was assured that Manuel had tenure of the lands covered by that endowment. Henry went on to justify the request by his concern that Alfonso might later seize the endowment – as Henry had heard that he had done to others. This apparently offensive suggestion of course referred back to Jeanne of Ponthieu and Enrique of Castile's disputes with Alfonso, and indicated that Henry was at the very least minded to give some credence to Eleanor's mother's complaints of Alfonso. He completely ignored Alfonso's request for aid against Aragon and made a very half-hearted offer to seek commutation of his crusading vow in six years' time, to allow him to get his second son established in Sicily.[8]

Unsurprisingly, in the light of this response, little progress was made. In due course, the distinguished ambassadors were replaced with men of less distinction – again conveying Henry's reluctance to accommodate Alfonso. These unfortunate ambassadors were the ones to reap the whirlwind: in the summer of 1256, Alfonso actually threatened to invade Gascony. Matters were very tense for some months in the wake of this threat, but, as Henry and his advisers had anticipated, Alfonso ultimately felt he was unable to do so – because of his sister's marriage. It may therefore be said that Eleanor exercised her function of last resort in averting war between the two countries, even if truly congenial relations had not yet resulted from the alliance. However, the position of brinkmanship was far from the comfortable relationship which had been anticipated on both sides, and would have been an appalling extra strain on a young girl already struggling to find her feet in a new country and environment.[9]

To make matters still worse, aside from the international strains which it evidenced, the Spanish embassy also played into the domestic issues, namely the question of 'aliens'. In the context of the existing problems with interloping royal relations, the Castilian marriage was already viewed with some suspicion by many; Paris makes plain that it was perceived as providing occasion for yet another group of foreigners to come to England and live off its wealth. Although the embassy actually offered little danger of this, from the outside these suspicions appeared to be well founded: Eleanor's half-brother Sancho was instrumental in recommending Henry to prepare the lavishly decorated rooms for her arrival and Henry offered land, money and benefices to Garcia Martinez and his son. Doubtless all of this made perfect sense in the context of attempting to have Henry's non-compliance with treaty provisions presented to Alfonso as favourably as possible. However, the appearance to a domestic audience was unfortunate.

What is more, the personal style of the envoys had also provoked negative reaction. It seems likely that in matters such as dress the Castilian envoys were very noticeable, emphasising their strangeness. Certainly pictures from this era of Castilian origin show women wearing 'horned' hats, which look utterly ridiculous to modern eyes and probably did likewise to Londoners, differing markedly as they do from anything depicted in English or French sources. Likewise, studies of textiles from Las Huelgas and Villalcazar show that the Castilian mode of dress frequently involved ornate repeated patterns in the textiles used, doubtless inspired by Arabic art. Eleanor's brother Felipe's tomb yielded a tunic with a repeated trellis-type pattern producing the effect of eight-pointed stars. That of her nephew Fernando de la Cerda at Las Huelgas is again ornately patterned, but this time with repeated iterations of his own coat of arms. It appears to have been designed for use with a biretta, also lavishly patterned with his arms. The effect is, to say the least, striking and there seems to have been no precedent for such patterning in England before this date. One can easily see that this style would have pointed up the strangeness or alienness of the Castilians, and produced even a degree of derision.[10]

To add fuel to the fire of the problems both of Anglo-Castilian relations and tolerance of foreigners, almost no sooner than one half-brother had disappeared (as Sancho did in early 1256), another one appeared at court. This was the dangerous and needy Enrique, who had finally pursued his rebellion against his brother to the point of defeat at the Battle of Moron in October 1255 and was subsequently banished from Castile. He had initially fled to France, where Louis IX refused to have anything to do with him. Quite where he lurked between late 1255 and August of 1256, when he surfaced in England, is not certain, but it appears likely that he found refuge with Jeanne of Ponthieu, who might be seen as an intercessor with Henry and Edward on the subject of providing a refuge for Enrique. Certainly Henry's raising of the issue of Manuel's prospective lands in early 1256 sounds as if it were prompted by some recent gossip from a trusted source; Henry would be unlikely to make so offensive a comment in the context of sensitive diplomatic relations without being quite sure of his ground. However it came about, Enrique arrived in England, notionally in hopes that Henry III and Edward could, through their relationship with Alfonso, bring about a reconciliation.[11]

However, as is perhaps not surprising, the fact of Henry III welcoming Enrique at more or less the very time that he was downgrading his mission to Alfonso, returning thoroughly unsatisfactory answers to Alfonso's requests and refusing to go on Crusade, was not conducive either to reconciliation or the amelioration of Anglo-Castilian relations. For months thereafter, the possibility of a renewed Castilian invasion of Gascony continued to hang fire, while Henry blithely bestowed gifts on Enrique and even threatened to support Enrique if Alfonso did invade Gascony. It cannot be doubted that Eleanor's position at this time would have been highly uncomfortable, both personally, given her fondness for both brothers, and politically.

Enrique remained more or less *in situ* for about three years, accepting numerous grants and favours. Henry did try to find things for him to do which could act as a useful olive-branch: in 1257 he sent him to act as an emissary to the papacy on the Sicilian business and in 1259 provided him with ships for an African venture, subject to an undertaking not to molest Alfonso's interests. But Enrique's presence seems in truth only to have exacerbated the situation. As for the hope that there would be a reconciliation, this was never to bear fruit.

However, it seems that, despite the political difficulties which Enrique's presence undoubtedly created, he was a likeable character, very probably having a good measure of the troubadour charm. Eleanor corresponded with him throughout her life, though, owing to his spending most of that time in prison, they never met again after his departure from England in 1259; in 1303, Edward himself acknowledged his warm feelings for him.[12]

As if this was not enough to complicate Eleanor's first year in England, yet another cause of friction with Alfonso and with key players at the English court soon made itself felt – the fight for the appointment as Holy Roman Emperor. No new Emperor had been appointed following the death of Frederick II in 1250, and by 1256 both candidates had died, leaving the way open to new candidatures. Soon after, Richard of Cornwall took his first steps towards seeking the job, paying a campaign agent and sending out an embassy to the Pope to try to gain his support. His candidacy was apparently quite well received, based upon his reputation as a diplomat, his wealth (essential to buy the votes of the electors) and his commercially important English connections. By 12 June 1256, his candidacy had been officially adopted as English foreign policy and he was sending out formal embassies. In addition, he was calling in loans to Henry and borrowing money to finance his candidacy.

By December, three out of the seven electors were bought. Two were established as hostile. All, therefore, turned on the decision of Ottokar of Bohemia, who could give Richard a majority. However, he refused to commit himself. Richard's team did not allow this to stand in their way. In London, on 26 December, the crown was solemnly offered to Richard by the Archbishop of Cologne, who pretended that the electors were unanimous. Richard accepted, and on 13 January 1257 he was elected 'King of the Romans' (the title of the Emperor designate) by his supporters. On 31 January, all remaining difficulties appeared to be clearing when it was announced that Ottokar of Bohemia had decided to support Richard's candidacy. Thereafter, Henry and Richard began to make plans for Richard's journey to Germany for his coronation, accompanied his family and by an impressive retinue of knights. At the Easter parliament, a variety of German magnates came to do homage to Richard. He left the country on 29 April, accompanied by these lords and a retinue of thirty-two English magnates on fifty ships.[13]

However, even as Richard was sailing, a significant storm cloud had formed. Ottokar of Bohemia had changed his mind in late March, and he had nominated an alternative candidate. By the time of Richard's arrival, this alternative candidate had the majority which Richard lacked. The candidate had other advantages, too. He could lay claim to direct descent from the Imperial line, and possessed a credible claim to extensive lands in Swabia. He had impressive outside support: that of the French king, the Duke of Brabant and the towns of Worms and Spier. That candidate? Alfonso X.

The net result was that, though Richard was crowned King of the Romans by his supporters in May 1257 and received the homage of large areas of Germany, and although Alfonso did not appear to take the field against him, Richard never did cement his position in Germany and his carefully conserved money was, to a great extent, wasted. The other result was that, by late 1257, having wasted large sums in political manoeuvrings against Richard, Alfonso was firing off a strong formal complaint to Henry that Richard's election was a wrong to him and a breach of the Treaty of Toledo, and he therefore called upon Henry to support him against Richard. Henry's reply of 14 December 1257 takes a pacific line, pointing out that he had known nothing of Alfonso's candidature until well after Richard's election, promising to send messengers to Germany to find out more and ending with a promise that when he does know more, he will proceed to do what is right by all parties.[14]

It can be imagined that this development hardly improved the already vexed Anglo-Castilian relations, particularly against the background of Enrique's continued presence in England and Henry III's continued foot-dragging over the Gascon issues: Henry had still not agreed to a commission to resolve outstanding suits, and in late 1257 he was pulling out of a planned meeting, citing Welsh and Scottish issues. All of these issues were still in play in 1258 when domestic issues flared up with the barons' revolt. In addition, this highly unfortunate coincidence led to open derision of Eleanor's marriage treaty by no less a person than Richard of Cornwall, who was regarded as a leader by much of the baronage: in 1256, he was openly blaming certain of Henry's advisers for the treaty – a sure sign that he was speaking ill of it to a wider audience.[15]

All in all, therefore, Eleanor's first years in England must have been frequently uncomfortable with the Anglo-Castilian alliance unravelling almost before she had arrived, and at breaking point thereafter. One can also be tolerably sure that the reactions of many at court would reflect this; a princess who encapsulates a popular, prosperous alliance will be respected and courted, whereas a princess whose alliance has fallen out of favour and whose relations are causing trouble for the powers that be would frequently be on the receiving end of slights and discourtesies. One cannot help but wonder if the fact that after the pomp of her arrival Eleanor makes only one appearance on the record in the period to late 1258 is a reflection of this; and indeed whether that appearance – a pilgrimage with Eleanor of Provence to St Albans in October 1257, following a serious illness of the queen – reflects a perceived need to bolster her position by open association with the queen.

What else was Eleanor doing in this period? We cannot be sure. But Edward's story gives us some clues. Edward returned to England on about 29 November 1255, and was welcomed back in a similarly lavish way to that in which Eleanor had been greeted. However, cracks in his relationship with his father appear to have opened up almost immediately. In part this may be put down to the fact that, as Morris points out, the physical appearance of the person who returned from

Gascony was probably very different to that of the boy who had gone. Edward had last seen his father in October 1254, when he was aged just fourteen. He was now approaching sixteen and had apparently reached, or very nearly reached, the height which was to mark him out all his life. He had also spent part of the last year in active campaigning and all of it shouldering the burdens of government. Doubtless his confidence had been increased by his successful tenure in Gascony. He had become a very imposing presence; he now looked like a threat.

His increased confidence translated into a willingness to stand up for his rights in relation to his territories against his father. Matthew Paris provides a very lively account of a row not long after Edward's return. Edward, embracing his duties as Lord of Gascony, took up with his father complaints which had been raised with him by Gascon wine merchants about forced seizure of goods by the king's agents. These Gascons had told Edward that they would rather trade with Saracens than with England because of the way in which they were treated. Henry (typically) felt the complaint to be an infringement of his sovereignty and produced an unreasoned tirade comparing himself to Henry II, rebelled against by his dearest son. The particular row was defused, but the seeds of division between father and son had been sown, and Henry was not a man to ignore a grudge. The atmosphere was not improved by Edward's subsequent decision to increase the size of his retinue considerably. The message of his return was clear – here was a new power at court.

Edward's next appearance is also in opposition to his father's wishes – and his inclinations. Paris recounts how, at about Whitsuntide 1256, a tournament was held for Edward at Blythe in Nottinghamshire. It was obviously quite an event, with many nobles who attended 'to gain renown' being crushed and unseated, and with William Longespée suffering injuries from which he never recovered. The obvious point which emerges is that Edward had acquired a taste for knightly pastimes in the real fighting in Gascony and wished to keep his hand in. Since neither actual warfare or tournaments were at all to Henry III's taste, this can only have been another source of friction. However, the more serious point lies in the many nobles who, despite Henry's well-known views, participated in order to gain renown; there is a real flavour of men trying to 'get in' with Edward in his new role as a force in his own right.[16]

Was Eleanor with Edward? It would be surprising if she were not present for such an event in Edward's life. Further consideration of what he was doing at the time and where he went indicates strongly that she was indeed with him. Eleanor had dower lands assigned to her on her marriage in the neighbourhood; the journey would put Eleanor in the way of looking at her dower property at Tickhill in Yorkshire and the towns of Stamford and Grantham, which even then formed part of the main road to the North.

Thereafter, there was a short visit to Scotland which suggests (as Morris has noted) a social call by Edward and Eleanor together on Edward's sister Margaret and her husband Alexander of Scotland. The two couples were of a similar age: Margaret was just over a year older than Eleanor and her husband some nine months younger than her. Alexander was also a connection of Eleanor's through his mother, Marie de Coucy, who had married Eleanor's cousin Jean de Brienne and whose brother had married Eleanor's aunt Philippa. The scope for common ground between the two couples was therefore considerable. The young couples apparently paid a visit to Whithorn in Galloway on the coast of Scotland, the site of the first Christian community north of the border.[17]

Shortly after this, Edward is heard of on a short visit to Wales, which would fit with a tour by the couple of their English properties: Edward had been invested with Chester and various Welsh properties as part of his appanage on the marriage. This again forms a very interesting contrast with Henry III, whose visits north of the medieval equivalent of the Watford Gap were few and far between. It is also another example of the way in which Edward and Eleanor were establishing a pattern which was to be theirs for life; one of the characteristics of Edward's reign became his constant travelling around his realm, accompanied by Eleanor, seeing to their respective businesses. The trip will have been pleasant. There was no sign of trouble; indeed, Edward's lieutenant in Wales, the Savoyard appointee Geoffrey de Langley, boasted that he held the Welsh in the palm of his hand.[18]

Following another stop in Chester, another rendezvous with Margaret and Alexander, now themselves en route for a visit to the English court, seems likely. The party of young royals will have travelled down to Woodstock together to meet with the main court party – who had commandeered every house nearby and still run out of room. Thereafter, the party progressed to Oxford and from there by different routes to London, where another of Henry's special shows was put on: the city was 'decorated with banners, chaplets and manifold ornaments'.

However the progress was managed, Edward, and in all probability Eleanor, had reached London in advance of the main party and came out to welcome them on the road on 28 August. Eleanor was therefore at court to welcome Enrique on his arrival, which Matthew Paris places as happening during the Scottish royal visit.

The Welsh rebellion which, in defiance of Langley's prediction, blew up just after this in late 1256, therefore took Edward away from Eleanor just at a particularly difficult point. It also marks a very significant point in Edward's political history – it is the point when he first openly breaks ranks with the Savoyards with whom his mother had surrounded him and forms his own political affiliations. It was also what is termed 'a valuable learning experience' – in other words, an absolute disaster. The starting point is that the rebellion was brought about only in part by the emergence in Wales of a viable political leader, Llywelyn ap Gruffudd, grandson of Llywelyn the Great, after a period of Welsh infighting. In part it was the product of insensitive handling of the locals by Langley – and in particular the taking of steps designed to bring the area known as the Four Cantreds within the same administration as the English lordship of Chester.

Through winter Edward (who, it will be recalled, had spent every penny he had and more in Gascony) was casting about desperately to find money to pay for forces to defend his lands. One might have thought that Henry's first instinct would be to provide lavishly for the support of his eldest son in defending lands which were held from him. However, the position was quite the reverse. Taunting Edward that they were his lands, and therefore his problem, he claimed to have problems of his own and offered a measly 500 marks. Edward next turned to Richard of Cornwall, who, owing to his own need for money in his imperial campaign, could only offer 4,000 marks and his services as a mediator (which were rebuffed by Llywelyn). Perhaps the final straw for Edward was that Eleanor of Provence was neither able nor willing to help at this time; her response was that she had no money. This was quite true, as she had just spent an absolute fortune in ransoming her brother and securing papal support for the Sicilian plan. All Edward got from his mother was an exchange – she and Peter of Savoy purchased the wardship of the Ferrers family from him for 6,000 marks and Boniface of Savoy lent him £1,000 on mortgage. Whether the Savoyard faction was genuinely out of cash, or whether this was a tactic designed to bring Edward back to heel after disturbing signs of independence, the effect was not at all one which they would have desired.[19]

Cut loose by his family, he turned to the enemies of the Savoyards and his natural allies in interest in the Marches – both of whom were more interested in war than politics and were therefore good allies for a campaign in Wales. The change of emphasis can be seen in a variety of ways. In mid-1257, Edward replaced the Savoyard constable of Montgomery with the Marcher Hamo Lestrange, and he was now fighting alongside not just Marchers like Roger Clifford but also Lusignan allies such as Eleanor's distant cousin John de Warenne (who had married a Lusignan) and Roger Leyburn (formerly of William of Valence's household). Interestingly, the only truly negative stories about Edward's behaviour date from this era and appear more to reflect the Lusignan 'robber baron' approach to provisioning for a campaign than any particular misbehaviour on his part. Paris tells of the carrying off of horses, carts and provisions, the seizing from a priory (while Edward was elsewhere) of food, fuel and fodder, and 'freebooting' in the form of seizing more horses and carts.[20]

Finally, and most clearly, by 1258 at the latest (and possibly by 1257, when his need for money was at its most acute) Edward had mortgaged Stamford and Grantham to William de Valence (both a Lusignan and a Marcher in his lordship of Pembroke) and the manor of Tickhill to Aymer de Valence. He had also incurred a large debt to their brother Geoffrey.[21]

Eleanor's link to this move in loyalties cannot be positively proved, but a variety of factors suggest that she was heavily involved. In the first place (and rather strikingly), it will be noticed that the properties mortgaged were precisely those which formed Eleanor's dower assignment; it is therefore overwhelmingly likely that she was at least consulted and consented to the mortgages. The pledging only of her dower does suggest an active role on her part in this realignment.

Once that step is taken, there are other points that suggest her involvement. The first is a general one – as we have seen, her upbringing had included a knowledge of the requirements of defence of disputed territories and the making of strategic alliances. This sort of thinking is demonstrated by the fact that the allies chosen were the Lusignans and the Marchers. The latter were the natural tactical allies of a non-Welsh lord in Wales and also experienced fighters in difficult territory. The Lusignans were not only valuable, experienced fighters of a less than scrupulous sort (and hence the right kinds of allies for war against the Welsh); they were also, perhaps crucially, strategic allies in another area. Edward and Eleanor would both have been well aware after their year in Gascony that in that region a Lusignan alliance was very valuable; indeed, Lusignan presence during their tenure is evidenced. Strategically, bringing them over to Edward's side in other areas might well pay dividends in Gascony.

Finally, the Lusignans were not simply Henry and Edward's relatives; they were also connections by marriage of Eleanor. Eleanor's family was twice linked by marriage to the Eu branch of the Lusignans, and Geoffrey de Lusignan would also shortly marry one of Eleanor's first cousins.[22]

However, Eleanor was almost certainly left behind when Edward went to attempt to deal with matters in Wales in mid-1257, with a complete absence of success. The counteroffensive funded by Edward in late May was a rout. When Henry finally assembled a royal army in August, the knee-jerk nature of the reaction showed. Although the army met with initial success in taking control of the easily accessible Four Cantreds, they quickly ran out of supplies. The campaign was over, with no real results, by October.

The best that can be said of the campaign is that it provided an opportunity for Edward to learn on the ground the difficulties of a Welsh campaign and that history reveals that, unlike his father, he did learn this lesson. In particular, the issues which had historically proved difficult for an English king to comprehend were the opportunities which the landscape provided for harrying raids by the Welsh and the phenomenal difficulties of victualling in a hard land when the inhabitants disappeared into the hills with all their cattle and provisions. Henry II struggled with this lesson, Henry III never began to grasp it, but Edward never again made the mistake of carrying a campaign into Wales without adequately planning for the conditions.

Given that his initial reported reaction, in the disappointment of the moment, was that Wales should be left to the Welsh, it is interesting to speculate how Edward ultimately came to turn his lesson to such good account. Certainly one can dismiss the idea that his father may take the credit. Possibly Simon de Montfort, with whom Edward soon afterwards came into close contact, is the person who induced Edward to evaluate what he could take from this major disappointment. But perhaps most likely is that Eleanor, bred at a court where campaigning was part of everyday life and whose father was well known for thinking through each campaign before it began, was able to plant the seed that no experience is ever truly wasted if it is learnt from.[23]

Regardless, one result was that, throughout the period when Anglo-Castilian relations reached their nadir and Richard of Cornwall was at odds with Alfonso, Eleanor was alone at an increasingly hostile court. It must have brought home to her the fickleness of court popularity and the importance of establishing a core group of people whose loyalty could be relied upon.

Interestingly, it is at this point that the records first disclose the foremost of those whom Edward and Eleanor recruited over the years from outside their immediate families to form part of their cadre – Robert Burnell. Burnell, who went on to be not just Edward's closest professional adviser but a close friend to Eleanor, was a priest and commenced royal service in the king's offices. He first appears in one of Edward's witness lists in April 1257. It has been plausibly suggested that he may have been recruited as a useful contact at about the time of the 1256 visit to Wales, since his home estate of Acton Burnell was in Shropshire, near the Welsh border.

Both his status and his interests – he was by no means of the warrior caste – make him an unlikely intimate for Edward, though perhaps more so for Eleanor. She and Burnell were also to share an interest in property acquisition – on his part probably fuelled by the need to provide for the family with which his mistress about now began to provide him. From this point in time he became settled in their establishment, from which he was to emerge as a major player in due course. Aside from the versatility and outstanding intelligence which his later years were to reveal, it was probably no small part of his success that he seems to have been a man of unusually happy manners, with an ability to endear himself to people in all stations of life – as not just one but two of the contemporary annalists remarked on his death.[24]

If Eleanor had indeed begun to be aware of the need to find people who would be properly loyal to her and Edward's joint interests, this was a lesson which would only be reinforced by the upheavals which were shortly to come, as a miscellaneous group of court powers coalesced into opposition to the king. The new alliance was based on a very diverse group of self-interests and grudges.

The first part of it was the Savoyard faction, always previously more or less in tune with the king because the queen's power came to her through him. Edward's move to the Lusignans had given rise to a determination in the Savoyard faction that something must be done, given that their main power at court came from controlling Edward as heir to the throne – particularly once news of the fact that Edward had mortgaged properties to the Lusignans came out in early 1258. The concern became more urgent once a fatal attack was made by Aymer de Valence's men on one of the queen's advisers and the king, when confronted about the matter, refused to act against his brother.[25]

The second element was that the Lusignans had roused Simon de Montfort to the point of action. Montfort had long cherished a particular grudge against the Lusignans. The most significant (but not the sole) element in Montfort's dislike was money. Throughout Montfort's career, however high flown the expressed ideals, his actions can usually be reconciled with his financial interest; perhaps understandably, given his need to provide for four sons and his shortage of transmissible land. In the case of the Lusignans, they trod on his toes in the very significant matter of his wife's dower assignment.

Eleanor Montfort had been entitled to a third of the value of the Marshal estates on the death of her first husband, William Marshal II. However, those lands were now in the hands of William de Valence (now styling himself 'Lord of Pembroke') in his role as husband to the remaining Marshal heiress, and he had defeated Montfort's attempts to get actual dower lands settled on Eleanor. As a result, Montfort had to wait for Pembroke to pay the equivalent fee, which he did not, so persistently that ultimately Henry assumed the obligation to pay the fee instead. He, too, consistently failed to keep up to date with payments, often using grudges against Montfort as a reason to refuse payment. Then, to add insult to injury, while remaining in arrears to Montfort, Henry could find money to pay yet more fees by way of presents to his Lusignan brothers. This was a very powerful grudge indeed – so powerful that it was later to lead to international complications. To add to this, Pembroke had 'taken out' one of the most valuable heiresses to come on the market in a generation, who (given the likely age of the respective parties) might have enriched one of Montfort's sons.

The bad blood between Montfort and Pembroke was notorious and extreme. In May 1257, the two quarrelled violently at court in front of the king. Pembroke accused Montfort of treachery, an accusation which reaped a predictably furious response given the work which Montfort had done for Henry in the past in Gascony and the ingratitude with which he had been repaid. A fist fight was only avoided by royal intervention. A similarly violent quarrel broke out a year later in April 1258 when Pembroke accused Montfort and Gloucester of giving aid and comfort to the Welsh. As a result, Montfort, adding up his grudges against the Lusignans and his almost equally strong sense of grievance over his treatment in relation to his efforts in Gascony, was ready to consider confrontation with the king.[26]

Yet the grievances of a party of foreigners brought to power by the king and another outsider, whose roots in England were very slight, would probably not have been enough. What carried these grievances over into crisis was their joinder to the less specific, but nonetheless strongly felt, discontentment of the powerful English nobles who joined with them. Two of these issues, the question of aliens and the Sicilian folly, have been outlined above. But to this were joined other, more fundamental questions – deriving from the way that Henry had driven the country into the ground by policies adopted and pursued without consultation with even his most powerful subjects. Added to this there were complaints more generally about heavy financial demands and a neglect of the local administration which gave rein to oppressive local officials and magnates.[27]

The confederation which came into place on 12 April 1258 therefore contained not just the foreigners Montfort and Peter of Savoy but also John FitzGeoffrey and Peter de Montfort, English lords who had allied themselves with the Savoyard faction, along with the earls of Gloucester and Norfolk and Norfolk's brother Hugh Bigod, representing the English high nobility. When the parliament convened in April was treated by Henry with his usual high-handedness, and no sign of amelioration in his approach to his siblings appeared, the decision was made to confront the king.

On the morning of 30 April 1258, Henry was confronted by a mass of knights and barons, swordless but attired as for battle, led by the confederation of magnates. Henry's first reaction was to ask if he was a prisoner. Instead, the barons outlined their terms – the expulsion of the Lusignans and a promise of consultation with the magnates in the form of a committee of twenty-four on future policies. The barons' revolt had begun; civil war would follow in its train.[28]

6

Dissent, Defeat, Victory

At the start of the revolt, Eleanor had been in England for two and a half years and was still only sixteen years old. By the time it drew to a close in 1265, she was twenty-three and had lived through a political storm and personal vicissitudes which marked her for life. Therefore, the revolt and the war which followed cannot be ignored. And yet for seven years the press of events and the constant realignments of loyalty and interest which took place at the English court push her almost entirely out of sight. Almost the only way to find Eleanor and understand what she was doing and the effect which this major event had on her is therefore to follow Edward, whose movements and political manoeuvrings are well covered.

On 2 May, Henry agreed to the Barons' terms. Edward, too, was required to consent, and his actions were very interesting – and revealing.

Putting the debate in context, when looking at the list of the main barons involved, it might at first seem probable that Edward would consent gladly – the list is thick with those who were or had been in his household, such as John FitzGeoffrey, Peter de Montfort and Peter of Savoy. However, Edward's recent move to the Lusignans was thorough enough for him to make it very plain that he did not support the moves of these men who were officially closely associated with him. It also appears more than possible that it was Edward, in concert with the Lusignans, who came up with the first scheme to frustrate the practical effect of the oath; when the time came to nominate his twelve councillors, the king nominated William, Aymer and Guy de Lusignan and their brother-in-law John de Warenne among his. Edward's involvement in this rather puerile gesture is certainly suggested by the nomination not just of Warenne, his friend and Eleanor's relation, but also Edward's cousin and friend Henry of Almain. Indeed, one of the complaints that was made against the Lusignans at Oxford two months later was that they had encouraged Edward to subvert the whole reform movement.[1]

Thus the Provisions of Oxford (as the results of the June parliament at Oxford have become known) provided for control of both Henry and Edward. The committee of twenty-four was replaced with one of fifteen, arrived at by a system of election designed to produce a pro-baronial/Savoyard result – including the queen's key men Boniface and Peter of Savoy. Everything done by the major officers of state, the Chancery or by way of grants had to be approved by the council. The clear implication was that Henry was incapable of running his own affairs and was back under tutelage. To keep Edward under control, it was ordered that all lands and castles alienated by Henry III were to be restored to the Crown. This included Henry's grants to Edward – the source of his money.[2]

Finally, everyone was to swear to uphold the Provisions – formally, in church, at a ceremony which involved the excommunication of all opposed to the Provisions and was supervised by Boniface of Savoy. When the Lusignans refused to take the oath, De Montfort made plain that the revolt had teeth, warning Pembroke,'You must know without a shadow of a doubt that you will lose your castles or your life.' In the face of this, the Lusignans, accompanied by Edward, fled to Winchester, where they were pursued by the baronial party. The Lusignans were escorted to the coast and forced to leave, which they finally did on 14 July. They were pursued by the evil wishes of Eleanor of Provence, who prevailed upon King Louis not to allow them to remain in his lands either, because of the fact that the Lusignans had 'defamed' her. Yet, even in the face of such open hostility from his mother, Edward still did not abandon them: on 28 June 1258, Edward appointed Geoffrey de Lusignan seneschal of Gascony and granted the Isles of Oleron and the Channel Isles to his brother Guy. However, within a few weeks he was forced to cancel the grants.[3]

In the face of this defiance, a council of four was appointed to supervise his affairs, with all correspondence requiring to be 'signed off' by the councillors. Interestingly, this period of quasi-supervision of Edward's affairs coincides with two more of Eleanor's rare overt appearances in the documents. In September 1258 we find her, like a good, dutiful princess, attending the consecration of Salisbury Cathedral in the train of her mother-in-law. And again, on New Year's Day 1259, she is to be glimpsed at Mortlake, receiving a knight from the Viscount of Béarn and giving him sapphire rings – provided by Eleanor of Provence. Put into context, these formal displays suggest that supervision was being exercised over Eleanor too, directly by Eleanor of Provence.[4]

The supervision of Edward's household appears to have been of short duration, as Edward repositioned himself politically over the next few months – improving relations with the Earl of Gloucester to the point of a formal alliance which he concluded in March 1259. Although the alliance was of short duration, it is interesting in showing Edward's focus at the time and also in listing his supporters. As to the first matter,

Edward's aim is expressly stated in the agreement to be the recovery of his lands – and Gloucester agreed to counsel Edward and to aid him in achieving this goal. Edward's concern at this time is therefore not the broader issues of royal control, but his own lands – his own present business. Secondly, however, the agreement lists supporters of Edward who Gloucester agrees to back. The people identified include Henry of Almain, Earl Warenne, Philip Basset, Robert Walerand, Roger Clifford, Roger Leyburn, Hamo Lestrange and William la Zouche. Aside from Henry of Almain and Earl Warenne, whose links to Edward and Eleanor have already been examined, this list contains a number of the Marchers with whom Edward had already allied in 1257 and who were to be his jousting companions in future. The list therefore shows signs of Edward continuing to surround himself with like-minded laymen whose prime loyalty was to him.

What is still more interesting about this agreement is its true likely motive. Aside from being useful if Gloucester could do anything to help Edward regain his castles, it probably represented a deliberate attempt to make common cause with Gloucester, not with a view to the welfare of the English properties but to that of Gascony. For Gloucester was slated to attend the last round of negotiations for the peace treaty with France, the Treaty of Paris. Edward's concern was that all the English royal family were supposed to renounce their rights to the Angevin inheritance of Normandy, Maine, Touraine and Anjou, which he perceived as weakening his current tactical position as Lord of Gascony as well as his future position as King of England with historical claims to these regions.[5]

This point of interest – opposition to the Treaty of Paris – was also to help bring Edward and Eleanor into closer communion with Simon de Montfort. De Montfort had an interest in Gascony by reason of family claims and his own long residence there as seneschal. He also had, through his wife, an interest in the claims in France which the Treaty of Paris was to put aside. He may well already have been planning to use the need for her consent to force Henry to deal with his financial claims in relation to her dowry and his own expenditure in Gascony. Until these were adequately dealt with, the Montforts, too, would oppose the Treaty of Paris.

It appears that it was at around this point that Edward ceased to focus solely on his lands and really began to grapple with the approach which he should adopt in relation to the more substantive issues of government. So from this time forward there is evidence of Edward putting himself forward as a supporter of reforms in justice and administration. For example, in August 1259 Edward wrote to his lieutenant at Chester arguing the necessity to maintain good government at all times 'if on account of the influence of anyone common justice is denied to anyone of our subjects by us or our bailiffs we lose the favour of God and man and our lordship is belittled. We wish therefore that common justice shall be exhibited to everyone.' This may, of course, be regarded as a cynical exercise in rebranding, but it is entirely consistent with Edward's later approach both in relation to the baronial reform movement and in terms of legal and administrative reform when king and should therefore be regarded as a more fundamental change.[6]

Whence had this shift in outlook come? I believe that this move can probably be traced, at least in part, to Eleanor. It is just possible that Edward himself came to consider the merits of the reformist approach, despite his early opposition. However, the likelihood is that some of his closest advisers – among whom we can number Eleanor and very possibly Robert Burnell (who would later play such an important part in the legal reforms which Edward introduced) – were involved in this change of heart. Eleanor's involvement particularly seems probable when one considers that the first and second parts of the *Siete Partidas* deal with the importance of lawmaking, indicating that a good legislator should possess mindfulness of God, a love of justice, a knowledge of the law and a willingness to change laws if necessary as well as model provisions for temporal and public law. They canvassed in detail the duties of the king towards God, the people, and the country.[7]

More evidence of Edward's change of approach is found at the time of the autumn parliament in 1259, when unrest was surfacing from the lesser nobility about the pace of reform – or more accurately the lack of pace of reform. Although the Crown had been neatly hamstrung, the wider concerns of the reformers, in particular as to administrative abuses by magnates, had gone next to nowhere. This was substantially because Gloucester was opposed to any inquiry into and reform of his own administration. De Montfort was unwilling to oppose Gloucester until his own concerns were addressed – one of which was an arbitration under Gloucester's aegis which was due to report by 1 November over the vexed question of the dower rights.

In any event, the parliament of October 1259 opened with a protest by a group picturesquely described as 'the community of the bachelors of England'. It was directed to the council and specifically to Edward and complained in terms about the failure to progress on the wider issues – which were of great practical moment to local society. No one knows who the 'community of bachelors' was. The likelihood is that it was a group of the knightly class, and this reading is supported by the fact that the term 'bachelors' was used to describe young men (knights) who were in attendance at tournaments. Still further support is given by the fact that Edward had recently become a keen participator in tournaments, and had attended three that year.

Edward's reaction to the protest was startlingly different to his response to the original reformist pledge – he swore immediately to support the bachelors to the death in fighting for the community of England and the common good. Putting all this together, the address to Edward and his response bear all the signs of being staged as an opportunity to let Edward publicise his change of position. The protest and Edward's intervention led to the promulgation of the Provisions of Westminster, which provide the high-water mark of the actual reform movement (as opposed to the anti-royalist elements of the disputes). These provisions abolished a number of abuses and dealt with a miscellany of practical grievances – rights of suit, distraint, exemption from jury service. It is significant that not until Edward's reign were such matters seriously considered again. Again, therefore, we can see that Edward's manifesto as future king is being 'trailed' by Edward and his team, among whom we must count Eleanor.[8]

To reinforce his move to the reformers, two days later Edward entered into a formal agreement to 'aid and counsel' Montfort and maintain the baronial enterprise. This agreement was witnessed by Henry of Almain, Earl Warenne and Roger Leyburn – all members of his clique. However, as with the earlier alignment with Gloucester, the alliance seems to have been of a multifaceted nature, and also to have had reference to Gascony, Montfort's financial issues and the threat to both posed by the Treaty of Paris, which was yet to be finalised. Finally, again as with the Gloucester Treaty, an alliance with one of the central members of the council freed Edward up to make moves to regain his English lands, and movement on this front soon followed. Between mid-October and mid-November, Henry, Eleanor of Provence, Montfort, Gloucester and Peter of Savoy all departed for France in preparation for the ratification of the Treaty of Paris on 4 December 1259, leaving England under the Bigod brothers, who were sympathetic to Edward's recent approach to reform.[9]

An interesting question at this point is where Eleanor went. Edward, we know, stayed in England. It has been suggested that on this occasion Eleanor did not remain with him, but instead went with her in-laws. The reason for this suggestion is the apparent meeting between Henry and Eleanor of Provence and Eleanor's mother Jeanne and brother Ferdinand, evidenced by their obtaining privileges for Ponthevin merchants. However, Eleanor was reported to be with Edward on Henry and Eleanor of Provence's return in spring. She did not, unlike her sisters-in-law (who are mentioned in correspondence as being with the king), receive any presents from Eleanor of Provence at Christmas 1259, which the king and queen spent abroad. Further, her health (unlike his and the queen's) is not mentioned by Henry in letters to Hugh Bigod to be transmitted to Edward. All this suggests powerfully that Eleanor passed up the opportunity to see her family in order to remain with her husband.[10]

Once his family and mentors had gone, Edward seized back his castles and replaced the council-appointed custodians with his own appointees.

This was not just a snub to the council, but to Eleanor of Provence, who was in alliance with the council, and some of whose Savoyard henchmen had been put in charge of these castles. Then, to further put fuel on the fire, Edward, in concert with de Montfort, began to argue that Parliament could be gathered in Henry's absence – in the face of Henry's clear prohibition on Parliament being convened while he was still in France. This was the touch point for a row between Edward (and presumptively Eleanor) and his parents which was never entirely resolved.

Within weeks, both sides were raising arms. Then Henry sent home as his representative none other than the Earl of Gloucester, with whom Edward was by now embroiled in a violent disagreement over their competing claims to Bristol Castle. The outcome was disastrous. Gloucester, possibly maliciously, reported back that Edward was planning to dethrone his father in a military coup. The king's party continued to prepare for war, with Henry summoning those barons and knights he thought he could trust, and Gloucester raising his own forces. Fortunately Richard of Cornwall, arriving back from his imperial interlude, took the sensible middle line and had the gates of London closed and guarded against both factions and arms issued to all men over the age of fifteen.[11]

At this point Edward and Montfort and their retinues (including Eleanor) holed up in the hospital of St John at Clerkenwell, where they stayed for weeks while the process of mediation inched forward. It seems plain that Edward was incandescent with Gloucester, but still more so with his mother, who he blamed for joining with Gloucester to create the situation. To make bad worse, Eleanor of Provence herself intervened to prevent reconciliation. Henry would have reconciled with Edward readily – indeed, he acknowledged that if he only saw Edward he would not refrain from embracing him – but his mother needed to get Edward back under control to maintain her own power base and would not reconcile short of capitulation by Edward.[12]

Pausing here for a moment, it is perhaps not a great leap to speculate that the situation brought about by a queen who took on an overtly political role and competed for power with her own husband and son was a very formative experience for the eighteen-year-old Edward; and may well have contributed to the role to which Eleanor was later to be confined by Edward (despite her stronger claims to a political role based on her greater intellectual attainments). Here, therefore, we see the origin of the fact that under Edward there would be absolutely no overt political role for Eleanor – and her consequent position in the shadows.

Edward found that, short of giving his parents the rebellion which they had imagined, he had no way back but capitulation. He was forced to eat humble pie – brought before his father in a set piece of contrition in St Paul's Cathedral – and to yield his castles back up to be run by new appointees. A month later, he was brought to sign up to a new reconciliation with Gloucester. Meanwhile, he had to stand by and watch while Montfort was put on trial by Henry, at the behest of Gloucester and Eleanor of Provence. The final straw came as the trial drew to a close. On 20 July 1260, news came that Edward's castle at Builth Wells – recently taken from the custody of Edward's Marcher appointee, the formidable Roger Mortimer – had been besieged by Llywelyn, had fallen and had been razed to the ground.

Edward's immediate reaction was fury that his property had been lost by the men appointed against his will and determination to go to war. He borrowed money and a month after the castle fell Edward was to be found in Chester preparing for action, with a muster planned for early September. Once again, however, his position was undermined by Henry, Eleanor of Provence and their advisers; on 1 September 1260, Henry agreed a two-year ceasefire and the attack was called off.[13]

While Edward prepared for war in Wales, Eleanor seems to have been being something of a trial to Henry in another way – hunting freely in the royal estates. One entry in the Close Rolls has her pardoned for taking no fewer than eight hinds without permission in the Forest of Dean while giving her permission to do likewise round St Briavel's Castle in Gloucestershire. Later, in November, she was given permission to take six hinds in each of the forests of Braden and Gillingham.[14]

Also at around this time news came of Eleanor's mother's remarriage to a Jean De Nesle, Sieur De Falvy et de Herelle. He was a connection of the de Coucy family into which Eleanor's aunt Philippa de Dammartin had married and seems, judging by the facts that he brought no notable alliance or property and that he outlived Jeanne by over a decade, to have been a handsome, and possibly younger, man. There is no sign that Eleanor took badly to this match; she will doubtless have borne in mind that it was prudent for any countess in her own right to be married. It is not clear how closely linked in time were Jeanne's remarriage and the death of her eldest son and heir apparent Ferdinand, which occurred at some point in the early 1260s, leaving Eleanor a potential heir to the county of Ponthieu, and increasing her political importance in English eyes.

Meanwhile, the Welsh ceasefire which his father had agreed left Edward in a very difficult position. He could not turn his attention to the Welsh question before 1262, in the face of the ceasefire. His relations with his parents and their advisers would inevitably lead to disagreements if he remained. At the same time, his interest in Gascony needed guarding in the light of the conclusion of the Treaty of Paris in the previous winter and the revival of hostilities between Gaston de Béarn and Esquivat de Chabanais. The obvious practical solution was, therefore, to remove himself from court to Gascony – but to achieve that he needed the co-operation of his father's (or rather his mother's) advisers, who, on the evidence of the Welsh affair, would be likely to sacrifice his interests to their own.

The result was an apparent volte-face of staggering proportions. In late September 1260, Edward and Montfort united with Gloucester, and with their combined power they were able to seize control of the council. There was no display of force or open political statement this time, but all the main ministers were replaced. Hugh Bigod was replaced by Hugh Despenser, a friend of Montfort, brother-in-law of Philip Basset and, like Peter de Montfort a member of Edward's household in Gascony. Montfort's trial was quietly dropped. However, the alliance came at a price dictated by Gloucester, which was a halt to the legal and administrative reforms which Edward had championed. The coup, though radical, was all but silent – the only overt sign of the new state of affairs was the ceremony in October when Edward knighted Montfort's eldest sons, Henry and Simon. Indeed, so silent was the coup that it has only fully come to light recently in Maddicott's research on Simon de Montfort.[15]

Some might suggest that this alliance, which committed Edward to Gloucester's essentially anti-reformist policy of allowing great magnates to investigate and correct abuses in their own territories, gives the lie to Edward's actual commitment to reform. It was indeed changes of this sort which gave Edward his second-best-known nickname 'the Leopard': a beast believed to be more cunning than a lion and thought to gain its way by deceit. However, it is more likely that the commitment to reform was real and that the change was truly one of practical necessity. Certainly Edward's discomfort with this alliance of convenience is strongly suggested by his immediate retreat from England. Rather than staying to keep the new junta in power, he instead decamped with his large retinue, to which the elder Montfort sons, Henry and Simon, were now added.[16]

In this one trip in late 1260 to early 1261 can be seen brought together three of Edward's major preoccupations in this period. The first was Gascony – consistently with his actions for the past year or more, once it became apparent that his position in England left him little to do, either for his lands there or the process of reform, Edward headed for Gascony to resume the reins of power and his administrative reforms there. His court was in Gascony before Christmas, and stayed there until March, missing a major family event – the wedding of his sister Beatrice to John of Brittany, which took place on Christmas Day in 1260. This gives the lie to the more usual account that Edward went abroad to participate in tournaments. He did participate in tournaments, it is true, but on the way down to Gascony. He also gave serious attention to the business of government.[17]

Nonetheless the tournament participation, which certainly did occur in these years, deserves to be counted in the list of priorities. It is not fair to say (as Matthew Paris tends to suggest, and subsequent commentators tend to accept) that participation in tournaments was a sign of irresponsibility or fecklessness. In context, it represents a commitment to establishing himself as personally skilled in arms and a leader in battle. In Eleanor's family this would be done in actual campaign, but for Edward, in the absence of actual war, in no other way were such skills to be learnt and practised until they came with facility. Richard I, England's most famous martial king, was a firm believer in the tournament's use as a training ground for knights, specifically licensing tournaments to improve the quality of English knights, and Alfonso's *Siete Partidas* recognises the role of tournaments in keeping fighters in training.

Moreover, whatever the view of Henry or Matthew Paris or the subsequent commentators, success in tournaments was far from a negative point in European society. It is, of course, well known that William Marshal first came to prominence as the great star of the tournament circuit of his era, and that the skills he honed here led to success in actual conflict in his later life, appointments and ultimately the bestowal of an earldom and lands sufficient still to be a point of vibrant debate between his heirs a century later. Nor had this route to distinction passed away – as we have seen, Eleanor's own uncle by marriage, John of Brienne, took exactly the same route to renown and even royalty. Accordingly, the derogatory tone directed to this aspect of Edward's life at this time should be discounted both as impractical and as out of step with broader perceptions of the time.[18]

Again, one may ask why Edward took this course – given that it was certainly not going to be at his parents' behest. The case for Eleanor's involvement in this is also quite compelling. It is perhaps natural, given Edward's later reputation as a warrior, to assume that his fondness for tournaments was innate; and it may be that he would have been keen on such pursuits without Eleanor at his side. However, the assumption is not necessarily a safe one. Three points are worth noting in this regard. The first is that he did take up the tournament circuit shortly after their marriage – despite the fact that he was brought up to despise tournaments. The second is that, consistent with that upbringing, he had never shown signs of any such interest prior to their marriage – unlike, for example, Henry the Young King. The third is that Eleanor, in contrast, was brought up among those who regarded training in arms as a vital accomplishment for a king, active participation in battle on his part as a *sine qua non*, and tournaments as the best substitute.

The final point of focus (in which we may again see Eleanor's hand) is that, on his way down to Gascony, Edward reunited with the Lusignans in Paris, where Aymer was on his deathbed, thereby making it plain that he had not abandoned them and that he continued to ally himself with them. To reinforce the point, he (as in 1258) appointed Guy de Lusignan his lieutenant in Gascony, and (almost certainly in concert with Eleanor) arranged the marriage of Geoffrey de Lusignan to Eleanor's cousin Jeanne, Countess of Châtellherault, the daughter of Eleanor's maternal aunt Mathilde.[19]

Thus, throughout the period from the beginning of the barons' revolt one can detect Edward working at acquiring particular skill sets that he would need in the future: in particular, learning the ropes of government and reform in a hands-on way and learning to be a military leader. Eleanor's hand in assisting in positioning Edward away from his mother's influence, maintaining their interest in Gascony and Wales and steering Edward in the direction of the skills which he would be required to exercise as a successful king and did not yet possess cannot be definitively proved, but seems to be strongly indicated, as one would expect, given her upbringing.[20]

Meanwhile, by April 1261, without Edward's retinue to hold them back, the Savoyards had moved to regain power and Edward, out of funds, was forced to return. It is plain that when Edward returned in April with Pembroke, he did so with the intention of maintaining the junta via the ties he had re-established with the Lusignans. Yet Pembroke was nobody's tool. Forming the view that he was more likely to get his estates in England and Wales restored via Henry than Gloucester and Montfort, he rapidly went over to the king's party.[21]

Edward's position was next to impossible. He had loyalties to his parents and his uncle, and yet also to Montfort and the cause of administrative reform. Within the erstwhile junta the aspects of administrative reform to which Edward was pledged were still being blocked by Gloucester, while his parents and the Savoyards were now claiming to espouse and to be the defenders of this aspect of reform. He had settled Gascony in concert with the useful Lusignan alliance, and to move away from that alliance would inevitably cause problems. As to money, Edward had considerably overspent in past years, both in defence of his lands and in the acquisition of his proto-army. On this point, he was much more likely to get funds from the royal–Lusignan alliance in power than the Montfortian one out of power: Montfort was always short of money himself and Gloucester was unlikely ever to assist.

Ultimately the bottom line won, and in May Edward defected to the royal party. But significant numbers of Edward's supporters, including some close friends, refused to defect with him. Most notable among these were Henry of Almain and Roger Clifford. If anything were needed to add bitterness to a very difficult period, it rapidly transpired that if Edward had made his move in belief that the Savoyard faction were indeed pledged to real reform, they and his parents had played him for a fool.

Henry simply procured a papal dispensation absolving him from his oath to uphold the Provisions of Oxford and annulled all the initiatives introduced under its aegis. Although Edward did not follow the stampede of those whose disgust at this move sent them into alliance with Montfort, there is strong evidence to suppose that he was appalled at this move. Apparently, when told that the king had obtained a letter of dispensation for Edward too, Edward's reaction was to renew his own oath. However, he was effectively stuck with the royalist side; as Morris points out, it was hardly practical for him to turn back to Montfort, having only defected scant weeks before, and all the financial imperatives for his defection still stood. It is also possible that he and those around him began to sense that the dispute would end in arms and with an actual challenge to Henry's rule, which Edward would be bound to defend, think what he might of his father as a king. But his action in leaving the country again at once surely marks his profound dislike of this move.[22]

So Edward, Eleanor and their companions set off again for Gascony in July 1261, where he returned to dealing with the problems of the duchy (never in short supply). Again, examination of what he did while there gives the lie to suggestions that this period of his life was idle and feckless and instead reinforces the impression of a king in training. He promulgated a new constitution for the city of Bordeaux, which gave him a better base for controlling the Colomb–Soler feud. He reformed the coinage and dealt with numerous issues of law and order.[23]

He also took some military steps to extend the territory under his control, in particular in the strategically important valley of Soule. In early November 1261, in an episode which has not attracted the attention of any of his biographers, he made a significant demonstration of force at the town of Mauléon which resulted in the submission of the troublesome viscounts of Soule. Certain lands, including Mauléon itself, were reluctantly ceded by the viscounts to Edward in exchange for other lands. Interestingly, Edward proceeded to fortify the town in bastide form – the very first evidence of Edward's interest in bastidisation. Supplementing the existing fortress, the 'haute-ville' was protected by an external wall and arranged around a central rectangular place, surrounded by arcaded houses or shops. A similar exercise was performed at Villeneuve-lès-Tardets (today Tardets-Sorholus).

This little-known interlude raises some fascinating questions. In particular, whence came the interest in fortifying towns? Richard I was the first Plantagenet to play with the concept in Gascony, with the foundation of Marmande in 1182, and Mont de Marsan and Nogaro had been locally founded even earlier. Since then little had been done in Gascony proper, though foundations had flourished in the Agenais under Louis IX's brother Alphonse of Poitiers – provocatively close to the Gascon border. Henry III was of course not interested in military building, and Simon de Montfort seems to have had little interest either. The first proper new foundations in Gascony were to be built by Edward in 1265 (Monségur and Montpouillan). The work at Mauléon therefore represents a new departure. While the new towns of the Agenais probably had some influence, it is also likely that Eleanor's own experience of the use made routinely in Castile of fortified towns, the emphasis placed on refortifying existing towns to a new user's requirements and the injunctions reflected in the *Siete Partidas* that a good king minds the walls of his towns will have had some influence in turning Edward's thoughts in this direction.

It seems possible that it is to this time, too, that we can trace the first evidence of Eleanor acting as a mediator or arbitrator in disputes between noble houses. A letter from Gaston de Béarn dating from around this time refers to her intervention in his dispute with Fortulus Ameravi. Apparently Eleanor was establishing her own reputation, at least outside England.[24]

Edward, Eleanor and their entourage remained in Gascony until February 1262, when he returned to fix a more long-term deal on his finances with his parents, who were meanwhile prosecuting some of Edward's erstwhile companions, such as Roger Leyburn and Roger Clifford – probably with a view to ensuring their alienation from Edward was final. As soon as the deal had been agreed, he returned to France, where he threw himself into the tournament circuit with a new team, the defectors to Montfort being replaced by new recruits from Burgundy, Champagne and Flanders. Eleanor's involvement in this move is seen in the presence of knights with Ponthevin names such as d'Abbeville and de Neel. The message to his erstwhile companions was stark – no one was indispensable to Edward.[25]

Again, most commentators see this period as one of frivolity or at best listlessness. However, another construction is possible. It may well be that Edward and his advisers, including Eleanor, were now readying themselves for an armed rebellion in England, not least given the knowledge that a number of their former allies, such as Roger Leyburn, were now in open revolt. If this came to pass, the vast bulk of the military experience and might was now with the rebels. Neither Henry or the Savoyards could be trusted as military leaders. If there was to be a fight, it would be Edward who would have to lead, and with the help of foreign troops. Viewed in this light, his tourneying takes on a very different colour – as being the best possible preparation for if the worst were to come about.[26]

Edward was back in England by spring 1263, brought back by the news that Llywelyn had overrun much of the March of Wales. It appears likely that it was on this return journey that his vessel encountered a terrible storm, which at first seemed likely to sink the ship. The ledger book of Valé Royal Abbey tells how the rigging was all torn and everyone was praying, but to no avail. Then Edward promised that if he were spared he would found an abbey of at least a hundred monks of the Cistercian Order. Although apparently the storm was calmed at once, the foundation of Vale Royal did not proceed as quickly; Edward's focus was on more immediate priorities. First he went to London, where his father ordered the men of London and the shires to swear fealty to himself and to Edward as heir. Interestingly, one key magnate refused. This was the new Earl Gilbert of Gloucester, piqued by Henry's refusal to allow him to enter on his estates before he came of age.

Thereafter Edward turned his attention to Wales, and this move proved the spark which finally ignited the rebellion. The chances are that it would have come at some point soon in any event, but that it came precisely at this time can be traced directly to Edward's return with his new army, and his consequent failure to ally with the Marcher lords who had previously formed the backbone of his military associates. This added fuel to the fire created by the Savoyard revival and the return of Pembroke.[27]

Edward commenced his campaign with a trip to Windsor Castle, where he settled Eleanor. However, his other action there – strengthening the defences of the castle – strongly suggests that war with Montfort was now inevitable; after all, Windsor hardly needed to prepare itself for a Welsh incursion. In April, Edward then moved off to campaign in Wales, where his strategy was sensible, but progress was grindingly slow.

Meanwhile, the Marchers and reformers were reviving the Provisions of Oxford, with their anti-alien mindset, and calling for the return of Montfort, who arrived in late April or May and rendezvoused with his supporters at Oxford. By the beginning of June 1263, while Edward was fighting in Wales, Montfort, Leyburn and Clifford rallied an army in the middle of England and began to attack the lands of the queen and her supporters and move to cut off aid from abroad. War had truly broken out. Entirely predictably, Edward was summoned to the aid of his parents, and had no alternative but to go, abandoning the Welsh war.[28]

Edward's first appearance outside of Wales comes in the middle of June, when he took an oath of loyalty from the ruling elite of Dover and the other Cinque Ports. Meanwhile, his former tutor in arms, Nicholis de Molis, was appointed to the key post of custodian of Corfe Castle.

By the time Edward reached London and took up residence with his followers at Clerkenwell, his parents were cowering in the Tower without military support or money, surrounded by a predominantly hostile city and deserted by many of their erstwhile supporters. Meanwhile, Montfort continued to attract more supporters from among the high minded, including, most upsettingly for Edward, his own cousin Henry of Almain and the young Northern baron John de Vescy.[29]

The situation was acute. Without money, many of Edward's army would defect; without the army there was no one to oppose the rebels. The crisis point came when Montfort put the Londoners to their election – were they for or against the Provisions of Oxford? The merchants in charge of London could see which way the wind was blowing, but tried to persuade Henry to go with it, sending a delegation to Henry asking him to endorse the Provisions of Oxford and send Edward's knights away.[30]

By now even more convinced that a military showdown was bound to come and well aware that the royal family's need for ready money was too urgent to await the outcome of protracted negotiations, Edward moved decisively. On 29 June 1263, in company with Henry's friend Robert Walerand, he raided the Temple, where ample funds were left on deposit with the banking order of knights, including some of the Crown Jewels. Gaining access under cover of a wish to inspect the jewels, he and his party then conducted a daring smash-and-grab raid which netted about £1,000 – enough to keep his army loyal for a while to come. He then sped to Eleanor at Windsor, grabbing further provisions as they went.

The raid unleashed a wave of violence in London against royalists and aliens, during which one particular key event took place. On 13 July, Eleanor of Provence, characteristically acting independently of her husband and taking the initiative, was ambushed and attacked by a mob while trying to escape to Windsor in her barge. While she emerged unscathed, there is no doubt that she was the subject of a very serious attack and was much shocked by it; pelted with stones and food as well as insults, she was in real fear for her life until rescued by the Montfortian Mayor of London. This was an outrage which incurred Edward's lasting wrath against the Londoners – but it also signified clearly that the barons had the upper hand, and that large swathes of the people no longer held the royal family in awe.[31]

Thus, by 4 July, Henry had to submit to the demands of Montfort that he agree that all foreigners be expelled, never to return. Henry remained, effectively under guard, at the Tower – which was now commanded by Edward's former companion, the Montfortian stalwart Hugh Despenser. Montfort then summoned the feudal host in the king's name, and (carrying Henry with him like a puppet) instructed them to expel the foreign knights at Windsor. Faced with this large army, Edward too had to capitulate, and his army left England in August 1263.[32]

However – and somewhat ironically – the departure of the resented foreign troops, together with the free hand which Montfort's actions in the rest of the country had given the Welsh to create havoc for all the English and Marcher lords in Wales, left the path free to reconciliation between Edward and his Marcher friends. This was still further eased by Montfort's suggestion of an alliance with Llywelyn, which was anathema to the Marchers.

At first sight, Eleanor seems completely irrelevant to these subtle political shifts in the revolt, but in fact closer scrutiny indicates that again she was, if not advising, at least integrally involved.

This can be seen from the fact that the first move which was made appears to have been a reconciliation of Edward with John de Warenne, sealed by the grant of Stamford and Grantham to him. These were towns to which Warenne had a claim though his father, and they were thus of great interest to him. It will, however, be recalled that these were also Eleanor's dower lands, and could not be alienated effectively without her consent. Similarly, Henry of Almain was reconciled by a grant of the honour of Tickhill – another part of Eleanor's dower. With Warenne and Almain back on side, the way was open for further covert diplomacy, and reconciliation with the Marchers. Quite how it was done is not clear – but the fact that, under the agreement reached, Warenne and Henry of Almain were to decide what security should be given by the returning friends suggests that the recapture of their loyalty had indeed been key. But certainly by 18 August the Marchers had once again sworn to be Edward's friends in all his affairs, and this compact was not made known to Montfort.[33]

So when, in mid-October 1263, Edward absented himself from London claiming he wanted to see his wife, no suspicions were raised. Nor, still, when Henry joined him shortly afterwards. The surprise came when the Marchers revealed their change in loyalty and came to Windsor in support of the royalist party, leading to a volte-face on the part of the magnates in Parliament, most of whom also declared for the king. Somehow Edward, using Eleanor's dower as leverage, had changed the balance of power – Montfort no longer had the majority of effective support.[34]

The two sides for the coming war were now constituted: on the one side was the king, supported by a disparate array of interests – Marchers, Lusignans, Savoyards and members of Edward's group of followers. Many of these hated each other, but all were now prepared to oppose Montfort, who appeared to wish to govern personally or even to replace the king. In support of Montfort were his own loyal band of followers, and a number of idealistic younger nobles, such as John de Vescy, who believed that Montfort was the only route to the reforms of the Provisions of Oxford. Balanced precariously in between was the new Earl of Gloucester, 'Red Gilbert' (a tribute to his flaming red hair).

Gilbert was at this stage twenty years old and, as a result of his famously unhappy marriage to Alix de Lusignan, was profoundly anti-Lusignan. There are strong hints in the documents that she suffered from depression, which may well have been exacerbated by the fact that Gilbert reputedly regarded the marriage as one which was beneath his deserts. It appears that Gilbert had a very well-developed sense of his own importance, which was of course considerable in right of his control over vast estates. One of the major factors disinclining him to both factions was his unwillingness to regard anyone as of greater importance than himself.

It is convenient to pause here, between the end of the political phase of the barons' revolt and the purely military phase, to consider Eleanor's life during these years of upheaval and what the evidence tells us about the developing relationship with Edward. The short answer to this inquiry is that everything points to this being a period where Eleanor became established as Edward's closest confidant and an essential part of his team. As has been seen, as the political manoeuvrings are traced through, Eleanor's hand can be detected supporting and guiding Edward at every turn of events. She can be seen encouraging his steps away from his parental guidance to independence, in establishing other political alliances for him and steering him towards roles which he could usefully perform in a politically trying period when his freedom of movement was limited. She can also be seen offering very real assistance in pledging her dower properties repeatedly to ensure Edward's best advantage.

What we also see is very powerful evidence of their mutual wish to be together. In the kind of life which Edward led over this period, it would have been very easy to leave Eleanor at home and travel without her. Yet Eleanor and Edward travelled together around Britain, and to Gascony and back repeatedly. It appears she passed up chances to meet her own family in order to remain with him. It also appears quite clear that everyone understood that Eleanor's safety was the concern of her husband, not her mother-in-law – when Queen Eleanor arranged a mass evacuation of noble ladies in the run-up to the seizure of Dover Castle in late June 1263, Eleanor was not among those for whom the queen made provision. Nor did Eleanor accompany her mother-in-law when she herself departed in September for the Continent, where she remained until 1265. Rather it appears that Edward, on his return in 1263, settled Eleanor at Windsor, effectively as hostess to the garrison which he established there, and she was expected to stay there – near, but not at that stage within the range of any anticipated battles – and await his visits as the fortunes of war permitted. Just, indeed, as Ferdinand III had settled her own mother, and his first wife, near his campaigns. The adoption of the Castilian modus operandi again implies an active role for Eleanor in deciding this strategy.[35]

One further point which indicates very strongly the closeness of the relationship and the extent to which this closeness was common property is Edward's action in using a wish to visit his wife as an excuse for making a break from London in 1263. This action is usually considered as an example of his slightly cavalier attitude to truth. However, when considered further, it actually becomes a very interesting revelation of the relationship. It was by no means common for husbands (even un-martial family men like Henry III) to give overt priority to wishes to see their wife or family. It is hard to think of another example of a prince, still less a prince later to be famed for his firmness, openly confessing to such a desire. Yet apparently Edward had no hesitation in deploying this reason. What is more, no one had any hesitation in accepting it as truth, and a truth unworthy of any particular remark. It follows, therefore, that the closeness of Edward and Eleanor had become a total 'given' for all those who knew them by 1263.

One other question about the relationship which necessarily comes to the fore is the question of sexual relations and children. Whether or not cohabitation was suspended for a period after the loss of the baby born in Gascony, one would expect it to have been resumed by the time Eleanor was eighteen in 1259, and very possibly before. If so, given her later fertility, where are the children? The earliest evidence of a named child is a daughter Katherine who was with Eleanor at Windsor in 1264, and who was described as an 'infant'. It is likely that Katherine was either a reason or *the* reason why Edward's old nurse Alice de Luton was with Eleanor in France in the summer of 1262. Given the travelling which Eleanor did in that summer and in July 1261 and February 1262, the most likely period for the birth of Katherine would be in either early or late 1261 while Edward and Eleanor were in Gascony. Parsons tentatively suggests 21 April 1261 for her birthdate, based on a difficult passage in one of the chronicles. However, this birthdate would involve Eleanor travelling to England when just about to give birth (she and Edward returned to England in April 1261) and hunting actively in her first trimester. Given her later active programme up to the birth of children this is a possibility, but at this early stage, with an heir not yet provided, it seems unlikely. I therefore incline to late 1261, and would tentatively place Katherine's birth on the saints' day of St Katherine of Alexandria on 25 November 1261 – this would also explain the use of the name, which had no strong family connotations on either side, other than its poignant association with Henry III's deceased daughter. This also fits well with Eleanor and Edward's remaining in Gascony for some weeks into 1262. Furthermore, a birth in Gascony would also account for the lack of any records of the birth in the English court accounts.[36]

Katherine can therefore be more or less accounted for. However, it is very possible that other children were born and died without trace in that period. A number of factors point to this conclusion. Assuming that full cohabitation resumed by 1259, and given that all the evidence suggests that Eleanor was able to conceive a child four years earlier, there would be no reason why she should not conceive. The pattern of her later pregnancies indicates that she conceived regularly at the rate of about two children every three years. In addition, as we have just noted, Edward and Eleanor were not apparently parted for long periods at this time. Accordingly, one would expect there to be some children – probably two or three – conceived during the period up to late 1263. However (also given the statistics of the later children), it might well be that one or more such children would be miscarried or not long survive.

The absence of any records of such children does not provide any particular indication that they did not exist – after all, there is no record of the birth of Katherine either. Further, the absence of any pregnancies would probably have been remarked upon – as it had been with Eleanor of Provence, who did not conceive until she had been married for several years. The absence of records of children other than Katherine indicates two things only. The first is that there was either no live birth of a boy or at least no live birth of a boy in England, as this would have been an event which the chroniclers would have noted. The second is that any children who survived to full term did not live long thereafter. There is certainly a possibility of the birth of a child in late 1262 or early 1263, while the couple were abroad. There may even be earlier children – in particular, the gift to Alice de Luton of lands in August 1260 may be in recognition of services at an earlier, unsuccessful lying in.[37]

However, by late 1263, with war arrived, we do know that Edward and Eleanor had started their family, with the birth of Katherine, probably in late 1261; and that Eleanor was at Windsor with the child and a substantial garrison and household, when Edward, his father and their allies arrived in October to make preparations for the second phase of the revolt – open warfare.

The last hope of peace was a mediation scheduled for Amiens in December, with Louis of France as mediator. In the run-up to this crucial hearing Henry struck at Montfort's own interests, recruiting the most redoubtable of the Marcher lords, Roger Mortimer, to take three manors in Hertfordshire which had been previously granted to Montfort by Henry in relation to the dowry dispute. Whether this indicated a lack of faith in the outcome, or was an attempt to keep Montfort from the hearing, is unclear. However, Montfort was indeed unable to attend, although for an entirely different reason: he suffered a fall from his horse which resulted in a broken leg. With Montfort's powerful personality and way with words in abeyance, the scale of lawlessness and destruction which the baronial cause had brought about weighed most powerfully with Louis. The baronial cause was rejected outright by him in the Mise of Amiens, and in particular he rejected the Provisions of Oxford in their entirety.[38]

Real war was now unavoidable. Montfort struck back against the royalist supporters at once, sending his sons to attack Mortimer's own castles in concert with Llywelyn – with some success – Mortimer's main castle at Wigmore (held by his family since 1075) was taken and his lordship of Radnor was ravaged. It seems likely that this attack also involved direct confrontation between the attackers and Mortimer's wife, Maud de Braose, who, as lady of Radnor in her own right, and a descendant both of King John's bête noire Maud de Braose and William Marshal, would be likely to be assertive in her own interests, and prone to resent insult. Certainly, in the longer term, this attack seems to have given rise to very unpleasant consequences for Montfort at the Battle of Evesham in 1265.[39]

Within weeks, the entire region was up in arms. Edward himself, moving to support Mortimer, came close to capture at the key town of

Gloucester following an incursion into South Wales, Hay and Huntingdon but was saved by making a truce with Henry de Montfort – which he then disregarded once Henry was out of reach.

Meanwhile, Montfort's position was strengthened by the rejection of Mise of Amiens by the Londoners and commonalty, as well as by Gloucester. It is perhaps worthy of note that much of the blame for the Mise was put at the door of Eleanor of Provence, who had been actively campaigning on the Continent and was the sister of Louis' queen. Beyond a doubt, at this stage Eleanor of Provence had a good claim to be the most unpopular queen in the history of England.[40]

However, the royalist cause was managed well – one suspects by Edward rather than by Henry or Richard of Cornwall. Under cover of preparation for a campaign against Llywelyn, a gathering of royalist barons was called to Windsor in late February. This force then marched on 8 March to Oxford, the royalist headquarters up until the Battle of Lewes.[41]

Meanwhile, London had settled under baronial control, with Montfort and Despenser in residence preparing the citizens to defend the city and to attack their chosen targets. Among these was Richard of Cornwall's manor of Isleworth, and properties of Pembroke and Philip Basset which were invaded by a mob led by baronial justiciar Hugh Despenser (Basset's own son-in-law).

In early April the royalist army moved from Oxford to Northampton, where the baronial forces had their headquarters. The French prior of the Cluniac house of St Andrew, who was a royalist sympathiser, allowed Edward's army to effect an entrance and take the baronial army by surprise. Numerous barons, including Simon de Montfort the younger and Peter de Montfort, were taken prisoner and subject to ransom. Edward saved Simon, his old tourneying friend, from royalist troops who would otherwise have killed him. Some of the prisoners were sent south to Windsor, where they were held, effectively in Eleanor's custody. The town was then sacked and the army moved on for more of the same at Leicester and Nottingham.[42]

The news of this victory would probably have been accompanied by the news of the grant to Eleanor by Henry 'at the Lord Edward's instance' of a manor at Ashford in the Peak – the first royal grant of lands to Eleanor since her dower assignment, and a thoughtful one as it was situated within the ambit of the castle and town of the Peak – the one remaining part of her dower which had not been granted elsewhere as a quid pro quo for the return of Edward's supporters. This was a key point in Eleanor's life – her first actual grant of lands, which meant her first acquisition of her own revenues. The grant was probably intended to assist in her maintenance while Edward and Henry were on campaign. But it seems possible that some of the revenues were immediately diverted by Eleanor to her pet interest

– books. Either at about this point or in early 1270, she commissioned the production of the beautiful illustrated apocalypse known as the Douce Apocalypse, possibly inspired by a Castilian Beatus apocalypse which it is thought likely that she brought with her to England on her marriage. As with later commissions, her own interests and instructions are manifest – some of the earliest illustrations completed show the forces of the Beast prominently including Montfort – and Gloucester.[43]

Meanwhile, from Nottingham, the royalist army was forced south by news of the baronial attack on Rochester, which was being held by John de Warenne and Roger Leyburn. Having relieved the siege of the castle, Henry and Edward moved on to Lewes, arriving on 11 May 1264.

The baronial army had tracked them there, rendezvousing with Montfort. A last-ditch offer to settle was firmly rejected, Henry sending a letter of defiance, and Cornwall and Edward one of challenge – making clear that on their side at least no quarter would be given in the future: 'From this time forth we will do our utmost to inflict injury upon your persons and possessions.' Montfort withdrew his allegiance the next day, as did his supporters.[44]

All was now ready for battle, and on the next day – 14 May – the two sides, numbering perhaps 7,000 men each, met. From Eleanor's perspective, the battle is significant in two respects. First, during the course of it Edward made a classic military blunder, pursuing the fleeing contingent of Londoners far from the field of battle. As Vegetius says, 'He who rashly pursues a flying enemy with troops in disorder, seems inclined to resign that victory which he had before obtained.' The truth of the maxim was amply proved by the event. When Edward returned some considerable time later, it was to find that the rest of the battle had taken a decidedly different course. Cornwall and Henry of Almain had been trapped in a mill on their right flank, and Henry III's horse had been slain under him in the baronial charge.[45]

The second significant point is that the result (by a process which is extremely unclear in the sources) was that Henry was effectively trapped in a priory, and Edward went with his Marcher companions to join him – at the cost of his own liberty.

At close of play, therefore, Montfort had the following credit/debit balance. On the credit side, he had definitely won the battle, and he had Henry, Edward and the Marchers trapped in the priory and Richard of Cornwall in his custody. On the debit side, he could not storm the priory, and a siege was almost as morally undesirable, as well as carrying the risk of attracting other royalist troops to oppose him. Also on the debit side were his own hostages in Eleanor's custody at Windsor – including his own son Simon, as well as those taken by Edward during the battle.[46]

The only way forward was compromise. Much of the night of 14–15 May was therefore spent in thrashing out a settlement, known as the Mise of Lewes. Montfort's gains in the settlement were the really big ones – custody of Henry and Edward, and the subjection of Henry to a council which would rule on his behalf. However, what he had to let go was the Marchers – for him a horrendously risky concession, given that they were now implacably opposed to him. Also released were the Northern and Scottish lords – whose presence was needed to forestall incursions on the border. Once terms were agreed, Henry was brought by Montfort to London at the end of May to be the figurehead of the Montfortian regime, and Edward and Henry of Almain were transferred first to Dover and later to Wallingford, where Richard of Cornwall was also transferred.[47]

This marks the beginning of what must have been a truly terrible period for the twenty-two-year-old Eleanor. Edward's capture was a disaster – Montfort was king in all but name and soon disregarded the provisions of the Mise of Lewes. Even historians with the perspective of hindsight tend to the view that Montfort seems to have regarded the Mise as no more than a ruse by which to get his hands on Edward and Henry, and this must certainly have seemed the case to the royalist faction at the time. This may well have been enough to raise suspicions, which gained credence as time passed, that he meant to move towards a formal claim to the crown. If he did so, Edward's continued existence would undoubtedly have been regarded by him as a danger which must be avoided. Eleanor would therefore have had very real fears for Edward's life. Certainly Henry seems to have considered that Edward was in danger; in one letter to Louis he speaks of his 'inestimable peril'. Further, at the time when news came to her, Eleanor was approaching the end of the first trimester of her second recorded pregnancy – she expected to give birth around the end of the year, the baby apparently having been conceived just before Edward commenced the Northampton campaign in April. As it was, however, Eleanor faced the entirety of this pregnancy alone.[48]

To make matters still worse, Edward's capture effectively left her all but destitute. Despite her notional dower assignment, she did not actually have the immediate right to any of this property or its revenues – these remained Edward's and she was effectively granted by him an annual allowance equivalent to the value of her dower. However, once Edward was in captivity, his lands passed into Montfortian control. Thus her one source of revenue was the manor at Ashford in the Peak granted to her earlier in the year. Whether she was able to collect these revenues or not, it is plain that what she received in the next year was inadequate to her needs – Henry III had to pay for medicines for her, and she was driven to borrow money from the Montfortian justiciar Despenser in April 1265.

It has been suggested that Eleanor's later behaviour in acting so assertively to acquire property can be traced to psychological scars caused by this period of poverty and powerlessness. This is probably a considerable exaggeration and oversimplification; Edward and Eleanor had been in financial difficulties ever since they married, and would continue to be so until her death. Furthermore, her later property acquisitions were not done entirely at her own instance, but as part of a concerted plan hatched with Edward. However, it is highly likely that the considerable financial difficulties of this period were never entirely expunged from Eleanor's recollection.

Her immediate concern, however, would have been the terms of her husband's captivity, and what her own actions should be. Once the terms of the Mise became clear, she would have understood that she held one of the major bargaining cards left to the royalist cause – the baronial prisoners. It was incumbent upon her, therefore, to hold them and Windsor as long as she could. This also appears to have been the instruction disseminated to other royalist strongholds, presumably via the released Marchers – Nottingham held out until December and Bristol (fortified by the Tonbridge garrison) until April 1265.[49]

Thus Eleanor remained at Windsor, faithful to her husband's orders despite his capture, with her young daughter Katherine, and Pembroke's pregnant wife Joan. Inevitably, as the senior person resident, she was also at least involved in the defence of the castle, which held out against the baronial forces for over a month after the defeat at Lewes, in order to maintain as strong a negotiating position as possible. However, in mid-June 1264 the castle was surrendered and she was ordered by Henry to leave Windsor, along with Joan. Further evidence of her active involvement in the defence for that month is suggested by the facts that the correspondence indicates that Henry and Edward left the castle specifically under her control, she refused to leave without a safe conduct and that, ultimately, she only went on positive orders from Henry, who promised to excuse her to Edward for her action: 'the king undertakes to excuse her to Edward her lord'.

The flavour which emerges is that she regarded herself as Edward's deputy in command of the castle under his orders – and that she had every intention of obeying those orders to the letter. As such, Eleanor acted very much in a small but significant tradition of militant English women: King Stephen's wife, Matilda, who summoned and commanded troops while he was captive; Nicola de la Haye, the defender of Lincoln Castle against Louis of France in 1217; and the two Mauds de Braose – the defender of Painscastle in 1198 and the current Lady Mortimer. One would, of course, expect nothing less of her father's daughter, but it shows once more that Eleanor was prepared to stray far from the paradigm within which she, as a princess, would be expected to operate.[50]

Where Eleanor went from Windsor is unrecorded – very possibly to Canterbury initially, where Henry III was then being kept in genteel captivity, and thence to London, where Henry appears to have spent the remainder of the summer, a supposition supported by the fact that Henry paid her expenses in November and for medicines for her in January. Certainly she was kept within the scope of close baronial supervision, and this fact also suggests that the barons did regard her as being untrustworthy and a threat in and of herself – Joan of Pembroke was simply ordered to withdraw to a nearby religious house and await her delivery. In part, concern to keep her close will doubtless have been due to the rumours which were current that Eleanor of Provence was raising an army abroad and that this army included Castilians, 'as Edward had taken to wife the sister of the King of that land', along with any rumours which also seeped out that Eleanor of Provence had obtained funding from, among others, Enrique of Castile. However, this approach also reinforces the probability that Eleanor had indeed taken a noticeably active role in the defence of the castle – to move a pregnant princess, and her young child, and send her any distance in the middle of the year was a fairly shocking thing to do, particularly in the unhealthy summer months.[51]

Whether either of these factors in fact influenced events, we can obviously never know. However, what is certain is that by 5 September 1264 Katherine was dead, aged around twenty months. She was buried around the end of the month and Eleanor was in such financial distress that she had to borrow the money to pay for the funeral. Eleanor (and Edward when he came to know of it) would hardly have been human if she had not laid this death at the door of the barons, as yet another item to be brought into an eventual reckoning.[52]

Nor did matters improve. With Eleanor now also in the hands of the Montfortians, the effective resistance to Montfort was left to the Marchers, with backup from the Savoyards abroad. In October they duly obliged, the Marchers sacking Hereford and taking castles in the South West, while some of Edward's knights attempted to free him from Wallingford. The latter aspect of the plan backfired spectacularly. As the would-be rescuers were held up in the inner bailey, Edward was seized by the guards, who threatened to hurl him from the castle on a mangonel. He was forced to order his friends to withdraw. Following this attempt, Edward and Henry of Almain were moved to the more secure Kenilworth Castle in Warwickshire, and Montfort, in alliance with Llywelyn, caught the Marchers in a pincer movement, forcing them to submit by mid-December. The price for this season of rebellion was the exile of the Marchers to Ireland for a year, and the annexation by Montfort of Edward's central lordship of Chester. Although notionally this deal was to involve Edward's release, it is unlikely that anyone on the royalist side now thought that a true release would be on the cards.[53]

At this low point, Eleanor was preparing for her next confinement. Her daughter Joan (presumably named after her mother) was born very late in December 1264 or very early in January 1265, as can be seen from the fact that Eleanor's churching was imminent on 3 February 1265. To add to the difficulties which Eleanor was already experiencing, it seems likely that the birth was not an easy one: medicines for Eleanor's use were bought (by Henry) on 25 January 1265, nearly a month after the baby was born. Incidentally, the birthdate provides further cogent evidence of Edward and Eleanor's devotion. The birth would indicate a conception date of early April – just days before Edward set off from Oxford for Northampton, and within the period when the royalist army was notionally stationed at Oxford. It therefore appears that Edward had sneaked off from camp to spend time with his wife in the last few days before the war finally began.[54]

Nothing had improved when Eleanor emerged from seclusion. In January, Montfort summoned a parliament to endorse the settlement of affairs following his defeat of the Marchers and to agree terms for a 'release' of Edward. Ironically, this parliament is celebrated as the first to which ordinary people were summoned, but it was at the time notable for the way in which Montfort utilised it to enrich himself and his family. He effectively annexed much of the vast wealth of Richard of Cornwall and took over a huge section of Edward's lands, also effectively removing Eleanor's sole property and means of support from her. He also took a further five royal castles as hostages for Edward's good behaviour.

A settlement to enable Edward's notional release was in place by March, and he was brought to London and officially handed over to the king in a grand ceremony at Westminster Hall on 11 March. The release, however, was a stage-managed farce. Edward remained in Montfort's custody, and following the ceremony Montfort left London with both King Henry and Edward in his train. And 'train' it very much was: Montfort had by this stage acquired a huge retinue of armed knights who formed his household – a greater number than was ever maintained by Edward as king.[55]

It is possible that Eleanor and Edward may have seen each other at this time – Eleanor had thus far been largely kept with Henry III, who had been brought to London to seal the deal, and it appears that she was at Westminster in January 1265 when she interceded with Henry to gain an exemption from jury service for a petitioner. Moreover, the agreement reached does seem to have had some regard for Eleanor's financial position. On 20 and 29 March, she was granted the revenues of three manors via a wardship of Cecily, daughter of William de Fortibus – one in Cambridgeshire, one in Somerset and one in Surrey. But certainly Eleanor will not have joined the Montfort party when they moved off; it was effectively a campaigning party. Therefore, if there was a meeting it was a brief one.[56]

Thereafter, it rapidly became apparent that Montfort did not intend Edward to be free in any real sense and that Edward and Eleanor's position was not actually improved by the March agreement. Edward's captivity was simply on a different footing, and Eleanor remained in genteel custody. Financially, she was even worse off than before – having lost the manor of Ashford in the March deal, her new grants were almost immediately seized by Gloucester and others. This left her completely destitute, and she was forced to borrow £40 for expenses from Hugh Despenser, Montfort's justiciar, in April.

It may be this step which caused Montfort to make some further provision for Eleanor: on 30 April she was granted the manor and hundred of Somerton, to be held at farm. It is ironic that this holding, which came to her at such a low point, was to be a key piece in her property acquisitions. But that may not be unrelated to the fact that Somerton was close to land held by her Fiennes relatives, who could, in the early years, help her to run it. It is tempting to speculate, therefore, that they suggested it to her, and she petitioned for it.

But until its revenues came in she was still penniless. It appears very possible that she was at this point driven to that well-known expedient of distressed well-to-do ladies – borrowing from her own tradesmen, notably her tailor. In the years just after the Barons' War, Eleanor was to put two pieces of land the way of her tailor, William, and to refer specifically, in petitioning Henry III for the land (itself a rarity), to the services William had performed for her.[57]

But events were beginning to turn. Gilbert de Clare had been annoyed by Montfort's failure to grant him sufficient recognition after Lewes, and the wealth and influence which Montfort acquired for himself and his sons was a further considerable vexation. Gloucester withdrew from court and retreated to the Welsh Marches, where an alliance was hatched with the royal party abroad, leading to two major events. The first was the landing of a royalist force in Pembrokeshire in mid-May, which drew Montfort (carrying Edward and Henry with him) off to Hereford to deal with the invasion. The second was Edward's escape.[58]

The escape, as it is described in the chroniclers, reads like a piece of theatre. The tale goes that, towards the end of May, Edward was permitted by Montfort to receive a number of visitors, including Clifford, Leyburn and Gloucester's brother Thomas de Clare. On 28 May 1265, Thomas and Edward, accompanied by guards, rode out to exercise their horses. Each horse (including those of the guards) was exercised thoroughly, under the pretence of a debate about which was the fastest – until only one remained fresh. At this point, Edward leapt upon the one fresh animal and galloped away, calling back a mocking message to his guards and a promise to return and release his father soon. Outside the woods, he met Mortimer by appointment and went with him to Gloucester at Ludlow, where a deal was struck for Gloucester's support.

The balance of power had now shifted emphatically in favour of the royalist party. In June Edward seized control of the River Severn, trapping Montfort. By the beginning of August, Simon de Montfort the younger had brought troops, destined to come to his father's aid, as far as Kenilworth.[59]

The fate of the Barons' War now turned on two facts. The first is that Simon the younger appears to have lacked his father's military sense – he permitted his army to camp outside the near-invulnerable walls of Kenilworth, rather than retreating within it. In the heat of August his decision was understandable, but it was nonetheless a mistake since Kenilworth was only thirty-five miles away from Edward at Worcester. The second fact was that Edward appears to have employed a good intelligence service, who rapidly brought news of this error to him.

Edward did not hesitate to capitalise on the slip. He took a cavalry force by an overnight march to Kenilworth, where he surprised the sleeping Montfortian relief force. A few (including Simon the younger) escaped into the castle, but many were captured and brought back to Worcester on the afternoon of 2 August – as were the army's battle standards.[60]

Meanwhile, Montfort had crossed the Severn. Believing his son's army to be more or less intact and on its way to join him, he made at once for Evesham on the evening of 3 August. Almost immediately their hopes appeared to be answered – the banners of the Montfortians were spotted. But within minutes it became apparent that these banners were actually being deployed by Edward's army, who had quietly followed them to Evesham through the night and who now commanded the heights above the town, while Montfort was trapped in the valley against the river.[61]

It is plain that the Montfortians knew that all really was lost this time. In the scant time available before the battle commenced, Montfort and his knights were shriven as if in the last rites. They knew well that the normal courtesies of warfare had been declared suspended by Edward – no quarter was to be given, and no surrenders for ransom would be accepted. More, so far as Montfort was concerned, in an unprecedented step, Edward had appointed a hit squad of twelve knights whose task was simple: to ensure that Montfort did not leave the field alive.[62]

On this occasion, the Montfortians did not buck the odds stacked against them. The battle was a bloody slaughter – at least thirty Montfortian knights died on the field, including Henry de Montfort, struck down in the first charge. Also dead on the field were Hugh Despenser and the Earl of Hereford's heir. Finally, Montfort himself fell to his nemesis Roger Mortimer. While other blades contributed to his death, Mortimer's was the blade that struck the first blow, and it was apparently he who took the lead in the desecration of the body which followed, cutting off Montfort's head and genitals and stuffing the latter into his mouth. The adorned head was then paraded on a pike (where it was seen by young Simon de Montfort as he arrived late at the battle) before being despatched off to

Wigmore Castle as a gift to Mortimer's wife, Maud de Braose. It appears that, in the light of her warlike Marcher ancestry and Montfort's raids on Mortimer and de Braose territory, Mortimer was entirely confident that his wife would take this thoughtful gift in the right spirit. The skull was indeed cherished at Wigmore Castle for many years.[63]

So, by the time night fell on 4 August 1265, the Barons' War was effectively over, and the royalists had won. Henry was notionally back in power, but since Edward had just established his credentials as an accomplished and ruthless military leader, there can be no doubt that he was now regarded not merely as 'the Lord Edward' but as a king in waiting.

And thus, overnight, Eleanor's fortunes turned. On the morning of 4 August, she was a penniless captive. By evening, she was queen in waiting.

7

Queen in Waiting

The Barons' War was decided, and in the royalists' favour, it is true. With hindsight we can see that, from this point, Eleanor's life moved into a new, more prosperous, phase, bringing her a huge change in fortunes and in activities as she started to acquire property and to manage it actively, as well as fulfilling her role as consort. However, the scale of the change which came about was not apparent at once. The outcome of the war might no longer be in doubt, but it was not actually over for months to come.

It is highly unlikely that the victorious Edward rode straight from the battlefield at Evesham to be reunited with his loyal wife, as a romantic view of history would dictate. As the military leader of the royalist cause, he had to attend immediately to what are now termed 'mopping up operations', superintending the surrenders of various Montfortian strongholds.

Meanwhile, for some time after the victory Eleanor remained in effective captivity, although quite where and with whom is unclear. It is tempting to suggest that after March she was sent with Eleanor de Montfort, staying with her at Odiham and then at Dover Castle. However, it seems highly implausible that Eleanor de Montfort would have let such a prize as Eleanor go freely when her world had just disintegrated at Evesham. And Eleanor was definitely free long before Eleanor de Montfort surrendered Dover Castle and her captives in October.[1]

Another possible custodian is Hugh Despenser, who lent Eleanor money in April, hinting that she was in his charge at that point. However, Despenser later moved to join Montfort, dying with him on the field at Evesham. It is possible that she remained at the Tower, in the custody of her near contemporary Aline Basset, Hugh Despenser's wife, who yielded the Tower in August. However, overall it seems most likely that Eleanor was sent back to Windsor at some point in early 1265 with the new warden of the castle, John Fitzjohn, the son of Edward's former governor

John FitzGeoffrey. Fitzjohn was thus a Montfortian with tie to both camps and he appears to have been a realist, surrendering the castle at once after news of the defeat at Evesham had broken.

Another possibility is that she was in Westminster throughout; and certainly it seems near certain that she was by 7 September 1265, when her baby Joan, who died in late August or early September 1265, was buried in Westminster Abbey with Henry III donating a gold cloth for her tomb. A location either in Windsor or Westminster would also be consistent with Eleanor's activities in September 1265, which show her commencing work as a landowner.[2]

What of the reunion between Edward and Eleanor? We know that Eleanor and Edward were reunited at least by late October, since their next child was born in mid-July of 1266, but it seems likely that they were together at some point in late September, since Eleanor's actions thereafter speak of a change in policy which was unlikely to have been arrived at independently.

Meanwhile, the way forward was a matter of debate among the victors. It is plain that Edward's inclination at this stage was to pursue a statesmanlike policy of mercy – he offered generous terms, promising that those surrendering would suffer neither in body or property. However, in mid-September Henry convened a parliament at Winchester and announced that all those who had stood with Montfort were disinherited and were to remain disinherited forever. Those of his supporters who had seized rebel lands were confirmed in their holdings, and inferentially all lands which had not yet been seized were up for grabs.[3]

The implications of Henry's approach must have been an important topic for discussion between Edward and Eleanor and with their supporters. It must be remembered that they had now been married for over ten years and had been hard up throughout that period, with Eleanor being destitute for the last year. Further, Edward had greedy supporters to please (notably Mortimer, who felt entitled to a good pay-off after his considerable exertions). They also had less prominent but loyal supporters who deserved a return, and for whom Edward and Eleanor could not provide themselves. The prime example would be Otho de Grandison, who had yet to see any advancement as a reward for his loyalty; now in his late twenties, he was still lacking the financial qualifications for knighthood.

It appears that the result of their consultations was a decision not to stand back from the awards of lands to Henry's supporters, which were to follow Henry's disastrous proclamation. In part this was a move of necessity, and in part it was probably guided by long-term self-interest. Both may well have appreciated that 'the Disinherited' would at some point have to be restored, but that Henry would feel obligated to those who were themselves the losers as a result. They and Edward's supporters therefore did indeed benefit largely from the grants of 'Disinherited' land made at this time. Roger Mortimer gained some grants at a very early stage, and then property at Aldermanbury in London. Roger Leyburn gained lands and wardships. And Otho de Grandison finally received the lands which would enable him to be knighted, being granted houses in Queenhithe in October 1265 and the property of William le Blund the next month.[4]

What is interesting in these grants, from the point of view of trying to ascertain Eleanor's position, is that the acquisition of lands for Edward and Eleanor did not simply proceed on the part of Edward, as it might well have done. Eleanor herself entered into the market, and actively so. A great deal as to the plans which she and Edward had arrived at for her future role and as to her personality and approach can be seen from one story which takes place in September 1265.

On 18 September 1265, Eleanor was granted wardship of a manor at Barwick in Somerset in the minority of Walter de Cantilupe's heir. This was a property quite near to her farm at Somerton. In the press of administration at the time, it was somehow granted again to someone else a few days later. Within days, Eleanor herself appears to have given considerable thought to the way forward. The letter which results is one of the very few of hers which survive, and this in itself justifies reproducing it in its entirety. It is just possible that it is in her own handwriting – the version which survives is clearly an informal draft, including interpolations and missing the formal recitals. But for present purposes, it shows three things quite clearly: Eleanor's personal involvement in her own financial planning, a thorough approach to strategy in acquiring lands, and an overwhelming concern that she gains the lands without acquiring a reputation for greed – as Eleanor of Provence had demonstrated was all too easy. It also shows the beginnings of her administration coming together.[5]

The letter reads as follows:

Eleanor, companion of the lord Edward, to her loyal and faithful Sir John of London, health and good love. Know that our Lord the King gave us the other day the manor of Barwick with its appurtenances, at the request of Sir Roger de Leyburn; and because the property is appurtenant to the guardianship of Cantilupe, my Lord has given it to another, so that nothing of it is now given to us. But there is another manor close by, in the county of Somerset, which is at the town of Haselbury, which belonged to Sir William le Marshal, who is dead, and who held it of the King in chief. We would like you to ask Sir John de Kirkby if the guardianship of that manor is granted, and if it is not, then you should request Sir Roger de Leyburn and the Bishop of Bath on our behalf, that they should ask our lord the King to grant us the manor until the coming of age of the heir of Sir William. And if it is already taken, there is another manor in the county of Dorset, called Tarrant, which belonged to Sir William de Keenes, who is dead, and who held it in chief of the King. So if we cannot have the other, we would ask you to request them on our behalf that they should apply to the King to allow us this one. The manor of Haselbury is worth less. And if nothing is possible, mention to Sir Roger that the manor of Barwick that the King gave us, at his suggestion, has been taken from us, for this will tend to make us seem less covetous; and say the same to the bishop of Bath. And if the letters which you have concerning it can achieve nothing, give them to the bearer of this letter, for he will carry them to Sir Walter de Kancia, our clerk. Be careful to dispatch this affair, for it will be to our profit; and deal with this matter in a way which ensures that they shall not set it down to covetousness. Farewell.

Before considering the results of this plea, it is worth breaking the letter down in some detail. The first thing to note is that the actual acquisition of lands was a new departure for royal women in England. In part this was because it was quite unusual for royal heirs to be married before their accession and queens had official sources of revenue such as 'queen's gold'. But even Eleanor of Provence, who concerned herself very actively with increasing her revenues, had not sought to involve herself in the details of landholding. Although it was well understood that a fortune could be built by the careful acquisition and management of property – as Richard of Cornwall had done – this was not a realm into which royal women had ever gone. It may be that the level of detail and active management required meant that it was seen as unsuited to women, whose responsibilities should lie elsewhere. If Edward had decided to add to his wife's assets by this novel means, one might therefore expect that it would be done under his aegis or at least by her clerks on his instructions. However, on the contrary, here we see Eleanor personally soliciting a land grant. It is therefore plain that she was wishing to be personally involved, and it is also fairly plain inferentially that this was approved by Edward.

The second important thing to note is that Eleanor is not merely soliciting an undefined or unnamed grant; she is soliciting a particular grant – and has even prepared a backup plan. However, the nature of the request reveals even more thoroughness than at first appears. Here, the locations of the properties are highly significant. It had become accepted that property empires should not consist of disparate properties over a wide geographical area, but should consist of properties which were relatively close to each other, so that economies of scale could be used. Eleanor thus far had two properties of her own, the Somerton farm and the manor of Ashford at the Peak (which was in the process of being returned to her). She also had three properties under management during the minority of Cecily de Fortibus: Dundon in Somerset (practically next door to Somerton), Woodmansterne in Surrey and Dullingham in Cambridgeshire. Barwick, the original September grant, was quite close to Somerton and Dundon, and it should be inferred that it had been sought for that reason. However, once Barwick had gone, Eleanor and her advisers sought about for another nearby property on the market. They decided that there were two possibles – Haselbury in Somerset itself and Tarrant in Dorset. Of these Haselbury, though less valuable, was preferable – and this would be because it was, like Barwick, close to Somerton and Dundon.

We can therefore see that this letter is based on research not just as to properties which would be up for grabs as part of the 'Disinherited' market, but also as to their location, to ensure efficient management. This is a level of preparation which indicates a real commitment to the process, and forewarns us that property acquisition and management is not to be a one-off departure for Eleanor.

The third point to note is that Eleanor knew the mechanics of getting the matter expedited. The request is to be made by Roger Leyburn and the Bishop of Bath; Leyburn was one of Edward's longest-standing associates, and the bishop (Walter Giffard) was a staunch royalist who became Henry's chancellor at about this time. However, to ensure that there were no slips, her clerk was to check with Sir John de Kirkby – a clerk in Chancery, who would be in a position to know what estates had been granted already – whether her first choice was still available. The conduits to the more major players are her clerk Walter de Kancia – already established in a role in her household and later becoming her steward for all her acquired property – and John of London, the treasurer appointed for her when she first came to England, who for obvious reasons had good contacts with the king's household.

Finally, we should note the repeated emphasis on avoiding any appearance of covetousness. It is therefore plain that Eleanor and Edward have perceived that the errors of Eleanor of Provence must not be repeated and that acquisitions by Eleanor must be defensible.

'Plan A', as it appears from this letter, seems to have borne fruit, for on 30 September Eleanor was granted the manor of Haselbury, to be held at pleasure for the Lady Eleanor's maintenance.

This was not the end of Eleanor's own acquisitions in this period. Later, on 17 October, Eleanor was granted manors in Derbyshire at Bakewell, Haddon and Codnor 'late of the King's enemies Ralph Gernon, Richard de Vernon and Richard de Grey' to be held for life. Again, the evidence of planning of an estate is evident – Bakewell and Haddon are practically next door to Eleanor's holding of Ashford, making effectively a single holding in what is now the Buxton–Chatsworth area, and Codnor is not far off. At around this time Eleanor also acquired forfeited manors at

Gayton le Marsh and Tothill in Lincolnshire, Martley in Worcester and Chesterfield in Derbyshire. Finally, in February, Eleanor was granted further rights over the manor of Somerton and, in April, full rights over it and two further manors, Pitney and Wearne, just to the west of Somerton, north of the current B3153.[6]

All the appearances therefore suggest that at this point Eleanor began to acquire an actual landholding of her own, which would of course in the long term enure to the benefit of the Crown. In addition she did so actively, rather than leaving it purely to her clerks to manage in consultation with Edward's staff. Finally she did so cautiously, making great efforts to avoid being characterised as greedy. All of this bears the stamp of a plan entered into with Edward and subject to his instruction to keep in the shadows, and this appearance will be borne out as the story of Eleanor's property business proceeds.

There is a strong impression that Edward, fond of his mother as he indubitably was, had well perceived how divisive an influence she had been as a queen, and had resolved that his own wife, however able, would never embarrass him or demean him as his mother had his father. Instead, Edward set Eleanor defined tasks to be carried out quietly and without notice – principally to enlarge their financial provision by acquiring property for herself, which would enlarge the royal holdings and make up for some of the alienations of the past in due course.

All of this business activity took place against a backdrop of a restored court and progress in dealing with the remaining rebels. Eleanor and Edward will have been with Henry III on his re-entry into London in early October, and present at the celebration of the Feast of the Confessor at Westminster Abbey on 13 October. Thereafter, Henry and Eleanor moved to Canterbury, where there is record of Eleanor soliciting a favour from Henry for William Taylor for his services specifically to her – he received houses in the parish of St Dunstan at her instance. This is the William Taylor who appears likely to have been the source of urgent financial relief during the war years.

Meanwhile, Edward proceeded to Dover, where he took the surrender of Dover Castle from Eleanor de Montfort and saw her off to exile. Following this, on 29 October, he welcomed his mother, accompanied by Edward's younger brother Edmund, who was now twenty years old. By the end of the month, the whole family was reunited in Canterbury.[7]

In December, the court moved to Northampton to prepare to deal with the rebels at Kenilworth. However, the resolution here was repeatedly delayed by other distractions. First, a division of the rebel forces meant that Edward had to go off into Lincolnshire to deal with Simon de Montfort the younger, while in the new year Edward moved on with Roger Leyburn to deal with the Cinque Ports. Still the rebel forces kept on reappearing in spots – in East Anglia, the Midlands and

Hampshire – forcing him and his associates to rush off to deal with each new group.[8]

In the end, Kenilworth was still under siege when, on 13–14 July 1266, Eleanor gave birth to her child at Windsor, where it appears likely she had been since spring. A large court was at this point assembled at Windsor. Prestigious prisoners (such as Robert Ferrers, the Earl of Derby) were despatched there upon capture, and visiting dignitaries, such as the Duke of Brunswick and John of Brittany, were also entertained there. She is therefore likely to have been kept busy with the responsibilities of a hostess right up until the last days of her pregnancy.

The child was a healthy baby boy, who must have been conceived very shortly after the couple were reunited in September of the previous year. This birth was the cue for national rejoicing. The Londoners, for example, took the day off work and danced in the streets. Henry III hailed the 'delightful news' of the birth, and rewarded the bringer with a pension of £20 annually. Eleanor could scarcely have timed the heir's arrival better – his birth was perceived as a new start after the years of faction and division.

Interestingly, the child was named John, not Henry after Edward's father and the saints' day (St Henry the Pious) on which he was born. The significance of this decision is tantalising, but elusive. St John the Baptist's feast day was 24 June, and the only possible religious reference is to the little-known St John Gaulbert, the merciful knight who became the patron saint of foresters. It may be that the name was in part a nod to the dead Joan, who had never even met her father, or to Eleanor's mother. However, one suspects that the name was at least in part a coded message to remaining baronial resistance, Edward's grandfather John having fought the barons until his dying breath.[9]

If this was the message, it is ironic that, in the wake of John's birth, Edward, together with Richard of Cornwall and the Pope's legate Cardinal Ottobuono, was busy persuading Henry to take a more moderate line with the defeated baronial opposition. Their success in this endeavour resulted in the policy statement known as the Dictum of Kenilworth of October 1266, whereby the Disinherited were offered the chance to be restored to their lands upon payment to the royalist occupiers of a fine of two or five years' income of those lands, depending on the degree of offence. The Kenilworth garrison surrendered in December and it appeared that all that remained was the suppression of rebels on the Isle of Ely.

However, in early 1267, John de Vescy raised a rebellion in protest against the terms of the Dictum of Kenilworth and in particular the sting in the tail of the Dictum, namely that the lands would only be returned to their former owners after the payment of the fines. Vescy and other former Montfortians pointed out the problem with this: how were they to pay the fines if they could not occupy the land and take its revenues? The apparently reasonable approach was, for many, forfeiture by the back door. Vescy and his supporters therefore retook their lands and vowed to defend them. Edward went north to deal with this threat, and succeeded, retaking Alnwick after some hard fighting. The interesting point about this rebellion is that it provided the occasion for the reconciliation between Edward and John de Vescy. After his victory, Edward pardoned Vescy, who became again one of his and Eleanor's closest friends.[10]

It may well have been Vescy's actions, as much as Gilbert de Clare's intervention, which prompted Edward later to support the crucial addendum to the Dictum of Kenilworth which enabled the former rebels to re-enter their lands before payment of the fine, thereby paving the way to a final settlement with the barons in mid-1267.[11]

Meanwhile, however, the Dictum of Kenilworth played merry hell with Eleanor's land acquisitions. All of the lands acquired in 1265, apart from those in Lincolnshire, were lost to her when the former owners paid their fines. Effectively therefore, she had to start again. However, with the birth of an heir, her position at court was improved and grants began to be made to her directly; again, it would seem, with an element of forward planning by Eleanor. For example, on 15 September 1265, Henry III had confirmed Edward's grant to Eleanor of a major acquisition: the manor of Ringwood in the New Forest and the issues and profits of the New Forest. In 1270, this grant of the stewardship of the New Forest was confirmed to her, along with a grant of the manor of Lyndhurst (adjacent to Ringwood), thereby giving her a large, valuable area of property which could be run as a single unit. In exchange, she transferred to Alan Plongenet (the previous holder of the New Forest stewardship) the manors of Pitney and Wearne.[12]

A second area in which property was acquired was Leicestershire, where, between 1267 and 1270, she acquired grants from the king of progressively greater rights over the substantial neighbouring manors of Great Bowden and Market Harborough, and these grants were supplemented in 1268 by the complementary hundred of Gartree – a property which included both these manors.

Again in Norfolk, in 1269–70 Eleanor acquired grants (eventually for life) of the manor of Aylsham, which carried with it rights in relation to the neighbouring North Erpingham hundred, and lands in Scottow. In Northampton, the manor of Kingsthorpe was granted at pleasure in 1267, rising to a grant for life in 1270, and this was supplemented by the grant of the surrounding hundred of Spelhoe. Meanwhile, in Stafford, Eleanor acquired lands at Leek and Densington, appurtenant to Macclesfield, in 1270.

Thus, by 1270, Eleanor had acquired seven areas of land, each of which contained more than one property which could be run in tandem for operational efficiency. In addition, in 1268, Henry permitted her to claim 'queen gold' in Ireland.[13]

Other instances of Eleanor's rise in status can be found in this period: in November 1267, Henry granted Castilian merchants at Southampton a seven-year exemption from murage (a tax for building or repair of town walls); her chaplain Bartholomew de Haya was granted the right to hold his houses free of livery obligations; she obtained a pardon for an indictment raised against a petitioner for the death of a relation; and she also obtained relief for another against outlaw status resulting from his involvement with a death. This last is particularly interesting as she first appears here as 'the King's daughter Eleanor, consort of Edward his son', a terminology implying a higher status. Other pardons and interventions, including one on behalf of the son of a delightfully named lady – Licoricia – succeed these. They show that Eleanor was using her influence in this respect on a regular basis; an interesting point when her very different operations as queen come to be considered. By 1269, she was in a position to get a licence for her own merchant to be permitted to trade in England. This merchant, Gil Martini, was later to source Castilian goods for her.[14]

Another way in which Eleanor's influence was felt, and which points the way forward to future operations, is that it was at this point that she first began to deal in debts owed by Christian debtors to Jewish moneylenders. In April 1268, Henry III gave her all the debts owed by William fitz William of Hartwell to Jacob son of Moses of Oxford and any other Jews in England. Similarly, in the subsequent years she was given the debts of Richard de Ernham of Froyle and Thomas Bassett of Welham. However, at this stage at least, these debts do not appear to have been used by her has a means of personally obtaining the debtor's lands. The fitz William debt was apparently conveyed to Alice de Luton. She also appears to have intervened to enable William, her tailor (probably the same William for whom she obtained lands earlier), to buy up the de Ernham debt to a Jewish moneylender and to claim the ransom for this debtor's lands, which had been placed in her hands. Interestingly, Eleanor also petitioned Henry III to assist favourites of hers who were hampered by Jewish debts themselves. In December 1269, she obtained Henry's promise that Benedict de Wintonia's debts would not be interfered with for ten years, and in February 1270 he paid off, at Eleanor's request, a debt owed by the father-in-law of her cousin Giles de Fiennes.[15]

There were also a number of other developments in the way in which Eleanor lived her life. One was the increasing size and status of her household. By the time of her departure on Crusade in 1270, Eleanor had built up a household of some size and significance.

We know that her household had its origins in 1255 with the secondment from Eleanor of Provence's household of the clerk John of London to head up her wardrobe (a term probably best translated these days as her private office) and William de Cheney from the king's household as her steward (butler). Certainly from the outset she would have had a group of waiting women; one of whom, Joan 'de Valle Viridi', was with her sometime before 1262, when she is recorded as marrying William Charles, who became one of Eleanor's knights. Both her 'ladies' and William Charles are mentioned as forming part of her household when Henry commanded her to vacate Windsor in the wake of the defeat at Lewes in 1264. Also traceable as a semi-regular part of the female side of the household is the nurse Alice de Luton – formerly Edward's own nurse.

Although not named at this stage, it appears likely that her closest waiting woman, Margerie, joined her sometime in the 1260s. This can be inferred from the facts that Margerie was married around 1270 to Robert de Haustede, then a groom in Eleanor's household, and that he was the beneficiary of two notable kindnesses from Eleanor at this period. In 1266, she procured his pardon from immediate payment of his father's debts to the Exchequer, arranging for him to pay by instalments, and in 1270 she had the outstanding £24 of the original £48 written off altogether. It appears most likely that such a significant favour was effectively done not for a mere groom, but for a closer attendant. Margerie remained with Eleanor to her death, rising to become her main damsel.

Also within the household and bearing 'yeoman' status (a subsidiary rank under the steward, approximate to a footman) in the late 1260s was John Ferre, whose brother was in the king's service. John appears to have been a trusted messenger, since he carried the news of the birth of young John to Henry III in 1266. In the succeeding years, he progressed up the household, being given custody of some of Eleanor's lands, and accompanying Edward and Eleanor on Crusade in 1270. He was knighted in later years, and became Eleanor's steward once she was queen. Another yeoman of this period was William de Meleford, who had come from the queen's household. There was also, from at least 1269, a certain John de Beaumes (recorded as bringing the good news of the birth of Eleanor's daughter Eleanor to the king). Apart from these, we have evidence of a cook, John of Woodstock, and the chaplain, Bartholomew de Haya, previously attached to Henry III.[16]

John of London had moved on by about 1265, being replaced by William de Yattenden, who had links to Edward's household, as well as that of Eleanor of Provence through his brothers. He too was to accompany her on Crusade in 1270, dying en route. At a similar period, her steward William de Cheney moves on, although his replacement is not clear. It may (as Parsons suggests) have been the businesslike Walter de Kancia, or John de Weston, mentioned in the Close Rolls as her steward in 1264. These changes reflect a move away from the influence of the king and queen and towards her own independent business interests, and are also reflected in the appearance in the records of her own bailiffs and a clerk (a relative of her cook). At the same period, a group of knights and archers also emerges: she had archers from Ponthieu in her service in 1263, as well as former archers of Henry III.[17]

The final feature of Eleanor's emerging household worth noting at this point is the matter of relatives. It might seem that Eleanor was rather unlikely to provide for her relations – there are no overt signs in the records of nepotism. The contrast with the problematic overt 'alien' approach of both Henry III and Eleanor of Provence is striking. However, closer examination of the record shows that Eleanor did indeed provide for her relatives from an early stage – but very cleverly and discreetly. What she did was favour not her relatives at large, but only those relatives who could prove a tie to England already; thus, while she was favouring her connections, she was emphatically not favouring aliens. Three families in particular can be highlighted as benefiting in this respect: the Fiennes, relatives of Eleanor through the Dammartin family, holders of land in England since the days of King Stephen; the de Pécquigny family, related to Eleanor through her Ponthevin family; and the de Brienne family, Leónese connections of Eleanor's, one of whom had married into the English de Beaumont family prior to Eleanor's marriage.

The beginnings of Eleanor's patronage emerge early, but become clearer as the years go by. William de Fiennes joined Edward's household at the time of the marriage. His brother Michael de Fiennes became Edward's chancellor shortly after the marriage (though his initial appointment to the household has also been suggested to result from a more distant connection to Eleanor of Provence). And, as noted above, Eleanor procured a relief from debt for another Fiennes cousin-in-law. Among Eleanor's other relations, Roger de Pécquigny was granted a yearly fee at around the same time. Further, advantageous marriages were brokered between different branches of Eleanor's extended family. In particular, at around this period the Fiennes family and Eleanor's Brienne relatives contracted a marriage alliance in which her hand can surely be traced. William, eldest grandchild of the Fiennes–Dammartin alliance, married Blanche de Brienne, the granddaughter of Jean de Brienne and Berengaria of León. Their family would become a particularly favoured group among Eleanor's relatives.[18]

Other signs of Eleanor's increase in status can be seen in Henry III's expenditure specifically on her account. He provided her with newly built chambers for her especial use at several royal castles, and paid for her and her ladies' outfitting at Christmas 1268 in identical manner to that provided for the queen and her ladies. Therefore, Eleanor was now truly recognised as the second lady of England.

Last but not least, there were domestic changes. This period was ushered in by the crucial birth of the heir, John, in 1266. The next few years of relative peace saw two further additions to the nursery – a second son, Henry, was born in early May 1268, cementing Eleanor's status as a successful royal wife in providing the necessary 'heir and a spare'. This arrival was duly celebrated by Henry III, who granted the messenger twenty marks' pension for the good news. Next arrived a daughter, Eleanor (referred to in this text as Eleanora), in June 1269 – attracting ten marks by way of present for the messenger.

However, even with the demands of the increasing family, Eleanor's peregrinations with Edward continued: in 1267, Edward, adopting Richard I's approach in seeing tournaments as a training ground for knights, persuaded Henry to revoke his ban on tourneys in England, and issued, with his brother Edmund and cousin Henry of Almain, an edict permitting them to be held. A rash of events followed, to which Eleanor will have followed Edward wherever possible.[19]

And her travelling was about to range rather further afield. From about mid-1268, Eleanor was part of the latest craze at court: Crusade fever. The papal legate had been preaching the Crusade in England since 1266 as part of a Europe-wide movement prompted by the loss of the fortified Crusader town of Saphet, near Acre, earlier in the year. At the time there had been few subscribers – the most notable early enrolments being Thomas de Clare, brother of the Earl of Gloucester and friend of Edward, and Teobaldo Visconti, the Archdeacon of Liège. The movement had gathered momentum in Europe in 1267, with Louis of France and his sons taking the cross, but was still not gaining ground in England.

However, as the post-war 'mopping up' drew to a close, the idea started to catch on, largely among Edward's circle, who had enjoyed the experience of war and did not look forward to returning to peaceful and often subsidiary roles. Thus, at Midsummer 1268, around 700 people, including Edward, his brother Edmund, Henry of Almain, John de Warenne, Gilbert of Gloucester, William de Valence and others, publicly pledged to go on Crusade. There is no doubt that Edward's commitment to going on Crusade was strong – despite papal advice that he should not go, he persisted in committing to the adventure. Of course, this determination may have been entirely his own – as Lloyd has pointed out, Edward was a classic example of a young man who wanted scope for his newfound skills, independence of action which (it was all too apparent already) would be lost to him in peacetime. There was, for example, no scope for exercising those skills in defence of his Marcher lands, since the peace of Montgomery, concluded in September 1267, precluded him from campaigning in Wales. He was also possibly driven by his own piety, by the example of Louis and his sons, and the past example of his uncle Richard of Cornwall and Simon de Montfort.[20]

There appears little doubt that Eleanor would have been equally enthusiastic – as the daughter of a great soldier and Crusader, she will have been firmly of the view that this was something which Edward ought to do. Still more would Eleanor have been in favour, since this was not the type of Crusade where ladies remained behind; since Eleanor of Aquitaine had caused scandal in accompanying her then husband the King of France on Crusade in 1147, the presence of women on Crusade had become quite the accepted mode. When Simon de Montfort and Richard of Cornwall had crusaded with Louis of France earlier in the century, Eleanor de Montfort and Queen Margaret of France had formed part of the party. So too with this new Crusade; Eleanor's cousin and Isabelle of Aragon, the wife of Louis' son Philip, was to go, as was Edward's sister Beatrice, to accompany her husband John of Brittany.

It is, of course, pertinent to ask about the children. This readiness to leave her young brood behind has been the cause of some fairly overt criticism of Eleanor's decision. But such an approach is hopelessly anachronistic. One can see, for example, from the list just given, that Eleanor's decision was hardly unique – Isabelle of Aragon had four sons under seven at the time of departure, while Beatrice of Brittany had three sons, a daughter and another on the way. It was usual for royal mothers of the era to have their children largely raised away from them in the early part of their life; Eleanor of Provence's approach was far more the exception than the rule. The approach which Eleanor's own family had taken would be one part of the cause – this would give an opportunity for the children to be raised away from likely sources of infection, and maximise their chances of growing to adulthood.

One may also suspect that emotional self-preservation played a role too – so many children died young that it may well have been considered best not to become too involved until the child had passed the main danger age. This certainly ties with what we know of Eleanor's relations with her children. Practicality, too, will have formed a part of many of the female Crusaders' calculations; their job was to provide heirs, and this would not be possible for years at a time if they did not accompany their husbands. Eleanor herself would bear two children during the course of the Crusade, and one on the way home. Put brutally, their job entailed their being by their husband's side. However, there seems little cause to doubt that, for Eleanor, inclination and her job marched here hand in hand – she would have wanted to be on the Crusade herself, she would want to be with Edward, and she would not want to be at home with a group of small children and her child-centred (and generally somewhat overbearing) mother-in-law.

But even once it was more or less settled that there was to be a crusading contingent from England, matters did not go smoothly. Cardinal Ottobuono had hoped to use the Crusade as a means of mending fences between the royal and baronial factions, seeing the shared opportunity to slaughter the infidel as a good route for reconciliation. But those who had just lost the war were, even after the adjustments to the Dictum of Kenilworth, in no position to find the money for the trip. It is therefore no surprise that the take-up from the former rebels was very slight – very few other than John de Vescy were among them. However, the Marchers were well represented: Roger Clifford, Roger Leyburn, Hamo Lestrange and William de Valence were pledged. So too was Gloucester – whose history might permit him to be classed with either side. Others who formed part of the party were Edward's brother Edmund and his friends and Henry of Almain, Thomas de Clare and Otho de Grandison.[21]

The main issue, however, was money. This was critical because Edward's own force would be the core of the expedition and Edward had to find 100 marks for each knight for a year's service, plus the transport costs. He also had to fund the costs of a considerable household. A grant from the Church was not forthcoming, which meant that the funds had somehow to be found from within England – no easy task when the country was still recovering from the war, and everyone's finances were accordingly straitened.

His solution was an interesting one, when Eleanor's business dealings are brought into the equation: he asked Parliament to grant him a tax, in return for legislation against the Jews. The particular grievance which made this legislation a popular measure was the fact that, in order to discharge their own obligations to the Crown, Jewish moneylenders had recently taken to selling on their loans at discounts to Christian investors. Some of these had an eye not to the interest on the loan, or even the principal, but the land on which it was generally secured. By these means, certain enterprising investors (William de Valence and Richard of Cornwall among them) had found a very cost-efficient way of adding to their own property portfolios.

Morris compares the practice of these speculators to a purchaser of a mortgage who refuses to respect the repayment terms and forecloses on the properties regardless. In fact, there was technically nothing wrong with the practice. The means by which money was lent will be familiar to readers of Victorian fiction: X borrows money from Y for a period of time at an agreed interest rate. But in reality, X and Y both know it is unlikely that X will be able to repay the principal at the end of the period. Both anticipate that, at that period, X will wish to renew the debt – that is, to borrow the same sum of money, plus or minus whatever repayments and interest are relevant. And so the matter might progress from year to year. However, technically (as one sees, say, in Trollope's *Framley Parsonage*) the lender is perfectly entitled, at the end of the period of each loan, to seek the repayment of the principal, and foreclose on the security if it is not forthcoming, rather than to renew the debt for a further period. This is what these Christian speculators did. The outrage from the 'victims' was a product of the tacit expectation that the debt would be renewed more or less ad infinitum. Edward's proposals, which advocated requiring permission of the king before such debts could be sold to a Christian, were not at this stage greeted with sufficient enthusiasm to attract a grant from Parliament. Possibly Henry was seen as an insufficient safeguard – and on the basis of past form, such doubts may well have been justified.[22]

In August of 1269, Edward therefore sought help from another source of funds – the French king, under whose aegis the Crusade was to take place. Louis agreed to lend about £17,500, with repayment secured on the revenues of Gascony over twelve years under fairly harsh terms, including a requirement that Edward and his force be ready to depart at Aigues-Mortes on the Mediterranean coast by 15 August 1270, and to hand over one of his sons (Henry) as hostage to guarantee the agreement. That Louis seems to have been playing rather tough is suggested by the fact that preparations were certainly made to send Henry to him, with the formal letters of protection being issued, and some accounts even suggest he was sent, but returned by Louis.

There is one other possible foreign trip in this period. There is a Spanish tradition that, in late November 1269, Edward attended the wedding at Burgos of Louis IX's daughter Blanche of France to Alfonso's heir Ferdinand de la Cerda. If he did go, it seems inconceivable that Eleanor would not have accompanied him. This event would have been a major opportunity for reunions for Eleanor, with most of her family and the Aragonese royal family present. It would also offer a good opportunity for discussing the Crusade with Philip, son of King Louis, who escorted his sister. And of course for Edward and Eleanor it would have provided a fine opportunity for sentimental reflection on their own wedding in the same location some fourteen years before. Sadly, the documents prove that this tradition is not based in fact: Edward is to be is found at Harrow on 23 November and at Windsor on 7 December.[23]

Shortly after Edward's return from his visit to France (which may have been a rare trip without Eleanor, given the birth of their daughter in June 1269), the entire royal family would have been busy with preparations for the moment which Henry regarded as the high point of his entire reign – the reinterment of the body of Edward the Confessor in the new Westminster Abbey – designed according to the new Continental-influenced English style. Again an element of emulation of the French monarchy can be discerned: Louis had finished his new cathedral at Reims in 1241. In fact, the church at Westminster was only partly built: the east end, the transepts and the radiating chapels were complete but the nave was only half-constructed, to the end of the choir; beyond that, the old Norman nave remained in place.

Apart from this slight oddity, the new abbey church was magnificent. The three master masons supervising the work appear to have sought inspiration from the new cathedrals at Reims, Amiens and Chartres, as well as from the Sainte-Chapelle for such features as an apse with radiating chapels, pointed arches, ribbed vaulting, rose windows and flying buttresses. But the long nave and single aisles retain the English idiom, as do the mouldings and sculptural decorations. The effect would have been far more dramatic and less restrainedly elegant than it seems in modern times: much of the decoration would have been brightly coloured, the wall arcades may have been decorated in vermilion and gold, and fine paintings – traces of which still remain in some places – decorated the walls. Stained-glass windows in bright reds and blues, with monochrome heraldic shields, added further colour – as did the bays in the aisles of the nave, which featured shields of the Confessor and the great nobles of England hung from projecting stone heads.[24]

Meanwhile, a new shrine had been constructed for the body of the Confessor, using workmen from Italy, principally Peter the Roman. The new shrine had three parts: a stone base decorated with Cosmati work – which may be loosely described as a kind of mosaic consisting of small pieces of cut stone, marble, glass and green-and-purple porphyry arranged in elaborate patterns. This base linked to a glorious Cosmati pavement and bore a gold feretory – a bier-like shrine – containing the saint's coffin. Above this was a canopy which could be raised to reveal the feretory or lowered to cover it. The shrine was decorated with gold images of kings and saints and featured a separate finely decorated Cosmati-work altar, which now marks the final resting place of the dead children of Henry III and Eleanor of Provence and Eleanor and Edward.

For Henry, this event was the culmination of years of planning. An especially large parliament and assembly of key magnates and prelates was summoned to witness this festival, which proceeded with the pomp and fanfare Henry so loved, only slightly marred by arguments over precedence between the Archbishop of York (officiating) and the bishops of the Canterbury province and between the citizens of London and Winchester. The monks celebrated Mass for the first time in the new abbey church. Henry himself, Edward, his brother Edmund and Richard of Cornwall were among those including 'as many of the greater barons as could put their hands' to the bier, who carried the saint's body to its new resting place. The church was duly admired and the feast awed the attendees – as it was intended it should do. The event was, in short, 'the admiration and wonder of all' – Henry III at his best.[25]

Following Christmas at Windsor, in the New Year Edward and Eleanor attended their own religious event, finally taking the first steps to fulfil the pledge which Edward had made in 1263 to found a monastery by way of thanks for his being spared from shipwreck. To be fair to him, the plan had not been in complete abeyance since that date. It had, for example, been decided that the foundation would be a daughter house of Abbey Dore in Herefordshire. The choice of Abbey Dore as the parent house was, according to Vale Royal's ledger book, owing to the kindness shown to Edward by members of that house during his captivity at Hereford in 1265 – and possibly, given that this is whence Edward made his escape from captivity, for some assistance in that escape. It is reported that in 1266 the general chapter of the Cistercian Order authorised an inspection of the site proposed for the new house, but certainly matters had not been proceeding apace, very probably owing to lack of funds from Edward. He will therefore have felt that before taking up his crusading vow to God, it would be sensible to balance the books on this other vow. Edward and Eleanor then seem to have met with the Cistercian authorities and decided on a site – at Darnhall in the Forest of Delamere in Cheshire. With this task completed, final preparations for the Crusade could begin.[26]

8

The Crusade

The early part of 1270 passed in a whirl of preparations for the Crusade. Edward was still short of funds, but in April 1270 the negotiations with the laity finally paid off, with there being agreement for the grant of a 'twentieth', or a levy of a twentieth of the value of all personal property and income, the quid pro quo for which may have been a promise by Henry to enforce Edward's proposed restrictions on Jewish moneylending. This yielded about £30,000, the greater part of which was paid to Edward, with sums also assigned at the rate of 100 marks per knight to the nobles accompanying him. So Henry of Almain, accompanied by fourteen knights, received 1,500 marks, William de Valence with his nineteen received 2,000, and so on.

Still, however, a major hurdle remained: the Earl of Gloucester. Certainly at this stage in their lives Edward and Gloucester could never stay in each other's good graces for long, and although Gloucester had pledged to go on Crusade, he and Edward had subsequently had another falling out – and a highly serious one, which provides the other possible dating for Eleanor's Douce Apocalypse depiction of him as Satan's minion. The row has been variously attributed to a number of different causes, but the result was that Gloucester had been refusing to make preparations for the Crusade or to attend court since autumn 1269. He had missed the translation of Edward the Confessor in the previous October and even pressure from Louis of France, the head of the Crusade, was not productive. However, in spring 1270, Richard of Cornwall brought his fabled diplomatic skills to bear on this difficult problem and brought about an apparent solution: it was agreed that the earl was to follow Edward on Crusade within six months. If he co-operated with Edward he would receive 8,000 marks; if not he would receive only 2,000 marks.[1]

Eleanor, meanwhile, had much to do on her own account. Her land business had to be brought to a position where it could be left in the hands of subordinates for a few years. Therefore, as was discussed in the previous chapter, previous grants in the New Forest, Leicestershire, Norfolk and Northampton were all 'tidied up' in the early months of 1270. This will inevitably have been a time-consuming business. In addition, she had to take decisions on her own provisioning and staff for the Crusade – in the end she took her steward, her valet, her tailor and two clerks (John of London and the lower-ranked clerk Mr Richard) as well as a number of women staff – it is likely that Joan de Valle Viridi and Margerie Haustede, as well as their husbands, will have been part of the group. There would also have been considerable business about who else should make up the group which was to provide the constant companions of the future king and queen for some years – and here, it is interesting to note that Eleanor's relatives William and Michael de Fiennes were both included.[2]

In addition, Eleanor and Edward had to agree on who should take charge of political and family matters while they were away. The former was primarily Edward's concern, of course, and it was a serious concern given that Henry seems never to have regained full health and vitality after the Barons' War and there was a real possibility that he might die while Edward was out of the country. When it comes to the family side, we see evidence that the relationship between Eleanor and her mother-in-law was not perfectly harmonious: despite Eleanor of Provence's excellent record as a devoted mother, and her closeness to her grandchildren, she was not left in charge of them. That job was given to Richard of Cornwall, along with the primary responsibility for minding Edward's political interests. Were Richard to die, his responsibilities were to devolve on his son Henry of Almain – a particularly odd choice, since he was pledged to go on Crusade with his fourteen knights.

Richard of Cornwall was to head up a committee composed of himself, the Archbishop of York, Philip Basset, Roger Mortimer and Robert Walerand. The latter was later replaced by Robert Burnell, who had, since about 1266, assumed the mantle of Edward's chancellor and assumed such importance that he was remunerated at a higher rate than the king's own treasurer. From a political standpoint this made perfect sense; though, as Howell notes, even politically the exclusion of Eleanor of Provence, a previous regent of the country, is a little surprising. But certainly the failure to commit the children to her care is striking. Howell rationalises the decision as one by Edward to avoid any appearance of 'alien' influence, in particular in the light of Gilbert of Gloucester's strong views on the subject and the need to keep him sweet. This may be the explanation for the political omission, although if it were the case then it would seem odd that Edward's brother Edmund made Eleanor of Provence his sole agent during his absence on Crusade.

Whatever rationalisations can be conjured up for the political side of the decision, they cannot adequately explain the omission to involve the queen in custody of the children. It seems likely that the exclusion of Eleanor of Provence was a joint decision by Edward and Eleanor. In the political sphere it did all that Howell says, and marked Edward out clearly as having emerged from his mother's and mother's family's tutelage. However, in the familial sphere it demonstrated the fault line which had begun between the two Eleanors shortly after Edward and Eleanor's marriage, and which was solidifying as Eleanor of Provence's day in the sun drew to a close and Eleanor of Castile was looked to as queen in waiting.[3]

Thus, at the parliament held in July 1270, Henry gave his blessing to Edward's fulfilment on his behalf of his crusading vows, and thereafter the final steps were taken to prepare for departure. The party, which comprised probably about a thousand soldiers (including knights) plus some wives and household staff, assembled in Portsmouth to sail to Gascony and then to proceed to Aigues-Mortes near Montpellier – the plan being for an August rendezvous. Whether this would in any event have been feasible must be open to serious doubt – as must the suggestion that Eleanor and Edward somehow planned to sandwich in a trip to visit Alfonso of Castile on the way. However, if the date had ever been achievable, other factors intervened. First the winds were unhelpful – the Crusaders were left twiddling their thumbs within reach of port. Edward and Eleanor seem to have based themselves at Winchester, where he tied up the last details of his administration for his absence, including the revised version of the committee to mind his affairs, and finally the charter establishing Darnhall (later Vale Royal) Abbey.

By about 7 August, now at Portsmouth and still waiting for favourable winds, it appears that the news had arrived of the death of the Archbishop of Canterbury, Boniface of Savoy. The plans for Burnell's travel were revoked and Edward rushed to Canterbury to try to persuade the monks to elect his chancellor as the new archbishop – without success. The monks of Canterbury were apparently less than enthusiastic about recommending a career clerk and pluralist whose dealings in Jewish debts were already beginning to be talked about.

While Edward was at Canterbury, the rest of the party reconvened in Dover and eventually started out on 20 August. They reached Aigues-Mortes in late September, to find that the French had already gone; in fact, Louis of France had not even awaited the appointed date. Doubtless aware that the English contingent would miss the 'sail-by' date agreed, he and his troops had left at the end of July. What is more, he had not headed for the Holy Land but for Tunis.[4]

The reason for this diversion was to assist his younger brother Charles of Anjou, who had taken the title of King of Sicily, which Eleanor of Provence had so expensively coveted for Edmund. Charles wished to strike against the Emir of Tunis, who had assisted Sicilian rebels and

ceased to pay tribute to him. Charles, probably with help from Louis'
Dominican advisers, had persuaded Louis that the arrival of the Crusaders
might convince the emir to convert to Christianity, thereby improving the
balance of power in the vicinity of the Holy Land, and that if this plan
did not come off, Tunis would provide both a good muster port and a
good base for attacking into Egypt – as Louis had done on his previous
Crusade in 1248. This was not a bad point – Charles would in fact later
lose Sicily via an invasion from Tunis – as would the Axis powers seven
centuries later, in the Second World War. Furthermore, Charles dangled
the carrot of adding his own considerable, and experienced, forces to
those of the other Crusaders. Faced with this change of plan, what were
the English Crusaders to do? Go ahead without the leader of the Crusade,
or follow him on a campaign which formed no part of their crusading
intent? They ultimately decided to do the latter, and the party set forth
again in October, headed for Tunis.

They arrived on 9 November 1270 to find yet another disaster. Louis,
along with many of his army, had been struck by dysentery caused by
poor drinking water soon after their arrival, and by the time the English
contingent reached Aigues-Mortes he was already dead, along with 400
of his force of 1,800, including his constable, Eleanor's cousin Alphonse
of Brienne. His heir, Philip III, struck by the same illness, was only just
on the road to recovery. To make matters still worse, such fighting as had
been necessary in Tunis had already been done by the French contingent.
Indeed, a peace had been concluded involving the payment of tribute and
liberty of worship and movement to Christians, and part of the French
army had already left – not for Crusade but for France. This final round
of bad news must have been inexpressibly disappointing to Edward,
Eleanor and their party; the entire future of the Crusade, which they had
planned for years to bring about, seemed in question.[5]

Interestingly, among the Sicilian rebels fighting against Louis and
Charles was Eleanor's brother Fadrique, who had been exiled from
Castile in 1255 at around the time of Enrique's rebellion. He had since
pursued a career of knight errantry alongside his brother. Whether
Eleanor re-established contact with him is uncertain, but given that
Alfonso and Fadrique reconciled after years of alienation in 1272, near
the time of Eleanor's return, it seems at least possible that she did so,
and then assisted in brokering some kind of deal between her brothers.
Indeed, given the timeline, he (and his sons) may even have joined the
crusading party; one of his sons has been tentatively identified as a
member of Eleanor's household in later years.[6]

Certainly, however, the much-delayed meeting of the crusading parties
will have brought one reunion for Eleanor. With the new King Philip III of
France was his wife Isabelle of Aragon, Eleanor's childhood acquaintance.
She, like Eleanor, was travelling on Crusade with her husband, despite

her pregnancy. Another likely reunion was with Jeanne of Châtellherault, Eleanor's cousin through her mother's sister Mathilde de Dammartin. Jeanne had, with Eleanor's probable encouragement, married Geoffrey de Lusignan, now part of the French crusading party.

The future of the Crusade was subject to a number of differing interests. At this point, the way forward for Philip, the new French king, was simply uncertain – he had unexpectedly lost not just his father but also his younger brother Jean Tristan, who had also died within days of reaching Tunis on 3 August, as well as his brother-in-law Theobald, Count of Champagne and King of Navarre – the former candidate for Eleanor's hand and now the husband of Philip's sister Isabelle. Mourning and administration therefore both called him home. However, what better memorial to his pious father could there be than to continue the Crusade which he had pledged to lead?

Edward, by contrast, saw matters in black and white – the Crusade must go on: 'This is only the beginning, and the highway shall be made plain before us so that we may go on to the holy city of Jerusalem!' Charles of Anjou was almost certainly not in favour of continuing the Crusade; he was already a notable Crusader, having fought with distinction at Damietta and Mansourah in the 1248 Crusade. Furthermore, his position in Sicily was still delicate and he was alive to the risk of spreading himself too thin by concentrating on Sultan Baibars, particularly with Aragonese naval power growing in the west. It is also possible that he considered keeping Baibars sweet a better political approach than antagonising him.[7]

With these various interests impossible to easily reconcile, Charles of Anjou proposed that all the Crusaders should convene in Sicily to plan the way forward. This plan resulted in a further stroke of bad luck for the Crusaders; the French fleet anchored on 14 November at Trapani on the west of the island, where they were struck on the next night by a huge storm which destroyed the fleet, killed many and resulted in the loss of much of the treasure and supplies needed to support the Crusade. This decided Philip: he announced his withdrawal from the Crusade and commenced a return with his relations' remains to France via Italy, trusting the sea no further. But even the land journey held perils: his wife Isabelle would die weeks later in Calabria, aged just twenty-seven, in premature childbirth brought on following a fall from a horse in the course of this already funereal journey. Whether Eleanor's cousin Jeanne and her husband Geoffrey returned with the French contingent is not recorded. Given the Lusignan links both to Edward and to the Crusader empire – a Lusignan cousin was King of Cyprus – there is a real chance that they pressed on with the fighting contingent. This suggestion appears to be supported by the familiar terms in which Jeanne was to address Edward, in 1276 asking for news of him 'because you are the man in all the world in whom I have the most confidence'.[8]

The English fleet's contrasting fortunes pointed them in a different direction to the French. They had anchored elsewhere and been unaffected by the storm. After the catalogue of disasters to date, Edward determined that this showed that God had spared them for the work of the Crusade; the English crusading force would go on alone. Some reports suggest that Charles was persuaded to join them by Edward's vow that 'if all my companions and all my fellow countrymen desert me I shall go onto Acre, if only with Sowin my groom, and keep my word unto the death!'. It is more probable, however, that Charles, with his Mediterranean interests, was always prepared to continue to offer some support, even without the French – but he was never seriously minded to commit to the extent of going himself.

In any event, the Crusade could not simply go on at once; mindful of the weather risk in the light of the Trapani disaster, the Crusaders would winter in Sicily and move on to the Holy Land in spring. Charles issued Edward with letters of protection, which safeguarded him and his force from external control. Meanwhile, Henry of Almain was sent back by Edward. A number of rationales have been suggested for this move – that it was in response to messages from home – or possibly (as Edward himself was to claim later) with a view to a rapprochement with the sons of Simon de Montfort – his former friends, and Charles's present employees. In reality, the reason was probably with a view to dealing with Gascon problems, as Henry was now uniquely qualified to do following his recent marriage to Constance of Béarn. But whatever the motivation, this was a decision which Edward was to regret.[9]

The Crusaders spent a pleasant winter in Sicily – possibly the more so without the company of the elder Charles, who accompanied the French northwards. Close association with the man who now employed the younger Montforts can hardly have been congenial to Edward. As far as Eleanor was concerned, to this was added the serious awkwardness caused by the fact that Charles had been a close associate of her brother Enrique, but was now his jailer. Enrique had supported Charles in the latter's campaign to become King of Naples, and lent him considerable sums of money. However, while Charles arranged for him to become a senator of Rome (hence his nickname – El Senador), he did not produce any larger reward, such as the kingship of Sardinia, at which Enrique aimed; nor did he repay the sums lent to him. There had been a serious falling out in 1268: Enrique had defected on the eve of the Battle of Tagliacozzo – and had picked the wrong side, being captured by Charles shortly afterwards. The victorious Charles was to have him held prisoner until at least 1291, in Castello di Canossa in Puglia from 1268 to 1277 and in Castel del Monte from 1277 to 1291. Typically, some accounts suggest Enrique finally escaped.[10]

For Eleanor, after fifteen years of English winters, the milder climate of the Mediterranean would have been a particular pleasure. They stayed in the beautiful palaces of La Ziza and La Cuba whose architecture, referencing Muslim, Roman, and Byzantine stylistic influences, and gardens, with their splendid parks featuring pavilions, tree-lined promenades and decorative Moorish watercourses, offered another echo of home. Further, despite the political bumps in the relationship, Charles would have ensured that their stay was made extremely comfortable. His eldest son, Edward's cousin Charles of Salerno, was at this point in his late teens and may well have acted as host in his father's absence. Certainly Edward and Eleanor at some point got to know Charles of Salerno well, and learnt to value him highly.

The lands surrounding the Sicilian palaces were also well adapted for hunting, and many afternoons will have been spent in this always beloved occupation. As for other preoccupations, it seems that reading and discussion of romances figured too, for at some point either on the outwards or return journey an Arthurian romance in the possession of Edward caught the eye of Marco Polo's secretary and ghostwriter, Rusticiano of Pisa, who borrowed it and used it as the basis for his French work *The Romance of King Arthur*. This, rather suitably, told the tale of Palamedes, a Saracen knight who joined the round table, as well as including the adventures of Banor le Brun, Tristan and Lancelot.[11]

Eleanor was also expecting a child and it is possible that this further delayed the progress of the Crusade – the date of birth of the child, again only known as Anonyma, is not known. Parsons, following the one chronicler to mention the child, gives her birth location as Palestine 1271. However, this seems unlikely once the calendar is considered. Given the arrival of Joan of Acre in spring 1272, she was conceived in June or July 1271. For Anonyma to be born in Acre, Eleanor would therefore have had to be travelling right up to her due date. Much more likely, therefore, is that the anonymous baby was born in Sicily in early 1271, and Eleanor and the baby then travelled to Acre a few weeks or months later. Not an ideal programme, but infinitely better than risking childbirth in the bowels of a military transport. As it is, it seems likely that the vicissitudes of such an early start on campaigning life may have contributed to the death of Anonyma shortly after the arrival of the Crusaders in Acre.[12]

Whatever the exact reason for the delay, the result was that the English Crusaders did not arrive in Acre until 9 May 1271, having stopped en route in Cyprus, where they had been entertained by the King of Cyprus, Hugh III – a member of the Lusignan family. It may well have been here that Edward and Eleanor received the appalling news of Henry of Almain's murder at the hands of the Montforts.

Since the end of the civil war, Simon and Guy de Montfort had done well in Charles of Anjou's service. Guy in particular had excelled, becoming governor of Tuscany and marrying into a rich and influential Italian family. In March 1271, they headed to Viterbo in northern Italy to rendezvous with the French royal party and Charles of Anjou. Quite how the murder came about is unclear – the circumstances suggest a lack of premeditation, but, on 13 March 1271, Guy and Simon found Henry of Almain hearing Mass in either the church of St Silvester or that of St Blaise. Guy attacked him, refusing Henry mercy when he pleaded for it: 'You had no mercy on my father and brothers.' One account, which has Guy cutting off Henry's fingers, which were clutching the altar for protection, and dragging his body from the church to better brutalise it, is particularly revolting. Whatever the precise details, the accounts agree that on leaving Henry dead, he claimed, 'I have taken my vengeance.'

If it was vengeance, it was an indirect one, since Henry was not even at Evesham. He and his father were in captivity at the time. Thus, if vengeance it was, it was directed straight at Edward – killing the cousin he loved as a brother. Whether, as some accounts claim, Henry's body was in fact later dragged outside and mutilated as Simon de Montfort's had been, is unclear. So too is the precise involvement of the hapless Simon the younger. What is clear is that the murder became an international scandal and cause célèbre – it was a devastating blow to Edward, whose companion Henry had been in the schoolroom, in captivity and in battle; and the attempt to bring Guy to justice was to be a feature of his foreign relations for years. Even Dante, a child at the time of the murder, shows how famed was the misdeed by the fact that he later immortalised Guy de Montfort as one of the murderers in the seventh circle of hell – submerged to his neck in a river of boiling blood – a fate which Edward would certainly have wholeheartedly endorsed.[13]

At this point it is necessary to try to summarise the position in the Holy Land, in late spring 1271, when the Crusade finally arrived. Following the fall of Jerusalem in 1244, a Crusade (the Seventh Crusade) had eventually been organised under the aegis of King Louis of France. The Crusade, which commenced in 1248 and lasted until 1254, was a costly failure. Good progress was made early on; Damietta in Egypt was taken in a single day as a promising base for an attack on Jerusalem, and the pregnant Queen Margaret was installed there. However, all went badly wrong thereafter. Both Louis and his brother Robert of Artois failed in an attempt to take Mansourah. The cost of the battle was heavy and included Robert's life, squandered in a foolhardy dash ahead of the main body of the army. Louis then tried to besiege Mansourah but ran out of provisions over the winter, with a resulting heavy loss of life for his Crusaders, who succumbed in their hordes to scurvy, dysentery and other diseases.

Louis tried to withdraw back to Damietta in April 1250, but, in scenes which suggest considerable similarities to the British retreat from Kabul in 1841, his army were harried, looted and picked off until finally forced into battle at Fariskur. The army was heavily defeated, and Louis himself taken prisoner and taken back in chains to Mansourah. It was during his imprisonment that Queen Marguerite bore the son Jean 'Tristan' (Sorrow), who died with his father in 1270. Louis was released following payment of a massive ransom – and the return of Damietta.

Hopes of recovering Jerusalem faded following this catastrophe, but the interests of the broader Christian territories in the Holy Land remained. However, in the 1260s these came under serious threat too. This threat has its origin in events in Syria, where the Mamluks (soldiers of slave origin) overthrew the Ayyubid sultanate and seized power themselves. The most prominent of the Mamluk generals was one of those who had defeated Louis at Mansourah: Sultan al-Zahir Baibars. He had, of recent years, been attacking and picking off the remnant of the Crusader states. By 1265, he had captured Nazareth, Haifa, Toron and Arsuf. Attacks continued at Caesarea in 1265, Athlith, Haifa, Ramla, Lydda and Saphed in 1266 and Jaffa in 1268. The fall of these cities was what had prompted the coalition which had set off on Crusade.

Nor was Baibars waiting quietly for the Crusade to descend upon him. In 1268, he also captured Antioch, thereby destroying the last remnant of the Principality of Antioch. Next he took Ascalon. Here, the citadel built by Richard the Lionheart, which had been refortified in 1241 by Richard of Cornwall, was demolished. Next, Chastel Blanc and Gibelcar fell to him. In spring 1271, just as the Crusaders arrived, the Crac de l'Ospital (now better known as the Crac des Chevaliers), the greatest of the Crusader castles, fell and Tripoli came under siege.[14]

Given the position, it was decided that Edward would take his forces onward to Acre, capital of the remnant of the Kingdom of Jerusalem and the final objective of Baibars' campaign. Awaiting them there was one of the cardinals principally responsible for the Crusade – Teobaldi Visconti. One of the current contenders for the papacy, he had accompanied Cardinal Ottobuono to England after the civil war and was consequently well known personally to Edward and Eleanor.

While some accounts suggest that Edward managed to attack Baibars' interior lines and break the siege of Tripoli, the reality is less impressive. Their arrival was certainly a great move in terms of morale, but the cause of the let-up in the siege was simply prudence on the part of Baibars. Unsure what sort of threat the new Crusaders offered, he was not prepared to be committed in one direction and possibly taken by surprise in another. Accordingly, Tripoli got a ten-year truce and Baibars moved towards Acre, where he performed a calculated show of strength: he took the castle of Montfort and then released its defenders before the walls of Acre, with all their belongings – a gesture to the Crusaders to indicate that he considered their force too small to be reckoned with. He then withdrew.[15]

And in indicating that the Crusaders could not hope to beat him, he was quite right. Precise figures for either side cannot be found, but given that the major part of the crusading army was the English contingent of a thousand, that Mamluk armies were very numerous and that we know Baibars had both trebuchets and engineering battalions (which indicates a very large army indeed), it was indeed a match the Crusaders could not hope to win.

It was apparent that more troops would be needed for any major inroads to be made in Baibars' gains, and these could only come from new allies. Edward therefore made some attempts to form a Franco-Mongol alliance, sending an embassy to the Mongol ruler of Persia, Abagha, the great-grandson of Genghis Khan and an enemy of the Mamluks. Meanwhile, Edward dealt with 'domestic' issues: preparing his horses and troops after the journey, and dealing with administrative problems in Acre, such as trying to ban trading with the enemy – with no great success, as it transpired that such trade had been licensed by Hugh of Cyprus.

One small raid was attempted alone in July 1271– on Saint-Georges de Lebeyne, fifteen miles east of Acre. The raid was not a success – the troops were unused to the heat and many of them were suffering from food poisoning. Consequently the results were limited to destruction of a few houses and some crops at the cost of quite a number of casualties. After this, Edward determined to await the arrival of reinforcements.[16]

In around September 1272, the arrival of the additional forces from England and Hugh III of Cyprus, under the command of Edward's younger brother Edmund, and a reply from Abagha agreeing to co-operate, put Edward into a position where a further raid could be contemplated. In October, a small force of Mongols arrived in Syria and ravaged the land from Aleppo southward. Baibars immediately moved to deal with this threat. In fact, by the time Baibars mounted his counter-offensive, the Mongols had already retreated beyond the Euphrates. This was the only help Abagha sent; he was occupied by other conflicts in Turkestan.

However, while it lasted, the raid left the way open for the Crusaders to mount an attack in Baibars' rear, and on 23 November (very possibly Eleanor's thirtieth birthday) the joined forces of England, Cyprus and the Hospitallers rode out against Qaqun, a town some forty miles distant, which Baibars had developed and which was a strategic objective on the road to Jerusalem. The result of this, the major engagement of the Crusade, was not exactly triumphant. Tactful commentators (such as Asbridge) call it a 'punitive raid'. Morris more realistically points out that it achieved nothing other than a bit of cattle rustling. The city was not taken. On the contrary, it appears likely that the Crusaders were chased off by a mere back-up relief force, left by Baibars when he took his main strength against the Mongols. Baibars' rather cutting, but realistic, comment was that 'if so many men cannot take a house it seems unlikely that they will conquer the Kingdom of Jerusalem'.[17]

On a personal level, it was probably at around this time that news reached Eleanor and Edward of the death of their eldest son, John. He had died at Wallingford Castle, the favourite residence of Richard of Cornwall, on 3 August 1271. He was buried in Westminster Abbey on the north side of the Confessor's shrine on 8 August. His death will naturally have been a blow to both of them, but it appears in personal terms to have been a moderate one; Edward's lack of mourning was later noted by Charles of Anjou. Of course, the loss of children was not new to Edward and Eleanor, and the evidence suggests that they were much more emotionally invested in relations with adults, particularly each other, than with their children. At this point, one slightly suspects Edward at least of the view attributed to William Marshal's father: 'I have hammer and anvil to forge other sons.' And, on this theme, Eleanor was again pregnant with their child.[18]

Another piece of news which can definitely be traced to this time is the receipt by Teobaldo Visconti of the news that he had been elected Pope on 1 September 1271. The new Gregory X therefore had to leave Acre before any real action was taken. Before he left, the Pope elect preached a sermon in the church of the Holy Cross on the text 'If I forget thee, O Jerusalem, let my right hand forget her cunning. If I do not remember thee, let my tongue cleave to the roof of my mouth, yea if I prefer not Jerusalem above my chief joy' – a sermon which reportedly went largely unheard for the weeping of the Crusaders.[19]

But the Crusade was at least bothering Baibars. Over winter, he came to suspect there would be a combined land-sea attack on Egypt and endeavoured to head off such a manoeuvre by building a fleet, with which he attempted to land on Cyprus, hoping to draw Hugh III of Cyprus and his fleet out of Acre, with the objective of conquering the island and leaving Edward and the Crusader army isolated in the Holy Land. However, in the ensuing naval campaign the fleet was destroyed and Baibars' armies were forced back.

Meanwhile, Edward was ensuring that the Crusader forces were ready for any attack. He arranged for a new tower to be built in the walls of Acre and tried to remedy disputes within the Crusaders' numbers, mediating between Hugh of Cyprus and his unenthusiastic knights. He also sent a message to Gregory X in March requesting that he continue to defend the Holy Land.

However, the English alone had real appetite for the fight. Early in 1272, less than a year after the Crusade's arrival, King Hugh began negotiating a truce with Baibars. The negotiations bore fruit: an agreement to last ten years, ten months and ten days was reached in May 1272, at Caesarea. Edward was furious, and refused to sign it. However, considering the lack of any real military success on the part of the Crusaders – Tyerman summarises Edward's actions as constituting 'a couple of military promenades' – the truce can be counted as a pretty good result. It must not be forgotten that on their arrival, Tripoli had been under siege and Acre considering surrender. The truce left both towns free for over ten years, and additionally allowed a right of pilgrim access to Nazareth.[20]

Pausing here, what can we know about Eleanor's experience of the Crusade? For a fact, very little, but by drawing on experiences of other Crusaders we can infer a good deal. The route taken by the Crusaders is not entirely clear, but it is clear that whichever the route, there would have been extensive sea and land journeys. The land journey would have been, except in the balance of the people attending, not hugely dissimilar to movements of courts to which Eleanor and Edward would be used. The differences would be that the numbers involved would be even greater and biased towards the military, as opposed to the domestic household staff who predominated on moves of court household, and that the length of the journey would have been much greater than any single move of a court would be.

However, in crusading terms, it would have been fairly straightforward – and unlikely to give rise to the kinds of violence which were seen in some of the earlier Crusades, where larger groups of Crusaders crossed countries that were not themselves involved in the Crusade. The main issue would have been simple fatigue, and the social problems which inevitably beset a group of people thrown closely together for a long period of time. While there would have been some stops of some days, the party would have been on the move fairly constantly for a lengthy period. For some of that time, Eleanor, the keen rider, would have ridden. But for some portions, she and the other aristocratic ladies would have been confined to an unsprung wagon or a litter – both unspeakably tedious and uncomfortable ways to travel – a mode of travel which would force the women into close intimacy for days at a time. For Eleanor, who seems to have dealt notably well with men, this was probably very trying, and we may imagine that she rode whenever she could. Nor, of course, was even riding without risk – as the departure of the French from this very Crusade had proved; Isabelle of Aragon had died as a result of a miscarriage, true – but it was a miscarriage brought on by a fall from her horse while she was fording a river.

Nor was the land journey without its dangers. The accounts which suggest that the crusading party commenced its expedition by land report that, although the party were under a safe conduct from King Louis, they were attacked by William de Tournon, who used his stronghold on the Rhône to make off with some of the Crusaders' stores.

However, the land portion of the journey would have had considerable advantages over the sea voyage. A sea voyage imported danger at any time – Henry I had famously lost his heir in the *White Ship* catastrophe of 1120, and Edward himself had been inspired to found Vale Royal by a sea voyage which left him fearing for his life. Likewise, Louis of France, after his terrible Crusade of 1254, nearly lost his life again on his return journey, when his ship ran onto a sandbank at Cyprus and part of the keel was torn off. The seaborne portions of the voyage would therefore have been cause for concern in themselves.

They would also have been cause for discomfort in no small measure, too. Eleanor and her ladies likely had the use of a few rooms below deck – the bishop elect of Acre, James of Vitry, had four rooms in 1216 – one to sleep, one to read and eat, a third for storage and a fourth for his servants and kitchen. But they would have been affected, as he was, by the darkness and dampness of below-deck rooms. What is more, if the weather turned lively and the hatches had to be battened down, their rooms would have been airless – and doubtless redolent of seasickness. Meanwhile, food was poor – provisions would (unsurprisingly) go off in the course of a voyage – and Crusaders even report the water becoming putrid and swarming with worms. Just how physically challenging the journey was can be seen from the fact that 250 companions of Louis IX supposedly died during a stop at Cyprus in 1248–9. Further evidence can be seen from the rapid and violent way the French Crusaders succumbed to dysentery after their disembarkation in Tunis on the 1270 Crusade.[21]

Once arrived, Eleanor of course did not get to see that much – her time will have been spent confined within the walls of Acre, with maybe an occasional short journey a few miles outside. Acre (now Akko) was the Crusaders' foothold in the Holy Land, a mighty fortress facing constant Muslim threat. It is one of the places on earth where human occupation can be documented most consistently: it is mentioned in Egyptian texts of the nineteenth century BC. It had played host to Alexander the Great and St Paul, among others. It was, therefore, even in 1271, a place deeply imbued with history. It was also stuff of Crusader legend, having been taken by King Baldwin I, retaken by Saladin and recaptured by Richard the Lionheart. What is more, it offered a hugely vibrant political and commercial environment: following the fall of Jerusalem, it served as the political and administrative capital of the Latin Kingdom and its port served as the Crusader states' link with Christian Europe, and also for trans-shipment westward of valuable cargoes originating in the East.

The city had expanded from its original base around a south-oriented peninsula with a south-east-facing harbour. This natural defensive position had been bolstered by very considerable fortifications by the first Crusader conquerors. Walls and towers were built all around the town, while the port was also rebuilt to boast an outer and an inner harbour. To the south was a breakwater with a massive tower, known (then and now) as the Tower of Flies, at the end. Along the east and north aspects of the city a double wall, further protected by a moat, warded off any landward attack.

The area near the harbour was dominated by trading interests. Merchant quarters or *communes* were the outposts of the great Italian traders, the Pisan quarter running from the southern breakwater, the Venetians facing directly onto the harbour and the Genoese slightly north-west of both. Each of these areas had a marketplace and boasted warehouses, shops and houses of the merchant families. Around this trading hub were the centres for the various military orders, on whom the Latin Kingdom depended for day-to-day protection. The Templars held the south-west corner of the peninsula, the Hospitallers the north-east of the original town and the Teutonic knights held the east face. The palace of the Crusader kings was located in the northern part of city, enclosed by massive fortifications. At the beginning of the thirteenth century, a new residential quarter called Montmusard had been founded north of the city. It was surrounded by its own wall. The city boasted numerous churches – St Laurence, St Brida, St Michael and the Holy Cross to name but a few – as well as hospitals and other civic amenities. In the middle of the century the city further benefited from sponsorship by Louis IX of France. By 1270, it was comfortably the largest city of the Crusader states and was probably home to around 40,000 people – not far off the size of London.

Eleanor will most likely have stayed in the citadel of the Knights Hospitaller or Knights of St John. They had a substantial building complex of nearly 5,000 square metres – about three times the size of the Tower of London compound. It housed an extensive range of buildings built into the original north wall of the city. It had thick sandstone walls, and was itself fortified with corner towers. Fortuitously, owing to the entire complex having been filled in for later building, considerable traces remain and continue to be explored by archaeologists. While much remains unclear about the complex, it was certainly not a bad base for a prolonged stay, offering halls and many rooms built around a broad, open central courtyard of about 1,200 square metres. The rooms were set out over two storeys, the upper storey of which was supported by arches and was accessed from a wide staircase on the eastern side of the courtyard. While blocked off from the outside, the rooms obtained light and air from broad openings in the walls of the courtyard. Water was well considered: a network of drainage channels carried rainwater from the courtyard to a main sewer, and in the south-western corner of the courtyard was a stone-built well that guaranteed the residents' water supply.

Within the complex were a number of impressive larger rooms. South of the courtyard was (and is) a hall, which was later misnamed the Crypt of St John. This 450-square-metre rectangular hall is in the Gothic style, with a ten-metre-high groin-vaulted ceiling supported by three large, round central piers. The carving of fleurs-de-lis in two corners of the hall suggest that it was built as part of the works sponsored by Louis IX, and it seems to have served as a kitchen and refectory.

The true crypt of St John (now known as al-Bosta), over which the church itself was built, lies to the south of this hall. Again it is a large hall with several enormous piers supporting a groin-vaulted ceiling. North of the central courtyard lay a row of long, parallel underground vaulted halls, ten metres high, known as the Knights' Halls, which were the barracks of the members of the order. To the east of the courtyard lay the 1,350-square-metre Hall of the Pillars, which may have acted as a storage room, hospital or dormitory. Above it probably stood the four-storey Crusader palace depicted in contemporary drawings. On the western side of the complex was a further building, where it seems likely that distinguished guests (such as Edward and Eleanor) would have been lodged.[22]

Less progress has been possible in recreating the appearance of the city outside the complex. There was certainly a broad road from the Templars' complex to the port. And apparently in the Genoese quarter there were roofed streets with shops facing the street, and courtyards behind. Overall, the atmosphere may well have been some way between the former Moorish cities familiar to Eleanor from her childhood and the Norman architecture with which she had become familiar in England since her marriage.[23]

However, as for that vagrant quality – atmosphere – the reports from earlier Crusaders suggest that Acre, despite its magnificence, may not have been the most congenial city in the world. James of Vitry called it a 'second Babylon' – citing the prevalence of murder, the easy availability of poison and the fact that certain clerics rented out their property to high-ranking prostitutes. Echoing this is Oliver of Paderborn, who called it 'a sinful city and one filled with all uncleanness'. Meanwhile, Joinville, who accompanied Louis IX on his earlier Crusade, spoke of the 'treacherous sins' committed in Acre – and predicted that the inhabitants' blood would be required to wash it clean. Edward's discovery that the Venetian merchants were trading with the enemy suggests that not much had changed.

With this in mind, it may well be that, after the first excitement of arrival, Acre rapidly palled on the party. Although the *Pelrinages et Pardouns de Acre*, compiled between around 1258 and 1264, listed forty places of pilgrimage within the vicinity of Acre, it is unlikely that many of these could be explored in what was, in 1271–2, a warzone; and without a congenial town to enjoy, time must have hung pretty heavy. Aside from religious services and the preparations for the two forays which were made by their small contingent of troops, there was probably relatively little to do. One suspects that much chess – a favourite pastime of Eleanor and Edward – was played in this period. Other accounts of the Crusades refer to Crusaders playing dice – indeed, Louis IX caught Charles of Anjou playing dice en route in 1248 and threw board and dice into the sea.

Plainly Eleanor had recourse to her books. Most notably, this period sees the production by Eleanor's clerk Mr Richard of the very first Anglo-Norman translation of the key Roman military handbook, Vegetius' *De Re Militarii*. It was a work with which Eleanor would have been familiar from her own childhood, since it formed the backbone of the military advice in the *Siete Partidas*. However, this book was destined for Edward, who would be unlikely to read it in the original Latin. It is also tempting to place the production of the book as a Christmas gift for 1271. Considerable efforts had clearly been made to make it attractive to and engaging for Edward. One illustration shows him approaching Vegetius, and receiving instruction. Another is a most spirited depiction of a naval battle, perhaps inspired by the recent rout of Baibars' fleet. It is also rather touchingly annotated with a note describing Edward's dash to Kenilworth before Evesham as a perfect example of Vegetius' principles.[24]

Eleanor would also have a chance to see at close range the recreations of the soldiers – there are, of course, recurrent stories of the Crusaders patronising prostitutes, but more innocently Joinville tells of soldiers building miniature versions of siege engines – with which they attacked each other's dinners. And again and again talk would fall to home, the missed greenness of England, and families – including chats about marriages past and future. Joinville tells of some knights, themselves shortly to fall at Mansourah, passing another knight's memorial Mass by discussing a possible remarriage for his wife.

Another absorbing topic of conversation will have been the history of the Crusades, and for the English this would involve tales of Richard the Lionheart. As Richard was a figure around whom many myths and romantic stories had aggregated over the years, there will have been much to hear. One aspect, however, can perhaps be traced into the approach which Edward and Eleanor later took to mythmaking domestically – the impact of Arthurian romance and chivalric approaches. Richard was closely associated with both of these. In particular, he was reputed to have taken Excalibur on Crusade and he organised the reburial of the reputed Arthur and Guinevere. Sadly, they were not inspired to imitate Richard's approach to telling his own story by means of newsletters or accompanying minstrels – one of the reasons why material for this Crusade is so thin on the ground. Richard had sent regular bulletins back home and maintained an 'embedded' minstrel, Amboise, to whose work we owe some of the more poetic stories about Richard.[25]

Edward and Eleanor will also have had much to discuss about the future at home – how to occupy themselves after the Crusade in Henry

III's twilight years, and how they would conduct themselves once the throne passed to Edward. It is most likely that it was at some point during the crusading years that Edward and Eleanor decided on the role which she was to perform as queen – not simply to support him as a traditional queen, yet not to usurp his authority (unlike Eleanor of Provence). Eleanor's role was to work as a businesswoman to build up a self-standing portfolio of property which could support a queen, as it was now apparent that at any one time appanages for two queens (the present and either the future or the past queen) would need to be available.

The need for such work would only have been emphasised as the bills for the Crusade racked up. Prestwich powerfully recounts the list of monies which Edward received (and obviously spent) on the Crusade: 70,000 livres from Louis of France, £31,000 by way of the grant of a twentieth, 6,000 marks from the Jewry, plus Edward's own revenues. And still, in early 1272, Edward was calling for further funds – he needed 3,000 marks in Acre as soon as possible and the total of his borrowings from his main financiers only, the Ricciardi, was £22,364. There are also references to debts of 2,000 marks to the Hospitallers' Paris branch, 7,000 livres owed to Italian merchants, plus nearly 28,000 livres owed to the Templars.[26]

The other matter which was, of course, central to Eleanor's existence during the Crusade was her role as child bearer – and practically throughout the campaign she was pregnant. By the time of the conclusion of the peace treaty in April/May 1272, it is likely that the birth of her next child was imminent. This is probably the reason why, although Edmund departed for England almost at once, Edward and Eleanor did not. Some accounts put it down to Edward's refusal to accept the peace, and there may certainly have been a desire on his part to pause a while and see whether the peace held; but realistically Eleanor and Edward simply could not move at once. The sensible thing was for them to await the birth of Eleanor's next child and head home in summer.

The new baby was a daughter known to posterity as Joan 'of Acre', in honour of her birthplace. As with so many of Eleanor's children, precise details for the birth are lacking and we know only that she was born sometime in spring 1272. Inferentially, however, it seems likely that she was born in May itself, since Eleanor makes her next – and most famous – historical appearance in June 1272, and at that time she was plainly neither about to give birth or awaiting churching.

Before this great event, however, was to come another piece of sad news: the death on 2 April 1272 of Richard of Cornwall, aged sixty-two. Richard was a great loss to the Royal family, and his death also provided a considerable family problem – Richard had, after all, been charged with the custody of Eleanor and Edward's children in their absence. Although backup plans had been made, they were to entrust the children to Henry of Almain, who was also dead. It would have been fairly obvious that Eleanor of Provence would move to fill the gap and assume the role which Edward and Eleanor had expressly denied her on their departure, as she did. However, it appears that in the circumstances Eleanor and Edward were content with this approach – there is no trace of their trying to put in place any other arrangement; nor did they hurry home. Doubtless they accepted that, as matters had transpired, Eleanor was the best option, both politically and for the children – as a devoted mother and grandmother, her household would have been a familiar one to the small children.[27]

But events at home were soon overshadowed by the one event in Eleanor's life which can properly be called well known: the assassination attempt on Edward – and Eleanor's reputedly heroic actions to save him. Here, the myth and fact (so far as it can be established) are regrettably at some variance. The backstory is as follows: if the authorities cited earlier are correct, Edward refused to sign the truce. He then also failed to vacate the area as the rest of the Crusaders did. Whether or not he had any warlike intent – and it seems unlikely that he did, given Baibars' huge military superiority – his presence was regarded with disquiet by Baibars. It may be that Baibars was concerned that Edward planned to stay and link up with the kings of France, Aragon and Sicily who had all spoken of resuming the Crusade in around 1273. Possibly also Baibars was vexed at the real check on his progress which the Crusade had achieved, and attributed it to Edward as the Crusade's leader. For whatever reason, it is certain that Baibars arranged to have Edward assassinated.

Quite how this took place will probably never be known – there are a variety of accounts. One tells us that the assassin had gained a position as a servant, another that he was a known emissary, a third that he was part of an embassy bearing gifts. One particularly complex version has the assassin pretending to betray the sultan to gain access to Edward. Some accounts are more circumstantial than others, with some suggesting that Edward was just rising from his siesta and that he was lured away from the members of his household who surrounded him by a suggestion that a further message was for Edward's ear only.

However, what does appear clear is that, on 17 June 1272, Edward's thirty-third birthday, an assassin got close enough to Edward to stab him, possibly with a poisoned dagger and probably in the arm. That the wound was no worse was down to Edward's own reactions – he is reported to have struggled with the assassin and killed him in doing so, or at least seriously injured him with a mighty kick, his own dagger being out of reach. There is no account from anyone who was present, but Walter of Guisborough, one of the main English sources, and probably the least unreliable, records that Edward was stabbed in the arm with a poisoned dagger and his life was despaired of until a surgeon cut inflamed flesh from the wound. Eleanor's only role in this version is to be led away weeping and lamenting by Edward's brother Edmund and John de Vescy, who is reputed to have tried to calm her with the remark, 'Better that you should shed tears than that all the English land should weep.' Of course (as the careful reader will have noticed), this account itself cannot be fully trusted – Edmund had left soon after the truce was signed. However, it is at least near-contemporaneous, whereas the account which elevates Eleanor's role does not emerge until the next century.[28]

The other versions of the story are threefold. The first is a short account in a book called *Historia Ecclesiastica* written in the 1320s by an Italian Dominican, Bartolomeo Fiadoni (also known as Ptolemy of Lucca), who recounts a 'popular tradition' that Eleanor 'showed great faithfulness; for with her tongue she licked his open wounds all the day, and sucked out the humour, and thus by her virtue drew out all the poisonous material'. This version was, perhaps unsurprisingly, picked up by the Spanish historian Sanctius and retold with variations in English in the late sixteenth century. From these comes the high romantic tradition of Eleanor's heroism.

Just to complicate matters, there is another late version of the story which gives Eleanor's role to Otho de Grandison. The bottom line appears to be that while we cannot be satisfied that Guisborough's version is quite accurate (a sensible reinterpretation would be to allocate the roles of friends who removed Eleanor from Edward's bedside to Vescy and Grandison, great friends of Edward and Eleanor and of each other), it is likely that it is his story which is at least roughly true. Thus, in all likelihood Edward was attacked and wounded, and, whether by reason of poison or lack of hygiene or otherwise, the wound festered and became dangerous. The possibility of poison is supported by the fact that he made a will on 18 June, which would suggest that within a day of the injury it was considered that he might die. The list of executors appointed by Edward is interesting: Otho de Grandison, John of Brittany, William de Valence, Roger de Clifford, Payn De Chaworth, Chaworth's son-in-law Robert de Tybetot, Robert Burnell and Antony Bek. With Edward's life in danger, an unpleasant operation to excise the affected flesh, which Edward might also not have survived, was necessary. Eleanor was at his bedside at this point and, unsurprisingly given their devotion and her recent childbirth, became hysterical and had to be removed by the couple's friends.[29]

The rough veracity of the Guisborough version, it should be noted, is also supported by the facts of the next few months – as will be seen, Edward and Eleanor's return was slow, and at some point this was ascribed by at least one friend to Edward's need to recuperate.

In August, William of Valence left Acre. On 14 September, John of Brittany left, presumably with his wife, Edward's sister Beatrice. Edward and Eleanor followed on 22 September 1272 for Sicily, leaving behind a small force under Jean de Grailly and Hamo Lestrange, one of the young Marchers, who had used his time on Crusade to arrange a marriage with the heiress of Beirut.[30]

Edward and Eleanor's party arrived at Trapani in October or November and stayed into the New Year. The prolonged stay which Edward and Eleanor made in Sicily may be attributable to the fact that Edward was still recovering from his injuries; this is certainly the suggestion of a letter from Gregory X to Eleanor at around this time. While they were there, however, it is clear that Eleanor took the opportunity to intercede for her brother Enrique – with rather limited success. In late 1272, Charles did order Enrique's prison to be cleaned and it was perhaps in this less rigorous confinement that the imprisoned knight errant wrote *Amadis de Gaula*.

Another contrasting intercession which the pair sought to make with Charles of Anjou was in respect of Henry of Almain's murderers, the young Montforts, who had not yet been handed over to justice and were understood to be hiding out somewhere in the Apennines. Again, the success of the intercession was rather limited. While Charles promised that his new vicar of Tuscany would do all in his power to bring the fugitives to justice, no concrete results eventuated.[31]

Late in December or very early in the year 1273 came major news: Henry III was dead. The news probably came in the form of a notification of Henry's death and burial, and a pledge of loyalty from the bishops and nobles of England. Henry had died on 16 November 1272 at the age of sixty-five, after fifty-six years as king. Although the news cannot have been much of a surprise – sixty-five was considered a very good age, Henry had been in ill health for some time, and Edward had been urged to come home earlier in the Crusade because of this – Edward was very upset indeed. Indeed, Charles of Anjou remarked on the fact that he grieved more for his father than he had the year before over the death of his heir. Edward's reply was that while children could be replaced, a father could not. For Eleanor, too, the loss of Henry will have been a grief. Henry had been in many respects a congenial companion to her, with their shared tastes for domestic comfort and finery, and he was the member of the family who had been closest to her in the dark days of de Montfort's victory and her daughters' deaths.[32]

Yet, too, for both, there must have been a sense of destiny fulfilled. Their crusading obligations discharged, they could return home – as king and queen.

9

The Triumphant Return

In 1273, Edward and Eleanor started their homeward journey as king and queen via Italy, Gascony and Paris. They had, in response to a letter from the regents in England urging their speedy return, promised to hurry back. But that was not how matters turned out.

In early January, the Pope wrote to Eleanor directly, asking her to induce the king to visit him. This direct contact and other direct letters from the Pope to Eleanor are interesting, demonstrating how Eleanor was regarded as a significant diplomatic contact by the papacy in her own right, and indicating, too, that she had built up a close personal relationship with the pontiff in his crusading and diplomatic days. In the light of Edward's desire to see the Montforts brought to justice, and the failure of Charles of Anjou to provide action on this front, this offered a valuable opportunity to pursue an alternative route to vengeance.

There was also an opportunity to eclipse the French king. In 1271, the new king, Philip III, had headed home with the remains of his father, Louis IX, in what was part funeral, part royal tour of acclamation. The route he had taken had been via Orvieto, Florence, Bologna, the Mont Cenis pass to Lyons and then on to Paris. Adopting the same route for their return offered Edward and Eleanor the chance to point up the contrast between the failed and successful Crusaders. For them, as Tyerman points out, this rather mediocre Crusade had paid fine dividends on the PR front: Edward was considered distinguished, as the sole king in Western Europe to have campaigned in the Holy Land itself. The truce was given its full value – particularly among the Italian merchants who had such good markets in Acre. And, of course, the attempt on his life added a considerable touch of romantic glory, particularly when combined with the emerging invention of Eleanor's role in saving her husband.[1]

Accordingly, the royal couple left Charles of Anjou in mid-January, accompanied by young Charles of Salerno, who accompanied them to the frontiers of the Regno. From there they pressed on, arriving in Rome on 5

February and at the papal court in Orvieto (where political and military conflicts had forced the papacy to withdraw) on 14 February 1273. The welcome was at once warm and magnificent – that due to a friend and to an acknowledged Crusader, with all the cardinals in attendance. It seems possible that on this occasion the Pope presented Edward with the papal accolade of a golden rose, traditionally given to the foremost prince in Christendom. While at the papal court, Edward at once began to campaign for sanctions to be imposed on Guy de Montfort for the murder of Henry of Almain. But the matter was not straightforward – Guy's father-in-law was very influential, and the younger Montfort brother, Amaury, was one of the pope's own chaplains.[2]

Nonetheless, Guy was summoned to appear. He refused to do so, on the grounds that his life would not be safe while Edward was at Orvieto – a suspicion which was probably justified. His refusal left the Pope had no real choice but to act. Thus, before leaving in late May, Edward had secured the excommunication and outlawry of Guy. He was deprived of the right to hold property or make a will, and also of the law's protections, making him a safe target for anyone. Moreover, the sanction was bolstered by a ruling that the lands of any men who aided him were also to be placed under interdict. The sanctions worked. Six months later, Guy submitted himself to the Pope and spent some years in prison. He was released, and taken back into service by Charles of Anjou in 1281, partly for his undoubted talents as a soldier and partly because of the family relationship between them. His story did not, however, end in prosperity: he was later captured by the Aragonese, and died in prison in 1291.[3] Meanwhile Eleanor made her own intercession – gaining permission for one of her clerks to hold multiple benefices.

After leaving the papal court, the new king and queen's journey north on the Via Emilia took on much of the appearance of a triumphal progress. Whatever the actual achievements of the Crusade, Edward was perceived as a great warrior and Crusader. There were acclamations and processions at every city. He was entertained at the episcopal palace at Reggio on 20 May. At Milan the citizens presented a number of selected chargers, richly caparisoned with scarlet trappings.

If a letter from Gregory X to Eleanor is to be believed, some of the slowness of the progress after Orvieto was, however, attributable to Edward's having fallen ill again. Finally, however, they reached the pass at Mont Cenis, where they were met by a party of English nobles who had set out expecting to meet the new king and queen in Paris. Also here to meet the royal party was Philip, Count of Savoy, and at his castle of St George near Vienne in late June Edward took his homage for various lands in Savoy which had come to the English Crown in Henry II's reign. He also took that of the impudent William de Tournon, who judged it best to make peace after having raided the party on their outward voyage. In all probability, Otho de Grandison parted from the company in Savoy, to assist his family in issues in his homeland. The stay at St George will have afforded Edward and Eleanor a chance to admire the work recently done there by the count – or, more accurately, his builders. Among these was Master James, later to be known as James of St George, who was to become Edward's architect in chief.[4]

At some point in June, Edward and Eleanor took the rare step of parting company. Quite when and how is unclear. Some accounts suggest that while he headed on to a tournament in Châlons and then Paris, she journeyed with a party to see her brother Alfonso in Seville. However, the letter cited for this proposition makes no mention of a visit and can be safely dismissed, not least because Alfonso's own timeline rebuts it.[5]

At this point it needs to be understood that Alfonso's position in Castile had deteriorated considerably since Eleanor's marriage. Despite his excellent inheritance, Alfonso had failed to live up to the standards of his father. His entry into the race to become the next Holy Roman Emperor had been an expensive fiasco. This election had hung fire for years, and had resulted in Alfonso taking up arms against the papal forces. This, and the large sums required to keep his case in the right minds over a period of years had carried a heavy financial cost. To obtain money, he debased the coinage and then endeavoured to prevent a rise in prices by an arbitrary tariff, which had a negative knock-on effect on external trade. This, in turn, affected his popularity with the middle and lower classes.

As for his relationship with his nobles, in the absence of continued focus against the Almohads, the traditional problems re-emerged, particularly with the de Lara and de Haro families. This was probably exacerbated by Alfonso's very obvious focus on the arts and sciences, rather than on the traditional warlike skills of a Castilian noble. Thus, while creating the reputation as a writer, musician and patron of the arts which was to earn him the title of Alfonso the Learned, he was constantly creating friction with those who should have been his most powerful supporters.

Finally, his attempts at legal reform and in particular his attempts to introduce a cohesive legal code which drew heavily on Roman law and gave minimal weight to the traditional Peninsular law, produced in 1271 a revolt on the part of the nobility – supported by his own brother Felipe. This was still not resolved in 1273, as Eleanor returned from the Holy Land. In fact, at the Cortes of Burgos in 1272, the nobles (including both de Haro and de Lara representatives) and Felipe withdrew their allegiance from Alfonso and went into exile under the protection of the Muslim Emir of Granada. Although a tentative accord was reached in March 1273 via the intercession of Queen Violante and Fernando de la Cerda, Alfonso's heir apparent, the accord was still in the process of being fleshed out, not assisted by serious illness on Alfonso's part in spring 1273. Thus when Eleanor suggested a late spring or summer meeting to Alfonso, Queen Violante told him to refuse because if he missed key negotiations on this account he would lose such limited ground with the nobles as he had made up. In late August, he was instead seeking help from Jaime of Aragon at Requena near Valencia. Following this meeting Alfonso was for some time seriously ill again with a tertian fever. He only returned to Burgos by December.[6]

So Eleanor simply cannot have met Alfonso until very late in the year. It seems most likely that Edward and Eleanor remained together until Lyons and Eleanor, who was expecting yet another baby in the late autumn, moved via Clermont Ferrand and Limoges into Aquitaine at an easy pace, rather than face travel later in her pregnancy, and risk confinement on the road.[7]

Meanwhile, Edward went on to a major tournament in Châlons. Such was the violence of this event that it was known as 'the little war of Châlons'. It featured what Guisborough recounts as a thoroughly dastardly attack by the Count of Châlons on Edward personally – perhaps hoping to gain renown by capturing the famed Crusader. But the attack was foiled by Edward's great personal strength, dragging the count bodily from his horse. Edward is then glimpsed in Paris from 26 July to 6 August, where he did homage to King Philip III for his French lands. There he received messengers from England, reporting that all was going on well there in his absence – a fact for which he expressed very great pleasure. But he also received the less good news that Gaston de Béarn was continuing to cause trouble in Gascony – reinforcing his decision to head to Gascony before leaving for England.[8]

It appears that on 26 July 1273, Eleanor had reached Limoges, which had been ceded to England by the 1259 Treaty of Paris. There she was received royally by the townspeople, who prepared a feast in her honour. They also asked her to intercede with Edward to protect them against the oppression of their viscountess's administration. Eleanor wrote to Edward for assistance, which was duly sent, and while he remained in Paris until early August, these troops – possibly under Eleanor's direction – gained a victory over the viscountess. Edward arrived shortly after this, and required the men of Limoges to swear fealty to William of Valence, who was to be left as his deputy in Gascony.

After spending the latter part of August at Saintes, the reunited party then moved on into Gascony, arriving at Bordeaux on 8 September 1273 with a view to dealing with the usual problems of disorder among the Gascon barons – as usual in particular Gaston de Béarn.[9]

Edward's immediate starting point in Gascony was to announce an inquest into tenures in Gascony. Though in part a forerunner of the *quo warranto* inquiries in England, it was specifically relevant to the Gascon issues, where the duke's authority was different as regards different vassals. An inquiry would enable him to have a good knowledge of his property and the rights and difficulties inherent in it. In particular, it would enable him to know, now that his authority was finally his own, who was prepared to recognise him and who was not. He could then judge how to deal with those who were not prepared to acknowledge his authority. A proclamation was therefore sent summoning vassals to do homage at various main locations and to declare the nature and extent of their obligations to the new ruler.

The party reached Louvigny on 18 September on their way to Saint-Sever, where the first of the grand courts had been convened. The chief absentee was, predictably, Gaston. Much of October was then spent trying to bring him to heel, resulting in a judicial assembly of the principal Gascon representatives, which granted Edward specific authority to proceed against him in arms. Edward immediately called his levies and marched in arms against Gaston.[10]

Thereafter, the focus moved temporarily to Eleanor and her imminent childbirth. The court moved to base itself at Bayonne, and on 24 November came the birth of Eleanor and Edward's next child – another much-longed-for son, who was named Alphonso, after Eleanor's brother, who stood godfather to him. The use of the name is highly unusual and signifies the close link between Eleanor and her brother – and also presumably Edward's own affection for him. The decision on the name has, however, had unfortunate ramifications for young Alphonso over the years. He appears in the records variously as Alfurnus, Aunfurs, Amfulsus, Amphur, Amphunsus, Alfundus, Anfours, Alfontis and Aufons – even his own roll of arms has him as Aunfons. He even appears in numerous reports to have been transmuted into a mythical daughter, Alice.[11]

As for the older Alfonso, the choice by Edward and Eleanor, the current stars of Europe, of him as a godfather will have been a much-needed piece of good news. It may even be interpreted as a deliberate gesture of support from Eleanor for the embattled Alfonso – a sprinkling of fairy dust from the current European golden couple. But certainly the meeting between Edward, Eleanor and Alfonso was thus one with a very different balance of power to the one which had occurred at the time of the marriage. However, Alfonso still was perceived as having some 'clout'. Eleanor, doubtless remembering his doughty work on her original settlement, asked him to speak to Edward about the need for a revised dower settlement now she was queen – a necessary starting point for her work of property development in the next few years.

Alfonso was not the only representative of the Spanish peninsula who was granted close audience with Edward and Eleanor. In October there had been a meeting with Pedro of Aragon, the heir to the Aragonese throne, at Sordes. The result of this meeting was a marriage agreement, matching the eldest daughter of Edward and Eleanor (Eleanora) with Pedro's eldest son, Alphonso. Another match was made in December between young Henry and his distant cousin Jeanne of Navarre, the daughter of Henry, King of Navarre and Count of Champagne and Brie, and his wife, Blanche of Artois. Henry of Navarre was a relative of both Edward and Eleanor, via Eleanor of Aquitaine; he was also the brother of the King of Navarre whose hand had once been considered for Eleanor.

These two matches show clearly the importance which was still assigned to maintaining a peaceful border into Gascony; as would the later time, attention and expenditure which was given to the maintaining of the Aragonese marriage. The reason for this can easily be seen. The difficulties which had to be dealt with in Gascony both in 1254 and at this time proved that the Gascons were vulnerable to mischief making. Castile might be counted out of the equation, thanks to Eleanor and its own internal difficulties. However, Aragon was an expansionist country with highly dynamic leadership, whose active influence on the far side of the Pyrenees had recently been shut off as regards Toulouse, Narbonne and surrounding areas under the Treaty of Corbeil of 1258. Absent a good, solid agreement, there was every chance that the Aragonese would at least make trouble in Gascony and at worst try to take control of lands there directly.[12]

The need for such precautions can only have been emphasised, as Gaston de Béarn provided occupation for the early part of 1274. He had been conducting guerrilla warfare against Edward's forces but with limited success. On 27 November 1273, his daughter Constance, the widow of Henry of Almain, had submitted on his behalf at Mont de Marsan and promised to yield his fortresses and castles on demand. However, no actual handover was forthcoming and early in 1274 Gaston appealed to the King of France, accusing Edward of doing damage to Gaston's property – and even seeking trial by combat. Although attempts were made to keep the dispute local, in the end Edward was forced to retire and to await the decision of their mutual overlord. This was likely to take some time, since a request came from the Pope to delay the hearing of Gaston's complaints, pending a General Council which he had summoned to Lyons on 1 May.[13]

The council, however, was of considerable interest to Edward and Eleanor for one very good reason: money. Although Edward now had access to royal revenues, the Crusade had been a crippling undertaking: even with the massive French loan, and all the monies which had been received before their departure, receipts had fallen a long way short of covering outgoings and massive debts needed paying. The Pope, who had witnessed much of this expenditure, was sympathetic – he had authorised a supplementary subsidy from the English clergy of 22,000 marks, to be split with Edmund of Lancaster, and he had still further plans for the Council of Lyons. There, he obtained a worldwide grant of a tenth from the clergy in aid of future crusading efforts. Edward, probably with his financial woes in mind, seems to have indicated that he would lead this Crusade; from this point on, he regarded the money thus raised as peculiarly his own.[14]

Edward and Eleanor thus began to move back north. At Limoges, the viscountess's administration was continuing, like Gaston, to create troubles; and matters were put on hold pending a reference to King Philip or her marriage into the friendly Brittany family.[15]

Towards the end of their Continental peregrinations, Eleanor and Edward found themselves in Ponthieu, her mother's county, with correspondence dating from Montreuil-sur-Mer in June and July of 1274. It may well have been the first time that Eleanor and her mother had met since the wedding, fourteen years before, though she may well have become acquainted with her new stepfather, Jean de Nesle, at Tunis, where he had fought under Louis' banner. A stay of reasonable length was made, perhaps because, since the death of her brother Ferdinand around 1264, Eleanor was now heiress to the county of Ponthieu, a place of which she would have had practically no knowledge. The stay with her mother will have offered an opportunity for Eleanor and Edward to familiarise themselves with her future inheritance and begin to plan how it would in due course be administered.

It also seems that, though Jeanne would have preferred Ponthieu to follow Ferdinand's line, relations at this time were altogether sunny. Otherwise, the decision to which Eleanor and Edward came – to leave their two-year-old daughter, Joan of Acre, to be raised by Eleanor's mother – seems peculiar indeed. Certainly, this future territorial acquisition cannot explain the decision to leave Joan behind – Joan as a younger child was never in line to inherit Ponthieu, which under local law went to the eldest surviving heir. It seems likely that there was a simple affinity between grandmother and namesake grandchild, and given the limited contact which the youngest would inevitably have with their parents, a long stay was not regarded as problematic by Edward and Eleanor. Perhaps too, it was hoped that fondness for Joan would smooth over any resentment at Ponthieu's destiny.[16]

By 28 July 1274 the king and queen are recorded for the last time at Montreuil, and on Thursday 2 August 1274 the couple arrived back at Dover. The arrival was not unexpected – indeed, it is apparent from the close space between the arrival and the coronation that considerable forward planning had been going on between England and France for some months. Nor were they in any sense alone – during their peregrinations they had been acquiring quite a mobile court, most of which will have crossed with them. Accompanying them also were John of Brittany and his wife, Edward's sister, who had left their son in the company of his cousins and would themselves attend the coronation.

The party was received with great state by the Earl of Gloucester – who, despite the troubles of past years, had been the first to declare his fealty to Edward on Henry III's decease – and John de Warenne, a prime candidate for being put in overall charge of organising their reception and coronation. They then proceeded, via stops at each of Warenne's and Gloucester's castles of Tonbridge and Reigate, towards London and the coronation. A prior stop, however, was Canterbury, where they were received by Eleanor of Provence. Eleanor's mother-in-law was now queen dowager, but it was perhaps symptomatic of her less than easy relationship with Eleanor that she tended to continue to call herself Queen of England (and Duchess of Aquitaine and Lady of Ireland) until her enclosure as a nun, some decade in the future. With the queen dowager were the surviving children: Henry, aged six; Eleanor, aged four; and the Brittanys' own John and Henry. Young Alphonso may well have awaited them in this company, too.[17]

By the time of their arrival, all was nearly in place; in February 1274, orders had been sent to various counties to supply some of the massive amount of food required for the epic feast that was to round off the coronation and to individuals who could supply some of the luxury items – swans, peacocks, lampreys, pikes and the rest. Westminster Palace was refurbished, temporary accommodation and catering facilities were built, and covered walkways erected. The coronation was to be particularly show-stopping for a variety of reasons. In the first place, there had been no coronation at all for many years – Eleanor of Provence was crowned in 1236, and Henry III's coronation even longer ago had been a hole-and-corner affair, which took place in a rush in Gloucester, amid the disorder of rebellious barons and invading Frenchmen. Secondly, it was to be a dual coronation – king and queen together. This had last occurred on the coronation of Henry II and Eleanor of Aquitaine in 1154. Thirdly, it offered an opportunity to celebrate Edward's new worldwide renown, and also to put the Barons' War firmly behind the country. Fourthly, it was the first coronation to take place in the revamped Westminster Abbey. And last but not least, that great showman Henry III had planned the whole thing himself.[18]

That is not, however, to say that the preparations went without a hitch – as at any major event, there were disputes as to people's roles – and, as with Eleanor of Provence's coronation, a court had to be established to consider these disputes. The role of Edmund of Lancaster was controversial; he claimed the right to carry the ceremonial sword Curtana. His right to do so was rejected, and it seems likely that he boycotted the ceremony in a fit of pique – which may have been heightened by a row which had developed between him and Edward over the division of Gregory X's crusading subsidy. It is likely that the ever-touchy Gloucester, who had to be rewarded for his good behaviour in Edward's absence, won the Curtana fight. Then there were fights between the archbishops of York and Canterbury about York's role in the ceremony – resolved with

York either being excluded or playing no active role in the ceremony. Meanwhile, the great and good of the kingdom – and many from elsewhere – made their way to London to participate in the coronation. While Edward and Eleanor brought his sister Beatrice and her husband John in their train, his sister Margaret and her husband Alexander travelled down from Scotland to be part of the great occasion.[19]

Coronation day was 19 August 1274. The day before this, Edward and Eleanor made a triumphal entry into London, which had pulled out all the stops to bedeck itself for the occasion. The accounts which are left to us are not as helpful as they might be – simply telling us that everything was grand or impressive beyond description – but the fragments which do make their way into the accounts, and the fuller accounts which the Tudors left us of similar occasions, give some idea of the kind of event which might have been expected.

We know that on coronation day the conduit at Cheapside ran with red and white wine for all to drink, and it takes no genius to infer from this that the crowd would have been loud and boisterous. This feature became a commonplace in later coronations, and was then accompanied by formal receptions of the royal party, with speeches and tableaux of welcome and congratulation. There were, apparently, 'multifarious inventions'. While the more extreme forms of these (Holbein's designs for a tableau of Apollo and the Muses on Mount Parnassus for Anne Boleyn's coronation springs to mind) are probably later accretions, they give some idea of the kinds of thing which greeted the couple. There will likely have been formal receptions by the mayor or guilds of London, with polite speeches in both directions, and possibly gifts to the new monarchs. For example, at the coronations of Mary Tudor and Anne Boleyn, the Recorder of London read out a speech professing the loyalty of the people of London and he gave a gold thread purse that contained a thousand gold coins.

The route would take in Cheapside, then St Paul's, Temple Bar and the Strand before heading to Westminster. All along the route, the streets were hung with rich cloths – and in places with cloth of gold – and so as not to let the spectacle down, the streets had actually been cleaned – a mammoth undertaking.

It would appear that the royal couple's necessary entrance to London, as they had been away for the entire lead-up to the event, was the very first such coronation procession, and set the precedent for the future. It became de rigueur for the king or queen to head, usually from Westminster, to the Tower along the river in order to be in the right starting position for the traditional procession from the City. However, while they were setting a precedent for coronations, they were keeping firmly to the Henry III book of extravaganzas – earlier such events, like Eleanor's own arrival in London, and the reception for the Scottish royals, have been described earlier and all featured some form of parade through the City. So too would Eleanor's own funeral procession.

One need only walk the journey now to see what a massive undertaking the parade was, how tiring it must have been for the ceremonially dressed participants, and how great an opportunity it afforded the much smaller population of medieval London of seeing their monarch. The route covers well over three miles, and effectively took the royal party in person through the heart of the thirteenth-century city.

The day will have ended with a great feast, and then Edward, at least, was expected to hold a vigil in his father's old room, appropriately decorated with a coronation scene, to prepare himself for the next day. Eleanor will meanwhile have taken over the luxurious rooms of the queen – formerly those of Eleanor of Provence – where the sad portrayal of winter was very out of keeping both with the festive mood and the time of year.[20]

On the day itself, there was a procession from the palace to the abbey for the first coronation to take place in the new church. Magnates and clergy all had places in the procession and – after doubtless countless disputes over precedence – very firmly fixed places. Edward and Eleanor were dressed in simple, flowing unbelted robes to evoke the continuity of kingship; these will coincidentally have hidden any signs of Eleanor's latest pregnancy. They processed over either the same carpet or a replica of the carpet used at Eleanor of Provence's coronation – a blue ray cloth, preceded by three earls bearing the swords of state, followed by the treasurer in a dalmatic carrying the paten (gold or silver plate) to be used in the coronation Mass, and the chancellor wearing full pontificals carrying the special stone chalice with the king's regalia. It is not clear to whom fell the job of carrying the queen's regalia. Two knights followed carrying sceptres – one for each of the king and the queen. Edward and Eleanor each walked under a silk canopy secured on silver lances, with a silver gilt bell at each corner, each lance being carried by a baron of the Cinque Ports. Unusually, Eleanor would have worn her hair loose, with just a circlet of gold to keep it in order.

At the door of the abbey came the first prayer. Although the heart of the coronation service was traditional, and had changed little since William the Conqueror, Henry III and his advisers, in planning for this event, had added new twists to improve the ceremony as theatre and bring it in tune with the new church. So, while Edward made the traditional promises to protect the Church, to do good justice and to suppress evil laws and customs, and the more recent innovation of protecting the rights of the Crown, new features appeared. For example, in order to increase visibility, much of the coronation spectacle took place at the crossing of the church where a huge stage was built – large enough for the magnates to ride under, for those whose roles required that they entered the church on horseback. Offerings were made at the altar of figures of St John the Evangelist and St Edward the Confessor.

In terms of order, the making of vows probably came first in time, followed by the anointing. For this, there was a further procession to the high altar, where the couple made their offerings and prostrated themselves on the beautiful new pavement, while a further prayer was said. The gold circlets were removed from their heads and then the king and queen were anointed with holy oil, or unction, which was deemed to exalt them to a new status and confer spiritual gifts. Edward was partially disrobed for this part of the event, so he could be anointed on the breast, shoulders and elbows, prior to being anointed with chrism on his head; Eleanor will only have received anointing on her head. This reflects the different roles which were evoked in the coronation. For Edward, his hereditary right to rule was evoked by analogies to biblical kings and patriarchs. Eleanor's role, however, was anchored in citations of Esther, the Blessed Virgin and the more fecund patriarchal wives. Nor was she blessed as a partner in royal power, as had been done in the eleventh century; the modern idiom was for exhortations and prayers to guide and limit her influence with the king.

It is then likely that the (re-dressed) king and the queen proceeded back to the stage for the coronation proper – the assumption of the coronation rings, the placing of a crown – golden lilies for Eleanor, the alleged crown of Edward the Confessor for Edward, and the bestowal of the sceptre and virge. Here, too, there was a difference in Eleanor's investiture – the purely ceremonial nature of the power she was supposed to wield was signified by the handing to her of the sceptre in silence and the requirement that she then bow to the king to honour his royal majesty. Her place, too, was at his left, not the traditional site of power on the right. The 'Laudes Regiae', an acclamation of Christ triumphant, was sung once those formalities had been completed, followed by acclamations of the established powers as vicars of God.[21]

The main point of novelty, however, was not one carefully planned by Henry III but one introduced by Edward. According to the chroniclers (who, of course, were unlikely to have been there in person), as soon as the crown was placed on Edward's head, he removed it, saying that 'he would never take it up again until he had recovered the lands given away by his father to the earls, barons and knights of England and to aliens'. While it seems implausible that this is exactly when Edward said – the idea of actually recovering all such lands was too provocative – it is a very interesting starting point for the reign. It seems likely that the reported speech amalgamates a broad statement of intent regarding lands – for certainly Edward had plans on this front – and a more specific statement regarding rights alienated by his father. This latter would tie in with his coronation oath to defend the Crown's rights, and also tie in with some of the legislation which Edward was later to introduce – in particular the inquiries into magnates' rights known as the *quo warranto* inquiries.

But the reference to regaining lands, if indeed it was made, does also chime with Edward and Eleanor's quieter agenda of reinvigorating the Crown's stock of lands. Some of this Edward did on his own account – and not always with the utmost scrupulousness – but much of it was left in Eleanor's hands; as we shall see, to great effect.

Meanwhile, after the coronation London's populace partied in the streets, and a major celebration was held at Westminster. The feast was of epic proportions, as the preparations suggested. However, at least according to a later tale of the event, it also had the jolly feel of a party headed up by the younger generation – Edward, Eleanor and their friends were all in their early thirties – right in the prime of life. According to this story, Alexander of Scotland (perhaps inspired by the riding of horses into the abbey?) arranged for one hundred mounted knights to ride into the hall, and then release their horses, to be taken by anyone who could catch them. This prompted a number of English earls, including Gilbert de Clare, to do likewise, in a classic piece of keeping up with the Joneses. While the veracity of the story must be open to serious doubt – at least in its scale – it does convey the impression of a vibrant celebration among a group of young friends.[22]

Another fact which testifies to the scale of upheaval and jollification is that, immediately after the hangovers settled, on 21 August, Edward and Eleanor and probably a good party of their friends decamped to Kempton near the river south-west of London – probably around the site of the modern racecourse, where there was a lavish royal residence, much updated and improved by Henry III and Eleanor of Provence; and appropriately featuring a statue of a crowned king on the roof. After a few days there, they moved on to Windsor where they remained, probably with the children, for some weeks, apart from a short visit to Eleanor of Provence.

In early October, they moved back to London where Edward had much to do in seeing to the commencement of the Hundred Rolls survey, by which commissioners went everywhere in England inquiring into 'the deeds and behaviour of all our sheriffs and bailiffs'. The idea was to inquire into the rectitude of all royal servants, but also to get a picture of the broader governance of the country, since people were asked to report issues with their lords or their lord's stewards and bailiffs. This was a masterstroke for the commencement of the reign, welcomed by the chroniclers as a sign that the king would come down on all those who were corrupt and that law and order generally would improve under the new king.[23]

But at the same time a terrible blow fell. Within months of the return, and the greeting of young Henry and Eleanora at Canterbury, Henry

– the heir to the throne – was gravely ill. The nature of his illness does not appear in the sources, but it seems that he had been unwell for some time, with payments made for candles to be burnt for his recovery and for widows to pray for him through the night. He died, aged six and a half, in October 1274 at Guildford with his grandmother. It is generally accepted that neither Edward nor Eleanor visited him, although there is a real possibility (based on the dating of a letter from one of the queens Eleanor to Robert Burnell, reproduced in Appendix 1) that Eleanor at least saw him in the final days before his death. The absence (if there was one) is a fact which is often invoked as evidence of the couple as uncaring parents, but it must be remembered that they had hardly seen the boy since his birth, owing to their absence on Crusade, and one of the reasons for separating younger children from their parents was to prevent suffering when, as was too often the case, those in their early years died.

It is possible, too, that Edward and Eleanor knew that he was dying and had said their farewells already; it is likely that he was with them for at least some of the month they spent at Windsor. For Eleanor, who was in the early months of another pregnancy, there may have been advice to avoid the sickroom. Certainly she should not be accused of indifference: she sent repeatedly to ask after Henry's health in the final months of his life, and, poignantly, in his last weeks sent him a white palfrey, which he was never to ride. Henry's body was brought to London and buried in Westminster Abbey along with all but the first of Eleanor and Edward's lost children – Katherine, Joan the first and John. England had a new king and queen, but was without an heir.[24]

1. The clearest picture we have of Eleanor; it characteristically invokes her heritage, in the repeated patterns of castles and lions on the cushion beneath her head.

Above: 2. Eleanor and Edward's common ancestors, the formidable Eleanor of Aquitaine and Henry II, buried together at the Plantagenet family burial site of Fontevrault Abbey.

Left: 3. The tomb of Eleanor's grandmother, Berengaria 'the Great'. A key adviser to her son, also accompanying him to war and managing politically vital properties, she will have been held up to Eleanor as the perfect model of a Castilian princess.

4. The resting place of Eleanor's great-grandparents Eleanor of England and her devoted husband Alfonso VIII of Castile at the Castilian necropolis of Las Huelgas Abbey. It was here that Eleanor and Edward married in 1254. The artistic link between this tomb and Eleanor's is clear.

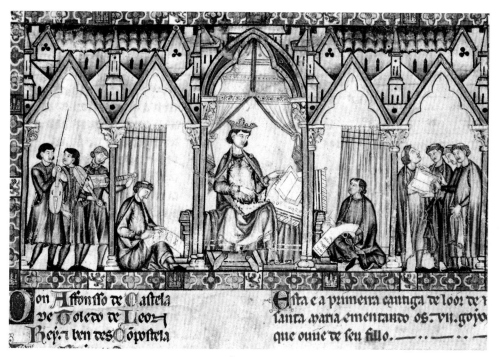

5. The court of Eleanor's brother Alfonso X 'the Learned', depicted, probably accurately, as a luxurious but work-hard-play-hard environment.

6. The man who bestrode Eleanor's childhood – her father, Ferdinand III, 'El Santo'. The hero of the Reconquista, but also a wise man and a scholar, who believed it was a king's duty to devote himself to the good of his country.

7. One of the wonders of the world – Eleanor was familiar with the fabulous beauties of such buildings as the Cathedral/Mosque of Cordoba, with its forest of pillars.

8. The famed Patio de Doncellas; stunning, but only a pale shadow of the beautiful gardens with which Eleanor grew up.

Above: 9. The unhappy king. Henry III lacked nearly all the attributes of a successful king.

Left: 10. Elegant, charming and determined to control her son Edward, Eleanor of Provence never entirely accepted Eleanor's place in Edward's life.

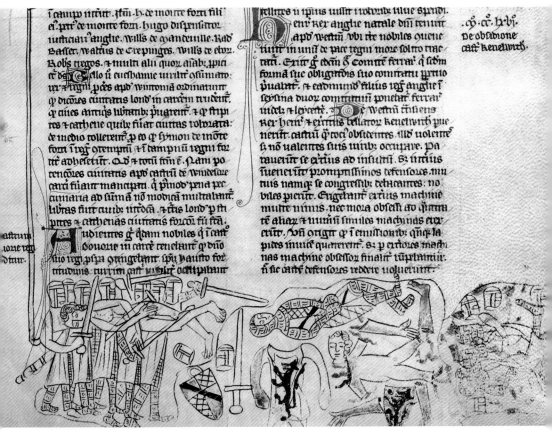

11. Richard of Cornwall, Henry's younger brother. A talented diplomat and businessman, his clash with Alfonso made Eleanor's first years in England miserable. He was, however, the person Eleanor trusted with her children when she departed on Crusade.

12. A man of exceptional abilities, Simon de Montfort brought England to civil war and held Eleanor captive for a year. His epochal death restored her to fortune, but cast a long shadow.

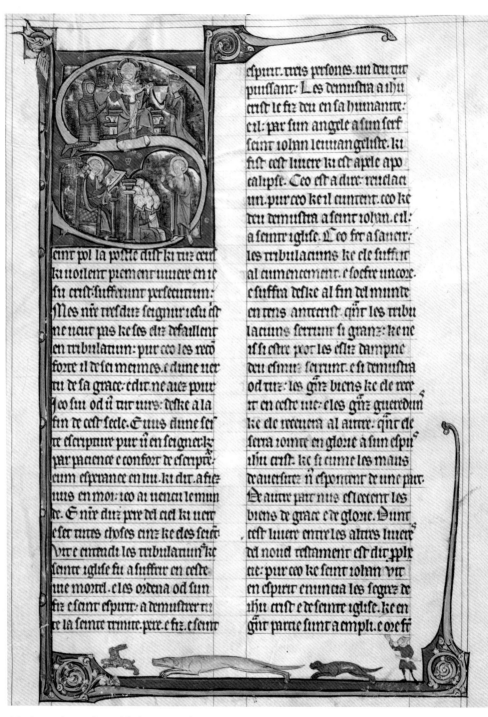

13. A product of troubled times – the Douce Apocalypse. Eleanor and her arms appear with Edward in the initial capital, proof that even with limited resources Eleanor could not resist commissioning books …

et uidi equos in uisione et qui sedebant super eos habebant loricas igneas et iacinctinas et sulphureas. Et capita equorum erant tanquam capita leonum et de ore ipsorum procedit ignis et fumus et sulphur ab hijs tribus plagis occisa est tertia pars hominum de igne et de fumo et de sulphure qui procedebat de ore ipsorum. Potestas enim equorum in ore ipsorum est et in caudis eorum. Nam caude eorum similes serpentibus habentes capita et in hijs nocent. et ceteri homines qui non sunt occisi in hijs plagis neque penitentiam egerunt de operibus manuum suarum ut non adorarent demonia et symulacra aurea et argentea et erea et lapidea et lignea que neque uidere possunt neque audire neque ambulare. et non egerunt penitenciam ab homicidijs suis neque a ueneficijs suis neque a furtis suis.

In hoc loco per equos insani pphi. per sessores auium equorum principes terre designantur. per loricas siquietes gladiorum a se repellunt. duricia condicio reproborum significatur. que ad corda eorum gladio spiritus quod est uerbum dei accedere non sinit. Et ueloce igneae iacinctine et sulphuree esse dicuntur. per ignem plane crudelitas mentis persecutorum. Per iacinctum qui celi figuram habet honor terrenus quibus suis se ferebant. per sulphur uero qui fetet blasphemie quas in xpm proferebant designatur. Per secutores igitur loricas igneas et iacinctinas. et cetera.

14. Or making jokes – here highlighting her least favourite people: Simon de Montfort (with his banner of a forked-tailed lion) fighting for the beast …

15. ... and Gilbert of Gloucester, whose arms fly above the forces of darkness. The later unacceptability of this joke may explain why the book was never completed.

16. The castle and town of the Peak (Peveril Castle and Castleton) was the only part of Eleanor's property empire to remain with her from the first dower to her death.

17. The Chateau of Mauléon. Acquired by Edward during a period of exile in the troubled years of the early 1260s, it was the location for his first venture into bastidisation. Eleanor and Edward would later return here with their son-in-law designate, the King of Aragon.

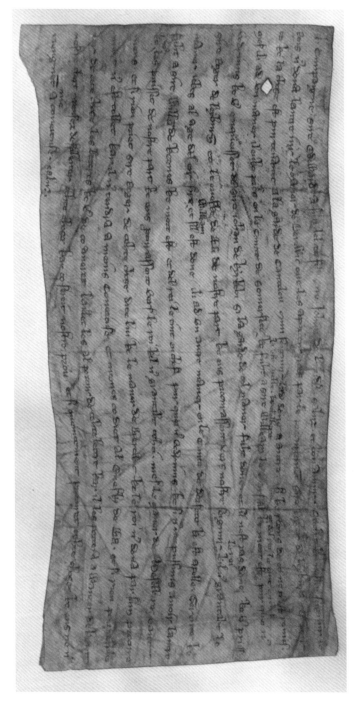

18. Eleanor commences her property business after the Barons' War. This is a draft letter explaining her planning and may even be in her own hand ...

19. Europe's foremost troublemaker – Charles of Anjou, younger brother of Louis IX. Diverting the Crusade to his own ends (with fatal results), holding Eleanor's brother prisoner and employing the young Montforts were just some of his sins.

20. Part of the immense complex of the Knights Hospitallers, where Eleanor spent over a year and gave birth to Joan 'of Acre'.

21. A thoughtful commission by Eleanor while at Acre, *The Lord Edward's Vegetius* is the first translation into Anglo-Norman of this key military manual. It conveys a subtle hint that Edward (pictured here with Vegetius) would learn from studying it. And the Welsh wars were to prove that he did just that …

22. This lively sea battle is possibly intended as a depiction of Hugh of Cyprus' rout of Sultan Baibars' fleet, and is characteristic of the books which Eleanor commissioned.

Above: 23. The Acre myth, at its most romantic, thanks to William Blake. There are plenty of other versions of the scene – some even more ridiculous …

Right: 24. These sketches in the Cotton Manuscript are not the most flattering depictions, but they are plainly intended to offer some form of resemblance.

Left: 25. These figures at Lincoln, however, though often referred to, are no safe guide. They have been restored extensively.

Below: 26. The hunting lady with dogs in the Alphonso Psalter – a commission by Eleanor for her son Alphonso – may well have been intended as a depiction of Eleanor. She shares face and eye shape with both the tomb effigy and the Cotton depictions.

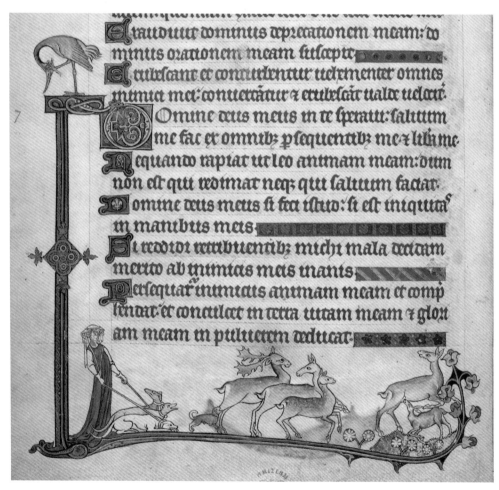

27. A marvellous testament to the tight ship Eleanor ran in business, this picture of one of her couriers explains their reputation for expedition. Note not only the speed, but also the use of Eleanor's Castilian arms.

Above left: 28. In contrast with earlier queens, Eleanor emphasised her power on her seal. Instead of the accepted floriated sceptre and an orb with peaceful dove, she adopts a position of power with a conventional sceptre, and the background is larded with references to her heritage. She is herself, not 'a queen'.
Above right: 29. Eleanor of Aquitaine's seal.

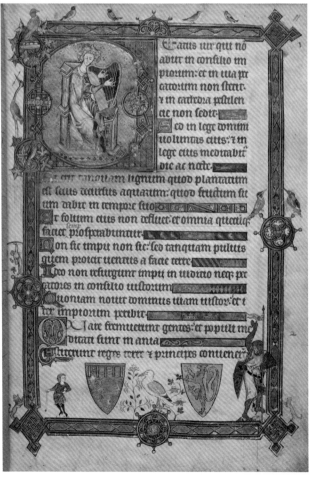

Above: 30. Eleanor's pet project – Leeds Castle. Though much changed over the years, her original concept of the 'gloriette', possibly derived from the 'pavilion on pool' type of Castilian garden, remains one of its notable charms.

Left: 31. The whole family loved birds – and Eleanor made sure that Alphonso would have enjoyment in his psalter, with amusing pictures of many varieties. The arms at the bottom reference Alphonso's projected marriage to the daughter of the Count of Holland.

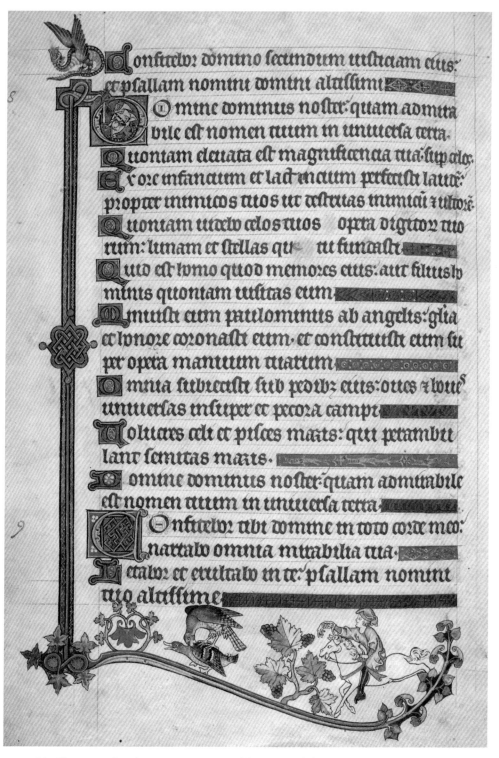

onfitelo2 domino fecundum iusticiam eius:
et pfallam nomine domini altissimi.
Domine dominus noster:quam admira
bile est nomen tuum in universa terra.
Quoniam elevata est magnificencia tua:sup celos.
Er ore infancium et lactencium perfecisti laude:
propter inimicos tuos ut destruas inimicu z ultore.
Quoniam videbo celos tuos opera digitoz tuo
rum: lunam et stellas qu tu fundasti.
Quid est homo quod memores eius: aut filius ho
minis quoniam visitas eum.
Minuisti eum paulominus ab angelis:gloria
et honore coronasti eum. et constituisti eum su
per opera manuum tuarum.
Omnia subiecisti sub pedibus eius:oues zboues
universas insuper et pecora campi.
Uolucres celi et pisces maris: qui perambu
lant semitas maris.
Domine dominus noster:quam admirabile
est nomen tuum in universa terra.
Confitebor tibi domine in toto corde meo:
narrabo omnia mirabilia tua.
Letabor et exultabo in te: pfallam nomini
tuo altissime.

32. The young boy hunting is very possibly young Alphonso, who was just emerging into
public view at the time of his death on the tenth anniversary of his parents' coronation.

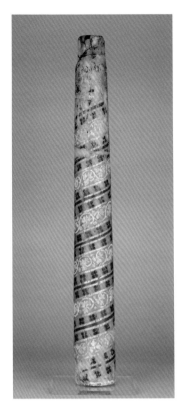

Above left: 33. He was buried at Westminster Abbey, and probably lies today here, where the bones of all Eleanor and Edward's dead children were joined with those of their aunt Katherine. The 'tomb' is in fact probably the original altar from St Edward the Confessor's shrine.

Above right: 34. Despite her taste for outdoor pursuits, and peripatetic life, Eleanor had a clear taste for domestic luxury. Records remain of her commissioning candles decorated in red and green, just like this one in the British Museum.

35. She even took her own goldsmith on campaign to Wales. This, however, is French work. The clasp, marked with Eleanor's arms, may have been a thoughtful Christmas gift from one of her inner circle.

36. Produced for an event in 1285 designed to encourage men to take up knighthood, the Winchester round table still graces the hall where it first was used. The Arthurian themes may well have been Eleanor's idea.

37. An unsubtle reminder that the Plantagenets had arrived, Conwy Castle played host to Eleanor during the course of its construction and was the site of one of the many gardens made especially for her.

38. But it is at Caernarfon that Eleanor's influence is most clearly felt. The Eagle Tower is plainly intended to reference 'The Dream of Macsen Wledig' in the *Mabinogion* (exactly the kind of tales in which Eleanor took an interest) – but it also bears a more than passing resemblance to the Castilian castle on Eleanor's arms.

39. Eleanor's wardrobe book shows the small doings of her household. Here we see them brought to a grinding halt by the words '*Decessus Regine*', marking Eleanor's death.

40. Eleanor's death continued to be marked by her family and friends for years to come. Here it is inserted into the calendar in the Alphonso Psalter, which passed to her daughter Elizabeth, and from her to Eleanor's faithful servants, the Haustede family.

Left: 41. The tomb of Eleanor's childhood acquaintance Isabelle of Aragon gives the lie to the suggestion that portraiture was not intended (note her sweet, dimpled hands). It also provides fascinating contrasts with Eleanor's tomb.

Below: 42. Eleanor's effigy is gilt bronze, like a great king, and she is presented as if for coronation, with flowing robes and loose hair. The full view of her tomb shows a striking resemblance between her seal and her final effigy.

Right: 43. This modern reproduction of the lost Lincoln viscera tomb provides an impression of how the shields would have appeared in the Westminster Abbey tomb.

Below: 44. Sheltered from public view, the ambulatory side of Eleanor's tomb echoes her tendency to hide away. But again, her full heritage is emphasised in the shields.

45. A few feet away and standing guard over Eleanor's tomb is that of Edward. Amusingly, he achieved the simple tomb to which Ferdinand, Berengaria and Louis IX had all aspired.

Right: 46. The one depiction which remains of the Stamford Cross: The Revd Dr William Stukeley's diary sketch of the excavated top portion, with its roses.

Below right: 47. The first and least obviously lovely of the surviving crosses, the Geddington Cross, situated near the site of one of Eleanor's favourite hunting areas as well as many of her properties, has an idiosyncratic charm.

Below left: 48. It is little changed from how it appears here, lovingly recorded by the Society of Antiquaries in their *Vetusta Monumenta* in the late eighteenth century.

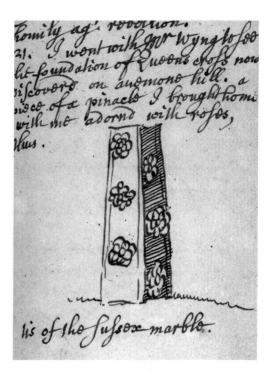

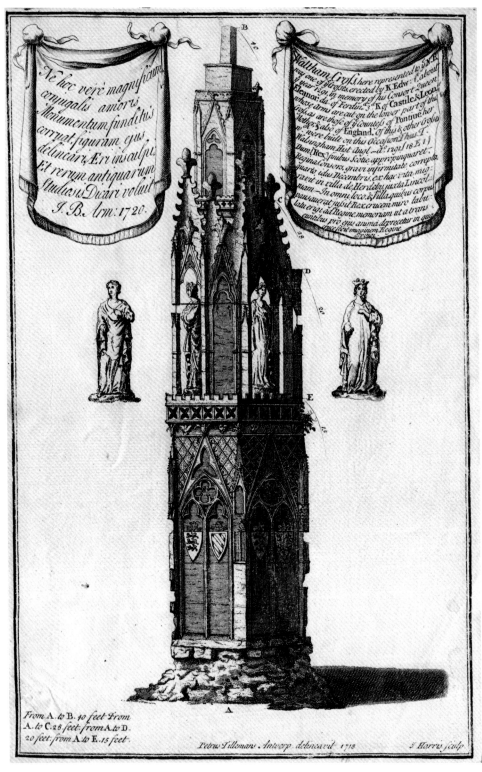

49. One of the first prints of an Eleanor cross, this 1716 depiction of the Hardingstone Cross marks the turning point for the fortunes of the crosses.

50. The record of the
Hardingstone Cross's
restoration in 1713, now
sited to one side of the cross,
with some of the remants of
the repaired statues.

51. By the end of the century
the crosses were fawned
over by antiquarians, as
Cruikshank mockingly
shows ...

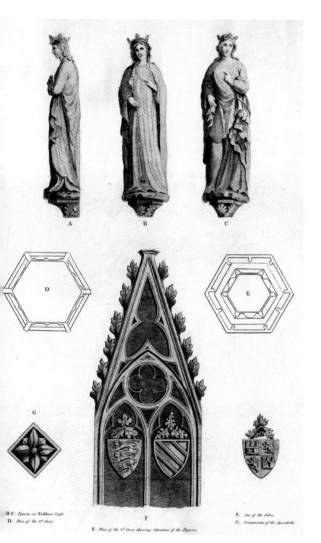

B.C. *Figure on Waltham Cross.*
D. *Plan of the 1st Story.*
E. *Plan of the 2d Story shewing Situation of the Figures.*
F. *One of the Sides.*
G. *Ornaments of the Spandrels.*

52 & 53. But restoration was needed: the tender attentions of the passing carriages are all too apparent in the *Vetusta Monumenta* depiction of Waltham Cross. Each *Vetusta Monumenta* depiction also showed details of the crosses, enabling the layouts to be discerned and details of the figures appreciated.

The 2 of May. 1643. y Croſſe in Cheapeſide was pulled downe, a Troope of Horſe & 2 Companies of foote wayted to garde it & at y fall of y tope Croſſe dromes beat tru pets blew & multitudes of Caper warre throwne in y Ayre. & a greate Shoute of People with ioy, y 2 of May the Almana ke ſareth, was y invention of the Croſſe. & 6 day at night was the Leaden Popes burnt. in the pla ce where it ſtood with ringinge of Bells, & a greate Acclamation & no hurt done in all theſe actions.

10 of May the Boocke of Sportes vpon the Lords day was bu rnt by the Hangman in the place where the Croſſe ſtoode, & at Exchange

54. The object of a hate campaign for years, the Cheapside Cross is destroyed – to great acclaim – in 1643.

55. But modern homages continue to be made. The nineteenth-century Charing Cross is the most famous, but this tribute in Stamford was raised at the start of the twenty-first century. The surviving rose detail on the original Stamford Cross forms the basis of the design.

56. And, now rescued from the more obtrusive attentions of restorers, the Hardingstone Cross still stands by the A45 (London Road), reminding passers-by of one of England's most remarkable queens.

10

The Queen's Work

With Eleanor installed as queen, the sources for her life become slightly more forthcoming. But this in itself presents a problem, as the years which were to follow were so crowded with a variety of events and interests that a chronological treatment cannot hope to do justice to the evidence which emerges. Left only in that format, it is hard for the woman and her interests to emerge from the welter of detail. The next three chapters therefore consider in turn three key aspects of Eleanor's life as queen: her work, her own personality and interests, and her family. This should enable the reader to see key themes which run through the remaining fabric of her life, and appreciate how they come together, when the story returns to a chronological format.

The story which this chapter tells is how Eleanor, more or less uniquely among English queens, managed to combine her day job as queen with carrying on another full-time professional job as a businesswoman dealing in property. In flat contrast to her later reputation as a modest and retiring queen, she was, in effect, an essential member of Edward's cabinet, dealing with an important and discrete job on his behalf. In so doing, she worked incredibly hard, driving her team mercilessly, and gained a reputation for being an implacable person who should not be flouted.

As this story takes us so far from the preconceived notion of Eleanor, it is obviously important to make the case good from the evidence; and herein lies a problem, for while a huge amount of material relating to the details of Eleanor's properties and dealings has been uncovered and analysed (principally by John Carmi Parsons in his magisterial *Eleanor of Castile, Queen and Society in Thirteenth Century England*), the details do not easily illustrate the overall picture. Each transaction is too small to be significant, but in getting into the details of the transactions, the overall picture recedes. One therefore has to effectively pan in and out from the detailed picture over a period of time to provide a synthesised perspective.

The best starting point for considering Eleanor's work is probably to step back and look at what she achieved overall and how she was perceived by contemporaries at the time. As to this, the bottom line is simple. The funds available to thirteenth-century queens had fallen way below the amounts which were required. Eleanor instituted a programme of land acquisition and management which effectively balanced the books, more than doubling the revenue available.

Eleanor and Edward had, of course, been plagued by financial difficulties since their marriage, and one might imagine that once he had acceded to the throne all such worries would be over. However, this was far from the case. The loss of the Angevin lands in France was a major blow to the financial position of the English monarchy, which had led to a pressing need to increase revenues from England. At the same time, Crown spending had increased sharply. Henry III had acquired a number of earldoms of greater or lesser financial use, but had granted them all away to family members. Edward himself, despite a highly aggressive policy of land acquisition in his own right, still had revenues in the 1280s of less than £19,000 per year and simply could not afford to follow the traditional route of allowing Eleanor to hold her dower lands during his lifetime.[1]

The difficulties facing them are illustrated by the fact that, even with Eleanor turning her attention actively to revenue generation and even as queen, it can be seen that from time to time she had recourse to the standard expedients to help her cash flow. So in June 1290 we find her selling a cup and a brooch, and in 1289 she borrowed funds from friends to cover some of her building works. Moreover we can see that she assigned debts and made substantial payments (over £2,000 between 1286 and 1290) to Edward's preferred bankers, the Ricciardi, which suggests that she had debts to them.

Why was Eleanor short of money? Some extent of the scale of the funds a Queen of England required can be seen by a consideration of Eleanor of Provence's position; even with her somewhat controversial and remunerative use of grants of wardship, Henry III still had to subsidise her heavily during his reign and acknowledged the kinds of amounts she would need (albeit on the smaller scale of a widow) by increasing her dower assignment to £4,000 per annum. This suggests that, as queen, with a greater household and responsibilities, Eleanor would be likely to need a larger sum even than that. Parsons suggests the figure required was somewhere in the region of £6,000 to £8,000 per annum and calculates her 1289–90 expenditure as being £8,800 once wardrobe expenses, alms, wages, household expenses and other miscellaneous payments are counted. While 1289–90 was probably an atypically expensive year, and the expenditure figures may be open to some argument, the material does suggest that some thousands of pounds per annum were required.[2]

On the other side of the balance sheet, the funds available to a Queen of England had become hopelessly inadequate. Since the change from the practice as to the holding of dower during the king's life, queens had been substantially reliant on 'queen's gold'; that is effectively a tax of 10 per cent of any fine above 10 marks or on any tax of the Jewry. This source produced wildly varying sums depending on the number and level of fines levied in a year – between the fourteenth and sixteenth years of Edward's reign they varied between just short of £500 and some £1,400 per annum – but at no time did they come close to the kinds of sums required.

While, in addition to queen's gold, a king would regularly grant his wife debts, reliefs or fines owed him, this source of income was erratic and unreliable – and highly unlikely to bridge the yawning financial gap. The same is true for simple cash gifts from the king or third parties. A combination of circumstances had meant that it was not until the thirteenth century that English queens were in a position to try to grapple with the problem, Eleanor of Aquitaine's freedoms being somewhat contracted by Henry II after her rebellion and Berengaria of Navarre and Isabella of Angoulême being placed by their respective husbands in a position of even more complete financial dependence.

Eleanor of Provence's approach to the problem had met with very mixed success and garnered her very considerable unpopularity. She had probed the very limits of queen's gold with her attempts to extend its ambit, leading to considerable complaint. She had also shown clearly that wardships and associated marriages were a politically dangerous source, and therefore they were an unsafe route for substantial revenue generation. Further, even with all their disadvantages, they still did not provide sufficient revenue.[3]

Eleanor therefore had to look for other means to bridge this gap. How she did so was to assemble, more or less from a standing start, a property portfolio of considerable extent and value. By the time of her death, her properties were bringing in somewhere between £2,500 and £2,600 annually, i.e. the most significant portion of her income; and, it will be recalled, roughly two and a half times the large dower which Eleanor de Montfort had from one of the largest estates in England. This landholding was kept intact as a separate estate after her death; run as 'Terre Regine' until Edward's second marriage to Margaret of France, the land then passed to her as dower and formed the backbone of English queens' dower assignment for the next century. Eleanor therefore created a great estate.

The extent of this achievement is underlined by how she was actually perceived. The clearest accounts which we have of Eleanor actually relate to her land-gathering activities, and are not flattering. The most straightforward is the simple ditty ascribed by Walter of Guisborough to the common people of the time: 'The king would like to get our gold/

The queen our manors fair to hold.' Also pithy is the epitaph provided by the Dunstable annalist: 'A Spaniard by birth, who obtained many fine manors.' So, even among those who had no direct contact with it, Eleanor's involvement in property acquisition was so extensive as to have become well known. When the annalists thought of Eleanor, they thought of business.[4]

One important point to note is that the queen herself was associated directly in the endeavour even by the gossips – and that gossip was true. There are numerous surviving pieces of correspondence which show Eleanor taking an active part in decision making, dealing with a variety of administrative details: the enclosure of a tract of land, a confirmation of a conveyance – even an allocation of wine or a recently arrived shipment. There are also letters which show her staff reporting to her, and plainly expecting her to be au fait with quite minor details, or apologising for not reporting to her in person – again indicating that she is expected to be keenly interested. There are letters from her most frequent man of business, alluding in passing to the details of the business 'which we spoke about', and advising her to consider the position in relation to specific portions of her holdings. The evidence, then, is quite clear – Eleanor was personally involved in her own business empire, right down to the level of fine detail. This is in sharp contrast with Eleanor of Provence, who did have land dealings herself, albeit on a smaller and more random scale. Her land dealings were seen (accurately) as being run for her by professionals. So Matthew Paris pictured Eleanor of Provence's estates steward William of Tarrant as a man who thirsted for money as a horse leech after blood, but he did not associate the queen with his misdeeds.[5]

More lengthy, but equally to the point, in particular in associating Eleanor as an active participant in the property dealings of her office, are two letters from the Archbishop of Canterbury, Archbishop Pecham: one in 1283 and one in 1286.[6] In the first, the archbishop focuses on dealings with the Jews and usury, referring to her property dealings in a sideswipe:

... for God's sake, my lady, when you receive land or manor acquired by usury of the Jews, take heed that it is a mortal sin to those who take the usury and those who support it, and those who have a share in it, if they do not return it. And therefore I say to you, my very dear lady, before God and before the Court of Heaven, that you cannot retain things thus acquired, if you do not make amends to those that have lost them, in another way, as much as they are worth more than the principal debt. You must therefore return the things thus acquired to the Christians who have lost them, saving to yourself as much as the principal debt amounts to, for more the usurer cannot give you. My lady, know that I am telling you the lawful truth, and if anyone give you to understand anything else he is a heretic. I do not believe that you retain in any other manner things thus acquired, but I would wish to know it by your letter, so that I can make it known to those who think otherwise ...

In the second letter, from 1286 to Geoffrey de Aspale, the keeper of Eleanor's wardrobe, we see that his mind has not been put at rest:

A rumour is growing strong throughout the kingdom of England and much scandal is thereby generated, because it is said that the illustrious lady queen of England, in whose service you are, is occupying many manors of nobles and lands and other possessions, and has made them her own property – lands which the Jews extorted with usury under the protection of the royal court from Christians. It is said that day by day the said lady continues to acquire property and the possessions of others by this means with the assistance (though we ourselves do not believe it) of certain clerics who are followers of the devil and not of Christ. There is gossip and debate about this in every part of England. Wherefore, as a gain of this sort is illicit and damnable, we beg you, and firmly command and enjoin you as our clerk, that when you see an opportunity you will be pleased humbly to beseech the said lady on our behalf, that she bid her people to abstain entirely from the these practices, and to restore what has been thus seized, or at any rate make satisfaction to those Christians who have been wickedly robbed by usury.

While the full extent of Pecham's assertions may be open to doubt – the evidence of the annalists tends to cast doubt on his suggestion of gossip and debate in every part of England – the picture is fairly clear. Eleanor acquired a very serious landholding – one sufficiently large to be the subject of talk which troubled the archbishop – and she did so via practices which some might regard as rather sharp or even morally reprehensible.

We can be sure that Eleanor did not do this on her own initiative. Her abilities and training may have enabled her to take a very active part in the business, and even made the role a fulfilling one for her, but the truth is that the plan to acquire a substantial and certain landholding to provide revenue and a source of patronage for a Queen of England was one which was authorised by Edward and which dovetailed very neatly with his coronation oath to regain as much of the land dispersed by his predecessors as was possible.

The plan may be one which was initiated well before Henry III's death – as evidenced by Eleanor's early dealings in property, and her close involvement in those dealings. But it is clear that, on return from the Crusade and after the coronation, the plan was picked up and put into action as swiftly as possible and with considerable business focus. Again the distinction between the two Eleanors, Castile and Provence, is clear in the evidence and was specifically noted by Eleanor of Provence's biographer.[7]

Having set the scene for what Eleanor was to achieve, one can now turn to look in more detail at how she went about this process. A good way in to this story is to consider the court's movements in the year which followed the coronation. This illustrates how Eleanor reacquainted herself with her existing properties and set about familiarising herself with potential acquisitions. The most straightforward aspect of it is neatly illustrated with one of the first bits of business of 1275: a visit to the New Forest.

The New Forest location reflects a part of the small property portfolio which Eleanor was nurturing before her departure on Crusade; between 1266 and 1270 she had acquired the manor of Ringwood and the issues and profits of the New Forest. So we see that one of her first interests, once the coronation and Edward's necessary business was seen to, was to get back in touch with her existing estates – in person if possible.

But there was far more going on than this simple story shows. As we know, Eleanor had turned her attention to getting a revised dower assignment. There were two reasons for this. The first was simply the need to keep pace with her mother-in-law – Eleanor of Provence had induced Henry III to increase her dower assignment to £4,000 in 1262. Eleanor would have been very unusual if she was not vexed to think that she had a quarter of the dower assignment which her mother-in-law had, and very imprudent if she had not looked ahead to the possibility of coping on such a sum if she were ever widowed (as she had so nearly been on Crusade).

Secondly, if a revision of the dower assignment was necessary, and if she was to commence work building up a property portfolio, practicality dictated that now was the time to revise the dower assignment; that way, the new dower assignment could form the nucleus of her future business dealings, so that her existing properties and those which she was to hold in dower would run well together administratively. So throughout this period, Eleanor and her team will have been liaising with Edward's team to audit which of the properties he had in his gift or which could be brought into play, could best be transferred to her to form part of her new dower and fit with her plans for future expansion.

This planning process for the revised dower can be seen from an even earlier trip – in fact the very first trip taken following the royal couple's return to England and coronation in December 1274. This excursion took them to Northampton, then on to Fotheringhay, King's Cliffe near Peterborough, and the hunting lodge of Geddington near Corby (later the site of one of the Eleanor crosses raised by Edward), looping back inland via Overstone. There at first appears no very good reason for this itinerary.

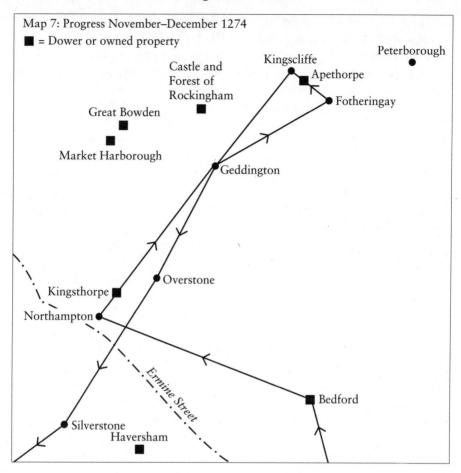

Map 7: Progress November–December 1274

■ = Dower or owned property

Peterborough

Kingscliffe

Apethorpe

Castle and Forest of Rockingham

Fotheringay

Great Bowden

Market Harborough

Geddington

Overstone

Kingsthorpe

Northampton

Ermine Street

Bedford

Silverstone

Haversham

However, before the Crusade, Eleanor had built up a decent holding at Great Bowden and Market Harborough, which lie just a little north of Geddington; and she had also acquired Kingsthorpe, which lies just outside Northampton and practically next door to Overstone. These original holdings were supplemented in the 1275 dower with properties nearby, but just over the Northamptonshire border: Apethorpe and the castle and forest of Rockingham. Fascinatingly, these two properties were cheek by jowl with King's Cliffe and Fotheringhay, where the court stayed. It therefore very much looks as if, on this trip, Eleanor and her team were not simply looking at existing properties, but actively scoping out suitable extra properties to be added to her dower. Also consistent with this is an early stop at Luton on the way north, which fits nicely with the later grant to Eleanor of the town of Bedford as part of her dower assignment.

Similarly, a stay which was made at the start of 1275 in Wiltshire offered an opportunity to review a grant to Eleanor in November 1274 of lands at Compton Chamberlayne and the grant to her in the 1275 dower assignment of the nearby farms of Bedwyn and Wexcombe. These were later to become the heart of one of her key property groups.[8]

Yet another example comes in immediately after the birth of the next baby, Margaret, in March of 1275, where we find in the itinerary a trip to Aylesbury, which later becomes part of the revised dower allocation. Also part of the revised dower allocation were the manor and forest of Brill and the farm of Wycombe – and these were probably viewed on this occasion from Risborough, where the court stayed briefly before reaching Aylesbury. The Aylesbury stop was followed by a stop in Balsham (more or less the location of the modern-day Gatcombe Park), Bury St Edmunds and Lavenham. These stops were suitable for pilgrimage, as was appropriate after a return from Crusade (and indeed replicate a round of pilgrimages previously pursued by Henry III); but they were also very convenient to enable Eleanor to inspect existing properties, in particular her holding at Dullingham in Cambridgeshire, some recent acquisitions at Badmondisfield, as well as Soham, which was to form part of the revised dower assignment. Piety and practicality could therefore be combined.

Once the requisite stay at Westminster for Parliament had been completed, the theme comes to the fore again. In August 1275, the royal progress went north. While a part of the trip constituted a stop within Edward's lordship of Chester, the journeys to and from Chester were so made as to enable the party to take in, along the way, Eleanor's future dower properties in Warwickshire, the very significant acquisitions via dower of Derby and Macclesfield and a second view of the Leicestershire and Northamptonshire properties.[9]

It is also possible to trace a certain amount of tying in of properties further afield. So, reverting to Eleanor's earlier holdings in Somerset, prior to Crusade, Eleanor had lands in the neighbourhood of Dundon and Somerton. To these, she immediately added on her return a further wardship at Barwick. A stay at Eleanor of Provence's manor in Gillingham in Dorset (a place which that lady abominated for 'the greasy smoky vapours which rise in the evenings') in December 1275 would have had Eleanor and her team well placed to visit those properties and that of nearby Camel and Kingsbury, which were added as part of the dower assignment in October 1275. In the dower assignment was also added a further block of properties further north in Somerset: the farms of Cheddar, Axbridge and Congresbury.[10]

It is therefore possible to see quite clearly, from the amount of time and effort taken, the work of the queen in putting together a property empire appearing as a priority for both king and queen in the immediate aftermath of the coronation; and it is also apparent that Eleanor must have been very hands-on in the management of this business. Property management could perfectly well have been deputed to staff. But instead we see the entire court traipsing around the country in her wake, as she inspected existing lands and assessed suitable future lands to add to her portfolio. Edward's approval of this paradigm is apparent in his bringing himself and the court along; it was of course open to him to let her go with her staff alone, or to insist that she relied on third-party assessments. The royal partnership might divide responsibilities, but it was a manifest partnership.

One can therefore see that Parsons is wrong when he says that there was little movement toward increasing Eleanor's estates between her return in August 1274 and the granting of the revised dower assignment in October 1275. There was in fact extensive work in the sense of planning – backed up by very active interest from both Eleanor and Edward.

The upshot of Eleanor's work was a revised dower assignment which was approved in October 1275. It amounted to £4,500 in English and Gascon lands, spread over twenty-two shires. So far as the English property was concerned, some of the more disparate elements of the 1254 dower were abandoned. To add to the blocks already outlined above, in Suffolk the castle and town of Orford and a number of farms (including Ipswich) were given. There was a huge grant of places in Derbyshire and Nottinghamshire (Ashbourne, Bolsover, Derby, Horston, Wirkworth, Clipston and Mansfield), which were added to complement her holdings around the Peak. There was also a significant block in Essex, the castles and towns of Bristol and Odiham and the city of Lincoln, accompanied by the town of Grimsby and the Soke of Caistor. Eleanor also received a considerable dower in Gascony: £2,000 per annum comprising Millan and Harbefaure and the castles, towns and forests there, with customs revenue from Bordeaux making up the shortfall.[11]

But Eleanor's work was far from done when the revised dower assignment was over. What followed thereafter was a careful acquisition of properties which complemented her existing portfolio and her dower. An example of how this seems to have been done can be traced through from a couple of examples pieced together by Parsons. The first example is her holding in Norfolk. It will be recalled that Eleanor had acquired the manor of Aylsham first at pleasure, and then in fee for life, together with some lands at Scottow, a little east of Aylsham. In late 1275 she acquired a manor at Scottow, with the advowson and member at Great Hautbois (then part of the hundred of South Erpingham). This was obtained via one of her Jewish connections. Having acquired these properties, Eleanor then arranged for her 1275 dower to include Cawston with the hundred of South Erpingham. This property was adjacent to Scottow and Aylsham and had been surrendered voluntarily to Edward by John de Burgh, the grandson of Henry III's regent Hubert de Burgh, to rid himself of an inherited debt to the Crown. In later years Eleanor would then build on this solid base, to add in 1278 Burgh 'next Aylsham'. Significantly, this

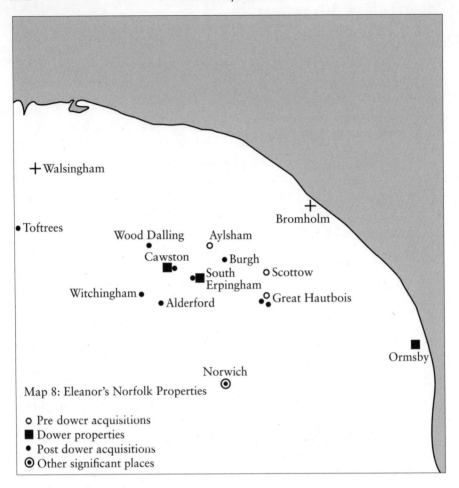

+ Walsingham

+
Bromholm

● Toftrees

Wood Dalling   Aylsham
● ● ○
Cawston   ● Burgh
■■ ● ■ South   ○ Scottow
■ Erpingham
Witchingham ●   ○
● Alderford   ●○ Great Hautbois
●

■
Ormsby

Norwich
◉

Map 8: Eleanor's Norfolk Properties

○ Pre dower acquisitions
■ Dower properties
● Post dower acquisitions
◉ Other significant places

was a move which was probably contemplated even at the time of the dower assignment, since Eleanor moved to acquire all John de Burgh's debts owed to the Jewry in November 1275 – just a month after the dower assignment.

Also interesting is the fact that Burgh was not finally acquired until after Edward and Eleanor had toured Norfolk in 1277. Again, as with the dower, it would appear Eleanor wanted, if possible, to view properties before any irrevocable steps were taken. This can be seen again when in 1281 (following another Norfolk trip) Eleanor added supplementary lands around Great Hautbois as the former owner's affairs went from bad to worse, following another acquisition of his debts owed to the Jewry in May 1275. Later still, in 1288, Witchingham and Alderford, lying to the south of Cawston, were added to the group. Eleanor also acquired some strategically placed wardships nearby in 1284 and 1285. Thus a core holding was in place to begin, and at the time of the dower both dower properties and future acquisitions were effectively marked down, with steps being taken to be ready to make acquisitions later. After that, any unrelated but convenient individual properties could be added.[12]

This set of acquisitions hints that one approach adopted was to monitor estates that were being dissipated and put herself in a position to reunite them. Further support for this theory is given by the situation in Eleanor's Kent holdings. Here the Crevequer family had held a barony based around Chatham, but it had been split into three parts – one being pledged by the heir, Robert, to the Jews, another part (including Leeds Castle) likewise pledged by William de Leyburn (son of Edward's old associate Roger), and a third (including Chatham itself) being in the hands of one Roger Loveday. Robert Crevequer was a part of Eleanor's household in 1290, being one of her household knights, and swapped other properties with Eleanor in 1283. It is at least possible that her knowledge of the details of the family's affairs came direct from him; it may be that he, like John de Burgh, alienated his inheritance willingly in order to free himself from inherited debts. In any event, Eleanor acquired an interest in the Crevequer debts in early 1275, and one in the Leyburn debts a month after the dower assignment was completed. There then seems to have been work behind the scenes to procure the transfer of these properties, and the purchase of the Loveday share, which resulted in transfers of all three parts of the barony to Eleanor in mid- to late 1278. Thereafter it would appear that Eleanor visited with her project managers in October of that year, while the court was nearby in Gillingham and Teynham en route for Canterbury; and then the builders were sent in.

A similar approach can be seen in her Leicestershire properties discussed above, where an acquisition of a convenient estate at Welham, near the Market Harborough grouping, was made in 1276, but Eleanor had already been the holder of debts owed to the Jewry by its owner.[13]

Another way in which Eleanor and her team went about building up her portfolio can be illustrated by her estates in Gloucester and Wiltshire. Here, she had a fairly limited dower assignment – the castle and town of Bristol and farms of Bedwyn and Wexcombe and no previous holdings. Additions were made to these assigned properties in 1279–80 when Eleanor purchased the manors of Great Sherston, which was about equidistant between her two holdings, and Woodrow, which was just south of Sherston. So far the story provides nothing remarkable, but this grouping yields two letters which show Eleanor and her team considering acquisitions specifically by reference to their location relative to her existing holdings. Thus, shortly after the Sherston and Woodrow acquisitions, follow these letters about a potential acquisition at Didmarton – in Gloucestershire, but just a few miles from Sherston. The first came from her bailiff John le Botiller – addressed direct to Eleanor – advising that he has heard from a local woman of a piece of land which would be a convenient acquisition for Eleanor, being close to Sherston, and has acted on the information, entering on the property. But within a few days a certain Sir Robert Burdon had ejected Botiller, claiming it was his land. Botiller suggests the queen get the king to act to get the land back.

A short while later comes another letter direct to Eleanor about this transaction, this time from the man who had sold Sherston and Woodrow to her. He is keen to pass on the news that, fortuitously, Sir Robert Burdon has died, leaving even more land in the vicinity; and a manor at Devizes, too. Anticipating her keen interest, he has taken custody of the small boy whose land this was to be, so that the queen could get the wardship of him, and thus the lands – since, as he notes, the wardship and marriage will be of great profit to her.

Following the initial misfire, Eleanor acted on the second tip-off and obtained the wardship of young Burdon and thus possession of the lands at Oldbury, practically next door to Didmarton and at Poulshot, similarly close to Woodrow. Young Nicholas Burdon was taken into Eleanor's children's household. However, it appears that Eleanor did take over Didmarton again following the death of Sir Robert and held it against her own ward until the inquest on her lands following her death, when it was proved that the original information from John le Botiller was false; the woman to whom he spoke held the land from Burdon and had no right to grant it to Eleanor. This story shows very clearly that those who dealt with Eleanor, either regularly or in relation to one-off transactions, knew she personally was actively looking for properties conveniently sited near her existing holdings and acted on that knowledge. It also shows that when such properties did become available, she acted with expedition to take them under her wing.

This Gloucester–Wiltshire holding was still further supplemented as the years went on. In 1284, a further acquisition of lands in wardship at Acton Turville added to the Sherston holding. Then in 1287 she gained Uley to add to the northern Sherston group and Erlestoke, Rowde and a manor at Yatesbury near to Poulshot in the southern group. Finally, in 1288, via a wardship in the Walerand family (considered further below), three further holdings were added to the southern group – another manor at Yatesbury, one at Market Lavington and one at Keevil. If one maps these acquisitions on a before-and-after basis, one can see clearly the impact of what has been achieved.

As for oversight by Eleanor herself, these two groups split neatly to be within range of places which she would visit regularly anyway: the northern Sherston group of properties was within reach of a favoured spring retreat at Quenington and Down Ampney, while the southern group was close to Marlborough and Upavon, where fairly lengthy regular stays were also made. So, for example, in 1279 Edward and Eleanor were

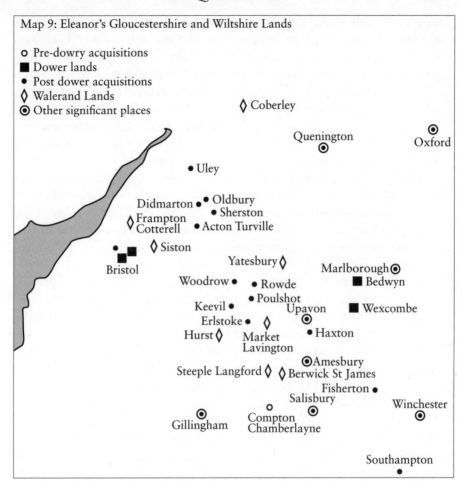

Map 9: Eleanor's Gloucestershire and Wiltshire Lands

○ Pre-dowry acquisitions
■ Dower lands
● Post dower acquisitions
◊ Walerand Lands
◉ Other significant places

Coberley

Quenington
Oxford

● Uley

Didmarton ● Oldbury
● Sherston
◊ Frampton
Cotterell ● Acton Turville

◊ Siston

Yatesbury ◊

Bristol

Marlborough ◉
Woodrow ● ● Rowde
■ Bedwyn
● Poulshot
Keevil ● Upavon ■ Wexcombe
Erlstoke ● ◊
Hurst ◊ Market ● Haxton
Lavington

◉ Amesbury
Steeple Langford ◊ ◊ Berwick St James
Fisherton ●
Salisbury
Winchester ◉
Gillingham Compton ◉
Chamberlayne

Southampton
●

at Quenington in March and December and in 1280 they were in Upavon and Marlborough at the end of February, and at Quenington and Down Ampney in March.[14]

One can therefore see a variety of different techniques being used by Eleanor and her team to put together a current landholding which was administratively streamlined, and which would sit well with her dower assignment. Crown grants formed a part of this, albeit a relatively small one. Otherwise Eleanor either acquired directly, or through debts owed to the Jewry, properties from individuals who wished or needed to sell portions of their lands.

The idea of acquiring lands via the debts of the person entitled to the land appears at first unattractive, and has been in part responsible for the rather poor press that Eleanor's land-gathering business has acquired over the years. At first blush, what it appears to suggest is the acquisition of debts and then rather ruthless foreclosure. However, closer examination shows that this hypothesis seems to be wide of the mark. In fact, the disposal of lands (and the redemption of their debt to the Jewry, on which compound interest was doubtless being charged) was often seen as a desirable step by those in question. For example, John de Burgh in Norfolk was keen to clear himself of inherited debt and had already voluntarily surrendered some of his properties to Edward, who included them in the dower assignment; and Robert de Crevequer remained on sufficiently good terms with Eleanor to be a knight of her household and be offered preferments in Wales as the years went by.

Indeed, this is something of a theme – while acquiring an endowment for herself, Eleanor's activities were capable of being positively helpful to those whose lands she acquired; Crevequer, for example, was given life tenure in other lands, which was presumably of more use to him than the rump of a fractured barony and a load of debt. So too with John de Camoys, who conveyed his lands at Torpel and Upton to Eleanor – he was granted life tenure in other lands. Gilbert Pecche, whose debts enabled her to acquire properties in Kent, Essex, Suffolk and Cambridge, was given rents worth as much as the lands he conveyed. Most emphatically proving that the transactions should not be seen as hostile takeovers is the transaction of Leeds Castle concerning William Leyburn. His father, Roger, was a key ally in the Barons' War, and had been involved in helping with Eleanor's early property transactions; exploitation of the son would therefore be most unlikely. But the mutually beneficial nature of the transaction is actually demonstrated by Eleanor obtaining pardons of William and Roger's debts to the Jewry and to the Exchequer.

Further supporting the view that Eleanor's acquisitions were, if anything, more 'white knight' moves than the converse, Parsons notes that in the inquiry into Eleanor's property affairs which took place after her death only one of the fourteen individuals whose debts Eleanor obtained from the Jewry raised any complaint; and that one, as discussed below, may well have been a 'try on'. This apparently tendentious section of her business was therefore much less controversial than it at first appears.[15]

A consideration of Eleanor's property transactions quickly conveys to the reader a sense that she and her team were a very businesslike outfit. Confirming this, it has been noted by one commentator that Eleanor's achievement in carrying forward a surplus in her accounts to 1286 is a feat almost unprecedented in medieval financial administration. Glimpses of the detailed planning involved in putting together the estate peek though the record repeatedly. One example, the letter at the outset of Eleanor's property dealings in 1265, has already been cited. Another is seen in the acquisition of debts to the Jewry secured on properties which marched with properties to be included in the dower assignment. Nor were they isolated incidents; between December 1274 and mid-1275, Eleanor was granted the Jewish debts of four other debtors. All of these debts shortly after resulted in property acquisitions in convenient places for Eleanor's portfolio.

But perhaps the best example of forward planning is the wardship of the Walerand family, where planning can be traced for over a decade before the properties materialised. In 1273, Robert Walerand, a notable supporter of Henry III, died, leaving a wife and no children. His heirs were the infant sons of his brother, both of whom were apparently mentally handicapped and unable ever to run their own affairs. The wardship of the heirs – an unusually long-term prospect – was in Edward's hand, and at least one of the boys was sent to reside with Eleanor's children. But meanwhile, Eleanor kept her eye on the dower manors enjoyed by Robert's widow, Maud, which would normally pass into the wardship on her death. Instead, all of these were granted to Eleanor on Maud's death in 1288; and meanwhile Eleanor had already acted. Maud Walerand's death brought Eleanor properties in five different shires. In each Eleanor had already acquired properties in the immediate vicinity of those manors, so that the new acquisitions slotted in without trouble to an existing structure. One example has been described in the Wiltshire area above. If this had occurred in one county it might be dismissed as coincidence, but five counties with key acquisitions in each is beyond the realm of happenstance.[16]

One complementary point, which emphasises the professionalism of the endeavour in which Eleanor was engaged, is the fact that she did not take up properties which did not march conveniently with her acquisitions and which were therefore uneconomic for her to run; or if obliged to take them as part of a package deal, she took the first opportunity to rid herself of them. So, when acquiring Robert Burdon's properties near Sherston, she did not seek the wardship of the Devonshire estates, even though she had the heir in her household. In another transaction in 1280, lands in Dorset and Somerset were taken into wardship, but inconvenient lands at Aust on the Severn were disposed of to Bishop Giffard of Worcester. Similarly, an isolated wardship holding of Weeting in Norfolk was granted to the mother-in-law of the king's household steward, some outlying lands in Somerset were leased out and the less convenient part of the Crevequer barony was first leased to a dependent, and later swapped for a better prospect – the custom and rent of the port of Sandwich.[17]

How was all this business done? In terms of the administration of her property empire, Parsons has uncovered a good deal of illuminating material. For example, Eleanor's household included at least eight messengers, of whom about half were given the formal title *nuncius* while the remainder were only entitled *cursor*. These messengers were kept very busy indeed. In 1290 alone they carried messages to her bailiff at Macclesfield, her steward Hugh de Cressingham, her seneschal in the New Forest, her manors at Lyndhurst, Leeds and Haverford and to the treasurer of the Bishop of Ely, the sheriffs of Northumberland and Worcester, and messages to London, Sandwich and Oxford. What is more, her couriers were astonishingly speedy – perhaps the best example is that one managed three visits to France in six weeks. We actually have what appears to be a joking eyewitness depiction of one of them on some documents relating to Eleanora's wedding: the courier, carrying Eleanor's arms, is shown proceeding at such speed that his hair streams behind him in the wind.

By way of aside, the evidence of the messengers also shows the additional range of work undertaken by Eleanor as queen – in 1289–90 alone there is correspondence with the Archbishop of Canterbury, the bishops of Ely, Durham, Lincoln and Salisbury, and the earls of Lincoln, Ulster, Gloucester and Cornwall; as well as the incumbent and dowager countesses of Lincoln. All of these (except possibly the Lincoln correspondence, which may well have been either property related, since Lincoln was part of Eleanor's dower, or based in friendship, as the earl and countess were close friends) suggests a considerable role in broader public affairs. So too does the frequent despatch of messengers to France.[18]

As for the administration of her properties specifically, it will readily be appreciated that this required a department of its own. This was headed by the steward and later stewards of the queen's lands. Walter de Kancia was the first, later (from 1276) holding the position together with Geoffrey de Piccheford. He was later succeeded by William de St Claro and then Hugh de Cressingham. There was a separate steward for the New Forest, but he ranked lower, with the queen's local bailiffs. These bailiffs were effectively the next step down, being the 'officer in charge' of lands within their geographical remit. They were in charge of trading as necessary with the produce of the estate and producing accounts, which would then be passed on to the queen's auditor, John de Lovetot.

Effectively, Eleanor's lands were divided up geographically and placed in the hands of a bailiff responsible for each area; thus a group of properties in the same locale would all be administered by the same man. The bailiffs were a mixed bunch. Some appear to have gained their places through contacts in Eleanor's household. So Robert de Bures may well have been related to Eleanor's 'garderobius', and John de Ponte was tied to Walter de Kancia. John de Cretingham came from a village near the homes of both Geoffrey de Aspale and the queen's knight Adam de Cretyng. Others, sensibly enough, were locals. The most obvious example is Thomas de Macclesfield, but Robert de Petra, the bailiff at Cawston, was from Aylsham, John de la Woderowe at Didmarton probably hailed from Eleanor's manor of Woodrow in Washlingstone and Brenchly, Walter de Chidecroft had been in the employ of the Crevequer family, and in Lincolnshire Roger de Walcote came from a family near Eleanor's holdings at Nocton. The local origins of John le Botiller at Woodrow in Wiltshire are suggested by the information conveyed to her by him.

Overall, there were effectively seven departments or bailiwicks in which Eleanor's lands were arranged under chief bailiffs. John de Horstede covered Somerset, Dorset, Gloucester and Wiltshire from a base at Somerton, one of Eleanor's first holdings; John FitzThomas covered Hampshire and the New Forest; Richard de Hoo controlled the properties in Oxfordshire, Buckinghamshire, Hertfordshire and Essex from Langley; Moses de Wautham dealt with Warwick; Hugh de Lyminstr covered Snowdon and Anglesey; and Thomas de Macclesfield covered Macclesfield and the Peak, together with the other Derbyshire properties and those in Chester and Stafford. Roger de Walcote had the substantial group of Northampton, Lincoln, Rutland and Leicester and was based at Market Harborough, again one of Eleanor's earliest acquisitions. There was then a Norfolk, Suffolk and Cambridge bailiwick. It is not clear how the holdings in Kent, York, Sussex or Surrey were managed, though certainly in the latter period the centre for the Kent holdings was at Leeds Castle.[19]

Consideration of the property portfolio and its management conveys a clear impression of a department working under considerable pressure to maximise revenue. The records show that wherever property was acquired, steps were taken quickly to assert rights and collect dues. The classic example of this is the abortive Barwick transaction of 1265, where Eleanor was only in possession for three weeks, but her bailiffs seized the full quarter's rent plus the relief due from the tenant. Examples can be found of administrative steps being taken within twenty-four hours of a grant being made to Eleanor. Another example is Sandwich in 1290, where Eleanor granted fairs, corresponded about the priory's rights and intervened with the town council on behalf of a Breton merchant, all within less than a month of the grant of the custom of the port being made to her. The queen's administration did not sleep.

Efficiency can also be seen in the records of management of the estates, with close attention paid to agricultural yield. As a major landlord, Eleanor was in a position to acquire substantial amounts of produce and sell them in the open market. To maximise profits in this respect, her staff tried to avoid agreements that involved payment in kind, such as a rent of grain owed to the Abbot of St Benet Hulme from the farm of Scottow, and the amount of grain to be enjoyed free by the Abbot of Muchelney; cash payments were negotiated in substitution. It is also reputed that Eleanor was the introducer of the more productive merino sheep to England; and while the tradition cannot be precisely verified, there is certainly a record of her importing some sheep. Her interest in efficient farming may also explain the possession by the royal family of a copy of Rutilius' *Re Rustica*, the Roman manual on agriculture.[20]

There was, however, a much less pleasant side to this nose-to-the-grindstone approach, and it is this which has considerably tarnished Eleanor's reputation. On her death, an inquest into her property affairs took place, and this turned up a number of complaints, some of which were held to be justified. However, the inquest and its results have to be kept in proportion. The holding of such an inquiry was not unusual; Eleanor of Provence instituted one in her own lifetime. Nor can it be considered surprising that such an inquiry, which involved hearings in four locations, designed to be convenient to the bulk of Eleanor's tenants, should turn up justified complaints over such a substantial and complex landholding. Nor that, when such an inquest was announced, a large number of complaints were made, some of them on a rather speculative or even dishonest basis.

The problem is that, of the contemporaneous records which survive of Eleanor, these are the largest in volume and the most cohesive. There is therefore a danger of inflating the importance of what was found simply because it is material which survived when other materials did not. Furthermore, just because a complaint was made does not mean that its validity should be accepted; while a number were overtly dismissed – for instance on the basis that those complained of were not in Eleanor's employ at all – a greater number of complaints (including some of the most damaging allegations) seem to have been withdrawn or abandoned. In such cases it may be inferred that these complaints probably were not soundly based. An example is the case of John de Wauton, regarded by Parsons as a fairly damaging accusation against Eleanor. De Wauton alleged that he was brought into Eleanor's council by her staff, that he asked for help in paying loans he had incurred to Aaron son of Vives without losing his lands and consequently entered into agreements with Hagin son of Cress, who collusively sold the debts to Eleanor – who then took the lands. While the charge was not formally dismissed, the implausibility of the story is apparent; and the fact that Edward granted the land in question to one of the members of the council named in the complaint indicates forcibly that it was considered unsustainable.

Having said that, what the records do show is that the bailiffs and reeves acted harshly on numerous occasions – there are any number of tabloid-worthy examples, of which perhaps the best is the case where one of Eleanor's reeves seized a house from its owners, falsely procuring their imprisonment and abandoning their baby in a cradle in the middle of the road. Another striking story is the family who were ejected from their home so that the local bailiff could use it to entertain a prostitute.[21]

One facet of the picture which emerges, which has modern corporate resonances, is that reeves and bailiffs in Eleanor's employ did not want to convey bad news up the line to a demanding superior. So when Eleanor took possession of properties and a review had to be made of what it would yield, sometimes stewards inflated the rents and services due from the properties, or overstated the size of the property. Thus at Overton a property was reported as nine acres, where previously it had been described as seven, and rents were stated to be 7*d*, not the 6*d* previously charged. Thereafter it seems that, under pressure to make good on the figures they had declared, bailiffs pressured tenants into paying the increased rents. In one case rent was exacted in what had been previously agreed as a rent-free period, in another case rents were extracted in full even though Eleanor had agreed to reduce them on account of the tenants' poverty. In yet another, previously free pasture was made subject to an annual charge of 1*d*. These are not isolated examples and show that Eleanor's team were keenly after every penny and often far from scrupulous.[22]

Another important fact which emerges is that a good deal of this can be put down to venal and opportunistic employees higher up the food chain, who took advantage of their own immunity from prosecution while on the queen's business. Archbishop Pecham – albeit no friend of Eleanor and her business practices – described them as coming of the followers of the devil, rather than of Christ. Walter de Kancia, for example, is considered by Parsons as notorious for his venality and viciousness. It may be that he was behind a number of sharp practices, such as the one where Richard Cole sued a certain Robert Baldwin, who owed nothing to the queen, having him fined £13 6*s* 8*d*, to cover which fine six of his oxen were seized and sold, and grain to the value of £20 was also seized. He then procured de Kancia and another authority, John de Budesthorn, to uphold him (presumably for a cut of the profits). Eleanor's decision to take Kancia's estate into her own hands on his death (his family only received its value after her own death) may reflect some suspicion on her part that he was salting away sums due to her.

Other examples which can be traced to Kancia include charging the Bokland family in the New Forest rent for eighteen years for a farm which had been surrendered some time before Eleanor took over the New Forest, and charging Richard de Burele 30*s* rent for a cow pasture he no longer needed, having lost his cows more than a decade before in the Barons' War. He also falsely asserted that another New Forest tenant had died intestate, seized goods worth £35 10*s* 8*d* and kept them himself, though he claimed to be acting in the queen's name. In a number of cases at the inquest it was found that Walter had acted dishonestly, that even his own colleagues had little to say in his defence, and the jury frequently found that sums had come into his hands and 'not to the profit of the lady queen'.[23]

Another example is Eleanor's own auditor, John de Lovetot. He was in her service by 1273–4 and became a justice of Common Pleas in 1275. This did not, however, stop him presiding on occasions when the queen's business was before the court; an approach which would somewhat surprise a modern judge. He also acted as a member of Eleanor's council in the 1280s and witnessed a large number of her acts, reflecting a considerable working closeness and degree of trust. He acted on commissions on her lands and audited Ponthevin accounts. His perceived influence is illustrated in a case where her bailiffs wrongfully sued someone on the orders of Lovetot, whom, they said, 'they dared not refuse'.

Lovetot seems to have been involved in the shady practice of inflating the amounts claimable on lands for rent and services. When defalcations on his part were proved, Eleanor did not defend him: he was one of the justices disgraced during inquiries against the justices in 1290. Nonetheless, in his case in particular, a degree of complicity or constructive knowledge on Eleanor's part may be suspected, in that employing an auditor who was so embedded in her administration seems to have run contrary to normal or at least best practice, which, even at the time, was to employ 'eminent men from outside the lord's entourage, men whose station commanded respect and whose lack of affinity to the lord's stewards and bailiffs postulated a capacity to do impartial justice to those … who might complain of the lord's officials during the audit'.[24]

This brings us to the crucial question: to what extent was Eleanor actually aware of or complicit in these misdeeds? Not entirely, we can be sure, since one example of her officials' wrongdoing involves the charging of rent to William and Iseut le Bruyn, former members of her personal household, who had actually been given lands in the New Forest by Eleanor herself; Eleanor had to certify in writing that she had remitted the rent when she made the grant before the bailiffs would desist. Nor was she likely to be aware of those examples given above, where Walter de Kancia abused his power to enrich himself, or similar cases where another bailiff ejected a tenant and had him jailed on the false accusation that he had broken into the house, or a reeve compelled tenants at Overton to give half of all their catch to the reeve's wife, who sold it and kept the proceeds. Nor would she be likely to know the facts underlying the inflation of rents and services (or the mirror image, withholding of rent from those from whom the queen held her manors); active as she was in her business, she will probably not have been able to master the minutiae of each property.

Further, on every occasion when injustices or hardships were drawn to Eleanor's attention, she acted to assist the person in distress. So, in 1289–90, one of Eleanor's team was told that a certain John de Folebourne owed money to the queen, and his lands were consequently taken into her administration. He proved he actually owed nothing and Eleanor restored the lands to him. Similarly, John de Budesthorne's lands were seized after his death based on information that he had been her bailiff, but were released when his wife proved that he had not been. In two cases which can be traced, Eleanor ordered repairs to be made to properties: one which she was granting to a dependant and another where her men had done damage to the property. Likewise, two different tenants at Overton were protected from the unjust actions of the queen's bailiff, and on Anglesey she reduced the rent of tenants who explained to her that they were reduced to poverty. The evidence suggests that, well before her death, Eleanor was keen not to act unjustly by her tenants – where injustice was brought to her attention.

However, tempting as it is to try to clear Eleanor entirely, the facts do not really permit it. The habit of inflating rents coming in and skimping on rents going out was probably not one which was profitable to her staff (unless a number of them were complicit in skimming profits from her, which is of course possible), and yet it was plainly common practice. Add to this the fact, noted by Parsons, that the only cause for which Eleanor dismissed or prosecuted her officials during her lifetime was for failure to produce revenue; and while Walter de Kancia's peculations in the New Forest were outed in 1277 and he lost his stewardship there, he was her gold keeper and overall steward until his death in 1283. Other malfeasant officials likewise kept jobs in her service.[25]

It therefore seems that these common wrongs were ones done, if not with Eleanor's knowledge, then at least in keeping with the fairly hard line being taken as to the need to maximise income, without much attention being given to the little people caught in the meshes, unless those little people actually managed to find a route to make representations personally to the queen. Eleanor can therefore probably be held guilty of at least some Nelsonian knowledge of her administrative staff's misdemeanours; and indeed, such knowledge would be consistent with her insistence on her deathbed that her estates' affairs be looked into, in case injustices had been done.

That there were doubts among those fairly close to her about her business practices is wonderfully illustrated by the story of Hugh Despenser 'the Elder' (in the sense of being the father of the Despenser famous under Edward II; he was, however, the son of the Despenser featured earlier who died at Evesham). A man with close ties to the royal family (his step-grandfather was Earl of Warwick, his stepfather was Earl of Norfolk and he was married to a sister of a later Earl of Warwick) he found himself owing Eleanor 1,000 marks in 1287 after he married Isabel Beauchamp, whose lands were under Eleanor's wardship, without royal licence. To secure the debt, he pledged a manor at Soham in Cambridgeshire – which was, of course, very temptingly close to Eleanor's own holdings there. He was obviously not entirely confident that this temptation would be withstood, since he asked for formal confirmation that the manor would be restored to him after he paid the debt. There is even a sting in the tail of the story: Despenser did indeed get Soham back, but he ended up surrendering lands at Macclesfield to Eleanor instead.[26]

It is actually in providing for her team of clerks that the greatest questions arise over Eleanor's own actual knowledge and approach. The principal means of providing for her clerks appears to have been via benefices in her gift or the gift of others she could influence – a route also explored by Eleanor of Provence, but with less success, owing to Henry III's tendency to grant her wardships while keeping the associated advowsons (rights to present the clerical benefice). So the invaluable but disreputable Walter de Kancia held a stall at Lichfield and at least six churches, including ones within Eleanor's property empire at Great Bowden, Macclesfield and Prestbury, as well as Little Billing (near Eleanor's holding at Kingsthorpe), presented to him presumably at Eleanor's behest by Henry III in 1270, and Taxal (near Macclesfield), presented by Edward. This need to provide for a department of hard-working clerks explains Eleanor's more than careful acquisition of advowsons with new properties whenever possible and the purchase of other convenient advowsons. In this way Eleanor provided for Edmund de Loundres, John de Caen and John de Berewyk among others, including her chaplain William de Windsore, who obtained St Peter's Northampton, with the chapels at Tring and Upton. Thus, too, Geoffrey de Aspale became one of the country's most prominent pluralists, holding fifteen benefices – including one described by Archbishop Pecham in a letter of protest as 'fat' – simultaneously.

However, some of the methods employed in making such provision were at least questionable. The records show a habit of usurping advowsons which were alleged to appertain to properties which she acquired, sometimes with success; though, again, she may not have received the accurate information from her clerks. She was also sometimes involved in collusive dealings to get others. So, having obtained lands from Robert de Camville in Fobbing and Shenfield in Essex via his debts to the Jewry, Eleanor agreed to make common cause with the prior and convent of Romilley in recovering various advowsons (including those of Fobbing and Shenfield), which Camville had detained from the convent. They then granted the advowsons to her for 250 marks in ready money. Another similar agreement was reached with St Osyth's Abbey regarding advowsons connected to the lands of William de Montchesny, which Eleanor was busy acquiring in her later years. Such an approach to litigation is certainly less than creditable, although it would appear that the priories were in the right and the underlying land transactions were not hostile; de Camville's son was in the royal daughters' household, and Eleanor paid for candles at his funeral, dowries for his daughters and made provision for his wife and daughter-in-law.[27]

But it is certainly the case that, in procuring such preferments, there is some evidence that Eleanor was very hard-nosed indeed. The classic tale – and, it should be noted, the sole case in the post-mortem inquiry where evidence emerged which implicated Eleanor directly in deliberate administrative vindictiveness – is that of Richard of Stockport. This gentleman had obliged Eleanor by presenting the egregious Walter de Kancia to his local living of Stockport and also that of Prestbury. On Kancia's death, Eleanor then required him to present another clerk, John de Caen, to the Stockport living. Stockport, however, had already given the living elsewhere. He was tormented, apparently on her orders, by her men for seven years, being sued and having property unjustly seized. The evidence implicating Eleanor personally came from her own bailiff at Macclesfield. While that alone might simply indicate an attempt to shift blame, the complainant asserted that Robert Burnell also knew the truth. There is no record of a finding in Stockport's favour and one can easily hypothesise circumstances which would excuse or mitigate the offence – for example if Stockport had sold the living to Eleanor, or was somehow in cahoots with the venal Kancia. However, there is no evidence for those possibilities and, at the very least, Eleanor's direct involvement in some fairly rough behaviour appears to be indicated by the fact that this case was ordered to be heard in camera once the accusation against her had been raised.[28]

But while it is the only case which ties Eleanor to actual wrongdoing, it seems to have been far from the only case where Eleanor made herself rather unpleasant in the search for good preferments for her men. In 1283, Bishop Godfrey Giffard of Worcester (a close connection of Eleanor's) advised the prior of Deerhurst to give a preferment to the queen's nominee, even though he had already given the nomination elsewhere; and Eleanor had not merely enlisted Giffard herself, she had also got Robert Burnell to take up the case. In another case in the early 1280s, the Bishop of Winchester was warned by Pecham not to run contrary to the queen's desire to have her Spanish physician presented to the church of Crondall. But in this sort of matter it would seem that not even close associates were exempt. In 1290, Giffard himself was concerned about his position with the queen when she asserted that he owed her £350. He sought assistance from Burnell, who reported back to him that the queen was indeed unhappy with him, and advised Giffard to meet her only in his (Burnell's) presence. The subtext is that Burnell might be able to speak a word to turn away the queen's wrath.[29]

A further story which reinforces Eleanor's own reputation for hard dealing is that of her acquisition of the two parts of the barony of Haverfordwest inherited by Humphrey de Bohun, Earl of Hereford, in 1286–8. It appears that young Hereford had been driven to distraction by that notorious robber baron, his guardian William de Valence, self-styled Earl of Pembroke. That Hereford sold the barony to Eleanor suggests that he and she considered that she was capable of dealing with the senior surviving Lusignan. And rightly so. Eleanor sent in her experienced and objectionable servant Hugh de Cressingham, a man whose reputation as a fat bully has survived to this day. The result, predictably enough, was litigation. Eleanor did not simply leave the matter to Cressingham, but superintended the dispute by correspondence. Despite complaints about Cressingham's behaviour, which involved ignoring royal mandates, and which Edward I described as 'unprecedented', Eleanor won the action.[30]

The conclusion to which one is inevitably drawn in considering Eleanor's business dealings is that, while she was scrupulous as to individuals who came to her attention, in general in business she played very hard, and occasionally overstepped the mark. Was this approach anything out of the way in the context of her times? There appears very little to suggest that it was. Certainly Eleanor of Provence's administrators were considered no better than Eleanor's and Pecham reprimanded other landowners, such as Earl Warenne, for similar shortcomings. Furthermore, while Edward was scrupulous as to matters of justice, his own approach to land gathering was very much on the ruthless side (or, as Prestwich calls it, 'devious and grasping') – his acquisition of the valuable honour of Aumale in 1278 and the Isle of Wight in 1293 still attract accusations of collusion and fraud. Nor, interestingly, do Eleanor's actions seem to have made her actively unpopular. It is true that the two contemporary summaries of her life focus on her land gathering, but in a factual way. As Parsons notes, comment would be likely to be generated by any lord who in the space of twenty-five years acquired lands worth £2,500 per year. Nowhere in the chronicles is there the sort of negative comment which Eleanor of Provence routinely attracted, or any protest directed at Eleanor. All in all, she was an active landlord, and to our perspective not a particularly model one; but to her contemporaries, the conduct of her affairs was not seen as particularly remarkable – save in the scale of her operations.[31]

The area of Eleanor's business dealings for which she has attracted most criticism since her time is that which involves dealing with debts owed by individuals to members of the Jewish community. Aside from Pecham's concerns about usury, such dealings do not seem to have concerned her contemporaries: it is notable that neither the Guisborough or Dunstable annalist refers to this aspect of her business affairs. One reason may be that, as has been shown above, a significant proportion of the dealings by which Eleanor acquired key properties have all the appearance of concerted acquisitions, in the sense that she was pushed towards them by the debtor in question, who could see a way to free himself from a debt to the Jewry and please the queen, with consequent benefits for himself.

However, her dealings in Jewish debt were not confined to property exchanges. Edward made somewhat of a habit of granting her issues of fines for coin clipping, the targets of which were predominantly Jewish. Thus in 1280 he gave her a grant from the issues of transgressions of coin and on 20 April 1283 a grant of all issues of concealed goods and chattels of condemned Jews and from all transgressions of coin. In addition, there are numerous debts granted to Eleanor which did not end up with her possessing the debtor's property. For example, in Trinity term 1275 she was granted debts owed to Hagin son of Cress in the amount of £1,207 13s 4d, where no property gain seems to have resulted. The inference is that she enforced the debts instead and received cash. Similarly, in November 1279 there was a grant of debts owed to Hagin son of Moses in the amount of £5,262 6s 8d. Some parts of this sum resulted in land transfers, though others did not, and it is to be presumed the debts were paid. The difficulty of enforcing some of these debts may have raised the profile of Eleanor's dealings in Jewish debts: some disputes about whether debts had already been paid dragged on for over a decade and were only finally thrashed out at the inquest into Eleanor's affairs after her death, and Eleanor had to summons the Abbot of St Mary's Abbey twice, in 1282 and again in 1284 when he asserted that the debt on which she sued was based on a forgery by the Jewish moneylender.[32]

So numerous were Eleanor's dealings with the Jewry that she had a specific contact, Hagin son of Cress, who was known as 'the queen's Jew'. However, this sort of association was not unique; Aaron son of Vives was known as 'the Jew of the king's brother'. Eleanor certainly obtained a significant number of debts and properties through her dealings with Hagin and his uncles Hagin son of Moses and Mr Elias. Further, a certain degree of closeness is implied by the fact that she persuaded Edward to name Hagin son of Cress as arch presbyter of the Jews, a move which would have been highly unwelcome to most of the community since he had been excommunicated from Jewish society. Another fact tending in this direction is that between 1268 and 1272 Eleanor nominated Jews to the custodianship of her Irish queen's gold revenues and tried to do so again in 1273 and 1276.[33]

Having said that, there is certainly no sign of open closeness; there is no evidence that Eleanor even met those Jews with whom she dealt frequently. Indeed, one may speculate that if she dealt openly and personally with the Jewish community, that would be likely to have attracted the attention of such a keen critic as Pecham. The mere fact of these dealings was enough to attract censure from those who took a very strict line on such matters. However, it would seem the Dominicans took a more nuanced or lawyerly view which relied on the Fourth Lateran Council's distinction between 'excessive' usury, which was condemned, and 'moderate' usury, which might be considered permissible. This would enable dealings in Jewish debts, so long as sums exacted were in some sense reduced. It appears very possible that this approach explains some of the compensatory transactions Eleanor entered into in relation to properties acquired, as well as explaining Pecham's stress that Eleanor may be being wrongly advised – and her apparent rejection of his approach.

But there is nothing in Eleanor's continued dealings with the Jewish community which particularly suggests any sympathy for them as a group. On the contrary, she seems to have had nothing to say against the ruination of the family of Jacob son of Moses, one of her first contacts in the Jewish community and formerly her gold keeper at the Exchequer of the Jews, nor did she intercede for Benedict de Wintonia, a long-term contact, nominee for her Irish queen's gold keeper and again former gold keeper at the Exchequer of the Jews, who was hanged for coin clipping in 1278. Moreover, in 1288, while abroad, Eleanor had no hesitation in appointing an agent to assist in the matter of enforcing seizure of the goods of a number of condemned Jews, to ensure all was dealt with efficiently. All the signs therefore point to the conclusion that Eleanor, while dealing extensively with the Jewish community, did so only in the way of business.[34]

The latter point links to another aspect of her Jewish dealings which is not irrelevant to Pecham's accusation of scandal. This is that they were predominantly in the earlier part of the reign, around the time of the dower assignment and the associated acquisitions. While there were some continued dealings with Jewish debts, most of the property acquisitions associated with these can be traced to conveyances of debt in the earlier phase of her business, before 1281. Only two property acquisitions fall outside this rule. The last grant of all a Jew's debts to her was in 1279, and there was no acquisition of a debtor's total debts to the Jewry after that. Why, then, was Pecham making such an assertion in 1286? Part of it may almost certainly be traced to the fact that he disapproved of Eleanor's theological independence, and her application of that to her unqueenly business dealings. Part, too, may be referable to the fact that Pecham, as a prominent Franciscan, was generally in favour of a more hard-line approach to dealing with the Jewish population than Eleanor and her Dominican advisers – Franciscan advice has been linked to Eleanor of Provence's expulsion of Jews from her dower lands. He also took a very strong line on pluralism – the backbone of Eleanor's financial provision for her more talented clerks.

But also there was tension from the fact that Eleanor and her administration were no respecters of the Church's asserted rights. Some of the disputes which arose concerned property issues, where Eleanor's administration seem to have made something of a habit of disputing rent or services owed to church landlords, including (and this is a far from exhaustive list) Clive Abbey, Southwark Priory, St Albans Abbey, Peterborough Abbey and even Amesbury Priory, home to Eleanor of Provence and Eleanor's own daughter Mary, and niece and goddaughter Eleanor. But other disputes had at least some link to Jewish debts in their purely financial incarnation. So Eleanor had disputes with the Bishop of Worcester about a debt to which both claimed title. Most particularly, it is tempting to see, in the dispute with St Mary's Abbey in York, grounds for church gossip and scandal and hence the genesis of his outburst. As recorded above, in this action Eleanor had the abbot before the Exchequer of the Jews on two occasions; moreover, provocatively, she claimed and was awarded not just the sum owed but also 'usury incurred'. It therefore seems likely that the archbishop's letter reflects a rather partial view, assisted by church rather than national gossip.[35]

One further topic should be dealt with while considering the queen's work. That is intercession, which (aside from childbearing) was the traditional job of the queen. In a society offering limited exercise of power for women, it had become traditional for queens to promote their profile by interceding with their royal husband, and procuring his exercise of power in favour of the object which they advocated. This role, where the obvious parallel is with the biblical Queen Esther, but a further strong parallel can be drawn with the intercessory role of the Virgin Mary, demonstrated actual influence and also associated the queen with powerful role models, giving power by association. Huneycutt has traced how effectively and prolifically Matilda, wife of Henry I, exploited her role as intercessor, but it can be seen echoed again and again by other queens both before and after Eleanor. For example, perhaps the best-known example of a queen's intercession is that of Philippa of Hainault for the burghers of Calais in the fourteenth century, a wonderful set piece of roleplay both for king and queen, which has duly received its tribute in artistic memorials by, among others, Rodin and Benjamin West. This intercessory role was of increasing importance to English queens as their roles in government lessened throughout the twelfth and thirteenth centuries, along with their control during their husband's lifetime over their dower properties. Eleanor of Provence, for example, was a great proficient in the intercessory art. At her own coronation she made a formal intercession with Henry for pardons. Among her surviving letters are numerous examples of intercessions with her husband while she was queen, and still more are addressed to Edward in her years as dowager queen.[36]

In this formal intercessory role there is almost a complete break during Eleanor of Castile's reign as queen. She did exercise her intercessory role under Henry III; and one example of this, on behalf of the de Haustede family in 1266, may well have won her loyal service from the family for two generations. However, this formal intercession practically stopped once she became queen. Aside from three intercessions for murder recorded in the Patent Rolls, there is not one single letter or account which demonstrates her interceding with her husband. Indeed, Eleanor of Provence was a far more prolific intercessor with Edward than was Eleanor the queen – as also was Margaret of France after Eleanor's death. Eleanor's behaviour is thus anomalous.

There is just one story which is generally cited as an example of Eleanor adopting an intercessory role. For a variety of reasons, however, it actually shows no such thing. The story in the records of St Albans Abbey goes thus: knowing that 'the queen' was about to visit the monastery, local people who were at odds with the abbot lay in wait to seek her help, forming a somewhat fractious mob. The abbot took the queen 'a private way' to avoid them, but the people nonetheless obtained access to her, running up shouting and crying. She rebuked the abbot for trying to keep the people from her. One of the queen's household then asked a poor woman all about the issue between the town and the abbot, but she was so overcome that she could not answer. In the end the issue was tried and found in favour of the abbot, which the chronicler of St Albans seems to find highly satisfactory.[37]

This somewhat inconsequential story is frequently cited as grounds for saying that Eleanor was looked to by the people as a benign queen to whom the common folk might look for intercession in the face of abuse from their superiors. It should be noted at the outset that even if this were a story about Eleanor, it does not actually demonstrate her interceding at all. But in fact, the story does not stack up as a story about Eleanor of Castile. The date given by the chronicler is around Maundy Thursday. It appears in the chronicle in a section which begins 'in 1274' and before a section which begins 'in 1275'; accordingly, Parsons originally considered that context of the story places it around Maundy Thursday 1274, at which point Eleanor was not even in the country. He later changed his view to suggest that the Maundy Thursday referred to is 1275, which is just about possible owing to the slightly thematic arrangement of the chronicle. However, the two possibilities for Eleanor's location on that date place her elsewhere. In March 1275, Eleanor had recently given birth to Margaret at Windsor. If Parsons' theory that Margaret was born on 15 March and Eleanor habitually lay in for twenty-nine days after birth is correct, on Maundy Thursday she was still at Windsor following the birth of Margaret. If, as I suggest in Chapter 11, Eleanor moved from Windsor with or shortly after Edward, she was spending Holy Week (including Maundy Thursday) at Weston, considerably further north in Hertfordshire; having followed a route well to the north of St Albans from Aylesbury. It is therefore more than likely that, whenever the incident took place, the queen in question was not Eleanor of Castile but Eleanor of Provence.

What is more, at this period Eleanor of Provence was far better known to the populace as queen than her daughter-in-law, and as we know, she continued to use the title of queen. The queen in question being Eleanor of Provence would also be consistent with the terms of the petition apparently presented to the queen on this occasion, which explicitly refers to 'your help, which you have often given to us'. There seems to have been no scope for the younger Eleanor to have given any help in the past at all. In contrast, Eleanor of Provence had close associations with the abbey at St Albans. Finally, identifying the St Albans queen as Eleanor of Provence is also consistent with the oddity of the story featuring a queen travelling alone. This is not at all remarkable if the widowed Eleanor of Provence is the queen, but highly anomalous if it is Eleanor of Castile.[38]

To the extent that Eleanor did intercede, she predominantly did so not directly with Edward, but with administrative staff. In this context, there are a number of letters from her to Edward's clerks in which she asks them to do something for a petitioner, and indicates that she will regard the doing of the thing as a favour to her. But are these properly categorised as intercessions? They are not intercessions in the accepted mode; they are not to the king and they are quiet, behind-the-scenes letters, which could gain no public advantage for Eleanor except through the (minimally useful) report of the individual petitioner. In fact, given the material regarding Eleanor's very considerable influence with Edward, and her dislike of being thwarted, one may perhaps better read these letters as gentle threats in the mode of a powerful 'Godfather'-style figure than actual intercessions; a command concealed under the courtesy of a request and a kind thank you. If that seems extreme, one may ask the question – where bishops tremble, would any clerk actually wish to cross Eleanor?

Further support for an inference that Eleanor actively rejected the role of intercessor may be seen in two other places. The first is that there is actually one classic example of Edward being procured to intercede with Eleanor, rather than vice versa. In 1287, the people of Southampton objected to paying a sum granted to Eleanor by Edward. They did not ask her to waive the sum or to intercede with Edward. Rather, they approached Eleanor of Provence, who held the town in dower, and she duly made a traditional intercession with Edward, asking him to remit the sum as it would reduce the town to poverty. The result? Eleanor peremptorily told Edmund of Cornwall, Edward's lieutenant in the area, that she had told the king that she would tell Edmund to give the petitioners short shrift. In effect, therefore, Eleanor of Provence interceded with Edward, who interceded with Eleanor – with no success.

The second piece of evidence which supports a vision of Eleanor as standing outside the traditional role as queenly intercessor is one of the surviving letters to her from Archbishop Pecham, which is considered further in the next chapter. This explicitly refers to 'those who say that you cause the king to use severity'. In other words, at least among a certain group known to him, Eleanor's reputation was the diametrical opposite of the intercessory queen; rather than moderating the king's wrath, she was seen as inclining him to greater harshness.[39]

Which comes first, the absence of intercessions or the reputation for harshness? At this distance, it is impossible to tell. However, if the correct answer (tentatively favoured by Parsons) is that Eleanor had a reputation for harshness leading to an absence of requests for intercessions, that reputation would have to have been established somehow; Eleanor as queen was an unknown quantity at Edward's accession and a body of evidence or rumour would take time to build. One would therefore expect to see a falling off in intercessions and consequently a pattern early in the reign of a number of people coming to Eleanor for intercession. Of course, an unsuccessful petition would be unlikely to show up. However, there is in fact no greater sign in the records of Eleanor interceding more earlier in the reign than she did later. There is therefore at least a suggestion in the air that the absence of intercession was a positive choice by her.

Furthermore, we will see later that such a non-standard approach to more or less accepted queenly practice can also be discerned when it comes to Eleanor's religious and charitable approach. It looks very much as if Eleanor, secure in her relationship with Edward (who would generally do as she wished), busy with her assigned role in putting the queen's financial affairs into order, and with no desire to be considered as affiliated with any other team than 'Team Edward', simply rejected the traditional intercessory role as being unnecessary to her. In doing so, she would of course know that an alternative route was available to would-be petitioners. The 'other' Queen Eleanor was still alive and well, with an established track record for and disposition much more inclined to the intercessory role, and she did indeed go on to play that role.

The picture which emerges is of Eleanor as a queen who carved out a unique and important role in the administrative side of government, which she pursued with vigour and considerable focus. With that important and fulfilling job available to her, and with constant additions to an already sizeable family materialising, as well as the necessary formalities of queenship, she had neither need nor time to expend much effort on other aspects of the traditional role of queen. So far as power was concerned, she had it in her financial autonomy and the influence on her husband which was well established and needed no advertisement to those around them. She therefore saw no need to adopt all the conventions of queenly behaviour. Eleanor did not simply accept the role of queen; instead she made her queenship in her own image.

11

The Queen and Her Interests

So far, we have seen the circumstances which took Eleanor to her thirty-third year and to her coronation as queen. This tells us much about the situations which formed her views and tastes. In addition, the preceding account of her work gives a better idea of her abilities and one of her major interests as a queen. But to date there has been no sensible place to stop and ask what Eleanor was like. What would those who actually knew her have told us about her?

The natural starting point is her looks. Here, one might imagine that the answer should be simple and that with all the commemorative statues of Eleanor one would be spoilt for choice. Sadly however, life is never that simple. We get very little assistance from the cross effigies; we cannot be sure that any real portraiture was even intended. Furthermore, they were not made by the most senior artist involved, Torel, but by more junior stone carvers. In addition, those which survive have been so affected by the passage of time that very little can be seen. So too with the stonework head supposed to be of Eleanor at Lincoln Cathedral; this has been restored from a degraded original.

The primary source to which one is driven, therefore, is the London tomb effigy by Torel. This gives some assistance, but it must be carefully weighed. One cannot take it that the effigy which we have of her is a true resemblance, since portraiture was not an established art. However, nor are tomb effigies completely anonymous. So, just as Edward's forceful chin seems to make it into just about every contemporaneous sketch of him, one can tell that some attempt at resemblance was made by effigy artists; for example, the slight droop of Henry III's eye which is contemporaneously reported is just about discernible in his effigy, also by Torel. At St Denis, Isabelle of Aragon's tomb effigy has softly dimpled hands, and Charles of Anjou's nose and massive forehead seem unlikely to be accidental. What is more, it appears likely that Eleanor visited Torel before her death, providing an opportunity for working sketches to be made from life. One can therefore expect that the figure who appears on Eleanor's tomb is not dissimilar from Eleanor as she was known to those around her. The question is of the extent to which particular aspects of the depiction can be trusted. This is a question which can be answered by comparing aspects of the image to other sources.

The face on the tomb is almost a pure oval, but with a rounded chin just breaking the symmetry slightly. There is a lively pair of sketches of Edward and Eleanor found in a document in the British Library (the Cotton Manuscript), each of which show clearly Edward's drooping eye, inherited from Henry, and they therefore appear to be a real attempt at portraiture. Eleanor's sketch in this document agrees with the tomb effigy on the shape of her face. There is therefore a case for accepting that this detail is from life. Interestingly, this facial shape also appears in the depiction of the elegant 'hunting lady with dogs' in the Alphonso Psalter. Although the book cannot be definitively traced to a commission by Eleanor, its origin in the London Dominican priory, which she favoured, and its purpose, for the marriage of her son Alphonso, raise a strong presumption that she was the commissioner of the work. If so, and given that Eleanor was a keen huntress and favoured hunting with dogs despite Edward's own preference for falconry, this is a picture which might well attempt some resemblance to Eleanor.

The effigy's mouth is small and somewhat secretive, but upturned, showing resemblance to the Cotton Manuscript sketch; and, again suggesting portraiture, the sketch of Edward suggests a straight or even downturned line for his mouth. Once again, the psalter illustration provides a match. Together with the chin it suggests a face that would be charming when smiling, and even more so when laughing.

On all depictions, Eleanor's nose is long, straight and slim. It is noticeably a slimmer nose than that of Henry III, or that shown on Eleanor of Provence's likely image in Westminster Abbey's Muniment Room (and hilariously more elegant than Charles of Anjou's effigy nose). Again, this suggests an element of real portraiture. Another point of interest is that there is considerable similarity as regards Eleanor's nose to that of Eleanor of Aquitaine, as depicted on her tomb at Fontevrault. In both sketch and tomb depiction and in the psalter there is a fairly high forehead, well-arched brows and large, almond-shaped eyes, not tilted upwards at the end but more sleepy in their setting.

As for colouring, this is always difficult to judge, since the chroniclers, only seeing the queens formally if at all, would never see their hair colour. The only occasion on which a decent queen's hair might be shown in public was on the occasion of coronation, and few of the commentators whose works survive (being generally monks) ever viewed a coronation. Eleanor's coronation was, of course, described by the chroniclers, but among the many wonders of the day the colour of her hair does not seem to have been reported back to the writers. One may infer, however, that if Eleanor had been the possessor of breathtaking blonde tresses it would have been considered worth mentioning. In fact with Eleanor, her own colour choices make it almost certain that her colouring was dark; as will be seen, she favoured reds and greens, colours which no blonde would be likely to choose but which are very becoming to brunettes. In relation to hair, the cross images are perhaps at last of some use: those which are not veiled show thick, wavy hair, worn long.

In terms of overall appearance, therefore, we can envisage a fine-looking Spanish lady, whose eyes and hair were probably her greatest beauty, with a determined chin and a winning smile. But, as we have already noted of the younger Eleanor, there is no sense that she was considered a notable beauty or that she presented herself to people as a woman remarkable for her looks.[1]

This obviously brings us to the question of the kind of person Eleanor was. On this point, little emerges openly from the records which we have; again Eleanor lurks in the shadows. Parsons concluded that the household records indicate a number of close ties and therefore no lack of affection and a person who was able to interact in a congenial way with those around her. However, rather more than this can be said. The records show us that Eleanor was plainly very much alive to the needs and wishes of the people who surrounded her. They repeatedly show small acts of kindness – paying for medical expenses, making provision for people's children, lending her valuable books to members of her household, giving her ladies leave to visit their families even when she herself was unwell, going out of her way to visit a friend who was sick, putting aside her own illness to honour a humble wedding among her servants. She was kind and considerate to those around her and those with whom she had direct contact, and that consideration was not limited to the more distinguished members of her acquaintance: servants and tradesmen could be assured of considerate treatment from her. What she was not was overtly or indiscriminately charming. There are no references (as there are with Eleanor of Provence) to her '*debonairité*'.

For all her kindness, however, the records show also a very different streak in her character, which most commentators have found difficult to reconcile with her traditional reputation as a sweet and merciful queen, and with the kind of documented details described above.

A good deal of this material comes from the evidence about Eleanor's work, and she was certainly somewhat hardnosed when it came to matters of business. The other evidence, substantially from two letters from Archbishop Pecham – one to Eleanor and one to a person involved in dealings with her – suggest rather more than this.[2]

The first letter runs as follows:

My lady, the saints teach us that women are naturally greater in pity and more devout than men are, and scripture therefore says 'he that hath no wife will wander about mourning'. And because God has given you greater honour than to others of your lordship it is right that your pity should surpass the pity of all men and women in your lordship. We therefore ask you for God's sake and our Lady's that you will incline the heart of our Lord the king towards our dear brother, the bishop of Winchester ... my lady we require you for God's sake that you will do so in this matter that those who say that you cause the king to use severity may see and know the contrary ... My lady, for God's sake, let pity overcome you and our Lord keep you, body and soul, forever...

This letter shows two important things. Firstly, Eleanor was perceived by the archbishop (who knew her fairly well) as being somewhat deficient in empathy or pity. Secondly, there was a view, presumably among those quite close to the royal family or the lords of the Church, being Pecham's likely focus groups, that she encouraged the king to harshness rather than acting as peacemaker and pacifying his wrath as she was exhorted to do in the coronation oath and by her confessors.

The second letter is one from 1279 to the nuns at Hedingham. This convent had refused to admit a lady whose application was supported by the queen. Pecham warned them in no uncertain terms that they would be ill advised to contest the matter: 'If you know what is good for you, you'll admit her' ('*si bene sapuessitis*'). The implication is clear; Eleanor was known to be highly intolerant of having her will contradicted and to be the kind of foe you do not want to have.

Two further letters, mentioned in Chapter 10, reinforce this impression, albeit indirectly. In May 1283, Bishop Godfrey Giffard of Worcester advised the prior of Deerhurst to present the queen's chaplain to a church, warning against incurring royal wrath. While it is not explicitly Eleanor's wrath which is mentioned, that is the plain implication. Equally, it is implied that, if Eleanor decided she wanted her way, Edward would almost certainly support her; thus the closeness of the marriage and everyone's knowledge of that closeness is again glimpsed in this sidelight.

In another similar case, very possibly a precursor to one of the letters to Eleanor quoted above, Pecham warned the Bishop of Winchester against the dangers of failing to appoint Eleanor's Spanish physician to a living. Although the indignation there mentioned is the king's, it again seems plain, particularly in the light of the plea in mitigation Pecham later addressed to Eleanor on behalf of the imprudent bishop, that it is actually Eleanor's wrath which is feared – and which duly followed.

As if this were not sufficient material, two other examples can be given. The first is a letter from the Count of Bigorre in 1283, reporting that he is regrettably unable to fall in with a request of Eleanor's, and asking to be excused and sheltered from her displeasure at his failure. The second is the exchange in 1285 when the people of Southampton sought to get

Eleanor of Provence to intercede for them with Edward, in relation to Eleanor's exactions from them. It is apparent that Edward did not press the matter, but effectively 'shopped' Eleanor's tenants and his mother to her instead; Eleanor writes in great displeasure to Edmund of Cornwall, telling him to make sure the townspeople pay up.[3]

There are two interesting points which emerge from this. The first is the complete contrast between the picture of Eleanor traditionally portrayed – gently submissive, pacific – and the woman who had bishops and abbots across the country shaking in their shoes. Indubitably Eleanor was no mouse but a formidable and sometimes terrifying woman. What is also interesting to note is that Eleanor was plainly capable of losing her temper quite dramatically and did so at least occasionally when crossed. This conjures up again Alfonso's injunctions for the raising of a queen: a princess should be prevented 'from yielding to anger for ... it is the one thing in the world which most quickly induces women to commit sin'; and it reinforces the inference that it was written with Eleanor in mind. Secondly, it shows that she kept this facet of her personality well hidden from the wider public; neither the abbey nor the convent – nor even the Bishop of Winchester, who was one of the major princes of the Church – had grasped what those who regularly featured in Eleanor's witness lists and hence knew her better were aware of: that it was foolish to cross her.

How do these two sides of Eleanor reconcile themselves? Some have seen this as impossible, but in my own view the answer is not particularly surprising. Very few real people fall simply on one side of the good/bad dichotomy. Eleanor, like any person we meet in real life, had good qualities and bad ones. It seems quite plain that she had, when roused, a sharp temper which impressed itself on those about her. It is equally plain that, like many executives or professionals performing high-pressure jobs, she liked to have things done her way and was intolerant of those who did not accommodate her. However, outside her professional sphere, she would switch off and concentrate on the more pleasant aspects of life. In this realm, it would appear, she was almost always a kind and considerate person to deal with.

A tantalising question is whether this fiery personality entirely confined itself to Eleanor's business doings, or if it sometimes made itself felt in the domestic environment. My own suspicion is that it did, albeit probably rarely. The facts which suggest this are indirect, and derive from the rather tempestuous behaviour of the royal princesses and Edward's somewhat surprising acceptance of such behaviour. Thus Joan once refused to accept any money from her own wardrobe keeper after a row, and ran up considerable debts as a result; Edward did not, as one might expect, make her face the consequences, but paid the debts. Joan (again) refused to get married until she had an equal number of servants as her sisters; Edward hired the requisite number on a 'temp' basis until her wedding day. Elizabeth threw a tantrum when certain jewels due to be prepared for her wedding were not ready on time – leading to generous monetary compensation from her father. She then flatly refused to leave England once married, leading to Edward himself losing his temper and throwing some of her jewels into the fireplace – but she got her way. Of course, the princesses' tempers may simply have been inherited from Edward; but, given the evidence of the letters, one suspects not. All in all, one may at least suspect that on occasion even Edward learnt to purchase peace on Eleanor's terms.[4]

Having said that, there seems no reason to suspect that anyone but Edward wielded ultimate authority in the royal household. All Eleanor's work was done very much under his aegis, with him assisting in providing funds both for purchases of and works at her properties. Eleanor's work came to a grinding halt repeatedly when it came up against the exigencies of Edward's own priorities. Furthermore, while an example can be found of Edward trying to intercede with Eleanor unsuccessfully on a matter of minor moment to him, there is at least one example of Edward putting his foot down when Eleanor sought to influence him in her favour. During the Gascon stay, Eleanor had word from one of her debtors, Geoffrey de Southorpe, that he had sold his manor of Southorpe to Stephen de Cornhill, who had (colluding with the Abbot of Peterborough) conveyed it to the king's clerk, Elias de Bekyngham. Southorpe was, as he reminded Eleanor, deliciously close to her existing manors of Torpel and Upton. Eleanor duly went to Edward, demanding that the manor be taken into his hands, with the intent that he would then grant it to her. But the abbey had despatched their own advocate, who said that the abbey were merely trying to buy the land through Bekyngham's agency. Edward is said to have told Eleanor that 'he would do nothing contrary to right' – a doubtless trying reminder of her own family's theory of kingship. He then ordered an inquisition into the facts. Southorpe was put into debtors' prison by Eleanor, and obtained his release by conveying to her some of his remaining lands. Peterborough Abbey obtained the land only after Eleanor's death, and the seller had to endow an anniversary service for the queen.[5]

As for the lighter side of Eleanor's personality, humour is, of course, something which is particularly hard to capture. But we can be almost certain that Eleanor had a very lively sense of humour. For one thing, she actually employed two fools, Robert and Thomas. Both seem to have been highly esteemed: Thomas received a horse from her executors and Eleanor bought Robert's wife an expensive furred robe. Furthermore, it is plain that humour of a fairly broad type was alive and well at the court generally. Some of these jokes will appear as the chronological story progresses but a few examples set the tone. The first is the story of the post-Lenten ambush. After forty days of abstinence, Edward, seeking to rejoin Eleanor in her bed, would every year be held hostage by her ladies until he paid them a sizeable ransom. The humour here is frankly racy – it is plain to everyone that Edward is madly keen to be back in bed with his wife, and it seems hilariously funny to them all for her ladies to pin him down, struggling, until he pays up.

Similarly slapstick is the story of Edward's bet with the laundress that she could not ride his horse, which has the woman leaping onto the mettlesome horse and galloping off, leaving him red faced. One might also think of the laughs involved in the riding of horses into the post-coronation feast, and a later party in Wales where the royal circle danced until the floor gave way. It is unlikely that any of this would have taken place if Eleanor did not enter into the fun also. She was therefore a person who was ready to laugh and to share a joke. There is also, as we shall see, evidence of Eleanor's humour manifesting itself in the books which she commissioned, and sometimes in little touches of wordplay or architecture; in passing, glimpses of 'in jokes' peek out at us. All in all, we can be sure that Eleanor was far from sober or implacable in her daily dealings with those close to her. She liked a joke, and liked a household which was full of jokes. Indeed, the evidence suggests that Eleanor enjoyed making her friends laugh in turn.[6]

This more informal approach also seems consistent with the picture which emerges of Eleanor as regards clothes. There is good reason to suppose that Eleanor (like Edward) was far from being absorbed by this subject, and this is perhaps not surprising given the evidence of her very strong interests in work and in sport in the form of hunting. The evidence begins early: Eleanor's arrival in England in 1255 without the right clothes speaks volumes; what remotely clothes-centred woman would face a new family and a new job without all the right clothes – and the best she could afford? This fact alone tells us that for Eleanor there were many things more important than appearances. But it does not stand alone; the picture is reiterated by the limited extent to which descriptions of clothes feature in the wardrobe accounts or in the chronicles. Under Henry III and Eleanor of Provence, royal clothes were noteworthy – and usually new. The directions for the clothes for the Scottish wedding provide a fine example, with colours, cloth of gold, and furs all being minutely specified even for outfits which were to be worn only for a few hours.

Under Eleanor, smart and seemly seems to have been the watchword; the pictures which emerge from the wardrobe accounts of Eleanor's daughters having to make do and mend, and trot their smart dress out for the fifth or sixth time, even if they had ripped most of the buttons off dancing last time, are both hilarious and revealing. Interestingly, too, there is less sign of this prudent approach after Eleanor's death: the royal princesses were rather more indulged in their fineries. However, that is not to say that the proper level of grandeur was lacking: clothes, when purchased, were clearly very good and serious thought was given to their fabrics and to their adornment. We can see that Eleanor (as queen at least) was far from being scruffy. The flavour is, however, that clothes were to be good and comfortable, and to be smart enough to do the job. Again Eleanor's early training under Alfonso echoes here: the *Siete Partidas* directs that a prince or princess should be taught to wear fine and elegant clothes, like accustoming a horse to harness. Eleanor accepted her fine harness, but never came to love it.[7]

When it comes to her domestic surroundings, however, a marked change of emphasis emerges. There is every evidence that Eleanor liked her surroundings to be comfortable to the point of luxury; the home which she created was a thoroughly pleasant place in all its appointments. What is more, it is plain that all around her understood that this level of comfort was very important to her and that she wished to maintain it, while also maintaining the very active programme which was hers and Edward's modus operandi. The fact that a high degree of comfort was absolutely non-negotiable is well illustrated by the fact that her living quarters in less prepared locations (such as Rhuddlan and Caernarfon) were subjected to considerable overhauls prior to her arrival. Proper roofs (lead), painted walls, glazed windows (sometimes with decorative or coloured glazing), coloured candles, and at least a simulacrum of a proper garden – with a lawn and some sort of water feature – were imperative.

The same message emerges from a consideration of the places where the court generally stopped. While not palaces, properly so called, these 'hunting lodges' tended to be ones which had been the subject of major renovations by that arbiter of domestic comfort and style, Henry III. Thus Clarendon was a favoured stop. Here, we know that the wainscoting of the queen's room was green, starred with gold, and that the walls were painted as green curtains. Geddington was another fairly frequent stop throughout the reign, from December 1274 right up until Eleanor's final trip north. A proper hunting lodge under Henry II, it was the subject of a substantial building programme under Henry III. The great hall was overhauled with decorative windows (some with columns, some round and some with stained glass), and further windows were added to the queen's gallery and another major chamber; the queen's rooms were enlarged and redecorated, while the king's room had decorative green panelling with small gilt shields. The king's and queen's chapels were painted green spangled with gold.

Even well-decorated venues, though, had to be adjusted to her taste: the chapel at Westminster (which was obviously frequently visited) had to be repainted and re-gilded, though it is unlikely that Eleanor of Provence left it in a state of disrepair. But the importance of such comfort can maybe best be seen by considering a location not previously honoured by Henry III; we know that Eleanor's chambers at the little-used venue of Banstead (visited only once, on 12 May 1278) had the walls painted with colours before her stay.[8]

Sadly, owing to the loss of Eleanor's accounts for the relevant years, the precise details of the work done by Eleanor at Leeds Castle, where her own taste will have directed the work, are not known. We can, however, be sure that domestic comfort will have been well attended to; the one well-known aspect of the works there effectively proves this. For at Leeds one feature was what was known as 'the King's Bath house', which was certainly tiled and probably included a system for piping water direct. This seems to have been the first such bath house in English history. This feature is also an obvious reflection of Eleanor's fond memories of the glories of baths in her home country – and a desire to approximate to them in her new home. Indeed, Eleanor may properly be credited with pushing bathroom civilisation in this country forward more generally, for she also ensured that proper bathrooms (albeit probably lacking the piped water) were installed at Langley and Westminster.

As for colours, the rich colours of red and green seem to have been favourites in terms of decor, as they are mentioned repeatedly. They also figure large in descriptions of accessories and jewels; for example, an inventory of the effects of the Earl of Hereford (Eleanor's son-in-law) included a great crown set with rubies, emeralds and pearls which had been devised by Eleanor to her daughter.[9]

Although interior design does not appear to have captivated Eleanor quite to the extent it did Henry III and Eleanor of Provence, the records do show that Eleanor had a taste for fine items, with a multitude of small luxuries being detailed in the wardrobe records – a fact which is reflected in Agnes Strickland's portrait of Eleanor and which Parsons amusingly suggests produces a version of Eleanor 'as a housewife with all the modern conveniences'. The joke conceals a truth, however – Eleanor did give great attention to the making of an elegant and comfortable home. Here, her early years, surrounded by fine items of craftsmanship, shine through. Thus, her wardrobe records describe purchases of basins of Damascene work. This probably reflects 'Damasquinado de Oro', the art of decorating non-precious metals with gold which had become very common in Castile, and particularly Toledo. In this tradition, an ornate gold leaf pattern is sunk into steel which is later treated to turn it a glossy black. Eleanor also sent for other, more informal, brightly painted bowls of Andalusian manufacture. Other items bought included cloths from Tripoli, Venetian vases (possibly Murano-type blown glass), tapestries from Cologne and enamel caskets from Limoges.

Key to Eleanor's style appears to be the fact that even small items were required to be beautiful; in 1284 she purchased knives with jasper handles, and in 1289 she had her goldsmith add enamels and ornaments to the hilts of some knives. She had candles decorated in her favourite colours of red and green. Her mirrors, glass and metal, were housed in ivory cases and she purchased silver ornaments for her books. In the list of her plate after death also figure a fork of crystal, and a silver fork handled with ebony and ivory, thereby lending some ballast to the tradition that Eleanor was the introducer of this *sine qua non* of elegant dining, some 300 years before it was described by Thomas Coryate, and 500 years before the idea really caught on in England. This supposition is reinforced by the fact that the next instance of a fork being recorded is after Edward I's death, when six silver forks and one of gold were recorded in his possession.[10]

And then there were jewels – a number of records show such items being purchased from Parisian or Florentine merchants. But at least some of her jewellery was made closer to home – in Rhuddlan Castle in 1282, the queen had a building made for her goldsmith.

Then, of course, there were the tapestries. It will be recalled that decorating a room in this manner (including, shockingly, placing carpets on the floor) was seen as particularly Spanish at the time of Eleanor's arrival. Eleanor's own records show that such decoration remained close to her heart – aside from the Cologne tapestries mentioned above, four green and three red carpets were purchased for her by Edward in 1278, and she paid £5 to a 'tapeciarius' called John de Winton in 1286. She even employed her own tapestry keeper and there are references scattered through the records to the carpets and tapestries of the queen's chamber.

Her taste in this regard apparently set the fashion for the court: one of the duties of Edward I's royal chamberlain was 'to ensure that the king's chambers and banquets are ... adorned with hangings'. Moreover, the records show her lending a set of tapestries to her close friend John de Vescy, and their having to be reclaimed after his death from Anthony Bek, the Bishop of Durham, who was plainly thought to be likely to keep his hands on such fine work.

Not all such decorative work was of foreign manufacture. John de Winton's supplies may well have been of domestic manufacture, and certainly England produced textiles of which Eleanor was proud; she sent her brother Alfonso hangings and vestments which she had had made which he later bequeathed to the cathedral of Seville.

Overall, therefore, a tone of considerable domestic luxury emerges when one considers Eleanor's taste. This is further emphasised when one considers that, after her death, those items of her carpets hangings and jewels which were not gifted elsewhere – in other words the less desirable portions of her collection – were sold for the staggering sum of £617 11s 10d.[11]

As for food, again Eleanor's early tastes acquired in Spain show through clearly. She was plainly pleased with the fruits which were available in England: apples, pears and quinces feature often, and though not shown in the records, grapes were available and are likely to have been enjoyed too. She was also sent gifts of fruit by the Earl of Lincoln on her return in 1289, and also by two poor women – suggesting that if anything about Eleanor was notorious, it was a taste for fruit. But it is also clear that she missed the more exotic fruits of home. Her accounts show repeated entries for fruit imported from Spain and indeed her eagerness for the fruit can be seen in the fact that she is recorded sending the messenger to meet the ship. The fruits purchased included figs, pomegranates, lemons and oranges and also dates and raisins. Vines and apples from France also feature as introductions in her gardens. Saffron seems also to have been missed; this is surely the 'strange colour' of which four earthen jars were purchased in November 1289. Unsurprisingly, too, there are records of purchases of olive oil for her. She also thought well of the onions of her maternal county – in 1280 she sent for seventeen large baskets of them. However, it seems she also developed something of a passion for soft cheeses, particularly those of Brie; there are repeated items in the wardrobe accounts for the purchase of such cheeses and the presentation of a cheese for Christmas for her in 1286 suggests her taste for them was something of a joke among her intimates.[12]

So far as anything about Eleanor's personality is well known, it is her taste for gardens and here, too, the influence of her childhood is strongly felt. Eleanor did not simply employ local men, but sent back to the Iberian peninsula for specialists who understood the idiom she sought to invoke. She thus employed a number of Aragonese gardeners at Langley, among whom was Ferdinand 'Ispannus', the gardener, and she left money in her will for them to return to Spain. A consideration of their work reveals why they may have been called for. The documentation shows that part of the extensive works undertaken in constructing the new gardens at Langley involved the digging of wells and ditches, and the documentation includes a layout of multiple wells. This is highly suggestive of some approach to the Spanish water gardens of her childhood.[13]

Langley is not the only place where the water gardens of Castile are referenced. There seems to be evidence of her having brought the Spanish/Arabic taste for water gardens with her to England, and created a number of homages to her native lands in her gardens. The most obvious influence of her home and its water gardens is perhaps the gloriette – the small structure which juts out into the water from the main castle at Leeds Castle, which may almost be a tribute to the famous garden of Ismail al-Mamun at Toledo. But also her garden at Westminster boasted a lead-lined pond, overlooked by an oriel window and filled by pipes from the river (hence running water rather than a static pond). There is also mention of a water channel at the Queen's Garden at Wolvesey Castle in Winchester. At Rhuddlan there was a garden with a fishpond and seats surrounding it.

There is also evidence of the erection in 1275 of a magnificent ornamental fountain at the mews near the site of the later Charing Cross, which had water brought by aqueduct from neighbouring land and pouring through four leopard-head spouts into a lead pool, the whole being surmounted by a bronze falcon. Pausing here, we may see two small private jokes – the use of the leopard's head rather than the maned lion used in Islamic gardens was doubtless a reference to the English coat of arms, which showed leopards, and the falcon on its summit was a reference to the location in the royal mews (mews then being associated with falconry rather than horses).[14]

Nor did her interest stop there. At Langley, Eleanor provided for a paved cloister, a garden and a park as well as the water features. Reflecting her interest in fruit, and the difficulties of obtaining enough for her taste in England, one feature of the extensive gardens planted there included apple trees (sent by Eleanor from Ponthieu and Aquitaine) and vines, which had their own 'vineator', the deliciously named James Frangypany. There was also apparently a summerhouse – a lodge known as 'little London' with a hall and chambers for recreation, again reminiscent of the garden pavilions of her homeland. At Westminster, the garden was replanted in 1277 under Eleanor's direction with vines and roses set around a lawn, and later improved with new cuttings and turves and a herbarium. A herbarium also featured in another of Eleanor's gardens at Mauléon in Gascony.[15]

There are also suggestions that Eleanor introduced Spanish plants; the hollyhock is one plant first reported in England at about this time which is commonly said to have been introduced by her, and its old-fashioned name of 'Spanish rose' does lend some colour to this tradition. Given the style of Spanish gardens, it is unlikely to have been a feature of a main garden, though its medicinal properties would qualify it to feature in one of Eleanor's herbaria. The suggestions that she introduced sweet rocket, wallflower, stock and perhaps lavender seem speculative – and the latter is far more likely to have been introduced by Eleanor of Provence. More certainly, there is evidence of her introducing certain French fruit varieties such as the apple varieties mentioned above and the cooking pear Cailloel.[16]

A keen interest thus is plain. But the very great importance to her of a garden is perhaps best indicated by the fact that when Eleanor was to sojourn in the building site that was Caernarfon Castle, arrangements were made to bring a garden to the castle. Likewise, in her earlier 1282 stay at Rhuddlan Castle, another garden was constructed – the details of which do not survive but some hints of which can be ascertained from the fragmentary accounts which remain for that period. So 6,000 turves were brought down by boat to turf the 80–90-foot courtyard (which still exists, albeit with no trace of the garden). Around the well, whose roof was boarded, Willemo le Plomer created a little fishpond with seats set around the pond. Landsberg calculates that the amount of turfing ordered, compared to the size of the space, indicates that the pool edging and seats were all turfed. Fencing within the garden was created from tun barrels. The amount of turfing employed here, at Caernarfon and at the Tower in fact also suggests that Eleanor came to appreciate that most English of gardening features – a lawn.

Even at relatively infrequently visited places, such as Banstead, gardens were put in order; there, for what appears to have been a single night's stay, a timber-framed cloister was constructed and a park enclosed with ditches and hedges. The sense which emerges is that one thing which was guaranteed to cloud Eleanor's temper was the absence of a decent garden.[17]

As one might expect from the fact that the court generally stayed at hunting lodges rather than urban castles or palaces, both Eleanor and Edward enjoyed hunting, but their tastes diverged as to the mode. Edward was an aficionado of falconry, while Eleanor preferred to hunt with dogs and maintained a number of different categories of hunting employees. It is probably no coincidence that the illustration in the Alphonso Psalter of a noble lady hunting shows her hunting with dogs (who look like greyhounds).

Some flavour of the extent of the hunting interest can be gained by looking at the provision made for it at some of the places where Eleanor and Edward stayed. So Geddington was the base for an extensive kennels for the royal greyhounds and also a mews for royal falcons, each of whose feed cost ½d per day (more, according to one calculation, than Eleanor de Montfort provided by way of alms to the poor), while Odiham had stabling for over two hundred horses.

It may well be this passionate interest in hunting which in part informs a curiosity noted by Marc Morris: every year from 1278 to 1282, in February/March (and again in 1289 after the upheavals of the mid-1280s), the royal family seems to have settled down for something approaching a holiday in the Cotswolds at Quenington near Cirencester. The timing of these visits might seem peculiar – it is a little early, even allowing for the effects of the Medieval Warm Period, for the delightful Cotswolds spring to be in full operation – until one recalls that hunting, of which both Edward and Eleanor were inordinately fond, is in full swing in February. Quenington is very close to the territory of the modern Beaufort hunt; their 2013 Boxing Day hunt commenced at Didmarton, one of Eleanor's nearby properties.

The possibility of this being the favoured royal hunting location is supported by the fact that there were also fairly regular stops in November or December (albeit usually only for two to three days) and the fact that it was unlikely that it was the most comfortable of the locations chosen for court stays. Quenington was not a royal manor but a preceptory for the Knights Hospitallers of St John, the manor having been given to them by the de Lucy family late in the twelfth century. It was therefore likely to offer a very good level of comfort in very congenial surroundings, but it would not be amenable to Eleanor's own preferences. There must therefore have been a very good reason for its favoured status, and hunting would seem the obvious answer.[18]

Eleanor was plainly a keen horsewoman, with her wardrobe records, especially those in Gascony, liberally featuring purchases of horses and harness and other riding impedimenta. She was also interested in the breeding of horses. This probably reflects her Spanish heritage, as horse breeding was taken very seriously there, with some monasteries applying a very scholarly approach to the subject; and Spanish horses had long been highly prized elsewhere in Europe. Thus, Eleanor employed a stud manager from Spain, one Garcia, and had studs at Hampton, Horsington (using this manor for this purpose was very possibly Eleanor's idea of a joke), Woodstock and Estwood. Tolley suggests that the employment of a Spaniard as stud manager reflects her use of Spanish jennets, which had a reputation for speed, strength and beauty through the cross breeding of European stock with the Arab horse, with which the Iberian countries were of course familiar as a consequence of the Muslim invasion.

Whether, as he also suggests, such high-status horses were used by Eleanor as mounts for her messengers may be more doubtful. However, as a good judge of horseflesh it is no surprise that her messengers had horses which could achieve the speedy correspondence shown in the records. She does seem to have promoted the use of Spanish horses by Edward's key supporters: most of his close circle purchased horses from Spain after the time of the marriage. Eleanor's influence can probably also be seen in Edward's introduction of studs for selective breeding: a younger Garcia was then employed in the studs of Edward II and Edward III.[19]

There is also considerable evidence that Eleanor was very fond of birds – a large aviary was included in the 1279 refurbishment of the Westminster gardens, and there are references in her accounts to swans, Sicilian parrots and nightingales. She also bought birds in Ponthieu and had them sent back to England. There are records of a further aviary at Leeds Castle. This taste is evidenced by the lavish use made of illustrations of birds in the Alphonso Psalter; as Yapp points out, it is unlikely that the artist would have gone this far unless requested to do so by the commissioner of the work. Looking at the illustrations, one suspects it was a taste which Eleanor shared with Alphonso or a taste of Alphonso's which she wanted to indulge, as the pictures seem designed to appeal to a child. Thus, a hunting scene is observed by an elegant crane, the royal coats of arms are separated by a very lifelike and rather comic seagull, a vivid woodpecker perches beside the text and one page is adorned by a most beautiful pair of peacocks being harassed by what appears to be a common or garden cockerel. Likewise in the Bird Psalter, also commenced for Alphonso's anticipated marriage, which cannot be directly proved to be commissioned by Eleanor but is probably linked to her, there are twenty-seven different species of birds carefully depicted. Again humour is notable in the pictures, such as the seagull who is managing to hide beneath a very large butterfly.

It seems likely that this taste for birds, aside from his hunting them, was shared by Edward too, since a reference to Eleanor's bird catcher has him taking birds 'for the king's amusement'. For those hunting birds, of course, Edward had his own lavish mews at Charing (approximately where Trafalgar Square now lies), with a lead bath for the birds and running water via the leopard's head fountain referred to above. He also had a probably even larger mews in Bicknor in Kent, where the chief falconer, John de Bicknor, lived.[20]

Turning away from outside pursuits, Eleanor had a documented enthusiasm for chess, and is likely to have gained it in childhood, her brother Alfonso being a noted chess patron, even being depicted playing chess. Her taste involved her in sending for a handbook of chess tactics from Alfonso. In 1286, Edward gave her a set of chessmen made of jasper and crystal, probably in her favourite colours of red and green, which seems to have had strong sentimental associations – he reclaimed it from her effects after her death and probably passed it to one of her children. Inferentially, her tastes influenced her children and other descendants: Edward III and his sister are both documented as possessing jasper-and-crystal chess sets. If she gambled on her chess games (as Edward did at least on some occasions) it would appear she was a good player, since, unlike him, her wardrobe accounts note very few losses. Aside from chess, Eleanor also played backgammon, or 'tables' as it was then known, and 'the game of four kings', which may well have been a four-hand chess variation.[21]

One other thing of which we can be quite certain is that Eleanor was very bookish indeed by the standards of her day. That is proved conclusively by the fact that she ran, as part of her household, a scriptorium wherein books she wished to read could be copied. This scriptorium – the only one documented for any royal court in Northern Europe in this period (even St Louis lacked one) speaks of a very powerful appetite for books indeed – way beyond the interests even among highly educated royal men of the time. Funding a scriptorium was, in essence, the act of a book addict and scholar. That it was Eleanor's own very personal interest and perhaps regarded as somewhat eccentric is demonstrated by the fact that it was disbanded by Edward on her death. In it were employed two scribes, Roger and Philip, and a 'pictor', Godfrey, who seems to have travelled with her, at least to Gascony. Another 'scriptor', Hugh of Hibernia, is also

mentioned in the records. The staff of the scriptorium purchased a full
range of materials needed to produce books: vellum, ink, quills, colours,
gold leaf, boards for binding books, glue and mucilage. This, and casual
references to their productions in the accounts – vellum being purchased
specifically for a life of St Thomas Becket, for example – prove conclusively
that it was a true scriptorium and not a mere correspondence office which
was being maintained. The importance which Eleanor attached to her
books is further shown by the fact that a chamber specifically for the
scriptorium was constructed at Westminster in 1289.[22]

Ironically, the existence of the scriptorium is in some sense a handicap
to ascertaining Eleanor's reading interests, because no correspondence
remains in relation to its works, which is not the case for commissions
outside the scriptorium. Thus we simply do not know how many books
the scriptorium produced, or what they were. But two commissions do
remain, and indicate a high degree of education on Eleanor's part. The
first is the commission for the copy of Vegetius' classic Roman military
handbook *De Re Miltarii* as a gift for Edward. The fact of the commission
shows that Eleanor knew what the contents of the book were, and her
familiarity with it is further evidenced by the comment inserted into the
commissioned work comparing his action at Evesham to the relevant
portion of the text. Apparently her education in Castile had covered
Vegetius (in Latin), and it had stuck in her mind as useful knowledge for
her solider husband. The other known commission is for a copy from
her brother of a translation of an Arabic chess manual, again a notably
highbrow choice.

In addition, among the forty-seven letters of Eleanor's which survive,
of which forty-six concern her administration and property empire, there
is one which is a letter of thanks to the Abbot of Cerne thanking him for
sending her a copy of a book which she wished to borrow. Again, it seems
almost certain that this book was a serious work, probably of theology.
This evidence for Eleanor reading and studying serious academic works
is also supported by one of her final recorded pieces of correspondence,
which was with an academic at Oxford about a point of theology, and
by Archbishop Pecham's exposition for her in his 'Jerarchie' of the
Hierarchia of Pseudo-Dionysius. The latter was a work of neo-Platonic
mystical theology which was influential on the scholastic approach to
theology and which, having been translated by Robert Grosseteste in the
early 1240s, was a subject for debate in the latter part of the century.
Pecham's work, which compares the hierarchy of angels to the ranks of
the king's officials, demonstrates that he appreciated that Eleanor sought
this work for her own information, and that his analogy was chosen to be
one which she would find familiar and useful. Her considerable interest in
theology is also indicated by her intimacy with the renowned theologian
William of Hotham.[23]

We can also see hints of Eleanor's love of learning even in her staffing of her office. It seems quite likely, for example, that Eleanor's strong taste for the academic was accountable for her appointment in 1277 of Geoffrey de Aspale as her wardrobe keeper – effectively her most senior household officer. He will have been familiar to her from the Crusade, which he joined in 1270, but is better known as a distinguished scholar of Aristotle, in particular his scientific works. Given the absence of any known qualifications for a financial career, and the fact that he left her accounts in considerable disarray when he died in 1287, it is unlikely that he was recruited for his skills as a financial manager. Rather, there is a sense that Eleanor's respect for his academic attainments, and possibly pleasure in discussing such subjects with him, encouraged her to admit him to a job for which he was not the most qualified candidate.

However, while relishing academic reading, there is evidence of a playful humour even in that; the amusing nature of the illustrations in the Alphonso Psalter have been alluded to above. Likewise, the copy of Vegetius now in the Cambridge Fitzwilliam Museum (which is probably a later copy of the original) features illustrations showing Lord Edward and his knights assembled at the feet of Vegetius, and of a lively sea fight involving different types of weapon. The Douce Apocalypse also shows signs of private jokes being inserted in the use of the arms of Simon de Montfort and Gilbert of Gloucester amongst the forces of the Antichrist.[24]

Nor was Eleanor's reading all highbrow. Certainly, it was not centred on the lighter Arthurian romances preferred by Eleanor of Provence, but it should by no means be assumed that Eleanor was above such interests. The wardrobe records show a purchase of a coffer *per romanciis regine* (in essence, for the queen's novels) which demonstrates that she liked to have some lighter reading to hand on her travels. Likewise, the fact that while on Crusade Edward gave Rustichello di Pisa a large volume of romance as the basis for the new work *Meliadus* suggests that he (and inevitably Eleanor too) had read *Palamedes* or the Prose *Tristan*, where the Meliadus story is touched upon.

But there are also two very interesting commissions by her. She was the dedicatee of Girard of Amiens' *Escanor*, and is specifically said by the author not only to have commissioned the work but also to have told him the outline of the story. The book is a very minor Arthurian work but its theme is not uninteresting, involving a Northumbrian princess and the enmity-turned-friendship between Escanor and Sir Gawain. The fact that *Escanor* appears to describe paintings of the royal palaces, which Girard would probably not have seen, tends to confirm his story of her positive input. If it is true that Eleanor told the story to Girard, it suggests a very thorough knowledge of the genre, and an interest in local variations of the canon. Moreover, that regional flavour suggests it may have been intended as a present for one or both of John or Isabelle de Vescy – or for their marriage; a particularly thoughtful present.[25]

The other fascinating commission is an illustrated copy of 'un romanz de Isembart' from France in 1281. Isembart was the hero of a French *chanson de geste* based on legends arising from the Battle of Saucourt in 881, and had been recently asserted by French historians to be a local Ponthevin hero, probably a count or duke of Ponthieu. In the tale, Isembart features as a rebellious young French lord who allies himself with a Saracen king, Gormont, renouncing his Christianity, and fights against the French king. There was an obvious family resonance for Eleanor, aside from the geographical association, given the Dammartin side of her family's history of opposition to the French king, and it is even possible that the commission had a political motive reflecting this. Certainly there are other commissions of essentially anti-Capetian work, notably translations of the *Historia Caroli Magna* (also known as the *Pseudo-Turpin Chronicle*) which are traceable to Renaud of Dammartin or his intimates; there is one by Renaud of Dammartin's chaplain and another commissioned by a Ponthevin lord taken prisoner with Simon of Dammartin at Bouvines. And again, the local link suggests someone had researched the local history. The Isembart song, but not the historical association with Ponthieu, is mentioned by Geoffrey of Monmouth; thus the inspiration for the commission cannot have come from there alone. This apparently light work therefore provides grounds for supposing Eleanor to have been familiar not just with the *chanson de geste*, but with what was then recent historical research; this would of course make sense, coming as she did from the Castilian court, which was enthusiastic about the historical record. It also provides some grounds for supposing that she knew of the *Pseudo-Turpin Chronicle* and the propaganda uses to which it had been put by her relations in the near vicinity of Ponthieu.[26]

Overall, there seem to be good grounds to suppose that Eleanor was an enthusiastic reader of light fiction, especially Arthurian, and of history as well as of more weighty works. The Arthurian enthusiasm was probably shared in some measure by Edward, brought up on Eleanor of Provence's Arthurian tales.

With her brother Alfonso, there appears to have been the lively give and take to be expected between two bookworms. Eleanor sent a copy of Rusticiano's *Meliadus*, which Edward commissioned while on Crusade, to Alfonso, and it then went on to influence the Arthurian tradition in Castile, in particular *Tristan de Leonis*, the first Arthurian Castilian romance. From him, in turn, she seems to have received at least a manual on chess, a very early copy of the first part of the *Siete Partidas*, and *The Ladder of Mohammed*, which had been translated from Arabic to Spanish by Alfonso's Jewish doctor Abraham and thence to French by Alfonso's clerk Buonaventura de Siena. It is also considered likely that she brought with her on her first arrival in England the *Primera Cronica General*, since this book was later found in her son's possession. The existence of this book in England, and the knowledge that another court was ensuring an 'authorised history', has been suggested to have influenced the 'official' continuation under Edward II of the *Flores Historiarum*.[27]

Certainly Eleanor seems to have been the intellectual driving force of Edward's court; as Binski notes, every book recorded in Edward's possession or that of his family can be traced back to Eleanor. Moreover, under her aegis, the entire thrust of literary production at court moved away from the rather 'vanilla' devotional verse and lives of the saints favoured by Henry III and Eleanor of Provence towards a genuine historical interest, sometimes in instructive prose works and sometimes in the forms of chivalric romances.[28]

Lives of the saints also appear to have figured in Eleanor's library – when a payment was made in 1288 for repairs to some of her novels and books, the ones specified are lives of St Thomas Becket and St Edward the Confessor (the latter presumably the copy given her as a gift on her arrival in England). But they are alone; there is no particular sign of enthusiasm for this portion of Eleanor's library. Eleanor also purchased religious works – records remain of her buying a 'portiferium' (akin to a breviary) in 1278 and a psalter and seven primers from Cambridge in 1289. She has also been credibly linked to the commissioning of two psalters – the Alphonso and Bird psalters – and to two Apocalypses – the Douce and the Trinity. The latter certainly shows signs of having been influenced by a Castilian-styled Apocalypse, which it seems may have formed part of her library on her marriage.[29]

As for the practice of religion, the simple approach would be to record Eleanor's charities and her extensive patronage of the Dominicans. However, if one digs a little deeper, an altogether more interesting picture emerges. A good place to start is with those basic facts. Eleanor was a very considerable religious and charitable patron. Of course charitable giving was absolutely expected of a queen, but there is evidence that Eleanor's contributions were over and above expectation. Thus, there was a set amount allowed in the king's accounts for almsgiving by the queen – 2s daily for distribution while travelling and 7s for oblations at religious shrines – but Eleanor's donations exceeded this and are recorded in her own *Liber Garderobe*. There are also a number of records in the king's expenses of his making extra donations at Eleanor's instance. So in winter of 1283–4, Eleanor asked Edward to feed extra poor men and women over the coldest weeks of the year and she asked for extra donations to be made on certain saints' days. No definitive reckoning can be made from the sources owing to their incompleteness, but Parsons has calculated that between April 1289 and November 1290 (the period of the surviving *Liber Garderobe*) Eleanor provided meals for 9,306 paupers at a cost of

1½*d* per meal. In other words, she was feeding about fifteen poor people a day. Overall, it would seem that Eleanor exceeded by a considerable factor the expected level of donation; for example, Eleanor de Montfort has been calculated to give 4*d* per day to Eleanor's approximate 60*d* (ignoring her donations while travelling).[30]

Secondly, Eleanor was a devoted patron of the Dominican Order, and has been called the 'nursing mother' and a devoted friend of the Dominican Order in England. There are ample records of donations to the friars at most of their English locations. Specifically one sees gifts of land to the Dominicans in Chichester, and substantial gifts to the Rhuddlan priory while she was in Wales. She is recorded as foundress or co-foundress of the Dominican priories at London (where her heart was to be buried), Chichester and Rhuddlan and she planned to settle Dominican nuns at Langley, though that plan was thwarted by her death. She enriched other houses such as Northampton, Salisbury and Saint-Sever in Gascony. She was also very generous to the Oxford chapter of the Dominicans; the wardrobe accounts for 1289–90 show that she provided money for food and drink at their provincial chapters of 1289 and 1290, sent salmon to the Oxford priory in Lent 1290, and provided food and drink there and at the Oxford Franciscans' priory for the anniversary of her brother's death in 1290. Indeed, so generous were her benefactions there that, in 1280, the Oxford chapter admitted Eleanor and her children to spiritual participation in the order's good works. While she also gave gifts to members of the Franciscan orders, to the Benedictine nunneries at Amesbury and Cheshunt and to two nuns at the Benedictine priory of Huntingdon St James, there is no doubt that the vast majority of her religious patronage went to the Dominicans; as such, Parsons has described her as being the most active royal foundress since Edith-Matilda, wife of Henry I.[31]

This aspect of Eleanor's religious and charitable giving provides a good point of entry for a more nuanced consideration of her religious interests. The very fact of her choosing the Dominicans as her main religious point of contact is not insignificant. They were, of course, familiar to her from her childhood, but represented a somewhat unorthodox choice for a queen. Generally, the Dominicans at this time received support from male members of the royal family, with the female members being patrons of the Franciscans. So Eleanor's patronage of the Dominicans was not a 'given', but represents a positive choice on her part; either in acknowledgement of her early education and training at their hands, or possibly reflecting her preference for their slightly more academic and less emotive approach to theology.

In concert with this piece of unorthodoxy, there is an absence of the other religious links which might be expected. Eleanor of Provence obviously had the advantage, denied to her daughter-in-law, of retreating to a convent in her old age; however, even as a young woman and throughout her years as queen, she was very embedded in the religious hierarchy of the English Church. Her brother, of course, became Archbishop of Canterbury, but she also corresponded with numerous bishops, including Edmund Rich of Canterbury, Richard Wych of Chichester, Nicholas Farnham of Durham and Robert Grosseteste of Lincoln. Letters survive from the latter in particular, seeking to advise her on how to use her queenly influence, and he supported her in her dispute with Henry III over the Flamstead appointment.

Nor was her reference to these bishops purely or even mainly on matters of business. Farnham, for example, was her moral guide and her doctor within her household until his elevation in 1241, and it seems likely that she continued to seek and to receive his moral guidance. She also sought spiritual and moral guidance from the celebrated Franciscan Adam Marsh – indeed, she appears to have positively bombarded him with letters, begging him to visit and provide guidance face to face, to which he occasionally had to return a plea of being too busy. She also kept a spiritual director within her household – William Batale, who was installed on Marsh's recommendation. Howell has even traced the influence of a third spiritual coach, Thomas of Hales, who may or may not have been the queen's chaplain for a few years, but who certainly specialised in providing moral guidance to aristocratic ladies via emotionally charged written works – the emotive appeal being very much the Franciscan style. Howell concludes that the fervour and lyricism of this style of piety was plainly very much to Eleanor of Provence's taste.[32]

Similarly, Eleanor de Montfort was fond of the Franciscan approach, and also sought a considerable amount of guidance from Adam Marsh, who directed her religious reading, and advised her on her moral conduct, including on the proper submission, restraint and passivity which a wife should show to her husband and adjured her to mind her temper, which he considered she governed less well than she should. She, too, retained a spiritual adviser in her household.[33]

With Eleanor of Castile, however, a very different picture emerges. She had no spiritual friendships with bishops at all. Those bishops to whom she was close, she was close as a matter of business. Thus the bishops with whom we can trace an intimacy are Burnell (of course), whose promotion she and Edward sought assiduously, precisely because he was their principal man of business, and John de Kirkby of Ely, who assisted her first property acquisitions and became her most regular correspondent on property affairs. There is perhaps half an intimacy with Godfrey Giffard at Worcester, but this was thanks to his family links to the royal family – his mother assisted at the birth of Edward, his father was Edward's tutor, and he had a niece among her ladies. Moreover, when Eleanor wrote to the Curia on his behalf in 1282, she spoke not of his spiritual qualities or advice, but of his advice in the business sense. The nearest one comes to spiritual advice flowing from a bishop to Eleanor is Pecham's 'Jerarchie'; but that is actually not advice, but effectively a scholarly précis, intended to assist private theological study. On occasion, Pecham may have (as can be seen above) sought to adjure Eleanor in respect of her behaviour, but this was not solicited advice. Nor, as we have seen, was it followed.

Her closest religious contact appears to have been Brother William of Hotham, a prominent Dominican and one of the foremost theologians of his day. Hotham is documented as being with the royal party in Wales in 1283, shortly before he clashed with Pecham on the fierce debate which had been underway for some years, and which was to simmer on until the Reformation, about the impact of Aristotelian thought on traditional Augustinian theology. This was a subject where the Parisian Dominicans, led by Thomas Aquinas and supported by Hotham, led the way. Given Eleanor's education, her employment of a prominent Aristotelian thinker in Geoffrey de Aspale, and her intimacy with Hotham, it seems hugely likely that she followed this debate closely, and sided with the Dominicans – against Pecham.

There are therefore distinct signs that Eleanor effectively rejected the established model for a queen's involvement in religion. Instead of building relationships with prominent bishops, she did so with the Dominican Order (which encouraged an intellectual approach to religion) generally, and particularly notably with their Oxford chapter, where some of their most distinguished and controversial theologians were based. Instead of relying upon moral and religious guidance from a spiritual director or adviser, Eleanor made her own study of theology and formed her own views. Both of these are, of course, entirely consistent with her upbringing under the Dominicans and the intellectual approach to religion which Alfonso X advocates in the *Siete Partidas*.

Further, and again consistently, what we can see of Eleanor's private devotions reinforces the impression of an independent and intellectual approach to religion. In 1278, she was given a dispensation to permit her to have a portable altar for her chapel. This altar and the two coffers full of furnishings which it required seem to have been a slightly comic theme in the royal court's peregrinations: some part or other of the furnishings was often missing, with the coffer having been left behind, or there having been no suitable cart to carry it. Then, as we have seen above, Eleanor had primers and books of hours, redolent of private devotions, and commissioned at least one psalter for her son. On the same theme and following the approach of the Dominicans, who are widely attributed with early fostering of the rosary, there are records of purchases of jet and coral beads for her own use. Finally her commemorations involved requirements, specifically stipulated by her, for prayer repetitions both by the clergy and by the objects of charitable donations in her memory.[34]

One point which Parsons has remarked upon is that, despite her considerable donations, Eleanor gained at the time practically no reputation as a charitable giver and her interests in this regard largely escaped the contemporaneous chroniclers and the historians who relied on them prior to his groundbreaking work. This is likely because of a noticeable difference in her approach to that of the noble lady patron paradigm, where ladies associated themselves personally with the donations. Thus Eleanor of Provence, like earlier queens, partnered her intercessory work with a broad range of charitable donations (including patronage of up-and-coming churchmen), and was seen as being a very charitable woman. However, Eleanor of Castile, while giving more, did so predominantly to the very poor and not directly but through chaplains and almoners. She otherwise gave almost entirely to purely religious causes. Again, this anomaly is consistent with the Dominican intellectual piety which she appears to have practised.

Parsons slightly shies away from the conclusion that Eleanor's approach to religious practice and to charitable donation was a deliberate one, and therefore an assertion of individuality. But it should be borne in mind that Eleanor was not likely to be unaware of the fact that her approach to this field of interest could, if she wished, be used to 'spin' her reputation and indeed to present herself in a conventionally pious light, broadening her appeal outside her own circle. The better view, therefore, is that, particularly when taken in conjunction with her unorthodox approach to the related subject of intercession, this approach was indeed deliberate. Eleanor had been raised to adopt a rigorous and intellectual approach to religion. She appears to have wished to be true to this, and she also appears to have seen no need to gild the lily to please anyone.[35]

Eleanor the queen was, therefore, not merely an intelligent and able woman, but a woman of many interests, which she pursued with considerable enthusiasm and determination. Her extensive reading ensured that she had much to contribute to discussions in many directions – be the conversation literary, historical, military or theological – and her sense of humour seems to have ensured that she wore her considerable scholarship lightly. She presents herself to us as a woman with a vibrant zest for life. Her vitality is reflected in her passion for hunting and even more so in her obviously notorious fondness for delicious food, which even had local poor women bringing fine items (or on one occasion 'a large loaf') for the queen's enjoyment. This last vignette also echoes the earlier evidence of her wardrobe accounts. Eleanor might have had a terrible temper when roused, but she seems to have exercised it on those who were in positions of power. To those who occupied a more humble position, she was a kindly and approachable queen; a real woman, not a figure of unimaginable glamour.

12

The Queen's Family

The next question to ask is, who was Eleanor's family? To whom did she look for support and affection in the busy and pressured years of her queenship? The answer is more complex than might be imagined.

The starting point for any consideration of Eleanor's family must be the most important constituent of it to her – her husband. The more time one spends looking at the life of Eleanor, the more apparent it becomes that she and Edward were genuinely incredibly close, and not really happy out of each other's company. Marc Morris concludes, and I entirely agree, that their shared tastes for horses, hunting, chivalry, romance and chess had provided a good base for a happy marriage. More than this, though, it is fairly clear that they shared a sense of humour – each was plainly ready to laugh and to find fun in amusing pictures and little wordplays and both also enjoyed the kind of boisterous fun which marked the coronation. Beyond these shared interests and tendencies, however, one can see in the household records the hallmarks of active respect, consideration and kindness which promote a happy marriage.

So repeatedly each can be seen paying attention to the interests of the other, and doing their best to help. Each helped the other financially – Eleanor gifting Edward with 1,000 marks when he and everyone else was out of cash following the Gascon expedition, and Edward helping with purchase monies and funds for improvements for her properties. For Eleanor, Edward was the centre of the world, and she identified herself completely with his interests – as she had been raised to do. Everything gave way to his interests and she would uproot herself from her work for years at a time to be with him in Wales and in Gascony, as well as on Crusade. Although Eleanor had her own office and power base of very able employees, there was no 'Team Queen' operating in opposition to 'Team King' as there had been under Eleanor of Provence and Henry III. Eleanor and her staff were parts of Edward's team, and never sought to be perceived otherwise. But it was far from being a one-way street.

Having charged Eleanor with a role in property management, Edward was supportive of Eleanor's very active interest in this role to the extent of inconveniencing himself in repeated dislocations.

Each can also be spotted in the records planning pleasant surprises for the other, and trying generally to make life more pleasant for their spouse. So in Gascony, Eleanor sent home to get Edward a particularly special hunting bird for his birthday, while on another occasion Edward, mindful of Eleanor's book obsession and vibrant theological interests, commissioned a psalter and book of hours as a present for her. Facing a social engagement too far, Eleanor agreed to go by herself, and made arrangements for musicians to be hired to amuse Edward while she was discharging their social obligations. Meanwhile, Edward made sure that everywhere they went, gardeners and decorators went ahead so that Eleanor need not face the shabby lodgings which were her aversion.

One surprising thing which emerges from the record is that Edward was surprisingly sentimental – rather more so, it would appear, than Eleanor. So the records of his charitable oblations for 1283–4 show him giving extra alms on the occasion of their wedding anniversary and also in those nervous days in the run-up to Eleanor giving birth to Edward, as well as the expected celebratory donations on the birth and christening of a prince. When Eleanor was ill and he could not actually be with her, he sent thoughtful gifts of food, with which he hoped to tempt her appetite or recoup her strength. The public face of his mourning is well known, but in addition to the well-known gestures after Eleanor's death of commissioning spectacular funeral monuments, he provided chantries at the place of her death and at Leeds Castle, where they had spent happy time together. He also took for himself the chess set with which they had played chess together.[1]

The next group to consider must be Eleanor's children. It might be thought that, with such a large family, Eleanor would find all the ties she needed here; but, as will become apparent, this was far from being the case.

So far as the children are concerned, the shape which the family was to take can conveniently be tracked by rejoining Eleanor just after the coronation, because to celebrate the return there was to be yet another baby. Shortly after Edward and Eleanor made it back to Windsor Castle from their spring tour, Eleanor gave birth to Margaret (reportedly on 15 March 1275), who must have been conceived during the journey home.

Within a few months of Margaret's birth, Eleanor was pregnant yet again – Berengaria, born 1 May 1276 at Kempton, must have been conceived in the summer of 1275 while Eleanor and Edward made their way northwards slowly towards a possible meeting with Llywelyn ap Gruffudd. And so the pattern continued: a daughter, born dead at Westminster in January 1278; another daughter, Mary, born at Woodstock in March 1279; another son who died young in 1280 or

1281; Elizabeth, born in Rhuddlan in August 1282; and finally Edward, famously born in Caernarfon in April 1284.[2]

There may even have been further pregnancies in Gascony in the years after 1286. That possibility is certainly suggested by the pattern of childbearing which one can see from this listing: there were sixteen months between Alphonso and Margaret, fourteen months between her and Berengaria, twenty months to the next anonymous daughter, fourteen months to Mary, eighteen months each for the anonymous boy and Elizabeth, and a further nineteen months to Edward. Thus, over this period Eleanor was bearing a child roughly every eighteen months or less. This is consistent with the pattern of births of the children born between 1265 and Margaret's birth: between Joan (born January 1265) and John was eighteen months (during some of which Edward was imprisoned). Between John and Henry was twenty-one months and then a gap of just thirteen months to Eleanor, another eighteen months to the birth of the anonymous daughter in Sicily, and barely a year then to Joan of Acre in spring 1272. She herself was followed by Alphonso eighteen months later. So for the best part of twenty years Eleanor bore a child every thirteen to twenty months.[3]

The absolute number of children which Eleanor bore is perhaps not important – on any analysis, she bore between fourteen and eighteen children in about twenty years. This bold statistic illustrates more than one point. The first is that Edward and Eleanor had, and continued to have, a thriving marriage. This tally of children would be regarded as pretty remarkable even in the modern era, without prescribed saints' day abstinences; in the context of those religious layoffs – and because of the story about the end of Lenten abstinence, and the dates of the children's births, we know that Edward and Eleanor observed this taboo – it becomes pretty staggering. The bottom line is that the two of them were plainly as little separated as possible.

The second fact it tells is that Eleanor had a very hard life physically. Although recent research has tended to suggest that what is termed 'great grand multiparity' is not necessarily an overall physical risk factor to the mother, no one can doubt that pregnancy is a physical strain on the body – and was probably still more so without modern supports and interventions in pregnancy and childbirth. Eleanor was more or less constantly pregnant, and combined this with a lifestyle which involved constant changes of residence in a period where, even for a queen, ensuring optimum nutrition would have been an impossibility. It may well be that the number of stillbirths which she endured can be in part ascribed to the physical effects of such a demanding lifestyle. However, despite this, she continued to participate fully in it, and to carry out both her role as queen and her job in managing her property empire. The evidence therefore establishes clearly that, at least until her latter years, she was a woman of fairly exceptional good health and physical robustness.[4]

As to her role as a property developer and manager, the challenge which her formal job as queen and mother to the royal children would have imposed on her routine was considerable. Every pregnancy meant a period of 'lying in', during which her access to business would have been restricted. This may be one reason why Eleanor appears to have broken with tradition and, at least with her girls, lain in not for the usual forty days but only for twenty-nine – and even, on occasion, less. One can see all these factors coming together in 1275 with the birth of Margaret.

So Eleanor undertook a tour of her lands late in her pregnancy, arriving back at Windsor not long before Margaret was born. Yet by at least 17 April she was back on her travels – this time at Bury St Edmunds, where a local chronicler notes her presence. Yet Bury is a good long way from Windsor, and Edward, at least, had proceeded there gradually via Cippenham (now part of Maidenhead), Risborough, Aylesbury, Weston and Royston. The conclusion seems inescapable that Eleanor left Windsor with Edward, and the only accommodation made for this was a slightly slower-paced journey than would otherwise have been the case – the stops were very moderately spaced. If Margaret was indeed born on 15 March, this would equate to a very short lying-in indeed. Rather more likely is that Margaret was actually born in mid-February, shortly after the arrival at Windsor; but even so the lying-in would have been considerably short of the traditional forty days. Perhaps the imminent end of Lent drove this move – the royal couple would certainly not have wanted to be parted at this point in the year. Another likely factor in this particular year will have been Eleanor's determination to get on top of her day job – the 1275 royal progress was closely linked to Eleanor's property interests and in particular the settling of her increased dower.

On other occasions, though, Eleanor maintained a fairly normal lying-in; Edward's itinerary shows him moving from Kempton, where their next child, Berengaria, was born in April/May 1276, to Westminster just days after her birth. Eleanor will have joined him later in the Westminster stay, around 29 May, giving time for preparations before the party set off into Sussex, Essex and Kent. And in early 1278, following Eleanor giving birth to a stillborn child, Edward undertook a short tour in Kent while she lay in for twenty-nine days, sending her venison to aid her recovery. Parsons hypothesises that Eleanor lay in for twenty-nine days for a girl and forty for a boy, but the material available does not provide firm support for this conjecture. What seems likely is that around thirty days was taken if convenient, but a full lying-in period was dispensed with if Eleanor considered other business more pressing. So in 1275 a short lying-in was probably taken. The final documented babies, Elizabeth and Edward, attracted full lyings-in, since Eleanor was on both occasions static in Wales while Edward campaigned there.[5]

As for her role as mother, we have seen earlier that Eleanor was not an overly fond mother to her very young offspring. To what extent that was innate, in that she was someone who found small children rather boring, and to what extent it was defensive, given the high mortality rate for young children, we cannot know. What seems quite likely, given her active memorialising of the first baby, her avoidance of or at best fleeting attendance at young Henry's deathbed, and 'farming out' of young Joan, is that it was at least in some measure a defensive and learned response, prompted by the trauma of the loss of the first baby. However, whichever is the case, there is much more evidence of her interest and concern for her children as they grew older, both in terms of their interests, their education and their future prospects.

Until about the age of seven the children lived in what was effectively a separate nursery establishment, which housed not just the royal children but wards and children of members of the household. To this establishment can be traced such a variety of people as the mentally deficient Walerand heirs, the children of Eleanor's ladies, the young Earl of Hereford, some of Eleanor's young de Beaumont relatives, some of the children of Edward's sister Beatrice and a number of Eleanor's wards, such as young Nicholas Burdon. The ages ranged from the very young, accompanied by their wet nurses or nurses, to the older children being prepared for military and court life or a career in the Church. Thus, the staff of Edward of Caernarfon's household included seven knights and nine sergeants and it was headed up by an ex-Crusader companion of Edward and Eleanor. It was, effectively, a small boarding school governed by rules such as those we have seen earlier about the number of servants, and amount of food, beer and candles to be provided to each child. As can be imagined, its provisioning requirements were considerable and even provoked negative comment in the chronicles. These problems were not assisted by the requirements of one member of the ménage – the King's Langley camel, for whom bushels of barley were required rather frequently.

Eleanor kept in close touch with the nursery establishment by messenger and sent treats to them – such as the salmon pies sent to young Edward in spring 1290. Toys were also sent: Alphonso, during the Welsh wars, was gifted with a detailed model castle – a complement for the toy soldiers of the era found at the Tower and now on display there. Young Henry had had toy arrows, a coronet and a toy trumpet. She also sent tutors – who were doubtless much less welcome. So in 1290, Eleanor arranged for Dominican friars and one of her scribes to join the household of young Edward of Caernarfon (then five and a half years old) to ensure his spiritual and intellectual formation. The nursery establishment was frequently uprooted in its entirety to place it more conveniently within reach of the king and queen – so while the Welsh campaign went on, the children were brought north. Likewise, in Eleanor's last months the nursery establishment moved north to Clipstone. Even when it was settled, it was not short of visitors – young Edward's household seems to have attracted distinguished visitors roughly once a week, including relations, other nobles, bishops and foreign dignitaries.

The middle children, and in particular Alphonso and Margaret, born in the mid-1270s, probably saw rather more of their parents than their older and younger siblings. The period from the return to England until the departure of Eleanor and Edward for Gascony in 1286 had a degree of stability about it; every year there were two lengthy stays in London. The main court would be housed at Westminster, but it appears that the nursery section was brought at the same time to the Tower. This was, of course, a very easy distance from Westminster, and it seems likely that Eleanor and Edward would make the trip across at least a few times a week, if not daily. Moreover, this period also sees fairly lengthy stays a few times a year at locations which were suitable for the younger royals to be part of the party. Windsor, of course, was well established as a location for the royal nursery, and Langley, under Eleanor's careful development, was to become the preferred base of young Edward of Caernarfon. However, Woodstock, Clarendon and Marlborough all have form as locations for the younger royal family under Eleanor of Provence, and still featured regularly in the royal itinerary; thus they too may have involved 'joined-up' parties of the whole family, adults and children.

As the children grew older, they were in fact tacked on to the court for at least some of the time as it moved. So in 1293 young Edward visited Westminster, Mortlake, Kennington, Canterbury, Windsor, Winchester, Salisbury, Bath, Clarendon, Melksham and Devizes. Thus, it seems likely that Eleanor did build close bonds with her children as they grew: Eleanora, Joan and Margaret were at court almost constantly once they had reached a good age to travel with the court, and even young Mary, who became a nun, came to court fairly frequently.[6]

A glimpse of how the regime worked can be gained by following the eldest surviving child, Eleanora. She seems to have joined the court in about 1276–7 – her age at this point was around eight, and she was already engaged to the prince of Aragon. Her mother would therefore have much to teach her in terms of the language and culture which she could expect to encounter, as well as the political issues of the Iberian peninsula. However, presence at court still did not denote constant proximity to her mother. She had an entire household of her own from 1277 – a chamberlain, keeper of the hall, groom of the bedchamber, and a sumpterer (seconded from her mother's household) among others. So in 1278 we find Eleanora and her household joining her royal parents at Devizes, and then proceeding with them to Easter at Glastonbury, and on to London in May. Furthermore, Eleanora maintained a close relationship with her grandmother Eleanor of Provence, interspersing her visits to court with stays with her grandmother until Eleanor of Provence took the veil in 1286. In 1282, Eleanora accompanied her mother to Wales, and by this point she had been joined at court by young Joan (now about nine or ten), returned from Ponthieu. By late 1284, the royal princesses at court numbered three, for Margaret (nine) had now joined the circle at court.[7]

Of course, the practice of bringing the children to court as they grew up does not necessarily reveal any strong affection for them on Eleanor's part; this might simply be done because it was deemed the best way to educate them. However, the story of Mary's veiling suggests differently. Mary became a nun at Amesbury as a companion to her grandmother Eleanor of Provence in August 1285 at the age of six. It is clear from the sources that Eleanor objected to this plan fairly strongly: the *Chronicle of Nicholas Trivet*, dedicated to the princess, notes that she was veiled by her sire, at the wish of her grandmother, and with the 'assent' of her mother. One very credible explanation for Eleanor's reluctance to go along with Eleanor of Provence's plan in 1285 for young Mary to join her as a nun there may be that Eleanor was reluctant to lose her daughter just at the stage of life when she would expect to be building a meaningful relationship with her. Certainly it seems unlikely that she objected to the project of Mary taking the veil per se, since a good deal of correspondence had already been conducted between Edward and the Abbey of Fontevrault as early as 1282 with a view to Mary ultimately becoming a nun there.

Fortunately for Eleanor, it is also clear that Mary's veiling was not a complete renunciation of the world; she paid a visit to her family in March 1286, and another in May of that year, which probably lasted a month. Mary was then at court again in early 1290, very probably again for about a month, culminating in the marriage of her older sister Joan. That she spent enough time with her mother to regard Eleanor with strong affection despite her enclosure is demonstrated by the decision of Mary and her younger sister Elizabeth to pay for a special Mass in honour of their mother in 1297.[8]

Further evidence for the affection in which Eleanora and her sisters were held by Eleanor as they grew up can perhaps be seen in Eleanor's attempts (in partnership with her mother-in-law) to delay the marriage of Eleanora in 1281 when she was rising twelve – the canonical minimum age for marriage, and the age at which Eleanor herself had been married. There are also records of her purchasing small items of jewellery for them in Paris, sending back to them other pieces gifted to her, and making offerings for their health at many of the major shrines visited.

However, although Eleanor was plainly fond of them and influential in their later upbringing, the sense of true closeness is missing; and Eleanora's choice to visit her grandmother at regular intervals, including in the run-up to the anticipated marriage in 1281, suggests that, certainly for her, emotional closeness lay more with the grandmother who had seen her through her early years than with her focussed and driven mother. Edward, who plainly did enjoy a very good relationship with his daughters in later years, seems to have purchased more personal presents for the girls, and to have been held in more demonstrative regard by them. All in all, it is fair to say that there is a flavour in the slim records which remain of Eleanor being fond of her children, but much more focussed on her marriage and her work.

There is also a sense that Eleanor was by some way the more disciplinarian parent – keen for the children to progress in the education to which none of them seems to have been very strongly inclined. Eleanor herself was, as we know, book mad, and unlike any of the English kings prior to Richard II she could write – that is the inescapable conclusion from her brother's view as to the utility of writing, the purchase which she made of writing tablets for Eleanora, and the despatch, shortly before her death, of a scriptor to help educate young Edward. Thus, either directly or indirectly, Eleanor saw that her daughter was, like herself, educated very much above the level of most educated noble men.

Eleanor's influence can be felt when Eleanora's abilities are contrasted with the youngest of the brood, Edward of Caernarfon, who was born too close to his mother's death to benefit much from her encouragement. In his case, there is no evidence of any primer being bought for him until his sixteenth year, he demonstrated no great fondness for books and there are certainly questions over the extent of his linguistic abilities, particularly as regards his ability to read Latin with facility. But we can see, from the despatch of the Dominicans and the scribe to Langley in the months before Eleanor's death, that she would certainly have had him commence serious study at an early age.

The difference of even a few years of influence can be seen when we compare young Edward to his sister Elizabeth of Rhuddlan, two years his senior, who was born in mid-1282 and was therefore just over eight when her mother died. Elizabeth is in some respects exceptional, appearing to have been the only child that Eleanor kept with her in the very early years – she either stayed with Eleanor full time or visited her frequently in her first two years, and was with her mother at Caernarfon when Edward was born. She nonetheless spent much of her childhood prior to her mother's death in her brother's establishment and received the basic education which would have been provided under Eleanor's running of that household. She would have come to court more or less on Eleanor's return from Gascony and thus have come under Eleanor's eye slightly more in that period, but even so, she spent a good proportion of her time still with her brother's household; she spent most of the summer of 1290 touring the countryside with him, rather than with the court, except for the royal weddings.

There is therefore relatively little ground for hypothesising any exceptionally close tie of affection or influence between mother and daughter; and this is reflected in the fact that Elizabeth was to call her first child after her stepmother. However, Elizabeth seems to have had a real fondness for books – service books are recorded as part of her marriage goods on her first marriage to the Count of Holland, and the Alphonso Psalter can be traced into her ownership at a later date.

As for Joan, while she herself offers very little evidence of academic attainments, a generation later her daughter Elizabeth de Clare/de Burgh was to become possibly the pre-eminent female artistic patron of the fourteenth century, inferentially inspired by a fairly full education organised by her mother.

Thus we can see that Eleanor did attempt to ensure that her children received a fine education, as she had done. But it is fair to say that the ground was a little stony: the daughters of Eleanor seem to have imbibed more of her taste for domestic finery than her appetite for books and scholarship. The surviving records of all the princesses describe a myriad of purchases of the kinds of luxurious small items which were such a feature of their mother's housekeeping – and no book purchases.[9]

So we can safely dispose of the myth that Eleanor had little contact with her children; though at the same time it is clear that her relations with them were less intense and more distant than the modern idiom expects. But this does not bring to a close a consideration of those whom Eleanor would have counted as family. The surviving *Liber Garderobe* for the 1289–90 period gives a vivid, though necessarily partial, indication of the members of her family with whom Eleanor corresponded. Relations with Eleanor of Provence were not notably affectionate – as can be seen from the fact that the older Eleanor was relatively seldom at court after her widowhood commenced and that the tone of her letters to Edward is obviously loving and warm, whereas the exchanges between the two Eleanors seem to have been confined to administrative detail, such as the loan of staff. But Eleanor had a wealth of other correspondents; for instance, within the immediate royal family, Eleanor corresponded with and sent gifts to her brother-in-law Edmund, Earl of Lancaster, and his second wife, Blanche of Navarre.[10]

Nor were her own brothers neglected. Eleanor maintained close contact with Alfonso until his death in April 1284 and with Enrique until hers (for all their contrasting fates, one suspects Enrique's letters were more fun than Alfonso's). For all his brilliance, Alfonso's story was not a happy one. Distracted, like Henry III, into a range of expensive sideshows at home and abroad, he bred discontent among his prominent nobles and, as we shall see, ultimately reaped the whirlwind. However, Eleanor continued to correspond with him and to fulfil her role by trying to persuade Edward to support him, or at least to let him down gently.

Thus we see, in 1275, Edward writing very politely to Alfonso, who had sought his help against the Moors, explaining that if he were to go on Crusade he had already been asked by the Pope to go again to the aid of the Holy Land, far from the Moors, but that while he could not help personally he was very content for his subjects in Bayonne to help if they were so minded, and following this up with letters to the Mayor of Bayonne offering ships for anyone who wished to serve. Even after his death, Eleanor maintained at least one of his illegitimate children in her household: Martin Alfonso, later Abbot of Valladolid, was with her throughout the Gascon stay of 1286–9. Another possible son of Alfonso is the gentleman known as Rotheric de Yspannia who was granted a legacy of £20 by Eleanor's executors in 1291 and who was acknowledged as a kinsman by Edward II. More likely, however, is that the latter was an illegitimate son of Fadrique, who did not return to Spain with his father and brother in 1272. These gentlemen were openly acknowledged as relations, albeit as 'cousins'.[11]

Further afield, Eleanor seems to have corresponded with a number of her female relatives on her mother's side.

The first of these ladies, Viscountess Jeanne of Châtellherault, has already appeared in the earlier chapters. She was the daughter of Eleanor's mother's youngest sister, Mathilde of Dammartin, and was demonstrably a close contact of Eleanor's over a number of years. It appears likely that Jeanne and Eleanor were born within a year of each other and that Eleanor was involved in arranging Jeanne's marriage to Geoffrey de Lusignan in around 1260, and the two possibly spent time together on Crusade. Further, there is correspondence which seems to demonstrate that she was also involved in Jeanne's second marriage, to the Sieur de Harcourt (a baron of Normandy), which occurred sometime between May 1278, when she appeared as a widow in litigation against one of her first husband's bailiffs, and March 1279, when Jeanne of Ponthieu died. Eleanor exerted herself to assist Jeanne; for example, she corresponded with Robert Burnell about her cousin's business in 1282. There is also material which shows Eleanor and Edward visiting her cousin in July 1289, and sending a thank-you present of scarlet cloth and some ermine furs after the visit.[12]

The second member of her maternal family with whom Eleanor corresponded (and who is referred to as her cousin) is the Countess of Gueldres. She was probably Marie of Flanders, the daughter-in-law of her aunt Philippa of Dammartin. Marie had previously been married to Edward's nephew Alexander of Scotland.

The presence of both of these maternal relations in her list of regular correspondents indicates that Eleanor also corresponded freely with her mother while her mother lived, and strongly suggests a wider correspondence with her maternal relations generally – an inference borne out by other connections discussed below.

But there was also correspondence with her paternal connections, and members of Edward's family: Eleanor's third correspondent in 1289–90 was Isabelle de Brienne, the daughter of Eleanor's cousin Alphonso de Brienne, who had married Marie de Lusignan, Countess of Eu. Isabelle married Jean de Dampierre, the Sieur of Dampierre. This correspondence with her wider family, including the Brienne connection, is consistent with the interest which she took in that family's careers.

The final lady mentioned in the 1289–90 records is Isabelle de Lusignan, the half-sister of Henry III who married Maurice of Craon, and later Geoffrey de Rancon, the seneschal of Poitou, who appears to have been managing Craon on behalf of her son, the heir to the lordship.[13]

As can be seen from this list of correspondents, Eleanor's family should not be regarded as confined to her immediate blood – cousins were close associates even when they were not likely to meet for years at a time.

But there is a whole further layer of family which has to be considered: Eleanor's household, often referred to in the records as her *familia*. A starting point here is a quick review of Eleanor's immediate attendants – men and women. Eleanor now stood at the head of a household that comprised around 150 people. In 1289–90, Eleanor had twelve knights, of whom one was the husband of her long-standing lady-in-waiting Margery de Haustede. Robert de Haustede himself had been part of Eleanor's household since at least 1266, when Eleanor interceded for him with Henry III. He went on Crusade with Edward and Eleanor and moved temporarily into Edward's household in 1280, before gaining promotion to the role of Eleanor's butler. He then accompanied the couple on the Gascon trip of 1286, and was knighted following their return. His close involvement with the whole royal family is shown by the fact that he was later to travel with Eleanor's daughter Margaret to her new home in Brabant.[14]

Two other knights in Eleanor's service were Guy Ferre junior and Giles de Fiennes, whose surnames echo those of some of Eleanor's connections in earlier years. Guy de Ferre was the son of John Ferre, who had served as Eleanor's yeoman as early as 1266. The family appear to have had connections in Gascony, each of John and Guy having been given postings there at some point in their career. John married one of Eleanor's ladies, Joanna, and the pair of them accompanied Eleanor and Edward on Crusade. John's brother, Guy, was the queen mother's steward and became magister to Edward of Caernarfon. The younger Guy was a 'scutifer' (a squire, and probably one of the more senior staff under the steward's direction) in Eleanor's service by April 1277. He seems to have impressed her, receiving grants of land from her in 1281 and 1289, a legacy of £100 on her death and further lands from the king. He also succeeded in marrying well, obtaining the hand of the daughter and heir of Roger Fitzosbert, with lands in Suffolk.

Giles de Fiennes was the nephew of the Michael de Fiennes noted in Edward's household in 1255 who had accompanied Edward to Palestine on Crusade together with his brother William. Eleanor had interceded with Henry III for him before their departure. He seems to have served in her household or Edward's throughout the period and by 1290 he had two children in the queen's household in addition to himself: John de Fiennes and Eleanor de Fiennes.[15]

Also on the knight's list are Philippe Popiot, a former servant of Eleanor's mother Jeanne, who appears to have come to England and into the queen's service after Jeanne's death and in company with his wife Edeline, who was Joan of Acre's governess until her marriage; and John de Hengham, whose wife Margerie was also a lady in the household of Joan, and whose son was brought up with Edward of Caernarfon at Langley. A relationship between this family and Edward's judicial right-hand man Ralph de Hengham seems possible, though if it did exist it was not a close one. Also in the list was Geoffrey de Piccheford, who was custodian over the person and household of both young Henry (until his death) and Edward of Caernarfon.[16]

Thus far, just looking at the senior male attendants who surrounded Eleanor, a picture begins to emerge of a family ethos around the queen.

This is reinforced by a consideration of her waiting ladies. Those who were actually related to her are considered separately later, but good examples of the household's family ethos can be found among those of the senior ladies who had no family link to Eleanor.

Chief among her ladies was Margery de Haustede, who was the lady in charge of Eleanor's jewels, and even apparently charged with shopping for pieces to be given as gifts. She accompanied Eleanor to Gascony (leaving at least one of her children in the care of another family), may well also have been on Crusade with her, and by 1289 was of such importance that she had a chamber built for her personally in the precincts of the palace of Westminster in the run-up to the Christmas festivities. Her daughter Joanna was a damsel to the royal princesses in 1289 and 1290, and her son Robert was sent to reside with Edward of Caernarfon in 1289 and later served him. Her third son, John, also passed into royal service and distinguished himself, serving in the prime position of seneschal of Gascony under Edward III. Margery and Robert's own good relations with the younger generation (and inferentially the closeness of the *familia* at court) is attested by the fact that their obituaries are inscribed in the Alphonso Psalter; in fact it seems possible that this valuable family memento was given to them by Elizabeth of Rhuddlan.

Another intimate of Eleanor's was Ermintrude de Sackville, the daughter of John de Chandos by Margaret FitzWalkeline. Although by reason of her status and single state she was unlikely to have been with Eleanor as early as the Crusade, she was a favourite by 1275, when she was married by the king's special precept to Andrew de Sackville, who was still a minor at the time of their marriage. The couple remained close to the court for most of the rest of Eleanor's life, with Andrew featuring on the witness lists in 1280 and 1281 and Ermintrude in a position of some authority over other ladies in 1289, when the queen sent her messages relating to their management. Towards the end of Eleanor's life, Ermintrude was accompanied at court by Eleanor de Sackville – likely her daughter and also almost inevitably Eleanor's god-daughter. Ermintrude was apparently so close to the queen that Eleanor went to stay with her in November 1289, when Ermintrude was ill: her itinerary shows her at Bindon near Dorchester in Dorset for about a week, and this appears to have been Ermintrude's home, since in January Eleanor had sent a messenger to her there with money to cover her expenses during her illness. Interestingly, and characteristically, Eleanor seems to have brought Edward with her most of the way on this personal diversion – he is recorded at Bindon for two nights and just up the road at Frampton for the remainder of Eleanor's stay.[17]

But the family ties and atmosphere did not stop with the immediate circle of upper attendants. Throughout the household can be found individuals with links to Edward and Eleanor's families, and with their own family links at Court. So Ebles de Montibus, a squire to Eleanor in 1289–90, was the son of Edward's former companion, who had died in around 1268. Young Ebles went on to be household steward to Isabella of France. Geoffrey, the kitchen ewer, had a brother Simon who was Eleanor's cook or sauser, and yeoman Richard had a brother in a similar post. Meanwhile, another yeoman, Raoulet, and one of her tailors, Gillot, had been in her mother's service, and her cooks John de Wodestock and Henry Wade had come from her in-laws' kitchens and were succeeded by one of Edward's cooks. In her administration, John of London, her first keeper of the wardrobe, came to her from Eleanor of Provence, and was replaced (until his death in 1270) by William de Yattenden, who was probably related to Bartholomew and Nicholas of the same name, who worked respectively for Edward and Eleanor of Provence.

Eleanor seems to have had a distinct preference for having married women in her household, presumably as they were unlikely to misbehave in a way which would reflect on her; a preoccupation directed by her education. Her apparent preference for finding husbands who were likewise part of the *familia* may be from the desire to have a family atmosphere surrounding her, but may likewise have been informed by the fact that seemly behaviour was more likely if couples were not separated. The results, however, are striking: of the women who formed part of Eleanor's group of ladies-in-waiting in 1289–90, two were widows of husbands chosen by Eleanor, most of the rest were married to knights and squires either in her household or that of Edward, and the small remainder of unmarried women had fathers at court in either Edward or Eleanor's household.[18]

A family or collegiate atmosphere was thus inevitable and was reinforced by the routines which were observed – all would attend church together regularly. They would also attend marriages and anniversary services for family and friends of the royal family, and services of commemoration for the deceased. Increasing the family atmosphere, these events were extended to those in the servants and attendants' families: weddings were celebrated at court (often financed by the royal family), pregnancies and childbirths were organised and often funded by the queen, and Eleanor stood sponsor to numerous offspring in the wider *familia* – such as the Eleanors de Sackville, de Beauchamp, de Cretyng, Ferre, de Hacche, de Burgh, de Caumpeden and de Ewelle.[19]

Eleanor's 'family', however, can be said to have extended beyond those who were part of her household. A consideration of the witnesses to her surviving deeds show a fascinating consistency, indicating a 'magic circle' of close friends around the king and queen, but also very close relations between Eleanor and some of the most prominent men in the country. For although certain key members of the royal household and administration appear again and again (Geoffrey de Aspale, John Ferre, Walter de Kancia, Giles de Fiennes, Andrew de Sackville, John de Lovetot), the witness lists range much wider than this. In particular Robert Burnell, the chancellor and Edward's closest adviser, is a regular feature on these lists, as is Hugh de Cantilupe, the Bishop of Hereford, and William de Middleton, Bishop of Norwich.

Indeed, Burnell seems to have been one of Edward and Eleanor's closest friends and, if the letter of October 1274 which appears in Appendix 1 is indeed hers, there is first-hand evidence of the ease and confidence with which they operated. Burnell is sent 'loving' greetings and the request is sent with affection. There is also a light joke about constantly boring him with requests for her friends and his being relied on to help. Whether or not that letter is Eleanor's, it is apparent that she corresponded with him frequently – a significant proportion of her surviving letters are to him – and that the two were on the warmest of terms. Ultimately he was to be one of her executors, and in the inquest on her properties he was referred to as the one person outside her administration who would know the details of her involvement in a specific transaction. Part of the rapport which grew up between Eleanor and Burnell was probably due to shared interests; Burnell, too, worked hard to acquire properties in parallel with his other duties – with notable success. This suggestion is lent force by the fact that Robert Burnell's attorney John de Berewyk emerged as a frequent witness to Eleanor's deeds well before he took up a new role as her last wardrobe keeper. Interestingly, Edward seems to have had no scruples about the very close association between his wife and Burnell, who, though a priest and therefore technically sworn to celibacy, was somewhat successful with the opposite sex, having at least one known mistress (Juliana) and five children by her. This evidences further the closeness between Edward and Eleanor, and his complete trust in her.[20]

Other very frequent appearances are Robert Tybetot; John de Vescy; Roger Mortimer; Otho de Grandison; Hugh Fitzothes; Richard de Clare, Earl of Gloucester; John de Warenne, Earl of Surrey; and Henry de Lacy, Earl of Lincoln. This list of the great and the good, essentially a list of Edward's closest associates, shows a regular core of long-standing friends often present at court. It is also – particularly when taken with other names which appear occasionally, such as a galaxy of bishops, the Bigods, and even the older and younger Bruces – in sharp contrast to the position as regards Eleanor of Provence's Acts, which were usually attested by members of her household or family, conveying the impression of actions performed very much as a private individual. The impression conveyed is that Eleanor was on very good terms with and was well respected by the major power players at court, and that her business was regarded as of significance and was approved by the king.

Beyond this, there is evidence for close friendship between Eleanor and a number of the core names in this list. So Henry de Lacy and his wife Margaret de Longespée (Countess of Salisbury in her own right and a relative of both king and queen through her descent from Henry II) appear to have been close friends of Eleanor's. As well as witnessing many of her Acts, Henry de Lacy was a frequent correspondent of the queen and was one of her executors. As for John de Vescy, Eleanor would arrange his marriage and that of his nephew; her affection for him is clearly seen on his death in 1289, when Eleanor arranged for his heart to be buried with her own and that of her son Alphonso in the London house of the Dominicans.[21]

A third member of Edward's male circle with whom a close friendship can be inferred is his childhood friend Otho de Grandison, who not only appears often as a witness but was a recipient of gifts from Eleanor. Earlier years cannot be spoken for due to the absence of records, but in 1290 she granted to him certain houses in London which she acquired via Hagin son of Moses, and in 1289–90 she gave him 1,000 marks. She also bequeathed him the manor of Turweston for life. Otho was to give her valuable personal gifts in return. His nephew John de Strattingen was in Eleanor's household as one of her knights by 1286 and she probably had a hand in arranging a marriage for him with the niece of Bishop Godfrey Giffard of Worcester. Another nephew, Peter d'Estavayer, was also among her knights. She patronised his nephew Gerard von Wippingen, later bishop of both Lausanne and Basel. Obviously Eleanor had no interest in anyone except her husband, other than by way of friendship. However, there seems a possibility that Otho's feeling for her was more tender.

Four facts point in this direction. The first is that, despite the fact that he ultimately made a considerable fortune in Edward's service, Otho did not marry. The second is that he is the one friend depicted on Eleanor's tomb, where he is pictured praying for Eleanor. The third is that he re-gifted the manor which she left him to the king to be used to endow her memorial service. Finally, he remained out of England for nearly six years following Eleanor's death. All in all, there seems some reason to speculate that he was devoted to her and was reluctant to return to England once she was no longer there.[22]

But perhaps the most interesting aspect of Eleanor's family concerns her ties to her female relations. The starting point for this is to look at her *domicille*, that is the women who surrounded her day to day. Among Eleanor's ladies were no fewer than four distant cousins: Joanna Wake, Clemence de Vescy, Alice de Montfort and Marie de St Amand. In these ladies we see clearly both an extended family being constructed and Eleanor's scheme of quietly advancing her maternal relatives.

Joanna Wake was a de Fiennes, and a 'double cousin' of Eleanor's, descending from the marriage which Eleanor arranged between her cousin William de Fiennes and her cousin Blanche of Brienne, granddaughter of Berengaria of Castile and John of Brienne. Joanna was particularly close to Eleanor, receiving new robes at the king's expense five times in the 1290 period (Christmas Easter, Pentecost and the two royal weddings), which was more than any other of the *domicille* received, and having her goods carried at his expense. What is more, her children were sent to be raised with the younger royals at Langley, and her expenses for visiting them there were paid by the Crown. She was therefore emphatically regarded as part of the family.

Her marriage to John Wake appears to have been another of Eleanor's matchmaking endeavours – Wake lands were granted to Eleanor after 1265 and were ransomed under the Dictum of Kenilworth, and John Wake and his brother were brought into the royal nursery establishment after the death of their mother in about 1283. John Wake's wardship was granted to Eleanor in 1285, and the marriage appears to have followed speedily upon this, as Joanna had two children by 1290. The marriage was a very good one for Joanna – the Wakes were of impeccable Norman descent and John also had connections via his mother to William the Conqueror, the Welsh royal family and to the earls of Salisbury. One of the younger Wake children, Margaret, was to marry Edmund of Woodstock, Edward's younger son by his second marriage; perhaps this was a match effectively made in the royal nursery, which both inhabited. Through this connection, Joanna Wake became the ancestress of the Fair Maid of Kent.[23]

The two ladies de Vescy were also cousins of the queen, and within her matchmaking ambit. John de Vescy's wife Isabella was part of the older Brienne line, descending from the marriage of Louis de Brienne to Agnes de Beaumont. Her marriage to John de Vescy in 1280 was very clearly brought about by Eleanor, with John promising to pay her £550 in silver if his new bride had no child (which she did not). The couple, as will be seen, remained very close to Eleanor and Edward, travelling to Gascony with them in 1286. Clemence de Avagour, later de Vescy, named as a *domicille* in 1290, married the nephew and heir presumptive of John de Vescy and was descended from the very same Brienne line, being Isabelle's own niece. Clemence's marriage, too, was a close concern of Eleanor's, with the groom's father (John de Vescy's brother William) making promises directly to the queen about what dower property would be assigned to Clemence, and the queen providing her with a coronet on the occasion of the wedding on 16 July 1290 at Westminster. Both de Vescy marriages were highly advantageous ones, since the Vescy family were at this time the great lords of the North – effectively the predecessors of the Percy family, who came to prominence in the North after the Vescy family line failed.[24]

The third *domicilla* mentioned, Lady de Montfort, was no relation to Simon de Montfort, but yet another of Eleanor's maternal relatives. Her grandfather-in-law was the Peter de Montfort who fell fighting in the Montfortian cause at Evesham. His son Piers reconciled with Edward in 1267 and it is the son of this Piers, John, who married Alice de la Plaunche, Eleanor's relative. The exact family connection between the two is hard to trace, though it is clear from the acknowledgement of her as a '*consanguine regine*' that such a connection did exist. The credible theory advanced by Parsons is that Alice was another connection of the de Fiennes family and hence a distant connection of Eleanor's on the Dammartin side. The connection was not a close one, so it is significant that Eleanor acknowledged the relationship, with Lady de Montfort being named as kin in her *Liber Garderobe*. It appears likely that the relationship was acknowledged during the Gascon trip, since in 1286 Edward is noted as giving a silver gilt cup to the lord de la Plaunche, also identified as a relative of the queen. Alice then joined Eleanor's household in Gascony and accompanied Eleanor to England on their return, with a suitable marriage being put in place for her before that return; the marriage appears to have taken place before March 1287, when Edward ordered Edmund of Cornwall to deal favourably with John de Montfort because he had married a relative of Edward's 'dearest consort'.

The Montfort marriage was not by any means as grand a marriage as those arranged for the other cousins, but it was more than respectable, and for a family which very probably descended from a bastard line it was something of a coup. Meanwhile, other members of this family were also looked after albeit to a lesser extent: James and John de la Plaunche had a tutor hired for them in Gascony in 1287. John de la Plaunche appears as a vallettus in Eleanor's wardrobe list and his brother James was married in 1289 to a ward of Eleanor, Matilda de Haversham. Matilda de Haversham/de la Plaunche was herself at court as *domicilla* to Eleanora from 1287 to 1290.

Also in attendance on the queen was Marie de St Amand, formerly Marie de Pécquigny, who was a distant cousin of Eleanor's, her great-grandmother having been a daughter of John I of Ponthieu (father of the William of Ponthieu who married Alys of France). Marie was married to Almeric de St Amand at Leeds Castle on 21 August 1289, a short time after she joined the royal household. The St Amands were not a particularly noble or rich family, but were close military associates of the English royal family: one of them was godfather to Edward himself, and then died on Crusade with Richard of Cornwall. Another served with distinction under Edward in the Welsh wars.[25]

These matches show Eleanor surrounding herself with maternal relatives, a natural extended family, and advancing them subtly at the same time. Such matches as we have seen within her own *familia* were far from being the limit of Eleanor's matchmaking, however. She arranged marriages for a couple of the younger de Fiennes relatives who were not in her own household but were being brought up in the nursery establishment with Edward of Caernarfon. From one of these matches, between John de Fiennes and Joanna Forester, descends the lines of the lords Saye and Sele and the lords Dacre – and in modern times the array of famous Fiennes.

But Eleanor also advanced her family in more marked ways, while at the same time keeping them within her extended family. These matches are not easy to trace – a contrast to Eleanor of Provence's profligate approach. However, when the records are closely examined, it becomes apparent that Eleanor almost certainly had a hand in at least two very high-status and ultimately significant marriages.

The first is the marriage, sometime in the early 1280s, of Joanna Wake's sister Margaret de Fiennes to Edmund de Mortimer, Lord of Wigmore. Margaret was therefore also a 'double' cousin of Eleanor's through the Dammartin family and the Castilian–Brienne link. Two things in particular indicate Eleanor's hand in this match. The first is that the arrangements for the wedding were made at royal expense, i.e. Eleanor gave the wedding, as might be expected if she had brought the match about. The second is that the history of Wigmore monastery reports the bride as being from a Castilian family – which, of course, she was not. However, a Castilian link was obviously perceived by onlookers, which indicates an association with the queen.

The significance of the marriage is not far to seek: Margaret de Fiennes, Eleanor's distant cousin, was the mother of the infamous Roger Mortimer (the lover of Edward II's wife Isabella, and bête noire of Edward III's minority), and she was also hence ancestress of the Yorkist kings. How the match came about is uncertain; there was no Welsh link, as was most usual for Mortimer marriages, though on the credit side the bride could boast descent from the famous warrior Jean de Brienne, as the Mortimers could from his English counterpart, William Marshal. Ultimately the most likely reason for the link is Eleanor herself; through the close ties that bound Edward to Edmund's father Roger Mortimer, a relative of Edward's adored and influential queen might well have been perceived by the Mortimers as a worthy or at least useful match, particularly in the difficult period after Roger's death.

The second match, even more prestigious and even more mysterious, is one between Margaret's aunt Maud/Mathilde de Fiennes, daughter of Enguerrand II de Fiennes, and Humphrey de Bohun, heir to the Earl of Hereford and Essex. This took place rather earlier, in 1275, and the blood link to Eleanor was later to be reinforced when their son, another Humphrey, married Eleanor's daughter Elizabeth after Eleanor's own death. As for the reasoning behind this first marriage, some link between the family and the Crown was probably felt to be politic after some years of uneasy relations – Humphrey de Bohun's father had died on the wrong side at Evesham – and again it seems likely that a link to Eleanor's family was seen as conveying its own prestige. This, of course, says much about the influence which she was felt to wield, even by major magnates. Another mild traditional justification might just be found in the Fiennes family's property holdings in Essex, the earl's own county.

There is also a suggestion in the documents that the marriage represented a rapprochement bought by Eleanor. De Bohun had bought from his guardian, Gloucester, the right to his own marriage in 1270, for a sum of £1,000. This sum had not been paid, and Gloucester had even commenced an action to recover it. This action was discontinued shortly after the wedding, the conclusion being that the sum was paid. On the other side of the transaction, we see that in 1270 Eleanor had acquired Martock, next to her farm of Somerton, from William de Fiennes on a six-year lease, and in 1275 she subleased it 'so the queen may recover a portion of the £1,000 she agreed to pay as a dowry for William de Fiennes daughter [sic], who is to marry the earl of Essex's heir'. The implication is clear – Eleanor bought de Bohun out of the litigation as the price of his taking her relative as a wife. Whatever the reasoning behind the marriage, the marriage was a momentous one – through this line was ultimately to descend the Lancastrian kings of England.

The third significant marriage in which Eleanor's hand can be traced is one between Margaret, daughter of Count Arnoul of Guines and Mathilde de Fiennes, and Richard de Burgh, 2nd Earl of Ulster. Again, too, there is a link to the royal nursery: Richard de Burgh was another of the children brought into the royal nursery after the death of his mother in 1274. He married Margaret in February 1281 and Margaret seems to have been a member of Eleanor's household from then until the Gascon visit. This was a high-status marriage for Margaret, but plainly had considerable advantages for Richard de Burgh too – courtesy of it, he was thereafter known as the king's kinsman and the extension granted of his tenure of his Irish lands was obviously related to this, being for the lifetime of his wife. In the longer term, this too was a significant marriage. Margaret's son John married Joan of Acre's daughter Elizabeth de Clare. Their granddaughter Elizabeth married Edward III's son Lionel of Antwerp, from whose line descends the Yorkist claim.[26]

As can be seen from this, Eleanor did not just surround herself with her wider family; some of the matches made by her put members of her family in the heart of some of the most prominent families in the country – and in future in the line for the throne. Yet Eleanor completely avoided the odium which was heaped on Eleanor of Provence. Indeed, one of the early chroniclers specifically praises her as being a queen in whose time the land was not troubled by foreigners, despite her own foreign birth. How was this coup achieved? The short answer is that Eleanor's matchmaking was a masterpiece of subtlety. Unlike Eleanor of Provence, she did not seek to marry relatives who were too obviously close to her. Unlike Eleanor of Provence, she did not choose as beneficiaries of her matchmaking impoverished male relatives, or girls with no connection to England at all; nor did she broker treaties encapsulating lots of matches, which were bound to be noticed.

Furthermore, she seems to have worked quite hard to make the marriages palatable in traditional English matchmaking terms as well. A very good example is that of the de Vescy marriages. The brides in those cases were from the Fiennes/Beaumont families, both of which were some little distance in terms of familial proximity from Eleanor, and both of which held English lands: the Fiennes family held lands in Somerset, Hertfordshire and Essex, given to Pharamus de Tingry by King Stephen; and the Beaumonts held lands granted to Raoul de Beaumont by Henry I on the occasion of his son Roscelin's marriage to one of Henry's numerous illegitimate daughters. Thus the Beaumonts and de Fiennes could by this stage pass muster as English – or at least 'non-alien'. In addition, however, the Vescy marriages had a subtle touch of kinship to recommend them even in traditional English matchmaking terms. The Vescys were related to the Scottish king, descending from a natural daughter of William the Lion of Scotland; meanwhile, the Beaumonts too were related to Alexander of Scotland, via Alexander II's mother Ermengarde de Beaumont, and held lands from him by reason of that connection. Therefore, while a marriage between the families was not an obvious dynastic choice, it was perfectly explicable in local terms and a world away from Eleanor of Provence's matches.[27]

Thus we can see that, very quietly, and without any of the outcry which Eleanor of Provence attracted for ultimately less influential marriages, Eleanor succeeded in inserting her relatives within touching distance of the royal house itself. At the time this was probably about securing loyal supporters for the royal house itself, in much the same way that she had done at a less elevated level within her own household. In the end, however, it maximised the chances of her family's bloodline occupying the top spot.

Parsons notes that one reason Eleanor avoided outcry was that she made no attempt to advance her male relatives; no heiresses were 'disparaged' and no Castilian or French relatives received baronial summonses to Parliament. Actually, Parsons slightly overstates the case – at least as regards her de Brienne relatives, who were related to her on her father's side. The Beaumont side of the family armoured by their descent from Henry I and Scottish connections not only received the marriage of Isabella to John de Vescy; the son Louis became Bishop of Durham in 1318 and another son, Henry, was Lord of Man, and through his marriage to Alice Comyn, the countess of Buchan, a conduit to the Lancaster line. However this marriage and his main honours (for example being made Constable of England) did not come until Edward II's reign. Probably Eleanor's main contribution to their advancement consisted in establishing them in Edward of Caernarfon's household, which facilitated their eventual promotion by him. Otherwise, advancement of male relatives, such as John de Fiennes and James de la Plaunche, was very limited and not at a level to create scandal.[28]

Eleanor's family can therefore be seen to be a very complex construct. Apart from Edward, the unalterable centre of her world, she assembled many layers of support and friendship, in which her children played a relatively small part. Her closest ties of blood created yet more responsibilities for her. But elsewhere she had a vibrant network of friends, most of whom were also Edward's intimates, providing a close support network as the royal couple went about their business. There was also a close extended family around the queen largely made up of families tied to her by blood and marriage and who also owed some portion of their advancement to her, although there was a small leavening of close blood family. The atmosphere will have been warm and familiar, many miles from the formalities of later court protocols. But also Eleanor will have been assured of the kind of loyalty which had been missing around England's royal family for some years – her household had multiple ties of interest with her and her family. The success of her strategy can be seen in the way that these families went on to support Eleanor's descendants for generations to come.

In addition, Eleanor carefully selected female relatives to advance her bloodline into Britain's foremost noble families. often choosing from among those who had played some part in that extended family at court. The aim was probably to seed loyalty into those houses as she did among her staff. The result would put her family on England's throne.

13

The Golden Years

I have called the period from the coronation in 1274 up to 1281 'the Golden Years' because this is how they appear from the outside, at first glance. The snapshot is the glorious Crusader king and queen, turning their hands to the work of peaceful government and business – and of course raising a family – with everything apparently going smoothly. However, looked at more closely, it becomes apparent that these years, which were to take Eleanor from her mid-thirties to her fortieth birthday, were a time of ceaseless work on many fronts for the king and queen, and also for those in their inner circle. While some sense of the individual jobs which fell within Eleanor's remit have been conveyed by the previous chapters, it is in following the chronological account that one can begin to grasp the intensity of the life which she lived over these years.

Following the completion of the first parliament of the reign, at the end of October the king and queen set off north via Luton for the trip into the Northampton–Leicester area of Eleanor's existing and dower lands discussed in Chapter 10. It was at Northampton that the king (in company with that notable denizen of Savoy, Otho de Grandison) renewed the pension of Count Philippe of Savoy for his homage in relation to the 'English' Savoyard lands. Officially, this tour was also originally intended to press on further to Shrewsbury, to meet with Llywelyn ap Gruffudd. But that part was called off, a little mysteriously, on the pretext that Edward was taken ill, possibly from a recurrence of his wounds – a suggestion not entirely borne out by the amount of travelling done.[1]

The party then moved back inland via Silverstone, convenient for a wardship just acquired by Eleanor at Haversham, along the modern A43 towards Woodstock. There, of course, lay one of the principal royal residences since the time of Henry II, which offered a congenial spot to spend the first Christmas in England as king and queen.

Once Christmas was over, Anthony Bek and Otho de Grandison were sent off to Paris to try to raise finance to pay off some of the more insistent creditors. The royal party was also on the move on the first day of the new year, after a bare week's rest – touring this time towards the west, taking in Marlborough, Amesbury and the palace of Clarendon – and the proposed Wiltshire holdings for Eleanor's revised dower. Some meeting with Eleanor of Provence, who held Marlborough as part of her dower, would have been inevitable during this visit, particularly since the elder Eleanor was about to undertake a visit to France and seems to have been in less than perfect health. Once this visit was completed, the party headed towards Eleanor's existing lands in Ringwood and Beaulieu and then back via Romsey and Wherwell to Windsor for Margaret's birth.[2]

This pregnancy would have been a doleful one for Eleanor – not only was there the loss of Henry, for whom there would have been considerable grief despite the absence of contact, but just weeks later Edmund of Lancaster's sixteen-year-old wife, Aveline de Forz, died in childbirth – a reminder of the risks which Eleanor was once again undertaking. Then, in late February 1275, Edward's sister Margaret of Scotland died. It seems beyond doubt that baby Margaret, whose birth occurred more or less exactly at this time, was named for this sister of Edward's, who had been one of Eleanor's early companions in her married days in England and who had so recently helped to make the celebration of the coronation such a joyous event. And then, while Eleanor was just emerging from her lying-in, came the news of the death of Edward's other sister, Beatrice, Eleanor's close companion from the Crusade. Beatrice died in London in late March, inferentially giving birth to a child named for Eleanor, Eleanor of Brittany (later Abbess of Fontevrault). When Beatrice's grieving husband left for his lands, their sons John and Henry remained to be raised by Eleanor and Edward with their children.[3]

As soon as Margaret had been born, the party were off again, on the combined pilgrimage and property-scoping visit via Aylesbury into Suffolk described in Chapter 10. They then rushed to return to London for the spring parliament, summoned for 22 April, but which did not actually commence until the 26th, since Edward had still been in Essex on 22 April. That parliament had a full programme, including the First Statute of Westminster, which reflected the materials gained during the Hundred Rolls inquiry. Thus the Hundred Rolls' theme of setting the country to right is prominently reflected in the Act's preamble. In the terms one can see both Edward's personal aim of restoring royal rights and his broader and more popular aim of improving law and order generally. The law and order agenda will actually have been much in the minds of the inner circle around Edward, following a serious incident at Canterbury in early 1275 when Otho de Grandison was attacked by a number of citizens, resulting in a heavy fine being levied against the citizens as a whole.[4]

Once Parliament had broken up in July, the royal party were off for the busy summer programme, commencing with small stops at Kempton and the children's main base of Windsor. The main summer programme had two themes: an attempt to take the homage of Llywelyn, and an assessment of Eleanor's properties and the proposed dower assignment. So through Buckinghamshire, with stops conveniently near Eleanor's properties at Risborough and Aylesbury, the party went, to Oxford, where a civic reception had to be met, and doubtless appeased, when Edward would not enter the town itself owing to the superstition that St Frideswide would exercise his displeasure on any king entering the town. Business came to join them there, in the form of Gaston de Béarn, who was committed to the custody of Sir Stephen de Pencestre, and a request from Philip of Savoy to be pardoned 1,000 marks owed to the late king. After a stop at Woodstock, it was North via Kenilworth to Eleanor's properties at Derby and the Peak and Macclesfield, and then on to Chester itself, where in September Edward had summoned Llywelyn to render his homage. There the court kicked its heels for a couple of weeks while Llywelyn refused to come over the border, and Edward refused to go to him. Edward issued a further peremptory summons for London in October 1275.

From Chester, the court moved across the country via Healey and Heywood in Lancaster, Lichfield in Stafford and Merevale in Warwickshire and Leicestershire to the heart of the Leicestershire–Rutland–Northampton territory which was to form one of the major blocks of Eleanor's property empire. This was combined with another stay at the royal hunting lodge at Geddington. From there the party headed back at top speed – reaching Windsor for a short visit to the children in less than a week and passing on to Westminster for the second parliament of the year. By the time of their return, Eleanor was pregnant yet again.[5]

This parliament is particularly interesting in that it saw the introduction of the Statute of Jewry, which was a quid pro quo for a much-needed injection of funds from Parliament into the royal pocket. The Act met the many complaints about Jewish moneylending, and more specifically the trade in debts to the Jews entered into by some rich Christian speculators (such as Richard of Cornwall, and latterly Eleanor herself), which had proliferated again since the deal which had been part of the price for Crusade funding. The means of providing a remedy went to the root of the problem: under the terms of the statute, Jewish moneylending was outlawed completely. Such satisfaction did this measure give that Edward was able to raise a fairly substantial tax to assist with his towering debts.

But the statute had other interesting features; contrary to the current trend in Europe, the statute made some efforts to assist the Jewish population in that it permitted them to live 'by lawful trade and by their labour' and officially offered them the king's peace and recorded his will that his sheriffs and bailiffs preserve and defend them. As such, it was a notably more broadminded approach that that of, say, Simon de Montfort, who believed in the virtues of encouraging his supporters to kill Jews, or Eleanor of Provence, who at about this time expelled all Jews from her dower property. However, along with the more tolerant approach, a considerable residue of prejudice remained: the statute also decreed Jews were only to live in the king's towns, and effectively in ghettos, with no Christian among them. It also notoriously put into law the Vatican's demand that all Jews over the age of seven wear a yellow felt badge (shaped like the Mosaic tablets) on their outer garment. Although this latter part of the legislation has been much seized on as demonstrating an anti-Semitic approach on the part of Edward, that is hardly a fair criticism, bearing in mind the fact that the Church had required such a distinction since the Fourth Lateran Council in 1213, that it had been officially enforced in England since 1218, and that even Alfonso X in Castile was by now beginning to yield to pressure on this item.[6]

Overall, the statute may be described as an attempt to find an acceptable modus vivendi for the Jewish population as contributors to the king's wealth. Can this middle way be traced at all to Eleanor's influence? Parts of it seem to find their inspiration in similar initiatives attempted by Louis IX, but there is certainly some reason to discern Eleanor's hand in its final form. Certainly it seems likely that, without Eleanor's influence, Edward would have been much more minded to follow his mother's approach; there are indeed some suggestions that he did consider expulsion at this time. Further, the provision in 1280 whereby the Jews were to listen to weekly conversion sermons preached by the Dominicans seems to hint at her influence. There is also something of the Castilian approach of encouraging broader Jewish participation in trade in the provisions of the Statute of Jewry, which enabled Jews to buy houses on behalf of the king or to take lands to farm. Finally, the overall thrust of the statute was commercial; in effect, the Jews were given a stay of execution on the basis that they were considered likely to have a continuing commercial utility to the Crown. This balance is consistent with Eleanor's own dealings with her Jewish contacts and also vividly echoes the approach of the Castilian monarchy during Eleanor's childhood, where the position of the Jews was stoutly defended because of their considerable commercial utility to the Castilian throne. Eleanor, of course, is not the only possible source of influence in this regard; there is certainly some evidence that Robert Burnell wished to make the affairs of the Jewish population workable. It is perhaps most likely that these two moderating influences worked together upon Edward in arriving at the approach which the statute encapsulated.[7]

The October parliament also coincided with a second refusal to render homage by Llywelyn, who refused to comply with Edward's summons on the grounds that he did not consider himself safe in England; he cheekily demanded that the Earl of Gloucester and Robert Burnell stand as hostages for his safety. At more or less the same time arrived the news that Llywelyn had married (by proxy) Eleanor de Montfort, daughter of Simon and Edward's aunt Eleanor. His defiance was now plain; the result was a vote in Parliament of funds to cover a Welsh war.[8]

Of course, the most important matter for Eleanor at this period will have been the finalisation of her revised dower assignment, which was approved in October 1275. Having visited key areas for that assignment and viewed potential properties during the tours made since their return, she and her advisers will have been spending considerable periods of time finalising exactly what was to be assigned in various areas; and where visits by Eleanor had not yet been possible, evaluating reports from the staff despatched to deputise for her in those areas. The result, as noted earlier, was a considerable block of property based in several different areas which was to form the nucleus of her acquisitions for the years to come.

Planning for those further acquisitions began at once, with assignment of various debts secured on strategically sited locations so that further purchases could then begin to be sought. Also, there would be planning for the revenue side of the acquisitions. So at this point, we find one Geoffrey de Lewknor writing apologetically to Eleanor, explaining that he can't find the certificate for the results of the Leicestershire eyre at this moment, but that he will send it as soon as he can lay hands on it. Interestingly, too, Eleanor's unusual head for business seems to have attracted personal petitions outside her own business – Lucy de Grey wrote to her in this period asking for help with her accounts.[9]

Another matter which claimed Eleanor's attention at this point was the crisis in Castile, where Alfonso's year had started badly and then deteriorated. Early in the year he had been forced by the Pope to drop his claim to the Holy Roman Empire. Glory in Germany was therefore off the menu. On his return to Castile, he therefore decided to resume the Reconquista against Granada, where there was a civil war going on. A concatenation of catastrophes followed. In autumn he sent a force to engage the Moorish and Moroccan forces. The resulting meeting was disastrous for the Castilians, whose general was among the dead. To add bad to worse, at around the same time Alfonso's eldest son, Ferdinand de la Cerda ('the Hairy'), died, leaving two small sons by his marriage to Blanche of France – and a highly sensitive inheritance issue between them and Alfonso's second son, Sancho. For a final touch, in October Sancho personally averted disaster in a second battle. The net result was that, by the end of the year, Alfonso had to sue for peace with the Almohads, rather than pursuing the Reconquista – the very obverse of his father's success. Yet it was the succession issue created by the death of Ferdinand and the rise in Sancho's prestige which was to haunt him longest and most seriously.[10]

Back in England, as soon as Parliament rose in November the court was off again. The first stop was the Tower of London itself, to oversee progress of the building works which had been started here soon after the coronation; the disrepair caused by the failure to progress Henry III's plans and the collapse of the great gate in 1240 doubtless was very apparent on Edward and Eleanor's return. How much of the current look of the Tower is owed to Edward's works and how much to Henry's original plans is a matter of debate. However, it seems clear that, as well as dealing with dilapidations, a considerable upscaling in size and defences – in particular the size of the moat – was part of the later works. It is also likely that its concentric pattern, which afforded multiple lines of defence and was familiar from Crusader castles, was an Edwardian innovation and may well have been linked to the architect in charge of the works, Brother John of the Order of St Thomas of Acre. While the works had an obvious purpose militarily, London was not actually under threat and the statement created by the building was more in the way of a manifesto by Edward that he was a strong king who would defend his rights. Such a message was of course pertinent to the historically troublesome Londoners, but it was also one worth making to the magnates, commons and foreign visitors alike, after a number of years when royal authority had been lacking. One can perhaps also sense Castilian overtones: the *Siete Partidas* adjures kings to preserve and defend castles for the good of the kingdom.

At the same time, the royal apartments themselves were undergoing a revamp: new apartments in St Thomas's Tower were created as part of the project and furnished in Eleanor's favourite colours of green and red. Tellingly, too, before Eleanor ever set foot in it Edward had spent considerable sums of money refurbishing the gardens of the Tower: at least 13,000 turves were laid and pear trees, rose trees and lily bulbs were all deployed.[11]

Once business at the Tower had been examined, in December 1275 the party moved off to visit more of Eleanor's properties. This time, after a stop at Marlborough and Upavon near the new dower acquisitions at Bedwyn and Wexcombe and Wimborne (next to her manor of Ringwood), it was on for another scanty Christmas holiday. This was a mere five days at the noxious Gillingham – which, we will be unsurprised to find, was very close to the lands which Eleanor had acquired in wardship at Compton Chamberlayne. The next move was to Charminster and Bindon, which were well situated for reviewing some properties which Eleanor had in mind to acquire (and did shortly thereafter acquire) in the neighbourhood of Dorchester before heading back to the New Forest property – which obviously had the added advantage of providing excellent hunting ground.

After all this movement, the party finally came to rest for a few weeks in January 1276 at Winchester, where the king's intervention was needed in a long-standing quarrel between the citizens. This was probably the venue for the wedding of Edward's brother Edmund to Blanche of Artois, the widow of Henri, Count of Champagne and King of Navarre and cousin to Eleanor through her grandmother Blanche of Castile. Blanche of Atrois had lost her only son in the most appalling circumstances – he was dropped from the battlements of a castle by a careless nurse. Her daughter Jeanne, heiress of Navarre, had been destined to marry Eleanor and Edward's son Henry, but after his death the previous year she had been snapped up by the French king as a wife for his son Philip. The marriage with Blanche was therefore very much second best; but it had its attractions, not least in that it brought Champagne and Navarre under English control during Jeanne's minority, since Blanche was regent for her daughter. It also appears to have been a successful and harmonious marriage on a personal level, with the Lancasters being close associates of Eleanor and Edward for the rest of Eleanor's life. Interestingly, the regency of Champagne and Navarre was exercised through Eleanor's cousin Jean of Brienne. While the Brienne family's good standing in the French court made this a politic move, Eleanor's influence seems possible in this appointment.[12]

In the interim, a great piece of excitement had occurred. Eleanor de Montfort was captured on the high seas on her way to join her new husband, Llywelyn, in Wales and was brought to England in genteel captivity. Her brother Amaury, who was escorting her, was despatched off into rather less genteel captivity, in which he was to stay for some years. It seems likely that Eleanor de Montfort was initially received at court during this period, before being banished to Windsor, where she spent the next three years as a bargaining chip between Edward and Llywelyn. Nor was she the only captive making her appearance at court at this time – Gaston de Béarn returned to make his submission to Edward and to be released. It is doubtful, however, whether anyone present thought that this was the end of his troublemaking. Meanwhile, the news of the death of their friend Gregory X, which occurred in early 1276, will have been a sadness, particularly to Eleanor, who had maintained a friendly correspondence with him. It was also a cause for concern going forward, since no replacement was likely to be as well disposed to them, in particular as regards disposing of the papal tenth, as their crusading companion; and so it was to prove.[13]

Late in February, the court passed to Marlborough and then to the favoured destination of Quenington, before heading up via Oxfordshire into Rutland and Lincolnshire for the entire month of March. Again the influence of Eleanor's property empire is manifest. The trip involved visiting her dower lands of Temple Bruerne and Sixhills, the former being just a mile or so from lands recently acquired by Eleanor at Nocton and Dunston and the latter being situated near her properties at Gayton le Marsh, Tothill, Lincoln and Caistor. Via a stay at Barton-upon-Humber, two properties from the dower in the East Riding of Yorkshire were accessible as well. Then, in an echo of the previous year, there was a rush back south. In April, the party passed back at speed via some of the northern Northamptonshire properties to Kempton, arriving just days before the birth of Berengaria, who arrived on 1 May 1276. The court thereafter moved to Westminster to attend Parliament throughout May, with Eleanor following once her lying-in was complete.[14]

With the dower and the immediate post-dower acquisitions now safely established and reviewed, the summer of 1276 offered the chance for a tour with very little reference to Eleanor's properties. The party ranged through Sussex, Kent and a little bit of Essex before returning to London in late July. However, this was not idle holidaymaking. It fulfilled at least two functions. While it provided an opportunity for Edward to survey the problems of the once prosperous port of Winchelsea, which was in the process of being overrun by the sea, the route chosen also reflected one of Eleanor's main preoccupations in the year of 1276 – the promotion of the Dominican Order.

As has already been mentioned, Eleanor's family had close associations with the order, and she was to demonstrate a clear preference for them throughout her life. Acting in their favour doubtless seemed particularly apposite at a time when the first Dominican Archbishop of Canterbury, Robert Kilwardby, was now incumbent, and the new Pope, Innocent V, was also of that order. It was therefore during this year that the London chapter of the Order moved from Holborn, where they had commenced their mission in fairly constrained surroundings opposite a tannery, though they had subsequently extended their holdings southwards through the area now known as Lincoln's Inn. In 1276, the mayor and aldermen of London gifted the order with property around two streets leading down to the Thames: the area now named Blackfriars after them. The Dominicans' London chapter was based there, at Baynard's Castle, from the completion of works in the 1290s. It seems that the impetus for this move came from the Archbishop of Canterbury and Eleanor. The works involved, however, were major and had required authority from Edward I to remove the city wall between the river and Ludgate and rebuild it around their precinct. Eleanor's influence can be seen in this permission and in later benefactions made directly by Edward to the chapter.

This Dominican theme was also featured in the summer tour, which featured a stay at Chichester to coincide with the translation of the body of the late bishop St Richard De Wych, the great supporter of the Dominicans in England prior to Eleanor's advent. Given that Henry III had refused to recognise Richard as bishop for many years, the hand of Eleanor as supporter of the order appears discernible in this decision. The foundation of the Chichester Dominicans, of which Eleanor was the major patron, probably occurred at the same time and with her support.[15]

After the Chichester visit, there was a stop in Lewes, which will have offered opportunities to look back to the stressful times of the war, before moving along the coast through Kent to Canterbury and then on to visit Eleanor's new dower properties in Essex, Rayleigh and Eastwood, before the return to London.

During the late summer which followed, Eleanor remained busy: in August the king and queen were back on the road in the vicinity of Eleanor's properties and dower lands in Hampshire and the New Forest, as well as Somerset (including Bristol) and Gloucestershire, before returning again to London for Parliament in October. At this point, the key issue was the continued refusal by Llywelyn to attend to render homage – at least not unless he was granted a safe conduct guaranteed by the Archbishop of Canterbury and the release of Eleanor de Montfort. In the face of what now appeared a contumelious refusal, it was inevitable that there followed in November a positive decision to call the feudal host and go to war the next year. The main Marcher lords were immediately ordered to take charge of affairs at the key points, Warwick being placed at Chester, Mortimer at Montgomery and de Chaworth at Carmarthen. The muster was set for July 1277, at Worcester. From then on, the focus of the court was around preparations for the war, with moves being limited around Windsor and the Gloucestershire–Worcestershire area until the end of February 1277.[16]

Around this time, further disquieting news reached Eleanor from Castile. Alfonso's position had been going from bad to worse over the succession issue. Philip III of France understandably wanted to see his nephews, Ferdinand de la Cerda's sons, acknowledged as heirs of Alfonso. This would have been the position had Ferdinand been king, and was the result under Alfonso's own revised legal codes. However, traditional Spanish law indicated that the correct heir was Ferdinand's younger brother Sancho, who was also of military age and had a proven track record. Alfonso's court, always prone to splits along party lines and already magnetised on the issue of reformed code versus traditional law, had polarised violently on this issue. One side, led by Blanche of France, Ferdinand's widow, and Queen Violante, upheld the cause of the child Alfonso de la Cerda. The other party, headed by Fadrique, who had been installed as his brother's adviser following their reconciliation in 1272, endorsed Sancho's claim. Alfonso was caught in the middle. Acting on Fadrique's advice, in 1276 Alfonso endorsed Sancho's claim. The result was a rapid deterioration in relations with France; Alfonso consequently fell out badly with Fadrique, and in 1277 (possibly in a fit of irrationality caused by his growing physical illness) actually had him assassinated. Both Alfonso's action and the acutely weak position which prompted it will have been a considerable grief and embarrassment to Eleanor.[17]

According to the chroniclers, the spring of 1277 was an utterly miserable one, with storms and floods in January giving way to wall-to-wall rain in March; all in all it was an unpleasant time to be on the move, still less to be trying to organise men and materiel. Over this period, the usual complement of the royal court on the move was boosted by what was effectively a recall of the crusading team of 1270. Among these were Roger Clifford, Otho de Grandison, John de Vescy, Payn de Chaworth and Robert Tybetot, as well as Edmund of Lancaster, himself a co-Crusader and Marcher lord by virtue of his holdings at Carmarthen and Cardigan. Other experienced names were the redoubtable Roger Mortimer, William Beauchamp, Earl of Warwick, and the young Henry de Lacy, Earl of Lincoln.[18]

So in February 1277, with the early stages of the campaign in the capable hands of seasoned battle commanders, the royal party left for a dual-purpose tour of East Anglia. On the one hand, Edward seems to have visited every shrine of note in the area and made offerings. The prominent venues of Walsingham and Bromholm, which Edward and Eleanor will have visited in Henry III's train, obviously feature; but so too do the lesser-known Augustinian priory in Cambridge and the Dominican house of Horsham, as well as the abbey of Hulme and the chapel of Worstead. On the other hand, many of the stops were convenient places for Eleanor to conduct a survey of her properties and potential acquisitions. Bromholm, for example, did not just boast a fragment of the True Cross – it was also excellently situated for her key Aylsham–Cawston group of properties. Indeed, additions at Burgh and Cawston were made very shortly afterwards. The Cambridgeshire stops in turn were close to her holdings at Soham and Dullingham, and there was actually a night's stay at the manor of Foulmire, which was later to be granted to her in wardship.[19]

Meanwhile, further preparations were still afoot. In particular, learning from the mistakes both of Henry II and Henry III, Edward placed massive orders to ensure that the supply chain for the army was well provisioned prior to the parliament in April. Even by this stage the campaign could be seen to be going well, with Llywelyn pushed back into Gwynedd and his support crumbling. The lords of South Wales agreed to pay homage by spring 1278 and the key castle of Dolforwyn (only just completed by Llywelyn) had fallen after only a week's siege. Thus the royal party was able to contemplate a stop at Windsor, where the unfortunate Eleanor de Montfort awaited the outcome of the war, probably with the royal nursery, before the departure to the final stage of the campaign in June.

In July, final preparations were made in Gloucester, Worcester (where the bulk of the invasion force mustered) and Chester. At the latter venue, a fleet of thirty-five ships, some from the Cinque Ports and others from a variety of locations including Gascony, was assembled. Towards the end of the month the king was at Basingwerk, near a spur of rock called the Flint, where a new castle was begun by late July. Characteristically, despite yet another impending baby, conceived some time in spring, Eleanor did not stay in Chester but parked herself at Shotwick Castle, halfway between Chester and the works at Flint – within easy reach of Edward.[20]

One point of interest in relation to the campaign are the echoes which we see of the principles of Vegetius, as set out in the book which Eleanor had given Edward on Crusade. So again the records show Edward's concern for the question of provisions and supplies, with further orders for grain going out as late as 17 July: 'An army unsupplied with grain and other necessary equipment will be vanquished without striking a blow.' Also borrowed from classic Roman principles (most famously deployed by Caesar, but also advised by Vegetius) was Edward's operation, which commenced in late July, to deforest either side of the route which his army would take to prevent ambush, an endeavour which involved transporting nearly 2,000 woodmen.[21]

With these final preparations in hand, in August Edward and Eleanor felt able to take yet another break from campaigning and head back into Cheshire for the ceremonies attending the foundation of the abbey of Vale Royal. The Mass of consecration, invoking divine assistance for the Welsh plans of the pious king, was performed by Robert Burnell, assisted by the Bishop of St Asaph. Edward laid the cornerstone, and Eleanor laid a stone for herself and one for Alphonso. Stones were also laid by the major figures in the royal retinue: the earls of Gloucester, Cornwall, Warenne, and Warwick, Maurice de Craon, Jean de Grailly, Robert Tybetot, Robert de Vere and Otho de Grandison.[22]

With the spiritualities seen to, on 23 August the army set out, proceeding as far as Rhuddlan, where work immediately began on another new castle. They then pressed on to Deganwy. From here, Edward was able to send the trusty pairing of John de Vescy and Otho de Grandison and a force transported by the sailors of the Cinque Ports to carry out another Vegetian strategy – to overcome the enemy by surprise and famine. The party did not engage the Welsh forces but instead occupied Anglesey, the breadbasket of Wales. At a stroke this deprived Llywelyn of his own supply store, and annexed to Edward's army an ample supply to remain in the field for the foreseeable future. The result was inevitable; Llywelyn had to submit before winter. Although his formal submission did not come until November, it is probable that he had conveyed his submission by mid-September, when the itinerary finds Edward back at Chester, albeit spending time on and off at Rhuddlan, doubtless supervising building works. Meanwhile, Eleanor divided her time between Chester, Shotwick and Shrewsbury.

By 9 November, the Rhuddlan castle had progressed sufficiently that Edward was able to take Llywelyn's submission there, in all probability accompanied by Eleanor. The terms of the submission, negotiated by Otho de Grandison, Anthony Bek and Robert Tybetot, effectively restored the high-water mark of English power over Wales, and thus marked a very successful and satisfactory campaign.[23]

However the accruing costs of the building programme which accompanied and outlasted the campaign should not be neglected. At Rhuddlan, the cost of the town was about £10,000, of which over £3,000 was spent in the first eighteen months. Much of this seems to have gone to ditch diggers and carpenters. The considerably smaller town of Flint cost £7,000.[24]

The royal party, boosted by Llywelyn and his entourage, left the emerging new castle on 20 November and headed back to Westminster for Christmas and the Welsh prince's formal public submission. Also on the agenda was the imminent birth of Eleanor's next child. The trip commenced with a week surrounding Eleanor's birthday at Shrewsbury and a visit to Robert Burnell's house at Acton Burnell, close to Watling Street and therefore convenient for the journey back to London. At this point, the house was probably no more than a well-built manor house; the red-sandstone house that substantially stands to this day was not commenced until 1284.

The party arrived in London around 23 December 1277 – as usual, only a few days before Eleanor's due date. On Christmas Day, Llywelyn submitted and swore fealty to Edward. Eleanor's next child (probably a daughter) was born on around 3 January 1278 at Westminster and either died at birth or very shortly thereafter, there being no mention of a child being born in any of the chronicles. Eleanor certainly lay in for a time, since records exist of venison being sent to her by Edward late in January from his tour of Kent, which followed on from a ten-day stay on his part at the Tower, probably with the younger children. However, given that Edward did not return until late in February, and then only for a two-day layover before the court was off into Gloucestershire, it is likely that at some point in early February Eleanor made her way down to Dover to join him, and thereafter moved with him to Northbourne, Wingham, where the archbishops of Canterbury then had a palace, and Canterbury before returning to London.[25]

Matrimonial plans were now in the air for the children. In particular, although she was only seven years old, Joan's marriage was already the subject of international planning. In 1277, Rudolph of Hapsburg, the new King of the Romans, had sent envoys to negotiate for Joan's hand at the behest of her great aunt, the dowager Queen of France, who had devised a rather complicated plan by which the marriage could be used to oust the ever-popular Charles of Anjou from his tenure of Provence. The plan was obviously fanciful, but the match with the Hapsburgs offered solid recommendations and the negotiations proceeded to some level of detail, with Edward stipulating for an allowance of 11,000 marks and the title of King of the Romans for young Hartmann if his father became Emperor. Indeed, plans were made for a wedding in 1279, including the issuance of a formal invitation, safe conduct and arrangements for accompanying guests. The Kent trip therefore also provided an opportunity to see off Stephen de Pencestre and his wife Margaret, who were to cross to France and bring back young Joan from her grandmother's custody, so as to ensure she would be back in good time before the date of her projected marriage.[26]

At the same time, the first steps were being taken for the marriage of the even younger Margaret – a commission from Duke John of Brabant arrived in January 1278 to negotiate her marriage with his son John, and by February emissaries were off to Compiègne to take the duke's oath to observe the provisions of a deal already negotiated. In modern terms, the match with Brabant sounds like an odd choice. Brabant (which sprawls across parts of modern Belgium and the Netherlands) was not actually a state bordering on England or any of England's Continental possessions. While it was not far from Ponthieu, it was not sufficiently close that there had been Ponthevin–Brabant marriages in the past. However, Brabant was a state which was seen as strategically key, with Louis IX's brother Robert marrying into it and a marriage into Brabant even having been proposed for Edward in his youth. It was very much on the rise at the time, under the direction of the impressive and charismatic Duke John I (also known as 'John the Victorious'). John descended on his mother's side from the powerful dukes of Burgundy and was the new star of the tournament circuit and one of the most admired leaders in Europe. Brabant was also an emerging market for England's key export – wool. More significantly, however, in 1274 Duke John's sister Margaret had married Philip III of France.

Therefore, despite the fact that Duke John bid fair to set a bad example of marital fidelity to his son, a counterweight alliance with Brabant was imperative. That the alliance was with John's second son and namesake rather than his first, Godfrey, is perhaps puzzling; however, it appears that Godfrey, who died young, was always considered unlikely to succeed to his father's duchy. These marriage negotiations were plainly serious: details such as the subsidy to be paid by Edward and the dower allocation to be made for Margaret were all dealt with and Edward's crack diplomatic team of John de Vescy, the Earl of Lincoln and Otho de Grandison were sent to take the Duke of Brabant's oath on Margaret's marriage contract.[27]

In March 1278, the court was off again into the Cotswolds. A letter of Edward's from Quenington/Down Ampney conveys a sense of a king in touch with affairs, but taking a step back for a short period. He writes to Burnell and Otho de Grandison, who had moved on to Paris to deal with Gascon affairs, expressing his approval of their actions, reminding them to get as many guarantees from the Gascons as possible and complaining that the Gascons are very unreliable, so everything needs to be put firmly in writing. He jokes that they should have the faith of Mary, mother of God, and not that of St Thomas, because he will back them in all their decisions. He also gives them a chatty general round-up: Llywelyn was behaving for once and Alexander of Scotland was coming to do homage at Michaelmas in London, and he hoped he would see them back in England by that time.[28]

It was at about this time that Alfonso's problems emerged again. At the Cortes in 1278, it was announced that Sancho would rule with his father. After the Cortes, Queen Violante, accompanied by her French daughter-in-law and the two de la Cerda boys, fled to the court of Violante's brother, Pedro of Aragon, who instantly began to make political hay out of his neighbour's dilemma. France, meanwhile, threatened war. As a result, there came an appeal from Alfonso to Edward for assistance, at the same time as a summons came from Philip III to aid him in his issue with Alfonso – a summons which he was perfectly entitled to make as Edward's feudal lord for Gascony. To Alfonso, Edward pleaded his engagement in Wales as an excuse and encouraged Alfonso to come to terms with France. To Philip, Edward replied that he would serve if he must, though he did not want to, but would do all in his power to settle the quarrel. In the event, the French summons was not pressed; Alfonso seems to have made terms on the basis of supporting the de la Cerda claim – a decision which was to prove unfortunate for him in the next few years. It would appear, however, that Eleanor was doing her best to drum up support for the beleaguered Alfonso – Edward's kind response to Alfonso reflects her influence. Further, Count Esquivat de Chabanais wrote to Edward, having heard that Eleanor held him in contempt for his failure to assist Alfonso the previous year in a crisis in Navarre, and begged Edward to excuse him to Eleanor. He evidently understood that Eleanor expected her friends to do what they could to assist Alfonso.[29]

At Easter 1278, the court went on through Wiltshire into the heart of Eleanor's Somerset property, with stays at her manors of Somerton and Queen Camel. The latter, just recently granted to Eleanor, was sited near the Cadbury fort that provided one of the speculated locations for Camelot, and was thus a particularly appropriate stop on the way to the next venue, Glastonbury, where one of the set pieces of the reign was staged – the reburial of the reputed remains of King Arthur and Queen Guinevere.

This rather bizarre incident needs to be put in context. It was not a 'discovery' of the remains – that had occurred in 1191, a few years after Glastonbury had first been suggested as a location for the Arthurian Isle of Avalon, when the monks of Glastonbury Abbey were doing some forced renovations in the wake of a major fire. There is a real possibility that

Henry II and Richard, who encouraged the 'discovery', were complicit in what seems likely to have been an opportunistic fraud by the monastery.

However, two forces made this a very worthwhile event for the Edwardian court. The first was that the lure of Arthur had by no means diminished in the years which had passed since the 'discovery'. Both Edward in England and Eleanor in Castile (and doubtless all their friends) were brought up on tales of Arthur and his knights and enjoyed them wholeheartedly. Thus, even if they did take the tales with a pinch of salt, Edward himself had been enthusiastic enough to commission an Arthurian work, and Eleanor was to be the dedicatee (and probable commissioner of) the Arthurian romance *Escanor*.

The alleged graves would be bound to have a romantic significance for any keen reader of Arthurian tales. But the event was not simply a bit of romantic byplay – if it had been inspired by pure Arthurian enthusiasm it could have been done earlier in the reign, for example as part of the Somerset trip in 1276. This event had a far more serious point. Arthur had been claimed by the Welsh, and therefore it made sense that, while Edward was settling Welsh affairs, as he was doing for much of the year in 1278, and trying to establish himself as the authority figure for that land, he should put to bed the idea that Arthur was located somewhere in Wales, or that he was going to return to assist the Welsh, as Welsh tradition insisted. So as Morris points out, this trip was not at all akin to the trip made to Glastonbury by Henry III and the then twelve-year-old Eleanor of Provence, eager to see the grave of her hero. This was far more a gesture of ownership.

This aspect of the performance is reflected in the ceremonies which were carried out: the bodies of the alleged king and queen were disinterred before a large audience at twilight. The chronicler reports that 'there in two caskets were found the bones of the said king of wondrous size, and those of Guinevere, of marvellous beauty' (though quite how bones are of particular beauty he regrettably does not explain). The next morning, Edward wrapped Arthur's bones in silk, and Eleanor performed the same office for those of Guinevere. The bones were then returned to the caskets, which were then sealed with a certificate of authenticity by Edward and Eleanor respectively and removed to the monastery's treasury until such time as a fit resting place could be prepared for them. The skulls, however, were left outside. The latter detail is not just faintly sinister, it also provides another powerful indication that the point of this event was not a romantic one but had a political purpose – to establish and publicise the deceased status and English location of the great Welsh hero. Any passing Welshman was to be left in no doubt that Arthur and Guinevere were very definitely dead.

However, there were also other resonances which the royal pair may have been positioning themselves to exploit. As mentioned above,

Arthurian mania was generally running high, and the next few years would see the commencement of the fashion for 'Round Tables', where knights effectively identified themselves with Arthurian knights of legend. In claiming and reburying Arthur and Guinevere, Edward and Eleanor positioned themselves to be perceived as the new Arthur and Guinevere; and indeed in the years which followed this characterisation was to be picked up by their entourage and by the chroniclers, with John of London asserting that Edward had exceeded Arthur as well as Alexander. If it is tempting to regard this as an overly cynical approach, it is worth reviewing the use which was to be made of Arthurian resonances in the second Welsh campaign and the interesting circumstances of the foundation of Caernarfon (both of which will be discussed in Chapter 14). It is also worth bearing in mind that Edward later went on to deploy the Arthur myth in his arguments over Scottish jurisdiction, and that of Joseph of Arimathea (also said to have been based at Glastonbury) in certain disputes with the Church.

Two questions necessarily present themselves: did Eleanor and Edward know that the remains were a fraud? And whose idea was the whole show? We can know the answer to neither question, but probabilities present themselves. For the former, despite the certification, there has to be a suspicion that Edward was sophisticated enough to be a little sceptical, and Eleanor, with her interest in history, may well have made the effort to uncover the truth. Indeed, one cannot help suspecting that if they thought the bodies were genuine they would not have desecrated them by removing the skulls for display. As to the latter question, different commentators incline in different directions. In fact, it seems likely to have been an idea which would appeal to both. Aside from some shared interest in Arthurian romance, Edward had seen his father pick a model for his kingship in the form of the Confessor and use publicity to promote it; Eleanor's family had form for exploiting myths to enhance family prestige. However, Eleanor's interest in Arthurian literature is more marked than that of Edward. What is more, there appear to have been other occasions – particularly later in Wales – where Eleanor's literary inclinations were used as a springboard for occasions which, though enjoyable in themselves, also had a considerable political point. It therefore seems very plausible that the driving force behind this occasion was Eleanor.[30]

Eleanor was never likely to miss a chance to visit her lands, so the period after this event was used for a whistle-stop tour which took in the northern Somerset properties and those in the New Forest before heading through Sussex and Chichester to the May/June parliament at Westminster. It was at this point that Joan of Acre rejoined her family, the elder portion of which was in residence at Westminster for the parliament, and the junior wing of which was then at the Tower. Thereafter in July there was time for a fairly decent stay at Windsor and a shorter one at Clarendon, before moving into the Marcher territories, presumably to review how the settlement was going, reaching Rhuddlan in September where, the results of the survey having been satisfactory, Llywelyn's hostages were released. In reply, Llywelyn sent four hunting dogs to Edward and two greyhounds to Eleanor, showing that he had got to know them well enough to appreciate their interests. From Rhuddlan, the court made its way via Vale Royal and Eleanor's dower property of Macclesfield to Worcester, where, in October 1278, the marriage of Llywelyn and Eleanor de Montfort finally took place, under Edward and Eleanor's aegis. Thus Edward provided the wedding fee, and Eleanor gifted the bride with an elaborate kerchief. As soon as the wedding was over, it was time to return again to London for the autumn parliament, albeit with a short stay at Windsor to visit the younger children.

While this unwanted Welsh wedding proceeded smoothly, problems were emerging in Joan's projected match. Rudolph, although crowned King of the Romans or King of Germany, was, like Richard of Cornwall before him, having difficulty in establishing his authority over the individual German territories. In such circumstances he could not afford to send his son, or the necessary accompanying guards, across to England for any period of time, and the match was put on hold. Young Berengaria, however, was not to reach even the precocious age at which a marriage could first be proposed for her: sometime in the period between June 1277, when a sum was paid to the woman who was her nurse, and the same date next year when the payment was to the woman who 'had been' her nurse, the youngest member of the family died, aged around eighteen months. She lies with her aunt Katherine and Edward and Eleanor's other dead children in Westminster Abbey.[31]

At the same time, it was necessary to take steps with reference to the archbishopric of Canterbury, Robert Kilwardby having been promoted to Cardinal Bishop of Porto in mid-September. This provided Edward with a second opportunity to try to get the trusted Robert Burnell installed here, confident that Burnell was no Becket. On this occasion, Edward did not find his wishes impeded by the monks of Canterbury and he despatched a lawyer from Bologna to the papal court to try to get this consensus approved by the papacy. Also sent to assist in the good work was one John Pecham. A distinguished theologian who had taught at Oxford and disputed with Aquinas, he was formerly head of the Franciscans in England and thus would be deemed likely to find favour with the new Pope Nicholas III, whose father had been a close friend of St Francis.[32]

After the parliament in the middle of November, it was necessary to visit Norwich for the dedication of the cathedral, which took place on 26 November. However, rather typically, the journey, taken over the period of Eleanor's birthday, was made via Newmarket, which was situated right between Eleanor's Cambridgeshire holdings of Soham and Dullingham. Interestingly, this journey commenced with a one-night stay at Waltham Abbey, where Eleanor was later to be commemorated. Norwich itself offered a good base for inspection of the Burgh–Scottow–Aylsham grouping of properties, which Eleanor had acquired just a few months earlier from John de Burgh and which were to be a major centre of her holdings. Indeed, the visit then progressed directly to Burgh and the court seems to have remained there for some time, with the party only returning to Cambridge in mid-December, before heading to Windsor for a family Christmas and New Year.

After a short stay in Westminster in January, the party proceeded to Woodstock, where the whole of February was spent awaiting Eleanor's latest baby. An interesting sidelight on this journey is that on the way there one of Eleanor's damsels exchanged promises of marriage with one of the king's marshals, a vignette which emphasises the familial nature of the peripatetic court party. So too does it show the high moral tone which was generally expected – this incident resulted in an episcopal inquiry later in the year.[33]

During this period, the news of the papal response to the request to install Robert Burnell in Canterbury was received – fairly unsurprisingly, Nicholas III was unwilling to accede to this plan. His solution, however, was both surprising and witty – he instead nominated John Pecham. Pecham's relations with both king and queen were to be, to put it politely, rather mixed. On the one hand, his academic distinction appealed to Eleanor, for whom he wrote a theological work; and his loathing of Welsh law, which he considered profoundly immoral, was very pleasing to Edward. Further, there are certainly signs of fairly friendly exchanges between them; for example, Pecham's 1283 letter berating Eleanor for her stance on usury is topped and tailed by kind words about a consolatory letter she had sent him, venison despatched to him and a pretty chapel he had just completed and which he was sure she would like.

However, as an archbishop who criticised usury and pluralism, both of which were intrinsic features of Eleanor's business dealings, he will inevitably have roused her anger on numerous occasions. Still more so, one cannot help thinking, did his habit of sending her letters of reprimand; a number of such letters survive, and more may well have existed. Nor did Edward find Pecham's first move on returning to England – ordering the display of Magna Carta in every church – much to his taste. For his part, Pecham was to find Eleanor's close association with one of his bêtes noires, the distinguished Dominican theologian William of Hotham, a matter for disapproval. Still more did he consider undesirable her habit of judging for herself on theological issues such as usury.[34]

The new baby, Mary, eventually arrived on 11 or 12 March 1279 and on this occasion Eleanor had to abandon the spring trip to Quenington, remaining at Woodstock with her household while the rest of the royal party moved into Gloucestershire, where the best part of the month was spent. But her lying-in was no peaceful event. Eleanor was busy acquiring new properties, in particular the wardship of some East Anglian lands proximate to her existing lands, and the inquiry into the marriage of her lady Amice de Weston was held in Eleanor's chamber on 9 April. Such peace as there was was soon to be brought to an end, however. On 16 March, Eleanor's mother, Jeanne of Dammartin, died. Eleanor was Countess of Ponthieu in her own right.

The news will probably have reached Eleanor and Edward at this point, or when they shortly afterwards reunited at or en route to Westminster. Jeanne had been in her fifty-ninth year and had made her will in 1276, so the news was probably no great shock; it was, however, of great significance for both, but particularly for Eleanor, who finally had a status in her own right. The importance of that status to her is evidenced by her later use of the Ponthevin arms, and Edward's use of them in her commemorations. The news was probably not very heartbreaking – although Eleanor kept in touch with her mother, the contacts had not been close or frequent. In fact, the evidence suggests that of latter years they had consisted largely of requests for assistance, often financial, from Jeanne.[35]

The position on succession to Jeanne's lands of Ponthieu and Aumale echoed the issue which arose in Castile. In Ponthieu, part of Picardy, customary law was that in the absence of an adult heir in the direct line the eldest living heir would succeed – to the exclusion of grandchildren in the direct line. Thus, so far as Ponthieu was concerned, it descended to Eleanor, regardless of the existence of her brother Ferdinand's children. In Aumale, which was in Normandy, customary law was different, requiring that the senior heir of the direct line must succeed regardless of age. It is perhaps not surprising, given Eleanor's fondness for property acquisition, that she and Edward initially tried to muddy the waters on this point by claiming Aumale as if it were part of Ponthieu. But it may actually have been a tactical step to strengthen their bargaining position, given that Jeanne had provided in her will for her eldest grandson, Jean, to inherit all the lands Jeanne had granted his father, all the lands she had purchased in her lifetime and the reversion of the lands held by her second husband for his life. It was also asserted by Jean that she had left him the maximum part of the county which she was able to leave by will under the law of Picardy (a fifth). Certainly, Eleanor and Edward's approach enabled the issue to be brought into the court of the French king, and the claim to the fifth share in the county was ultimately defeated.

However, the inheritance was, quite apart from the succession dispute, not an unmixed blessing. Ponthieu had been in debt ever since Marie de Dammartin's submission 1225, which involved ceding part of her lands.

This had not been helped by the Dammartin ladies' tastes for expensive second husbands. Marie's had run up debts which had resulted in the sale of more land and Jeanne's, Jean de Nesle, had assisted her to run up considerable debts to tradesmen – over £700 to the merchants of Arras alone. To avoid these debts ending up before the French king, Edward and Eleanor had to agree to assume the widower's share of them, as well as Jeanne's. It appears that considerable work was needed to sort through and reconcile all the debts: in 1279 and 1280, Eleanor's auditor, John de Lovetot, with John de Vescy and Otho de Grandison, put in considerable work on an audit of the county's finances.[36]

For the present, however, the news necessitated a trip to France; and fortunately one was already in the diary. Since late the previous year Robert Burnell and Otho de Grandison had been working on a treaty whereby the remaining issues from the 1259 Treaty of Paris could be resolved. This was scheduled for May. The royal couple crossed the Channel in early May, meeting up with Edward's cousin Philip III and the returning John Pecham, en route from the papal curia, at Amiens. Also present, and completing the cousinly theme, was Charles of Salerno, who seems to have been a much more endearing character than his father, though plainly lacking his talents and force of character. It is notable that he even attracted positive reviews as a good and just man from an Aragonese chronicler, who was naturally disposed against the Angevin family. The fondness which Edward had for him was very clearly demonstrated by the fact that Charles continued to intercede with Edward on behalf of Guy de Montfort, the principal in Henry of Almain's murder, even seeking the return of the Leicester lands to Guy, without receiving a rude or even a plain rebuff. Edward stonewalled with the utmost courtesy and even suggested that Guy's representatives propose a deal to Otho de Grandison for consideration – and sent the various horses and dogs which Charles also requested. Given that Edward was continuing to hold Amaury de Montfort in captivity on the grounds of his alleged complicity, when it was plain that he had been a student in Padua at the time of the murder, this surely evidences affection between the two.[37]

So at Amiens, on 23 May, the Treaty of Paris of 1259 was ratified and the key territory of the Agenais made over to Edward as provided for in that treaty, twenty years before. Eleanor's claim to Ponthieu was recognised by Philip, and Eleanor did homage to Philip as the new countess. The diplomatic accord was celebrated with the usual feasts and jousts, though Edward and Eleanor did not go on to the truly magnificent tournaments held in Charles of Salerno's honour by the French king at Senlis and Compiègne, during the course of which the king's brother Robert suffered life-changing head injuries.

Thereafter, Edward and Eleanor made a short tour of Ponthieu, staying in Abbeville and Crécy, before returning via Montreuil. Arrangements were made for the administration of the new territory thus joined to the English Crown, with Edward and Eleanor jointly appointing one Pierre Aucoste as their receiver, Sir Thomas de Sandwich as seneschal and her cousin William de Fiennes, who held most of his lands in the county, as custodian of the county. Administratively, the transition to the new rulership seems to have been relatively unproblematic, at least as regards the nobility, a fact which can probably be substantially put down to Eleanor's extensive familial connections to the most important families of the region; she could claim kinship to the counts of Eu and Dreux, the lords of Pécquigny and Roncherolles, as well as the Fiennes.[38]

During this period, there is evidence that Eleanor, never one to miss a financial trick, continued her property acquisitions, this time in Ponthieu itself, where many of the noble class were financially straitened and welcomed the chance to dispose advantageously of some land. Such acquisitions continued for some period; in May 1281 the king and queen sent £1,000 from England to help pay for the purchase of new land there. Over the period from her accession to her death, Eleanor acquired no fewer than twenty-four properties in Ponthieu. Smaller purchases were also made while the royals were in Ponthieu – Blandurel apple trees (this apple still being much esteemed for the making of apple tarts), pet birds, silver ornaments for the queen's books, and most notably the commissioning of the quasi-dynastic romance referred to as 'un romanz de Isembart'. Probably, too, it was at this point that Eleanor made contact with Girard d'Amiens, who was to produce *Escanor* for her. At the same time, she did not neglect her English properties: one of the surviving letters from her concerns the church at Fordingbridge on the edge of her New Forest property and is dated from Le Gard in France.[39]

The return brought the party via Dover and Canterbury to Leeds Castle, acquired the previous summer. Rather typically it would appear that the royal party was actually on the road between Montreuil and Dover on Edward's fortieth birthday on 17/18 June 1279; the 17th and 18th are blank days in the itinerary sandwiched between these destinations. Although Morris suggests there may have been celebrations at Dover Castle, there seems little sign of this – the stay there was only one night and the memorandum of the king's arrival is dated 19 June. However, there seems little sign of the court paying much mind to birthdays at any point.[40]

If there were celebrations, they will have been at Leeds, to which the royal family was paying its first visit. After its acquisition in 1278, given that it had been passed from one debtor to the other, it obviously needed plenty of work doing to it to make it a suitable venue for the court. In all likelihood, it was still very substantially a building site in 1279 when the visit was made. After the break at Leeds, there was a stay in London for the summer parliament and then a lengthy stop at Windsor Castle, presumably with the children, for the rest of July.

It was apparently either in July or at Michaelmas that the first famous Round Table, that of Kenilworth, was held. Although it is often reported that Edward was present at this event, which was organised by his brother and sister-in-law and was designed to honour Roger Mortimer, who was retiring from tourneying, his presence and that of Eleanor seems unlikely. In July, the itinerary shows a succession of orders of business conducted at Windsor throughout late July and a progress thereafter through Buckinghamshire. At Michaelmas, the royal party are vouched for in Essex. No stop at or near Kenilworth appears. Moreover, the contemporaneous chronicler mentions the presence of innumerable knights at this 'famosissimus' tournament staged at the most profuse expense, but fails to mention any appearance by king or queen. One may doubt whether, after the carefully staged reburial of Arthur the previous year, either approved an event which was predicated on the supposed Welsh descent of Mortimer from Arthur.[41]

In August, Eleanor was back at work on her Buckinghamshire properties, using as a base the Confessor's palace of Brill. This lay at the heart of the royal hunting forest of Bernwood, which extended almost to Oxford, and therefore would provide good hunting for those with leisure. The manor and forest were part of Eleanor's dower assignment. Little is now known of this palace, but from the fact that Henry III, on his visit, brought at least thirteen carts and over forty packhorses, it was plainly a sizeable palace; and a few records remain which indicate that he modernised it considerably. Brill was also almost exactly equidistant between Eleanor's two very recent acquisitions in Oxfordshire: Thrupp, where Eleanor had acquired a share of a wardship, and Godington, where she had acquired a manor.

The party then moved on via Buckingham to territory familiar from the 1274 trip: from Silverstone and Overstone to Geddington and Eleanor's dower property of Rockingham, near the Leicestershire and Market Harborough properties. Then to Liddington and Oakham, near the Apethorpe dower properties, and Buckden, near her Brampton and St Ives properties in Huntingdonshire. While in the area, she was able to deal with a troublesome tenant at Gartree near Market Harborough: having failed to pay his dues to Eleanor, the property was repossessed at this time. Again, direct correspondence with Eleanor shows that she was personally concerned in the business.[42]

The autumn was again spent largely at Westminster, where Parliament was sitting until November. However, in September, Eleanor managed to seize a few days to visit her dower properties in Essex and inspect new acquisitions made that year nearby at Barstable, Fobbing and Shenfield. The former was an acquisition made from the Giffard family. The latter was part of the lands of the Camville family and was one of Eleanor's last dealings in Jewish debt.

Meanwhile, as Eleanor's position went from strength to strength, Alfonso's position in Spain kept getting worse. Sancho obtained his mother's defection from the de la Cerda cause by offering to pay her enormous debts. Since he did not have the money himself, he procured one of Alfonso's tax gatherers to divert to him money intended for a siege at Algeciras. Queen Violante returned to Castile; but the diversion of the funds led to the failure of the siege. Enraged, Alfonso committed another public relations disaster by having the tax collector dragged to his death, with Sancho as witness to the execution. Despite this, he still continued to support Sancho as heir; consequently, war with France was hovering. In June 1279 he had sought reassurances of support from Edward, which were sent, along with some grey gerfalcons. More helpfully, Edward despatched William de Valence and Jean de Grailly to negotiate with France, getting Alfonso a year's truce.[43]

The decision to spend Christmas 1279 at Winchester probably reflects the imminent demise of its bishop and the royal desire to procure the support of the monks for Robert Burnell as his successor. On the death of the bishop in early February, the nomination of Burnell was speedily made, duly approved by the diocese and referred to the Pope with strong support from Edward and Eleanor. However, the Pope was again unwilling to see Burnell advanced further and the nomination was quashed. The question of a replacement then hung fire for some years, with John of Pontoise finally being enthroned late in 1282.

This episcopal mess might not seem to have much relevance to Eleanor, but again it provides an interesting glimpse of her hard at work. Within three days of the death of the bishop, she had had a manor at Ringwood (neighbouring her holdings there) granted to her by Edward at pleasure 'during the voidance of the see of Winchester'. It was still in her hands at her death. This single transaction offers a characteristic picture of not a moment being wasted to identify and acquire a suitable property, and a reluctance to part with that property, regardless of the terms of the grant.[44]

The remainder of 1280 was, in English domestic terms, a quiet year, but financial questions continued to hover. It would seem that most of the proceeds of the 1275 vote of funds had been spent by now – doubtless assisted by the cost of the Welsh war. A substantial payment on account of the crusading debt to the French Crown had been made in 1279, and was due to be completed by 1281. There seemed little prospect of this, unless the crusading tenth ordered in 1274 could somehow be tapped. Edward was obviously not in a position to go himself for some time to come, and in 1276 he had written to Pope John XXI promising that if he could not go, he would send his brother in his place. With the matter becoming urgent, in July 1280 Otho de Grandison was despatched to the papal curia to try to get agreement to this arrangement – only to find himself awaiting a new papal election, as Nicholas III died before he arrived.[45]

Meanwhile, the problems of Alfonso were never far from the agenda of Edward and Eleanor. It was agreed that Alfonso and Philip should meet, under Edward's aegis, if not in his presence, in Gascony in 1280. Instead, in July 1280, Alfonso authorised Charles of Salerno, with his closer French connections, to act for him. By the end of the year, he had come up with a proposal which was to cause him trouble on both sides: the ceding of the territory of Jaén to Alfonso de la Cerda. This was not considered sufficient by Philip, while Sancho opposed any partition of Castile. With Alfonso in a worse mess than ever, Edward agreed to meet him on the Gascon–Castilian border at around Easter 1281.

For some reason, this plan never got off the ground. Certainly Edward was not in Gascony – much of the early part of 1281 before the May parliament was spent in Gloucestershire and Wiltshire. Another odd point is that in this period the court, quite atypically, never moved any very great distance for over three months. This therefore is a very likely date for the delivery of the stillborn son which Parsons hypothesises for some time in the 1280–81 period. It is therefore quite probable that Edward was kept from his plan to help Alfonso by a traumatic stillbirth or a late miscarriage which left Eleanor below par for a considerable period.[46]

However, Eleanor was certainly sufficiently recovered to make a very interesting appearance in partnership with Robert Burnell in early June 1281. The Close Rolls reveal that she acted with Burnell as an arbitrator appointed to decide disputes between Edward's cousin Edmund, Earl of Cornwall, and Walter Brunscombe, the Bishop of Exeter. The disputes seem to have been part of a complicated and long-standing feud, with writs flying in each direction and a dash of cattle rustling. The importance of the event, however, is that it demonstrates Eleanor being looked to by two of the most powerful men in England as a figure of authority and a person capable of mastering the intricacies of a difficult dispute. It also demonstrates her taking on a role in active justice making, which was highly unusual for a queen consort. Her abilities and her stature among England's executive powers are both implicitly recognised by this event.[47]

The main feature of the year in terms of touring was the most extensive Northern tour yet, which took place from July to October. This took the court via the usual route through Eleanor's holdings in Hertfordshire, Bedfordshire, Northamptonshire, Leicestershire and Nottinghamshire to York, where there was a stay sufficient to enable Eleanor to inspect some recent acquisitions which she had made in 1279 in that town. Thereafter the court performed a loop, proceeding via the Bowes Moor Road to Carlisle before coming back across to Newcastle and Durham, before returning south to Westminster for the October parliament.

This northernmost loop will have had two justifications. The first is that Edward will have wanted to inspect the state of affairs in the far North in company with John de Vescy, who had joined a Scots expedition to put down an uprising on the Isle of Man in 1275. The second is that the wedding of John de Vescy to Eleanor's cousin Isabella de Beaumont took place at this time, and as part of the arrangements for that wedding Edward granted John lands in Northumberland, to add to his existing patrimony. This journey will also, however, have afforded Eleanor the opportunity to inspect her northernmost dower property – Corbridge in Northumberland. After the November parliament, the end of the year was spent predominantly in Norfolk, particularly near Eleanor's new acquisitions around Burgh, to which she actually added further during the stay, acquiring on 5 January 1281 a package of lands in and around Scottow. Another trip to Walsingham was also fitted in, before the court moved off into Suffolk and thence into Gloucester to enjoy the Cotswold spring and hunting.[48]

In this period the children's marriages were also under consideration. First was young Alphonso, betrothed in July 1281. The bride selected for him was Margaret of Holland, daughter of Floris, Count of Holland, and Beatrix of Flanders. But the question of young Eleanora's marriage also moved to the fore. She, of course, had been engaged to the son of Pedro of Aragon in 1273, but in early 1281 she was now approaching twelve, the age when both her mother and grandmother had been married. An alliance with Aragon was now, of course, a somewhat vexed question, given Aragon's intervention in the Castilian succession issue. It may even be this political dimension, as much as concern over Eleanora's youth, which led to Eleanor and her mother-in-law staging the famous intercession with Edward, asking that Eleanora's marriage be delayed on account of her youth: 'The queen her mother and our dearest mother are unwilling to grant that she may pass over earlier on account of her tender age.' John de Vescy and Anthony Bek were charged with the difficult job of keeping the marriage on the cards, while procuring a delay of at least a year and a half, and preferably two and a half years, before the marriage took place.[49]

Nor should it be supposed that Eleanor's property empire slept in this notionally quiet time: during 1280 and 1281 Eleanor acquired properties in twelve different counties, including additions to her core property areas in Northampton, Gloucestershire, Southampton and Norfolk, but also including a new outpost in Kent, a farm at Westcliffe which was presumably convenient as a victualling point for trips to Ponthieu or Gascony, being only a couple of miles from Dover Castle. Other acquisitions included Headington, on the edge of Oxford, and Weymouth, Lyme Regis and the Cobb.

The process of these acquisitions and the activity which surrounded them again bears eloquent testimony to the professionalism of the outfit which Eleanor was heading up. In the first place, a number of these transactions take place on the same days in November 1280 or July 1281. This indicates a portfolio being presented for completion at one time. Secondly, the movements of the court can often be seen to reflect these acquisitions. The coincidence of timing of the Norfolk stay with Norfolk acquisitions has already been remarked. But the long Gloucestershire stay in early to mid-1280, too, was followed by the addition of three new Gloucestershire properties (including the Burdon lands) and two in the nearby Wiltshire grouping. The slightly earlier Bristol stay, near the northern Somerset group, is followed by an acquisition at nearby Uphill. The later Hampshire stay offered an opportunity to inspect the dower property of Odiham and acquisitions in Hampshire in early 1280. In 1281, recent acquisitions at Fobbing and Shenfield could be viewed from Havering-atte-Bower in July.[50]

Further, Ponthieu required attention, and its affairs were not left entirely to Edward. Throughout the rest of her life, Eleanor sent a succession of letters of credit to Ponthieu to finance further purchases and make good the shortfalls in the revenue from the county.

In general, though, all seemed to be progressing well. There was time for a further visit to monitor progress at Leeds, and also one to Langley, which Eleanor had acquired in 1275 and was likewise transforming, though on a less extravagant scale. There was time for a lengthy autumn stay in the New Forest, and after Parliament concluded in November, the royal party spent the late part of 1281 and the early part of 1282 in the slightly unusual surroundings of Pershore and Worcester, before proceeding for the usual Quenington spring break.[51]

This period therefore reverts to the image of the royal family with which the chapter commenced – peaceful, prosperous and enjoying their business. But by this stage storm clouds were in view on the horizon. Both sides of the family were providing cause for concern. Alfonso's position continued to deteriorate, putting Edward under unwelcome pressure to support him. While Aragon and Castile had signed a treaty of friendship in March 1281, it had not brought an end to Alfonso's problems. He remained under pressure from Philip of France and a rift was opening up between him and Sancho as to the best way to manage the de la Cerdas. By November, Sancho was starting to drum up support within Castile, which by spring 1282 resulted in his calling an assembly at Valladolid – with a full cast of the disaffected, including Alfonso's estranged Queen Violante, Alfonso's brother Manuel (up to this time one of the king's most trusted advisers) and discontented nobles. The stage was set for civil war.[52]

Meanwhile, dowager Queen Marguerite of France, ably supported by her sister Eleanor of Provence was stirring up trouble with the family of Charles of Anjou in relation to her claims to Provence. The presence

of Edmund of Cornwall and Edward's Gascon seneschal at a meeting
concerning this issue led to a formal complaint from Charles of Salerno
to Edward. Edward was forced to issue a letter, effectively outing his
mother's involvement and explaining the difficulty of his position given
his own closeness to his mother. Further tension was probably felt in
the relationship owing to Eleanora's engagement to the heir of Aragon;
her betrothed's father, Pedro, married to the most immediate heir to the
Sicilian throne and himself a claimant through an older line of succession,
was stirring up trouble for the Angevins in their other territory, the
Kingdom of Sicily.

Then, right at the end of 1281, there came the tragic news, via Otho
de Grandison's brother, the Bishop of Verdun, that Joan's fiancé had been
killed in a boating accident on 21 December. Setting off to visit his father
in a thick fog, Hartmann's boat struck a rock midstream and he and most
of his companions were drowned.[53]

Finally, perhaps unnoticed by the royal party amid the whirl of foreign
diplomatic letters and pleas of assistance from both sides of the family,
was perhaps the real reason behind the period spent in Worcester: a cloud
was gathering above Wales.

14

The Welsh Years

The years 1282 to 1285 have to be known as the Welsh years, because Welsh affairs were to dominate them, and Eleanor herself was to spend a very large proportion of her time in that principality. But as with the late 1270s, the summary fails to do justice to the range of Eleanor's experience – or to the other issues which required attention from her during that time.

Two themes in particular run through these years, in partnership with the dominant Welsh one. The first is the continuing crisis endured by her beloved brother Alfonso, now seriously ill and at odds not just with the King of France but also with his own family. In spring 1282, a staged Cortes would depose him from his throne and launch a civil war which would see each side desert the Reconquista and take Muslim allies to defeat the other.

The second theme, which was to last out Eleanor's life, was the affairs of Aragon's monarchy – Eleonora's future family. Here, a shocking turn of events in Sicily created a problem which was to convulse Europe. On Easter Monday, 30 March 1282, just before Vespers, a major uprising began. Discontent about Charles of Anjou's autocratic style of government and wider ambitions had been fostered for some time both by the Byzantine Emperor and Pedro of Aragon – who had his own claims to Sicily. As is often the case with this sort of event, a small row escalated unimaginably. Thus, in most traditions, the sparking point was disrespect shown by a French soldier to a Sicilian girl, which resulted in fatal violence on the part of the girl's protector or husband. The indubitable outcome of these 'Sicilian Vespers' was days of slaughter, the seizure of the island, and the destruction of Charles' fleet at Messina. By the end of May, Ferrante of Aragon was reporting that 'five Sicilian cities have risen against King Charles and killed all the French living in them'. By mid-June, the accounts which were reaching the English court from Orvieto suggested that Aragon planned to go to the support of the people of Sicily, while Charles, supported by the Pope, was gathering a large force at Naples. Shortly afterwards, Pedro of Aragon confirmed that he had been offered the crown of Sicily by the people – and he intended to take it.[1]

But these major events elsewhere in Europe could only be second and third themes for the English royals, who were faced with a major rising of their own in Wales. The upheaval slightly predated both European convulsions and, for all its sudden manifestation, had been long in the making. It had much to do with the day-to-day conditions which were imposed on the Welsh following the terms of the 1277 peace, particularly in the border regions. Border trespasses, disputes about fugitives in both directions, and attempts to assert English jurisdiction over Welsh residents all formed part of these complaints. The most immediate cause which can be found was a spat between Llywelyn and his neighbour Gruffydd ap Gwenwynwyn over the county of Arwystli, which had been rumbling on for years. The reason for the persistence of both sides was doubtless partly historic, but also, although it mostly consisted of moorland unsuitable for raising crops, it was a strategic route between Mid Wales and the Marches.

The point at issue at this time was the question of proper law. Given that Arwystli was part of Wales and the 1277 treaty entitled Llywelyn to have disputes over property in Wales decided by Welsh law, should the right to the county be decided by English law (as Gruffydd argued) or Welsh law (as Llywelyn claimed)? The point was not actually as simple as it might seem, since there were issues of what law should be used to determine the question of proper law; and moreover, Gruffydd's claim was as a Marcher lord, not based on Welsh law. But to muddy the waters further, Edward, naturally unwilling to reach a conclusion detrimental to his own lordship and to Gruffydd, who had allied with him in 1277, insisted that the proper forms of litigation be observed, rather than granting Llywelyn the right to have his complaint heard directly by him. This dispute was just one of many which raised similar issues, where original disputes were considerably complicated and delayed by lawyers' arguments about procedure and proper law. Fundamentally, too, the Welsh considered that the English attempts to define and establish laws was alien to their way of doing business; while Edward and later historians might say that he respected Welsh law where established, the very cage of establishing precedent was inimical to Welsh sensibilities.

By the end of 1281, there had been markers of likely trouble ahead. Llywelyn on his side had reached an agreement with the great Marcher lord Roger Mortimer, an alliance of past enemies which might suggest trouble. In November, frustrated by Llywelyn's constant complaints, Edward removed the Justiciar of Chester and replaced him with the hardliner Reginald de Grey. While this move would have limited effect on Llywelyn, it directly impacted Llywelyn's impulsive younger brother Dafydd, who had been given border lands in 1277. The appointment of de Grey was perhaps more than a knee-jerk reaction to the complaints; the combination of this appointment, de Grey's actions thereafter and the decision of Edward to spend such a period of time in the vicinity of the Marches in late 1281 raises some suspicions that Edward had himself concluded that the deal of 1277 would not work in the long term, and was looking to provoke a decisive fight.[2]

If that was Edward's intention, the storm broke shortly after he had returned into the English heartlands. On 21 March 1282, Dafydd decided to communicate his discontent directly and led a band of attackers on Hawarden Castle. A number of men were killed, the castle was burned and its castellan, Roger Clifford, an old and close friend of Edward's, was taken prisoner. Meanwhile, copycat raids were launched in the south of Wales and against the English border town of Oswestry. This left the recently widowed Llywelyn in an impossible position; he could refuse to join the rebellion and lose all credibility with his countrymen, or he could join what he must have known was a doomed rebellion. He chose the latter option, and commenced attacks on the new castles of Flint and Rhuddlan – the symbols of English oppression.

The news of the rebellion reached Edward and Eleanor on 25 March, on the Wednesday before Easter, when they were observing Holy Week from the Abbey of Malmesbury. Eleanor, now just over forty, was approaching the end of the first trimester of yet another pregnancy. Moving to Devizes Castle for the Easter weekend, all plans for the next months had to be cancelled and new plans for a move into Wales made. The royal party stayed put for nearly a month, sending out streams of messengers and orders, and summoning all necessary advisers to consult from there. The usual suspects were put in place: de Grey took the Chester command, with Roger Mortimer in the central Marches and Robert Tybetot on the west.[3]

As far as Eleanor was concerned, this move to a war footing will have involved finishing off such transactions as could be completed at once, and otherwise putting her properties into holding status. As she was a hands-on manager of her property empire, acquisitions (except in Wales) almost shut down for the next two years. Two final transactions were closed off before the court moved to Gloucester: the acquisition on 29 March of an advowson and some land in Norfolk and on 8 April 1282 of some land in Derbyshire, near her existing holdings. Oddly enough, this land came indirectly from the loyal Welsh lord Gruffydd ap Gwenwynwyn.[4]

Summonses having gone out for a muster of forces at Worcester on 17 May, the royal party moved to Gloucester at the end of April, arriving in Worcester itself just ahead of the date set. Further writs were then issued for feudal levies to be at Rhuddlan at the start of August – about the time Eleanor's baby was due. In fact, Edward and Eleanor – accompanied by Eleanora and Joan – reached Rhuddlan in early July, after a stop in Chester for most of June. Rhuddlan Castle, begun in 1277, was already complete, the bulk of work having been finished by 1280. The site on the banks of the River Clwyd had been connected to the sea by turning the final stretch of river into a canal by straightening and dredging it – a hugely time-consuming and expensive task. The siege which Rhuddlan Castle had faced had been thrown off in June, but it is likely that some damages were still being made good on the royal party's arrival – certainly Edward borrowed some money from Eleanor for the Rhuddlan works at about this time.[5]

In early August, Eleanor gave birth to Elizabeth, who would be consequently known as Elizabeth of Rhuddlan. Despite the efforts which had gone in to civilising the place for Eleanor, with the installation of the garden, decorative seating and fishpond and the presence of her resident goldsmith, it would hardly have been a peaceful venue for childbirth. Apart from the constant round of messengers, Edward was using Rhuddlan as the base for troop assembly; by the end of August there were 750 cavalry and about 8,000 troops based there. However, Eleanor appears to have taken the bustle in her stride, making a gift of £10 to some minstrels who helped celebrate her churching and buying a range of small necessaries for Elizabeth – a basin, some tankards, a storage chest and a bucket.

While the troops assembled, issues further afield were not forgotten. In particular, on 15 August, Eleanor's eldest daughter, Eleanora, now nearly fourteen, was married by proxy to Alphonso of Aragon, with John de Vescy playing the part of the bride. This event indicates that while Edward and Eleanor had initially been disquieted by the Aragonese role in the Sicilian Vespers, they were nonetheless minded to proceed with the match. It seems that Eleanor's views were very influential in the conduct of the marriage negotiations: the documents were kept in a group, and one bears a depiction of the figure of a speedy courier holding in his hand a banner – of Castile. So it was Eleanor's messengers, it would seem, who were doing the legwork on this tricky diplomatic issue. But the rushing of the marriage seems to have been a tactical move on the part of the Aragonese. Pedro of Aragon landed in Sicily at the end of the month, being proclaimed king on 4 September. Within weeks, he had been excommunicated by the Pope. Eleanora had thus been married into a family at war with the papacy.

Meanwhile, Eleanor was also busy exercising her influence in relation to Alfonso's problems. In June 1282, Alfonso had written to Edward asking him to give Eleanor full credence in relation to matters she would discuss with him – indicating that she had had detailed correspondence with Alfonso. Later in the year she wrote to the King of Aragon on Alfonso's behalf, and persuaded Edward, despite his own needs, to arrange for Gaston de Béarn to take a hundred Gascon knights to Alfonso's assistance. Even so, Alfonso continued to seek assistance.[6]

But these problems would have to await resolution; the requirements of the Welsh war were more imperative. The retaking of Anglesey, such a success in 1277, was prioritised under former Crusader and Gascon seneschal Luke de Tany. To ensure shock and awe, this time a different strategic twist was used; it was decided to construct a pontoon bridge from Anglesey to the mainland in order to give a further attack route which would outflank Llywelyn's defences. This approach is interesting because this use of pontoon bridges was far from orthodox. It was not unheard of, dating back many centuries, but was an approach which had somewhat fallen into disuse in the Middle Ages. Given that fact, it is perhaps interesting to note that it is (again) a technique commended by Vegetius, who suggests the use of small, light boats lashed together to form a bridge. Although the scheme was not without difficulty – since the technique was unfamiliar, the boats originally brought were too heavy to be transported, and new ones had to be purchased at Chester – the bridge was completed by November 1282.[7]

Meanwhile, Edward was elsewhere, leading the forces moving inwards from Rhuddlan. In late August and early September he led an attack on Ruthin and Llangernyw. Following the success of this attack, he returned to Rhuddlan in late September before setting off again against Dafydd's bases in mid-October, returning victorious in early November. But the good news will have been seriously offset by the news of the death of Roger Mortimer in early October, possibly as a result of his exertions in his sector of the campaign. Mortimer was about eight years older than Edward, and his formal retirement from tournaments in 1279 indicates that his health may not have been good, but it will nonetheless have been a memento mori for the crusading group now gathered in Wales – Mortimer was still only about fifty at his death.

And the return to Rhuddlan brought even worse news, this time from Anglesey. The pontoon bridge scheme had misfired horribly. An English force either chanced an attack in the hope of catching Llywelyn, who was nearby, or were ambushed while on a routine sortie. Trying to regain the pontoon bridge, they were either prevented from reaching it by a change in the tide or the bridge was damaged in the force of the tide and the retreat. The result was catastrophic. Luke de Tany and Roger Clifford's son both drowned, Robert Burnell lost two brothers and Otho de Grandison barely escaped with his life. The disaster at Anglesey predictably gave new heart to the Welsh, and Edward had no choice but to redouble his efforts. So, on 24 November, more writs were despatched around the country.[8]

But even as troops began to arrive at Rhuddlan, the Welsh suffered their own, even larger disaster. On 11 December 1282, Llywelyn himself was killed. Save that he was killed at some point close to the River Irfon at a little place called Cilmeri (where a memorial stands to this day), the story is unclear. He may have fallen in battle or in the process of returning to join his troops. He may have been there in hopes that if the fight in Mid Wales could be turned – its leadership being in a state of flux following Mortimer's death – the entire war could be brought to a successful conclusion before Edward could gain traction in Gwynedd. One interesting version has his death occurring as a result of a conspiracy led by Roger Mortimer of Chirk, the second surviving son of Roger Mortimer, who is said to have pretended that he would come over to Llywelyn's side and bring his men with him. Certainly, if Mortimer of Chirk's reputation is justified, such a ruse might not be beyond the bounds of possibility; he had lost two wards in suspicious circumstances in 1277 and was later to win a reputation for unscrupulousness. Another version points the finger at his bookish older brother, Edmund. He had originally been the second son, destined for the Church, and became the heir to his formidable father only on the unexpected death of his older brother. Edward clearly had reservations about his ability to stand in his father's shoes, and had delayed confirming him in his lands. He therefore had a point to prove – and was present sufficiently close to the death to have items from the body to pass to Robert Burnell. But whatever the reason Llywelyn was there, the result was simple: the end of the Welsh war was in sight. Having lost their one acknowledged leader, there could be only one outcome.[9]

The death of Llywelyn was therefore the cause of great celebrations in the royal party. His head was brought to Edward, who sent it to be displayed to the army at Anglesey before it was sent to London, where it was carried through the streets and pilloried. Finally, it was displayed on the Tower battlements, where it apparently remained for some years. Within days, Dafydd had sent his hostage Roger de Clifford to seek peace terms. Equally speedily, Edward rejected the offer; only surrender was acceptable.[10]

Meanwhile, the Aragonese marriage again provided cause for discussion and concern. The proxy marriage having been performed, the Aragonese sought Eleanora's actual marriage, tactfully not via the excommunicate Pedro but instead by letter from Queen Constance. Edward's reply, on 12 January 1283, makes clear that the English monarchs were troubled both by the prospect of sending Eleanora into a family at odds with the papacy and by the conflict now inevitable between Aragon and France. Edward therefore politely but firmly refused to send his daughter before at least the beginning of the next year. Trapped between obligations both to Aragon and France, it may well have been a relief when a papal

Bull emerged shortly thereafter, effectively preventing the marriage by expressly excluding descendants of Pedro from the dispensation allowing Eleanora to marry any person within the fourth degree of consanguinity and enjoining Edward to make no connections with enemies of the Holy See. Pedro, however, continued to correspond with Eleanor in a friendly fashion. He wrote to her in February 1283, plainly in answer to a letter of her own expressing anxiety for her brother, to report on the state of negotiations between Alfonso and Sancho and to promise his best endeavours to reunite the pair.[11]

Meanwhile, the Welsh resistance gradually crumbled – with some active encouragement from Edward's team. In January, the key castle of Dolwyddelan was placed under siege and soon surrendered. It is apparent that Eleanor was keenly waiting to hear news of her husband's success and welfare, because the records show her paying two messengers who brought rumours of the castle's fall on 4 January. By March 1283, Edward felt secure enough to move his headquarters to Conwy, which was the principal residence of the princes of Gwynedd and therefore represented a hugely significant move in PR terms. With him went Eleanor. Her presence there is testified by the emergency provision of hangings for her rooms, the laying of a lawn, and the construction of a garden structured, as at Rhuddlan, around fencing from tun barrels. To make certain that all was ready to an acceptable standard, she even sent ahead one of her squires to make sure the new planting was well watered in. Even in war, Eleanor expected domestic standards to be maintained.

At once plans were laid to largely dismantle the existing palace and build a castle which was an unequivocal statement of the power of the English king. The castle which was built here is a massive edifice of roughly rectangular shape arranged around two baileys and set with eight substantial round towers. Built from rubble masonry, it was originally rendered and whitewashed, like the White Tower in London, thereby ensuring that all eyes must be drawn to it. But a new castle was not enough. To emphasise further the defeat of the Welsh, the ancient priory of Aberconwy, where the kings of Wales (including Llywelyn the Great) were buried, was dismantled and administrative offices were built over it, and while the great hall of the Welsh kings was left intact, it was now inconsequential, attached to the side of the new town walls and in the shadow of the grand new hall.

The approach taken with Conwy marks an appropriate point at which to consider the Welsh new towns more generally. In 1277, Edward had begun the process of seeding new towns into the Welsh conquered territories with the building of Rhuddlan and Flint; this he now continued with Conwy, Caernarfon and others. Rhuddlan and Conwy together demonstrate some key points. First, in both, a decision was taken to move the castle and town to some extent, thereby obliterating features which were totems for the local population. Secondly, although what is most notable in the records and the survivals is the castle, the castle was only a part of the building programme – the construction of a new town, built to be prosperous, was equally important. Thirdly, attention was given to privileges which were to attach to the town, both to boost its chances of economic survival and to attract to it new inhabitants, who would themselves assist in this endeavour. Thus in Rhuddlan, a charter of liberties to encourage new burgesses was issued in November 1278, granting them essentially the same privileges as Hereford. This charter of liberties was then in turn granted to Flint, Conwy and Caernarfon. Immigrants were encouraged, and taxes were remitted in the early years to encourage the building and improving of the town. Similarly, Aberystwyth, commenced by Edmund of Lancaster at about the same time as Rhuddlan, was chosen with a view to supplanting existing Welsh castles and was quickly granted the rights of Henry III's town of New Montgomery: a market, two fairs and a gild merchant.

Edward's inspiration for the programme of town building has been considerably debated, with the bastides of Gascony usually posited as the source. Stylistically, there is of course much to be said for this theory. However, the bastides of Gascony were not associated with war or conquest, and the treatment of conquered territory was something of a novelty for recent Plantagenet kings, who had lost far more territory than they had gained. Nor were the Welsh new towns pure new towns, built on bare ground; the majority, like Rhuddlan, Conwy and Aberystwyth, were reincarnations of existing towns. Similarly, while plainly some of the architectural idiom for the castles can be found in Savoy, in particular St Georges d'Esperanche, that was a peaceful *villa nova*.

Here, it seems, there is a noticeable parallel with Eleanor's experience. Her childhood had featured close contact with the business of conquest and its aftermath, and in particular the development of existing conquered towns into stable and prosperous units of their new nation. She had experience of a paradigm which saw a conquering king turning his administrative attention to a newly acquired town, reclaiming or amending key features of that town in line with his own vision and putting in place economic measures to encourage settlement of new townspeople to dilute the existing population and boost the economic success of the town. It is suggested that this experience, conveyed to Edward and his other advisers, whose experience was unlikely to have offered them such insights, was at least a part of the thinking which lay behind these developments and fed into the perspectives offered by the foundations of Gascony and Savoy.

Residence at Conwy, where both builders' and military bills will now have been pouring in, will only have brought home the financial difficulties which the war had caused. While some voluntary loans had been made by towns, further funds were needed urgently. Parliament voted for a tax in January, but money trickled in slowly. So in March, with the evidence of financial need before his eyes, Edward simply ordered the seizure of the crusading monies gathered years before and which had so long hung fire. While Pecham eventually persuaded him to return it, the forceful gesture did achieve what was probably intended – a sizeable grant from the clergy.[12]

Meanwhile, with war effectively over, Eleanor was once again taking up the reins of her property business to a limited extent. In late February, Edward conveyed to her Dafydd's castle at Hope – a modern castle, building having commenced in 1277. Over the succeeding months, Eleanor and Adam de Cretyng, who was to be her bailiff in this area for a year or so, seem to have sought out a useful package of nearby properties over the summer: a manor in May, followed by the whole of the *Maelor Saesneg* or English-speaking border lands east of the Dee and associated hamlets, pasture and advowsons. The latter was acquired by an exchange with Robert de Crevequer for her Soham and Ditton holdings in Cambridgeshire, which were slightly detached from her main holdings geographically. Other than this local work, the only property business Eleanor conducted was to take a wardship near her Hampshire lands.[13]

But the war was not quite over. Although the last major castle, Llywelyn the Great's castle of Castell y Bere, surrendered on 25 April after a ten-day siege, one task still remained: to find Dafydd.

While the searchers were out, a fantastic distraction appeared: in May, a Roman sarcophagus was found at the coastal town of Arfon, near the Roman fort of Segontium. Folk memory associated the site with Magnus Maximus, reputedly the father of the Emperor Constantine and the husband of Empress Helena, the discoverer of the True Cross. Folk tales and Geoffrey of Monmouth also posited Magnus Maximus as the first independent ruler of all Britain. Of course, both folk tales and Geoffrey of Monmouth were very wide of the mark. Magnus Maximus was the Roman leader in Britain in the late fourth century for a few years before leaving to pursue his imperial ambitions – unsuccessfully. What happened to his family after his execution is unclear, but there is no evidence to suggest a connection to Constantine's father Constantius Chlorus, or to his mother. What may have occurred is a conflation of folk tales, which had Magnus Maximus finding his true love in a Welsh girl called Elen and being succeeded in Britain by a leader called Constantine, with the facts of later and unconnected history. Regardless, this romantic tale will have provided fuel for the misidentification of the owner of the sarcophagus as Magnus Maximus or Constantine. So in mid-May Edward and Eleanor headed to Dolwyddelan Castle, where they stayed until the beginning of June, and the reputed body of Magnus Maximus was reinterred in the local church on Edward's orders. It will have been during this visit that plans were first hatched for the building of a new castle on the site, since by June work had already started at what was to be known as Caernarfon.[14]

This little-known vignette helps to make sense of much that has been regarded as puzzling about Caernarfon: why Edward, having started a massive project such as Conwy, would then change his mind about the main power base for Wales; why he choose this lesser site; and why, unlike Conwy, the structure is very much Roman in design terms, with strong echoes of the Roman Pharos tower at Dover. There is a parallel with the annexation of the supposed graves of Arthur and Guinevere: a supposed King of Britain was being claimed by Edward, and his resting place turned into the centre of English power over Wales. Past kings were gone; it was Plantagenet power which had to be respected. The message is repeated in the massive and highly fortified gatehouse which was erected in the latter phase of building, which features above the doorway a life-size statue of an enthroned king.

However, there are perhaps traces of Eleanor's involvement in the design of the castle too. Dominating the outer ward of the castle stands the Eagle Tower, which was the first part of the castle to be built. This has two interesting features, both of which can be linked to Eleanor. Firstly, it features three tall projecting turrets emerging out of the main polygonal tower; this is an exact echo of the castle depicted on the arms of Castile, and, although they were not completed until well into Edward II's reign, there seems a possibility that they were part of the original design inserted at Eleanor's instance or as an 'in joke' for Eleanor's benefit. The shape and structure of the tower, after all, had to be planned from the outset.

The second interesting feature is the tower's eyrie of birds, which originally comprised three eagles, one for each of the turrets. There is a very obvious Roman link in the inclusion of the eagles, symbol of Rome's victorious legions, and they can therefore be seen simply as another imperial statement. But they can also (with a bit of manipulation) be linked to a story called 'The Dream of Macsen Wledig' in the Welsh *Mabinogion* – a collection of quasi-historical folk tales which was emerging in written form at the time. In that story, Magnus Maximus (or Macsen Wledig as he is in the Welsh version) had a dream in which he travelled to a great city in Wales with a castle with coloured walls, and turrets and a throne decorated with golden eagles, where he found his true love, Elen. The parallel with Caernarfon is striking – was it intended? It seems very possible that it was, and by Eleanor.

Eleanor, after all, can be shown to have had an interest in local myths; this is seen both in her apparent recounting of the Northumbrian Escanor story to Girard of Amiens and in her commissioning of the Ponthevin Isembart romance. What is more, there is further evidence, to which we shall come, that someone in the royal party – again most likely to be Eleanor – had been making themselves familiar with the Welsh folk tales.

There is another resonance in the Eagle Tower which suggests Eleanor's design input. The eagles also echo Edward's love of birds and falconry – which also appears to have been possessed by young Alphonso, judging by the clever and repeated depictions of birds in the Alphonso Psalter. These, of course, were inserted at Eleanor's instruction – as was the bird on the top of the Charing mews fountain. The eyrie therefore may well also have been intended as a joke for the benefit of Edward or Alphonso – or both.

All in all, it seems that the Caernarfon trip provided an entertaining and fruitful diversion while news of Dafydd was awaited.[15]

And in June, not long after work had commenced at Caernarfon, the long-awaited news arrived. Dafydd was taken at the foot of Mount Snowdon; triumphant messages were despatched at once to Edward's supporters. In defeat, the Welsh princes' treasure was also yielded up. In June, Edward was presented with the Cross of Neith, a fragment of the True Cross which thereafter accompanied him on all his travels, gaining in luxurious adornment as the years went by. It would also be at around this time, with the Welsh war apparently finally over, that the future Edward II was conceived.[16]

But there remained plenty to do – on more than one front. In proper military style, July and most of August then constituted mopping-up operations: the royal party returned to Conwy to take possession of Dafydd (destined for a horrible end) and numerous hostages to ensure Welsh good behaviour, and a further trip was undertaken to Caernarfon to see how the initial works were progressing. Meanwhile, though Eleanora's match was on ice, others were not. Alphonso would turn ten years old in November 1283 – an event marked by Eleanor with special offerings of alms – and plans could be made seriously for his marriage. Accordingly, his bride's dowry was agreed in August 1283 and work was proceeding on the beautiful illustrated psalter which Eleanor commissioned to mark the wedding.

And naturally Eleanor wanted to view her new properties. So on the way to Chester in late August there was a two-day stop at Hope Castle, formerly property of Dafydd. Since Eleanor had selected her properties carefully, a stop here would have her well placed to survey the other five of the six properties she had acquired, all grouped tidily, as was her wont, on the road between Flint and Whitchurch (the modern A541). However, the stop was hardly the uneventful one planned. On the second night of the stay, 27 August, the castle caught fire; and it was no small blaze. Eleanor, Edward and their party barely escaped with their lives. The castle was reduced to rubble and never rebuilt.[17]

From Chester it was back into the more usual routine of the royal court for a short time. A stay of a few weeks in and around Macclesfield enabled Eleanor to review her dower property there, as well as some new acquisitions just on the English side of her new Welsh properties and her easterly Derbyshire properties, before the court headed back in a south-westerly direction to Shrewsbury, where Parliament had been summoned. The first act of the Parliament on convening on 30 September 1283 was the trial of Dafydd for treason. On 2 October, he was hanged, drawn and quartered, meaning he was dragged by horses to the scaffold, hanged alive (part strangled by a small drop insufficient to break the neck), his bowels were removed and burned before his eyes, and he was finally cut into four pieces. This sentence is probably well known to the reader, since in later years it became fairly formulaic. But at this point in time it actually reflected four separate sentences, for Dafydd's four crimes against the English king: treason, homicide, committing crimes at the holy season of Easter and plotting the king's death. It reflected the genuine outrage felt by Edward at what he perceived to be Dafydd's ingratitude and the horror felt by many at a revolt timed to coincide with the holy season of Easter. As with the receipt of Llywelyn's head, it is likely that the pregnant Eleanor observed this novel horror; certainly non-participation in the event seems to have been viewed with disapproval, judging by the fine which the people of Lincoln incurred for refusing to take one of the quarters of the late prince. Dafydd's head, mockingly crowned with ivy, was sent to join that of his brother at the Tower.[18]

Following this, the rest of the year was spent in touring the Welsh Marches and giving thanks for the victory. Along the way, remembrance of Roger Mortimer was not forgotten: special alms offerings were made for the anniversary of his death and a stay – perhaps coinciding with the wedding of Edmund Mortimer to Eleanor's cousin Margaret de Fiennes – was made at his castle of Wigmore, before they headed back to Rhuddlan for Christmas. Here, 500 extra paupers were fed on Christmas Day on the advice of William of Hotham. As usual, there was little in the way of a holiday; by 28 December the party were off again – this time through the winter cold to York. The purpose of the trip was to be present at the consecration in York Minster on Sunday 9 January of Anthony Bek as Bishop of Durham and to play a personal part in the translation of the body of St William of York to a more elevated burial place behind the high altar. Edward was one of the bearers of the saint's remains. As usual, it would appear that Eleanor's mind was not far from work; she was to acquire a manor north of York later that year.

Care was taken to mark respectfully the death of the heir to Alexander III of Scotland, an event which left Alexander's baby granddaughter, daughter of Erik II of Norway and Margaret of Scotland, heir presumptive to the throne of Scotland. Eleanor herself marked separately the death of one of Dafydd's daughters, taken captive after his defeat, who would otherwise have been destined with her sisters to a life in an English abbey.[19]

The party then passed south to Eleanor's properties in Nottinghamshire and Lincolnshire and what would appear to have been a general review of her business to see what acquisitions could be made in the near future. It would seem that each of her local agents will have met her, and produced their reports and suggestions. By 11 February at Lincoln, Eleanor (now well into the third trimester of her latest pregnancy) had conducted enough of a review to carry out a very busy day's business acquiring convenient wardships, advowsons and knights' fees in Cambridgeshire, Essex, Gloucestershire, Somerset, Suffolk, Sussex and Wiltshire. Business complete, in March the party then returned to Wales via Chester. Here, Eleanor was obviously impressed with the recluse of St Martin's church, later giving money to the recluse and paying for work at the church.[20]

The year 1284 was marked out for consolidation and publicity in Wales. Having won the war, the territory needed to be settled – another echo of Eleanor's childhood. So the 1284 Welsh tour commenced in mid-March at Rhuddlan. Here, consolidation was on show – building was plainly going on in the town around the castle – and Eleanor was seen to encourage it, giving wood, nails and hinges to assist in the construction of the church of St John, as well as a donation for Rhuddlan's own recluse. Donations also flowed from her to the Rhuddlan Dominicans and those of Bangor, while the friars and clergy who visited court were liberally looked after.[21]

It was also at Rhuddlan that the main administrative tool of settlement, the Statute of Wales, was passed on 19 March 1284. The purpose of this statute was to set out clearly how Wales would be governed, defining the hierarchy of royal officials who would govern and where Welsh law would continue to be permissible (in a number of circumstances as regarded civil claims). Interestingly, and again suggesting Eleanor's influence in Wales, it was in a sense a parallel to Ferdinand III's *fueros* for conquered territories in the Spanish peninsula, and followed the same format, trying to harmonise the laws and procedures of the new territory with those of the conquering nation. It also avoided the problems which Alfonso X had encountered in trying to impose an overarching legal code without regard to local customs. Therefore, while the wording of the statute and the balance drawn between Welsh and English law was almost certainly predominantly the work of Robert Burnell, with assistance from the members of the commission which had been appointed to report on Welsh law, it seems quite likely that Eleanor was involved with the discussions which led up to the statute and the overarching question of the balance to be struck between harmonisation and maintaining facets of law and practice familiar to the local inhabitants.

From Rhuddlan, the royal party moved at the end of the month to the two building sites, first to Conwy and then to Caernarfon. Conwy, of course, had already been civilised for Eleanor. Now Caernarfon, too, was made as congenial to her tastes as a building site could be, with a ready-made lawned garden in which she could pass any fine days as she waited for the arrival of the next baby.[22]

It was at the latter location that Eleanor received the news of the death, on 4 April 1284, of her brother Alfonso. His health utterly broken, anathematised by his son as a mad leper, the terrible effects of his illnesses meant that he spent the last months of his life almost alone in Seville. From his deathbed he laid a curse on the undutiful Sancho and sent bitter reproaches to Edward for his failure to provide any assistance. One of the few items of value which he still had to leave in his will was some fine brocade, sent to him in better times by Eleanor. As Eleanor arranged with Edward for their son Alphonso to present the reputed crown of King Arthur at the shrine of St Edward at Westminster, it will not have been lost on her that his godfather and namesake had been so desperate and without help that he was forced to sell their father's crown to the Emir of Morocco. Yet for all this, to the very end, Alfonso earned his title of the Learned King: he was still finalising the *General Estoria*, the *Cantigas de Santa Maria* and his handbook on chess in his final days, and writing of the solace which the pleasures of the mind give against life's miseries.[23]

Still mourning Alfonso, Eleanor prepared for the birth of her next child. It was at Caernarfon, either in temporary apartments or in the partially constructed Eagle Tower (which had been built to three storeys and given a temporary roof), that Eleanor gave birth on 25 April 1284 to the son who was to become Edward II but until his accession was known as Edward of Caernarfon. It seems fairly clear that the birth of the next child at this historically resonant site was fully intended as a further symbolic annexation of the Welsh mythology: young Edward annexed the role of Constantine. Although the famous story of Edward presenting the Welsh with an heir who knew no word of English is plainly untrue (not least because Edward was only a second son), the birth of Edward at Caernarfon marked Wales as the territory of the English Crown even more powerfully than that of Elizabeth at Rhuddlan. It also seems very likely that the decision to bear Edward in this location was Eleanor's own. Other options – such as Conwy and Rhuddlan – were obviously available, and the location must therefore have been deliberate. Edward seems unlikely to have exerted pressure; but Eleanor, with her understanding of mythmaking, would be likely to appreciate the value of the gesture.

Almost at once, a destiny seemed to await this new baby. Alexander III of Scotland had a female heir presumptive: Margaret of Norway, known to history as the Maid of Norway. Her age (one year old) was perfect for Edward of Caernarfon, and would enable him, although only the second son of the English king, to rule Scotland and Norway. At present, the project remained provisional, but the idea that through young Margaret 'much good may yet come to pass', to quote the practically minded Alexander in his correspondence with Edward, remained in the air.

Despite its likely shortcomings as a residence, the king and queen stayed at Caernarfon until June, when, over Edward's birthday, a two-week break was taken at the remote manor of Baladeulyn. This had two attractions which harmonised with recent themes: first, it was on the site of a Roman palace; and secondly, it was close to the supposed burial place of Mabon ab Madron, a hero who features in the *Mabinogion*, and also to the site where another hero of those tales, Lleu, was supposed to have transformed into an eagle. During this period, the court seems to have properly got away from the cares of the world, with the manor surrounded by royal tents and pavilions supplied from Chester and Edward getting lost in the woods at night (the payment to the local lad who set him right remains in the records). Amusingly enough, local tradition has it that during this visit the local lord Tudor ap Einion was dispossessed of all his lands by the greed of King Edward's wife 'Matilda' before being restored to them by the king. Needless to say, there is no evidence which supports this story.[24]

But outside affairs, in particular Eleanora's marriage, continued to press. In May, Edward had announced to the Pope his intention of going on Crusade again, subject to two small riders: a deal on financing and the procuring of peace in Europe. In other words, Edward and Eleanor were keen to prevent Pope Martin from exacerbating the European position – and Eleanora's prospects – by declaring a Crusade against Aragon. This seemed likely to be his next move unless distracted, since he had already offered Aragon to Charles of Valois, Philip III's second son, and had invested him as king in May 1284. The ploy failed; Martin, a Frenchman, owing his elevation to the French king's interest, nonetheless declared the Crusade against Aragon on 4 June. To add to the intractability of the Sicilian–Aragonese problem, the very next day, during a major naval engagement off Naples, an epochal event occurred: Charles of Anjou's son Charles of Salerno was captured by the Aragonese. The capture of the heir to Sicily by the excommunicate Aragonese provided further escalation where none was needed, and was to prove a sticking point for peace for years to come. The wider Crusade – and Eleanora's match – was consequently stalled for the foreseeable future.[25]

In July, another break was taken at Nefyn, where Edward and Eleanor held their first Round Table. Much has been made of the fact that this was a location resonant in Welsh mythology: the prophecies of Merlin were said to have been found here. However, despite the description of the tournament by the chroniclers and the Arthurian connection, there appear to have been no very striking Arthurian aspects in the staging; the event was simply a jousting tournament, with one team captained by the Earl of Lincoln and the other by the Earl of Ulster. It was, however, a major tournament into which much organisation will have been put, and involving many knights (apparently both domestic and foreign) in considerable travel, expense and inconvenience. It therefore plainly had a point. Part of that point will have been to again reinforce the position of Edward as King of England and Wales, and any location in Gwynedd could have made this point. But also, as with Conwy and Caernarfon, Edward chose in Nefyn the site of a Welsh princely residence. It was also, tellingly, the location from which Llywelyn and Eleanor de Montfort had written their last letters to Edward in early 1282. So while the Arthurian connection did also help to offer a parallel between Edward and King Arthur, the predominant point was a straightforward political one. The event itself seems to have been very hearty, and very heartily enjoyed. Aside from the jousting, there was also apparently dancing, which was entered into with such enthusiasm that the floor of the hall collapsed.[26]

Once the crowds of visitors had departed, the main royal party passed onwards along the coast to the end of the Llŷn peninsula, including taking a trip to Bardsey Island. Extra offerings were made for this trip both prior to departure and while on the island.[27]

However, the triumphant and light-hearted mood of the summer changed in an instant shortly after their return to Conwy in mid-August. Messengers reached the king and queen with the worst possible news: Alphonso was dead, having died on 19 August 1284 – the tenth anniversary of Edward and Eleanor's coronation.

The cause of Alphonso's death is not recorded, and the chroniclers hardly mention his death, perhaps out of tact; or more likely because he had, to date, been more or less invisible in the nursery. The extent of this tragedy for Eleanor and Edward is difficult to gauge at this distance in time. Dynastically, of course, it was close to their worst nightmare; the succession now hung on the life of young Edward, barely four months old and subject to all the illnesses of childhood. There was no guarantee that, with Eleanor now forty-two years of age, any more pregnancies would be viable or successful – or that they would result in boys who would live. The irony of the timing will have seemed particularly bitter, coming as it did both at the moment of their greatest triumph, when Edward had established himself as a conquering king in fact; and also almost exactly at the time when Alphonso, aged nearly eleven, would have been reckoned to have weathered the highest-risk period of childhood. Indeed, his presentation of the alleged crown of Arthur at the tomb of the Confessor shows that he had begun to carry out some public duties, as was only the case once a prince or princess was deemed to have emerged safely from childhood.

What doubtless made the loss even worse was that the very limited material available suggests that Alphonso had promised well; a poignant thought, given that young Edward turned out to be a real candidate for England's worst king. That evidence is contained in a letter of condolence from Archbishop Pecham which described Alphonso as 'the hope of us all'.

While Salzman dismisses the tributes of the chroniclers ('flower of youth', 'hope of knighthood', 'comfort to his father') as the kind of flannel which would have been applied to any youthfully deceasing prince, the tribute from Pecham, with his high moral standards and unrelenting tendency to call a spade a spade, is worth noting. It suggests that that scrupulous academic himself thought well of Alphonso; else he would have confined himself to expressions of sympathy for Edward's grief, or kept quiet, as he appears to have done in due course on the death of Eleanor.

Personally, too, it is likely to have been a huge blow. Alphonso was the child who had spent the greatest portion of his childhood with his parents, having been born en route from the Crusade and in the nursery during their most domestic years, when time with the younger children was feasible and obviously frequently achieved. There also seems every sign of his having developed tastes which gave him common ground with each parent. Thus a castle and a siege engine had been carefully made for him, while the psalter prepared for him indicates that he was taking pleasure in reading from an early age – very probably under Eleanor's personal tutelage. As he grew older, his tastes in hunting reflected the preferences of both his parents – he had both hawks (like his father) and hounds (like his mother) – and the eager-looking hunting boy in the psalter may well be intended as a depiction of him. Altogether, it would be astounding if his loss were not a huge source of personal grief to Eleanor – almost certainly more than any of her other deceased children, all of whom died younger and had had much less contact with her. It is therefore no surprise to find her stipulating that his heart be reserved for burial with hers at the London house of the Dominicans.

Some might suggest that the absence of Eleanor and Edward from his funeral indicates (as with the death of young Henry) a lack of concern for his fate. However, on this occasion attendance was absolutely not feasible; it was the height of summer and the king and queen were over a week's journey from London. The exact date of the funeral is unknown, but it appears likely to have been on or around 27 August and presided over by Archbishop Pecham, who on this date wrote reassuring the Abbot of Westminster that whenever he officiated there at the request of the king, the queen consort or the queen mother, no infringement on the exemptions of Westminster was intended. The right thing to do was what they did, ensuring that his funeral was conducted appropriately and soldiering on with the work which they had in hand. Alphonso's heart was duly buried according to Eleanor's wishes at the house of the London Blackfriars. His body joined those of his lost siblings, Katherine, Joan, John and Henry, at Westminster Abbey.[28]

It is hard to imagine that either Eleanor or Edward took any joy in the remainder of the triumphant program for the rest of the year. It is a mark of their joint determination and sense of duty that the program went ahead without apparent alteration. So in early September the king and queen visited Vale Royal, where they presented the monks with a chalice of silver made from the seal matrices of Llywelyn, Dafydd and Eleanor de Montfort the younger. They even maintained their plans for a big celebration at Overton in late September, lasting for the best part of two weeks, at which a thousand Welsh minstrels were assembled to help celebrate the end of an independent Wales.

In another ironic touch, this celebration coincided with a further personal blow. Henry of Brittany, a younger child of Edward's sister, who appears to have been part of young John and Henry's establishment and to have joined the court as he grew, died in September. He was buried at Bangor and lavish arrangements were made for masses in his memory, while his horses were despatched to Eleanor of Provence, who had minded the nursery when he was small. The arrangements for this foster son's mourning rebut the accusations levelled at Eleanor and Edward as unfeeling parents – as also do the preparations which were made to ensure the visit of the surviving children. The nursery party was at Acton Burnell in September, and Robert Burnell was authorised to get plenty of venison in for them. Moving the children's household this far was a major undertaking; it would only have been done if their parents had a strong wish to see them.

More sentiment can be seen towards the end of October. On 1 November, Edward and Eleanor would have been married for thirty years; it seems likely that it was in memory of their first meeting that one of them arranged for baby Edward to make special donations throughout the last week in October.

The final part of the 1284 tour was a massive procession around the coast of Wales – beating the bounds on a national scale. To commence, the new castles at Conwy and Caernarfon were inspected, plus the other northern Welsh castles. At Harlech, as with Conwy, the original hall of the Welsh princes was to be retained as a subsidiary part of the new imperial structure, pointing up for all eternity the superiority of the English style and resources. In November, the progress moved out of North Wales through Bere and Llanbedr and then followed the coast via Aberystwyth to Cardigan and south to Haverford. At Haverford, the party turned inland to Carmarthen, Kidwelly and Oystermouth in Glamorgan.[29]

All along the way, free boroughs were created around key castles, encouraging commercial development and prosperity around the new marks of power. Meanwhile, Edward and Eleanor's closest associates were appointed to positions of power in the new Wales: Otho de Grandison became Justiciar of North Wales and Robert Tybetot occupied the equivalent position in West Wales.

Finally, in mid-December, the party reached Cardiff. There the official court reception began, with a festivity at Cardiff Castle hosted by the

Earl of Gloucester. This was a particularly important and sensitive event
– and not just because of Gilbert the Red's notorious touchiness. For
during the Welsh years there had first evolved a new idea for binding
this most powerful and prickly of characters safely to the Crown: Joan,
now without a foreign match, was to become Gloucester's wife, and the
annulment of his marriage was now pending before the papal court. So
the celebrations at Cardiff marked not just the final round in the triumph
of the campaigners, but also the formal welcome of Joan to her future
home.

Following this grand event, further receptions were hosted by two
further magnates with whom relations had been not entirely easy. The
first was held at Caldicot by the Earl of Hereford, he whose dubious
heritage was being atoned for by his marriage to Eleanor's cousin
Mathilde de Fiennes. The final reception was by Roger Bigod, the Earl
of Norfolk. His family's involvement in the Barons' War had been partly
prompted by a sense of being outside the royal magic circle, and nothing
had changed in this respect; there was an uneasy state of truce between
him and Edward, who would later pursue him for his debts to the Crown.
As with the Herefords, Eleanor may well have provided a means to easier
relations – she had shared Geoffrey de Aspale's services with Bigod for
some time. The party took place at Chepstow, where the refurbished
castle of the Bigods perched on a clifftop above the River Wye, and
considerable expenditure was undertaken by the host to please the king,
with Bigod's steward being sent as far as Sussex to provision the feast.

After this slightly minatory series of visits, the court crossed to Bristol
to rejoin the children for the Christmas season. Wales was declared
settled. The most difficult earls had shown their adherence. It was time
to move on.[30]

15

Gascony

With Wales off the agenda, and Alfonso X now beyond help, the issue which cried out for attention was the Sicilian crisis. This was to occupy the bulk of the next five years, and was to prove a thoroughly frustrating business.

The first question was to decide what action should be taken in response to Philip III's summons to Edward to assist him in his Crusade against Pedro of Aragon, which summons could not now be put off on the plea of business in Wales. The outcome of discussions over the holiday seems to have been a decision to cross to France for a face-to-face meeting with Philip; either to assist him, or more likely to try to stop the war. So the party performed a sweep through the south of England, arriving at Dover in late January. The plan seems to have been abandoned – perhaps because Philip was not easily accessible, or perhaps because of news of the death of the key protagonist, Charles of Anjou on 8 January 1285. The party waited at Canterbury and Leeds until mid-February, making offerings for peace and reconciliation at the altars of St Thomas and St Adrian of Canterbury. As news was still awaited, they moved on, spending the time until mid-April in Suffolk, Norfolk and Cambridgeshire.

This stay, as usual, afforded access to Eleanor's current and contemplated properties in the area. These included new properties in each county which had been acquired as part of the February 1284 review and further Cambridgeshire properties of Robert de Crevequer, which would be acquired later in 1285. It is therefore hardly surprising to see a two-week stay at Eleanor's property at Burgh – or indeed a one-day stay at her new Foulmire property. The trip also permitted a visit to Walsingham and Bromholm, again in hopes of assisting the prospects of peace in Sicily and Aragon. But the international question was still further complicated by the death of another player in the Aragonese crisis: Pope Martin IV died in March, and was replaced by Honorius IV in April.[1]

While nothing was plainly happening fast in Europe, the May parliament provided an opportunity to celebrate the Welsh victory with the people of London and a huge show was accordingly put on. On 4 May 1285 the king and queen, led by the Archbishop of Canterbury carrying the Cross of Neith, set off on foot from the Tower for Westminster Abbey, accompanied by the major magnates and fourteen bishops. At the abbey the cross was offered on the high altar. After the official celebration, it was the turn of Parliament, which dealt formally with the issue of the French summons to serve in the campaign against Aragon. It was concluded that service should be delayed until the French had made good on their treaty obligations and, so that there should be no further opportunity offered to them to fudge that issue, that a commission should be appointed to resolve outstanding issues.[2]

With this settled, plans began to be made for the crossing to France. But for some reason the departure was again delayed. It seems likely that news reached England that the French king had already set off on his Crusade, having plundered Elne in late May. The party was again left waiting in the South: the feast of St Thomas Becket in July was marked at Canterbury Cathedral by the presentation at the shrine of gold figures of St Edward the Confessor, St John, St George and his horse, and a week was taken at Leeds Castle. There was also time for a short excursion into Sussex to inspect new acquisitions in the county and in Chichester. During this stay, Eleanor bought a sizeable strip of land adjoining the grounds of the Dominican friary, which was then in the process of being established, and gave it to them. A further grant of land was made to them before departure to France the next year.

Her own property affairs also bear every sign of being readied for immediate departure if that became necessary, because there are two groups of acquisitions – one in June and one in July. In June, we see Eleanor acquiring Washlingstone and Littlefield in Kent for her life. In July, Robert le Crevequer seems to have surrendered a piece of his own property in Cambridgeshire and arranged for the sale of a neighbouring piece of land with it. At the same time, Eleanor acquired a manor in Rutland, near her north Northampton holdings, and was appointed to the custody of the counties of Dorset and Somerset.[3]

Then the family moved on into Wiltshire, visiting Henry III's favourite palace of Clarendon and Amesbury Abbey. There young Mary – only just seven years old – was veiled as a nun on 15 August 1285, accompanied by thirteen other girls from aristocratic families. Among them was probably her cousin Eleanor of Brittany, who showed more aptitude than Mary for the religious life; she would later become Abbess of Fontevrault. The timing of this enclosure was perhaps partly brought about because Eleanor of Provence was apparently ill at Amesbury at this time; since she was now sixty-two years of age, it may have been felt that she was not long for the world. But equally it seems likely that Edward and Eleanor wanted to be present for this major event in their daughter's life, before they departed for a lengthy stay in France.[4]

Autumn was spent predominantly in the Hampshire area. There were two special points of interest in this period. The first was the stay in Winchester for which the great Winchester Round Table was created. In fact, there were two Winchester stays this autumn, the one in September apparently providing the occasion for the tournament – the Worcester annalist records that on the Feast of the Nativity of the Virgin (8 September) the king created forty-four knights at Winchester. While the event has acquired a romantic Arthurian patina, it had, like most of the other Arthurian events, a more hard-edged practical side. Edward had been seeking to boost the numbers of men taking up the status of knighthood, following a drastic fall in knights, from around 4,000 at the start of the century, to somewhere around 1,500 in the 1280s – of whom only a minority were actual fighting knights. To achieve this, he had adopted a mixture of carrot and stick tactics. Thus he made an order that all men with lands worth more than £100 per year and so eligible for knighthood should come before him to be knighted; but he sweetened the pill by making it an extremely high-status occasion.

So the beautiful new table – five and a half metres in diameter and three quarters of a ton in weight – was crafted and put into place. The royal family was put under a three-line whip: the king and queen, the older princesses, John of Brittany, John of Brabant and the new nun, Princess Mary, were all present. It is interesting, given Eleanor's impending forty-fourth birthday, that the number of knights made echoed her age; perhaps another of the thoughtful gestures in which Edward improbably excelled. The Statute of Winchester was promulgated later, on 8 October 1285, in a second and separate stay. The intervening period was spent between Micheldever, Wootton and Woodmancott – close to some of the Walerand manors which Eleanor had in her eye for future acquisition, and which were duly acquired in her absence in Gascony.[5]

The second notable event of the period was the royal party's first stay on the Isle of Wight. If one were perhaps to wonder what sent the royal party to the Isle of Wight at this time, the reader may by now guess the answer. In 1284, Eleanor had acquired a manor at Swainstone on the Isle of Wight. This manor was duly the royal base for the stay on the island.

The latter part of the year took the royal travellers into the West Country, Eleanor having been appointed to custody of the counties of Dorset and Somerset in summer, and having both long-standing and more recent acquisitions in those counties, as well as dower properties to inspect. Another stay was made at Eleanor's property of Camel as part of this trip. Edward will also have been interested to inspect progress on his new town (daringly called Newton) on the shores of Poole Harbour;

orders for the detailed laying out of the town were given in January 1286, before the royal party left Exeter. The primary impetus for this latter visit seems to have been an appeal to the king for justice from the family of a murdered precentor of the cathedral at Exeter. The case, in which the Mayor of Exeter and the Dean of the Cathedral were among the accused, had mysteriously failed to progress, and the family sought justice from the top. The king, reflecting his coronation manifesto of law and order, came to hear the trial personally, taking off only Christmas Day itself. However, Edward did not neglect his domestic duties either: for Christmas, Eleanor received from him a cup of gold worth £24, and a gold pitcher decorated with jewels and enamels.[6]

But among this domestic business, international news came at last: Philip III of France died of dysentery in early October 1285 in the course of his disastrous 'Crusade'. It was closely followed by the death on 11 November 1285 of Pedro of Aragon. Eleanora was now, in name at least, Queen of Aragon. What is more, in the course of 1285, all the principal players – Philip of France, Pedro of Aragon, Charles of Anjou and Pope Martin IV – had died. There was now, therefore, a natural point at which attempts could be made to settle the disputes between the parties. Edward, who had been appealed to earlier in the dispute by both sides to act as a mediator, was the ideal person to try to bring about an accommodation. Further, he was now at liberty to so; and with a number of very real incentives.

The first was that of saving his eldest daughter's marriage and thus providing Gascony with a good neighbour. The second, effectively the correlate of the first, was keeping France out of Aragon. The Aragonese marriage had been recommended by the need to keep a potentially difficult neighbour sweet; however, even at their worst, the Aragonese would hardly be so undesirable as neighbours as a French fief. Were the Crusade to succeed, and France to take Aragon, Gascony would effectively be encircled by France – a position not to be contemplated if anything could be done to avoid it. The third incentive, of course, was to save his amiable cousin Charles of Salerno from captivity.

So the arrangements for diplomatic activity began to be reanimated at once, and before the end of 1285 Edward had made arrangements for the despatch of Otho de Grandison and Henry Cobham to Rome. This time, there was no evasion from France. On the contrary, an embassy came early in the year, urging Edward to come to France as soon as he could and attempt to bring about a peace. The long-delayed trip was therefore back on.[7]

For Eleanor, this naturally meant trying to tidy up her various landholdings and bring into ownership any purchases which could be finalised in good time. February seems to have been the prime period for this, although a few deals trickled on into the later months.

In the January–February period, Eleanor acquired new properties in Buckingham, Essex, the Isle of Wight, Oxfordshire and Sussex.[8]

There was time for a trip in February to Langley to the younger children, and then a move to London (probably accompanied by the nursery party) for the parliament at the end of February. This parliament had eyes cast abroad in anticipation of the royal visit, for the status of Gascony formed part of the topic of debate. Also coming to the fore was the question of the proposed Scottish match for young Edward: Alexander III died on 19 March 1286, and once it was clear that his young widow, Yolande de Dreux, would not provide a posthumous heir, young Edward's intended bride, Margaret of Norway, was confirmed as Queen of Scotland, opening the vista of a peaceful annexation of Scotland, to complete the conquest of Britain.

Within this period the royal family, despite the press of business, found time for what at first appear to be two boating trips for simple pleasure: one at the end of February to Brentford, for which two barges were handsomely fitted up, and a more substantial trip in April to Gravesend, in which the king and queen travelled by barge and the princesses by ship.

It may be, though, that the limited programme of this period and the boat trips are both markers of the beginnings of Eleanor's move into the ill health which was henceforth to plague her. Until 1285, despite almost constant childbearing and a busy programme of national and international travel, she seems to have enjoyed robust good health. From this point on, however, her health seems to have become decidedly unsatisfactory. Certainly there are signs that she had an illness in the winter of 1285–6, as medicines were provided for her several times, including in February. The illness seems to have lingered: in March a *mensura* – a wax candle of the same height as the subject, which was burned before a favourite saint – was purchased. This could indicate continuing illness or recovery, but in April there is another record of medicines being sent for, which indicates the former is more probable.[9]

Despite ill health and all the preparations, there was the usual spring trip to Quenington and Down Ampney in the Cotswolds, emphasising the fondness which the king and queen had for this location, plus short stops in Chichester, Langley and Westminster. At the latter stop Edmund of Cornwall, Edward's double cousin – Richard of Cornwall's son by Eleanor of Provence's sister – was placed in charge of the realm. Then, after stops at Leeds and Canterbury, the party reached Dover, where the queen mother and princesses assembled to see them off. The party finally departed for Wissant, still a favoured crossing point from England, on 13 May 1286 – about a year later than originally intended. The plan was probably to make a stay abroad of no more than a year; in fact they were not to return for over three years – and the group which returned would be sadly diminished.

The party was substantial and included key friends and advisers such as Robert Burnell and John de Vescy, as well as the Lancasters, and the earls of Lincoln, Gloucester and Pembroke. The transfer was conducted over a period of about four days, with some of the ships making three crossings in that time. The need for this becomes clearer when one appreciates that the core group was supported by a thousand horses and eight ships of kitchen equipment. On arrival, Edward collected the recent communications to him from Charles of Salerno's sons and his people of Provence, as well as news of his designation as Alphonso's agent for making a truce. Less welcome was the news that Pope Honorius had stated that the dispensation which had been granted for Eleanora's marriage did not apply to a union with the family of the late King of Aragon. For Eleanor, there seem to have been family meetings: the wardrobe book reveals gifts to her French Fiennes relatives and to her distant cousin the lord de la Plaunche, whose children now joined Eleanor's household.[10]

On arrival, the royal party proceeded to Amiens to meet the new eighteen-year-old French King, Philip IV 'le Bel' (the Fair) of France. This was in some ways quite a family occasion. Philip was the son of Edward's cousin, and, as the son also of Isabelle of Aragon, the nephew of Eleanora's fiancé. His thirteen-year-old wife, Jeanne of Navarre, was the daughter of Blanche of Lancaster by her first marriage. But there was a generation gap: Edward and Eleanor, now in their mid-forties, were old stagers by comparison. The conjoined royal party proceeded to Paris, where the English royals lodged at the monastery of St Germain-des-Prés, on the left bank of the Seine. June and July were then spent in Paris with much socialising, including a banquet on the Feast of the Trinity which cost £151, and also, it would seem, plenty of shopping – jewels were sent home to the princesses and a crown of sapphires, emeralds, rubies and pearls, given by the King of France, was sent on to Eleanora. Edward gave Eleanor some gold cloths and the crystal and jasper chess set which the Master of the Temple gave him.

The party also probably took the opportunity to visit the Sainte-Chapelle where France's kings and some of their privileged great were buried. Isabelle of Aragon had received a lovely tomb here – a sparkling white marble effigy evoking her youth and beauty. Alphonse of Brienne also lay here; as did his sister Marie. Most of the kings had received similar treatment to Isabelle – striking tomb effigies in marble or polished stone, arranged in orderly ranks. But the greatest of them, including Philip Augustus, Charles the Bald and Louis VIII, were given a special treatment: their tombs featured gilded bronze images.

As well as pleasure and sightseeing, there was plenty of business. Homage had to be performed to the new king for the lands held from him, including Eleanor's territory of Ponthieu, and more carefully, in the light of the position under the Treaty of Paris, for Gascony. And, of course, there was the small detail of a truce between France and Aragon which had to be ironed out. However, with plenty of willingness on both sides to create a period for discussion of the issues, Edward received all the authorities he needed and a year's truce was duly agreed in late July.[11]

Immediately with the prospect of negotiations for peace, there also came discussions about the fulfilment of Eleanora's marriage; Alphonso, looking to rivet English interests to his, wrote to Edward to seek his co-operation in bringing this about as soon as Edward arrived in Paris. Edward, in turn, promised that once the truce was in place he would seek a dispensation from the Pope, with a view to sending Eleanora to her husband, and a meeting then took place between Edward and his nominal son-in-law. But when Otho de Grandison reappeared from Rome, carrying a yet further reiteration of the papal veto against the Aragonese marriage, it was plain that the dispensation was unlikely to be forthcoming, at least until Alphonso made peace with the papacy. The focus therefore shifted to negotiating a treaty which could bring this about.

There were also, as always, issues in Gascony, which were brought to Paris for the purpose of getting a head start on the business of the Gascon part of the trip. But here there was not only business for the king. It would seem that Eleanor was actually conducting Gascon business for Edward on her own – the Gascon Rolls report Edward ratifying an agreement reached between the Crown and the Viscount of Fronsac through 'our dearest consort Eleanor' – the result of yet another of Eleanor's forays as an arbitrator. It seems that a dispute between Edward and the viscount had resulted in a decision on liability, and the question of the assessment of the amount of the claim, which concerned property values, was remitted by consent to Eleanor. Away from her property interests, Eleanor was therefore making herself useful effectively as Edward's deputy in business concerning Gascony, and obviously was considered sufficiently knowledgeable on property matters to reach an appropriate result.

This overt exercise of royal power came at a time when Eleanor will finally have felt her position as queen to be unchallenged; Eleanor of Provence, now aged sixty-two, had finally taken the veil at Amesbury on 7 July. From this point on, her correspondence (though still active and demonstrating a will to exert influence) is almost always commenced 'Eleanor, humble nun of the order of Fontevrault of the order of Amesbury'; the claim to be Eleanor, Queen of England, is dropped at last. Yet not quite all was rosy; July also saw medicines being paid for on Eleanor's behalf.[12]

The Paris visit also offers one of the most interesting vignettes of the royal couple. Apparently, one day Edward and Eleanor were sitting by a window and chatting together in a room with some of their attendants when a bolt of lightning passed through the window between them, and actually struck two attendants, who were killed instantly. Trivet, writing for Mary, regarded the incident as interesting mostly from the perspective of the royal couple's escape as a sure sign of divine favour. However, more compelling is the intimate domestic portrait painted by the incident: the royal couple, together among a crowd and absorbed in each other's company, present an irresistibly romantic picture which verifies the existence of a continually engaging and interesting marriage.

In August, having achieved the truce, Edward and Eleanor took their leave of the French court and began to make their way to Gascony, at no great pace. Part of the delay is attributable to a certain amount of sightseeing; the route took them via Pontigny, where Edmund of Abingdon, the Archbishop of Canterbury who baptised Edward, was buried and thence along the beauties of the Loire via Blois, Amboise and Langeais to the family burial centre at Fontevrault. The party reached Saintes around the middle of September and the remainder of that month and the first part of October were spent in inspecting the territories reclaimed under the finalised Treaty of Paris – principally in the area between Saintes and Saint Pierre d'Oleron.[13]

Yet part of the delay in reaching Gascony was apparently attributable to ill health generally among the travelling party: the wardrobe records evidence repeated purchases of medicines for its members and provision for care for those who had to be left behind, though the nature of the malaise is not clear. And Eleanor did not escape: in among the other medical expenses there are payments for medicines and syrups bought for Eleanor 'at Saintes and elsewhere', implying a fairly lengthy period of illness or repeated episodes of illness within a short period.[14]

Thus it was only in late October that the group reached Libourne, a bastide founded by the late Roger Leyburn in 1270, during his tenure as Seneschal in Gascony. From there the party continued touring the newly conceded lands: the itinerary which can be reconstructed for November shows stops in and around Bergerac, before heading further inland and south via Cadouin and Monpazier. The latter is a bastide which has, over time, proved one of the best advertisements for Edward's scheme of 'bastidisation' – the seeding of new bastide towns throughout the region. It survives in charmingly picturesque fashion to this day, and visitors can even explore it from the Hotel Edouard Ier. At the time of Edward and Eleanor's 1286 visit, however, it was simply one among a number of fledging bastide towns; Edward had founded it only the year before and it was presumably still in the course of construction – though sufficiently far advanced for an overnight stay. From there, the party went on to Agen via Villeneuve-sur-Lot, arriving late in the month, before exploring the eastern borders of the Agenais at Roquecor and Montsempron, returning to Agen in the middle of the month.

The mobile nature of the trip provides an opportunity to mention an ongoing theme in the household accounts throughout the time in

Gascony: horses and their equipment are key. Again and again, horses (white, bay, 'morello' or dark bay and more) are bought and sold, harness is repaired, or new harness bought. On one occasion Eleanor even sends all the way to England for some particularly favoured piece of harness; the keen horsewoman's conviction that a particular mount will go best under the guidance of a key piece of kit speaks to us clearly. The impression conveyed, when glancing through the household records, is that the mobile court was akin to a travelling hunt, with the officers in charge of the horses very much the heart of day-to-day business, and discussion of all matters equine being a running theme.

The mobile nature of this phase of the trip also seems to indicate that the health of the party generally and Eleanor in particular had improved. But the respite was temporary; again at Agen there are records of medicines and syrups being purchased for the queen, revealing that her health was again giving trouble. The travelling and her ill health did not, however, stop Eleanor from keeping up with her work; her correspondence with her office in England proceeded alongside her despatches for harness, and in November there are records of her acquiring a wardship in Essex. It was probably also at around this time that Eleanor learnt that Hugh Despenser, the stepson of the Earl of Norfolk, had married Isabel Beauchamp without royal licence. As Eleanor had the wardship of the lands of Isabel's first husband, this affected her business; and out of sight was emphatically not out of mind: she demanded recompense in the sum of 1,000 marks from Despenser – a debt which he acknowledged early in the new year, pledging lands as security.[15]

Christmas was spent in the familiar surroundings of the priory of Saint-Macaire near Bordeaux. The holiday was observed with the usual celebrations, with the priory hall serving as the king's great hall and a large bill for candles being run up. The incorrigible Gaston de Béarn (now in his early sixties) gave a vastly suitable present of chargers for the king and queen, and Anthony Bek gave a hound – a present more likely to please Eleanor than Edward. So too was Edmund of Lancaster's gift effectively a gift for Eleanor – a quantity of Brie cheese, doubtless sourced through his wife's contacts. All of these tend to indicate that pleasing Eleanor was very much a priority for the court. It was perhaps on this occasion that the pleasing Limoges-made clasp featuring her arms was given to Eleanor. And more general jollification was plainly in order, too. Echoing the parties of the Welsh tour, there was much music; 125 minstrels were paid for performing over the holiday period. It would seem likely that the peaceful routine of the abbey was much disturbed by their distinguished guests. Among these was a new face – Marie of Brittany, daughter of Edward's sister Beatrice, who seems to have joined the court (with her substantial household) following the death of her father and to have stayed mostly at court until Eleanor's death.[16]

January 1287 was spent in and around Bordeaux, in particular at Blanquefort, slightly north-west of Bordeaux, where there appears to have been a congenial residence, at some point conveyed to Eleanor, to which the party were to return repeatedly. In February, there was a trip beginning along the left bank and progressing to the mouth of the great river at Soulac opposite Royan. As with the similar Llŷn peninsular trip in Wales, offerings were made at the great altar of the Virgin Mary. This trip, or part of it, apparently involved hunting rather unusual prey: wolves. Although Eleanor's presence at the wolf hunt is not specifically mentioned, she was obviously part of the group involved in this tour, and, particularly given her own fondness for hunting, it is likely that she participated.

At around this time, there are reports in the English chronicles that Edward fell seriously ill but was restored by the good offices of his physicians; however, the absence of matching references in the household books and the existence of the February tour tend to contradict this story.

The first part of March was spent in Bordeaux, followed by another mini-tour, with a river trip from Barsac to Langon, before heading inland to Bazas (where the king and queen made donations at the great altar) and Uzeste, after which they returned to Bordeaux. April and May then appear to have been spent in or around Bordeaux, again with a good deal of time spent at Blanquefort. The king and queen are spotted in the wardrobe accounts passing a place called Lesparre on their return from an excursion, giving gifts to people of the village for losses which they had sustained through the passage of the court through their lands.[17]

In spring (reportedly on Easter Sunday, 6 April), there was another piece of high drama. Edward was standing with some others in a solar at the top of a tower when the floor beneath them suddenly gave way, and they fell a distance somewhat improbably described as being eighty feet. Three knights were killed and Edward was recovered, with a broken collarbone, from beneath a Gascon knight.

It seems likely that the three dramatic incidents so far described for this year (Paris lightning, Edward's illness at Blanquefort and the collapsing building) are accounts of two incidents, not three, with the illness being a misreporting of some indisposition following the Easter fall. Indeed, it would actually be tempting to say that only one could be true and that either this fall or the earlier Paris lightning strike is accurate, but not both; two such dramatic incidents in under a year would seem like outrageous bad luck. However, the Trivet account should probably be believed, since Trivet wrote for Mary and he is likely to have had accounts of dramatic incidents at least in the direct family oral tradition.

As for the collapse, the records of the household certainly lend credence to something dramatic happening, albeit a little earlier than Easter – they show Eleanor paying John de Montfort's sick bill at Bordeaux in

April, and making offerings for the funeral of Morris ap David of Wales at Bordeaux in March 1287. There is no record, however, of Edward's illness at this time, and it seems permissible to infer a much smaller fall, with fairly minor cuts and bruises to Edward. All the same, this incident must have added to the sense of high drama, and perhaps misfortune, that was gathering about the party involved in this expedition.[18]

The next phase of the diplomatic circus began in early April, showing that throughout this hiatus period the diplomatic process had been moving on. Ambassadors arrived from Aragon in a delegation of over eighty men. Progress was made, and in May the embassy departed with John de Vescy to arrange a face-to-face meeting with Alphonso. At around the same time, news arrived that financial terms had been reached with Pope Honorius for Edward's Crusade; and thus on 12 May, either at Bordeaux or Blanquefort, he and his companions made crusading vows to the Archbishop of Ravenna.[19]

At about this time, in accordance with papal views or with a view to assisting directly in the financing of the Crusade, Edward ordered the arrest of the Jews in England, who were later released on payment of a fine of 20,000 marks. Also at this time, and probably with similar motives, Edward ordered the expulsion of the Jews from Gascony and the seizure of their assets by the Crown. The crackdown on the Jews by Edward, of which this really marks the beginning, has attracted to him considerable odium. It should be noted, however, that neither the expulsion or the arrest was a unique occurrence; as well as the expulsion by Eleanor of Provence from her dower lands, Jews in France were coming under increasing pressure owing to papal influence, with expulsions from Poitou and Moissac in 1249 and 1271 and from Maine and Anjou within a short space of time. Even Alfonso X had arrested his Jewish population while under financial pressure in the political upheavals towards the end of his life. Given her own approach in business and the trend even in Castile, it seems likely that so long as the financial case pointed to the expediency of the new approach, Eleanor was untroubled by its implementation.[20]

For a few weeks, the party was doubtless exalted by the favourable crusading prospect which had opened. But almost at once it transpired that Pope Honorius had died before the oath was taken, and an agreement would have to be made with the new Pope – once he was eventually chosen.

Alongside the diplomatic circus and the crusading preparations, Eleanor was still maintaining her business interests. In May, she plainly had an emissary from her office at home, as on 17 May she acquired a fairly extensive package of properties in Devon, Hampshire, the Isle of Wight and Wiltshire. A few further properties in Buckinghamshire and Macclesfield were then added early in June, presumably before the return of the same emissary to England.

Yet still there was time for more personal issues. Poignantly, on 29 May 1287 we find Eleanor observing the anniversary of the death of her first daughter in the church of the Friars Preachers – and thereby providing the one record of that child's existence. This event provides a suitable point for asking whether Eleanor had any further pregnancies during the Gascon trip. Her age certainly doesn't make it impossible, and the fact that she had borne young Edward so recently might seem to suggest that more children might yet be expected. But the household records seem to negate such speculation. There are records of other childbeds being paid for by Eleanor; three members of her household gave birth during the final year of the trip. But no such records exist for Eleanor. It seems likely that Eleanor's increasingly frail health either precluded conception or had tipped her into the menopause. It is unlikely that the end of her childbearing years, after the bearing of some sixteen children and the loss of ten of them, was any great grief to Eleanor; there is a strong sense that (save as to the conception) this was the least congenial of her roles as queen. However, both she and Edward will have been concerned that the result was to leave the throne dependent on the health of the worryingly young Edward junior.[21]

While the major preoccupation for the Gascon stay was the question of Aragon, genuine Gascon issues of moment also demanded attention. One major topic was the charge of misconduct which was brought against Jean de Grailly, Edward's long-time trusted associate and co-campaigner in the Crusade of the 1270s, as seneschal of Gascony. A full commission, featuring the Bishop of Norwich, John de Vescy, Otho de Grandison and Robert Burnell, inquired minutely into the charges in late spring and early summer of 1287, and found them proved. De Grailly was ordered to make full restitution and to lose all his lands in Gascony.

Eleanor and Edward, though doubtless kept up to date by regular bulletins, were not present for this inquiry. They spent the early part of June at Blanquefort before moving towards Bayonne and then inland to Lucq de Béarn in the Pyrenees in early July.

During this period, Eleanor's ill health reappeared – there are again records of medicines for her being purchased in June and July 1287 – and, unusually, it appears that Edward was also ill in June, since electuaries and syrups were said to be for both king and queen. While it is tempting to translate the mention of syrups into modern terms and hypothesise a summer cold or flu, this is not a safe assumption. Syrups were the means of delivering any number of unpalatable medicines, just as they are now for children. Eleanor's illness appears to have been more serious and worrying, for in late June payments were made for two boys to hold vigil around *mensura* candles for the queen at the chapel of St Thomas in Bordeaux. It was therefore perhaps to tempt the elusive appetite of the invalid that one of her staff purchased a number of damson plums for her at this time.[22]

Meanwhile, the negotiations for a French–Aragonese peace were progressing, the chief sticking point being the release of Charles of Salerno. Following the return of John de Vescy in early June, preparations began to be made for a meeting at Oloron-Sainte-Marie in Béarn in July. The records of the household contain endless small details of the planning which went into the meeting – the transporting of furniture, the guiding of the royal party, the provision of supplies and so forth. Amusingly, and consistent with practice elsewhere, this involved a degree of planning for Eleanor's gardening interests; in readiness for her arrival, work was proceeding in June on a herbarium for her garden at Mauléon. This garden was presumably sited at the strong fortress which gives its name to the town, strategically placed on the road to Spain and dominating the valley of Soule, which Edward had bought from a reluctant Viscount of Soule back in 1261.

The meeting commenced in the middle of the month. Alphonso of Aragon and his party were given the local monastery for their lodging, while the English royal party roughed it in such other lodgings as the little town afforded. Ten days were spent in lavish hospitality – feasting, dancing and jousting all played a part, with gardens and vineyards being levelled for the games and melees. Edward even sourced a lion from somewhere (for what purpose history does not relate), and it escaped and killed a horse. Meanwhile, two of Alphonso's Saracen followers ran away.

To some extent, all this sweetening of the Aragonese paid off: on 25 July a treaty was signed which gave a three-year truce and provided for the release of Charles and his procuring of the recognition of Alphonso as King of Aragon by the King of France and the Pope. Despite the marriage link, and all Edward and Eleanor's work, there was little romance in Alphonso's approach. It can be seen from the terms of the treaty that he was playing rough about the return of Charles; the terms demanded the surrender, before his release, of two of Charles' sons (Louis, the future saint and Bishop of Toulouse, and Robert, the future King of Naples), the additional surrender of his eldest son, Charles Martel, within ten months, with the fifth son, Raymond Berengar, standing hostage for his brother in the interim. Provence was pledged against the securing of the necessary recognitions. Nor was this all. There were to be hostages in the form of sixty firstborn sons of the nobility of Provence. Charles was also to deposit securities to the value of 50,000 marks, of which 30,000 was to be in cash and the remainder provided by Edward. The marriage did creep into the terms: Edward was also to seek the consent of the next Pope to Eleonora's marriage to Alphonso, and the terms of the marriage contract were finally drawn up.[23]

The strength of Edward's desire to see the marriage brought about can be gauged by his agreement to these terms, in particular the hard-cash element, when he was himself as pressed for money as ever; mere fondness for Charles of Salerno is unlikely to have prompted Edward to such generosity. Quite why the treaty did not bear fruit is unclear; a number of reasons seem to have been in play, including Charles' difficulties in finding the requisite cash, Philip of France's vehement opposition to the pledge of Provence, and the eventual papal opposition once the new Pope Nicholas was installed in February of the next year. But as a result, in late 1287 or early 1288, the English mediators were back somewhere very close to square one.

Of course, this was all in the future when, in the wake of the treaty, the royal party left Oloron on 5 August. They then stayed at Mauléon (complete with herbarium) until 19 August. Local records suggest that this was a visit of considerable size and moment, marking the agreement of Eleanora's dowry, with carpenters and masons preceding the party by some weeks and making considerable improvements, before the royal suite, and finally the royal party themselves, arrived. During the stay there were a number of festivities – jousts, tourneys and banquets, plus a pilgrimage to the shrine of St Engrace. Gifts were given by Alphonso, including two superb Arab stallions for Edward; one may perhaps doubt whether Eleanor, that keen connoisseur of horseflesh, was overjoyed with her present – a mule.[24]

After the festivities were over, the party moved on to Sauveterre-de-Béarn and Dax in September, before visiting the Abbey of Saint-Sever for October. From here Eleanor despatched her knight Richard de Bures on her behalf to visit the shrine of Santiago de Compostela. It may well be supposed that he was charged to ask for the saint's intercession both in the matter of Eleanor's health and the continuing political crisis. Meanwhile, they king and queen continued to conduct the business of Gascony, receiving petitioners and issuing charters from the abbey.

A meeting of this sort, which probably was of little moment to Eleanor or Edward at the time, but which casts an interesting shadow over the future, also took place on 27 October; they received one Arnald de Gaveston, who had served Edward in the Welsh wars and was now seeking to establish his claims to his late wife's lands. The records do not say whether Arnald brought his son Piers, a boy of about the same age as young Edward of Caernarfon, to be presented to the king and queen. However, the close contact which Edward and Eleanor had with Arnald will have paved the way for this ill-fated addition to their son's household in due course.

In late 1287 Eleanor's health seems to have been more robust, since in November a further tour was made in the direction of Pau before returning to Uzeste and then to Blanquefort in December. It was in December, however, that signs re-appear of Eleanor's illness; she is then described as suffering from a 'double quartan fever'. This is a fever pattern where two days of fever symptoms are followed by one day of remission, in contrast to a traditional quartan fever, which would give a single day of fever with two days of remission, the fever recurring on the fourth day. Parsons suggests that this was probably malaria, which was not uncommon in France in the period, but in the light of the time of year and previous illnesses, this is by no means certain.[25]

Despite her distance from home and her ill health over winter, Eleanor was again reviewing her properties in England. In January she acquired a package of farmland in Norfolk. Sometime later in the year this was supplemented with the substantial acquisition of the Walerand lands, useful holdings over five counties for which she had already acquired complementary properties. And she had also, in November of the previous year, effectively enforced her claim against Hugh Despenser, taking his property at Bollington near Macclesfield.[26]

In spring 1288, with little to do while negotiations still dragged on, one can find what may be one of the most sentimental gestures which remain in the records of Edward and Eleanor's time together: according to most scholars, during this period Edward built Eleanor a bastide. The evidence for this is that in the early part of the year messages cease to be directed from Bordeaux and start to be directed 'Burgum Reginae' (in French Bourg La Reine); and there are certain entries in the household accounts which refer to the queen's bastide of Burgus Reginae. The problem is that no one knows where this is. Various suggestions have been dismissed. Trabut-Cussac's suggestion is that it probably denotes the hamlet known as La Bastide, in the commune of Labarde on the west bank, directly opposite the junction of the Garonne and the Dordogne. Yet there is no real material in its favour: nothing remains on this site to show whether a town ever lay here, and analysis of aerial photos and historical maps has proved completely undemonstrative. Generally, scholars have adopted his suggestion in default of a better one, since there is no lack of 'disappeared' bastides – Robert Burnell's 'Baa', for example.

It is, however, possible that there was no new bastide at all, and that this was a joke. There are three factors which suggest this as a possibility. The first is that there is no practically record of work on Burgus Reginae before the court is apparently settled there and doing business. The first mention of the town in despatches comes in March 1288; the first records of expenditure on building are only in January of the same year. It is hard to believe that even Edward and Eleanor, with a tolerance for building sites unusual in royalty, could have set their court down, practically in a field, and operated from there for months at a time, with the first building works going on around them. This is still more so in that Eleanor's health was, as we have seen, not as robust as it once had been, and there were plenty of more comfortable places within easy travelling distance of the speculative site of the town where the court could have based itself.

The second is the relative paucity of builders' bills for the town. If Edward was building a town from scratch, one would expect many references to expenditure within the household records – or even an assigned roll, as there was for some of the work in Wales. However, there are relatively few references to works at Burgus Reginae – and there is relatively little money heading in that direction. Indeed – and this is significant – there are about four or five times as many records of work at Bonnegarde en Chalosse, a town founded remotely by Edward in 1283 and on which further work was commenced in the period of the royal stay of 1286–9.

The third is a potential alternative location for Edward and Eleanor's stay: the town of Bourg-sur-Gironde or Bourg-sur-Mer, a strategic and ancient town fifteen miles north-east of Bordeaux, near the point of land formed by the junction with the River Garonne, possessed of a tidal harbour and the recent recipient of works on its fortifications which involved a bastide-like closing of the walls. This town's name would readily lend itself to the joke of Burgus Reginae (literally translated 'the town of the queen'), a reflection of the court's favourite spring venue in England of Quenington – now being missed for the second year in a row.

Bourg, which was visited by Edward and Eleanor on their first visit to Gascony in July 1255, is now partially subsumed in the sprawl of Bordeaux, but still exists, with some beautiful medieval stonework. Three factors other than its name suggest it as the place mentioned. First, there is one reference in the records during the 'Burgus Reginae' period to documents being issued at Bourg-sur-Gironde. Secondly, later materials establish that Burgus Reginae had a port, at least by 1301. Thirdly, there are references to Burgus Reginae sending wine to England, and Bourg-sur-Gironde has had a thriving wine trade almost since time immemorial. The evidence from the Gascon Rolls is ambivalent. There is a reference to sending wines to 'nove bastide Burgum Reginae', but at the same time the message refers to Pierre de la Roquetaillade – who was castellan of Bourg-sur-Gironde. Moreover, the absence of any other reference to Burgus Reginae in the Gascon Rolls, when there was plainly a considerable stay, is suggestive.[27]

The remainder of spring 1288 was spent in the vicinity of Bordeaux, with a few small visits nearby; but again the court returned to the city in time for the anniversary of the death of Anonyma, before moving off southwards in June via Dax and Bayonne back to Oloron, where most of July was spent.[28]

Eleanor continued to correspond regarding her properties throughout this period, and in June she acquired further lands: manors at Lockerly and Avon in Hampshire. However, the indications are that, despite this and despite the healthy location high in the Pyrenees (which now abounds in spa towns), Eleanor's health was deteriorating further. From early August we find her based in Asasp-Arros on the road to Urdos near the border, where she was again unwell – syrups and other medicines bought in Bayonne were brought to her by her doctor, Peter of Portugal. Significantly, while Edward went on to Urdos, arriving on 28 August, and thence to Jacca in Aragon, Eleanor is recorded from 30 August to late September in a place variously described as Montyor, Montoyar, Montyor, Mountinor. This location is mysterious. It could be, as Trabut-Cussac suggests, Montaner, just north of Tarbes, but in context such a significant move seems unlikely, particularly when we next find Eleanor with Edward at Oloron at the end of September. More likely, particularly given one reference in the household records is to 'Montan de Aspe', is that it is a small place on or near the road somewhere between Asasp-Arros and Oloron which has since ceased to exist.[29]

On 28 October 1288, the waiting finally came to an end; a replacement for the Treaty of Oloron-Sainte-Marie was signed at Canfranc in Aragon, just on the far side of the Gascon border. Edward certainly attended. Whether Eleanor accompanied him is unclear, but in the absence of any references to her elsewhere, and in the light of the fact that this was a major event, it is probably safe to infer that she did. Under this treaty, the Sicilian question was ignored and the bulk of the liabilities of Charles as to hostages and financial securities were to be discharged initially by Edward. Charles was put under an obligation to procure peace for Aragon with the Pope and the King of France within three years. Seventy-six hostages, including three of Charles's sons, numerous important Gascons (among them Gaston de Béarn and Arnald de Gaveston) and some leading lights of the English court (including Otho de Grandison and John de Vescy) were to be sent to Aragon as hostages. Edward was to provide 23,000 marks of silver at once and Gaston de Béarn was required to pledge most of his lands as security for the payment of the remaining 7,000 marks.

At Oloron in mid-October a grand cavalcade was formed up and marched down to the road towards and past Urdos and over the border to Canfranc, where they were received by Alphonso – doubtless with his own extensive retinue. In the days which followed, there was a series of meetings, at which the completed web of agreements, guarantees, counter-guarantees and payments were put into place. The money (in a variety of currencies, which cannot have helped matters) had to be counted and receipted. The locations and conditions of the hostages' custody were finalised and they bade farewell to any members of their families who had accompanied them.

Finally, however, the treaty and its subsidiary documents were completed – and this was sufficient to win the liberty of Charles of Salerno. He then returned with Edward and Eleanor and their much-diminished party to Oloron, where he executed subsidiary agreements (themselves guaranteed by an array of French and Italian nobles) to perform his obligations to the English Crown. Charles then left to return to Provence and make arrangements for the provision of the rest of his hostages, taking with him John de Vescy, who had been released early by Alphonso – very probably as a recognition of his personal work in bringing about the treaty.[30]

The next few months, awaiting the return of the hostages, were spent predominantly at the recently improved town of Bonnegarde on the border of Béarn. The hostages were much in Eleanor's mind – during this period she sent gifts of Brie and fruit to the families of the local lords who had stood hostage. In early February, a trip was taken to Lucq de Béarn near Oloron, where the court made offerings on the Feast of the Purification of the Blessed Virgin Mary, and the king and queen pressed on to Abos near the border, perhaps to meet with Aragonese representatives.

It was during this period, on 10 February 1289, that John de Vescy died at Montpelier. He was still only forty-four years old. The distressing news apparently reached the royal party – and his wife, who was in attendance on Eleanor – on 13 February, and immediate arrangements were made to send members of the household to bring back his bones to the royal party at Oloron to enable them to be taken home for burial in Alnwick Abbey. Arrangements were also made to send a priest to pray for him at the shrine of the Blessed Virgin of Rocamadour and to the monks at Oloron to say Masses for his soul. The urgency with which these steps were taken conveys something of the shock and distress which the loss of this closest of close friends must have had on Edward, Eleanor and the entire party. It was also, probably, that key point at which the first of their close contemporaries died, a point which inevitably brings intimations of mortality to those left behind. Edward, of course, was some years older than John de Vescy – approaching his fiftieth birthday. Eleanor, too, was older than de Vescy by a few years, and not in the best of health.[31]

To add bad to worse, Edward and Eleanor had to part very shortly after this, for a rare period apart. He was to press on to the border to meet the hostages. It seems to have been a mark of her own ill health that, on this occasion, Eleanor did not accompany Edward; presumably the journey through the high mountain passes in winter was considered inadvisable for her. The separation seems to have been a difficult time for the pair – one of their longest separations, coming on top of the news of John de Vescy's death and Eleanor's own protracted illness. Touchingly, the records show Edward sending Eleanor not just letters but also 'gingembras' while he was away. It is tempting to equate the latter with gingerbread, which was apparently first baked in France in the thirteenth century. However, gingembras is more likely a reference to preserved ginger, which was used as one of the more palatable medicines in the physicians' repertoire of the time. Whichever it was, however, it bespeaks a thoughtful concern for his absent wife.

On Eleanor's side, there is ample evidence of her missing her husband – letters to him are recorded as being sent repeatedly. But alongside this, she was plainly avid for news of the hostages – messengers were sent again and again for any rumours about the hostages, and both Edward and Robert Burnell sent her messengers back with the latest rumours they could find. Clearly Eleanor and the court around her were concerned lest more bad tidings were heading their way. And, as always, even with illness and concerns for the hostages, Eleanor continued to work: the wardrobe records contain evidence of her correspondence with her staff in England, and on 7 February 1289 she acquired a wardship of lands near Huntingdon.

Yet all was well. On 9 March, the English and Gascon hostages were released, being met at the Spanish border by Edward. And while Eleanor had held them firmly in her thoughts, it would appear that one of them, at least, Otho de Grandison, had likewise thought of her amusement while separated from her – he gave her the slightly troublesome present of a lion and a lynx, for which carriage, goat meat and a keeper had to be provided. They and their keeper, Jakemyn, were later to find their way to the Tower of London.[32]

The party could now begin to make plans for a return. Unsurprisingly, after three years and the various illnesses and losses that they had brought, there seems to have been no desire to stay. William of Hotham, who appears to have been attached to the royal party for a considerable portion of the stay and who had actually turned down the honour of a second regency at the University of Paris in favour of supporting Edward and Eleanor, reported to his friend Henry Eastry, Prior of Canterbury, that the king's stay 'in these parts has seemed too long to both him and his'. Given William's affiliation with the Dominicans, Eleanor's devoted support to their order, and his previous intimacy with the pair in Wales, it seems probable that he was reporting Eleanor's own feelings, related direct to him. It would hardly be surprising if she were keen to return home from this trip. While Edward had gained stature as a mediator, it had been at a near-ruinous financial cost; despite Charles of Salerno's best intentions, there is no record of his ever repaying the 30,000 marks paid on his behalf by Edward.[33]

The party spent April in Condom, where Eleanor, still in correspondence with her office, acquired another wardship in Kent. But judging by the wardrobe reports, which show payments to a Doctor Leopard 'when the queen was ill in this region', Eleanor was still not recovered. From Condom, the party began to break up, with Otho de Grandison and William of Hotham departing to negotiate with the Pope, Charles of Salerno and the leader of the Pope's forces. The main royal party moved back into the Dordogne, staying in St Emilion and Libourne before passing on to Saintes. At Libourne there are plenty of records of loose ends being tied up – the Gascon Rolls show tens of decisions by Edward being published in mid-June.

Among them is another evidence of Eleanor's own conduct of local business during the stay; Edward ratifies a peace which Eleanor (again 'our most beloved consort') had 'made and decreed' between two warring families, that of Amanieu de Fosse and William Raymond de Pinibus. The clear picture is that Eleanor herself was the person deputed to deal with the details of this, and authorised to effectively state terms agreeable to the Crown, with Edward ratifying the decision at a later date. Taken together with the earlier settlement negotiated by Eleanor and the absence of any remark as to these dealings, this suggests that during their Gascon stay there was a fairly active role for Eleanor in mid-level diplomatic issues, which was accepted by those around the royal couple and by petitioners. Again, as with the property transactions, Eleanor assumed an executive role in Edward's administration without fuss and without outcry; she acted independently, but was always perceived as acting for the king.[34]

The starting point for the return journey was to pay a short visit to Eleanor's cousin Viscountess Jeanne at Châtellherault, after which Eleanor sent her cousin a charming guest gift of scarlet cloth and some furs. After this, in July 1289, the party set off for home, on the way taking in a number of famous shrines and relics: the relics of St Leonard at Brou near Noyant, the tear of Christ at Vendome, Sancta Camisa (or tunic of the Blessed Virgin Mary) at Chartres, unnamed relics at the Abbey of Coulombs, the Crown of Thorns and a nail from the feet of Christ at St Denis, and the head of John the Baptist at Amiens. At many of these stops, offerings were made on behalf of the royal couple's children, proving that the family was much in their mind.[35]

While making this pious tour, however, the patience of Edward and Eleanor with the institution of the papacy must have been sorely tried; news came just at this point that the Pope had abrogated the Treaty of Canfranc, absolved Charles of Salerno of his vows under it, crowned Charles King of Sicily and renewed the excommunication of Alphonso. To add insult to injury, he had also granted to Charles, in aid of his Crusade against Aragon, the papal tenth which had been previously collected in aid of Edward's own proposed Crusade. All the efforts (and expense) of the past three years had apparently been for nothing. It is hardly surprising that Otho de Grandison, Edward's ambassador to the Pope, upbraided him in round terms, stating that his king was amazed that the Pope should have encouraged the dispute rather than making some effort to bring about peace. The diatribe had some results: the Pope agreed to send an envoy to try to bring about peace. But, for the present, Canfranc remained a dead letter and Eleanora's marriage no nearer.

The end of the month finally brought the party into Eleanor's own county of Ponthieu, where a stay of a couple of weeks was made between the capital city of Abbeville and the Cistercian abbey of Le Gard at Picquigny (between Abbeville and Amiens). Here, the affairs of her county were reviewed, a new seneschal appointed – and Eleanor acquired a new attendant in the form of her cousin Marie de Pécquigny, before moving to Boulogne. However, even with such a pleasant family addition, it can have been with little sense of satisfaction that the party finally left France from Wissant on 12 August.[36]

16

The Last Year, Death and Remembrance

When Eleanor arrived back in Dover on 12 August 1289, she had just over fifteen months to live.

She and Edward were greeted by their family, two of whom – Edward and Elizabeth – would hardly recall their parents after a three-year absence in their five- and six-year-old lives. The older girls, perhaps under the influence of their grandmother, had decked themselves out in brand-new cloth of gold dresses trimmed with green velvet. The next day, the family proceeded to Canterbury, where they were joined by a large assembly and sumptuous celebrations of their return were staged. During the course of the party which ensued, Edward sent to invite Archbishop Pecham to join in, but the archbishop refused because archiepiscopal ceremonial required that he be preceded by a procession and cross which, with the precedent of Henry II and Becket in mind, he felt might not be taken kindly. When Pecham's concerns were explained to Edward, he summoned a clerk and, tongue firmly in cheek, had drawn up and sent straight back a formal sealed proclamation permitting the pompous archbishop to have his cross borne before him in the presence of the king.

The general situation which confronted the returning royals was considerably less light-hearted. In the prolonged absence of the king, general lawlessness had increased, with armed gangs roaming the countryside. Nor were these malefactors all of lower castes – in 1288 the regent warned four earls about riding around the country and causing trouble. There were also considerable bodies of clergy, merchants and townspeople who considered that they were being hemmed in by government.

Edward's solution was to implement measures which indicated that the king was minded to deal with all forms of malfeasance. So, in October, he announced that there would be a general review of grievances. He then set in train an examination of the justices for corruption, which examination revealed considerable cause for concern, with many justices, including Chief Justice Thomas Weyland, being convicted and losing their jobs. There was, therefore, in late 1289 a perceived need to make sure that one's deputies were doing a good job and not acting unfairly.[1]

Eleanor thus faced a dual imperative on her return. The first was to make sure that her property business yielded as much as possible, given the Crown's desperate need for money. The second was to review the way in which her estates were being run, in the light of her long absence and the current climate of feeling regarding abuses.

The royal party's first stop was for a break of two weeks or so at Leeds Castle, where at least some time for pleasure was found: the party celebrated the marriage of Eleanor's cousin Marie de Pécquigny to Almeric de St Amand. But it should not be supposed that the stop was all leisure. The likelihood is that Leeds, as department centre for the Kentish properties, offered a good location for Eleanor to catch up with her local interests. That this was in her mind is put beyond doubt when one traces the royal party's next steps, which were to Rayleigh and Eastwood, both parts of Eleanor's dower assignment; and then to Nayland in Suffolk, another part of the dower assignment. On the way, she contrived to make stops through Essex near to all but one of the groups of properties which she held in that county. From Nayland the southern Suffolk properties could be inspected, and the next destination was Melford, convenient for the middle and western Suffolk lands, followed by Bury St Edmunds, close to both the northern Suffolk lands and the Cambridgeshire holdings.

At this point, however, rather than striking back to London, or making direct for Eleanor's Norfolk holdings, the party moved on (at no great pace) to Walsingham, home to the famous shrine. It is more than likely that the purpose of this visit was to seek intercession in relation to Eleanor's health. This inference is supported by the surprisingly long time taken on the Essex leg, with over a week spent at Rayleigh, and by the circumstances surrounding the next stage in the tour. This did indeed take the party to Eleanor's Norfolk properties, starting with Burgh, the administrative centre for that area; but after another unusually long stop of five days, we find two boatmen of Spalding being hired to row the king, queen and attendants from West Dereham in Norfolk to Ditton in Cambridgeshire, by way of the Isle of Ely. Green saw this as a medieval boating holiday. It seems more likely that the cause was Eleanor's increasing ill health. But naturally, it finished right in the middle of Eleanor's Cambridgeshire properties.[2]

Despite Eleanor's frailty, after a short stop in London the party was off again in mid-October, again via locations convenient for Eleanor's properties – but again at a rather slower pace than of yore, and with a long stop in early November at Clarendon. There, on 6 November 1289,

Edward of Caernarfon's fate was decided at a meeting with Norwegian and Scottish representatives: he would marry Margaret of Norway within twelve months. In late November, Eleanor made a visit to her sick friend Ermintrude de Sackville in Dorset. The court then headed back to Westminster for the Christmas period via Lyndhurst, part of Eleanor's New Forest property, and Odiham, part of Eleanor's dower assignment. Then, in the February of 1290, the court was off again for what was to be Eleanor's final stay at Quenington.[3]

It seems probable that by this stage Eleanor and those who surrounded her suspected that her illness was terminal. Her hunting expenses, until now regularly incurred, cease altogether in February 1290. She would appear to have been constantly taking medicines for some time – in April 1289 the queen's wardrobe provided Peter of Portugal, who was attending her, with a silver vessel 'wherein to place the queen's syrups', a phrase indicating that use of syrups was now habitual. Further, Peter of Portugal himself seems to have been brought back to England on the return from Gascony. By February 1290, a court goldsmith was making images in the queen's likeness for intercession when she was ill. Tellingly, too, Eleanor gave £100 to have a chapel prepared for the burial of her heart at the London Dominican priory and arranged for the purchase of stone for her tomb – steps which plainly intimate that she was considering that they might be needed in the near future. Parsons suggests credibly that the number of other donations to religious houses in the same year tell the same story: land given to the canons of Chatham to enlarge their garden in May, land and advowsons in Kent to Christ Church Canterbury in June, and two manors to Holy Trinity Canterbury in the same month.[4]

Interestingly, the *Liber Garderobe* lets slip these facts almost grudgingly. With hindsight, we can know that Eleanor was ill and had been so for some time. But there is no overt mention of her illness until almost the day of her death, only administrative arrangements for dealing with it and contingency planning for her death. This, together with her continued travels with the king, and still more her travels by reference to her properties, indicate that Eleanor refused to have a fuss made. She soldiered on.

Another indication that there was an awareness of her impending death can be read in the fact that not only were arrangements for young Edward's marriage being expedited, but two of the princesses were married in this period, after weddings had hung fire for some time. Joan's wedding to the Earl of Gloucester had been arranged in 1283, and by spring 1290 Joan was well over the customary age of marriage, being nearly eighteen. Similarly, Margaret's match with the heir to the Duke of Brabant had been in preparation since 1278, when Margaret was only three years old, and her groom had been resident in the kingdom for five years already in 1290 – notionally completing his education, but from the evidence of the wardrobe books, principally hunting and spending money.

There is therefore a sense that Eleanor wanted to see her children settled before she died and hurried on the marriages. This would explain the rather startling fact, remarked on by Green, that at Joan's wedding on 30 April 1290 Joan and her sisters did not have new dresses for the occasion – rather their dresses had required nine days of work in the mending.

Whether the weddings were at Eleanor's wish or not, the bustle and stress surrounding them was probably no great help to her health; and these weddings were certainly not without their stresses and strains. Joan, for example, in the run-up to her wedding took exception to the fact that she had fewer attendants than her older sister. While this was dealt with by the expedient of hiring in temporary staff, one can envisage the family scene which led up to this solution. Nor was this the only row which surrounded the weddings. After her wedding, Joan initially refused to stay at court for Margaret's, and retired to her husband's estates. Enraged at her decision, Edward and Eleanor took back seven dresses she was to have had from them, and decided to make them part of Margaret's trousseau instead. It would therefore appear that tempers were running high all round.[5]

After the Cotswolds spring stay the court was off again, this time into Worcestershire, to Eleanor's new acquisition of the forest of Feckenham (resigned to her by Eleanor of Provence in 1286 on her taking the veil) before a return in early April to Woodstock, where Edward of Caernarfon was then based.

After a ten-day stop here, there was time for a quick review of the Berkshire, Buckinghamshire and Wiltshire properties, before a stop at Amesbury, where Gilbert de Clare's pre-marriage oath to uphold the succession was taken. The location was probably chosen for a variety of reasons: the previous movements of the king and queen, a natural desire to see Eleanor of Provence prior to Joan's wedding and to pick Mary up for her visit to court for the wedding. At the same time, plans for Edward of Caernarfon's projected marriage to Margaret of Norway were being moved on, with Edward writing to Norway asking for Margaret to be sent to England without delay. Again, this reinforces the impression that Eleanor was keen to see her children settled as quickly as possible.

After Amesbury, there was no simple return to court. First, the Hampshire properties were taken in review via Winchester, where a celebration in honour of the various weddings was held. As usual, the return to Westminster was therefore rushed, with the royals arriving just two days before the wedding. Despite Joan's bridal nerves, the wedding seems to have been an enjoyable occasion. Although she was dressed in a second-hand dress, Edward and Eleanor gifted her with a 'magnificent zone [belt], all of gold with emeralds and rubies' and a matching headdress, sent for from France. While the wedding was private, the wedding party was held in a temporary hall lined throughout with cloth – perhaps a nod to Eleanor's taste, and an obvious precursor to modern faux silk-lined marquees – and one guest enjoyed himself so much he broke several tables (sadly history does not relate quite how).[6]

The family then appears to have been fixed in Westminster for some time. Part of this was due to the fact that, for most of May, Parliament was in session. In part this was due to the fact that it was during this period, on Ascension Day, 11 May 1290, that the translation of Henry III at Westminster took place, moving his body from his temporary grave in the old grave of Edward the Confessor to its current resting place alongside the Confessor's shrine. It was here that his descendants, and Eleanor, were to rest with him. It was reported that the king's body appeared intact, with a luxuriant beard. During this period, Eleanor seems to have attended yet another wedding – that of the daughter of the king's steward to John de la Mare.

The fact that the royal party then remained in London throughout the rest of May and most of June may indicate that Eleanor was again unwell. Certainly when they moved it was not far – only to Havering-atte-Bower, Brentwood and Thurrock in Essex – close to those of Eleanor's properties in Essex which had not been particularly convenient for the earlier Essex circuit. There is another resonance at Thurrock, however. It was the home of a family by the name of Torel – and it was William Torel who produced the image of Eleanor for the Westminster Abbey tomb. It thus seems quite likely that Eleanor, aware of impending death, was making her own arrangements for her memorials. Some further indication of ill health may be taken from the uncharacteristic length of time then spent at Havering. Usually Eleanor's stays were no more than a day or two; but the Havering stay was nearly two weeks. It also featured a further wedding, that of the Earl of Norfolk, Roger Bigod to Alix of Hainault, a member of a family closely associated with both the Brabant and Holland families. In relation to this wedding, Edward seems to have reached the end of his tolerance for company – he refused to attend the service and we find Eleanor, the amused and long-suffering wife, arranging for some minstrels to keep him happy, while the rest of the family did the polite thing and attended the service. It also appears from the wardrobe records that the marriage of Margaret was privately celebrated – and consummated – here on 2 July.[7]

In July came the formal wedding of Margaret, and once again Edward and Eleanor arrived at the last moment – reaching London the day before the wedding. This wedding was well covered by the chroniclers and seems to have been an altogether bigger affair than Joan's – with a distinct 'royal wedding' flavour. Again there was a zone and headdress of gold – in this case of pearls and rubies, with the royal leopards in sapphires. Another headdress, studded with 300 emeralds, formed part of her trousseau. Her sister Eleanora, attending her down the aisle, wore a costume decorated with 'fifty-three dozen' (in other words 636) silver buttons, which Green rightly points out sounds rather heavy. Edward of Caernarfon attended with eighty knights, while the Earl of Gloucester (possibly put up to this by Joan) was accompanied by 103 knights (but only six ladies). Edmund, Earl of Cornwall also limited himself to six ladies, but brought 100 knights. The groom, on the other hand, brought sixty ladies and only eight knights, and set a precedent for the more extravagant modern brides by changing his outfit three times in the course of the day. An additional 700 knights and ladies formed a mobile party, at first assisting the celebrations at the palace and then moving off to join the citizens partying in the streets. For those in the palace, there were plenty of fools and minstrels, harlequins, harpists, trumpeters and violinists. For the wider populace, there was a massive illumination for which it had taken four days to prepare the candles. Meanwhile, Edward again seems to have been on a somewhat short fuse, perhaps angry at the toll which the constant round of socialising was taking on Eleanor: at this wedding he is recorded as having struck and injured a squire.

After the wedding, Archbishop Pecham preached the cross and many nobles and bishops pledged to go, including Gloucester and Joan. Also taking the cross was Otho de Grandison, now nearing his sixties. He, as an experienced Crusader, diplomat and trusted friend, was to go as advance guard for the Crusade and make on-the-spot preparations. He would return only after Eleanor's death and the fall of Acre.[8]

The royal family remained in London for another two weeks. With the tail end of wedding celebrations, various political affairs and the presence of the Duke of Brabant, there would clearly have been a huge amount going on. In addition, the Avagour–de Vescy wedding was celebrated at this time, on 16 July 1290. And while we know from the records of Sandwich that Eleanor was continuing to work at her property business, her health was still giving concern – Edward of Caernarfon sent 'medicinal waters' to his mother. It may be partly because of concerns over Eleanor's health that Margaret and her new husband did not yet depart.

These weeks also saw the passing of the Edict of Expulsion of the Jews from England. This was hardly a surprising move, given the expulsion from Gascony in 1287, Edward's financial crisis and the fact that the compromise promoted by the Statute of Jewry had not paid off in financial terms for the Crown. At this point there was more to be gained from expelling the Jewish population, which would ease a grant of taxation from Parliament, than from keeping them. There is no sign that on this occasion Eleanor interceded for the Jewish people, with whom she had done so much business. As noted earlier, her relations with them had been based purely on economic considerations; if there was no economic case to be made, she was not the person to resist the tide. Moreover, as she made her preparations for death, it is more than likely that the advisability of aligning herself with Church teaching began to loom larger.

At the end of the month there was a week's stay at Eleanor's manor of Langley – the administrative centre for Eleanor's properties in Oxfordshire and Buckinghamshire as well as Hertfordshire and Essex. It may be that this visit doubled as a chance to see Edward of Caernarfon, whose favoured residence it was, although Edward's wardrobe books suggest that he returned to Woodstock; Elizabeth of Rhuddlan accompanied her parents as far as St Albans, where she, her father and her sisters Eleanora and Margaret all made offerings at the shrine and relics of the abbey church of St Albans.[9]

In the closing days of July, Eleanor's final journey commenced. Since this trip took in the Clipstone parliament of October to November 1290, it is tempting to say that the journey was made with this in mind. But it actually seems unlikely that Parliament had been summoned as early as this; summonses under Edward were usually no longer than about a month and a half in advance of the session. Further, the Clipstone parliament is unique in not taking place in a city. Clipstone was a hunting lodge in the middle of Sherwood Forest in Nottinghamshire, and was apparently ill adapted for holding a parliament, with attendees being lodged in every nearby abbey and great house and clerks being stationed as far afield as Warsop.[10]

It is therefore likely that the summoning of Parliament to Clipstone was an afterthought and the journey was commenced with some other purpose. A number of writers, puzzling over the Clipstone venue, have suggested that Edward was there on his way to harass the Scots – or that he was journeying north to meet Margaret of Norway. But harassing the Scots was off the menu given the impending marriage, and Margaret's arrival was not imminent. She was initially bound for the Norwegian territory of Orkney, before a formal entry into Scotland. Consequently, neither of the popular theories provides a satisfactory explanation.

But with our greater familiarity with the modus operandi of the court under Edward and Eleanor, and the locations of her properties as well as the stops along the way, one purpose is clear. The journey was one of Eleanor's property-monitoring trips, and was commenced at her instance. Thus, the party, including Eleanora and Margaret and her husband, set off immediately after the wedding for a review of her extensive properties in the North. The itinerary shows the usual ceaseless round of work: a trip to Ashridge in the middle of her southern Buckinghamshire properties during the Langley stay, then on to Leighton Buzzard, well placed for the northern Buckinghamshire and Bedfordshire properties, before a month spent around the properties in Northamptonshire, Nottinghamshire, Rutland, Derbyshire and Chester.

The itinerary also shows clearly that the tradition which had Eleanor lying ill for several weeks at Harby, where she later died, is completely wrong. The confusion is caused by the fact that there were two stops at two different places called Harby. Harby in Leicestershire was visited in September, en route between the Midlands properties and those in Derbyshire and Chester. Following the Clipstone parliament, Eleanor reached the other Harby in Nottinghamshire (on the border of Lincolnshire) only in late November.[11]

But by autumn, Eleanor was certainly ill. It may even be this factor which led to Parliament being summoned to Clipstone rather than London; Eleanor was simply too unwell to travel at anything like their usual speed, or to face a trip back to London and then another north to meet Margaret of Norway later on in the year. As early as the start of August, the party seem to have required a stop at Silverstone even to get as far as Northampton from Leighton – and they remained there some days.

By this stage, Edward and those used to travelling with Eleanor must have been becoming very concerned. This may well explain the rather peculiar passage in Edward's wardrobe records which show him making some thoroughly over-the-top donations – feeding of 300 poor men and additional alms to be distributed by John of Brabant – to make up for Margaret and her husband failing to attend Mass on 6 August at Silverstone. Things did not improve, however; the moderate eighteen-mile leg from Northampton to Geddington required a stop at Pytchley. The longer Rockingham-to-Nottingham leg now took three days and required stops at unfamiliar houses, including Newstead Abbey, without any apparent reason in the property portfolio. By 23 September, Eleanor's health had deteriorated to the extent that Peter of Portugal was sent for; but she still set off for a further excursion into her Derbyshire and Chester properties on about the same date, returning in mid-October for Parliament.[12]

During the course of the Clipstone parliament, news reached the royal party that Margaret of Norway, who had set off by boat a few weeks earlier, had died on her journey. This was a blow to Eleanor's hopes to see young Edward married. But Eleanor will doubtless have been interested to know that, with no clear successor to the Scottish throne, one of the main contenders, John Balliol, was not only a loyal supporter of Edward's family, his father having fought at the Battle of Lewes; he was also a lord of Ponthieu, his family hailing originally from Ballieul-en-Vimeu, near Abbeville. Indeed, he himself seems to have spent rather more time in Ponthieu than in Scotland.

Further medicines were purchased for Eleanor at Lincoln on 28 October. Joan appears to have been summoned to see her mother; she came north in November under the escort of her wayfarer Robert, with her expenses paid for by the king. This strongly suggests that those around Eleanor considered it likely she would never reach London again. So too does the fact that the younger children were summoned north – a plan which drew a protest from Eleanor of Provence, on account of the risk to the children's health. It was, however, proceeded with – Edward and Elizabeth are recorded at Clipstone in October.[13]

By the end of the parliament, the deterioration in Eleanor's health can be pretty clearly reckoned by the court's slow progress. Leaving Clipstone on 13 November to travel the fifteen to twenty miles to Lincoln – usually a short day's journey and, tellingly, a considerably shorter distance than some of those covered by her funeral procession, they made it as far as Laxton (roughly halfway) on the first day, and were obliged to stay there until 17 November. The desperation of the situation is made clear when one sees that they then proceeded only a couple of miles up the road to Marnham, a manor in the family of Eleanor's former chaplain Payn de Chaworth, where another two days were passed. Still the queen was working, sending a letter to the Bishop of Rochester, concerning a disputed advowson granted to her by the priory of Canterbury, in exchange for the Sandwich port revenues. While she worked, however, it would seem the household surrounding her were distraught – this letter was not recorded in her own records, surviving only in the Canterbury archives.

The royal party arrived at Harby on 20 November. It is highly unlikely that this was a planned stop – Harby is and was a tiny village and had never been part of Eleanor's round in this well-trodden area. It was only a few miles from Lincoln. The only permissible inference was that she was simply too ill to travel further. It was fortunate that Harby had a house in the ownership of a member of the de Weston family, local justice Sir Richard de Weston, a connection of John de Weston of the royal household.

On 23 November – probably Eleanor's forty-ninth birthday – a member of the household bought parchment for wardrobe accounts and letters, indicating that Eleanor intended to keep at her work. On 24 November comes the first open acknowledgement in the *Liber Garderobe* that the queen was ill ('at that time having become infirm'). A rider was sent to Lincoln to buy *urinalli*, which Parsons speculates was some sort of bowl for preparing medicines, but which more strongly suggests Eleanor was now too weak to leave her bed. The next day, another messenger was sent to London with all speed 'on account of the queen's illness'. A message was sent to Robert Tybetot, Edward's long-time friend and ally, the only one of Edward's close friends not at court who was available to be summoned. Then for four days the records are silent.

On Tuesday 28 November, another messenger was sent to buy *specia* – ingredients for medicines. It is not clear whether he arrived in time for the medicines to be made, but in any event it was to no avail. The *Liber* concludes its entries for 28 November with the words 'Decessus Regine' – the queen died. The timing at which Westminster Abbey later observed her death, on St Andrew's Eve, which ran from 6 p.m. on 28 November to 6 p.m. on 29 November, indicates that she died at some time after 6 p.m.[14]

Perhaps characteristically, some of Eleanor's last thoughts were with her work: 'After she had devoutly received the last rites she earnestly asked her lord the king, who was agreeing to her requests, that everything taken from anyone unjustly by her or her staff should be restored and damage repaired.' This was, of course, in keeping with the current political climate – in the summer of 1290, Eleanor of Provence had requested a similar inquest into the conduct of her officials. But it might also reflect questions raised by her recent journeys through her properties and the sense which she was bound to have, in the light of Archbishop Pecham's remonstrances, that theologically she was treading a very difficult line.

What is also clear from this account is that Edward was, as one might expect, fixed firmly at the side of the wife to whom he had been so devoted since their teens, listening to her every word and promising what relief it was in his power to offer. The circumstances of Eleanor's death mean that she will have had a chance to bid farewell to the close household which had surrounded her for years, and to her daughters. Almost certainly her friend Robert Burnell will also have been in attendance, and the proximity of Lincoln suggests strongly that her friends the earl and countess of Salisbury also were enabled to say their last goodbyes. Some reports also suggest that the local priest, William de Kelm, and the Bishop of Lincoln, Oliver Sutton, were at her deathbed also.

What killed Eleanor? At this distance of time we shall never know. Parsons, taking the view that she was gravely ill only from about 20 November, favours the theory that she died from an opportunistic infection or septicaemia, consequent on malaria contracted in Gascony. Most other commentators defer to his opinion, but in my own view the history of illness demonstrated by the records over a period of three to four years and the timing of the supposed 'malarial' infection in the cold Pyrenean December militate against this view. Another commentator suggests tuberculosis. However, this diagnosis rests on some unreliable assumptions.

Although the possibility of coronary or circulatory problems was dismissed by Parsons in his early work, he noted a significant point – that on her paternal side her father and grandfather had apparently suffered from such problems and that her own brother Alfonso may have done likewise. This medical history would certainly be regarded as a risk factor for heart disease today. It seems quite possible that some form of heart malady – even something as simple as coronary artery disease – could account for a fairly long period of reduced vitality, with intervals of illness requiring medical intervention, leading to a final complete breakdown of health over her final year.[15]

Eleanor's body was removed to Lincoln. By 2 December, her body had been eviscerated, embalmed and stuffed with barley, preparatory to a progress back to London which was unprecedented in English history and which has formed much of the myth of Eleanor which survives. The process of embalming was probably performed by the Lincoln Dominicans, who had their own water supply and were situated close to the North Gate of the city, through which a cortege from Harby could most safely access the city. The body would then have been carried to the cathedral to lie before the high altar, with priests keeping vigil. The ceremony observed probably reflected that when King John brought the body of St Hugh to Lincoln; the body was carried by his magnates to the porch of the cathedral, where it was received by the archbishop and bishops. Thence it was carried to the choir on the shoulders of priests.

For this, and for the procession south, Eleanor's body was not coffined but exposed, dressed in loose robes as for a coronation. She wore a crown and carried a sceptre, a parallel with the approach taken on the death of Henry II and probably Richard I, and also the approach taken more recently by the French in 1252 with her great-aunt Blanche of Castile, who was 'attired completely as a queen with a crown on her head' and carried in a litter of gold. This approach, according Eleanor honours previously bestowed on ruling kings and France's greatest and most powerful queen, surely reflect a tribute by Edward to her active role in assisting him, as well as of affection.

Eleanor's viscera were buried in the cathedral on 3 December. This meant that she ultimately received what is termed a 'triple' burial, with heart, viscera and body all in different places. This was the first recorded instance of such a burial in England, although double burials were plainly fashionable – examples were those of John de Vesci and Alphonso, both of whose hearts awaited Eleanor's at the house of the London Dominicans. Henry III had also received double burial, his heart being sent to the Abbey of Fontevrault. Further, there was a growing trend in the European monarchies for triple burials. After Louis of France was so divided after his death on Crusade, this approach was followed by his brother Charles of Anjou and one of his sons, Peter of Alençon. Interestingly, the practice, which was not conformable with the usual Spanish burial practices, was also adopted by Eleanor's brother Alfonso on his death in 1284. However, it appears likely that, although Eleanor's burial was to be an unprecedented event in English history, this triple burial was not specifically a part of the plan to provide a funeral of inimitable grandeur; rather, as with the other 'triple burial' in English history (that of Richard I), the inconvenient fact of dying far from the destined grave rendered separate burial of the viscera expedient, particularly if the plan for a prolonged procession was already in play.[16]

The next day, 4 December, a magnificent cortege departed. Eleanor's bier, on which the royally clad body was clearly visible, was accompanied by her chaplain, a cross propped on his saddle. Some distance behind rode Edward, giving primacy to the wife who had so loyally supported him. Accompanying him were the household (including presumably Eleanora and Margaret), the chancellor and 'numerous magnates'.

Unprecedented as it was, there is no full account of the procession in the chronicles. The timing and course of the journey is reconstructed from the evidence of the business of the court, which still went on at each stop. Thus we can see that halts were made by the bier as follows:

Monday 4 December: Grantham
Tuesday 5 December: Stamford
Weds–Thurs 6–7 December: Geddington
Friday 8 December: Hardingstone near Northampton
Saturday 9 December: Stony Stratford
Sunday 10: Woburn
Monday 11: Dunstable
Tuesday 12: St Albans
Wednesday 13: Waltham

The cortege arrived at the priory of the Holy Trinity Aldgate on 14 December before moving to St Pauls, convenient for the Dominicans' house at Blackfriars on 15 December. The final stop was at Charing on 16 December, leaving a short, final distance to Westminster. At each overnight stop, Burnell and the attendant nobles chose out a fitting place for the bier to rest and the place was sprinkled with holy water. These then became the sites of the memorial crosses.

Edward followed the procession until St Albans and probably proceeded direct via Watling Street (the modern A5) while the cortege passed across country to Waltham, entering through the city, thereby allowing his wife to be honoured in her own right throughout the city of London.[17]

It will be noted that most of the stops had a resonance with Eleanor's landholdings, past or present. Thus Lincoln was part of her 1275 dower and she had acquired houses there, whereas Stamford and Grantham had been part of the original dower and again she had properties in the vicinity of each. Dunstable, Geddington and Northampton were all places at which Eleanor had stayed while on tour examining her properties, actual or prospective; indeed, Geddington had been one of the first places the royal couple had stayed on return from Crusade, and had been visited in 1275 and 1279 as well as earlier in 1290. Stony Stratford was a couple of miles from her Haversham holdings – now held by one of her de la Plaunche relatives, who had married the heiress in May 1289. Woburn was the closest point on Watling Street to Eleanor's Bedfordshire

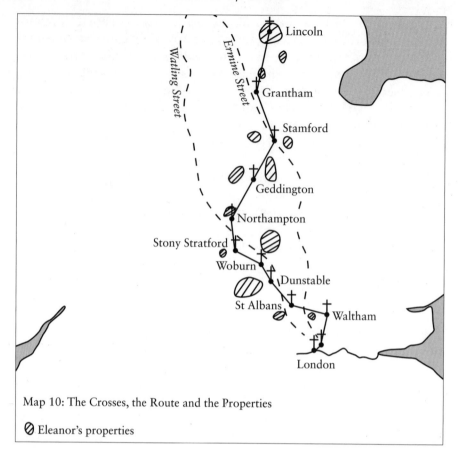

Map 10: The Crosses, the Route and the Properties

⊘ Eleanor's properties

landholdings, St Albans was close to Langley and Waltham was near to her property of Shenley.

It should not be thought that this coincidence of properties and stops was entirely fortuitous. The cortege started out, and finished, on Ermine Street (which approximates to the A1 in its northern reaches and to the A10 closer to London), entering London at its north-eastern corner. However, it moved from Ermine Street to Watling Street after the Stamford stop, and then looped back after St Albans. Given the detours involved in the two changes of route, there has to have been some good reason for this. Powrie suggests a variety of possible reasons, but her suggestions are not compelling. Yet when one looks at the route taken for the move to Watling Street, one likely reason becomes very apparent: that route, following the modern A43, enabled the cortege to process right through one of the most crowded areas of Eleanor's holdings, past most of her Northamptonshire holdings, and close to her property centre for the area at Market Harborough. After that, Watling Street would bring the cortege close to the Bedfordshire holdings and within reasonable distance of the most easterly of the Buckinghamshire properties. Following Ermine Street would, after Stamford, have exposed the cortege to relatively little of Eleanor's property – her Cambridgeshire properties were some way off Ermine Street, and her Norfolk and Suffolk properties still further away. Given Eleanor's devotion to her work, and the amount of time she and Edward had consequently spent in the area, the fact that the move to Watling Street enabled them to 'take in' the heart of Eleanor's property empire is surely no coincidence. Essentially, therefore, someone ensured that Eleanor progressed to London within sight of her own lands, and readily accessible for all her tenants and dependents on those lands to pay their last respects.

The Dunstable annalist, giving a first-hand account, recorded how precious cloths and a stunning eighty pounds of wax for candles were provided on the night when she rested there. He also describes how 'her bier lay in the centre of the market place until the king's chancellor and the nobles who were there with it chose a suitable place, for there to be built ... a wonderfully large cross; and our prior sprinkled holy water to bless the chosen place'. The St Albans witness, in turn, gives a sense of the grandeur of the event, with the entire abbey, dressed in their finest vestments, going to the edge of town to meet the bier and escort it to the abbey before a massive service and night-long vigil.[18]

Edward was not as prone to great pieces of showmanship as his father had been, but on this occasion it is clear that he had learnt the lessons of how to stage such an event well – and to use it with focus and subtlety. The act of returning the body to Westminster, and creating a lavish funeral there, continued the tradition which Henry III had begun of marking Westminster as a royal 'centre' akin to those of the French royal family at Sainte-Chapelle and the Castilian royal family at Las Huelgas, and hence elevating the status of his royal house both at home and abroad. The magnificent procession did not just honour Eleanor; it also inflated the importance of the entire royal family. At the same time, after a period which had been politically difficult for Edward, it marked him out as a focus for sympathy and support. Undoubtedly deep grief was there, but he had managed to pull off a truly excellent piece of political theatre in the midst of it.

Whether the plan of the memorial crosses had been reached at once is unclear; very probably it had, since the idea almost certainly came from the Montjoie memorials erected in France to mark the resting places of the body of King Louis on its return from the Crusade; a lavish procession would therefore fit with the creation of monuments in its wake, and by Dunstable, certainly, sites were being marked. Still more interesting is the question of whether the planning was all Edward's, or if it had been pre-concerted with Eleanor. The Torel meeting and her ordering of material for her own tomb-chest suggest that at least some planning had gone into Eleanor's funeral at her own behest. The Westminster tomb can therefore be inferred to be at least in part Eleanor's idea. There is nothing, however, which links her to the crosses, save to the extent that they took their styling in some measure from the main tomb. It is more probable that these, which do contain more touches of sentiment, were genuinely Edward's own idea, albeit inspired by ideas which he knew were important to Eleanor.

On Sunday 17 December, the queen's body was buried in Westminster Abbey. The funeral was conducted by Oliver Sutton, the Bishop of Lincoln, since Archbishop Pecham was ill. The event was so splendid that Walter of Coventry thought the like had not been seen in England since the coming of the Christian faith. It records that she was interred 'with royal vestments, crown and sceptre, dust on forehead and breast in the form of a cross, and a wax candle with certain writings'. In terms of position, it is interesting to note that Eleanor effectively usurped Eleanor of Provence's position opposite Henry III, possibly because the latter had decided that she wished to be buried at Amesbury's mother house of Fontevrault or because preparations had already begun on her grave and tomb, since her decease was naturally to be expected within a few years, and Eleanor's untimely death required the grave to be annexed.

On 19 December, Eleanor's heart was deposited at the Blackfriars church, together with those of John de Vescy and Alphonso. Once the ceremonies were over, Edward retreated until the end of January to the hermitage which Edmund of Cornwall had founded at Ashridge in Buckinghamshire. From here came his best-known tribute to his lost wife; writing to the Abbot of Cluny, he refers to the wife 'whom living we dearly cherished, and whom we cannot cease to love, now she is dead'. At Easter, three months later, her absence from his bed was still a powerful grief as he paid the traditional fine to her ladies, which in previous years had restored him to enjoyment of his conjugal rights after the loneliness of Lent.[19]

The tombs and memorial crosses were obviously some time in the making; each of them was a work of art in its own right, and together they may be seen as the highest flowering of arts under Edward's reign. The Westminster tomb survives gloriously to this day, and is widely regarded as one of the best medieval tombs. On top of the tomb an effigy of Eleanor reclines in gilt bronze, cast by William Torel in 1291. The use of the bronze image rather than the more orthodox marble was surely a nod to Capetian practices – Eleanor was given the treatment accorded only to their most glorious kings. Dressed in flowing robes, whose loose folds suggest luxury and softness even in their brazen form, one hand, which would once have held a sceptre, rests gently along her right flank while the left is raised over her chest, in a gesture which now suggests blessing but in fact reflects the fact that she is pulling gently at the cord of her mantle – in a similar way to the established fashion at Sainte-Chapelle, also depicted in the English context in *L'Estoire de Seint Aedward le Rei*.

Eleanor's head rests on two pillows, her hair flows free as for a coronation, and she wears a full circlet crown. This, the sceptre and the mantle would at the time have been gilded and borne paste jewels. Overall, the pose – and even the gable which surrounds her head – is very reminiscent of the pose in which she appears on her own seal. Her face is thoughtful, meditative even – no sign remains of the fiery personality which we know resided within the real woman. Parsons notes how the pose mingles the sacred and the secular, and could equally be a model for a statue of the Virgin Mary or the goddess Diana. But to the contemporary viewer, the secular message would have been very clear. The coronation references in the effigy – including the wearing of unadorned clothes, as was then considered appropriate to such a ceremony – would emphasise her status as a crowned queen and evoke the continuity of the monarchy. The tomb slab and the pillow beneath her head are carved with a patchwork effect of castles and lions, signifying Castile and Leòn and reminding the viewer of Eleanor's elevated birth and thus her status in her own right.

Interestingly, Eleanor did not disclaim the less elevated sides of her ancestry either. The sides of the tomb have an arch-and-gable motif and are richly carved with heraldic shields, suspended from foliage. These shields state Eleanor's full pedigree. So, while the arms of Castile and Leòn are there, so too are those of Ponthieu, flanked by the royal leopards of England; an acknowledgement of her mother's family and perhaps a sly nod to the families she had successfully seeded into England's highest aristocracy. But also, the combination of these three shields identifies Eleanor precisely: no one else was entitled to exactly these arms. Her tomb identifies her as a particular individual in unambiguous terms.

What is more, the message at the time would have been even clearer than it is now. Not only would the audience understand the arms, but they screamed out from the side of the tomb in Technicolor. The facsimile version of the viscera tomb at Lincoln Cathedral gives something of the effect which the painted shields would have had: the rich red and gold of the English shields, bold blue and gold diagonal stripes of Ponthieu and the martial black lions and gold castles of Castile and Leòn. But the Lincoln tomb is a slightly muted version; it has only four shields (two English coats of arms and one each of Castile and Leòn, and Ponthieu), where the London tomb has six, two of each. Again Eleanor's heritage and uniqueness is referenced by the Norman-French inscription around the tomb: 'Here lies Eleanor, sometime Queen of England, wife of King Edward son of King Henry, and daughter of the King of Spain and Countess of Ponthieu, on whose soul God in His pity have mercy. Amen.' In this mixture of the messages of majesty, spiritual power and domestic context, in death, as in life, Eleanor presented herself ambivalently.

On the ambulatory side of the Westminster tomb is a fine carved iron grille by Thomas of Leighton Buzzard, which shields Eleanor from prying eyes behind a screen which evokes a garden trellis with plants growing up it – possibly intended again as a personal reference to her tastes. Also on the ambulatory side is a painting (now hard to discern) which is thought to depict Otho de Grandison, arrayed in chain armour, praying for Eleanor in the Holy Land before the Virgin and Child. The floor of the ambulatory by the tomb was apparently set with tiles depicting the queen between St Edmund and St Thomas Becket.

Overall, the tomb appears to have been a groundbreaking work. While there was a precedent for a gabled, arcaded tomb chest embellished with coats of arms – that of Jeanne, Countess of Toulouse, at Gercy Abbey – that tomb appears to have been much simpler and to have involved a more formal praying effigy. There are also echoes of effigies of the French royal family at Sainte-Chapelle and at the abbey of Royaumont, but those tombs lack the surrounding detail and magnificence. The shield work best recalls the striking dual tomb of Alfonso VIII of Castile and Eleanor of England. But that, it seems nearly certain, was not in place at the time. Indeed, there is a powerful case to be made, inter alia by reference to such details as the form of the castles and the lions on that tomb, that it was not installed until around 1330, and that it was deliberately intended as an homage to Eleanor's tomb, using the prestige which she and Edward still had to add to the glamour of a venue which had fallen out of fashion. In fact, the repeated shield work may best be seen as referencing Castilian fashions, in a way which was unprecedented.

The tomb therefore captured the best and most up-to-date trends in royal burials and harmonised them into a major work which was to inspire other notable tombs for years, including that of Edward's brother Edmund, his first wife Aveline de Forz and Aymer de Valence, all at Westminster Abbey.[20]

The Lincoln tomb was apparently a replica of the London tomb, since two large images were ordered from William Torel. The tomb itself, of marble, was made by Dymenge de Leger and Alexander of Abingdon between 1291 and 1292. The tomb visible today is not the original, but a copy produced in 1891 and sited on the opposite side of the church from the location of the original.

The London heart tomb was rather different. The nature of the monument is unclear and has been considerably debated. It stood on the north side of the choir, in a chapel, possibly the lady chapel. It appears clear that it was a smaller monument than those at Lincoln or Westminster, more in the nature of a reliquary than a full tomb; though, given the amount of wax and metal ordered for the image, it was certainly not small. It featured three metal images made by William of Suffolk and a figure of an angel holding a representation of the queen's heart made by

Adam the Goldsmith. The heart tomb was surrounded by some decorated stonework by Alexander of Abingdon. It also had paintings by the same artist as provided the London tomb painting (William de Dunolmia). There was a crest carved by one William de Hoo above the tomb, and, in keeping with Eleanor's love of wall hangings, there was a cloth painted to hang above the queen's heart. Although parallels with Aymer de Valence's heart tomb at Winchester and that of Thibaut of Champagne at Provins have been suggested, it seems more likely that St Louis' lost heart tomb would have been the inspiration, or perhaps the viscera tomb of Isabelle of Aragon at Cosenza, which features three relief figures beneath a tracery arcade above an altar.[21]

As for the memorial crosses, which have come to be known as 'Eleanor crosses', their derivation from the St Louis Montjoies has been noted briefly above. The idea of a memorial cross was not unprecedented. In France, some memorial crosses had been erected along part of the route of Philip Augustus' funeral and Henry III raised one in Merton for the Earl of Surrey in 1240. Edward and Eleanor themselves had erected one at Reading in memory of his sister Beatrice. But these were simple crosses. The Montjoies, of which Eleanor and Edward may well have seen a sample on the 1286 trip, redefined the genre. Named after the traditional French war cry of Charlemagne, 'Montjoie!', they were elaborate structures with detailed sculptural decoration and included statues of the king – or, according to some theories, 'a' king.

The images were lodged beneath an ornate gable, on each of the road-facing sides. None survive today, and so we are reliant on seventeenth-century pictures of them for information as to how they looked. It appears that they were two-storey constructions, the base being a hexagonal gabled structure with statues in niches between the gables. The second storey was a rod, about the same height as the first storey, topped with a cross. The statues were in a variety of fairly standard postures, similar to those seen on tomb effigies. The king toyed with a glove, or held a sceptre, or raised his hand to the fastening of his cloak. Interestingly, some scholars have interpreted the memorials as being fairly unsubtle reminders of the power of the king – a point which would have resonance, given the law-and-order problems which faced Edward on his return from Gascony.[22]

The tributes erected in Eleanor's memory built on all these aspects. They are essentially bigger and better than the Montjoies, being three storeys high and tiered like a wedding cake. The base is solid, generally with a foliate cornice easing the transition to the open storey; the second layer is open, with statues of the queen bordered by pinnacles and again topped by a foliate gable; and the third (again arched and decorated) is solid, topped with a cross. As with the Montjoies, the focal points of the crosses are statues of Eleanor, in what at first blush appear to be somewhat formulaic positions – again evoking the coronation idiom, with flowing robes, unbound hair and circlet crown, and, in some images, sceptres.

However, a closer inspection of the detailed sketches made in 1791, when the statues were in better condition than they are today, indicates an interesting variety and hints of personality in the poses. In some, her mantle is clasped and her hands are by her sides; in another, echoing the tomb effigy, there are remains of a sceptre and one hand toys with the cord of her cape. In another, her robe is looped up on one side and she appears to be stepping forward, on the verge of speech. These details would probably have presented more clearly at the time with the new images, each of which would have been painted, than they do on the weathered versions which survive today. Furthermore, unlike the Montjoies, the crosses were larded with references to Eleanor as a person, separate from her role as queen. Her arms appeared again and again, including those of Castile, Leòn and Ponthieu. They are a celebration of a unique individual.

With Louis it is generally considered that the crosses were intended, at least in part, as part of a bid for sainthood – ultimately, of course, successful. The purpose of the Eleanor crosses is altogether more obscure. In the light of the Montjoies' existence, they cannot be taken simply as a tribute of love and grief on Edward's part. Some, therefore, see them as essentially an invocation of the dignity and prestige of kingship, without personal overtones. Others consider them as part of an attempt to rehabilitate Eleanor – that the quasi-religious imagery (for even sceptres carried Marian overtones) represents a bid to refashion her as the compliant intercessory queen she had not been, and to do away with her alleged unpopularity. From the distant perspective of the twenty-first century, this seems perfectly rational.

However, as discussed above, Eleanor was in fact by no means an unpopular queen. Further, this approach ignores the repeated personal references which would not have been lost on a contemporary audience – and the placing of the crosses, which were positioned in the heart of areas where Eleanor was best known. Overall, in the trouble taken to invoke the actual woman and her personal identity, one is entitled to see the crosses as a very personal tribute. Another factor which tends in this direction, largely unremarked to date, is the preponderance of roses in the decoration of the crosses. The Geddington cross's elaborate tracery is principally composed of roses, and at Waltham the arches containing the shields are surrounded by a background composed of roses. We know, too, that some of the other crosses featured roses, since this is one part which survived at Stamford. This decorative feature should not be taken as a mere standard filler, for such decoration was by no means common – indeed, the crosses' lavish use of miniature features was something entirely new. Nor was the rose as well associated with the English Crown as we, brought up on the Wars of the Roses and Tudor history, instinctively think. In fact, the rose as a royal symbol was new – it had first been adopted in the form of the golden rose by Edward I himself, perhaps based on his mother's badge, or on the papal golden rose. Thus, it seems plain that, while Edward may have been making some propaganda points along the way in the concept of the crosses, the tribute was very personal.[23]

Otherwise, the crosses showed an interesting variety. All were three-layered, and all the surviving crosses appear to be about forty feet tall, minus the cross which it is considered likely originally surmounted them – raising the tantalising possibility that, with the cross, each was forty-nine feet tall – echoing Eleanor's age at her death. However, all the three surviving crosses are subtly different in shape. The Geddington cross is most noticeably different and, aesthetically speaking, divides opinion. It is the most delicate of the three which survive and is, in its uniqueness, enigmatic. It has a hexagonal base but rises to be triangular and bears three images of Eleanor. It also features 'stone lacework', which it has been suggested may reference Moorish architecture, although there are echoes in the decoration of Westminster Abbey's choir, too. This decorative feature is richer than what is discernible on the other surviving crosses, or the illustrations of lost crosses. The images of the queen are generally considered inferior in quality to those of the other surviving crosses both in anatomical treatment and in the handling of the draperies. Each image of the queen (here wearing a headdress under her crown) is set in a gabled recess, but her feet appear to stand on a lace-decorated column which features a shield – in each case one out of England, Castile/Leòn and Ponthieu, reinforcing her descent. Above the second layer is a slender, spire-like storey with finials adorned with oak leaves and flowers. One particularly striking feature of the cross is that the narrowness of the base means that the statues cannot sit opposite the gable openings and so the statues hide behind a pillar of the gables, affording the viewer only a side-on glimpse. In purely aesthetic terms, this is probably a fault; but to anyone who has pursued the elusive Eleanor through the record, it seems remarkably apposite.

Some commentators have suggested that the Geddington cross is the work of a mason called 'Garcia of Spain' because of the differences to the other remaining crosses and surviving illustrations of Cheapside and Charing. However, the reference to Garcia of Spain in the records is to a cross 'given to the Queen' by John de Berewyk (one of her executors) and costing only 30 shillings. Such a cost could have nothing to do with the Geddington memorial, and this entry must sensibly refer to some smaller cross either given to Eleanor on her deathbed and buried with her or left on one of her tombs.

The other two remaining crosses are polygonal and resemble each other more closely. The Northampton cross is actually more properly called the Hardingstone cross, for it stands on a hill, some little way south of the town on the London road (the modern A508), just on the borders of what was then the village of Hardingstone. The site was apparently chosen because of its proximity to the abbey of De la Prie of St Mary's de Pratis, a Cluniac foundation of King Stephen, which held the church of Fotheringhay. It was in the chapel of this foundation that Eleanor's bier rested overnight.

The cross was originally perched on twelve steps, though now only ten are visible. It has an octagonal base supporting eight gables with lacework, in each of which a pair of shields appears. Beneath the shields on alternate faces is a stone book, which it has been suggested were painted or carved with prayers to be said for Eleanor, but again these also reference the real woman behind the tribute. The pinnacles and gables of the first layer are adorned with blind tracery and foliage. Above this layer the monument steps in, and becomes four sided, with another set of fancy gables with finials and foliage protecting recesses, in each of which a statue of Eleanor appears. The images (one of which has a headdress, like the Geddington images) are to some eyes inferior to the Waltham images, but time and restoration have to be considered here, and certainly both sets of images were made by key workers in royal employ – William of Ireland in Northampton and Alexander of Abingdon in Waltham. The third layer is a square layer, somewhat lower than the Geddington third layer, with Gothic arches. The top, originally bearing a large cross, which will have seemed to float above the monument, is lost.[24]

The Waltham cross is effectively the first of the London crosses. Although it survived the Civil War, it has not passed through the centuries unscathed. The antiquarian and Eleanor cross expert Revd Dr William Stukeley, writing to the Earl of Oxford in 1728, stated that 'Waltham is pretty perfect, but this last summer Mrs Robinson has rebuilt part of her house and encroached upon the road and broke down a good deal of the cross to make way for her roof'. Another reporter, Gough, writing in 1796, says that the pub 'the Four Swans' (later the Falcon) has built almost into the cross, 'whereby much of its beauty is concealed and many of its ornaments disfigured.' Stukeley also reports a good deal of damage from carriages running against the cross, which can be seen fairly clearly in numerous eighteenth- and nineteenth-century prints and sketches (including some by J. M. W. Turner). Two restorations consequently took place in the nineteenth century.

One cannot, therefore, be very confident about the extent to which the remains actually reflect the original cross. However, overall it appears to be a somewhat scaled-up version of the Hardingstone cross. It is reputed to have boasted six images, but, while this is consistent with the shape of the second layer, the arrangement of the arches in that layer appears to make this unlikely; and certainly the _Vetusta Monumenta_ survey shows only three. Thus the cross commences with a hexagonal base, with gables ornamented with rosettes and heraldry, a foliate cornice and battlements, and on the second storey a hexagonal layer of hollow gables fitted with images of the queen in one face followed by a double gable supported by a pillar in the next face. There is then a smaller, hexagonal top layer with another round of arch-and-gable carving and a mini-parapet, above which a cross, which may or may not have resembled the one which now sits there, would have sat. Caen stone was bought for the images on this and the Charing cross.

As for the images, there certainly seems to be something to recommend the view that they are the finest of the survivals. The version which has Eleanor grasping the cord of her cape bears a striking resemblance to the tomb effigy. Meanwhile, the one with the looped-up draperies seems both on the point of movement and of speech – the most lifelike of the entire lot, and a strong argument against the theory that no portraiture was intended in the representations. That Alexander was also deemed the more accomplished workman to thirteenth-century sensibilities is implied by the fact that he was the person commissioned to make the ornaments for the final, most upmarket, cross at Charing.[25]

As for the lost crosses, a certain amount can be inferred from the surviving evidence. The Lincoln cross, which probably stood outside Wigford by St Catherine's Priory, utilised rods, rings and hoods, and also statues of the queen made by William 'Imaginator'. The Grantham cross does not figure in the accounts and no part of it is known to survive to the present day. All that we do know is that it featured heraldry, since Stukeley refers to having 'one of the lions' – presumably from the arms of Castile – in his garden.

The Stamford cross, which the more reliable witnesses place on the Casterton Road on the way out of Stamford towards Geddington, had (depending on which account you prefer) a hexagonal or octagonal base thirteen feet long, with steps of 'squared Barnack stone'. Again heraldry was a major feature. Captain Richard Symonds in 1645 and Richard Butcher in 1646 refer to shields, and Symonds describes the arms of England, Ponthieu and Castile and Leòn carved repeatedly – presumably on each face of the cross. It was topped with a piece described and drawn by Stukeley as being pyramidal and carved with roses. As to its details, the Stamford cross was considered 'not very splendid' by Camden. It may be that the lack of splendour reflects that it was on the more simple Geddington pattern – and the surviving sketch by Stukeley, though very rough, tends to support this theory. But it may equally reflect a comparison with the London crosses, or the state of its repair when Camden viewed it.

Stony Stratford was built by the same builder as the Hardingstone cross and obviously featured images of Eleanor, but has otherwise disappeared. Of the Woburn cross no trace or description remains, but given that it was made by the same builder as the other Watling Street crosses, it is likely to have been stylistically consistent. The Dunstable cross, also from the same stable, is described as 'having engraven on it arms of England, Castile and Ponthieu and adorned with statues'. Likewise, the St Albans cross (the original long lost – the cross in existence is a modern copy) was made by the same builder, who supplied the rings, rods and hoods which indicate the presence of statues. Overall, therefore, it seems clear that all the crosses shared the theme of repeated statues of Eleanor, and repeated iterations of her arms.[26]

As for the lost London crosses, the first of these was the cross known as 'the Cheapside cross', which stood outside St Peter's, Cheapside, opposite the entrance to Wood Street. It appears to have been made under the direction of one man, Master Michael of Canterbury. Over the period early 1291 to late 1292, he charged £226 13s 4d for this cross – nearly twice the traceable cost of the Waltham cross. Other than that Walter of Guisborough considered the cross (and that at Charing) to be 'most beautiful' and described them as being made of marble, very little clue remains as to what the Cheapside cross looked like. If its shape remained consistent after its first renovation it would seem likely to have been hexagonal, but an octagonal shape has also been suggested. However, consistent with the theme thus far, the fragments which remain in the Museum of London bear Eleanor's arms – the shields of England and Castile quartered with those of Leòn, apparently displayed in gables as were those in Northampton and Waltham.

The final cross, at Charing, is perhaps appropriately controversial. The first point to make is that, contrary to popular tradition and a sense of romantic fitness, Charing was not so called after Eleanor as *chère reine*. Charing had existed for some time before Eleanor's bier rested there. Its name probably derives from the Saxon *cierre*, which means to turn, as it fronted on to a bend in the River Thames. There is, consistent with this, another 'Charing' at a bend in the Pilgrim's Way to Canterbury. The second point to note is that the cross did not stand where the modern version stands, but where the equestrian statue of Charles I is located, on the south side of Trafalgar Square. One may ask why a cross was needed here, so close to Westminster. The answer again emphasises the very personal element in the tribute: Charing was the site of Eleanor's beloved royal mews, which she had beautified with a remarkable fountain in the Spanish style and where she will have spent many happy times with the like-minded Edward.

This cross, made under the supervision of Richard and then Roger of Crundale, seems to have taken an implausibly long time to create, with the payments preceding and outlasting the payments for all the other crosses – indeed, Eleanor's executors accounts are liberally littered with entries simply entitled 'Charing'. The total construction cost exceeded

£700, of which the majority was labour cost. It was said to be constructed of marble, and certainly some payments for Purbeck marble can be identified, but was probably actually constructed in part at least of Caen stone, polished to look like marble and only part faced with marble. The cross is reputed to have been based on an octagonal design with eight images of the queen, though the later sketches of it which survive suggest six as the more likely number.

One possibility, which does not seem to have been much canvassed to date, is that the crosses formed a progression, with the simplest at the start of the journey, and the most ornate nearest her grave. On this hypothesis it may be that the 'puzzling' Geddington memorial is actually the last in a lost set running from Lincoln to Geddington and that Lincoln, Grantham and Stamford were also all hexagonal with three images, like Geddington. This would be consistent with one description of the top part of the Stamford cross as being 'pyramidal', and with the substantial absence of any records of the construction of all these crosses from the surviving records. The fact that the Charing cross is reported to have been the most magnificent of the series would be consistent with this, as would the fact that Waltham cross, which effectively bridges the move from country to town, is considerably more ornate than either of the preceding surviving crosses (though possessing one fewer image than Hardingstone).[27]

Most of the crosses were worked on by the same teams, with pedigrees on royal sites. So John of Battle, a mason and undermaster at Vale Royal, worked on the Hardingstone and St Albans crosses, including lifting into place the images of the queen, and also worked on the crosses of Stony Stratford and Dunstable. The images of the queen for the later crosses were mass produced by Alexander of Abingdon (also known as 'the image maker') and William of Ireland, at a cost of £3 6s 8d each. Both of these artists have been identified as working at Westminster. Meanwhile, Dymenge de Leger and Roger Crundale, who worked also at Westminster and the Tower, worked on Waltham cross before being transferred to work on the Lincoln tomb. Work appears to have commenced in 1291 and to have been substantially completed by 1293. There is no conclusive evidence for the process by which the designs were arrived at, but there seems reason to suppose that an overall plan of the shape of each cross and its significance in the procession were agreed, as were authorised types of pose for images of the queen. The workmen for each cross were then given a limited amount of scope in which to express their artistic instincts and produce a cross which was coherent with the plan, but at the same time unique.[28]

However, while the crosses are indubitably glorious, perhaps the depth of Edward's mourning may be best judged not in those politically charged memorials but in his ongoing commemoration of Eleanor. For the first year after her death, he made a special distribution of alms each Tuesday to as many as might approach him. There seems to have been a wide understanding that Edward encouraged commemorations of the queen: less than six months after her death, the Archbishop of York reported that over 47,000 Masses had already been said for her and a forty-day exemption from penance had already been granted there for anyone who said the paternoster and Ave Maria for the queen. A similar indulgence was granted at Lincoln in 1291.

On the first anniversary of her death, there were very glorious memorial services in both the abbey and the London Dominican priory. Each featured a special Mass and an elaborate hearse, and in total 3,000 pounds of wax was used for candles. So elaborate were these memorials that the clergy were reported to be exhausted by the ritual. The memorial service seems to have been a national talking point, being picked up by almost all of the annalists. Judging by one of the later celebrations, the abbey would have been ablaze with light, with each member of the congregation holding a candle, large candles round Eleanor's tomb and smaller ones round those of Henry III and the Confessor, and a framework constructed above the shrine on which candles were placed at regular intervals. At the same time, services were held at the manors which were the hubs of Eleanor's estates: Market Harborough, Burgh, Somerton, Lyndhurst, Leeds, Langley and Haverfordwest.

Thereafter, Edward endowed a yearly observance at Westminster for Eleanor's soul, granting the abbey seven of Eleanor's properties to fund the service. The extent of the grant itself shows how magnificent the remembrance was to be, but the terms of the grant, which survives, make matters even clearer. Eleanor's tomb was to be surrounded by thirty large candles at all times. All were to be lit on great feasts, and two were to be kept burning at all times. Every Monday, the eve of the day on which she died, the entire convent was to gather in the abbey and sing Placebo and Dirige with nine lessons and a tolling of bells. On the Tuesday, the convent would celebrate Mass with the tolling of bells, and 140 paupers (or such lesser number as appeared) were to receive a silver penny – but each was to recite the paternoster, credo and Ave Maria before and after receiving the coin, for Eleanor's soul. It is interesting to note that, by this provision, two of Eleanor's own interests, the recitation of prayers and alms for the poorest in society, were thoughtfully combined.

As for the annual memorial, it began on the vigil of St Andrew, and one hundred candles, each weighing twelve pounds, were to be lit. The weight of the candles was calculated to allow them to burn without interruption from that time until after High Mass the next day. Bells were to be rung incessantly throughout this period and divine office chanted hourly with Placebo, Dirige and nine lessons. At the end of the commemoration, alms were to be given to the poor, the mendicant friars and the London hospitals. To ensure proper observance of all the details, the entire letter patent was to be read out annually in chapter and all the goods of the abbot, prior and convent of Westminster were pledged to compliance. It would appear that this was complied with until the Dissolution: in around 1500, a visitor to the abbey was told that candles had never ceased to burn on Eleanor's tomb since her burial there.[29]

In addition to all these more ceremonial and politically resonant memorials, Edward also endowed a chantry chapel in the church at Harby. Lands were made over to Lincoln Cathedral to provide 10 marks paid annually to a chantry priest to pray for Eleanor's soul. Edward also founded chantries at Maidenheath, the London Dominicans priory and at Leeds Castle. Nor did he rely on these donations to keep Eleanor in mind: in 1300, when in York, he specially arranged with the sacristan of York for the ringing of a knell on the anniversary of her death.

And Edward was not alone in remembering Eleanor; it was apparent to all that the commemoration of Eleanor was likely to be well received by the king, and thus from 1291 we find records of other people endowing chantries or chaplains in her memory. A move to Peterborough by one of Edward's clerks was granted on condition that two chaplains celebrated Mass daily forever for her soul. Three celebrated her anniversary in the controversial manor of Southorpe, and two hundred paupers were fed. Henry Sampson, who had sold Eleanor another rather controversial piece of land in Rutland in 1285, endowed a chapel there for her soul and that of his parents.

Less seemingly charged dedications followed: St Albans founded a yearly service in 1294 and the Archbishop of York provided a chaplain for the Harby chantry. In the same year, William and Juliana de Copstone arranged for a celebration at the altar of St Edward the Confessor in Coventry Cathedral. In 1305, Edward II asked the Abbot of St Albans to take in John le Parker, a servant of Eleanor's from her manor of Langley, who wished to spend his last days in prayer for the queen's soul. A chantry was founded by the Friars of the Sack in London in 1305 for the king and both his queens and their children, and in 1315 a chaplain was provided for at Lincoln Cathedral to pray for Edward II, his family and his parents. There is also some evidence of alienations of land by religious houses to support chantries in honour of Eleanor as late as 1323. Finally, and rather touchingly, the William Somerfeld for whom one of Eleanor's earliest acts of patronage took place as far back as 1269 gave several vestments to St Paul's, London, in her memory; and Alice Wisman, Eleanor's laundress, petitioned Edward to be allowed to give fifty-two acres of land in Elm to a chaplain to chant for Eleanor's soul.[30]

Eleanor, then, was not just mourned by her nearest and dearest – she was also remembered fondly among those who had known her across the spectrum of society.

17

Afterlives

Actual memory of Eleanor died in the 1340s, over fifty years after her death. By then, Edward too was long dead: he lived on until 1307. Still celebrated as England's greatest medieval monarch, Eleanor's death is seen as a turning point in his reign by many scholars. It was, of course, after 1290 that the issue of Scotland, which was to occupy so much of his time, came to the fore. So too did new problems with France, whose young monarch, Philip IV, bitterly resented the fact that Edward was seen as a greater statesman and knight than he was. The combination of these troubles was essentially to force Edward into his second marriage, to Philip of France's sister Margaret in 1299; proof, if proof were needed, of his devotion to Eleanor, particularly when the succession hung only on the life of young Edward of Caernarfon.

Aside from these major political issues, some have seen in Edward's latter reign a loss of the deftness of political touch which marked the years before Eleanor's death and, given the closeness between the two throughout their marriage, it is hardly too much to see a causative relationship there. The advice of Eleanor, for so long an integral part of Edward's inner circle, was bound to be felt. In her, more, perhaps, than any of his other advisers, was the voice he knew he could trust – and hers was also the one voice he could not escape. Morris suggests that it is hard to imagine the disastrous 1294 treaty with France – which was negotiated by Edmund of Lancaster, his wife Blanche and her daughter the French queen and resulted in the forfeiture of Gascony to the French Crown – being allowed to proceed if Robert Burnell had been there to stop it. Equally, it is hard to imagine that Eleanor, so exigent in relation to her own administration, would have contemplated a situation where such a treaty was agreed – or even where such a diplomatic team was put forward.

But Edward was gradually deprived of many of his key advisers in this period, and it would be wrong to say that it was Eleanor's loss alone which caused the change of approach. Since their early years together, Edward and Eleanor had been surrounded by three other key players: Robert Burnell and, when diplomatic duties allowed, John de Vescy and Otho de Grandison. Interestingly, the latter had in fact been sent to help Edmund of Lancaster on the previous occasion when he had been entrusted with solo diplomatic work – and found it too much for his abilities. John de Vescy, of course, had died in Gascony. Otho de Grandison was to head off to the Holy Land to make preparations for the Crusade and was not to return for six years. Robert Burnell in turn died in 1292. Edward was, therefore, left very much alone within a short period of Eleanor's death, and deprived of most of the wise voices who had earned the right to influence him.[1]

There was some consolation to be found in his family. While Eleanor of Provence outlived her daughter-in-law by only a few months, dying in autumn 1291, Edward continued to have the company of a number of his daughters. The unfortunate Eleanora was not long among them. She was never united with her notional husband, Alphonso of Aragon. He died in mid-1291, and in 1293 she married Henry, Comte de Bar, to whom she gave two children before her death in 1297, thereby creating the line which would in due course produce Elizabeth Woodville. She is often credited with a daughter, Eleanor, who was claimed as an ancestor by the Tudor dynasty to thicken their royal blood; sadly, she is entirely mythical.

Joan, of course, was settled in England with Gilbert of Gloucester, though spending much of her time in Gloucester's Marcher lands. She gave birth to her first child, Gilbert, the future earl of Gloucester and Hertford, the May after Eleanor's death. In the short years before her widowhood in 1295 she also produced three daughters: Eleanor (later Lady Despenser) Margaret (later Lady Gaveston) and Elizabeth (later Countess de Burgh). Edward's affection for her and them can be seen in some lavish grants of land to Joan, and arrangements for the children. Characteristically, and one might suggest showing her true descent from the Ponthevin countesses, Joan succeeded in scandalising society by her secret second marriage to the handsome young squire Ralph de Monthermer in 1297. Thereafter, although she succeeded in reconciling Edward to the match, assisted by Monthermer's very solid abilities, she kept prudently close to him. This was an expensive proximity for Edward, because, although richly dowered, she seems forever to have been in need of loans from her father. She predeceased Edward by a few months.

Mary, too, despite her conventual vows, managed to be frequently at court throughout her father's life. As with Joan, she appears to have possessed a talent for spending money and a taste for gambling – generally paid for by her father. The scandal of her alleged affair with Earl Warenne was, thankfully, not to arise until after Edward's death.

Elizabeth, only eight years old on her mother's death, was reputedly her father's favourite and was so attached to him that, after her first marriage in 1297 to the Count of Holland, she refused to accompany him to the Netherlands for some time – despite written pleas from her husband to her father. In the circumstances, her husband's early death in 1299 (fairly shortly after she was finally prevailed on to take up residence with him) provided her with a welcome opportunity to return to England, which she quickly took. In 1302 she married Humphrey de Bohun, the Earl of Hereford, her cousin through the marriage of Mathilde de Fiennes. She bore him ten children, dying aged thirty-four in 1316 while bringing the tenth into the world. Her granddaughter Mary married Henry of Bolingbroke, later Henry IV.[2]

Otho de Grandison's story still had forty years to run at the time of Eleanor's death, but he spent little of that time in England. He led the English forces in Acre at the time of the fall of that city in 1291, and saved the life of Jean de Grailly. After making a pilgrimage to Jerusalem, he returned to England briefly in 1296–7 and was present with Edward at the Battle of Dunbar. Thereafter, he campaigned with the Templars and the Hospitallers before returning for the final years of Edward's reign. He left England after the accession of Edward II, but continued to do some diplomatic work for the Crown. Towards the end of his life he finally settled in his ancestral lands of Grandson, where he died in 1328.[3]

Enrique of Castile was finally released from prison by Charles of Salerno in 1291 – one would like to think in recognition of the kindness shown him by Eleanor and Edward. Ironically, he did in fact come to exercise power in Castile, some fifty years after he had first challenged Alfonso. In the turbulent minority of King Ferdinand IV, Enrique became regent along with the king's mother, until his own death in 1204.[4]

The longest survivors among those who had known Eleanor well were among Eleanor's ladies. Eleanor's faithful waiting woman Margerie de Haustede was one of the last to die, in 1338, outliving her own sons. She herself was outlived by one of the younger ladies-in-waiting, Clemence de Vescy, who died in 1343.

From this point Eleanor's story entered the territory of mythmaking – with some surprising results.

The first and most important influence on Eleanor's post-mortem reputation must be the funeral commemorations. The means by which Edward commemorated her inevitably focussed attention on Eleanor the Queen, standing alone, in a way which she had resolutely avoided in life. And those tombs and monuments are beautiful, gracious items of artistic endeavour, embellished with elegant figures which are almost interchangeable with representations of the Virgin Mary. There are, to the knowledgeable, a number of features which invoke Eleanor's temporal power and suggest a more assertive person; but to the majority of the viewers the picture is clear – a gentle and gracious lady. This impression is even more likely to communicate itself to anyone viewing a cross or a tomb only in passing, and to later viewers to whom the artistic references of the time are lost. The funerary monuments therefore offer a massive piece of disinformation echoing down the centuries.

Nor was there a contemporaneous verdict of the chroniclers to pass down with the more solid memorials. Aside from the throwaway characterisations which have been mentioned earlier, there is silence on Eleanor's character until Matthew Paris' successor in the *St Albans Chronicle*. This work, known as the *Opus Chronicorum*, is dated to 1308; that is, eighteen years after Eleanor's death – and during the reign of the son who quartered Eleanor's Castilian arms with his own. Its tone as regards Eleanor is adulatory, describing her as surpassing 'all women of that time in wisdom, prudence and beauty; indeed except that it would appear to be flattery I would say that she was not unequal to a Sybil in wisdom'. Assessing her in connection with the account of her death, he goes on to say that 'her passing was tearfully mourned by not a few. For she was a pillar of all England, by sex a woman, but in spirit and virtue more like a man ... As the dawn scatters the shadows of the darkness, so by the promotion of this most holy woman and queen, throughout England the night of faithlessness was expelled ... of anger and discord cast out.'

Parsons considers the account to be astonishingly positive – to the point of rewriting the record. So far as the tone is concerned, this may be true. But the account of Eleanor of Provence is equally cloyingly approving, and there was now no call to reinvent Eleanor of Provence, whose retreat to a convent for the last five years of her life had already whitewashed her reputation. The tone is likely simply to be one adopted to gain the approval of the new young king by referring to his family with unqualified approval. But the substance which lurks under the thick veneer of flattery is not without interest. Firstly, consider what is not said. It is not said that Eleanor was a gentle, pacific queen, a reconciler of arguments and a stayer of her husband's hand – the queen Pecham urged her to be. Secondly, there is interest in what is positively chosen to be said. Three points are made. First, she was wise. Here, we may see some knowledge and recognition of Eleanor's intellectual attainments. Secondly, she was more like a man in 'spirit and virtue' than a woman. Here, we see a tactful allusion to both her active role in business, her implacable tendencies and her rejection of a traditional feminine intercessory role as queen. Thirdly, her role in religious foundations (and possibly also her wider encouragement of prayer chanting) is acknowledged, as it was not at the time of her death. In essence, therefore, the author, while sugar-coating the message thickly, does suggest that some picture of the real Eleanor had permeated England's premier abbey, which had considerable ties to the royal court. But one might say that, for the readers of this description, 'if you didn't know, you wouldn't know'; a familiar would see the glimpse of the real woman, but a stranger would take a fairly formulaic positive impression away.[5]

The process of movement to that impression can be seen in an updated version of this account written in 1327, also at St Albans, which was repeated in Thomas Walsingham's *Historia Anglicana* (after 1392). This starts the transformation of Eleanor into what might be termed the rosewater version:

> She was the most pious, modest and merciful woman, a lover of all the English, and was like a pillar of the entire realm. In her time foreign favourites did not afflict England. The people were not troubled by royal officials, if the slightest suggestion of oppression came to her ears in any way. As her rank permitted, she consoled the afflicted everywhere, and wherever she could, she reconciled those in discord.[6]

So by the time that Eleanor's friends were dying out, the process of development of a myth was well under way. At the same time, the negative publicity in the areas where Eleanor held her lands in the wake of the inquest into her business dealings, and the litigation which sometimes followed, fizzled out into nothing. There may have been a few families for whom the version of the loss of their lands told among themselves involved wrongdoing on Eleanor's part, but they were few and far between, and frequently proved wrong when put to the test in litigation. The Camvilles, for example, having failed to pursue any claim at the inquest, alleged in 1341 that Eleanor took against Robert de Camville when he refused to sell Westerham to her, trumped up charges of failing to answer a military summons to serve in Wales and imprisoned him until he made the conveyance. Poetically, in this version (his health doubtless shattered by imprisonment) he died nine months later. In fact, as was proved in court, he lost his lands through his debts to the Jewry, conveying them to Eleanor quite voluntarily; and he retained Westerham until his death – some seven years later.

So Eleanor's memory passed into the unreliable hands of the chroniclers and the loaded images of the crosses and the tombs. Within a few more decades, Eleanor had receded back into near-total obscurity, with one rare mention of her misidentifying her as Alfonso's daughter rather than his sister.[7]

The decay of the crosses echoes the falling away in recollection of Eleanor. By the 1530s, John Leland could not identify the queen remembered at the Hardingstone cross and other reports in the sixteenth century speak of decay to the crosses at Stony Stratford and elsewhere, with tops in particular showing a tendency to go missing.

As for the historians, no one seems to have paid much mind to Eleanor's character. Some accounts mention her travels to Palestine and Gascony with Edward, while others confine themselves to her coronation, death and children. With Polydore Vergil came the misapprehension that Eleanor brought Ponthieu as her dowry. Later, in Elizabeth I's reign, came the translation of Walsingham's eulogistic description of Eleanor. A highly coloured Spanish version of the Acre legend, which gave full credit for Edward's recovery to Eleanor's love, followed in 1579.

By the end of the sixteenth century, Camden, in his 1605 book *Remains of a Larger Work Concerning Britain*, links the Acre story to the crosses:

> This good Queen Eleanor his wife who had accompanied him in that journey endangering her own life, in loving affection saved his life and eternized her own honour. For she daily and nightly sucked out the ranke poison, which love made sweet to her, and thereby effected that which no Arte durst attempt; ... so that well worthy was shee to be remembered by those crosses as monuments, which in steade of Statues were erected by her husband to her honour.

Here we find, therefore, the source and the essence of that picture which has transmitted itself – 'good Queen Eleanor', the rescue of her husband from the assassin's poison and her deserved immortalisation through her husband's loving tribute.[8]

One might imagine that the story of Eleanor's reputation effectively stops there, and that this view simply became tradition. However, before this was to happen, Eleanor's reputation was to take one further, rather unexpected turn, scrupulously unearthed by John Parsons and traced out in the latter part of *Queen and Society*.

At more or less the same time as Camden's *Britannia*, a dramatist called George Peele, now best known as the possible author of parts of *Titus Andronicus*, was penning his play *Edward the First*. The first version of this, written in the early 1590s, is now effectively lost, later accretions having formed the more popular, and therefore long-lived, version of the play. This first version appears likely to have presented a rather endearing picture of Eleanor and Edward ('sweet Nell' and 'sweet Ned' between themselves). However, the more popular version is given a very different flavour. This version features a haughty Eleanor, who delays the coronation by a desire for Spanish-made gowns which will need over twenty weeks to make and says she will keep the English in a 'Spanish yoke'. And these are simply her milder faults; her more appalling crimes include demanding that the women of Britain be ordered to lose their right breasts, the murder (by serpent) of the lady mayoress of London and confession to adultery with Edmund of Lancaster and a French friar.

Why, one may ask, was Eleanor suddenly traduced in this remarkable manner? The answer appears to be partly a question of politics and partly a question of facility. So far as politics are concerned, there seems a real likelihood that, while there may have been a mischievous desire to play flat against the saccharine picture of Camden, the main reason behind the reworking was a serious suggestion in the latter part of Elizabeth I's reign that her throne might descend to Isabella of Spain, the daughter of Philip of Spain. When looking for candidates to take the English throne after the death of Elizabeth I, there were always bound to be those who would look back into the Plantagenet family tree, in preference to opting for Mary Stuart with her predominantly French descent and training and her poor track record as a monarch. Where the Tudors could claim male descent only through the legitimised line of John of Gaunt (the Beauforts), bolstered by Elizabeth of York, Isabella of Spain was descended from both of John of Gaunt's legitimate daughters Philippa of Portugal and Katherine of Castile, who were his daughters by Blanche of Lancaster, heir to Edmund of Lancaster (and hence doubly royal). Thus the play appears to have been used as a means of spinning thought against foreign and specifically Spanish queens come to lord it over Englishmen – and also, it will be noted, to suggest that Isabella's descent through Blanche of Lancaster was not all it was cracked up to be.

The story was facilitated by the existence of two ballads. The first, and source for most of these inventive fabrications, is a ballad called 'The Lamentable Fall of Queen Elenor who for her Pride and Wickedness by Gods Judgment sunke into the ground at Charing Crosse and rose up again at Queen Hive'. Its origins are obscure, but it seems likely that it dates from the virulent bout of anti-Spanish feeling which accompanied the later reign of Mary Tudor (and her marriage to Philip of Spain). The second is a ballad called 'Queen Eleanor's Confession', which seems to refer (via a confession of the murder of Fair Rosamund) to Eleanor of Aquitaine, but also has references apposite to Eleanor of Provence.[9]

With continued performances of Peele's play and continued publications of 'The Lamentable Fall' in the late sixteenth and early seventeenth centuries, this entirely hostile portrait of Eleanor was probably more widely known at the time of the Civil War than the romantic one put together by Camden. Of course, it is likely that the war would in any case have seen the destruction of a number of the crosses, with their obvious Marian overtones, but it seems likely that the absence of a widely disseminated sense of 'Good Queen Eleanor' played a part in the loss of most of the crosses, which can be documented or inferred to have been lost in the years 1643–6.

The Lincoln cross disappears without any documentary record, leaving behind just one relic – a part of one of the statues of Eleanor which was found doing duty as a footbridge in the mid-nineteenth century and now stands in a flowerbed in the grounds of Lincoln Castle. The cross was definitely in place as late as 1542, when it is mentioned by John Leland, one of the first English antiquaries. Prior to that, it had acted as a meeting point for pilgrims and also a rallying point for Henry VI's forces in 1445–6.

As for the Grantham cross, there is powerful evidence that the cross was thrown down in the Civil War. The minutes of 1646–7 meetings record the collection of stones from the cross and another cross known as the Apple cross for the Corporation of Grantham's use and a prosecution of someone for involvement in the destruction of the cross, and using stones from it to repair a wall. It seems likely that some stones from this cross, and the other cross in the town (known as the Apple cross) now form part of the current Grantham Market cross, parts of which have been dated to 1290.

The fate of the Stamford cross is mysterious. It was reported as being in need of repair in the Stamford administrative records of 1621, and was noted in situ by the Royalist Captain Richard Symonds in 1645. But in 1646 a survey by the town clerk reported it to be in a parlous state, with the only discernable decorations being those of Castile and León, the rest defaced by 'envious time'. By 1745, however, it had long fallen, with its remains being discovered in a tumulus, enabling Stukeley, who attended its rediscovery, to carry off numerous fragments, including a 'stone adorned with roses' – probably part of the pyramidal top storey which he sketched – to decorate his garden.

The Stony Stratford cross, described by Camden as 'not very splendid', has left practically no record of itself behind. It appears that it was long since gone when, in 1697, a distinguished traveller and chronicler of English historical remains, passing the cross site, makes no mention of it. That it would have rated a mention is demonstrated by the description given by the same traveller of the Hardingstone cross. That distinguished traveller was one Celia Fiennes, a descendant of Eleanor's favoured relatives. Poignantly, she appears to have had no knowledge of the relationship which existed between the two of them, for when she does encounter the Hardingstone cross, she merely remarks on the statues of 'some queen'. All that we do know of the Stony Stratford cross is that, in 1735, William Hartley, who was then nearly eighty, could recall the time when the base of the cross was still discernible. This strongly suggests destruction in or around the time of the Civil War.

Woburn cross disappears from sight without even a mention after its initial construction; and that of Dunstable, attracts only one brief mention, by Camden. It is reputed to have been demolished by troops under the Earl of Essex in 1643.

St Albans cross has no clear fate. It was described as 'verie stately' in 1596. Stukeley shows its location on a plan dated 1721, but it seems likely that all but the base, demolished to make way for the Market Cross in 1701, had been destroyed in the seventeenth century, probably in 1643.[10]

It is the London crosses whose fate can be most easily traced. The Cheapside cross in particular had become quite a controversial site. A key landmark in the later medieval period, it saw the start of races under Edward III and the start of Henry V's victory procession in 1415. In 1441, the city denizens had considered the Cheapside cross to be in need of works, having been 'by length of time decayed' – possibly not assisted by the fact that it was apparently re-gilded for every event of note in the city. Henry VI gave the Mayor of London licence to 're-edify the same in a more beautiful manner' and a committee was formed to decide how it should be smartened up. No precise record of their decision remains, but the later depictions of the cross, together with Stow's *Survey of London*, which contains a description of the 'improved' cross, indicate that it had been very considerably changed and possibly entirely rebuilt. In its second incarnation, the lower layer incorporated much more religious imagery – the resurrection of Christ, the Virgin Mary with the Christ child in her arms and St Edward the Confessor. Following attacks on such 'popish' images the statues were replaced, with one replacement being a rather indelicate fountain of Diana the Huntress spouting river water. A cupola appears to have been added between the main body of the monument and the cross, drawing attention to the statuary.

Three objections seem to have been taken to the cross. The first was practical. Standing, as it did, in the middle of Cheapside, it was seen as a traffic hazard, and various citizens sought to have it removed on this ground. Anyone driving along Cheapside today can readily appreciate the force of this objection. Secondly, its timber cross, covered in lead – and itself repeatedly gilded for special occasions – apparently rotted and was considered dangerous. Thirdly, as the Reformation gained ground, its imagery was regarded as objectionable, and was defaced repeatedly in the late sixteenth century. To the Parliamentarian forces it became a focus of anti-Catholic and anti-Royalist feeling, and was the subject of vandalism and an active pamphlet campaign, during which it was even described as the Antichrist. It was therefore pulled down on 2 May 1643 by the local citizens, with the approval of Parliament and an accompaniment of celebratory bells from St Peter's Wood Street, songs from the city waits, volleys of musketry and acclamations of joy. The great event was witnessed by John Evelyn and recorded for posterity in pictures and pamphlets, including the delightfully named 'The Down-fall of Dagon, or the taking down of the Cheapside Cross'. One of these says that 'a troop of horse and two companies of foot waited to guard it and at the fall of the top cross drums beat, trumpets blew, multitudes of capes were thrown in the air and with a great shout of people with joy'.

The Charing cross, which had survived in its original, unimproved form, did not attract the same level of odium, though it was apparently looking rather weather-beaten and down on its luck by 1590, when it was described as being 'defaced by antiquitie'. It was condemned by the same vote of Parliament, but its destruction was not actioned until 1647, and was greeted with something of regret by Londoners, who joked that the lawyers would never be able to find the courts at Westminster now that the cross was no longer there to guide them.[11]

It is ironic that it was just at this point, when the majority of the crosses were torn down, that the tide for Eleanor's reputation began to turn again. Sir Richard Baker's *A History of the Kings of England* of 1643, which went on over the next years to become a bestseller – indeed, the front-running manual of English history of its day – brought Eleanor back into the light of popularity with its telling of the romanticised version of the Acre story. This was reinforced in 1695 by a new edition of Camden's *Britannia*.

By early in the eighteenth century, sketches and prints of the remaining crosses begin to appear, and a first attempt was made to restore the Hardingstone cross. By 1720, Good Queen Eleanor's reputation was firmly established; the last publication of 'The Lamentable Fall' features a disclaimer from the printer excusing himself from publishing a version so much at variance with what was 'known' to be the truth.

The remaining crosses were gifts to the cult of the picturesque emerging in the eighteenth century, and romanticised renditions of the survivors appeared in some numbers. By the end of the eighteenth century, the crosses were considered important historic monuments and featured on the Society of Antiquaries' *Vetusta Monumenta* of 1780 and 1791. This round-up of notable and endangered items involved scrupulous drawings of each, accompanied by renditions of notable points of detail; by the end of the century, Cruikshank was mocking antiquaries admiring the Hardingstone cross.

Some hint of the frantic attentions of those antiquarians can be traced in the history of the Hardingstone cross. The first recorded restoration was in 1713, when the justices of the county, 'seeing its dilapidated condition', made an order for its repair. A cross three feet high was erected on the summit (to replace that which had been lost before 1460), four sundials with mottoes were placed on the third stage, and on the west side of the bottom stage was placed a white marble tablet surmounted by the royal arms, with a long Latin inscription. More repairs were performed in 1762. A further extensive 'restoration' in 1840 under the direction of Edward Blore undid the 'improvements' of the 1713 restoration. However, he made his own additions: the picturesque broken shaft which is still visible today was substituted for the cross, and one of the gables was completely rebuilt.[12]

Meanwhile, in 1739 Eleanor appeared on the London stage again – in a very different guise to her earlier appearance. James Thomson wrote a play based on Baker's saccharine and inaccurate version of the Acre myth. *Edward and Eleonora: A Tragedy* was intended to support the campaign of his patron Frederick Louis, George II's son, to be given a greater role in public affairs. The by-product of Thomson's intent was that Eleanor was explicitly presented as 'a Princess distinguish'd for all the Virtues that render Greatness aimiable' as well as her 'endearing goodness'. For those who are wondering where the tragedy comes into the play, in this version the price for saving Edward's life is for a willing victim (Eleanor of course) to suck the poison from the wound in certain knowledge that he or she will be poisoned instead. Those of delicate sensibilities will be relieved to hear that, his heart wrung by such devotion, the evil sultan supplies an antidote in the last few minutes of the play.

Appalling as the play sounds, it was considered perfectly reasonable at the time – at least by those on one side of the political argument. Better still, the play was a *succès de scandale*, achieving the accolade of being the second play banned from performance by the Lord Chamberlain under the Licensing Act of 1737 – and accordingly selling very well indeed in hard copy and being performed frequently in the latter years of the eighteenth century, when its political overtones were no longer audible. Its reflection can be seen in the repeated depictions of the Acre myth in the art of the late eighteenth century, with Blake and Kaufmann, among many others, giving us touching depictions of Eleanor's heroics.[13]

It was against this background that, in 1842, Joseph Hunter, the Assistant Keeper of Records at the then Records Commission (precursor to the Public Records Office), wrote a scholarly article on Edward's commemorations of Eleanor. He did highlight the falsity of the Acre myth, but simply repeated the character sketches of Eleanor provided by Walsingham, *et al.*, which effectively served to authorise those accounts.

But of course the most prominent and influential author to deal with Eleanor's life was Agnes Strickland, in her 1840–48 publication *Lives of the Queens of England*, a work which was hailed as a *sine qua non* for all those pretending to an accurate knowledge of English history. The huge success of this publication has made it the source material for depictions of medieval queens well into the twentieth century, and sometimes even to date.

In fact, the earlier queens' lives (including that of Eleanor) were probably the work of Agnes' sister Elizabeth. Her account, although occasionally referencing some of the medieval chronicles, is substantially based on the Tudor historians and later antiquarians and, putting it with the utmost of charity, evidences little evaluation of the materials available. A starting point in the now accepted vision of Eleanor the dutiful wife and mother having been adopted, what was added was only that material which was conformable with this picture. Thus, the picture of Eleanor is fleshed out with references to her literary interests, her wardrobe and her taste in items of personal refinement. Interestingly, references exist in some of the sources used (such as Botfield and Turner's edition of Eleanor's executors' accounts) to the more hard-edged aspects of Eleanor's personality, and yet these were ignored. Parsons concludes, and it is hard not to agree, that the case for deliberate suppression of this evidence is compelling. However, to be entirely fair to Strickland, Botfield and Turner themselves had introduced their work with a pen portrait which was still more emphatic in its assertion of Eleanor the sweet peacemaker. One suspects that the picture of the fertile and compliant consort queen was so very much in tune with Victorian sensibilities that it seemed a pity to 'spoil' it by painting a picture of a much more complex personality, particularly when the materials were very fragmentary.[14]

There was also a degree of synchronicity in the 'setting' of Eleanor's image. At the same time as the Strickland image disseminated itself, in the wake of the fantastic success of the *Lives of the Queens of England* publications, the artistic style which characterised the Eleanor crosses entered again into vogue, bringing a new round of appreciation for the surviving monuments. Thus the use by Gilbert Scott of the crosses as models for the Martyr's Memorial in Oxford and the Albert Memorial in London focussed attention back on Eleanor, as the inspiration for this medium of artistic and emotional expression. So too did the parallel between Queen Victoria's overpowering grief for the premature loss of a beloved consort and that of Edward's mourning for Eleanor.

This revival of interest in Eleanor and her crosses is what gave rise to the erection of the modern Charing cross, intended as a replica of the destroyed Charing/Whitehall cross in 1864. Ironically, although a fake, and put in place as an advertisement for a the newly built Charing Cross Hotel, it has served the purpose of the original perhaps better than all the others put together, through the accident of its location outside one of London's busiest railway stations.

Illustrating the strength of the fashion for the crosses, in 1840 Jesse Watts Russell raised a replica of an Eleanor cross at his home town of Ilam in Staffordshire in commemoration of his wife Mary, and another was raised in 1869 in Walken in honour of Lady Ellesmere. There are other local crosses which are plainly inspired by the Eleanor cross model at Sledmere in East Yorkshire and Glastonbury.

Most recently, in 2008 a reinterpretation or homage to the lost Eleanor cross of Stamford was erected in the town's sheep market as part of Stamford's Gateway project. Based on the one verified survival from that cross, the cross is essentially a tapered spike or needle composed of bands carved with a repeating spiral pattern of roses which tapers into a bronze point.

As for Eleanor's reputation, while the early part of the twentieth century saw her famed in Hutchinson's *History of the Nations* as one of the 'Famous Women in History', along with Mary, Queen of Scots, and Lady Jane Grey, her fame soon began to fade. As the century progressed, scholarship around her land acquisitions, the inquest into their management and Pecham's letters provoked a somewhat revisionist attitude in historians. So, recently, Lisa Hilton's precis of Eleanor saw her as a horrible woman with a vile temper. Yet in the absence of a full work on Eleanor, most scholars have stopped somewhat short of wholesale condemnation, tending to echo the Dunstable annalist and simply categorise her as being somewhat rapacious in her land acquisitions. John Carmi Parsons, who set out to produce that full work, seems to have been troubled by the binary nature of the images which emerge from the details. He at once sees in the household record a gracious and generous spirit and also, from the business records, a person whose admirable resolve and tenacity displayed itself in some very unpleasant ways.

At the same time as scholars have grappled with the difficulties of the fragmentary nature of the sources, and the ambivalent picture which emerges, the accepted portrait has continued to exist in the popular mind. Of that portrait, one facet stands clear. Aided by the crosses, and most of all the replica at Charing Cross railway station, now boosted by a 100-metre mural depicting the cross's construction on the Northern Line platform and a cocktail bar named after Eleanor, her story has become set in romance. If Eleanor exists at all in the consciousness of most people, she is seen as Edward's *chère reine*. It is perhaps appropriate that, through all the twists and turns of Eleanor's afterlives, the deep love of Edward for Eleanor is the one point at which the historical record and popular myth actually do now coincide.

Oddly enough, it may be that Eleanor, trained to regard her greatest glory as coming to her from her husband, would not object to this being her immortality. But surely, having considered Eleanor's life fully, she deserves rather more than this. Certainly, she should at least be remembered as a queen who lived a most remarkable life. Eleanor of Aquitaine is often identified as having led an exceptional life, by dint of her travels and her captivity. But Eleanor of Castile had experience of far more countries, both to live in (Castile, Gascony, England, Wales, Sicily, the Holy Land) and to visit (Scotland, Aragon, France, Italy, Tunisia). She too faced a rather more real, though shorter, captivity and far greater want of resources. But Eleanor was so much more than even this allows. She should be celebrated for her truly remarkable abilities. She was a woman who was highly intellectual and who promoted intellectual and artistic endeavour; England would not see another queen of similar abilities until the Tudors sat on the throne. She was a woman who ran a massively demanding property business alongside discharging her job as both queen and mother of sixteen children. She was also a woman who advanced the cause of civilised life in the rather unpromising ground of medieval England. As the champion of decent bathrooms, forks, culinary variety, well-decorated rooms and exquisitely designed gardens, she was a woman much in tune with modern sensibilities.

But finally, Eleanor should now be given credit for her role as Edward's consort/adviser. Those who have concluded that she had no political role were surely wide of the mark. Close examination of the record shows again and again the traces of her subtle touch in directing his political and even his military endeavours. While it would be wrong to suggest that she was in any sense the sole power behind the throne, or a dominating force over her husband, the material gives grounds to believe that she was a highly influential adviser to Edward throughout their marriage, that she helped to develop in him the abilities which he had and that she assisted him with much relevant knowledge as his career progressed. Indeed, one cannot help but wonder whether, without Eleanor, Edward would have become such an outstanding king that the accolade of greatness is often bestowed on him.

Eleanor thus deserves to be remembered in the modern world as a remarkable woman and an exceptional consort. Truly, she was a queen who fully deserved the unique and beautiful series of monuments which have kept her in the public eye in the many years in which almost all detailed memory of her life and abilities was buried.

Appendix 1

The Robert Burnell Letter

This letter, dated 'October 14 Guildford', from the Tower of London Collection is now in the National Archives under the reference SC 1/22/29. It runs as follows:

> Eleanor, by God's grace queen of England, lady of Ireland and duchess of Aquitaine, to Lord Robert Burnell, sends loving greeting.
>
> We require and affectionately entreat you to give counsel and assistance in this affair that the transgression injuriously committed against the bearer of these presents, the servant of the lady Constance our cousin, which Master John Clarell will show you, may be reasonably redressed. For the confidence which we have in your benevolence is the cause why we so often direct our prayers on behalf of our friends. And do you for love of us give such diligence in this affair, that we may henceforth be bound to you by special favour.

It has been published twice: Wood, Letters of Royal and Illustrious Ladies pp. 46–47 and Crawford, Letters of the Queens of England p. 74. In both sources it is ascribed to Eleanor of Castile and given the date of 1274–8. The reason for the ascription appears to be (i) that Eleanor of Castile was then queen and (ii) that if it was written after 1278 Eleanor would be using the title of Countess of Ponthieu, to which she succeeded in March 1279.

The National Archives, however, have until recently filed the letter as belonging to Eleanor of Provence with a date of 1273–4. The only other source offering a view as to ascription is Parsons, who seems to accept that the letter is one by Eleanor of Provence, although the precise chain of his reasoning is not clear.[1]

There are reasons to sympathise with the ascription to Eleanor of Provence: the location (Guildford) is one more associated with Eleanor of

Provence than Eleanor of Castile, and in broad terms the very lively style is perhaps more consistent with the surviving letters of the older queen. Moreover, Constance of Béarn was a closer cousin by blood of the former than the latter (though she was a direct cousin of Eleanor of Castile by marriage to Henry of Almain), and Eleanor of Provence is documented as assisting her in her pecuniary difficulties over her dowry.[2]

However, on further consideration some questions hang over this ascription. One is the content: Eleanor of Provence was not an intimate of Burnell, and therefore one might suppose that she would be unlikely to address him informally or send him 'loving greeting'. By contrast, Eleanor of Castile was a very close friend indeed of Burnell. Moreover, Eleanor of Castile has 'form' for sending love to her regular business correspondents: 'health and good love' to John of London, 'her beloved clerk, Sir John de Kirkeby', 'greetings and good love' to Richard Knout. Having said that, Eleanor of Provence was herself prone to fairly warm addresses to her correspondents: 'discreet and well-beloved' to Burnell's predecessor as Chancellor Walter de Merton, or 'her beloved Peter of Bordeaux, seneschal of Gascony'. The letter's 'loving greeting' to Burnell would therefore be a little warmer than expected from Eleanor of Provence, but not completely out of the way.[3]

The reference to frequent requests might again be said to favour Eleanor of Castile, who worked closely with Burnell. However, both queens corresponded with Burnell regularly, and there is certainly quite a bulk of surviving correspondence between Eleanor of Provence and Burnell over the mid-1270s period as she took up the reins of her dower. Indeed Huscroft, Burnell's biographer, has concluded that Eleanor of Provence was Burnell's single most prolific correspondent based on the surviving letters. The reference to frequency of correspondence cannot be determinative. The playful terms in which the reference to repeated requests is couched is again ambivalent. On the one hand, it seems more consistent with the intimate friendship between Burnell and Eleanor of Castile than with the older queen. The latter part is also quite similar to the terms in which Eleanor of Castile asked other administrators to do favours for her. On the other, the playfulness could be just an aspect of the older Eleanor's famous charm.[4]

It would initially appear that the matter could be put simply to rest: if the letter is dated 1273–4, it cannot be by Eleanor of Provence, as Henry III died in November 1272 and after that date she would have written as dowager queen. But Eleanor of Provence certainly did write letters after that date as 'Queen of England' – all her numerous letters to Edward prior to her taking the veil are commenced 'Eleanor by the grace of God Queen of England', and she sometimes used the Irish and Aquitaine titles too; for example, a letter to William de Merton which must date from early 1273 or 1274 (the period of Merton's chancellorship) and which cannot be from Eleanor of Castile, who was abroad at the time, commences with 'Eleanor by the grace of God queen of England, Lady of Ireland, Duchess of Aquitaine'. There are also a number of other later letters which for reasons of location or content seem unlikely to be those of Eleanor of Castile and which are similarly commenced. An example is a letter to Robert Burnell of 1275–85 which deals with a jail at Milton Regis within the older queen's dower properties. Indeed, looking through Eleanor of Provence's correspondence after her widowhood, it looks very much like one clerk simply continued to use the form of address to which he was used, while another adopted the more correct 'Eleanor by the grace of God Queen of England and mother of the King'. The introductory words therefore offer no real guide as to which queen is writing.[5]

The fact that Eleanor of Provence did have direct involvement in financially assisting Constance of Béarn in November 1274 (referred to above) may be said to turn the scales in her direction. This appears to have been the factor which inclined Parsons' ascription. However, the payment (covering non-payment of dower revenues) seems to have nothing to do directly with the subject of the letter (a wrong done to one of Constance's agents). Further, another later letter in the National Archives from Constance of Béarn to King Edward prays the king to listen to the Bishop of Bath and Wells (Robert Burnell) and Otho de Grandison, the implication being that they were themselves au fait with the subject of her dower problems. The involvement of two such close associates of Eleanor of Castile's rather suggests her involvement in Constance's ongoing difficulties.[6]

The only other indication is the despatch reported in the letter of one John Clarell on this business to Robert Burnell. John Clarell was a clerk in the king's service. In 1277, we find him going to the French court on the king's business. Although Clarell did previously serve Henry III, he would, at least from Edward and Eleanor's return in 1274, be more likely to be despatched by them than by Eleanor of Provence.[7]

Therefore, ascribing the letter with any degree of confidence to one queen or another seems almost impossible.

The only other point which may assist is tying down the date; i.e. determining to what year it should be allocated. If it were dated 1273, this would determine the matter in favour of Eleanor of Provence, since Eleanor of Castile was not present to make the representation. Similarly, if it could be dated to the early 1280s, Eleanor of Castile could not conceivably have authored it, since she was then in or around Wales.

The filing location in the National Archives is of no assistance in narrowing the field, as this grouping of letters runs from 1272 to after Eleanor's death. The basis for the tentative year designation given to it of 1273–4 by the National Archives is not clear.

The year 1273 can be eliminated. It seems that the letter must date from 1274 or later, since if it were written earlier it would be inconsistent with its filing in a series of chancery letters, since Burnell was only appointed chancellor in 1274.

The point made by Wood and Crawford – that it must predate Eleanor's accession as Countess of Ponthieu – is tempting, but flawed. The other surviving letters of Eleanor as queen show that she did not in fact use her Ponthevin title. Exactly the same preamble as commences this letter also appears in letters of Eleanor dated 1283, 1288 and 1289. The absence of the Ponthevin title therefore cannot be regarded as significant in terms of ascribing the letter to one queen or the other, or of dating.[8]

However, the letter referred to above from Constance of Béarn to King Edward dealing with her dower actually provides 1279 as the *terminus ad quem* for the letter, regardless of which queen was the author. That letter can be dated 1279 by reference to other records in *Foedera*, which show her dower situation being resolved prior to her remarriage. This would indicate that the letter under consideration predates this 1279 letter, with the consequence that the field narrows to 1274–8.[9]

There appear to be no further references to Constance's dower problems, which enable a better fix to be had. Only one fact provides a tentative indication. The letter is addressed simply to 'lord Robert Burnell'. It does not cite him as Bishop of Bath and Wells, as the accepted mode would have required. Of course, between good friends this is not necessarily determinative. However, when one takes into account that Burnell was not made a bishop until 1275, and therefore in 1274 he would actually correctly have been addressed as lord Robert Burnell, there is at least some ground for saying the most likely year for dating the letter is 1274 – the year of young Henry's death.

In logistical terms, if that date is correct, either of the queens could have authored the letter. Eleanor of Provence is documented as being at Guildford then, and Eleanor of Castile is inferred to have been at Westminster, within easy reach of Guildford, where her son was ill.

However, if the letter is a 1274 letter, this may provide one final small factor in favour of an ascription to Eleanor of Castile, since she and Edward had been in direct contact with Constance during their stay in Gascony the previous year. Constance, it will be recalled, had submitted to them on behalf of her father.

Overall, the evidence therefore probably points towards a 1274 date for the letter. On authorship, the evidence is almost too close to call, but in my own view it inclines by fractions to an ascription to Eleanor of Castile. If this is so, it rebuts the suggestion that she did not visit young Henry on his deathbed in October 1274.

Notes

Further materials including supplementary maps and family trees can be found at www.saracockerill.com

Preface

1. Jones The Tower p. 53
2. Botfield and Turner, Manners II, i
3. Parsons C&H, p. 17
4. Parsons C&H p. 3, Hilton, Queens Consort, pp. 199, 203

1 The Backdrop

1. Foedera 209. On marriages as a means of autonomy see Parsons 'Mothers Daughters' and authorities cited there.
2. Parsons Q&S p. 7, Warren Henry II p. 42–5, Warren King John p. 19, Poole Domesday Book to Magna Carta p. 163, Turner Eleanor of Aquitaine p. 103, 105–6, 108
3. Turner p. 109, Warren King John pp. 21–3, Warren Henry II p. 47
4. Warren p. 117, Poole p. 329 Turner p. 194, Green Lives of the Princesses Vol I p. 264, 270–3, 278
5. Green, 1 pp. 284–287 Turner p. 289. On the dowry debate, the suggestion that Gascony was an actual part of the dowry is unlikely given Eleanor of Aquitaine's influence and the later abandonment of the claim by Alfonso X. Given the destruction of key documents at the time of Eleanor and Edward's wedding, the true facts are unlikely ever to be known: Cerda in Cahiers De Civilisation Medievale 54, 2011 p. 225.
6. O'Callaghan Alfonso X and the Cantigas de Santa Maria p. 39, Green Vol 1 pp. 287–289 Turner King John: England's evil king? pp. 102–3, Bowie The Daughters of Henry II and Eleanor of Aquitaine pp. 119–122 gives the best available account of the Alfonsine invasion.
7. Bianchini The Queen's Hand p. 5, Lomax The Reconquest of Spain pp. 119–20, 122, Green Vol 1 p. 279–282, 293, Parsons QCB p. 203–5, 207, Pratt, Gorey, The Battles that Changed History p. 104
8. Green Vol 1 299–300, Lomax p. 126–7, Pratt, Gorey p. 106–110,
9. Ridder Simoens, A History of the University in Europe Vol 1 p. 92 Green p. 283. Eleanor's grandfather Alfonso IX of Leon founded the stadium of Salamanca in 1218, presumably in imitation of Palencia. On troubadour patronage: ed. Akehurst A Handbook of Troubadours p. 273, McCash Cultural Patronage of Medieval women pp. 15–16,. Bowie, The Daughters of Henry II and Eleanor of Aquitaine pp. 165–7 considers Eleanor's promotion of the Becket cult.
10. Green Vol 1 p. 283–4, 286–7 289 Labande, Les Filles de Aliénor pp. 106–8.
11. HMS p. 38, 224, 242, 244, 338, CSM 1: 229

12. HMS p. 244–5, Bianchini p. 7, 73. For arras generally see Institutes of the Civil Law of Spain Vol 1 Title VII del Rio, Rodruiges, Palacios Women in Medieval Society ed. Bolton Stuard p. 77

13. HMS p. 245, Green Vol 1 pp. 289–90, O'Callaghan p. 245, Bianchini p. 71–77

14. Martinez Alfonso X p. 33, Szabolcs de Vajay (1989), p. 379,.

15. Green Vol 1 p. 303, 305, Martinez p. 29, Bianchini p. 238, 246 Lomax p. 131, O'Callaghan p. 335, Shadis 34–5, 41,.

16. Martinez p. 35–36 PCG II 718a. The children of the match were: King Alfonso X of Castile (November 23, 1221–1284) Fadrique (September 1223–1277), Fernando (1225–1243/1248) Leonor (1227–?,)Berenguela, (1228–1288/89), Enrique 'El Senador' (March 1230–August 1304) Felipe (1231–1274), Sancho, Archbishop of Toledo and Seville (1233–1261), Juan Manuel (1234–1283) Lord of Villena.

17. On John of Brienne see generally Perry John of Brienne King of Jerusalem, Emperor of Constantinople c 1175–1237. In particular see pp. 29–30, pp. 40–6, pp. 79–80, pp. 128–31

18. Shadis, p. 1; Martinez Alfonso X p. 32–3, O'Callaghan Reconquest and Crusade in Medieval Spain p. 84, 87, 88, HMS p. 339–340, 344.

19. Warren Henry II p. 109, Warren King John pp. 43, 65 Churchill, History of the English Speaking Peoples Vol 1 p. 181

20. Monicat, M.J. Recueil des Actes de Philippe Auguste Roi de France, 1996.

21. Du Fresne Histoire des Comtes de Ponthieu p. 144. Baldwin, The government of Philip Augustus: Foundations of French Royal Power p. 201, Malo Un grand Feudataire: Renaud de Dammartin et le coalition de Bouvines

22. Poole From Domesday to Magna Carta p. 453, Powicke Loss of Normandy pp. 190–5, Baldwin The Government of Philip Augustus pp. 201–203

23. Malo p. 224. There is an eerie parallel between the story of Renaud's fate and one of the versions of the fate of that other military man and seducer of heiresses Lord Bothwell. He too is reported to have spent the rest of his days chained in a dark hole to a chain of miniscule length. It gives one pause to wonder whether a moralist's wish is father to the thought in such details.

24. Du Fresne p. 145, Malo pp. 220–3, Baldwin p. 342

25. DRH Book IX, C, XVIII, Foedera 216.

26. Foedera 217, 219, CM iii 327–8 Martinez p. 41. HIII vol 1 178–9,

27. Parsons Q&S p. 8, 260, Laurentie Saint Ferdinand p. 104–5. De Rebus Hispaniae reports concern that Ferdinand might involve himself with 'illicit women' and 'dissipation in … wantonness' which predated Ferdinand's first marriage (9.10). This apparently resurfaced when he was widowed (9.80).

28. The other children of the marriage were Luis (1243–1269) Ximen (1244) and Juan (1245).

2 Eleanor's Early Years

1. Strickland Lives of the Queens of England Vol 1 p. 79, Parsons Mothers, Daughters, pp. 66–68

2. DRH Book 9 Chap 18. He describes the last two children as 'parvulus' or very young. DRH 9.12, Laurentie p. 107, Parsons Birth/Children pp. 247–8, Botfield & Turner p. 99

3. PCG II 1057.

4. Gonzalo Conquistas 86–87, DRH book 9 ch 1, PCG II 1059

5. For the campaigns see the PCG,II 1045–47, 1057, 1052, 1065, 1069–72, 1075–1131; Gonzalo, pp. 515–631, Ballesteros, p. 67, Martinez p. 43, Laurentie p. 126–7, 130, 137–8, Lomax p. 149.

6. Laurentie pp. 141–2. PCG II p. 718a. Martinez p. 20

7. PCG 1077 1125–1131, Laurentie p. 148, 150, 158–9, 160, 162–5, Lomax p. 150–1, 153, 155

8. PCG II 1132, Martinez p. 95, Laurentie pp. 169–70. 171–2. The list of attendees replicates the order given in De Rebus Hispaniae, reinforcing the inference made above that Eleanor was the middle child.
9. PCG II 1132–3, pp. 772–3. Martinez pp. 97–98, 99–101, Ballesteros pp. 55, 60, Laurentie p. 173–5, 177 179,184–5
10. PCG, II 1046–7, 1125–30 1131–2. Paris is quoted in Lomax p. 156. See also Lomax p. 136 dealing with the admiration caused by the taking of Cordoba in 1236.
11. Laurentie p. 130, 165, 170, Macdonald Chapter 7 in Ed Burns The Worlds of Alfonso the Learned …
12. González, Fernando III, vol. 1, p. 418. O'Callaghan p. 65, Macdonald, Burns Iberia and the Mediterranean World in the Middle Ages pp. 119–20
13. Siete Partidas Part II, O'Callaghan Learned King pp. 135–6. The chronology of the Setenario as compared to the Siete Partidas and Ferdinand's role in the former is still a matter of considerable academic debate.
14. O'Callaghan The Learned King p. 136 Lourie A Society Organised for War: Powers A Society Organised for War: Contamine War in the Middle Ages 55–56. On Vegetius: Allmand The De Re Militari of Vegetius: The Receptions, Transmission and Legacy of Roman text in the Middle ages pp. 96–104.
15. Barton The Aristocracy in Twelfth Century Leon and Castile pp. 168–170, Glick From Muslim Fortress to Christian Castle pp. 13–29, 105–113. Scott History of the Moorish Empire in Europe vol 3 467–8, 522–3. The role of the castle in medieval times is still hotly debated. As regards the size of Cordoba, some think 350,000 is a safer figure to use: Crow, Spain the Root and the Flower p. 56–7
16. Abulafia Christian Jewish Relations 1000–1300 p. 111 114, Ray The Sephardic Frontier 93–4 Martinez pp. 4-, Baer A History of the Jews in Christian Spain p. 122.
17. Abulafia p. 112–4 Baer p. 122. Todros Ben Judah wrote poems in Hebrew praising Alfonso 'the poet king'.
18. Ray pp. 1–71, 98–104, Abulafia p. 115
19. Scott p. 518–21
20. Crow, The Root and the Flower p. 55, 66–7, 70
21. Tabaa The Medieval Islamic Garden: Typology and Hydraulics p. 304, 313 Stoksad and Stannard pp. 27–9, Gardens of the Middle Ages. The image of paradise as a garden beneath which a river flows occurs no fewer than twenty four times in the Koran, Tabaa p. 320.
22. Tabaa pp. 304–5, 318–9. Gardens Landscape and Vision in the Palaces of Islamic Spain D Fairchild Ruggles p. 157, Dickie, Islamic Garden in Spain pp. 96–8,
23. Tabaa p. 315, 321, 324, Stuart p. 42, Al-Maqquarï, quoted in Bargebuhr, The Alhambra, A cycle of Studies in Medieval Spain p. 144, See also Ruggles p. 50, 147–8, Stoksad/Stannard p. 28.
24. Stuart Gardens of the World p. 35, Ibn Khaqan quoted at Thacker p. 36.
25. Burns in Castle of Intellect, Castle of Force in Ed Burns The Worlds of Alfonso the Learned, O'Callaghan Alfonso and the Cantigas de Santa Maria p. 46, CSM 1: 122.
26. Alfonso's presence is noted at Cordoba, Murcia, Jaén and the Algarve and in the siege and capture of Seville: PCG, chaps. 1048 1060, 1065; Gonzalez, Fernando III, vol. 1, pp. 101–7
27. Chronique de Guillaume de Nangis records that in 1244 the Emperor of Constantinople sent 'ses trois fils, Alphonse, Jean et Louis, encore enfants' to Louis IX of France. For the later contacts between Alfonso and the younger Briennes see Perry John of Brienne p. 165
28. Martinez p. 40, 45, 50.
29. Martinez p. 47, 74–75 77
30. Alfonso Cantigas de Santa Maria, Enrique Almadis de Gaula
31. Martinez p. 49, Siete Partidas Part II Title VII Law xi, Law ii-iv, vii, vii, x
32. Part II Title VII Law xi, Part V

33. Setenario p. 13, O'Callaghan Alfonso and the Cantigas de Santa Maria 43, Snow in Akehurst ed. A Handbook of Troubadours p. 274 Martinez p. 57
34. Law x
35. C47/4/5 Parsons Q&S pp. 23–5, C&H p. 104

3 The English Side of the Equation

1. Trivet Annales Sex Regum Angliae p. 282, Carpenter, The Minority of Henry III p. 1, C13 p. 19, Howell Eleanor of Provence p. 15
2. HIII Vol 2 p. 573 C13 p. 19
3. CM v 269–270, Staniland 'The Nuptials of Alexander III of Scotland and Margaret Plantagenet' 20–45, HIII Vol 2 p. 573
4. CM v 335, Wilkinson Eleanor de Montfort p. 9, Walker, Medieval Wales 113, 115–6, Carpenter Reign p. 97
5. Carpenter Reign p. 97, 202, 209, Kanter Peripatetic and Sedentary Kingship. His favourite locations were London, Windsor, Woodstock, Reading, Kempton, Marlborough, Clarendon, Winchester, Gloucester and Marwell
6. HIII p. 196 C13 p. 19
7. Carpenter Minority p. 153, 193, C13 p. 89, Weir Eleanor of Aquitaine p. 177, Church King John New Interpretations p. 171
8. Howell 2, 23–4, HKW I 125, 501–2
9. Howell pp. 27, 30, 35, 45, 65–7. Later chronicles do float the possibility that there were two other sons between Edmund and Katherine, and two more after her. But see Howell: 'The Children of Eleanor of Provence and Henry III' convincingly rebutting this suggestion.
10. Howell p. 32–3, 55, 99, Ridgeway The Lord Edward pp. 90–3
11. Howell 94, 167, 194, 196 274–7, Parsons QI p. 150
12. Crawford Letters pp. 54–67. See also Howell p. 75
13. Foedera 253, Denholm Young 43, 47–48, HIII p. 196
14. Denholm Young pp. 15, 21, 27, 49, 51, Appendix 2 HIII pp. 196–7, Howell p. 38
15. CM v pp. 295–6, Rishanger p. 6, Maddicott p. 9, 109, 350–1, Mon franc I p. 124, C13 pp. 113–4
16. Maddicott p. 5,17–18, HIII pp. 203–4. Montfort had first courted Renaud of Dammartin's daughter Matilda of Boulogne, who was instead married to the King of Portugal: Wilkinson Eleanor de Montfort p. 62
17. Wilkinson p. 65, Maddicott pp. 25–6
18. CM iv 213, v 290, Maddicott p. 31, 49–51, 121 HIII pp. 205–6, C13 p. 114, Carpenter Reign p. 223
19. Carpenter Reign p. 238, Wilkinson p. 91, Maddicott pp. 120–2
20. Howell pp. 25–6, 30–33
21. Ridgeway King Henry III and the 'Aliens' p. 89, Howell p. 49–50 Jobson p. 8
22. Howell p. 52, 78
23. CPR (1272–81) p. 188, Clifford Knight of Great Renown 11–12
24. CM iv 598, 628, Ridgeway Aliens p. 85, 88, Howell 53–4, DBM pp. 80–1
25. Carpenter Reign p. 190, Jobson p. 10
26. Ridgeway 'Politics' 245–6
27. CM v 348–51, vi 222–5, Carpenter Reign p. 191, Howell p. 67
28. CR 1251–3 272–3, 283, 431 CM v 351–3, 359 vi 222–5, Howell p. 67–9,
29. Jobson 12–13, Weiler Henry III and the Staufen Empire 133, 147–9 Carpenter Henry III and the Sicilian Affair
30. CR 1237–42 476, 1242–7, 5, 45, 118, CLR 1240–5 174, E 101/349/17, 24, Howell p. 76
31. Green Vol 2 p. 297
32. E101/349/18, CPR 1237–42 523, Parsons Q&S p. 55, Prestwich pp. 6–7, Howell 81.

33. Prestwich p. 7
34. Kanter p. 25, Prestwich p. 111, Prestwich 'The Piety of Edward I' pp. 120–8
35. CLR 1240–5 286, CLR 1245–51, 65, AM ii 337, CM iv 639
36. CLR 1240–45, 31, 60, 90, 323, Wait Household and Resources 1–8, 203–6, Ridgeway The Lord Edward 91
37. Wilkinson p. 89, Maddicott p. 95. It is just possible that Simon junior and Guy, were part of his household, but it seems more plausible that they had a military education within their own household in Gascony.
38. CR 1242–7 30, 141 Prestwich p. 5, Morris pp. 10, 19
39. Prestwich p. 6
40. Howell 82
41. CM iv 147, 166–7 Morris 13

4 The Marriage

1. CM v 277–90, Powicke C13 pp. 108–9 Maddicott p. 107, Prestwich pp. 8–9
2. CM 368, 370, Studd The Marriage of Henry of Almain and Constance of Bearn, Goodman, Alfonso X and the English Crown, p. 41, Marsh English Rule in Gascony p. 36, Linehan Spain a Partible Inheritance 1157–1300 Ch 4, Trabut-Cussac L'Administration Anglaise en Gascogne, xxix-xxx, Parsons Q&S p. 12
3. Foedera 290.
4. CM v 365, 370, 513, CR 1254–1256, 240, Henry III 232, Marsh, English Rule in Gascony 135, 143, 151, Lodge Gascony under English Rule 42–43, 48, Ballesteros Alfonso X 92–96, Trabut-Cussac xxix-xxx, HMS 361–362, Goodman 41–2, Parsons Q&S p. 12
5. CM v 397–8, CPR 1247–58, CIR 1251–3 37–8, 191, 442–3, 465, 471, 475, 486,508–9, CHEC 44–46, 219.
6. CPR 1247–58 291, CIR1251–1253, 486, CHEC 44–46
7. Bianchini p. 244–5
8. O'Callaghan p. 223, 346, 361, Ballesteros 89, 96–99 Tolley Eleanor of Castile and the 'Spanish Style' pp. 181–184
9. Foedera 292, Maddicott 121–3, Lodge p. 42
10. Foedera 295
11. Foedera 296–8, CPR 1266–72 736–7, CChR ii 192–3. Berengaria and Isabella of Angoulême's dowers can be found at Foedera 84, 161, 219 CChR ii 218
12. Foedera 299–301, CM v 450, Prestwich 11, Powicke Henry III and the Lord Edward vol 1 p. 232–3, Studd The Lord Edward, 4–19
13. See Chapter 13 where the rules of inheritance in Ponthieu are considered.
14. RG p. lxviii, Foedera 300, 304, Parsons Q&S p. 15 and footnote 27 as to the anomalous fact of a male *ayo* for a princess
15. Other examples of Alfonso's pride in his descent can be seen when he castigated his brother Felipe in 1272 by reference to the lineage which he had and his duty to it, by reference to both mother and father and in the Siete Partidas where he emphasises that one of the two most important qualities in a queen is high birth.
16. Bensch Barcelona and its rulers 234–76 esp 262 Hughes From Brideprice to Dowry 262–96, Barton Aristocracy 53–55, Dillard Daughters of the Reconquest 46 Adair Countess Clemence at 63–4 in ed. Vann Queens Regents Potentates, Scott, Siete Partidas Vol IV p. xx; Alfonso's reforms: Siete Partidas Part IV Title XI law vii.
17. Bianchini p. 343, Laurentie p. 173, Parsons Q&S p. 16, Martinez 41, 111–112
18. Martinez pp. 111–112
19. Parsons Birth 250–253
20. Macdonald pp. 187–8
21. Parsons Q&S p. 16
22. CR 1253–4 74–5, 156. CLR 1251–60 158, 162–70, CR 1253–4 121 CM v 446–7

23. Trabut-Cussac 3 n 1, 7 RG p. lxix, no 3658,
24. Trabut-Cussac p. 3–8, Prestwich 14, RG vol I no 4275, 42788 p. lxix
25. Trabut-Cussac p. 5, 7, Parsons Q&S p. 16 note 29, RG p. xxix, lxix, 3463, 3472, 3479, 3439, 3478, 3573, 4552
26. Foedera 310 Trivet pp. 282–3, Shadis Berenguela of Castile (1180–1246) and Political Women in the High Middle Ages
27. Trabut-Cussac 7, 11, RG p. xxix, Foedera 310, Lodge p. 49
28. Trabut-Cussac p. 7, RG p. xxix, Howell p. 130, 135
29. Parsons Mothers, Daughters p. 66
30. Macfarlane 1972: 13, 16–17 quoted in Parsons Mothers Daughters. Numerous other examples can be cited – see Parsons Mothers Daughters p. 67
31. Parsons Birth p. 256–7
32. Parsons Birth p. 257, Itineraire 178, RWH 1285–1286. Trabut-Cussac and Parsons favour the view that the commemoration is for Anonyma 1255, Salzman p. 85 inclines to the view that the commemoration was for an Acre casualty.
33. RG Vol IV (Supplement) pp. 24–28
34. RG II no 597, Prestwich p. 127–8
35. Trabut-Cussac p. 10, HIII vol 1 pp. 208–13
36. Maddicott pp. 110–111
37. Howell p. 145, Ridgeway Politics 170–6, Reg Innocent IV no 7683
38. Trabut-Cussac p. 8 RG Vol IV, which covers the period of the 1254–55 stay.
39. Trabut-Cussac p. 11, Lodge p. 50
40. Powicke p. 211, CM iv p. 594. v p. 368.
41. Trabut-Cussac p. 11–2
42. Trabut-Cussac pp. 11–14
43. RG Vol IV pp. xxvii-ix for Henry III, pp. xxx–1 for Edward
44. Trabut-Cussac p. 8
45. Prestwich pp. 11–12 RG pp. 35–52
46. CR 1254–6 p. 219–20

5 The First Years in England

1. CPR 1247–66 381 CCR 1254–56 128, 136, 144–5, Jobson p. 13, Carpenter Sicilian Business, Bowie Daughters pp. 165–7
2. Ackroyd London Under 2011 pp. 41–43, 53–5 Jones Tower p. 19–22, Benham Old St. Paul's Cathedral pp. 6–8
3. Gater & Wheeler Survey of London Vol 16 158–164, Vol 18 pp. 1–2, 51–60 Thornbury Old and New London Vol 1 149–158, Vol 3 p. 98–100 Page ed. History of the County of London Vol 1 London within the Bars p. 507
4. CM v 513 CCR 1254–6 p. 225 RG 3968
5. Howell 74–5
6. Parsons Q&S p. 139
7. CPR 1247–58 389–90, CCR 1254–56 114, 132–3 212, 391.
8. CIR 1254–6 389–90 Shirley Royal letters 506, Foedera 372
9. CCR 388–91, 318, CPR 458, 506 CM v 585–6
10. CPR 1247–58 324, 385 Tolley Spanish Style
11. Ballesteros 117–8, 191–2
12. CM 575–6 CCR 1254 368, 1256 23 1251–60 318, 320, 330 336, 339 348 352 410 469, CPR 1247–58 567, CPR 1258–66 34 Johnstone Edward of Carnarvon pp. 88–9
13. Foedera 353, Denholm-Young pp. 86–9,
14. CCR 1256–9 284–5 CCM 649 657–9 Denholm-Young pp. 95–6, Martinez pp. 180, 308
15. CCR 1254–56 389–91, Denholm Young p. 84
16. CM v 538–9
17. Studd Itinerary p. 30, Morris p. 25

18. AM vol. 3 p. 200 Prestwich p. 17, Howells p. 146
19. CM v 539, 597 Prestwich pp. 17–18 Jobson pp. 13, 16 Lloyd History of Wales ii 717–22, DBM 175–7,
20. CR 1256–59, Wait Household and Resources 287–9 Howell 148 Jobson 16–17, Prestwich 23.
21. CM 679, CPR 1247–58, 644, CCR 1279–88 180, Howell 148, Jobson 17 Ridgeway The Lord Edward and the Provisions of Oxford 95
22. Bracton vol 2 p. 268–272 makes plain that a person receiving property designated as dower without the consent of the wife would not be entitled to hold it against her.
23. CM v 640 Smith Llewelyn 94, 101–6, Jobson p. 16
24. Prestwich p. 23 Huscroft pp. 16–20, 187–196, 219–220 Studd thesis p. 43
25. Carpenter Reign pp. 192–3, Jobson 17–18
26. Paris v 634, 676–7, Maddicott p. 145, 154, Jobson 10, 18,
27. Jobson 10–14
28. Carpenter Reign pp. 187–8, Jobson 20. Peter de Montfort was of a Worcestershire family and linked to the Savoyard interest. The Norfolk siblings probably had an additional grudge against Pembroke: their mother was the daughter of William Marshal and would have had claims on the estate following the death of the male line in 1245: Morris Bigod Earls p. 52

6 Dissent, Defeat, Victory

1. CPR 1247–58 641, DBM 4, 66–7, 72–4, Jobson 20–1, Carpenter Reign 187–90, Burt Chapter 4, Howell p. 154–5.
2. Flores iii 253–4, DBM 90–3 104–5, 258–9 Prestwich 25, Howell 157 Jobson 24 – 25.
3. CPR 639, 641, Foedera 374, 378 Flores iii 253–4, DBM 92–3, 258–9. CM v 697–8 Jobson 26
4. CM v 653–4, HIII I 385, Jobson 34, Morris 39, Prestwich 27–8 Parsons Q&S p. 17
5. Prestwich p. 28 Jobson 34–5, Morris 40, 43
6. Carpenter Reign pp. 235–7, 250 Burt Ch 4
7. Siete Partidas 1,1,11
8. CM v 744–5, Flores ii 424–5 Maddicott 185, Morris 40–41 Jobson 34, 37, Jobson 34 Barker The Tournament in England 1100–1400 23, HIII I, 400–401
9. HIII I 408–9, Bémont p. 173, Howell 162–3 Jobson 38
10. Shirley Royal letters ii 802, CCR 1259–1261 259 Parsons Q&S p. 17, HIII II 693 Howell 165
11. DBM 220–3 Prestwich 32, Maddicott 194, Howell 163–4 Jobson 48–51 Studd Acts of the 742, 715, 733–4 Parsons Q&S 17, 263
12. CM 46–7, Ann London I 54–5, DBM 228, 230, 232 Jobson 49 Howell 164 Morris 45,
13. Prestwich 33, Studd 790–2, Jobson 52–4 Maddicott 199, Morris 45, 47 Smith Llywelyn 127–31
14. CCR 1259–61 134, 301
15. Maddicott 200, Morris 46–7, Jobson 54–5.
16. CPR 1258–66 126, 181, Prestwich 24, 34, Jobson 55 Huscroft Thesis p. 19
17. Annales London p. 54, Prestwich 34, Jobson 55, Morris 47
18. Saul For Honour and Fame p. 36 Crouch Tournament 44, 53–4, Willam of Newburgh ii p. 422
19. Morris 48, Jobson 61, Parsons Q&S p. 22
20. Maddicott p. 194 and Burt Chapter 4 confirm.
21. CR 1259–61 467, Howell 179–80, Jobson 62, Prestwich 35
22. Flores ii 466–7, Howell 180 Jobson 62–3, Morris 49–50 Maddicott 207, 209, Prestwich 35,
23. Howell 180–1, Studd Itinerary 57–8 Prestwich 37, Trabut-Cussac 22–7

24. Larroque, Le Chateau Fort de Mauléon, Beresford New Towns of the Middle Ages 352–3. On Eleanor's intervention: SC 1/11/3
25. Gerv Cant ii 211, Prestwich 32, Morris 52–3, Jobson 78 3 Howell 181 Carpenter Reign 271
26. CR 1261–4 133, Morris 53 Prestwich 38, Howell 188
27. Ann Dunstable 220 Morris 53–4, Prestwich 38 Jobson 79–80, 83, 86 HIII II 437, Howell 187–8, 193–4
28. Flores ii 478, Prestwich 39 HIII II 438 Jobson 84 86–7
29. CPR 1258–66 264–6 Jobson 88 Prestwich 39, 91 HIII II 439
30. Morris 55, Jobson 90–1
31. Flores ii 482, Prestwich 39, 41, HIII II 439, Morris 56, Jobson 91, 93
32. CR 1261–3 308-Flores 482–3, HIII 440, 9, Prestwich 40 Jobson 95
33. Foedera 430, Flores ii 484–5, Prestwich 41 Parsons Q&S 196 Maddicott 245–6 Denholm Young 142 Jobson 102
34. CIR 1261–64 308–9 Dunstable 225 Howell 199 Jobson 102
35. Howell 195, 197
36. CCIR 1256–59 2–3, CPR 1258–66 p. 220, CChR 2.84 Parsons Birth
37. Parsons notes the absence of gossip as to the lack of an heir as a mystery and favours 1280–1281 for the birthdate of the 'missing' son: Birth p. 264. On the possible 1260 birth: Studd Acts 824
38. CPR 1258–66 325. Dunstable 227, DBM 266–7, 333–6, Maddicott 257, 259 Jobson 104–5, Prestwich 41,
39. Maddicott 263, Jobson 108 Carpenter A Noble in Politics p. 324
40. AM iii 227, Flores ii 487, Gloucester ii 743–6, Shirley Letters Vol II p. 253–4, CM 61 Ger Cant ii 234, HIII II 456–8 Jobson 108, Maddicott 26–5 Morris 60 Howell 151,
41. Maddicott 265 Denholm Young 125 Jobson 108–9
42. CPR 362 AM iii 232, Denholm Young 126–7 HIII II 459–61 Jobson 108–10 Prestwich 43
43. Parsons Q&S p. 164 McKitterick, Trinity Apocalypse p 20.
44. Carpenter Battles of Lewes and Evesham 17–18, 20, 22–3, Jobson 109–114 Carpenter 20–1, Jobson 112–4 Denholm Young 128 Powicke 464, Prestwich 44
45. AM iii 232 Sadler Second Barons War pp. 53–4, 61–2 Denholm Young 128, Jobson 115 Morris 62, Vegetius p. 91 Carpenter 33.
46. Wykes 151–2, Maddicott pp. 272–5, 282, Jobson 117
47. CPR 318, 343, 364, 374, Flores iii 261, CM 63, AM iii 232–3 Ann Lond 64, Carpenter Battles 35, Jobson 117, 121 HIII II 465, Prestwich 45 Maddicott 272–5
48. Maddicott 287, Carpenter Reign pp. 281–291.
49. Hilton Royal Consorts p. 191 Maddicott 282
50. CPR 324–9
51. Jobson 123 Howell 214
52. CLR 5.142–43
53. Maddicott 307, HIII II 486 Jobson 130
54. CLR 5.150, Parsons 'Birth' p. 258
55. Maddicott 309–10 318, 321 Jobson 133–5
56. CPR 1258–1266 p. 400 Parsons Q&S p. 161, 188, 192
57. Flores iii 264 CPR 1258–66 420, CR 114 Maddicott 322, 330 Parsons 24
58. Maddicott 329–333 Jobson 135–6 Morris 65
59. Prestwich 49, Jobson 136–40 Maddicott 334–9
60. Maddicott 339 Jobson 140–141
61. Morris 67, Carpenter, Battles 50–4, Jobson 140–2
62. Jobson 141, 144 Cox Battle of Evesham 13–14, Carpenter Battles 58–9, Carpenter last hours of Simon de Montfort 395–406
63. CM 80, AM iv pp. 173–5, Jobson 144, 146 Maddicott 342

7 Queen in Waiting

1. Shirley Royal Letters 440, Morris 71, Jobson 150
2. CClR 1264–68 pp. 70–71, Maddicott 326, 335–6. Botfield & Turner pp. 9–10, 65–6. AM iv 175, Jobson 150
3. Jobson 150-2
4. CIM I nos 609–940 CPR 1258–66 465, 466, 467, 493, AM ii 367, Robert of Gloucester ii 768, AM iii 239
5. CPR 1258–1266 453 Parsons Q&S 146–7, 188 Shirley Royal letters no 647 Translation author
6. CPR 1258–1266 458 466, 476, 522, 555, 578, Parsons Q&S p. 164, 180, 188, 189. Haselbury was only held for a few weeks.
7. CPR 1258–66 492 Prestwich 55, Howell 234, Jobson 153–4,
8. CPR 1258–66 653, Prestwich 55, Jobson 154 Powicke II 518–9, Morris 73–4
9. CPR 1258–66 617, Howell p. 235, CR 1268–72, 49, De Antiquis Legibus Liber p. 87.
10. Powicke II 532–8, Jobson 157–8 Morris 78
11. Morris 79, Jobson 159–60
12. CPR 1258–66 638, CPR 1266–72 460, 484, CChR ii 149–50, Parsons 170, 188
13. Leicestershire: Parsons 126 179, CPR 1266–72 168, 179, CChR I 133. Norfolk: Parsons 182, CPR 1266–72 372, CChR I 133. Northampton: Parsons 184, CPR 1266–72 168, 179, CChR ii 133. Spelhoe was a now defunct district which contained several villages including Kingsthorpe and Overstone: Weston Favella A History of the County of Northampton: Volume 4, pp. 63–64. Stafford: CPR 1272–81 471–2, Parsons 190. Queen's Gold: CPR 1266–72 p198
14. CPR 1266–72 p. 169, 243, 262, 305, 317, 343, 391, 401, Parsons Q&S p. 101
15. CPR 1266–72 pp. 360, 402, Parsons Q&S p. 126
16. CCR 349, Parsons C&H 33, 36
17. CCR 349, Parsons C&H 26, 86–7, 97, 98–9
18. Howell 145, 168
19. CLR 6 no 272, CPR 1266–72 p. 349, Parsons C&H p. 28, AM iv 212, Coss The Knight in Medieval England 120
20. Flores iii 14 AM iv 217–8 Prestwich p. 68, Powicke 562
21. CPR 1266–72 425, C Ch R (1257–1300) 177 149, Lloyd English Society and the Crusade 113–5, Prestwich p. 70, Howell 246
22. Lloyd The Lord Edward's Crusade 126–7, Morris p. 87
23. Prestwich p. 72 Morris p. 89, Studd thesis pp. 826–7 Powicke 2 576, Johnstone Wardrobe p. 12, CPR 1266–72 412, Martinez pp. 185–6
24. Powicke p. 570, Lethaby Westminster Abbey and the King's Craftsmen A Study of Medieval Building p. 119, Wilson Westminster Abbey p. 27
25. AM iv 27, 226–7 Carpenter Reign pp. 409–25 Howell The Children of Henry III and Eleanor of Provence p. 67 Powicke 2 p. 569, 575 Carpenter Westminster Abbey in Politics in TCE vii 48–59
26. CR 1268–72 p. 162, Parsons Q&S 28 C&H 53 Morris 91, Ledger book of Vale Royal pp. 1–19

8 The Crusade

1. Morris p. 90, 92, Lloyd 116–24 Powicke II pp. 577–9 Prestwich p. 70
2. Parsons Q&S pp. 26, 97, 170, 179, 182, 184
3. Prestwich p. 73, Powicke II 583, Foedera 484 Howell p. 250 Huscroft Thesis pp. 20–22, 24–26
4. CPR 431 CR 1268–72 211–2, 290–1, Liber de Antiquibus Legibus 125 Hilton p. 192 Wykes 236 Prestwich p. 73 Ann Winchester 109 Powicke II p. 580, Huscroft thesis p. 22. 26–32

5. Tyerman God's War pp. 810–812, Powicke p. 598–9 Morris 93–4, Dunbabin Charles 1 of Anjou 3–5, 57, 195–7 Clifford 19, Prestwich 73–74

6. Fadrique was back in Castile by March 1272, counselling the king during the early phase of the nobles' conspiracy The World of Alfonso the Learned and James the Conqueror Chapter 7

7. Powicke pp. 598, 608–9 Dunbabin pp. 194, 196–7

8. Tyerman God's War p. 812, Sainte-Chappelle p. 815, Clifford p. 42, Parsons Viscountess Jeanne p. 141

9. Foedera 501 CPR 1266–72 528, 611 AM iv 239–241, CM 131, Salzman p. 31 HIII II 599, 607–8, Denholm Young p. 150 Prestwich p. 74–5 Morris 106, Studd Marriage of Henry of Almain pp. 175–7

10. Martinez, pp. 181–2, Ballesteros 460–475

11. Clifford 22 Tomasi *et al.* Palaces of Sicily, 46–55. Caronia, *et al.* La Cuba di Palermo, Lacy, The New Arthurian Encyclopedia, p. 392.

12. Parsons Birth p. 260, Liber de Antiquibus Legibus p. 171

13. Denholm Young pp. 150–151 Maddicott 370–1, Morris 106, Inferno xii 118–20.

14. Tyerman The Crusades 45–46, Tyerman God's War pp. pp 784–799. 807, Runciman A History of the Crusades pp. 314–329,

15. Prestwich p. 75, Asbridge The Crusades p. 643

16. Liber de Antiquibus Legibus 143 HIII II p. 600–602 Prestwich pp. 75–6 Asbridge p. 643

17. Asbridge p. 643 Morris p. 98–9 HIII II p. 602

18. Denholm Young pp. 151–2 Parsons Birth p. 259, Crouch William Marshal: Knighthood War and Chivalry 1147–1219 p. 20. Rishanger 78 suggests the news was not obtained until landing in Sicily on the return journey, but this seems implausible.

19. Clifford p. 27

20. Powicke p. 602 Prestwich p. 75–6. Ibn al furat 157–9 in Riley Smith, Levillan Encyclopedia of the Papacy p. 657 Tyerman God's War p. 813. There is an isolated suggestion based on a fairly liberal reading of a single letter of 1275 that Edward did consent, but this seems implausible. As Clifford p. 28 notes, if he had done, there would have been no motive for the later attack on him.

21. Salzman p. 35 Houseley Fighting for the Cross – 86–8

22. Israel and the Palestinan Territories Thomas/Kohn p. 235 Itineraria Phoenicia Lipinski p. 304, http://www.akko.org.il/en/, http://www.jewishvirtuallibrary.org/jsource/Archaeology/Akko.html The websites give a detailed account of the buildings. The former also provides a number of photographs of the Hospitallers' compound

23. http://www.mfa.gov.il/MFA/History/Early%20History%20-%20Archaeology/Akko-%20The%20Maritime%20Capital%20of%20the%20Crusader%20Kingdom

24. Vegetius: The timing can be fixed courtesy of the inscription 'Maistre Richard, votre clerc, que vostre livere escrit, En la ville d'Acre sans nul contredit'. Lewis Thorpe, 'Maistre Richard, A Thirteenth-Century Translator of the 'De Re Militari,' of Vegetius.' Scriptorium 6 (1952) 39–51. M. D. Legge, 'The Lord Edward's Vegetius.' Scriptorium 7 (1953), 262–65. The Polos: Travels of Marco Polo Chs 1–9 (Yule and Cordier 1902, Project Gutenberg) detail the travels of the senior Polos.

25. Houseley pp. 174–176 Saul For Honour and Fame p. 35

26. Prestwich p. 80–81, 240–1 Tyerman God's War p. 813, Tyerman England and the Crusades pp. 126–30

27. Denholm Young p. 152

28. Morris p. 100 Guisborough 208–10, Holinshead Vol II p. 474–5 Ibn al-Furat xi-xii 157–9, Gestes des Chiprois 779.

29. Foedera 495, Parsons Q&S 29–30 Hilton p. 193

30. HIII p. 603, 605–6

31.　Salzman 32 Foedera 497 Les Registres de Gregoire X et Jean XXI ed. Guirard and Cadier no 817, Powicke p. 608
32.　Foedera 497, 488 Parsons FW, p. 210, HIII p. 606 Morris p. 102–3, Prestwich p. 82 Salzman p. 33

9 The Triumphant Return

1.　Foedera 497, 499 Powicke ii p. 589, Tyerman God's War p. 813
2.　Liber de Antiquibus Legibus 158, Rishanger 78 Registres de Gregoire X nos 209, 326, 814, Prestwich p. 83, HIII ii 608–12 Ormrod Edward III p 15. Simon the younger had died.
3.　Foedera 499, 500, 501 Prestwich 83, HIII II 608, Salzman 34–5, Dunbabin 186–7 Parsons Q&S p 30
4.　Foedera 504, HIII II p. 612, Prestwich p. 83–4 Salzman p. 35, AJ Taylor Master James of St George EHR LXV 1950 433–57
5.　Foedera 503 Salzman 36 HIII p. 614
6.　O'Callaghan Alfonso X and the Cantigas Santa Maria, pp. 128–133, Ed Valladolid The Chronicle of Alfonso X p. 3, HMS, p. 374 Martinez p. 242–6, 354
7.　Morris p. 108, Parsons Q&S p. 31
8.　SC/1/18/88–90, Guisborough pp. 110–11, Prestwich p. 85 RG vol iii p. x, Trabut-Cussac p. 41
9.　Trabut-Cussac p. 41, 42–4, 47, Prestwich 85, Salzman 37 RG vol iii p. x Morris p. 109. Studd The Marriage of Henry of Almain p. 162–177
10.　Foedera 505, 506, Lodge p. 54–6 RG iii p. x, Salzman 37 Trabut-Cussac p. 43. One of Gaston's sureties was Sir Arnald de Gaveston
11.　Chron Bury p. 56, AM ii 385 Parsons, Birth p. 252–3
12.　Foedera 506 Salzman 37 Trabut-Cussac p. 45 Chaytor, A History of Aragon and Catalonia Ch 6
13.　Foedera 506 Morris 109, Trabut-Cussac p. 42–5 Huscroft Thesis p. 87
14.　Powicke p. 615
15.　Itinerary, Foedera 507 Morris p. 110, Trabut-Cussac pp. 46–7 Salzman pp. 38–9. RG vol 3 p. x
16.　CCIR 1272–1279 70–71 Liber De Antiquis Legibus p. 170 Parsons Q&S p. 31 Parsons English Administration, p. 388
17.　CCR 1272–9 97, CPR 1272–81, 55–6, Foedera 513, 514, Flores iii, 43, HIII II p. 616–7, Salzman pp. 39–40 Itinerary, Parsons Q&S p. 31, Morris p. 110 Howell pp. 288–9
18.　CCR 1272–9 68–71, Prestwich p. 89,
19.　Foedera 515, Prestwich p. 90, Howell p. 290, Richardson The coronation of Edward I 97–8
20.　CLR 1226–40, 444, AM iv 259–60, Morris 111–112 Liber de Antiquibus Legibus p. 13, Howell 23
21.　Parsons Q&S p. 70, 73, Morris 113–115, Howell 18–20 266–70
22.　Morris 129
23.　Itinerary, Foedera 517, Morris p. 119
24.　Parsons Q&S 39 Johnstone Wardrobe p. 397 Prestwich p. 126

10 The Queen's Work

1.　Parsons Q&S 122, McFarlane Had Edward I a Policy p. 248–67, Spencer Nobility and Kingship in Medieval England p. 6–7, 28, Wolffe Royal Demesne 45–6, 52–5, 65–66
2.　Parsons Q&S 85. I am indebted to Michael Prestwich who has pointed out to me that the figures arrived at in this passage may not be bomb proof. In particular,

some of the figures used may be post mortem expenditure on items such as the crosses, which were obviously exceptional.

3. Parsons Q&S p. 72 78, 80–81, 83, 122, Howell 164, 262–3, 273–4. On Eleanor of Provence's approach: Paris CM 299, Howell p. 155–6, Treharne 78–9
4. Parsons Q&S p. 84, 123, Guisborough 216, AM iv 363
5. Examples of correspondence can be found at SC 1/30/54, 1/10/54, 1/11/51, 1/29/190, 1/29/205, 1/10/50, 1/10/53, and other examples can easily be found. Parsons pp. 114–6 Howell 116, 140
6. Reg Pecham ii 619–20, trans 767–8, iii 937–8, translation author, with help from Tout Chapters v 270–1, Parsons Q&S pp. 120–1
7. Parsons Q&S p. 123 Howell p. 278
8. Itinerary, Howell p. 294 Parsons Q&S 184–5, 159, 195
9. Itinerary Parsons Q&S pp. 164, 194
10. Itinerary Parsons Q&S 188–90, Letters of the Queens of England 60, quoted by Howells at p. 294
11. CChR ii 143, 192–3, Parsons Q&S p. 127. A further assignment of Gascon property followed in June 1280: CPR 1272–1281
12. Parsons pp. 128, 182–4, *Blomfield History of Norfolk volume 6,* pp. 297–302. Powicke II p. 704
13. Parsons Q&S pp. 127–9 176–179, Parsons C&H p. 154
14. The letters SC 1/11/11 SC 1/29/190 are set out at Parsons p. 129–131. The acquisitions are summarised at Parsons p169–70, 195 and are analysed by Parsons at pp. 129–131. See also Itinerary
15. Parsons Q&S p. 128 134–6 HIII II 704 RWH 1286–9 xv
16. Parsons Q&S p. 127, 136–7 Johnstone Wardrobe and Household of Henry 390
17. Parsons Q&S pp. 107, 130–1, 176–7
18. Parsons C&H pp. 18–19, 20
19. Parsons Q&S p. 103–8
20. Parsons Q&S pp. 76–7, C&H p. 20, Costain p. 39,
21. Parsons Q&S p. 103, 144–5, 192 LR p. 40, C&H 75n 93n Manners 100–1, Tout v 236–7, 271n, Prestwich 124
22. Parsons Q&S p. 108, 110 Some other examples are summarised at L&R p. 35
23. Parsons Q&S p. 110, 112 Tout p. 238
24. Parsons Q&S pp. 104–105, 181 Denholm-Young Seignorial Administration 140–1
25. Parsons Q&S p. 109–10, 113–14 Adam Bassett lost his post because he was £30 in arrears
26. Parsons Q&S pp. 74, 152, 163
27. Parsons Q&S p. 74 101, 135, 250
28. Parsons Q&S p. 102, 156, 272 Rolls of Chester ed. Stewart-Brown 214, 215, 230, 239 L&R 37
29. Parsons Q&S p. 43–4
30. Parsons Q&S 104, 109, 187, 305 C&H 21, 93 LR 35, Spencer Nobility and Kingship 188, 199, 202, 209. Cressingham, whose talents were snapped up by Edward after Eleanor's death, died at Stirling Bridge and was skinned by the Scots: Guisborough p. 303
31. Parsons Q&S p. 154 C&H p. 22, Reg. Pecham 1 38–9 Spencer, p. 28, Prestwich p. 105
32. CCIR 1279–1288, 18, CPR 1281–92 62, 173, 184, 193, 213 CCLR 1288–96 91 224–5, Parsons Q&S p. 78–80
33. Huscroft Expulsion p. 133–4 Parsons Q&S pp. 79, 140 L&R p. 30, 48
34. SC 1/30/53, Parsons Q&S p. 139–141, Howell p. 299
35. Parsons Q&S 79–80, 139, 142 150
36. Huneycutt The High Medieval Queen, Parsons Intercession p. 148. Rodin's sculpture is in Victoria Gardens
37. CPR 1281–92 38 (with Edmund the King's brother) 194, 218. Parsons Intercession p. 147, 149, 156

38. Gesta Abbatum Sancti Albani ed. Riley pp. 410–11 Parsons C&H p. 8 Q&S p. 153 Howell 86, 91–2, 161. The petition of the townsfolk is at SC 1/11/90 reproduced and translated at Transactions of the St Albans and Hertfordshire Architectural and Archaeological Society (1929), p.263.
39. Parsons Intercession p. 151 Q&S 4–5, 38, 44 SC 1/30/44 Reg Pecham ii 555, 765–66

11 The Queen and Her Interests

1. Cotton Nero D II f 179v Morris 142–3 Binski The Early Portrait pp. 211–15. I differ from Binski on the extent to which Henry III's effigy shows his sleepy eye. Readers will be able to form their own view.
2. Reg Pecham ii 56–7, 555, 765–66, Parsons Q&S pp. 4–5
3. SC 1/15/66, 1/30/44 Parsons Q&S 43–4, Intercession p. 152
4. Green Vol 2 325, 335, Vol 3 p. 14–15
5. CPR 1281–1292 414, Parsons Q&S 132, 134, 309 L&R p. 28, Raban Mortmain Legislation and the English Church 1279–1500 p. 76
6. Parsons C&H 66, 76, 159, Botfield and Turner Manners p. 97
7. Part II Title VII Law 8
8. Parsons Q&S p. 51, 275 Powrie p. 102, Gee Women Art and Patronage p. 60, Steane The Archaeology of the Medieval English Monarchy
9. Martin The History and Description of Leeds Castle, HKW ii 695–8, 973, 504, Tolley p. 175–6 Gee p. 59 Parsons Q&S p. 246
10. Parsons Q&S 53, C&H p. 11, English Administration p. 376, 397. Re forks: In the delightfully named 'Coryat's Crudities Hastily Gobbled up in five months travel in France Italy etc' (1611). The use of a fork was considered a laughable Italian affectation by Ben Jonson in Volpone Act IV Scene 1.
11. Landsberg the Medieval Garden p. 128 Parsons Q&S p. 51–2 C&H p. 12, Tolley p. 184–5.
12. RWH 3243, 3224, 3245, Parsons C&H 12, 100, 124, 150 QS 54 English Administration p. 376, Tolley p. 176, Harvey Medieval Gardens p. 78 McLean Medieval English Gardens pp. 102, 228
13. Parsons Q&S p. 53 C&H 70,104 Manners, 102 Harvey, p 78 Landsberg, p. 86, Tolley p. 176
14. Parsons Q&S p. 53 HKW ii 695–8, Harvey pp. 82, 103–6 Tolley p. 176 Gee p. 61, Landsberg p. 60
15. Gee p. 60 Parsons English Administration p. 376, 398, HKW II ii 970–2, McLean 1981 p. 102, Harvey p. 78
16. Harvey pp. 127–30, Hobhouse plants in Garden History p. 78 Taylor Global migrations of ornamental plants p. 26 AM Coates Flowers and their histories pp. 11–12, Tolley p. 176 RHS Gardening p. 159 McLeod In a Unicorn's Garden p. 199. The Cailloel is also referred to as Cailhou and Kaylewell
17. Landsberg p. 128 Gee p. 61, HKW II 53
18. Foedera 568 Prestwich 115–7 Parsons Q&S 55, 276 Morris p. 174, Steane Archaeology, Almond Medieval Hunting Chapter 3. On Quenington see A History of the County of Gloucester: Volume 2 (1907), p. 113. In all probability the two names of Quenington and Down Ampney represent one event – a holiday with the substantial party divided between a couple of premises in the neighbourhood. Down Ampney at that stage appears to have been less of a place than Quenington, and began to acquire a church of its own only in the 1260's and courtesy of the Quenington preceptor
19. Tolley p. 173–5, Parsons C&H p. 19 Davis Medieval Warhorse pp. 9–11
20. Parsons Q&S p. 53, 276 English Administration p. 376, 398 QCB p. 178 Harvey p. 106 Yapp Birds of English Medieval Manuscripts 343, Hutchinson 'Attitudes towards Nature' 5–37 Prestwich p. 115
21. Chess: Ancient precursors and related games (Encyclopædia Britannica 2002)

Vale, The Princely Court: p. 177 Parsons Q&S p. 12 Gee Women Art and Patronage p. 63

22. Branner Manuscript Painting in Paris pp. 3–7 Parsons QCB p. 178.179, 94 Tolley p. 170
23. Parsons Q&S p. 3 C&H p. 13 note 39.
24. Tolley p. 170–171, Thorpe 'Master Richard: A Thirteenth Century Translator of the 'De Re Militarii of Vegetius" 39–50, Legge 'The Lord Edward's Vegetius', Morgan The Douce Apocalypse pp9, 41, 96
25. Parsons C&H p. 13 QCB 179, 195, Escanor lines 15597–15746, The paintings are described at HKW 129, 502, 760, 914, 916
26. Parsons English Administration p. 376, QCB p. 181–2 Spiegel 'Pseudo-Turpin, the Crisis of the Aristocracy …' 207–23, Romancing the Past: pp. 71–74, 78–80
27. Entwistle The Arthurian Legend in the Literatures of the Spanish Peninsula 109, 113 de Malkiel Arthurian Literature in Spain and Portugal in Arthurian Literature in the Middle Ages pp. 406–7 Hilton p. 197 Parsons Q&S p. 28, 265, QCB 182, Procter Alfonso X 15–19 113, Keller Alfonso X 150–2
28. Binski The Painted Chamber at Westminster, Parsons QCB p. 184 Green 2: 284
29. Parsons QCB p. 179, C&H pp. 63–4, 190 Botfield & Turner p. 136. The link to the Trinity Apocalypse is more controversial: see Gee 46–48. Suzanne Lewis will be making the full case in favour of the link to Eleanor in a forthcoming book.
30. Parsons C&H p. 8, 17 Taylor Alms and Oblations pp. 107–108 Wilkinson p. 119
31. Hinnebusch The Early English Friars Preachers 34–7, 44–5, 78–9, Parsons C&H p. 16–17, PPR p. 114, 116–117
32. Parsons PPR p. 111, Howell pp. 23, 44, 65,93–6 258–9
33. Howell pp. 94–5 Wilkinson p. 12, 83
34. Parsons PPR p. 108, 113, C&H 30–1, 63–4 71bis, 74, 78, 94, 95, 102, 117, Botfield & Turner p. 136, New Cambridge Medieval History V Abulafia pp. 274–5 Traditionally the rosary is attributed to St Dominic, but the material does not support this attribution. However, it is certainly the case that prayer counting by reference to paternoster and ave beads was a developing practice, and one encouraged by the Dominicans: Binz Mysteries of the Rosary p. 3, Reinburg Prayer and the Book of Hours pp. 39–40 Dodd, Musson The Reign of Edward II new perspectives p. 227, Parsons p. 41–2, 271
35. Parsons PPR pp. 118–9, 121–2

12 The Queen's Family

1. Morris p. 231, Taylor Alms and Oblations pp. 108–9, HKW ii p. 698
2. Parsons Birth p. 262 irons out the difficulties in the sources which suggest a later date, or a different name. Richardson & Sayles 'The English Parliaments of Edward I' 136, CCR 1272–9, 197–8, AM iv 263 Parsons p. 263 Prestwich p. 101.
3. Green Vol 2 pp. 402–403. The upheavals of the Barons' war and Eleanor's early insignificance from the chroniclers point of view disrupt the statistics prior to 1265
4. Prestwich p. 126 opts for the figure of 14 based on the strict evidence, Parsons for 16, including the child of the first year of the marriage and the unnamed boy hypothesised for 1280–1. On grand multiparity see Bugg, G.J., Atwal, G.S. and Marchs, M. (2002) Grand multipara in modern setting. *British Journal of Obstetrics and Gynaecology*, 109, 249–253, Humphrey, M.D. (2003)
5. Itinerary p. 46 Parsons Birth p. 257, 263
6. Phillips Edward II 47–8, 50, 51–2 Tout ii 166 AM iii 392 Johnstone 24, 26–7
7. Parsons C&H p. 10, Green Vol 2, 282–5, 303–4, 414

8. Trivet 310, Parsons Q&S p. 4 note 4, 9 Green Vol 2 p. 406–7, 412, 414, 420, 421, 423
9. Green Vol 3 p. 4, 19, 39 Gee pp. 19, 22–24, 49, 149–50
10. Parsons C&H p. 10–11, 75, 82, 96, 105, 108, 111, 116, 119, 124
11. Salzman p. 47, Manners p. 96, Johnstone Edward of Carnarvon 76, Szabolcs de Vajay (1989), p. 393. Parsons C&H p. 76 was unable to trace the lineage of Rotheric, and there still appears no obvious candidate amongst Alfonso's numerous illegitimate progeny
12. Parsons C&H pp. 11, 64 65, 114, 77, 68–9, 101 Viscountess Jeanne p. 283–4, 286. Mathilde de Dammartin was also known as Agathe in some records
13. Parsons C&H p. 11, 69, 77, 114 Countess Margaret pp. 669–680
14. Parsons Q&S p. 87 C&H 158–60 p. 35–6. The butler's role was not quite the superior one it was in the Victorian era; there were also heads of the pantry, the kitchen, the wardrobe, the chamber and the treasury
15. Parsons C&H 33–35, 53, 55
16. Parsons C&H 38–9, 155
17. Parsons C&H p. 14–15, 37–8, 139
18. Parsons Q&S p. 89
19. Parsons Q&S p. 90, 91 Ch1 n 87; RWH 1286–9 p. 108
20. Moorman Church Life in England p. 169. Parsons Q&S 97 Morris p. 117, Huscroft PHD, Prestwich p. 234 Reg Peckham I, 46–7; AM iv 373
21. Parsons C&H 19, 77 Q&S p. 47, 143
22. Parsons Q&S p. 35, 160, 182, 268 C&H 61, 74, 110, 155. Parsons describes the relationship with Grandison as 'intriguing'.
23. Parsons C&H p. 42–44, 45–6, Countess Margaret p. 671–3
24. CClR 1279–1288 67–68, Parsons C&H p. 15, 44, 46, 48, 97
25. Parsons C&H p. 49–52, 76 Morris pp. 118, 133, 159, 161
26. CChR ii 190–1, 214, Parsons C&H p. 33, 53 Q&S 189, Spencer p. 187 202
27. Parsons Countess Margaret 670–1, 676–8
28. Fryde, *et al.* Handbook of British Chronology p. 242, DNB John de Vescy

13 The Golden Years

1. Itinerary Foedera 519 Clifford 47, Smith Llywelyn 367–9, Morris 138
2. CPR (1272–81) pp. 77, 85, 98, Foedera 520, Clifford 47 Howell p. 294
3. CCR 1272–9, 197–8, AM iv 263
4. Itinerary, Foedera 521 CFR (1272–1307) p. 45 Clifford 42
5. Foedera 527–8 Itinerary, Prestwich pp. 174–5, Salzman p. 48–9
6. Morris p. 125 Mundhill The King's Jews p. 133, Watt The English Episcopate the state and the Jews p. 141 Abulafia p. 116
7. Each of Abulafia p. 102, Roth History of the Jews p. 71, and Huscroft Expulsion p. 120 see the Statute as a well meaning but highly imperfect attempt to provide a commercial modus vivendi for the Jewish population. See also Mundhill The Kings Jews p. 138, 153–4. On Burnell's views, see his attempts to impede Archbishop Pecham in his aggressive stance against the Jews in the 1280s: Mundhill The King's Jews pp. 139–40
8. Prestwich p. 175, Salzman p. 49–50 Morris 141
9. Chapter 10 above, SC 1/30/135, SC1/30/97
10. World of James of Aragon Chap 7,. Ballesteros, Alfonso X, chap. 15.
11. Morris p. 127–8 HKW ii 715–23, Jones p. 51, Goodall pp. 200–201, Siete Partidas II.XI.ii
12. AM iv, pp. 266–7, FW, p. 216, Itinerary, Prestwich p. 316, Salzman 49, Perry p. 165
13. Maddicott p. 371, Morris 141, Salzman 50–51
14. Itinerary, AM ii p. 122
15. Beresford p. 15 The Parish of St Andrew Holborn pp. 11–12. AM ii p. 122

16. J Morris Welsh Wars p. 115–116
17. Ballesteros pp. 818–27, Macdonald 'Alfonso the Learned and Succession' 647–53 The World of James of Aragon..., chap. 3, n. 46 González, Fernando III, vol. 2, 107–9
18. AM ii p. 123 Morris p. 121, 145 Clifford p. 49.
19. Itinerary, Kanter p. 40
20. Morris p. 147 Parsons Q&S 272
21. Morris p. 150, 154 Vegetius p. 91 see also p. 56 J Morris 130, 138–9. See Caesar's deforestation of the holy grove of Massillia Bellum Civile book 3, Vegetius p. 62 advising the opening of safe ways without regard to the labour involved.
22. Ledger book of Vale Royal Abbey p. 5, Clifford p. 51. As usual, Alfonso's name is wrong: Alfunso.
23. AM p. 124 Vegetius p. 91 J Morris p. 142
24. Beresford pp. 37–8
25. Itinerary, Parsons Birth p. 263 Green vol 2 p. 321 CChR 209,
26. Foedera 536, 544, 545, 554, Green Vol 2 p. 321
27. Foedera 549–50, Prestwich p. 317, Lloyd The English Wool trade in the Middle Ages 66–69 Clifford p. 52. Re the selection of the younger son: John's elder brother Godfrey died in puberty and no distinguished match appears to have been made for him. He was betrothed, but only very shortly before his death, to Margaret, daughter of the Count of Berg, as part of which transaction the Count's claim to the Duchy of Limburg was sold to John of Brabant; it seems more than likely that this was a death bed match made to lend colour to the financial transaction
28. Foedera 554
29. Ballesteros, Alfonso X, pp. 786, 860–66 Foedera 540–1, 607 Flores iii, 48, Prestwich p. 316 Parsons QS 43, 272
30. Prestwich 120, Morris 162 Salzman 54–5, Saul pp. 78–9
31. Green Vol 2 p. 321. Salzman p. 56 Green p. 322 Parsons Birth p. 263
32. Bellenger, Fletcher, Princes of the Church: p. 173
33. Itinerary Parsons Q&S 89, 291
34. Prestwich 249, 250–1, Registrum Peckham vol ii pp. 795–6 Larsen The School of Heretics: Academic Condemnation at the University of Oxford p. 44
35. FW, p. 221 Parsons Q&S p. 33 Brunel Recueil des actes no 466
36. Parsons English Administration pp. 388–9, Plucknett A concise History of the Common Law 5th ed. 1956 pp. 716–18, Pollock & Maitland The History of English Law before the time of Edward I 2d ed. 1898 2.283–6. For the sides' positions: CPR 1272–81 p. 306, Parsons English Administration p. 389–90, 392. On the debts of Ponthieu: Parsons English Administration p. 374–5
37. Foedera 566, 568, 584 Clifford 64–5, 92, Tournament, Crouch p. 45
38. Lettres de rois, reines et autres personages au cours de France at Angleterre pp. 225–6, 232–233 Parsons English Administration p. 382
39. Parsons English Administration p. 376, 377, 383, 397, 398
40. Foedera 575, HKW vol 2 pp. 695–9 Morris p. 172
41. Loomis Arthurian Enthusiast 116–7 Saul p. 80, Spencer p. 39 Crouch Tournament pp. 66–67
42. Steane Archaeology, Parsons Q&S p. 179, SC1/11/51
43. Ballesteros, pp. 919–20 Salzman p. 62
44. CPR 1272–1281 362, 426, 445 CCIR 1272–1279, 80, Huscroft Thesis p. 93, Parsons p. 171
45. Foedera 584, Clifford p. 61
46. Foedera 586, 589, 590, Trabut-Cussac 67–8 C13 242–5, 248, Foedera 580–6, 594 Prestwich p. 319 Ballesteros, pp. 928–29.
47. CCR 1279–88 59–60
48. Itinerary Parsons Q&S 183
49. Foedera p. 593, Green Vol 2 p. 286 Chronologia Johannis de Beke 74e, p. 227,

50. Itinerary Parsons Q&S p. 143, 167, 171, 177, 190. Westcliffe, the property which attracted Archbishop Pecham's particular reproach is near St Margarets at Cliffe, approximately the site of Walletts Court Hotel
51. Parsons English Administration p. 389, Itinerary
52. Ballesteros, pp. 935–41 948–50 966–71, 975–77
53. Prestwich p. 319, Foedera 600, 611, Powicke C13 248, Green vol 2 p. 323, Clifford p. 60

14 The Welsh Years

1. Foedera 609 Runciman Sicilian Vespers p. 212–20, Clifford pp. 77–8
2. Prestwich pp. 185–7 Powicke 13C pp. 415–7 J Morris 150 Morris pp. 175–6 Smith pp. 455, 470
3. Morris p. 177–9 Prestwich p. 182, 183,189 Powicke 419 J Morris 153–5 Smith 460–1, 467.
4. Parsons Q&S p. 164, 184
5. Salzman p. 70 Morris p. 179 Prestwich p. 189 HKW 1 318–27 J Morris 158–9 Goodall The English Castle pp. 215–6
6. Foedera 606, 615, 620–1, 625, 629, 634, 638, Parsons Q&S p. 48 Birth p. 265, J Morris pp. 160–1, 174, Prestwich p. 190 Green Vol 3 p. 3, Vol 2 p. 288 referring to document E36/24 (112), Chaytor, p. 103
7. Vegetius Book III Dispositions for Action, HKW I 354–7, Prestwich p. 190 Morris p. 181, J Morris pp. 176–177
8. Itinerary, Prestwich p. 190, 192–193, Morris p. 181–3, J Morris 173–4 178–80, 188–9 Smith 537–42, 550, Inquisitions Post Mortem, Vol. II, Edward I, 446, p. 265, Huscroft thesis p. 95 (proving that the Burnells who died were not nephews or 'nephews' of Robert)
9. Prestwich pp. 190–191, 193–4. pp. 185–6 J Morris 181–3 Mortimer The Greatest Traitor pp. 10–12 Smith p. 552
10. Prestwich p. 194, 202, Salzman p. 73 Morris p. 186
11. Foedera 625, 665 Green p. 290
12. Itinerary, Prestwich p. 195, 327 J Morris 186, 190–1, Clifford 81, HKW 1 338 Goodall pp. 218–20 Beresford, 37–40, 42, 93–5.
13. Parsons Q&S pp168–9, 171
14. AM ii 401 J Morris 192–5 Goodall p. 218 RR Davies The First English Empire p. 32
15. HKW 1 369–72 Mabinogion p. 104. On Eleanor's recounting of the tale see lines 8–29 of Escanor.
16. AM iii 293, Prestwich p. 196, Morris p. 188 Taylor p. 119
17. Taylor p. 108 Pettifer Welsh Castles p. 71, Parsons Q&S p. 33
18. Ann London 92, Parsons Q&S 162–3 Prestwich p. 202–3, Salzman p. 74–5, Morris 190 Smith 568, 578–9, Pollock and Maitland ii 501 n 1
19. Trivet p. 309 Morris p. 190, Taylor pp. 99, 100, 113, 120, Parsons Q&S p. 197
20. Parsons Q&S pp. 161, 168, 169, 189, 193, 195, 211, Taylor p. 124
21. Taylor p. 112, 117, 121
22. Prestwich p. 206 C13 p. 437, Morris p. 190, Salzman p. 75, L Beverley Smith 'The Statute of Wales 1284', Macdonald, Abulafia p. 119 Beresford 42–44
23. Martinez pp. 500–520
24. Itinerary Safford gives Llyn Cwn Dulyn, which is followed by Morris p. 192. However, the Gough itinerary, and the original documents are clear that the location is 'Baladeulyn' which approximates to modern Nantlle, a little further north; which used to have two lakes 'Deu Llyn'. Taylor 97, 124,125, An Inventory of the Ancient Monuments in Caernarvonshire: III West cxliii, http://www.nantlle.com/history-nantlle-baladeulyn.htm. The Mabinogion pp. 61–2, 202–5, 214.
25. Foedera 626, 627, Green Vol 2 p. 291 HMS p. 388

26. AM ii 402, iii 313, Flores iii 62, Prestwich p. 120, Morris p. 192, Davies p. 31–2, Smith p. 504, Denholm Young The Tournament in the Thirteenth Century 353–5 Saul p. 80 Wickham Early English Stages Vol 1 p. 17
27. Itinerary, Morris p. 193 Taylor 109, 115
28. Parsons Birth p. 261–2 concludes that there is no reason to doubt 19 August as the date or Windsor as the location. Salzman 78–9 Reg Pecham 2.233
29. Morris p. 195 Taylor p. 108–9, 115, 122, Prestwich p. 126, J Morris p. 199–201 Huscroft p. 98
30. Itinerary, Prestwich p. 206–7 Morris p. 195, Salzman p. 76, Morris Bigod Earls 52–3, 130, 144

15 Gascony

1. AM iv 300, Prestwich pp. 321–2, Morris 199, Dunbabin p. 232, Parsons Q&S pp. 161–2, 183, 192 Itinerary
2. Flores iii 63, AM ii 402, Prestwich p. 323, Taylor p. 119
3. Morris 202, Q&S 143 162, 165, 175, 187, 189, 193 Page History of the County of Sussex Vol 2 p. 94
4. Howell 302, 304 Parsons Birth p. 264
5. Itinerary, Morris pp. 202–3, Morris Edward I and the Knights of the Round Table (preferring the 1285 date to the usual 1290 date) Saul pp. 80–1, 86–89
6. RWH 1285–6 424, Itinerary, Parsons Q&S pp. 188–9, Beresford pp. 295, 297–8, Rose-Troup Exeter Vignettes pp. 38–53
7. CPR (1281–92) p. 213 AM ii 403, Prestwich p. 322 C13 p. 255 Morris p. 203
8. Parsons Q&S p. 160, 167, 168, 172, 186, 193
9. RWH 1285–6 56, 226, 346, Green Vol 2 p. 295, Parsons C&H p. 23. On the mensura Johnstone Wardrobe and Household of Henry p. 15, note 1
10. Foedera 664, 665, RWH 2005–6, Parsons C&H p. 50, Itinerary, Salzman p. 83, Prestwich p. 323, Morris p. 204
11. Foedera 667, 668, 669, truce 670, AM ii p. 403–4, RWH 2004, 2009, C13 255–6 Prestwich p. 323, Clifford p. 86
12. RWH 1285–6 596, 611 Foedera 678, AM ii p. 404 Flores p. 65, RG vol 2 No 916, C13 pp. 311–2, Green vol 2 p. 301, Clifford p. 91, Howell 300 Crawford Letters pp. 66–7
13. Salzman p. 83 Trivet 313. This story is missing from AM ii 404, and Flores iii 65–6 which simply have Edward falling ill later in the trip. Foedera 668–70 Morris p. 207, Prestwich p. 323–4, Itineraire p. 168
14. Prestwich p. 324 RWH 1285–6 pp. 66–8, 70–4, 147–56, 200–1 RWH 1287–89 E36/201 no 64, Parsons C&H p. 24
15. Itineraire p. 171 Examples of horse related trivia: RWH 22, 59, 91 On Eleanor's illness: RWH 3244 Parsons Q&S pp. 163, 168, 171
16. Itineraire RWH 1286–9 xii, 66 Parsons C&H 130, Salzman p. 83
17. Itineraire, RWH 785, 1618, Salzman p. 84 apparently based on AM ii p. 404 Flores p. 65–6
18. Chronica Johannis de Oxenedes 269–70, RWH no 31 849, 1619, Morris p. 368
19. AM ii p. 404Prestwich p. 324 Morris p. 209
20. Salzman pp. 84–5 94–5 Prestwich Plantagenet England pp. 136–7 Huscroft Expulsion p. 146, Mundhill England's Jewish Solution p. 66, 280, Trabut-Cussac p. 313, Richardson 225–6, Korlach Masters of the World Vol 2 p. 177 C13 p. 282–4 Martinez pp. 419–20. Although Prestwich rejects a financial motive for the Gascon expulsion, the fact remains that Edward was as usual pressed for money; and that he did take the money liquidated by the expulsion. However, he and Huscroft are obviously right to reject the argument that the expulsion was to fund Charles of Salerno's ransom; the chronology simply does not fit.

21. RWH 1619, 1767, 3239, 4343, Parsons Q&S pp. 160, 163, 172 195, Salzman p. 85 Itineraire p. 178
22. Itineraire p. 179–80 Parsons C&H p. 24 E 36/201 pp. 18, 20, RWH 295 381 384
23. Foedera 677–9 RWH 108, 367, Prestwich p. 324–5, Morris p. 209–10, C13 p. 259 Salzman p. 85, Trabut-Cussac p. 87, Clifford p. 94
24. Foedera 680, 681, Powicke p. 260, Izpegi Le Pays de Soule, Larroque Le Chateau fort de Mauléon
25. Itineraire p. 181–5 RWH 1639.
26. Parsons Q&S p. 163, 165, 170, 171, 173, 184, 195, 196. Technically Despenser was pardoned the 1000 marks in June 1287 and Eleanor took over a claim which Edward had against Despenser, but it is hard to see the acquisition as unrelated to the original claim.
27. Foedera 684 Morris p. 212, Itineraire 161, 164, 187–9, Beresford pp. 593–4, 602 Drouyn Blaye/Bourg-sur-Mer pp9–10, RG vol I supp pp. xxxi, Baker, Man made the Land p. 82, Revue Historique 175–6 p. 581. Bémont's suggestions of Labastide Chalosse and Labastide-Bordeaux as locations have been rejected. The listings of work for Burgus Reginae are at RWH 2143, 3208, 3211–2, 3214, 3217, 4254, 4318–9. The listing for Bonnegarde is at p. 569 of RWH 1287–9.
28. Itineraire p. 190–1 E 159/61 m 9d
29. Itineraire p. 192 Parsons Q&S p. 172 RWH 1731, 2179, 2499, 3223–8 Montan de Aspe is at RWH 2499.
30. C13 pp. 260, 282–4, Salzman p. 86 Prestwich p. 325, Clifford p. 96
31. RWH 1719–1722, 1730 2491, Itineraire p. 196 Morris p. 216 Beresford 187, C13 C13 284
32. RWH 1737, 1755,2665–2669,3230, C13 p. 261, Prestwich p. 325 Parsons Q&S p. 175. The lion and lynx seem to have been counted as a present from Alphonso at a later date: 2894–9. The lynx actually appears in the wardrobe accounts as an 'uncie' or ounce; but the beast which appeared at the Tower after the Gascon trip was a lynx. Michael Prestwich has kindly referred me to E 101/4/10–11 which gives Jakemyn's name and some details of the animals' life at the Tower.
33. Prestwich p. 325, C13 p. 261, Roensch Early Thomistic School pp. 31–2.
34. Foedera 708–9, RWH 4345, Parsons Q&S p. 175 Itineraire RG Vol 2 1064
35. RWH 2535, 2537, 2539, 3239, 3240, 3241 Parsons Viscountess Jeanne, C&H p. 65, Itineraire p. 202, Salzman p. 87.
36. Clifford p. 99 Parsons C&H 52 English Administration p. 379, Itineraire, Itinerary

16 The Last Year, Death and Remembrance

1. Guisborough 216, Prestwich 262, Morris 222, 224
2. Itinerary, Parsons Q&S p. 161–2, 166, 191–2, C&H 52
3. Morris p. 236 Duncan Kingship pp. 165–70, 175–9 Itinerary Parsons Q&S 170–3, 195–6
4. CChR 1257–1300 411, 357, Parsons C&H p. 12, 24,
5. Foedera 551, 553, Green vol 2 p. 330–1, 366–370
6. Foedera 742, Green vol 2 p. 330, Howell 305. The brevity of the Winchester stay militates against it being the occasion of the great 'Round Table' celebration.
7. Annales London p. 98, Chron Bury 94, FW, p. 243, Howell 306, Parsons QS 53 C&H 16, 103
8. Green vol 2 p. 15, 372 Cotton p. 177, Stacey Expulsion p. 90–1, Morris p. 227, Clifford p. 109, 111–13
9. Prestwich p. 343, Parsons C&H p. 24
10. The 15 July 1290 parliament was summoned on 13 June, the 13 October 1275 Parliament on 1 September. There are some suggestions that Clipstone's famous Parliament oak reflects a meeting at the time of King John. However, if any council did take place at Clipstone under John, it was not a formal parliament.
11. Parsons C&H p. 25, Itinerary

12. Itinerary, Morris p. 237 Green vol 2 p. 373
13. Green vol 2p 336, Johnstone p. 24
14. Parsons C&H p. 25–6 Q&S 89, Powrie p. 21–2
15. Flores iii, 71, CPR 1281–92 405, Howell p. 303, Parsons Q&S p. 58,C&H p. 23, Powrie p. 22–3 Linehan p. 173
16. Powrie p. 32–34, 62 Parsons Q&Q 324 Q&S 206, Woodward pp. 65–6 Giesey The Royal Funeral Ceremony p. 22–3 Hallam, in D Parsons ed. Eleanor of Castile p. 17–18
17. The course of the procession has been reconstructed by Powrie and is summarised at p. 192. Powrie suggests (p 142) the reason for the resumption of the Ermine Street route was to take in Waltham Abbey and Abbot Reginald.
18. AM iii p. 362, Opus Chronicorum 50, Powrie p. 98, 142, Galloway 12–13 Parsons Q&S 60
19. Foedera 743 Barnwell p. 226 Flores iii 171–2,Hallam p. 18 in D Parsons, Giesey p. 32, Galloway 131–2, Parsons 60 Parsons C&H 133 Huscroft Thesis p. 108 Parsons Q&S 50
20. Cambridge University Library MS Ee.3.59, fo. 9 Parsons Q&S 207 Coldstream p. 57, Lindley Romanticising Reality p. 72 in D Parsons Gee p. 112 Leonor of England and Eleanor of Castile pp. 77–83
21. Powrie records the payments made at p. 63, 163, Hinnebusch p. 45, HKW I p. 482, Botfield and Turner pp. lxxvi-vii, 98, 100, 1–2–3, 108–9, 111, 113
22. Parsons Q&S p. 209, Perkinson, p. 97–98, 107, Binski, Medieval Death 110. Perkinson p. 107 has a good picture of a montjoie.
23. Coldstream Commissioning and Design p. 57 in D Parsons, Parsons Q&S p. 209, 212, Steane Archaeology p. 169
24. Lindley Romanticising Reality p. 76–78 Powrie p. 124 Coldstream Commissioning and Design p. 57
25. Rimmer's Ancient Stone Crosses of England 1875 Powrie p. 148–9 Coldstream p. 57 Lindley p. 75, 77
26. Powrie p. 65–8, 80–3, 136, Vallance, Old Crosses and Lychgates p. 96
27. Powrie p. 148, 165, Vallance p. 102, 107 Coldstream p. 57
28. Powrie p. 125, 129, 148, Lindley pp. 80–1Coldstream p. 59
29. Guisborough 227–8, AnnPaulini 225, AM iii 366, Worcester 506, Parsons Q&S p. 213–5, 324, Manners 137 Lathbury Denham 79–83
30. SC 8/280/13964, Parsons Q&S p. 132, 215, 218, 324, C&H pp. 65–6, 134, Johnstone Letters 115–6, Powrie p. 23, Manners 108, 135

17 Afterlives

1. Prestwich 125, 355, Morris 269, Vale Edward I and the French Rivalry and Chivalry TCE ii p. 166–8
2. Prestwich 128–9 Morris 375
3. Clifford pp
4. Martinez p. 181–3
5. Parsons Q&S p. 207 216–8, Opus Chronicorum 26, 49–50
6. Rishanger 120–121, Gesta Abbatum sancti Albani 411–12, Walsingham Historia Anglicana I 32, Parsons Q&S pp. 219–20
7. Parsons p. 177, 218–219, 221, 320
8. Parsons p. 221, 223 citing Holinshead Chronicles of England ii 431, 435, 439, Camden Britannia I 390–1 trans Gibson 1695 col 320–1, Camden 'Remains of a Larger Work ...' p. 236–7
9. Parsons p. 224–6, 232 The play is available at Internet Archive: https://archive. org/stream/kingedwardfirst00peeluoft#page/n11/mode/2up
10. Powrie 66–7, 80–1, 82–4, 130 135–6, 141, Vallance p. 101, Celia Fiennes Journey 1697 London to Coventry: http://www.visionofbritain.org.uk/travellers/ Fiennes

11. Stow 1 215, 266, Keen English Society p. 115, Powrie 165–167179 Vallance 106 108.
12. Parsons p. 237 Ed Salzman, A History of the County of Northampton Vol 4 pp. 252–259, Vallance pp. 98–100
13. Parsons pp. 237–40, Sova Banned Plays pp. 87–89. The play can be found at: http://ota.ahds.ac.uk/text/3539.html
14. Parsons Q&S p. 240, 245–6, L&R p. 24, Pope-Hennessy Agnes Strickland 303–4

Appendix 1 The Robert Burnell Letter

1. Parsons L&R p. 51
2. CPR 1272–81 pp. 58, 63–4 November 1274. Her grandmother was Garsende of Provence, Eleanor of Provence's paternal aunt. However, Constance was betrothed at one point to one of Eleanor's brothers, and previously married to one of her Aragonese cousins (the son of Alfonso VIII's daughter Eleanor)
3. Crawford p. 73 SC 1/10/50 SC 1/30/50 SC 1/7/98
4. Huscroft Thesis p. 137. 40 of the total of 160 surviving letters are from her. Parsons QI p. 151
5. SC 1/7/98 SC1/23/27 The mother of the King formulation is found in numerous letters in the chancery SC 1/23 series eg. 8–12, 17 as well as in the 1/10 series: 40–2, 46–7
6. Royal letter No 1454 in Wood p. 47–8
7. CPR p. 226, CPR Henry III vol 6 p. 662
8. Crawford p. 73, SC 1/10/50, RG, Crawford p. 75 SC 1/30/50
9. Royal letter No 1454 in Wood p. 47–8 Foedera 569 (date April May 1279), 576 dated November

Bibliography

Primary Sources

Annales Halesiensibus

Annales Londoniensis: Chronicles of the Reigns of Edward I and Edward II ed. W. Stubbs (Rolls Series, 1882) (**AL**)

Annales Monastici ed. H. R. Luard (Rolls Series, 1864–9) (**AM**)

de Cotton, Bartholomaeus *Historia Anglicana* (AD 449–1298) ed. H. R. Luard (Rolls Series, 1859)

Lettres de rois, reines et autres personages au cours de France at Angleterre eds Brequigny and Champollion-Figeac (Paris, 1839)

Calendar of Ancient Correspondence relating to Wales ed. J. G. Edwards (Cardiff, 1975) (**CAC**)

Calendar of Chancery Rolls 1277–1326

Calendar of Charter Rolls (**CChR**)

Calendar of Close Rolls (**CClR**)

Calendar of Fine Rolls (**CFR**)

Calendar of Inquisitions Miscellaneous (**CIM**)

Calendar of Liberate Rolls (**CLR**)

Calendar of Patent Rolls (**CPR**)

Cantigas Santa Maria (**CSM**)

Paris, Matthew *Chronica Majora* ed. H. R. Luard (Rolls Series) (**CM**)

Chronica Johannis de Oxenedes ed. H. Ellis (Rolls Series, 1859)

Chronicle of Bury St Edmunds 1212–1301 ed. A. Grandsen (1964)

Chronicle of Walter of Guisborough ed. H. Rothwell (Camden Society lxxxixx, 1957)

Chronicle of William Rishanger of the Barons' Wars ed. J. O. Halliwell (Camden Society, 1840)

Chronicon de Lenercost ed. J. Stevenson (Matland Club, 1839)

Close Rolls (**ClR**) 1237–42, 1242–471251–1253, 1253–4 1261–4 Cr 1268–72

De Rebus Hispaniae (**DRH**)

Flores Historiarum ed. H. R. Luard (Rolls Series, 1890) (**Flores**)

Foedera, Conventiones, Litterae, et Acta Publica I. ii, ed. T. Rymer (Record Commission ed., 1816) (**Foedera**)

Historical Works of Gervase of Canterbury ed. W. Stubbs (Rolls Series, 1880)

Florentii Wigorniensis monachi Chronicon ed. Bohn (London, 1854)

Gerald of Wales *The Autobiography of Giraldus Cambrensis* trans. and ed. H. E. Butler (London: J. Cape, 1937)

Gervase of Canterbury ed. W. Stubbs (London, 1880)

Gesta Abbatum Sancti Albani ed. Riley (London, 1867)

Les gestes des Chiprois, Recueil des Historiens des Croisades (Paris 1841–1906)

Holinshead *The Chronicle*, 1577 (Dent 1955)

Al-Furat, Ibn *Ayyubids, Mamlukes and Crusaders: Selections from the Tarikh al-Duwal wa'l-Muluk of Ibn al-Furat* ed. Riley-Smith (Heffer, 1991)

John of Salisbury *Letters* ed. W. J. Millor & H. E. Butler, vol. 2

The Ledger Book of Vale Royal Abbey ed. Brownbill (Lancashire and Cheshire Historical Society, 1914)

Liber Feodorum/Testa de Nevill (HMSO 1920)

Liber De antiquis legibus: Cronica maiorum et vicecomitum Londoniarum ed. Stapleton (Camden Society, 1846) *Mabinogion*

William of Newburgh *Historia Rerum Anglicarum* ed. C. Johnson (London: SPCK, 1920)

Primera Cronica General (**PCG**)

Records of the Wardrobe and Household 1285–1286, 1286–1289 eds B. F. & C. R. Byerly (1977, 1986) (**RWH**)

Les Registres de Innocent IV

Les Registres de Gregoire X ed. G. Cadier (Paris, 1892–1906)

Roles Gascons ed. M. Bemont (Paris, 1885–1906)

Royal and other historical letters illustrative of the reign of Henry III ed. W. W. Shirley (Rolls Series, 1862–6)

Robert of Gloucester's Chronicle ed. Hearne (Oxford, 1724)

Roberti Grosseteste Epistolae ed. H. R. Luard (Longman, 1861)

Siete Partidas ed. S. Burns (University of Pennsylvania Press, 2000)

Robert de Torigny *Chronicle in Chronicles of the reigns of Stephen, Henry II, and Richard I* ed. R. Howlett (London, 1889)

Trivet, Nicholas *Annales Sex Regum Angliae* ed. T. Hog (1845)

Vegetius, *De Re Militarii*

National Archives:
E 101/349
SC 1/7/98
SC 1/10/50
SC 1/11/11, 51, 90
SC 1/15/66,
SC1/16/20
SC/1/18/88–90
SC1/23/27
SC1/29/190
SC 1/30/44, 50, 53, 97 135
SC8/280/13964

Secondary Sources

Abulafia, A. S., *Christian Jewish Relations 1000–1300* (Routledge, 2008)

Ackroyd, P., *London Under* (Vintage, 2012)

Adair, P., 'Countess Clemence' in Vann, T. (ed.), *Queens Regents Potentates* (Boydell and Brewer, 1995)

Ailes, A., 'Heraldry in Medieval England' in Coss & Keen, *Heraldry, Pageantry and Social Display in Medieval England* (Boydell, 2002)

Akehurst, F. R. P. (ed.), *A Handbook of the Troubadours* (University of California Press, 1995)

Alfonso X, *Setenario* ed. K. H. Vanderford (Buenos Aires, 1945)

Allmand, C., *The De Re Militari of Vegetius: The Receptions, Transmission and Legacy of Roman text in the Middle Ages* (CUP, 2012)

Almond, R., *Medieval Hunting* (History Press, 2003)

Asbridge, T., *The Crusades* (Simon & Schuster, 2010)

Baer, Y., *A History of the Jews in Christian Spain* (Varda, 2002)

Baker, Manley & Harley, *Man Made the Land* (David & Charles, 1973)

Baldwin, J. W., *The Government of Philip Augustus: Foundations of French Royal Power* (University of California Press, 1986)

Ballesteros y Beretta, *Alfonso X el Sabio* (Barcelona: Salvat, 1963)

Barker, J., *The Tournament in England 1100–1400* (Boydell, 2003)

Barron, C., *The Parish of St Andrew Holborn* (London, 1979)

Barton, S., *The Aristocracy in Twelfth-Century León and Castile* (CUP, 2002)

Bellenger & Fletcher, *Princes of the Church: A History of the English Cardinals* (Sutton, 2001)

Benham, W., *Old St Paul's Cathedral* (London: Seeley & Co, 1902)

Bensch, S., *Barcelona and Its Rulers 1096–1291* (CUP, 2002)

Beresford, M., *New Towns of the Middle Ages* (Farrar, Straus & Giroux, 1999)

Bianchini J., *The Queen's Hand: power and authority in the reign of Berenguela of Castile* (University of Pennsylvania Press, 2012)

Binski, P., 'The Early Portrait, Verbal or Pictorial' in Schmidt (ed.), *Europaische Kunst um 1300* (Wien: Bohalu, 1986)

Binski, P., *Medieval Death: Ritual and Representation* (Cornell University Press, 1996)

Binz, S., *Mysteries of the Rosary* (Twenty-Third Publications, 2005)

Blomefield, F., *History of Norfolk* (1807)

Botfield & Turner, *Manners and Household Expenses of England in the Thirteenth and Fifteenth Centuries* (London, 1841)

Bowie, C., *Daughters of Henry II and Eleanor of Aquitaine* (Boydell & Brewer, 2014)

Branner, R., *Manuscript Painting in Paris during the Reign of Saint Louis* (Berkeley, 1977)

Brewer (Vol. 1) & Howlett (Vol. 2) (eds), *Monumenta Franciscana* (1858/1882)

Bruch, H. (ed.), *Chronologia Johannis de Beke* (The Hague, 1973)

Brunel, C., *Recueil des actes des contes de Ponthieu: 1026–1279* (Paris, 1930)

Bugg, Atwal & Marchs, 'Grand multipara in modern setting', *British Journal of Obstetrics and Gynaecology*, 109 (2002), pp. 249–253

Burns, R. I. (ed.), *The World of Alfonso the Learned and James the Conqueror: Intellect and Force in the Middle Ages* (Princeton, 1985)

Burns, R. I., 'Iberia and the Mediterranean World in the Middle Ages' in Simon & Chevedden (eds), *Iberia and the Mediterranean World of the Middle Ages* (Brill, 1996)

Burt, C., *Edward I and the Governance of England 1272–1307* (CUP, 2012)

Camden, W., *Britannia* (London, 1616)

Camden, W., *Remains Concerning Britain* (Smith, 1870)

Caronia, N., *La Cuba di Palermo (Arabi E Normanni Nel XII Secolo)* (Palermo: Linee D'Arte Giada S. R. L., 1988)

Carpenter, D., *The Battles of Lewes and Evesham 1264–5* (British Battlefield, 1987)

Carpenter, D., *The Minority of Henry III* (Methuen, 1990)

Carpenter & Maclean (eds), *Power of the Weak: Studies on Medieval Women* (University of Illinois Press, 1995)

Carpenter, D., *Reign of Henry III* (London, 1996)

Carpenter, D., 'A Noble in Politics' in Duggan (ed.), *Nobles and Nobility in Medieval Europe, Concepts, Origins, Transformations* (Boydell, 2002)

Carpenter, D., 'The Last Hours of Simon de Montfort', *English Historical Review* 165(461) (2000), pp. 378–412

Carpenter, D., 'Westminster Abbey in Politics' in TCE vii

Chaytor, H. J., *A History of Aragon and Catalonia* (London: Methuen, 1933)

Church, S. D., *King John New Interpretations* (Boydell, 2007)

Clifford, E. R., *Knight of Great Renown* (University of Chicago Press, 1961)

Coates A. M., *Flowers and Their Histories* (Black, 1968)

Coldstream, N., 'The Commissioning and Design of the Eleanor Crosses' in Parsons, D., *Eleanor of Castile*

Colvin, H. (ed.), *History of the King's Works* (1963–1982) (**HKW**)

Corfis, I. A., *Al Andalus, Sepharad and Medieval Iberia: Cultural Contact and Diffusion* (Brill, 2009)

Coss, P. & S. Lloyd (eds), *Thirteenth Century England vols I-IV* (Boydell & Brewer, 1985–1989) **(TCE)**

Coss, P., *The Knight in Medieval England 1000–1400* (Sutton, 1996)

Coss, P. & M. Keen, *Heraldry, Pageantry and Social Display in Medieval England* (Boydell, 2012)

Costain, T. B., *The Three Edwards* (Popular Library, 1983)

Cox, D., *The Battle of Evesham* (Vale of Evesham Historical Society, 1989)

Crawford, A., *Letters of the Queens of England* (History Press, 2002)

Crouch, D., *William Marshal: Knighthood War and Chivalry 1147–1219* (Routledge, 2002)

Crouch, D., *Tournament: A Chivalric Way of Life* (Hambleden Continuum, 2005)

Crow, J. A., *Spain, the Root and the Flower – an Interpretation of Spain and the Spanish People* (University of California Press, 2005)

Davidsohn, *Forschungen zur Gesch von Florenz* (Berlin, 1898)

Davies, R. R., *The First English Empire Power and Identities in the British Isles* (USA: OUP, 2000)

Davis, R. H. C., *Medieval Warhorse: Origin, Development and Redevelopment* (Thames & Hudson, 1989)

de Malkiel, L., 'Arthurian Literature in Spain and Portugal' in Loomis, R. S. (ed.), *Arthurian Literature in the Middle Ages* (Oxford, 1959)

Denholm Young, N., *Seignorial Administration in England* (OUP, 1937)

Denholm Young, N., *Richard of Cornwall* (Blackwell, 1947)

Denholm Young, N., 'The Tournament in the Thirteenth Century' in Hunt (ed.), *Studies in Medieval History presented to F. M. Powicke* (Oxford, 1948)

Dickie, J., 'The Islamic Garden in Spain' in Ettinghausen & MacDougall (eds), *The Islamic Garden* (Washington DC: Dumbarton Oaks, 1976)

Dillard, H., *Daughters of the Reconquest: Women in Castilian Town Society 1100–1300* (CUP, 1990)

Dodd, M. (ed.), *The Reign of Edward II: New Perspectives* (York Medieval Press, 2006)

Downey, D., *Spanish-Irish Relations Through the Ages* (Four Courts Press, 2008)

Drouyn, L., *Blaye/Bourg-sur-Mer Histoire* (Militaire Editions des Regionalismes, 2003)

Du Fresne du Cange, C., *Histoire des Comtes de Ponthieu* (Paillart, 1916)

Dunbabin, J., *Charles I of Anjou: Power, Kingship and State-Making in Thirteenth-Century Europe* (Routledge, 1998)

Entwistle, W., *The Arthurian Legend in the Literatures of the Spanish Peninsula* (Phaeton Press, 1925)

Gater & Wheeler (eds), *Survey of London Vol 16–18 (St Martin in the fields/Charing Cross)* (London, 1935)

Gee, L. L., *Women Art and Patronage from Henry III to Edward III* (Boydell, 2002)

Giesey, R., *The Royal Funeral Ceremony in Renaissance France* (Droz, 1960)

Glick, T. F., *From Muslim Fortress to Christian Castle: Social and Cultural Change in Medieval Spain* (MUP, 2002)

González Jiménez, M., *Crónica de Alfonso X* (Murcia, 1998)

González, J., *Reinado et Diplomas de Fernando III* (Cordoba, 1983)

González, J., *Las conquistas de Fernando III en Andalucía* (Maxtor, 2006)

Goodman, A., 'Alphonso X and the English Crown' in Rodruigez, Fernandez & Graino (eds), *Alfonso El Sabio: Vida, Obra e Epoca* (Madrid, 1989)

Gough, H., *Itinerary of Edward I 1271–1307* (Paisley, 1900)

Green, M. A. E., *Lives of the Princesses* (Colburn, 1854)

Hallam, E. M., 'The Eleanor Crosses and Royal Burial Customs' in Parsons, D. (ed.), *Eleanor of Castile 1290–1990: Essays to commemorate the 700th Anniversary of her death: 28 November 1290* (Watkins, 1991)

Harvey, *Medieval Gardens* (Batsford, 1981)

Hilton, L., *Queens Consort: England's Medieval Queens* (Pegasus, 2010)

Hinnebusch, W., *The Early English Friars Preachers* (Rome, 1951)

Hobhouse, P., *Plants in Garden History* (Pavilion, 1999)

Holinshead, R., *Chronicles of England, Scotland and Ireland* (Johnson, 1807)

Houseley, N., *Fighting for the Cross: Crusading to the Holy Land* (Yale, 2008)

Howell, M., 'The Children of Eleanor of Provence and Henry III' in TCE iv

Howell, M., *Eleanor of Provence: Queenship in Thirteenth Century England* (Blackwell, 2001)

Hoyt, *Royal Demesne in English Constitutional History, 1066–1272* (Greenwood, 1968)

Hughes, 'From Brideprice to Dowry in Mediterranean Europe', *Journal of Family History*, 3 (1978), pp. 262–96

Huneycutt, L., *The High Medieval Queen: the Esther Topos* in Carpenter & Maclean (eds), *Power of the Weak: Studies on Medieval Women* (University of Illinois Press, 1995)

Huscroft R., *The Political Career and Personal Life of Robert Burnell Chancellor of Edward I* (London: PhD thesis, 2000)

Huscroft, R., *Expulsion: England's Jewish Solution* (Tempus 2006)

Jobson, A., *The First English Revolution: Simon de Montfort Henry III and the Baron's War* (Bloomsbury, 2012)

Johnstone, H., 'Wardrobe and Household of Henry, son of Edward I', *Bulletin of the John Rylands Library,* vii (1922–3), p. 397

Johnstone, H., *Edward of Carnarvon* (MUP, 1946)

Jones, N., *The Tower* (Hutchinson, 2011)

Kanter, J., 'Peripatetic and Sedentary Kingship', *Thirteenth Century England*, XIII (Proceedings of the Paris Conference, 2009)

Keen, M., *English Society in the Later Middle Ages, 1348–1500* (London: Penguin, 1990)

Labande, 'Les Filles de Aliénor' CCM, 29 (1–2) (1986), pp. 101–8

Lacy, N. J., *The New Arthurian Encyclopedia* (New York: Garland, 1991)

Landsberg, S., *The Medieval Garden* (British Museum Press, 1998)

Larroque, *Le Chateau Fort de Mauleon, Le Pays de Soule* (Baigorri, 1994)

Larsen A. E., *The School of Heretics: Academic Condemnation at the University of Oxford* (Brill, 2011)

Laurentie, J., *St Ferdinand* (Paris: J. Gabaldoa, 1910)

Legge, M. D., 'The Lord Edward's Vegetius', *Scriptorium*, 7 (1953), pp. 262–65

Lethaby, *Westminster Abbey and the King's Craftsmen: A Study of Medieval Building* (London: Duckworth, 1906)

Levillan, P., *Encyclopaedia of the Papacy* (Routledge, 2002)

Lewis & Thacker, *A History of the County of Chester* (University of London, 2005)

Lindley, P., 'Romanticising Reality: The Sculputual Memorials of Queen Eleanor and their Context' in Parsons, D. (ed.), *Eleanor of Castile 1290–1990: Essays to commemorate the 700th Anniversary of her death: 28 November 1290* (Watkins, 1991)

Linehan, P., *Spain: A Partible Inheritance 1157–1300* (Wiley, 2008)

Lloyd, S. D., 'The Lord Edward's Crusade 1270–1272: Its setting and significance' in Gillingham & Holts (eds), *War and Government in the Middle Ages* (Woodbridge, 1984)

Lloyd, T. H., *The English Wool Trade in the Middle Ages* (CUP, 2005)

Lodge, E. C., *Gascony under English Rule* (Methuen, 1926)

Lomax, D. *Reconquest of Spain* (Longman, 1978)

Loomis, A., 'Edward I, Arthurian Enthusiast', *Speculum*, 28(1) (1953), pp. 14–27

Lullin & de Fort (eds), *Regeste Genevois* (Geneva, 1866)

Macdonald, 'Law and Politics: Alfonso's program of Political Reform' in Burns (ed.), *The World of Alfonso the Learned and James the Conqueror: Intellect and Force in the Middle Ages* (Princeton, 1985)

Maddicott, J. R., *Simon de Montfort* (CUP, 1996)

Makrizi, A., *Histoire des Sultans Mamlouks* (Paris, 1837)

Malo, H., *Un grand Feudataire Renaud de Dammartin et la coalition de Bouvines* (Paris: Champion, 1898)

Marsh, F. B., *English Rule in Gascony 1199–1259* (Ann Arbor: Wahr, 1912)

Martin, C. W. *The History and Description of Leeds Castle, Kent* (Nichols and Sons, 1869)

Martínez, H. S. & Cisneros (trans.), *Alfonso X, the Learned* (Brill, 2010)

McCash, J. H., *The Cultural Patronage of Medieval Women* (University of Georgia Press, 1996)

McFarlane, K. B., 'Had Edward I a Policy towards the Earls?' in McLeod (ed.), *The Nobility of Later Medieval England* (USA: OUP, 1981)

Monicat, M. J., *Recueil des Actes de Philippe Auguste Roi de France* (Paris, 1996)

Morand, S., *Histoire de Sainte Chapelle Royale de Paris* (Paris, 1790)

Morgan N., *The Douce Apocalypse Picturing the End of the World in Medieval England* (Bodleian, 2006)

Morris, M., *The Bigod Earls of Norfolk in the Thirteenth Century* (Boydell, 2005)

Morris, M., 'Edward I and the Knights of the Round Table' in Brand & Cunningham (eds), *Foundations of Medieval Scholarship: Records Edited in Honour of David Crook* (Borthwick, 2006)

Morris, M., *Edward I: A Great and Terrible King* (Windmill, 2009)

Mortimer, I., *The Greatest Traitor: The Life of Sir Roger Mortimer, 1st Earl of March* (Jonathan Cape, 2003)

Mugnier, F., *Les Savoyards en Angleterre au XIII' siècle et Pierre d'Aigueblanche* (Chambery, 1890)

O'Callaghan, J. F., *A History of Medieval Spain* (Cornell University Press, 1983) (**HMS**)

O'Callaghan, J. F., *Alfonso X and the Cantigas Santa Maria, a poetic biography* (Brill, 1998)

O'Callaghan, J. F., *Reconquest and Crusade in Medieval Spain* (University of Pennsylvania Press, 2011)

O'Callaghan, J. F., *The Learned King: The Reign of Alfonso X of Castile* (University of Pennsylvania Press, 1993)

Ormrod, W. Mark, *Edward III* (Yale University Press, 2012)

Page, W. (ed.), 'House of Knights Hospitallers: The preceptory of Quenington', *A History of the County of Gloucester*, 2 (1907), p. 113.

Page, W. (ed.), *History of the County of London Vol. 1: London within the Bars* (London, 1909)

Page, W., *London, its origin and early development* (London: Constable & Co, 1923), p. 192

Parsons, D. (ed.), *Eleanor of Castile 1290–1990: Essays to commemorate the 700th Anniversary of her death: 28 November 1290* (Watkins, 1991)

Parsons, J. C., *Court and Household of Eleanor of Castile in 1290* (PIMS, 1977) (**C&H**)

Parsons, J. C., 'Eleanor of Castile and the Countess Margaret of Ulster', *Genealogists Magazine*, 20(10) (1982)

Parsons, J. C., 'The Year of Eleanor of Castile's birth and her children by Edward I', *Mediaeval Studies*, XLVI (1984)

Parsons, J. C., 'The Beginnings of English Administration in Ponthieu', *Medieval Studies*, L (1988), p. 369

Parsons, J. C., 'Eleanor of Castile and the Viscountess Jeanne of Châtelleraut', *Genealogists Magazine*, 23(4) (1989), p. 283

Parsons, J. C., 'Eleanor of Castile: Legend and Reality through seven centuries' in Parsons, D. (ed.), *Eleanor of Castile 1290–1990: Essays to commemorate the 700th Anniversary of her death: 28 November 1290* (Watkins, 1991) (**LR**)

Parsons, J. C., 'Mothers, Daughters, Marriage, Power: Some Plantagenet Evidence 1150–1500' in Parsons, J. (ed.), *Medieval Queenship* (New York: St Martins, 1993)

Parsons, J. C., 'Piety Power and the Reputations of two thirteenth century English Queens' in Vann, T. (ed.), *Queens Regents Potentates* (Boydell and Brewer, 1995)

Parsons, J. C., 'The intercessionary patronage of Queens Margaret and Isabella of France' in TCE vi

Parsons, J. C., 'The Queen's Intercession in Thirteenth Century England' in Carpenter & Maclean (eds), *Power of the Weak: Studies on Medieval Women* (University of Illinois Press, 1995)

Parsons, J. C., *Eleanor of Castile: Queen and Society in Thirteenth Century England* (New York: St Martin's Press, 1995) (**Q&S**)

Parsons, J. C., *Of Queens, Courts and Books: Reflections on the Literary Patronage of Thirteenth Century Plantagenet Queens* in McCash, J. H., *The Cultural Patronage of Medieval Women* (University of Georgia Press, 1996) (**QCB**)

Perkinson, S., *The Image of the King: A Prehistory of Portraiture in Late Medieval France* (University of Chicago Press, 2009)

Perry, G., *John of Brienne: King of Jerusalem, Emperor of Constantinople c. 1175–1237* (CUP, 2013)

Phillips, S., *Edward II* (Yale, 2010)

Plucknett, T. F. T., *A Concise History of the Common Law* (Butterworth, 5th ed., 1956)

Pollock & Maitland, *The History of English Law before the time of Edward I* (CUP, 2nd ed., 1898)

Poole, A. L., *The Oxford History of England: From Domesday Book to Magna Carta* (Clarendon Press, 1951)

Powicke, F. M., *Henry III and the Lord Edward* (Clarendon Press, 1966) (**HIII**)

Powicke, F. M., *The Loss of Normandy* (Manchester, 1963)

Powicke, F. M., *The Thirteenth Century* (Clarendon Press, 1962) (**C13**)

Powrie J., *Eleanor of Castile* (KAFB Brewin Books, 1990)

Pratt, F., *The Battles that Changed History* (Doubleday, 2013)

Prestwich, M. C., 'The Piety of Edward I' in Ormerod (ed.), *England in the Thirteenth Century* (Woodbridge, 1986)

Prestwich, M. C., *Edward I* (Yale, 1997)

Ray, J., *The Sephardic Frontier: The Reconquista and the Jewish Community in Medieval Iberia* (Cornell University Press, 2013)

Reinburg, V., 'Prayer and the Book of Hours' in Pearson (ed.), *Envisioning Gender in Burgundian Devotional Art* (Ashgate, 2005)

Richardson & Sayles, 'The English Parliaments of Edward I', *BIHR*, 5 (1928), p. 136

Richardson H. G., 'The coronation of Edward I', *BIHR*, 15(44) (1937), pp. 94–99

Ridgeway, H., 'King Henry III and the "Aliens"' in TCE ii

Ridgeway, H., 'The Lord Edward and the Provisions of Oxford (1258): A study in faction' in TCE i

Roensch, F. J., *Early Thomistic School* (Domincans, 1964)

Roth, C., *A History of the Jews in England* (Clarendon Press 1989)

Royal Commission on the Ancient and Historical Monuments of Wales, *An Inventory of the Ancient Monuments in Caernarvonshire* (1956–64)

Ruegg & Ridder-Simoens, *A History of the University in Europe* (CUP, 1994–2011)

Ruggles, D. F., *Gardens, Landscape and Vision in the Palaces of Islamic Spain* (Penn State Press, 2002)

Runciman, S., *The Sicilian Vespers: A History of the Mediterreanan World in the Late Thirteenth Century* (University Press, 1960)

Runciman, S., *A History of the Crusades* (CUP, 1987)

Sadler, J., *The Second Barons War* (Pen and Sword, 2008)

Salzman, L. F. (ed.), *A History of the County of Northampton* (1937)

Saul, N., *For Honour and Fame: Chivalry in England 1066–1500* (Bodley Head, 2011)

Scott, S. P., *History of the Moorish Empire in Europe* (Lippincott, 1904)

Shadis, M., *Berenguela of Castile (1180–1246) and Political Women in the High Middle Ages* (Palgrave Macmillan, 2009)

Smith, J. B., *Llywelyn ap Gruffudd: Prince of Wales* (University of Wales Press, 2001)

Smith, L. B., 'The Statute of Wales 1284', *Welsh History Review*, X (1980–1), pp. 127–54

Spencer, A., *Nobility and Kingship in Medieval England: The Earls and Edward I, 1272–1307* (CUP, 2013)

Spiegel, G. M., 'Pseudo-Turpin, the Crisis of the Aristocracy and the Beginnings of Vernacular Historiography in France', *Journal of Medieval History*, 12 (1986), pp. 207–23

Spiegel, G. M., *Romancing the Past: The Rise of Vernacular Prose Historiography in Thirteenth-Century France* (Berkeley, 1993)

Stacey, R. C., *Politics, Policy and Finance under Henry III* (Oxford, 1987)

Staniland, K., 'The Nuptials of Alexander III of Scotland and Margaret Plantagenet', *Nottingham Medieval Studies*, 30 (1986), pp. 20–45

Steane, J., *Archaeology of the Medieval English Monarchy* (Routledge, 1993)

Stoksad &Stannard, *Gardens of the Middle Ages* (Lawrence: Spencer Museum of Art, University of Kansas, 1983)

Strickland, A., *Lives of the Queens of England* (Lea and Blanchard, 1852)

Stuart, R., *Gardens of the World: The Great Traditions* (Frances Lincoln, 2010)

Studd, J. R., *A Catalogue of the Acts of the Lord Edward, 1254–1272* (Leeds: PhD Thesis, 1971)

Studd, J. R., 'The Lord Edward and Henry III', *BIHR*, XLX (1977)

Studd, J. R., *The Marriage of Henry of Almain and Constance of Bearn* in TCE iii

Tabaa, Y., 'The Medieval Islamic Garden: Typology and Hydraulics' in Hunt, *Garden History* (Dunbarton Oaks, 1992)

Taylor, A., 'Royal Alms & Oblations in the later 13th century' in Emisson & Stephens (eds), *Tribute to an Antiquary* (Leopard's Head Press, 1976)

Taylor, J. M., *Global migrations of Ornamental Plants* (Missouri Botanical Gardens Press, 2009)

Thacker & Escobar (trans), *The Chronicle of Alfonso X* (University of Kentucky Press, 2002)

Thorpe, L., '*Maistre Richard*, A Thirteenth-Century Translator of the *De Re Militari* of Vegetius', *Scriptorium*, 6 (1952), pp. 39–51

Tolley, T., 'Eleanor of Castile and the 'Spanish' Style' in Ormerod (ed.), *England in the Thirteenth Century* (Woodbridge, 1986)

Tomasi, Z., *Palaces of Sicily* (New York: Rizzoli, 1998)

Tout, T., *Chapters in the Administrative History of Medieval England: the Wardrobe, the Chamber and the Small Seals* (Manchester, 1920–33)

Trabut-Cussac, J. P., 'Itineraire D'Edouard 1er en France 1286–1289', *BIHR*, 25 (1952), pp. 166–73 (**Itineraire**)

Trabut-Cussac, J. P., 'Le finacement de la croisade anglaise de 1270', *Bibl de L'ecole de Chartres*, cxix (1961), p. 114

Trabut-Cussac, J. P., *L'Administration Anglaise en Gascogne* (Droz, 1972)

Transactions of the St Albans and Hertfordshire Architectural and Archaeological Society (1929)

Treharne & Sanders (eds), *Documents of the Baronial Movement of Reform and Rebellion, 1258–1267* (Oxford, 1973) (**DBM**)

Turner, R. V., *King John: England's Evil King?* (History Press, 1994)

Turner, R. V., *Eleanor of Aquitaine, Queen of France, Queen of England* (Yale, 2009)

Tyerman, C., *England and the Crusades, 1095–1588* (University of Chicago Press, 1997)

Tyerman, C., *The Crusades: A Very Short Introduction* (OUP, 2005)

Tyerman, C., *God's War: A New History of the Crusades* (Allen Lane, 2006)

Vajay, S. D., 'From Alfonso VII to Alfonso X, the first two centuries of the Burgundian dynasty in Castile and Leon – a prosopographical catalogue in social genealogy, 1100–1300' in Brook (ed.), *Studies in Genealogy and Family History in tribute to Charles Evans* (APSGL, 1989)

Vale, M. G. A., *Edward I and the French Rivalry and Chivalry* in TCE ii

Vale, M. G. A., *The Princely Court: Medieval Courts and Culture in North-West Europe, 1270–1380* (OUP, 2001).

Vallance, A., *Old Crosses and Lychgates* (Batsford, 1920)

Walker, D., *Medieval Wales* (CUP, 1990)

Walker, R., 'Leonor of England and Eleanor of Castile: Anglo Iberian Marriage and

Cultural Exchange in the twelfth and Thirteenth Centuries' in Bullon-Fernandez (ed.), *England and Iberia in the Middle Ages* (New York, 2007)

Walsingham, T., *Historia Anglicana* ed. Riley (Longman, 1864)

Warren, W. L., *King John* (Yale, 1997)

Warren, W. L., *Henry II* (Yale, 2000)

Weiler, B., *Henry III and the Staufen Empire, 1216–1272* (Woodbridge, 2006)

Weir, A., *Eleanor of Aquitaine by the Wrath of God Queen of England* (Random House, 2011)

Wickham, G., *Early English Stages 1300–1660* (Psychology Press, 2002)

Wilkinson, L., *Eleanor de Montfort: A Rebel Countess in Medieval England* (Bloomsbury, 2012)

Wilson, C., *Westminster Abbey* (New Bell's Cathedral Guides, 1986)

Wolffe, B. P., *Royal Demesne: The Royal Estate in English History* (London, 1971)

Woodward, J., *The Theatre of Death: the Ritual Management of Royal Funerals in Renaissance England* (Boydell & Brewer, 1997)

Yapp, B., 'Birds of English Medieval Manuscripts', *Journal of Medieval History*, 5(4) (1979)

Yule & Cordier, *The Polos: Travels of Marco Polo* (Murray, 1902)

Online Resources

Cassidy & Clasby, 'Matthew Paris and Henry III's elephant', *Henry III Fine Rolls Project*, http://www.finerollshenry3.org.uk/redist/pdf/fm-06-2012.pdf

Carpenter, 'Henry III and the Sicilian Affair', *Henry III Fine Rolls Project*, http://www.finerollshenry3.org.uk/redist/pdf/fm-02-2012.pdf

Old Acre Development Company, *Secrets of Old Acre*, http://www.akko.org.il/en/

American-Israeli Cooperative Enterprise, 'Archaeology in Israel: Ancient City of Akko', http://www.jewishvirtuallibrary.org/jsource/Archaeology/Akko.html

Israel Ministry of Foreign Affairs, 'Akko: The Maritime Capital of the Crusader Kingdom', http://www.mfa.gov.il/MFA/History/Early%20History%20-%20Archaeology/Akko-%20The%20Maritime%20Capital%20of%20the%20Crusader%20Kingdom

List of Illustrations

36. Produced for an event in 1285 designed to encourage men to take up knighthood, the Winchester round table still graces the hall where it first was used. The Arthurian themes may well have been Eleanor's idea. (Photograph by Mike Peel, www.mikepeel.net)

37. An unsubtle reminder that the Plantagenets had arrived, Conwy Castle played host to Eleanor during the course of its construction and was the site of one of the many gardens made especially for her. (Courtesy of David Benbennick under Creative Commons Attribution-Share Alike 3.0 Unported license.)

38. But it is at Caernarfon that Eleanor's influence is most clearly felt. The Eagle Tower is plainly intended to reference 'The Dream of Macsen Wledig' in the *Mabinogion* (exactly the kind of tales in which Eleanor took an interest) – but it also bears a more than passing resemblance to the Castilian castle on Eleanor's arms. (Courtesy of Albert Istvan under Creative Commons Attribution-Share Alike 3.0 Unported license)

39. Eleanor's wardrobe book shows the small doings of her household. Here we see them brought to a grinding halt by the words '*Decessus Regine*', marking Eleanor's death. (© British Library)

40. Eleanor's death continued to be marked by her family and friends for years to come. Here is it inserted into the calendar in the Alphonso Psalter, which passed to her daughter Elizabeth, and from her to Eleanor's faithful servants, the Haustede family. (© British Library)

41. The tomb of Eleanor's childhood acquaintance Isabelle of Aragon gives the lie to the suggestion that portraiture was not intended (note her sweet, dimpled hands). It also provides fascinating contrasts with Eleanor's tomb. (Author)

42. Eleanor's effigy is gilt bronze, like a great king, and she is presented as if for coronation, with flowing robes and loose hair. The full view of Eleanor's tomb shows a striking resemblance between her seal and her final effigy. (© Dean and Chapel of Westminster)

43. This modern reproduction of the lost Lincoln viscera tomb provides an impression of how the shields would have appeared in the Westminster Abbey tomb. (Courtesy of Richard Croft under Creative Commons Attribution-Share Alike 2.0)

44. Sheltered from public view, the ambulatory side of Eleanor's tomb echoes her tendency to hide away. But again, her full heritage is emphasised in the shields that decorate the sides of the tomb. (© Dean and Chapel of Westminster)

45. A few feet away and standing guard over Eleanor's tomb is that of Edward. Amusingly, he achieved the simple tomb to which Ferdinand, Berengaria and Louis IX had all aspired. (© Dean and Chapel of Westminster)

46. The one depiction which remains of the Stamford Cross: The Revd Dr William Stukeley's diary sketch of the excavated top portion, with its roses. (© Bodleian Library)

47. The first and least obviously lovely of the surviving crosses, the Geddington Cross, situated near the site of one of Eleanor's favourite hunting areas as well as many of her properties, has an idiosyncratic charm. (Author)

48. It is little changed from how it appears here, lovingly recorded by the Society of Antiquaries in their *Vetusta Monumenta* in the late eighteenth century. (Author's collection)

49. One of the first prints of an Eleanor cross, this 1716 depiction of the Hardingstone Cross marks the turning point for the fortunes of the crosses. (Author's collection)

50. The record of the Hardingstone Cross's restoration in 1713, now sited to one side of the cross, with some of the remnants of the repaired statues. (Author)

51. By the end of the century the crosses were fawned over by antiquarians, as Cruikshank mockingly shows … (© The Trustees of the British Museum)

52 & 53. But restoration was needed: the tender attentions of the passing carriages are all too apparent in the *Vetusta Monumenta* depiction of Waltham Cross. Each *Vetusta Monumenta* depiction also showed details of the crosses, enabling the layouts to be discerned and details of the figures appreciated. (Author's collection)

54. The object of a hate campaign for years, the Cheapside Cross is destroyed – to great acclaim – in 1643. (© The Trustees of the British Museum)

55. But modern homages continue to be made. The nineteenth-century Charing Cross is the most famous, but this tribute in Stamford was raised at the start of the twenty-first century. The surviving rose detail on the original Stamford Cross forms the basis of the design. (Courtesy of Bob Harvey under Creative Commons Attribution Share Alike 2.0 license)

56. And, now rescued from the more obtrusive attentions of restorers, the Hardingstone Cross still stands by the A45 (London Road), reminding passers-by of one of England's most remarkable queens. (Author)

Index